중학영어듣기 만점 솔루션

24회

듣기는 실전이다 중학1 24회

저자 강보배, 김대성, 서성용, 소원석, 육상태, 윤진섭, 이수윤, 장정근, 전광훈

펴낸날 [초판 5쇄] 2022년 6월 30일

펴낸이 이기열

펴낸곳 (주)디딤돌 교육

주소 (03972) 서울특별시 마포구 월드컵북로 122 청원선와이즈타워

대표전화 02-3142-9000

구입문의 02-322-8451

내용문의 02-325-3224

팩시밀리 02-335-6038

홈페이지 www.didimdol.co.kr

등록번호 제10-718호

출간 이후 발견되는 오류는 "디딤돌 홈페이지 ⇨ 영어 ⇨ 정오표"를 통해
알려드리고 있습니다.

중학영어듣기 만점 솔루션

24회

듣기는 실전이다

듣기만점 실전공부법

1 단계 나를 진단한다!

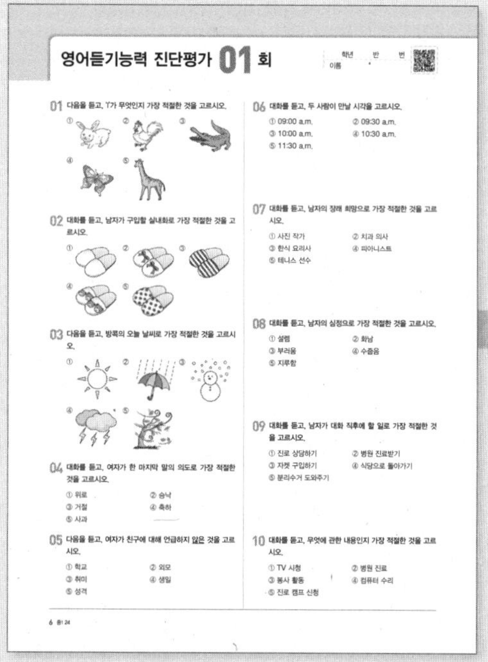

최근 3개년 기출 문제로
나만의 듣기실력 진단!

2 단계 듣기는 실전이다!

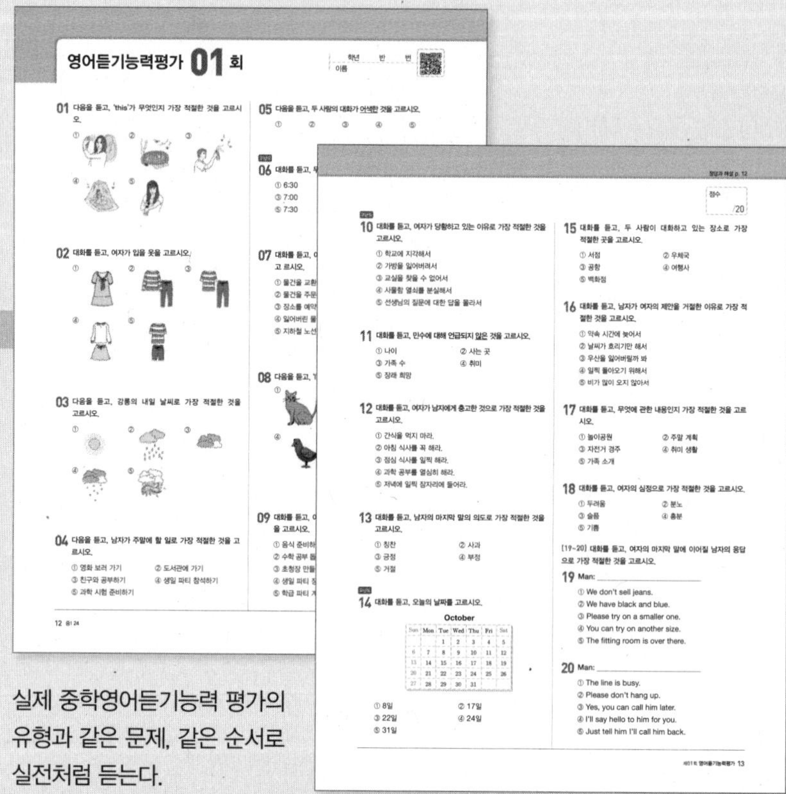

실제 중학영어듣기능력 평가의
유형과 같은 문제, 같은 순서로
실전처럼 듣는다.

만점 듣기전략

교육과정 성취 기준에 맞춰 듣기능력평가 출제 유형을 제시, 각각의 유형을 잘 드러내는
기출문제로 유형별 실전 솔루션을 익힌다.

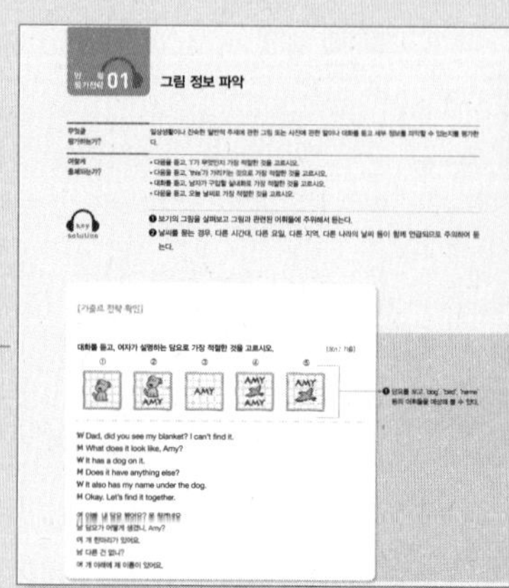

3 단계
만점 듣기 PLUS BOOK

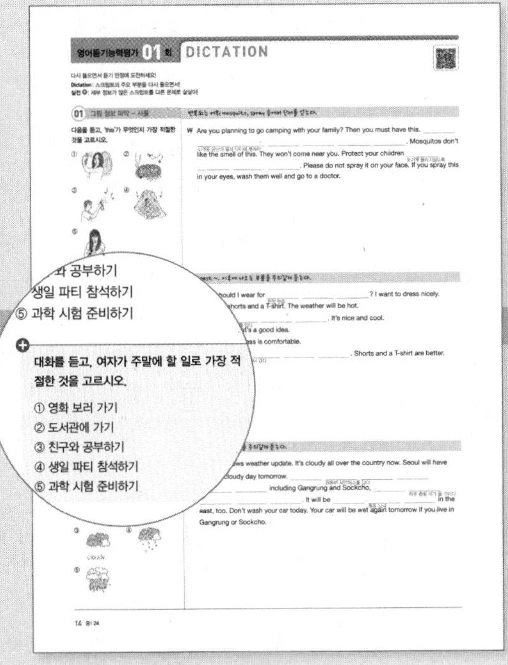

- **듣기 만점으로 가는 DICTATION과 실전 PLUS!**

DICTATION 스크립트의 주요 부분을 다시 들으면서!

실전 Plus 세부 정보가 많은 스크립트를 다른 문제로 샅샅이!

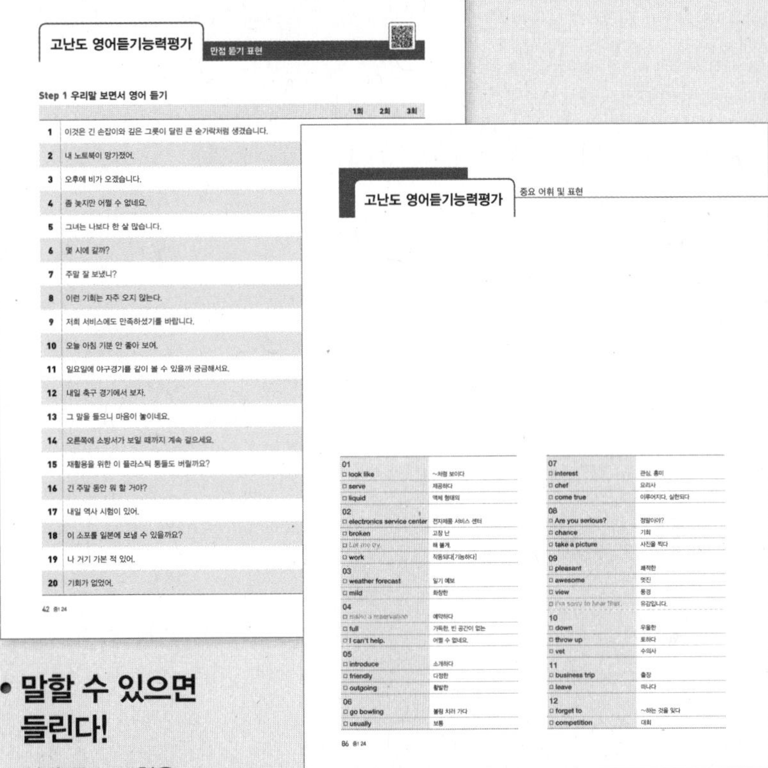

- **말할 수 있으면 들린다!**

회별 주요 표현을 우리말을 보면서 영어로 듣고 또 듣고 영어를 보면서 듣고 따라 말하고

- **주요 어휘 및 표현**

회별, 문항별 주요 어휘와 표현을 시간 날 때마다 반복, 또 반복! 사진처럼 저장한다.

꼼꼼한 해설로 듣기 만점에 도전!

유형 안내부터 스크립트, 해석, 만점 솔루션, 어휘와 표현으로 이어지는 꼼꼼 해설로 듣기 만점에 도전하세요!

듣기는 실전이다

CONTENTS

중학영어듣기 진단평가

· 01회 06
· 02회 08
· 03회 10

중학영어듣기능력 평가

계획을 세워 매일 정해진 양을 공부하고,
공부가 끝나면 공부한 날과 맞힌 문항 수를 체크해 보세요.

찾아가기		공부한 날		맞힌 개수
01회	12	월	일	/
02회	20	월	일	/
03회	30	월	일	/
04회	38	월	일	/
05회	48	월	일	/
06회	56	월	일	/
07회	66	월	일	/
08회	74	월	일	/
09회	84	월	일	/
10회	92	월	일	/
11회	102	월	일	/
12회	110	월	일	/
13회	120	월	일	/
14회	128	월	일	/
15회	138	월	일	/
16회	146	월	일	/
17회	156	월	일	/
18회	164	월	일	/
19회	174	월	일	/
20회	182	월	일	/
고난도	192	월	일	/

만점 듣기전략

01 그림 정보 파악 ········· 28

02 대화 내용 파악 ········· 46

03 어색한 대화 찾기 ········· 64

04 이유 · 의도 파악 ········· 82

05 장소 · 관계 · 직업 · 심정 파악 ········· 100

06 적절한 응답 ········· 118

07 위치 · 언급 유무 파악 ········· 136

08 특정 정보 파악 ········· 154

09 할 일 · 부탁한 일 · 제안한 일 파악 ········· 172

영어듣기능력 진단평가 01 회

학년 반 번
이름

01 다음을 듣고, 'I'가 무엇인지 가장 적절한 것을 고르시오.

① 
② 
③ 
④ 
⑤ 

02 대화를 듣고, 남자가 구입할 실내화로 가장 적절한 것을 고르시오.

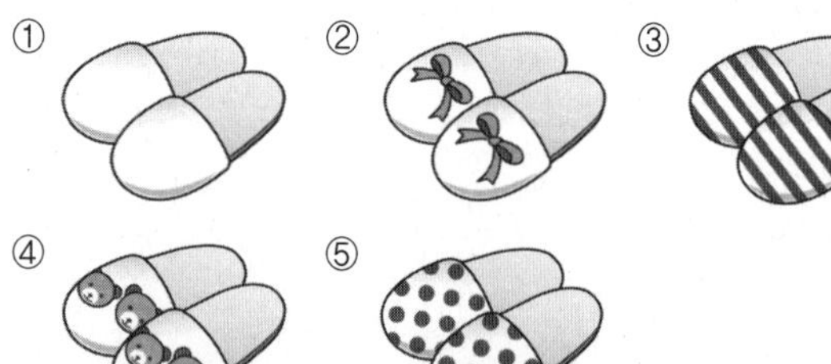

03 다음을 듣고, 방콕의 오늘 날씨로 가장 적절한 것을 고르시오.

04 대화를 듣고, 여자가 한 마지막 말의 의도로 가장 적절한 것을 고르시오.

① 위로
② 승낙
③ 거절
④ 축하
⑤ 사과

05 다음을 듣고, 여자가 친구에 대해 언급하지 <u>않은</u> 것을 고르시오.

① 학교
② 외모
③ 취미
④ 생일
⑤ 성격

06 대화를 듣고, 두 사람이 만날 시각을 고르시오.

① 09:00 a.m.
② 09:30 a.m.
③ 10:00 a.m.
④ 10:30 a.m.
⑤ 11:30 a.m.

07 대화를 듣고, 남자의 장래 희망으로 가장 적절한 것을 고르시오.

① 사진 작가
② 치과 의사
③ 한식 요리사
④ 피아니스트
⑤ 테니스 선수

08 대화를 듣고, 남자의 심정으로 가장 적절한 것을 고르시오.

① 설렘
② 화남
③ 부러움
④ 수줍음
⑤ 지루함

09 대화를 듣고, 남자가 대화 직후에 할 일로 가장 적절한 것을 고르시오.

① 진로 상담하기
② 병원 진료받기
③ 자켓 구입하기
④ 식당으로 돌아가기
⑤ 분리수거 도와주기

10 대화를 듣고, 무엇에 관한 내용인지 가장 적절한 것을 고르시오.

① TV 시청
② 병원 진료
③ 봉사 활동
④ 컴퓨터 수리
⑤ 진로 캠프 신청

점수 /20

11 대화를 듣고, 남자가 이용할 교통수단으로 가장 적절한 것을 고르시오.

① 배 ② 자동차
③ 비행기 ④ 지하철
⑤ 고속열차

12 대화를 듣고, 남자가 여자를 도와줄 수 없는 이유로 가장 적절한 것을 고르시오.

① 집에 가야하기 때문에
② 시험을 봐야하기 때문에
③ 청소를 해야 하기 때문에
④ 우체국에 가야하기 때문에
⑤ 동아리 모임이 있기 때문에

13 대화를 듣고, 두 사람의 관계로 가장 적절한 것을 고르시오.

① 가수 – 팬 ② 호텔 직원 – 고객
③ 기자 – 발명가 ④ 도서관 사서 – 학생
⑤ 여행 가이드 – 관광객

14 대화를 듣고, 서비스 센터의 위치로 가장 알맞은 곳을 고르시오.

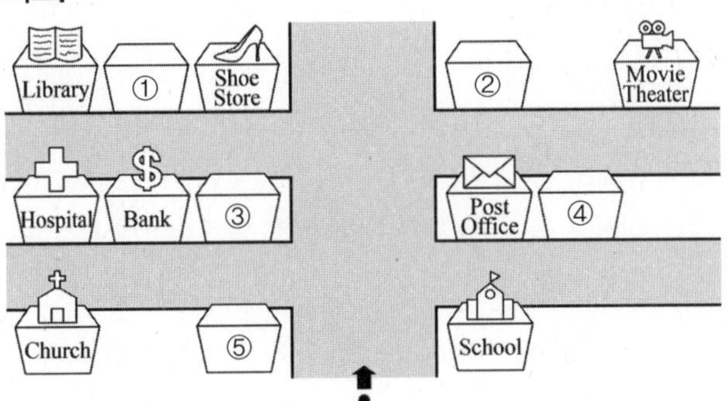

15 대화를 듣고, 남자가 여자에게 부탁한 일로 가장 적절한 것을 고르시오.

① 꽃 사오기 ② 풍선 장식하기
③ 케이크 가져오기 ④ 음료수 준비하기
⑤ 축하 노래 부르기

16 대화를 듣고, 여자가 남자에게 제안한 것으로 가장 적절한 것을 고르시오.

① 과학 실험하기 ② 축제 참가하기
③ 배드민턴 연습하기 ④ 미술 작품 감상하기
⑤ 댄스 동아리 가입하기

17 대화를 듣고, 두 사람이 구입할 과일을 고르시오.

① 사과 ② 포도
③ 딸기 ④ 바나나
⑤ 파인애플

18 대화를 듣고, 남자의 직업으로 가장 적절한 것을 고르시오.

① 화가 ② 식당 점원
③ 방송 작가 ④ 버스 기사
⑤ 안과 의사

【19~20】 대화를 듣고, 남자의 마지막 말에 이어질 여자의 응답으로 가장 적절한 것을 고르시오.

19 Woman: ______________________

① Nice to meet you.
② I'd love to, but I can't.
③ No, I don't have one.
④ Thank you for your advice.
⑤ Oh, I'm sorry to hear that.

20 Woman: ______________________

① I'm 14 years old.
② I'll go there by train.
③ I'm doing my homework.
④ I had some delicious seafood.
⑤ I'll join the swimming camp.

영어듣기능력 진단평가 02회

학년　　반　　번
이름

01 다음을 듣고, 'this'가 가리키는 것으로 가장 적절한 것을 고르시오.

02 대화를 듣고, 여자가 설명하는 담요로 가장 적절한 것을 고르시오.

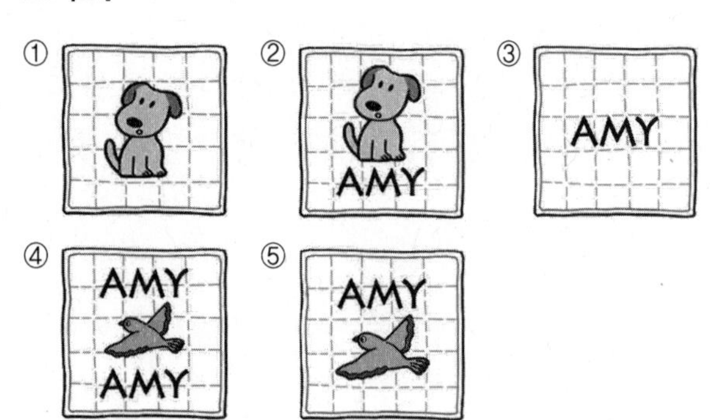

03 다음을 듣고, 일요일의 날씨로 가장 적절한 것을 고르시오.

04 대화를 듣고, 남자의 마지막 말의 의도로 가장 적절한 것을 고르시오.

① 제안　② 의심
③ 거절　④ 부정
⑤ 허락

05 다음을 듣고, 남자가 동아리 활동에 대해 언급하지 않은 것을 고르시오.

① 다양한 책 읽기　② 책 포스터 만들기
③ 작가에게 편지 쓰기　④ 독서 캠페인하기
⑤ 책 읽어 주기

06 대화를 듣고, 요가 수업이 시작되는 시각을 고르시오.

① 3:30 p.m.　② 4:00 p.m.
③ 4:30 p.m.　④ 5:00 p.m.
⑤ 5:30 p.m.

07 대화를 듣고, 여자의 장래 희망으로 가장 적절한 것을 고르시오.

① 작곡가　② 피아니스트
③ 공연 기획자　④ 뮤지컬 배우
⑤ 성악가

08 대화를 듣고, 남자의 심정으로 가장 적절한 것을 고르시오.

① sad　② angry
③ shy　④ worried
⑤ excited

09 대화를 듣고, 남자가 대화 직후 할 일로 가장 적절한 것을 고르시오.

① TV 시청하기　② 축하 전화하기
③ 약속 시간 정하기　④ 대회 일정 확인하기
⑤ 말하기 대회 참가하기

10 대화를 듣고, 선생님의 무엇에 관한 내용인지 가장 적절한 것을 고르시오.

① 고향　② 취미
③ 생일　④ 결혼
⑤ 애완동물

점수 /20

11 대화를 듣고, 두 사람이 함께 이용할 교통수단으로 가장 적절한 것을 고르시오.

① 자전거 ② 버스
③ 비행기 ④ 택시
⑤ 지하철

12 대화를 듣고, 남자가 공원에서 자전거를 탈 수 없는 이유로 가장 적절한 것을 고르시오.

① 자전거가 고장 나서 ② 다리를 다쳐서
③ 자전거 도로가 아니어서 ④ 공사 중이어서
⑤ 축제 기간 중이어서

13 대화를 듣고, 두 사람이 대화하는 장소로 가장 적절한 곳을 고르시오.

① 교실 ② 복도
③ 행정실 ④ 화장실
⑤ 운동장

14 대화를 듣고, 여자가 찾고 있는 휴대전화의 위치로 가장 적절한 것을 고르시오.

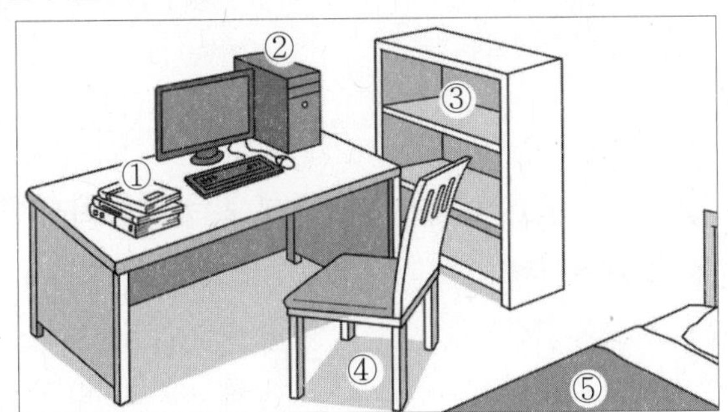

15 대화를 듣고, 남자가 여자에게 부탁한 일로 가장 적절한 것을 고르시오.

① 블록 찾기 ② 블록 주문하기
③ 블록 교환하기 ④ 블록 설명서 가져오기
⑤ 블록 상자 가져오기

16 대화를 듣고, 여자가 남자에게 제안한 것으로 가장 적절한 것을 고르시오.

① 부산 여행하기 ② 할인 쿠폰 찾기
③ 바다 수영하기 ④ 버스 시간 검색하기
⑤ 조부모님 찾아뵙기

17 대화를 듣고, 두 사람이 토요일에 할 일로 가장 적절한 것을 고르시오.

① 분리수거 하기 ② 동물 사진 찍기
③ 클럽 가입하기 ④ 포스터 그리기
⑤ 지구에게 편지 쓰기

18 대화를 듣고, 여자가 언급한 엄마의 직업으로 가장 적절한 것을 고르시오.

① 잡지 기자 ② 패션모델
③ 요리사 ④ 웹 디자이너
⑤ 아동복 디자이너

【19~20】 대화를 듣고, 여자의 마지막 말에 이어질 남자의 응답으로 가장 적절한 것을 고르시오.

19 Man: ______________________

① It's not fair. ② It's my fault.
③ That's my book. ④ For here or to go?
⑤ That's a good idea.

20 Man: ______________________

① Yes, I like dancing too.
② No, I can't dance very well.
③ I'm not interested in dancing.
④ I practiced at a dance school.
⑤ I want to join the dance contest.

영어듣기능력 진단평가 03회

학년 반 번
이름

01 다음을 듣고, 'I'가 무엇인지 가장 적절한 것을 고르시오.

02 대화를 듣고, 남자가 구입할 양말로 가장 적절한 것을 고르시오.

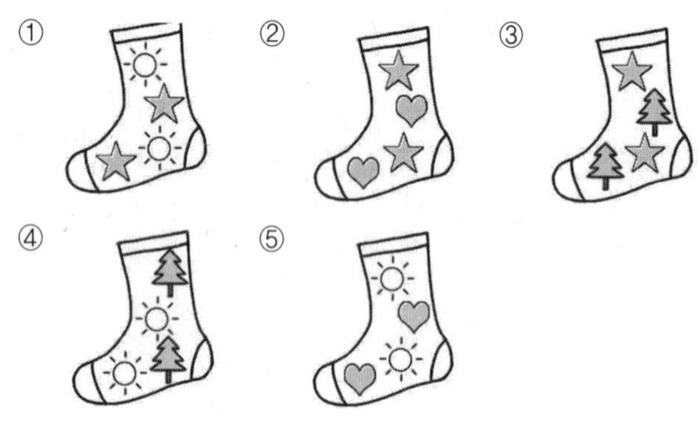

03 다음을 듣고, 내일의 날씨로 가장 적절한 것을 고르시오.

04 대화를 듣고, 남자가 한 마지막 말의 의도로 가장 적절한 것을 고르시오.

① 사과 ② 승낙
③ 거절 ④ 축하
⑤ 감사

05 다음을 듣고, 남자가 엄마에 대해 언급하지 않은 것을 고르시오.

① 직업 ② 귀가 시간
③ 외모 ④ 고향
⑤ 취미

06 대화를 듣고, 두 사람이 만날 시각을 고르시오.

① 2:30 p.m. ② 3:00 p.m.
③ 3:30 p.m. ④ 4:00 p.m.
⑤ 4:30 p.m.

07 대화를 듣고, 남자의 장래 희망으로 가장 적절한 것을 고르시오.

① 화가 ② 가수
③ 정원사 ④ 수의사
⑤ 동물 조련사

08 대화를 듣고, 남자의 심정으로 가장 적절한 것으로 고르시오.

① 기쁨 ② 지루함
③ 부러움 ④ 걱정스러움
⑤ 자랑스러움

09 대화를 듣고, 여자가 대화 직후에 할 일로 가장 적절한 것을 고르시오.

① 양초 만들기 ② 종이접기 배우기
③ 티셔츠 만들기 ④ 페이스 페인팅하기
⑤ 물풍선 터뜨리기

10 대화를 듣고, 무엇에 관한 내용인지 가장 적절한 것을 고르시오.

① 체육 대회 ② 합창 대회
③ 봉사 활동 ④ 영어 캠프
⑤ 박물관 방문

점수 /20

11 대화를 듣고, 남자가 이용할 교통수단으로 가장 적절한 것을 고르시오.

① 도보 ② 기차
③ 자동차 ④ 자전거
⑤ 지하철

12 대화를 듣고, 남자가 밤에 잠을 늦게 잔 이유로 가장 적절한 것을 고르시오.

① 축구 연습을 했기 때문에
② 수학 숙제를 했기 때문에
③ 컴퓨터 게임을 했기 때문에
④ 축구 경기를 보았기 때문에
⑤ 수학 시험이 걱정되기 때문에

13 대화를 듣고, 두 사람의 관계로 가장 적절한 것을 고르시오.

① 의사- 환자 ② 교사- 학생
③ 요리사- 손님 ④ 버스 운전기사-승객
⑤ 자동차 정비사- 고객

14 대화를 듣고, *Smile Shop*의 위치로 가장 알맞은 곳을 고르시오.

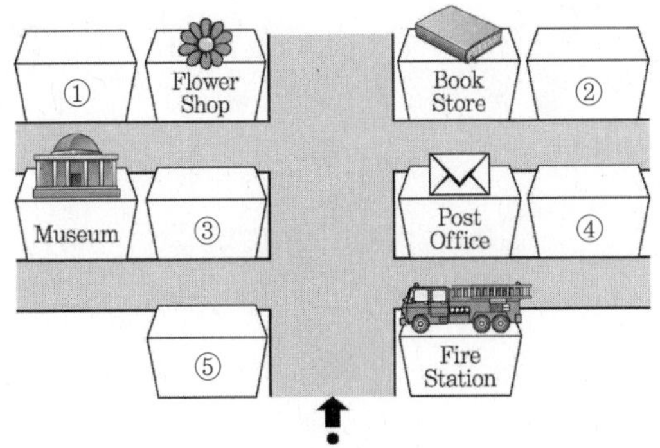

15 대화를 듣고, 남자가 여자에게 부탁한 일로 가장 적절한 것을 고르시오.

① 책 사주기 ② 책 빌려주기
③ 퍼즐 맞추기 ④ 게임CD 빌려주기
⑤ 삼촌에게 전화하기

16 대화를 듣고, 남자가 여자에게 제안한 것으로 가장 적절한 것을 고르시오.

① 설거지 하기 ② 꽃다발 만들기
③ 쿠키 함께 굽기 ④ 감사 카드 쓰기
⑤ 생일 케익 사오기

17 대화를 듣고, 남자가 잃어버린 물건을 고르시오.

① 자 ② 필통
③ 연필 ④ 볼펜
⑤ 지우개

18 대화를 듣고, 여자의 직업으로 가장 적절한 것을 고르시오.

① 경찰관 ② 은행원
③ 작곡가 ④ 소설가
⑤ 도서관 사서

【19~20】 대화를 듣고, 남자의 마지막 말에 이어질 여자의 응답으로 가장 적절한 것을 고르시오.

19 Woman: ______________________

① It's my fault.
② I can't believe it.
③ Nice to meet you.
④ Long time no see.
⑤ That's a great idea.

20 Woman: ______________________

① Don't worry about it.
② Sorry to hear that.
③ Three times a week.
④ I play it at the gym.
⑤ Of course. Here you are.

영어듣기능력평가 01 회

학년 반 번
이름

01 다음을 듣고, 'this'가 무엇인지 가장 적절한 것을 고르시오.

02 대화를 듣고, 여자가 입을 옷을 고르시오.

03 다음을 듣고, 강릉의 내일 날씨로 가장 적절한 것을 고르시오.

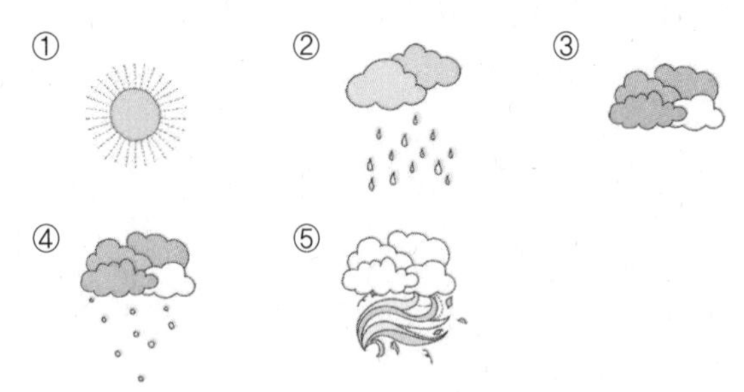

04 다음을 듣고, 남자가 주말에 할 일로 가장 적절한 것을 고르시오.

① 영화 보러 가기 ② 도서관에 가기
③ 친구와 공부하기 ④ 생일 파티 참석하기
⑤ 과학 시험 준비하기

05 다음을 듣고, 두 사람의 대화가 어색한 것을 고르시오.

① ② ③ ④ ⑤

고난도

06 대화를 듣고, 두 사람이 영화관에 도착할 시각을 고르시오.

① 6:30 ② 6:50
③ 7:00 ④ 7:10
⑤ 7:30

07 대화를 듣고, 여자가 전화를 건 목적으로 가장 적절한 것을 고 르시오.

① 물건을 교환하려고
② 물건을 주문하려고
③ 장소를 예약하려고
④ 잃어버린 물건을 찾으려고
⑤ 지하철 노선을 문의하려고

08 다음을 듣고, 'I'가 무엇인지 가장 적절한 것을 고르시오.

09 대화를 듣고, 여자가 남자에게 부탁한 일로 가장 적절한 것을 고르시오.

① 음식 준비하기
② 수학 공부 돕기
③ 초청장 만들기
④ 생일 파티 장식하기
⑤ 학급 파티 계획하기

점수 /20

고난도

10 대화를 듣고, 여자가 당황하고 있는 이유로 가장 적절한 것을 고르시오.

① 학교에 지각해서
② 가방을 잃어버려서
③ 교실을 찾을 수 없어서
④ 사물함 열쇠를 분실해서
⑤ 선생님의 질문에 대한 답을 몰라서

11 대화를 듣고, 민수에 대해 언급되지 않은 것을 고르시오.

① 나이 ② 사는 곳
③ 가족 수 ④ 취미
⑤ 장래 희망

12 대화를 듣고, 여자가 남자에게 충고한 것으로 가장 적절한 것을 고르시오.

① 간식을 먹지 마라.
② 아침 식사를 꼭 해라.
③ 점심 식사를 일찍 해라.
④ 과학 공부를 열심히 해라.
⑤ 저녁에 일찍 잠자리에 들어라.

13 대화를 듣고, 남자의 마지막 말의 의도로 가장 적절한 것을 고르시오.

① 칭찬 ② 사과
③ 긍정 ④ 부정
⑤ 거절

고난도

14 대화를 듣고, 오늘의 날짜를 고르시오.

October

Sun	Mon	Tue	Wed	Thu	Fri	Sat
		1	2	3	4	5
6	7	8	9	10	11	12
13	14	15	16	17	18	19
20	21	22	23	24	25	26
27	28	29	30	31		

① 8일 ② 17일
③ 22일 ④ 24일
⑤ 31일

15 대화를 듣고, 두 사람이 대화하고 있는 장소로 가장 적절한 곳을 고르시오.

① 서점 ② 우체국
③ 공항 ④ 여행사
⑤ 백화점

16 대화를 듣고, 남자가 여자의 제안을 거절한 이유로 가장 적절한 것을 고르시오.

① 약속 시간에 늦어서
② 날씨가 흐리기만 해서
③ 우산을 잃어버릴까 봐
④ 일찍 돌아오기 위해서
⑤ 비가 많이 오지 않아서

17 대화를 듣고, 무엇에 관한 내용인지 가장 적절한 것을 고르시오.

① 놀이공원 ② 주말 계획
③ 자전거 경주 ④ 취미 생활
⑤ 가족 소개

18 대화를 듣고, 여자의 심정으로 가장 적절한 것을 고르시오.

① 두려움 ② 분노
③ 슬픔 ④ 흥분
⑤ 기쁨

[19~20] 대화를 듣고, 여자의 마지막 말에 이어질 남자의 응답으로 가장 적절한 것을 고르시오.

19 Man: ____________________

① We don't sell jeans.
② We have black and blue.
③ Please try on a smaller one.
④ You can try on another size.
⑤ The fitting room is over there.

20 Man: ____________________

① The line is busy.
② Please don't hang up.
③ Yes, you can call him later.
④ I'll say hello to him for you.
⑤ Just tell him I'll call him back.

DICTATION

다시 들으면서 듣기 만점에 도전하세요!
Dictation: 스크립트의 주요 부분을 다시 들으면서!
실전 ⊕: 세부 정보가 많은 스크립트를 다른 문제로 살살이!

01 그림 정보 파악 – 사물

반복되는 어휘 mosquito, spray 등에서 단서를 얻는다.

다음을 듣고, 'this'가 무엇인지 가장 적절한 것을 고르시오.

① ② ③ ④ ⑤

W Are you planning to go camping with your family? Then you must have this. ________ ________ ________ ________ ________ ________. Mosquitos don't like the smell of this. They won't come near you. Protect your children ________ ________ ________ ________. Please do not spray it on your face. If you spray this in your eyes, wash them well and go to a doctor.

이것을 당신의 팔과 다리에 뿌려라 / 모기에 물리지않도록

02 그림 정보 파악 – 사물

I suggest ~. 이후에 나오는 부분을 주의깊게 듣는다.

대화를 듣고, 여자가 입을 옷을 고르시오.

① ② ③ ④ ⑤

W What should I wear for ________ ________ ________? I want to dress nicely.
현장 학습
M I suggest shorts and a T-shirt. The weather will be hot.
W I want to ________ ________ ________. It's nice and cool.
원피스를 입다
M I don't think that's a good idea.
W Why not? My dress is comfortable.
M Yes, but you will ________ ________ ________. Shorts and a T-shirt are better.
많이 걷다
W Okay.

고난도

03 날씨 파악

'강릉'이 언급되는 부분을 주의깊게 듣는다.

다음을 듣고, 강릉의 내일 날씨로 가장 적절한 것을 고르시오.

① ② rain ③ cloudy ④ ⑤

M 9 o'clock news weather update. It's cloudy all over the country now. Seoul will have another cloudy day tomorrow. ________ ________ ________ ________ ________ ________ including Gangrung and Sockcho, ________ ________ ________ ________ ________. It will be ________ ________ ________ in the east, too. Don't wash your car today. Your car will be wet again tomorrow if you live in Gangrung or Sockcho.

동부 지역 / 하루 종일 비가 올 것이다 / 추운 날씨

04 할 일 파악

대화를 듣고, 남자가 주말에 할 일로 가장 적절한 것을 고르시오

① 영화 보러 가기
go to see a movie see, go for a movie
② 도서관에 가기
③ 친구와 공부하기
④ 생일 파티 참석하기
⑤ 과학 시험 준비하기

대화를 듣고, 여자가 주말에 할 일로 가장 적절한 것을 고르시오.

① 영화 보러 가기
② 도서관에 가기
③ 친구와 공부하기
④ 생일 파티 참석하기
⑤ 과학 시험 준비하기

M Soyoung, what are you going to do this weekend?

W Miran and I are going to study together at my house. Will you join us?

M Well, I wanted to ask you to ______ ______ ______ ______ ______ together.
영화 보러 가다

W There will be a science quiz on Wednesday. Did you finish studying?

M Well, not exactly, but I really ______ ______ ______ ______ ______ ______.
영화를 보러 가고 싶다

W Well, enjoy it.

M Thank you.

05 어색한 대화 찾기

질문의 의문사(Do, What, Where)와 대답이 어울리는지 주목하며 듣는다.

다음을 듣고, 두 사람의 대화가 어색한 것을 고르시오.

① ② ③ ④ ⑤

What does your brother do?는 직업을, What is your sister like?는 성격이나 생김새, 특징을 묻는 표현이다.

① **M** Do you have any brothers or sisters?
W No, ______ ______ ______ ______.
나는 외동이다

② **M** What does your brother do?
W He's a college student.

③ **M** ______ ______ ______ ______ ______?
너의 언니는 어떤 분이시니
W She ______ ______ ______.
요리하는 것을 좋아하다

④ **M** What is your favorite food?
W I like *bulgogi* most.

⑤ **M** Where can we meet?
W Let's meet at the bus stop.

고난도

06 숫자 파악 – 시각

대화를 듣고, 두 사람이 영화관에 도착할 시각을 고르시오.

① 6:30 ② 6:50
③ 7:00 ④ 7:10
⑤ 7:30

M When does the movie start? I don't want to be late.

W It starts at 7 o'clock. We ______ ______ ______ ______, don't worry.
시간이 많다

M Should we leave at 6:30?

W Sure. Then we'll get there ______ ______ ______ ______.
10분쯤 일찍

M Good. We'll have enough time to ______ ______ ______.
좋은 자리를 잡다

W Yes, and we can buy some snacks.

07 전화 목적 파악

전화를 건 목적은 주로 앞부분에서 밝혀지므로 대화의 시작 부분에 집중하여 듣는다.

대화를 듣고, 여자가 전화를 건 목적으로 가장 적절한 것을 고르시오.

① 물건을 교환하려고
② 물건을 주문하려고
③ 장소를 예약하려고
④ 잃어버린 물건을 찾으려고
⑤ 지하철 노선을 문의하려고

[Telephone rings.]

M Good afternoon. Green line Lost and Found. How can I help you?

W I _________ _________ _________ _________ on the subway this morning. (내 가방을 두고 내렸다)

M What station did you get on and get off at?

W I got on at Suyoung station and got off at Seomyeon station.

M _________ _________ _________ _________ _________ about the bag? (좀 더 설명해 주시겠습니까)

W It's a black school backpack. A small teddy bear is hanging on the zipper.

M I'll check _________ _________ _________. Hold on, please. (그것이 여기에 있는지)

08 그림 "I" 파악(담화)

다음을 듣고, 'I'가 무엇인지 가장 적절한 것을 고르시오.

① ② ③ ④ ⑤

M I have a short tail and long ears. I also have soft fur. I _________ _________ (채소 먹는 것을 좋아하다), green grass, and flowers. But I don't eat meat. I _________ _________ (집단으로 사는 것을 좋아하다) _________ in the woods or forests. But sometimes, people have me _________ (애완동물로) _________ _________. What am I?

09 부탁 파악

Can[Could] you~? 이후에서 부탁하는 일을 알 수 있다.

대화를 듣고, 여자가 남자에게 부탁한 일로 가장 적절한 것을 고르시오.

① 음식 준비하기
② 수학 공부 돕기
③ 초청장 만들기
④ 생일 파티 장식하기
⑤ 학급 파티 계획하기

I would be glad to.는 '기꺼이.'라는 의미로, 상대방의 부탁을 수락하는 표현이다.

W I'm really busy these days. I have _________ _________ _________. (여가 시간이 없는)

M Why? Are you studying for a test?

W Actually, I am _________ _________ _________. It's hard work. (학급 파티를 계획하고 있다)

M You mean the end-of-semester party?

W Yes, and there's so much to do. We are inviting the parents and siblings as well.

M That sounds like a huge responsibility. Could I help you with anything?

W That would be great. Can you _________ _________ _________ _________ _________? (부모님을 위한 초대장을 만들다)

M Sure, I would be glad to. Please email the information to me.

➕ 대화를 듣고, 여자가 대화 후에 할 일로 가장 적절한 것을 고르시오.

① 시험공부하기 ② 이메일 보내기
③ 초대장 만들기 ④ 부모님께 전화하기
⑤ 휴식 취하기

고난도

10 이유 파악

여자가 처한 상황과 두 사람의 관계를 파악한다.

대화를 듣고, 여자가 당황하고 있는 이유로 가장 적절한 것을 고르시오.

① 학교에 지각해서
② 가방을 잃어버려서
③ 교실을 찾을 수 없어서
④ 사물함 열쇠를 분실해서
⑤ 선생님의 질문에 대한 답을 몰라서

M What are you doing here? The bell already rang. You should go to your classroom.

W Well, I ________ ________ ________ ________ ________, sir.
어디로 가야 할지 모르다

M Where is your classroom?

W I think I have English now and the room is over there. But it's locked. Nobody's in there.

M Are you a new student?

W Yes, sir. Today is my second day here.

M Come to the teachers' office with me. I'll find out ________ ________ ________ ________.
네가 어디로 가야 할지

11 언급 및 비언급 파악

다음을 듣고, 민수에 대해 언급되지 않은 것을 고르시오.

① 나이 13 years old
② 사는 곳 moved to Seoul
③ 가족 수 There are ~ in my family
④ 취미 play soccer and basketball
⑤ 장래 희망

M I'm Minsu. I'm ________ ________ ________. I lived in Incheon when I was young. When I was 10, my family ________ ________ ________. My relatives and my close friends live in Incheon, so I sometimes visit my hometown. There are my parents, one sister and one brother in my family. We have a dog, whose name is Mimi. ________ ________ ________ ________ ________ ________ with my friends.
13살 / 서울로 이사왔다 / 나는 축구와 농구하는 것을 좋아한다

12 특정 정보 파악

대화를 듣고, 여자가 남자에게 충고한 것으로 가장 적절한 것을 고르시오.

① 간식을 먹지 마라.
② 아침 식사를 꼭 해라.
③ 점심 식사를 일찍 해라.
④ 과학 공부를 열심히 해라.
⑤ 저녁에 일찍 잠자리에 들어라.

W Is something wrong? You don't look well.

M I'm very hungry. I can't wait until lunchtime.

W But it's only 10 in the morning.

M I ________ ________ ________. I usually get up late and ________ ________ ________ ________ ________.
아침을 못 먹었다 / 먹을 시간이 없다

W That's too bad. All scientists say that breakfast is important for your brain. It's ________ ________ ________ ________.
그것을 거르는 것은 좋지 않은

13 의도 추론

Who doesn't?의 숨겨진 의미를 파악한다.

대화를 듣고, 남자의 마지막 말의 의도로 가장 적절한 것을 고르시오.

① 칭찬 ② 사과
③ 긍정 ④ 부정
⑤ 거절

I'm tired of ~.는 '나는 ~이 질렸다.'는 의미로, 싫증을 나타내는 표현이다.

W What should we have for dinner?

M Let's ________ ________ ________. How about fried chicken?
뭔가를 주문하다

W I'm tired of fried chicken. I had that last night.

M Then let's have pizza.

W Sounds good. And I already ________ ________ ________ ________, too.
후식으로 먹을 것을 만들어 놨다

M That sounds great.

W Do you like chocolate cake?

M ________ ________ ________? Who doesn't?
농담해

고난도

14 숫자 파악 – 날짜

요일에 집중해서 듣고 Tuesday와 Thursday를 혼동하지 않도록 주의한다.

대화를 듣고, 오늘의 날짜를 고르시오.

October

Sun	Mon	Tue	Wed	Thu	Fri	Sat
		1	2	3	4	5
6	7	8	9	10	11	12
13	14	15	16	17	18	19
20	21	22	23	24	25	26
27	28	29	30	31		

① 8일 ② 17일
③ 22일 ④ 24일
⑤ 31일

M What are you going to do after school?
W My friends and I are practicing a dance for the school festival.
M A dance for school festival? That's great. When is the festival?
W It's on the ______ ______ ______ ______.
10월의 마지막 주 목요일
M Today is Thursday. You ______ ______ ______ ______ to practice.
일주일밖에 안 남았다
W That's right. We're doing great. Come and see us.
M Of course.

15 장소 추론

대화를 듣고, 두 사람이 대화하고 있는 장소로 가장 적절한 곳을 고르시오.

① 서점 ② 우체국
③ 공항 ④ 여행사
⑤ 백화점

M Good afternoon.
W Hi, ______ ______ ______ ______ ______ ______ ______ Sydney.
~로 이 소포를 보내고 싶다
M ______ ______ ______ ______ ______?
항공 우편으로 보낼까요, 해상 우편으로 보낼까요
W By surface mail. The package has books in it.
M Put the box on this scale, please. Let me check how much it weighs.
W All right.
M Well, it'll cost $37.

16 이유 파악

대화를 듣고, 남자가 여자의 제안을 거절한 이유로 가장 적절한 것을 고르시오.

① 약속 시간에 늦어서
② 날씨가 흐리기만 해서
③ 우산을 잃어버릴까 봐
④ 일찍 돌아오기 위해서
⑤ 비가 많이 오지 않아서

M I'm going out, honey. See you in the evening.
W Dan, ______ ______ ______ ______ ______ ______? It looks like it's going to rain.
우산을 가져가지 그래요
M It won't rain today. The weather forecast said that.
W The weather forecast might be wrong. Look at the sky.
M I really ______ ______ ______ ______ ______. Don't you remember I lost one the other day?
우산을 가지고 다니고 싶지 않다
W All right. If you insist.

17 대화 내용 파악

대화를 듣고, 무엇에 관한 내용인지 가장 적절한 것을 고르시오.

① 놀이공원 ② 주말 계획
③ 자전거 경주 ④ 취미 생활
⑤ 가족 소개

W Finally, it's Friday!
M You look happy. Do you have ______ ______ ______ ______?
주말을 위한 좋은 계획
W Yes, I'm going to Wonderland with my family.
M Wow, that sounds interesting. You will have fun!
W Yes, I'm very excited. ______ ______ ______, Minho?
너는 어때?
M We're just going to go biking in the park.
W We? Who are you going with?
M With my brother. We ______ ______ ______ have a race.
~할 것이다

18 심정 추론

대화를 듣고, 여자의 심정으로 가장 적절한 것을 고르시오.

① 두려움 ② 분노
③ 슬픔 ④ 흥분
⑤ 기쁨

반복되는 어휘 sick, upset 등을 단서로 이용한다.

M Are you OK? You don't look very good today.
W Yeah, just __________ __________ __________ today, that's all.
마음이 약간 우울하다
M Why? Did something happen to you?
W It's my puppy. He is very sick.
M Oh, no. Is it something serious?
W I hope not. I feel upset because he's sick.
M I'm sure he'll get better. __________ __________ __________.
속상해 하지 마
W I will try not to.

19 알맞은 응답 찾기

[19~20] 대화를 듣고, 여자의 마지막 말에 이어질 남자의 응답으로 가장 적절한 것을 고르시오.

Man: __________

① We don't sell jeans.
② We have black and blue.
③ Please try on a smaller one.
④ You can try on another size.
⑤ The fitting room is over there.

마지막 질문이 Where로 시작하고 있으므로, 장소와 관련된 대답이 나와야 한다.

M May I help you?
W Yes, I'm __________ __________ __________.
청바지를 찾고 있다
M Jeans for ladies are in the next row. Is there any particular style you want?
W I'd like a classic style with no decorations on them.
M These jeans over here have a basic design. What size do you wear?
W Size 4. __________ __________ __________ __________ __________?
어디에서 그것을 입어 볼 수 있나요
M __________

20 알맞은 응답 찾기

Man: __________

① The line is busy.
② Please don't hang up.
③ Yes, you can call him later.
④ I'll say hello to him for you.
⑤ Just tell him I'll call him back.

Can I take a message?는 메시지를 남기겠냐고 묻는 표현이고, Can I leave a message?는 메시지를 남기겠다고 요청하는 표현이다.

[Telephone rings.]

W Hello. Jacobson and Brown. How may I help you?
M __________ __________ __________ Mr. Robinson?
~와 통화할 수 있을까요
W __________ __________ __________, please?
누구세요
M This is Mr. James Callman.
W I'm sorry, Mr. Callman. He's talking on the phone right now. __________ __________ __________ __________?
메시지를 남겨 드릴까요
M __________

영어듣기능력평가 02회

학년 반 번
이름

01 다음을 듣고, 남자가 그린 그림을 고르시오.

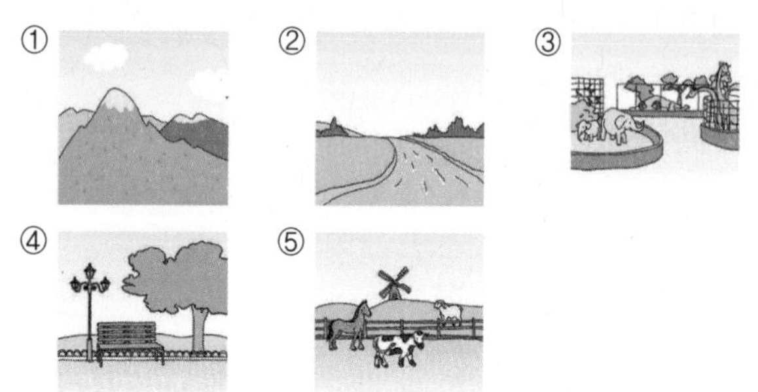

02 대화를 듣고, 팝콘이 있는 곳을 고르시오.

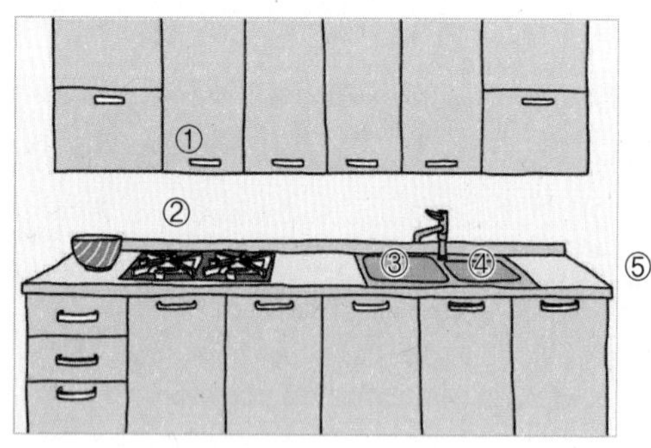

03 다음을 듣고, 강원도의 내일 날씨로 가장 적절한 것을 고르시오.

04 대화를 듣고, 여자가 여름 방학에 할 일로 가장 적절한 것을 고르시오.

① 공부하기
② 테니스 배우기
③ 여행하기
④ 아르바이트 하기
⑤ 스쿠버 다이빙 배우기

05 다음을 듣고, 두 사람의 대화가 어색한 것을 고르시오.

① ② ③ ④ ⑤

고난도

06 대화를 듣고, 두 사람이 만날 예상 시각을 고르시오.

① 2시 10분
② 2시 30분
③ 2시 40분
④ 2시 50분
⑤ 3시 10분

07 대화를 듣고, 남자가 전화를 건 목적으로 가장 적절한 것을 고르시오.

① 컴퓨터를 주문하려고
② 디지털 카메라를 빌리려고
③ 포토 프린터를 주문하려고
④ 가전제품 수리를 의뢰하려고
⑤ 홈쇼핑 회사의 위치를 확인하려고

08 다음을 듣고, 'this'가 가리키는 것으로 가장 적절한 것을 고르시오.

09 대화를 듣고, 여자의 장래 희망으로 가장 적절한 것을 고르시오.

① 프로 게이머
② 보석 디자이너
③ 패션 디자이너
④ 메이크업 아티스트
⑤ 컴퓨터 프로그래머

10 대화를 듣고, 여자가 꽃집에 간 이유로 가장 적절한 것을 고르시오.

① 큰 화분을 구입하려고
② 천연 비료를 주문하려고
③ 꽃꽂이 수강 신청을 하려고
④ 꽃집의 일자리에 지원하려고
⑤ 고무나무 재배법을 물어보려고

점수 /20

11 다음을 듣고, Patrick에 대해 언급되지 않은 것을 고르시오.

① 나이 ② 가르치는 과목
③ 좋아하는 동물 ④ 사는 곳
⑤ 취미

12 대화를 듣고, 남자가 대화 직후에 할 일로 가장 적절한 것을 고르시오.

① 숙제하기 ② 집에 가기
③ 방 청소하기 ④ 저녁 식사 준비하기
⑤ 저녁 식사하러 나가기

13 대화를 듣고, 여자의 마지막 말의 의도로 가장 적절한 것을 고르시오.

① 항의 ② 감사
③ 거절 ④ 부탁
⑤ 충고

고난도
14 대화를 듣고, 남자의 생일 날짜를 고르시오.

① November 1 ② November 30
③ December 1 ④ December 30
⑤ December 31

15 대화를 듣고, 두 사람이 대화하고 있는 장소로 가장 적절한 곳을 고르시오.

① 집 ② 병원
③ 서점 ④ 교실
⑤ 백화점

16 대화를 듣고, 두 사람의 관계로 가장 적절한 것을 고르시오.

① 아빠와 딸 ② 의사와 환자
③ 교사와 학생 ④ 상사와 직원
⑤ 손님과 점원

17 대화를 듣고, 여자의 직업으로 가장 적절한 것을 고르시오.

① 의사 ② 가게 점원
③ 약사 ④ 영양사
⑤ 요리사

18 대화를 듣고, 무엇에 관한 내용인지 가장 적절한 것을 고르시오.

① 여자가 어제 한 일
② 친구들과 싸운 이유
③ 남자가 보고 싶은 영화
④ 두 사람이 영화를 볼 날짜
⑤ 여자와 친구들이 오늘 한 일

[19~20] 대화를 듣고, 여자의 마지막 말에 이어질 남자의 응답으로 가장 적절한 것을 고르시오.

19 Man: ____________________

① Sorry, we don't have any rooms left.
② Good! Let me teach you how to swim.
③ Okay! Then, let's go to the hotel right away.
④ How long does it take from here to the beach?
⑤ Well... I want to eat spaghetti. What about you?

고난도
20 Man: ____________________

① Then, you should buy a textbook.
② No. I don't want to learn this program.
③ Can I use your computer for a minute?
④ Thank you. Please fill out this form first.
⑤ Really? When did you buy this computer?

영어듣기능력평가 02회 DICTATION

다시 들으면서 듣기 만점에 도전하세요!
Dictation: 스크립트의 주요 부분을 다시 들으면서!
실전 ⊕: 세부 정보가 많은 스크립트를 다른 문제로 샅샅이!

01 그림 정보 파악 – 사물

I drew ~. 이후에 나오는 부분을 주의깊게 듣는다.

다음을 듣고, 남자가 그린 그림을 고르시오.

① ② ③ ④ ⑤

M Today, we drew pictures in art class. We had to draw pictures of the country. Some students drew mountains. Others drew rivers or lakes. But I ________ ________ (농장을 그렸다) ________. It was my uncle's farm.
I went there last summer vacation. There were many different kinds of animals. There were lots of cows. ________ ________ ________ (그곳에는 양이 있었다), too.
I ________ ________ ________ (나의 삼촌이 먹이 주는 것을 도와드렸다) the animals.

02 그림 정보 파악 – 위치

위치를 나타내는 전치사에 유의한다.

대화를 듣고, 팝콘이 있는 곳을 고르시오.

① ② ③ ④ ⑤

M Where did you put the popcorn?
W It's in a bowl.
M Is it ________ ________ ________ (조리대 위에)?
W Yes, beside the stove.
M I don't see the bowl. Is it next to the sink?
W No, it's on ________ ________ ________ ________ (~의 다른 옆쪽) the stove.
M Oh, I see. There is ________ ________ ________ (큰 그릇).
W Right, that one.

03 날씨 파악

'강원도'가 언급되는 부분을 주의깊게 듣는다.

다음을 듣고, 강원도의 내일 날씨로 가장 적절한 것을 고르시오.

① showers ② ③ snow ④ sunny ⑤

W It's time for the weather report. ________ ________ ________ (전국적으로 눈이 내리고 있다) ________ ________ including Jeju Island. The snow will continue until tomorrow for most of the country. However, in the Gangwon area, ________ ________ ________ (내일 화창할 것이다) ________ with no snow. There will be showers in the some southern part of Gyoungsang province. And that's all.

04 할 일 파악

원래 계획에서 마음이 바뀐 이후의 말을 잘 듣는다.

대화를 듣고, 여자가 여름 방학에 할 일로 가장 적절한 것을 고르시오.

① 공부하기
② 테니스 배우기
③ 여행하기 take a trip
④ 아르바이트 하기
⑤ 스쿠버 다이빙 배우기

W In two weeks, we'll have summer vacation.

M That's right. So, will you really __________ __________ __________ __________ during this vacation?
스쿠버 다이빙과 테니스를 배우다

W No. I __________ __________ __________. I'll __________ __________ __________ to Asia.
마음이 바뀌었다 / 여행하다

M Really? That's a wonderful plan. But I think you'll need a lot of money.

W Don't worry. I already saved enough.

05 어색한 대화 찾기

다음을 듣고, 두 사람의 대화가 어색한 것을 고르시오.

① ② ③ ④ ⑤

① **W** Oh, this jacket looks nice. Where did you buy it?
M At the Sunshine Shopping Mall. It was only $30.

② **W** What are you reading, Sam?
M A detective story. It's very interesting.

③ **W** Excuse me, can you __________ __________ __________ __________ me?
~의 사진을 찍다
M Sure, no problem.

④ **W** Please __________ __________ __________ __________ before riding your bicycle.
헬멧을 착용하라
M Okay, I'll __________ __________ __________.
이 헬멧을 사다

⑤ **W** I'd like to send this package to Seattle.
M I see. Please put it on this scale.

고난도

06 숫자 파악 – 시각

현재 시각(two forty)에 소요 시간(ten minutes)을 더하면 만날 예상 시각이 된다.

대화를 듣고, 두 사람이 만날 예상 시각을 고르시오.

① 2시 10분 ② 2시 30분
③ 2시 40분 ④ 2시 50분
⑤ 3시 10분

How long is it going to take ~?는 How long will it take ~?와 같은 의미로, 소요 시간을 묻는 표현이다.

[Cellphone rings.]

W Hello? Angela speaking.

M Hi, Angela. Where are you now? __________ __________ __________ __________.
거의 2시 40분이다

W I'm passing City Hall now.

M How long is it going to take from where you're at?

W Well... it will __________ __________ __________ __________, I think. I'll be there soon.
약 10분 걸리다

M Okay, see you soon.

07 전화 목적 파악

I'd like to ~. 이후에 나오는 부분을 주의깊게 듣는다.

대화를 듣고, 남자가 전화를 건 목적으로 가장 적절한 것을 고르시오.

① 컴퓨터를 주문하려고
② 디지털 카메라를 빌리려고
③ 포토 프린터를 주문하려고
④ 가전제품 수리를 의뢰하려고
⑤ 홈쇼핑 회사의 위치를 확인하려고

[Telephone rings.]

W Hello, Seven Star Home Shopping. How may I help you?

M Yes, please. __________ __________ __________ __________ __________ __________ showing on TV now.
나는 컴퓨터를 주문하고 싶다

W I see. It costs $800. And you can get either a digital camera or a photo printer as a free gift.

M Well... I'll take the photo printer.

W I see. __________ __________ __________ __________ __________?
어떻게 지불하시겠어요

M Credit card, please.

08 그림 "this" 파악(담화)

다음을 듣고, 'this'가 가리키는 것으로 가장 적절한 것을 고르시오.

① ② ③ ④ ⑤

M You ride this to go to a place. This has ________ ________ ________ ________ (두 개의 바퀴). You don't need any fuel. But you need to ________ ________ ________ (다리를 사용하다). It can be hard to go up a hill, but it's really ________ ________ ________ ________ (내려가기 쉬운). What is this?

09 특정 정보 파악

남자가 원하는 것과 여자가 원하는 것을 구분하여 듣는다.

대화를 듣고, 여자의 장래 희망으로 가장 적절한 것을 고르시오.

① 프로 게이머 pro gamer
② 보석 디자이너 jewelry designer
③ 패션 디자이너 fashion designer
④ 메이크업 아티스트
⑤ 컴퓨터 프로그래머 computer programmer

W What do you want to be in the future?

M Well... I ________ ________ ________ ________ ________ ________ (프로 게이머가 되고 싶다) or a computer programmer.

W I'm sure you'll be one of them. You're very good at computers.

M What about you, Stella? Do you still want to be a fashion designer?

W No, I changed my mind. Now I ________ ________ ________ ________ ________ (보석 디자이너가 되고 싶다)!

10 이유 파악

남자가 원하는 것과 여자가 원하는 것을 구분하여 듣는다.

대화를 듣고, 여자가 꽃집에 간 이유로 가장 적절한 것을 고르시오.

① 큰 화분을 구입하려고
② 천연 비료를 주문하려고
③ 꽃꽂이 수강 신청을 하려고
④ 꽃집의 일자리에 지원하려고
⑤ 고무나무 재배법을 물어보려고

W Hi, do you remember me?

M Yes, I do. You bought a rubber tree last weekend, didn't you?

W Yeah, that's right. You ________ ________ ________ ________ (기억력이 좋다).

M Is it doing well?

W Yes, it is. But I think the pot is ________ ________ ________ ________ (약간 작은) for the tree. So, ________ ________ ________ ________ ________ ________ ________ (나는 좀 더 큰 화분을 사고 싶다).

M I see. Follow me, please. Pots are inside.

11 언급 및 비언급 파악

다음을 듣고, Patrick에 대해 언급되지 않은 것을 고르시오.

① 나이 30 years old
② 가르치는 과목 mathematics
③ 좋아하는 동물
④ 사는 곳 Green Apartments
⑤ 취미 playing tennis

M Let me tell you something about myself. My name is Patrick Johnson and I'm ________ ________ ________ (30살). This year, I'll ________ (여러분에게 가장 어려운 과목인 수학을 가르치다) ________ ________ ________, ________. I live in Green Apartments just next to the school. ________ ________ ________ ________ (내 취미는 테니스 치는 것이다). I was a tennis player when I was in high school. I was pretty good and won a few medals at local competitions.

12 할 일 파악

저녁 식사하러 나가기 전에 할 일을 주의깊게 듣는다.

대화를 듣고, 남자가 대화 직후에 할 일로 가장 적절한 것을 고르시오.

① 숙제하기
② 집에 가기
③ 방 청소하기 cleaning your room
④ 저녁 식사 준비하기
⑤ 저녁 식사하러 나가기

➕ 대화를 듣고, 남자가 집에 와서 한 일로 가장 적절한 것을 고르시오.

① 숙제하기
② 집에 가기
③ 방 청소하기
④ 저녁 식사 준비하기
⑤ 저녁 식사하러 나가기

W Peter, ________ ________ ________ ________ ________ (네 숙제 다 했니)?
M Yes, I did it as soon as I came home.
W That's good, son. ________ ________ ________ ________ ________ (네 방 청소를 하는 게 어떠니)? I think your room is a little bit messy.
M OK. ________ ________ ________ (지금 그것을 하겠다).
W Good! After cleaning your room, let's go out for dinner. I'll take you to a nice Chinese restaurant.
M Really? Oh, I like Chinese food.

13 의도 추론

반복되는 어휘 Sorry의 의도를 추론해 본다.

대화를 듣고, 여자의 마지막 말의 의도로 가장 적절한 것을 고르시오.

① 항의　② 감사
③ 거절　④ 부탁
⑤ 충고

How about ~?은 '~하는 게 어때?'라는 의미로, 제안을 나타내는 표현이다.

➕ 대화를 듣고, 여자가 내일 할 일로 가장 적절한 것을 고르시오.

① 놀이공원 가기　② 생물 보고서 쓰기
③ 일요일 계획 짜기　④ 양로원 방문하기
⑤ 자원봉사 하기

M Judy, how about going to the amusement park with me tomorrow?
W Tomorrow? Sorry, ________ ________ ________ ________ (난 ~을 작성해야 한다) my biology report.
M Didn't you finish it yet? Poor Judy. Then, how about Sunday? If you don't have any plans, let's go there on Sunday.
W ________, ________ (또 미안해). ________ ________ ________ ________ (난 일해야 한다) as a volunteer at a senior center.

고난도

14 숫자 파악 – 날짜

대화를 듣고, 남자의 생일 날짜를 고르시오.

① November 1 ② November 30
③ December 1 ④ December 30
⑤ December 31

W John, you won't forget my birthday, will you?

M Sure! How can I forget your birthday? It's ______ ______ ______ ______ .
(11월의 마지막 날)

W Right! And your birthday is ______ ______ ______ ______.
(바로 그 다음 날)

M That's right! Hey, why don't we have a birthday party together?

W That's a good idea.

15 장소 추론

두 사람의 관계를 파악하여 장소를 추론한다.

대화를 듣고, 두 사람이 대화하고 있는 장소로 가장 적절한 곳을 고르시오.

① 집 ② 병원
③ 서점 ④ 교실
⑤ 백화점

M Did you ______ ______ ______?
(네 숙제를 다 하다)

W Yes, but I need your help.

M OK. What is it?

W I don't understand number 9.

M Oh, don't worry. I'll ______ ______ ______ to everyone later in class.
(숙제를 설명해 주다)

W Then I'll just ______ ______ ______ to you now.
(그것을 제출하다)

16 관계 추론

대화를 듣고, 두 사람의 관계로 가장 적절한 것을 고르시오.

① 아빠와 딸
② 의사와 환자
③ 교사와 학생
④ 상사와 직원
⑤ 손님과 점원

W What should I do now?

M Did you clean the storeroom?

W Yes. Should I ______ ______ ______ ______?
(매장 선반을 청소하다)

M That's a good idea. And then please open all the boxes here.

W Are they ______ ______?
(신상품들)

M Yes, they are. You need to put them on the shelves afterwards.

W When can I ______ ______ ______?
(쉬다)

M In about half an hour.

17 직업 파악

대화를 듣고, 여자의 직업으로 가장 적절한 것을 고르시오.

① 의사 ② 가게 점원
③ 약사 ④ 영양사
⑤ 요리사

W Okay, you don't ______ ______ ______. That's good news.
(열이 있다)

M Really? Does it mean I don't ______ ______ ______?
(독감에 걸리다)

W Yes, that's right. But you are coughing a lot.

M Yeah, and I ______ ______ ______ and a stuffy nose.
(두통이 있다)

W You have a cold. You should drink lots of water, and you should get lots of rest.

M Are you going to give me any medicine?

18 주제 파악

대화를 듣고, 무엇에 관한 내용인지 가장 적절한 것을 고르시오.

① 여자가 어제 한 일
② 친구들과 싸운 이유
③ 남자가 보고 싶은 영화
④ 두 사람이 영화를 볼 날짜
⑤ 여자와 친구들이 오늘 한 일

Kind of.는 '어느 정도는 그렇다.'는 의미이다.

M Did you ________ ________ ________ yesterday?
(재미있는 일을 하다)
W Kind of. We ________ ________ ________.
(영화를 봤다)
M Was it a good movie?
W Not really. It was kind of boring.
M What movie was it?
W It was called *Battle of Planets*.
M I'm sorry to hear that you did not enjoy it.
W It's okay. I still ________ ________ ________ ________ ________ my friends.
(~와 어울리며 즐거운 시간을 보냈다)

19 알맞은 응답 찾기

[19~20] 대화를 듣고, 여자의 마지막 말에 이어질 남자의 응답으로 가장 적절한 것을 고르시오.

Man: ________________

① Sorry, we don't have any rooms left.
② Good! Let me teach you how to swim.
③ Okay! Then, let's go to the hotel right away.
④ How long does it take from here to the beach?
⑤ Well... I want to eat spaghetti. What about you?

M Wow, look at the sea!
W Oh, it's really beautiful. The sea ________ ________ ________.
(매우 멋있어 보이다)
M That's right. Anyway, hurry up. I want to swim in the sea right away.
W Me too. But we ________ ________ ________ ________ the hotel first.
(체크인해야 한다)
M ________________

고난도

20 알맞은 응답 찾기

학원 수강 신청 과정을 떠올리며 대화를 듣는다.

Man: ________________

① Then, you should buy a textbook.
② No. I don't want to learn this program.
③ Can I use your computer for a minute?
④ Thank you. Please fill out this form first.
⑤ Really? When did you buy this computer?

W How much is this computer program course for beginners?
M It's $80 a month.
W Well... that's not very cheap. Ah, ________ ________ ________ ________ ________ a textbook?
(사야 하나요)
M No, you don't have to. We'll give you one ________ ________.
(무료로)
W That's good. Okay, ________ ________ ________.
(그 과정을 수강하겠다)
M ________________

그림 정보 파악

무엇을 평가하는가?	일상생활이나 친숙한 일반적 주제에 관한 그림 또는 사진에 관한 말이나 대화를 듣고 세부 정보를 파악할 수 있는지를 평가한다.
어떻게 출제되는가?	• 다음을 듣고, 'I'가 무엇인지 가장 적절한 것을 고르시오. • 다음을 듣고, 'this'가 가리키는 것으로 가장 적절한 것을 고르시오. • 대화를 듣고, 남자가 구입할 실내화로 가장 적절한 것을 고르시오. • 다음을 듣고, 오늘 날씨로 가장 적절한 것을 고르시오.

❶ 보기의 그림을 살펴보고 그림과 관련된 어휘들에 주위해서 듣는다.

❷ 날씨를 묻는 경우, 다른 시간대, 다른 요일, 다른 지역, 다른 나라의 날씨 등이 함께 언급되므로 주의하여 듣는다.

[기출로 전략 확인]

대화를 듣고, 여자가 설명하는 담요로 가장 적절한 것을 고르시오. [2017 기출]

①

②
AMY

③

④

⑤

❶ 담요를 보고 'dog', 'bird', 'name' 등의 어휘들을 예상해 볼 수 있다.

W Dad, did you see my blanket? I can't find it.
M What does it look like, Amy?
W It has a dog on it.
M Does it have anything else?
W It also has my name under the dog.
M Okay. Let's find it together.

여 아빠, 내 담요 봤어요? 못 찾겠네요.
남 담요가 어떻게 생겼니, Amy?
여 개 한마리가 있어요.
남 다른 건 없니?
여 개 아래에 제 이름이 있어요.
남 좋아. 같이 찾아 보자.

그림 정보 파악 유형의 발문과 보기

다음을 듣고, 일요일의 날씨로 가장 적절한 것을 고르시오. [2017 기출]

오답 찍는 문장 It will rain all day long today.
만점 잡는 문장 On Sunday it will be sunny.

다음을 듣고, 'this'가 가리키는 것으로 가장 적절한 것을 고르시오. [2017 기출]

만점 잡는 문장 ① You can watch video clips, take pictures, and play games on this.
② We can talk on this.

그림 정보 파악에 쓰이는 어휘 및 표현

● 사물

You can use this to wash the dishes or clothes. 설거지를 하거나 세탁할 때 이것을 사용할 수 있다.
This is round and has a handle. 이것은 둥글고 손잡이가 있다.
It shows twelve months and three hundred sixty-five days. 그것은 12달과 365일을 보여준다.
You can see this in a bathroom. 이것은 욕실에서 볼 수 있다.
We have to be careful because it breaks easily. 깨지기 쉽기 때문에 조심이 다루어야 한다.

● 동물

I have very strong and sharp teeth. 나는 아주 강하고 날카로운 이빨을 가지고 있다.
I can live both in the water and on the ground. 나는 물과 땅 양쪽에서 살 수 있다.
I have black lines on my body. 나는 몸에 검은 줄무늬를 가지고 있다.
I am a member of the cat family. 나는 고양이과에 속한다.

● 날씨

There will be rain all day long. 하루 종일 비가 오겠습니다.
Paris will be windy and very cold. 파리는 바람이 불고 매우 춥겠습니다.
It's raining a lot now, but it's going to stop tonight. 지금 비가 많이 내리고 있지만 오늘밤 그칠 예정입니다.
It'll be sunny and windy on Monday. 월요일은 화창하고 바람이 불겠습니다.
On Friday, the temperature will go down. 금요일은 온도가 내려가겠습니다.

영어듣기능력평가 03 회

학년 반 번
이름

01 다음을 듣고, 'this'가 가리키는 것으로 가장 적절한 것을 고르시오.

① 
② 
③ 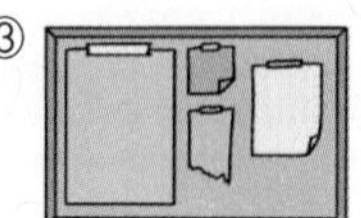
④ 
⑤ 

02 대화를 듣고, 메모리 스틱이 있는 곳을 고르시오.

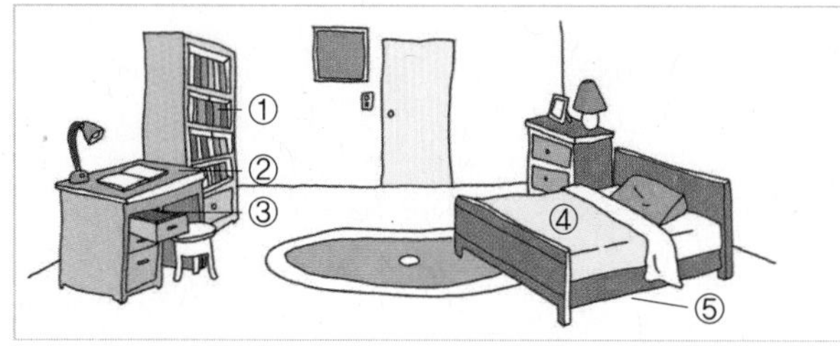

03 다음을 듣고, 내일 오후의 날씨로 가장 적절한 것을 고르시오.

① 
② 
③ 
④ 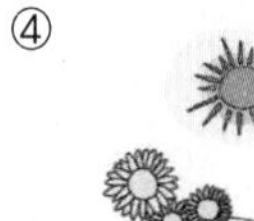

⑤ 

04 대화를 듣고, 여자가 언급한 아빠의 직업으로 가장 적절한 것을 고르시오.

① 의상 디자이너　② 기자
③ 건축가　④ 잡지 편집자
⑤ 시청 직원

고난도

05 대화를 듣고, 두 사람이 파티에 초청할 사람의 수를 고르시오.

① 18　② 20　③ 21
④ 22　⑤ 24

06 대화를 듣고, 남자가 여자를 위해 할 일로 가장 적절한 것을 고르시오.

① 상자 열기　② 상자 만들기
③ 상자 버리기　④ 상자 옮기기
⑤ 상자 포장하기

07 대화를 듣고, 남자가 내일 의사를 만나기로 한 시각을 고르시오.

① 1시 30분　② 2시
③ 2시 30분　④ 3시
⑤ 3시 30분

08 다음을 듣고, 두 사람의 대화가 <u>어색한</u> 것을 고르시오.

①　②　③　④　⑤

09 대화를 듣고, 두 사람이 대화하고 있는 장소로 가장 적절한 곳을 고르시오.

① 주차장　② 콘서트 홀
③ 자동차 안　④ 자동차 판매점
⑤ 전자제품 대리점

10 대화를 듣고, 남자가 내일 친구의 집에 가야 하는 이유로 가장 적절한 것을 고르시오.

① 책을 빌려야 해서
② 시험공부를 해야 해서
③ 게임을 같이 하기로 해서
④ 생일 파티에 참석해야 해서
⑤ 생일 파티 준비를 도와야 해서

점수 /20

11 대화를 듣고, 여자의 마지막 말의 의도로 가장 적절한 것을 고르시오.

① 수락 ② 요청
③ 사과 ④ 용서
⑤ 거절

12 다음을 듣고, 유라의 가족에 대해 언급되지 않은 것을 고르시오.

① 가족 수
② 즐겨 보는 운동 경기
③ 부모님 직업
④ 자주 가는 식당
⑤ 가족 식사 요일

13 대화를 듣고, 여자가 전화를 건 목적으로 가장 적절한 것을 고르시오.

① 학교 축제에 초대하려고
② 축제가 시작되는 날을 알려 주려고
③ 축제 포스터 붙이는 일을 부탁하려고
④ 포스터를 만들어 줄 것을 요청하려고
⑤ 공연을 함께 보러 갈 것을 제안하려고

14 대화를 듣고, 두 사람의 관계로 가장 적절한 것을 고르시오.

① 남편 – 아내
② 서점 주인 – 고객
③ 부동산업자 – 세입자
④ 가구점 점원 – 손님
⑤ 이삿짐 센터 직원 – 집주인

15 대화를 듣고, 남자가 가려고 하는 장소를 고르시오.

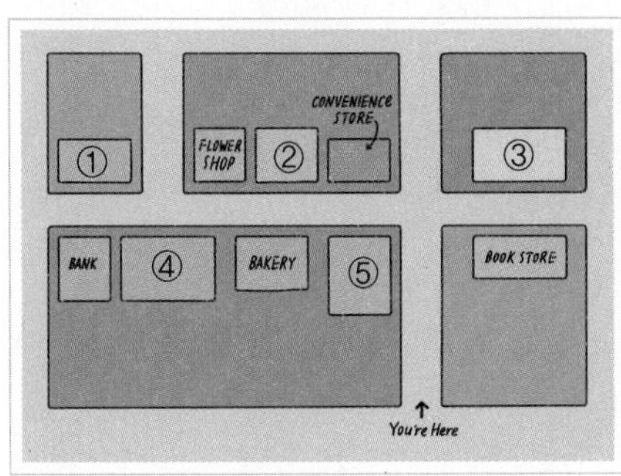

고난도

16 다음을 듣고, 무엇에 관한 내용인지 가장 적절한 것을 고르시오.

① 복습의 중요성
② 발표를 잘 하는 요령
③ 수업에 임하는 올바른 자세
④ 시험공부 계획을 세우는 방법
⑤ 교실 분위기를 좋게 하는 방법

고난도

17 다음을 듣고, pretzel에 대한 설명으로 일치하지 않는 것을 고르시오.

① 만들기 어려운 빵 간식이다.
② 매듭 모양이다.
③ 반죽은 하루 동안 숙성시킨다.
④ 반죽을 긴 줄로 만든다.
⑤ 긴 줄로 된 반죽을 꼬아서 굽는다.

18 대화를 듣고, 여자의 심정으로 가장 적절한 것을 고르시오.

① 화남 ② 슬픔
③ 행복함 ④ 무서움
⑤ 피곤함

[19~20] 대화를 듣고, 여자의 마지막 말에 이어질 남자의 응답으로 가장 적절한 것을 고르시오.

19 Man: ______________________

① Will you run today?
② Yes. I'm so hungry.
③ Sure. I'll go with you.
④ Are you gaining weight?
⑤ No, I don't enjoy eating.

20 Man: ______________________

① You're so kind.
② That's a good idea.
③ Let's get off the bus.
④ I like to walk in the park.
⑤ Thank you for helping me.

DICTATION

다시 들으면서 듣기 만점에 도전하세요!
Dictation: 스크립트의 주요 부분을 다시 들으면서!
실전 ⊕: 세부 정보가 많은 스크립트를 다른 문제로 샅샅이!

01 그림 "this" 파악(담화)

다음을 듣고, 'this'가 가리키는 것으로 가장 적절한 것을 고르시오.

① ② ③ ④ ⑤

M You can use this to ________ ________ ________ (편지를 보내다) or a postcard. You put your letter or postcard in this, and then someone will pick it up later. The color of this ________ ________ ________ (보통 빨간색이다). But not many people use this nowadays, because they ________ ________ (이메일을 사용하다). What is this?

02 그림 정보 파악 – 위치

대화를 듣고, 메모리 스틱이 있는 곳을 고르시오.

① ② ③ ④ ⑤

M Mom, I can't find my memory stick.

W Did you check on your desk or on the bed?

M Yes, I did. I even checked ________ ________ ________ (침대 아래), but I ________ ________ (그것을 찾을 수가 없었다).

W Then ________ ________ ________ (책장 위를 확인하다). You usually put your things on it.

M Oh, here it is. Thank you, Mom.

03 날씨 파악

tomorrow afternoon이 포함된 날씨 정보를 주의깊게 듣는다.

다음을 듣고, 내일 오후의 날씨로 가장 적절한 것을 고르시오.

① rain ② snow ③ wind ④ clear, sunny ⑤

W Here's the channel 9 weather report. Today ________ ________ ________ ________ ________ (청명하고 맑았다) and not too cold. I think you had a great day if you did something outdoors. However, ________ ________ ________ ________ (내일 아침에는 비가 올 것이다). And it will start to get very cold. The rain ________ ________ ________ ________ ________ (내일 오후에 눈으로 바뀔 것이다). So don't forget to wear your coat.

⊕ 다음을 듣고, 오늘의 날씨로 가장 적절한 것을 고르시오.

① rainy ② snowy ③ windy ④ sunny ⑤ foggy

04 직업 파악

대화를 듣고, 여자가 언급한 아빠의 직업으로 가장 적절한 것을 고르시오.

① 의상 디자이너 ② 기자
③ 건축가 ④ 잡지 편집자
⑤ 시청 직원

M Jihye, look at this photo. Isn't this your dad here?

W Yes, that's him. ________ ________ ________?
이게 뭐야?

M It's this month's city magazine. I got it from city hall.

W Cool, I didn't know he was in it.

M I didn't know he is a famous person. It's awesome.

W Yes, he ________ ________ ________ ________ in our city.
유명한 건물들을 디자인했다

M Wow, that's great.

고난도

05 숫자 파악

처음 초대장을 보낸 사람의 수와 잊고 보내지 않은 사람의 수를 계산한다.

대화를 듣고, 두 사람이 파티에 초청할 사람의 수를 고르시오.

① 18 ② 20
③ 21 ④ 22
⑤ 24

W Honey. Did you send invitation cards to people for our party?

M Yes, I did.

W How many invitation cards did you send?

M I sent the invitation cards ________ ________ ________.
20명의 사람들에게

W Did you send one to Tom and Mary?

M Oh, I forgot to send one to them. I'll ________ ________ ________ ________ ________ ________ tomorrow.
그들에게 각각 하나씩 보내다

W OK.

06 할 일 파악

Could(Can) you ~? 이후에 나오는 부분을 주의깊게 듣는다.

대화를 듣고, 남자가 여자를 위해 할 일로 가장 적절한 것을 고르시오.

① 상자 열기
② 상자 만들기
③ 상자 버리기
④ 상자 옮기기
⑤ 상자 포장하기

M What are you doing now?

W Can you help me with this box? It ________ ________ ________.
시간이 오래 걸리지 않을 것이다

M Sure. What do you want me to do with it?

W Could you move it for me? It's ________ ________ ________ ________ ________.
내가 들기에는 너무 무거운

M No problem at all. Where should I put it?

W Can you ________ ________ ________ ________ ________?
탁자 위에 그것을 놓다

M Of course. It's easy.

W Thank you.

07 숫자 파악 – 시각

대화를 듣고, 남자가 내일 의사를 만나기로 한 시각을 고르시오.

① 1시 30분　② 2시
③ 2시 30분　④ 3시
⑤ 3시 30분

Is that OK with you?는 상대방에게 자신의 의견이 괜찮은지 묻는 표현이다.

[Telephone rings.]

W Hello? This is Kim's Medical Clinic.

M This is Mr. Morgan.

W How can I help you, sir?

M I'd like to ________ ________ ________ with Dr. Kim tomorrow at two o'clock. (약속을 하다)

W I'm sorry. He has an appointment with another patient at that time.

M Then, how about three o'clock?

W I'm sorry. He isn't free then. ________ ________ ________ ________ ________. (그는 3시 30분에 시간이 있다) Is that OK with you, sir?

M Well, it's fine with me.

08 어색한 대화 찾기

다음을 듣고, 두 사람의 대화가 <u>어색한</u> 것을 고르시오.

①　②　③　④　⑤

How's it going these days?는 안부를 묻는 표현이다.

① **W** What subject do you like best?
M I like history best.

② **W** ________ ________ ________ ________ for America? (언제 떠날 거니)
M I ________ ________ at the airport. (막 도착했다)

③ **W** How's it going these days?
M I'm feeling good.

④ **W** Shall we ________ ________ ________ ________? (저녁 먹으러 밖에 나가다)
M Really? I'd love to.

⑤ **W** You look tired. What's wrong?
M I ________ ________ ________ ________ yesterday. (밤새 깨어 있었다)

09 장소 추론

도로 표지판을 보면서 대화를 나누고 있음을 파악한다.

대화를 듣고, 두 사람이 대화하고 있는 장소로 가장 적절한 곳을 고르시오.

① 주차장
② 콘서트 홀
③ 자동차 안
④ 자동차 판매점
⑤ 전자제품 대리점

W Honey, ________ ________ ________ ________ ________. (도로 표지판을 보다) We have to turn left.

M But the navigation system says we have to turn right.

W ________ ________ ________ ________, honey. (표지판을 믿어 보자)

M OK. *[Pause]* The sign was right. I can see the parking lot of the concert hall over there.

W We are almost there. ________ ________ ________ ________, honey. (운전해 줘서 고맙다)

10 이유 파악

대화를 듣고, 남자가 내일 친구의 집에 가야 하는 이유로 가장 적절한 것을 고르시오.

① 책을 빌려야 해서
② 시험공부를 해야 해서
③ 게임을 같이 하기로 해서
④ 생일 파티에 참석해야 해서
⑤ 생일 파티 준비를 도와야 해서

What's bothering you?는 상대방의 걱정거리나 아픈 곳을 묻는 표현이다.

W Do you have any plans for tomorrow?
M Yes, I am going to my friend's house tomorrow.
W Are you going to play games with him?
M No, he ________ ________ ________ ________ ________. (생일 파티를 열 것이다)
W But you don't seem so happy. What's bothering you?
M I have a big test next week so I ________ ________ ________ ________ ________ ________ ________ (집에서 공부하고 싶다). But I can't miss the party. He's my best friend.
W Just enjoy. You can study later.

11 의도 추론

I'd love to ~.의 의도를 파악한다.

대화를 듣고, 여자의 마지막 말의 의도로 가장 적절한 것을 고르시오.

① 수락 ② 요청
③ 사과 ④ 용서
⑤ 거절

I'd love to ~.는 제안을 수락하는 표현이다.

M Nora. Do you have a minute to talk with me?
W Sure. What do you want to talk about?
M Well, Tony and I are going to visit a hospital to ________ ________ ________ ________ (환자들에게 노래를 몇 곡 불러 주다). Would you join us?
W ________ ________ ________ ________ (나는 함께 하고 싶다) you guys.

12 언급 및 비언급 파악

다음을 듣고, 유라의 가족에 대해 언급되지 <u>않은</u> 것을 고르시오.

① 가족 수 four family members
② 즐겨 보는 운동 경기 baseball game
③ 부모님 직업
high school teacher, nurse
④ 자주 가는 식당
⑤ 가족 식사 요일 every Sunday evening

W Hi, my name is Yura. There are ________ ________ ________ (네 명의 가족) in my family: My father, my mother, my younger sister, and me. My family likes to ________ ________ ________ ________ (야구 경기를 보다) together. My father is a high school teacher. My mother is a nurse. Everyone is very busy, but we ________ ________ ________ ________ ________ (근사한 가족 저녁 식사를 하다) every Sunday evening.

13 전화 목적 파악

Can you help me ~? 이후에 나오는 부분을 주의깊게 듣는다.

대화를 듣고, 여자가 전화를 건 목적으로 가장 적절한 것을 고르시오.

① 학교 축제에 초대하려고
② 축제가 시작되는 날을 알려 주려고
③ 축제 포스터 붙이는 일을 부탁하려고
④ 포스터를 만들어 줄 것을 요청하려고
⑤ 공연을 함께 보러 갈 것을 제안하려고

[Telephone rings.]
M Hello?
W Hello, Daniel. This is Julie.
M Hi, Julie. ________ ________? (무슨 일이니)
W Actually, I ________ ________ ________ (네 도움이 필요하다). Can you help me ________ ________ ________ ________ (축제 포스터를 붙이다) around the school?
M No problem. Did you make the posters already?
W Yes, I did.
M Then, I can do that.
W Thank you.

14 관계 추론

대화를 듣고, 두 사람의 관계로 가장 적절한 것을 고르시오.

① 남편 – 아내
② 서점 주인 – 고객
③ 부동산업자 – 세입자
④ 가구점 점원 – 손님
⑤ 이삿짐 센터 직원 – 집주인

➕ 대화를 듣고, 대화 직후 남자가 할 일로 가장 적절한 것을 고르시오.

① 청소하기 ② 책상 옮기기
③ 소파 놓기 ④ 이삿짐 정리하기
⑤ 결과 보고하기

M Where should I ________ ________ ________, ma'am? (이 소파를 놓다)
W Put it over here, please. Be careful.
M This sofa is the last thing. ________ ________ your desk, books, and everything else. (우리는 이미 옮겼다)
W You did a good job!
M Thanks. ________ ________ ________ is very nice. (당신의 새 집)
W Thank you.

15 지도, 위치 파악

대화를 듣고, 남자가 가려고 하는 장소를 고르시오.

W Hi, Ujin. Where are you going?
M Well, I want to ________ ________ ________ ________, but I'm lost. (도서관에 가다)
W You have to walk one more block to the main street, and turn left.
M Oh, is it next to the bank?
W No, it's ________ ________ ________ ________. It's between the flower shop and the convenience store. (반대쪽에)
M Now I got it. Thanks!

고난도

16 주제 파악

수업과 관련된 어휘들, 즉 classroom, notes, class, lesson 등에서 단서를 얻는다.

다음을 듣고, 무엇에 관한 내용인지 가장 적절한 것을 고르시오.

① 복습의 중요성
② 발표를 잘 하는 요령
③ 수업에 임하는 올바른 자세
④ 시험공부 계획을 세우는 방법
⑤ 교실 분위기를 좋게 하는 방법

W You should sit at the front seat ________ ________ ________. (교실에서) And pay attention to your teacher. ________ ________ (필기를 하다) when the teacher speaks. Don't think about other things ________ ________ ________. (수업 중에는) Think only about the lesson. These things will help you get a good grade.

고난도

17 내용 일치 파악

남자가 하는 일과 여자가 하는 일을 구분하여 듣는다.

다음을 듣고, pretzel에 대한 설명으로 일치하지 않는 것을 고르시오.

① 만들기 어려운 빵 간식이다.
② 매듭 모양이다.
③ 반죽은 하루 동안 숙성시킨다.
④ 반죽을 긴 줄로 만든다.
⑤ 긴 줄로 된 반죽을 꼬아서 굽는다.

M Soft pretzels are ________ ________ ________. (맛있는 빵 간식) They have ________ ________ (매듭 모양의) and they are a little difficult to make. First, make dough. Let it sit ________ ________ ________. (그것이 더 커질 때까지) Then roll the dough into long strings. Then ________ ________ (그 반죽을 꼬아라) and bake it. Pretzels are hard to make, but easy to eat!

18 심정 추론

여자가 회사에서 처한 상황을 파악한다.

대화를 듣고, 여자의 심정으로 가장 적절한 것을 고르시오.

① 화남 ② 슬픔
③ 행복함 ④ 무서움
⑤ 피곤함

W Finally the day is over.

M What's up? Did you have a hard day?

W Yes. My boss ________ ________ ________ ________.
내게 화를 냈다

M Were you late for work?

W No, but I ________ ________ ________ ________ ________.
실수로 컴퓨터를 망가뜨렸다

M Oh. Was it an accident?

W Of course. But he was still angry and ________ ________ ________.
나를 울게 만들었다

M That's too bad. Well, sit down and rest now.

19 알맞은 응답 찾기

[19~20] 대화를 듣고, 여자의 마지막 말에 이어질 남자의 응답으로 가장 적절한 것을 고르시오.

Man: ____________________

① Will you run today?
② Yes. I'm so hungry.
③ Sure. I'll go with you.
④ Are you gaining weight?
⑤ No, I don't enjoy eating.

M Where are you going?

W I'm going to run. Nowadays I'm afraid ________ ________ ________.
나는 살이 찌고 있다

M Me too. So we ________ ________ ________ every day.
운동할 필요가 있다

W Right. So I'm running around the park now. ________ ________ ________ ________ ________ ________?
나와 함께 할래

M ____________________

20 알맞은 응답 찾기

여자가 How about ~?으로 제안하는 말을 주의깊게 듣는다.

Man: ____________________

① You're so kind.
② That's a good idea.
③ Let's get off the bus.
④ I like to walk in the park.
⑤ Thank you for helping me.

I've never been there.은 '거기에 가 본 적이 없어요.'라는 의미로, 경험을 나타내는 표현이다.

M It's already 2 o'clock. ________ ________ ________ ________ ________ the City Park?
언제 ~에 도착할까요

W I don't know. This is ________ ________ ________ ________ go there. How about you?
내가 ~하는 처음

M Me too. I've never been there.

W ________ ________ the bus driver?
~에게 물어보는 것이 어떨까요

M ____________________

영어듣기능력평가 04회

학년 반 번
이름

01 다음을 듣고, 'this'가 무엇인지 가장 적절한 것을 고르시오.

① 
② 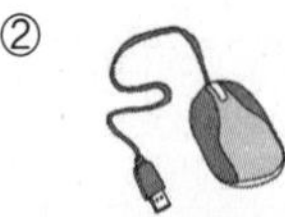
③  
④ 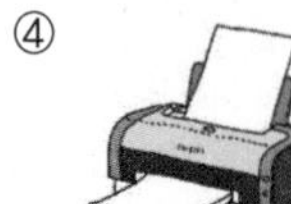
⑤ 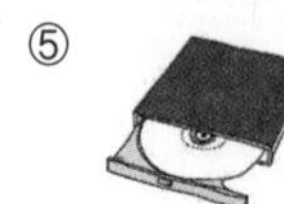

02 대화를 듣고, 두 사람이 보고 있는 물건으로 가장 적절한 것을 고르시오.

① 
② 
③  
④ 
⑤  

03 다음을 듣고, 내일의 날씨로 가장 적절한 것을 고르시오.

①  
②  
③  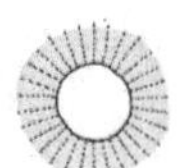
④ 
⑤  

04 대화를 듣고, 남자의 마지막 말의 의도로 가장 적절한 것을 고르시오.

① 초대
② 사과
③ 거절
④ 칭찬
⑤ 요청

05 대화를 듣고, 남자에 대한 설명으로 일치하는 것을 고르시오.

① 팔이 부러졌다.
② 주말에 스키를 타러 갔다.
③ 스키를 타다가 부딪쳤다.
④ 집에 오는 길에 넘어졌다.
⑤ 다리에 붕대를 감고 있다.

06 다음을 듣고, 두 사람의 대화가 <u>어색한</u> 것을 고르시오.

① ② ③ ④ ⑤

07 대화를 듣고, 두 사람이 출발할 시각을 고르시오.

① 6:00
② 6:15
③ 6:30
④ 6:45
⑤ 7:00

08 대화를 듣고, 여자가 전화를 건 목적으로 가장 적절한 것을 고르시오.

① 소풍을 같이 가려고
② 소풍 날짜를 물어보려고
③ 사진 촬영을 의뢰하려고
④ 이메일 주소를 확인하려고
⑤ 사진을 보내달라고 부탁하려고

09 대화를 듣고, 두 사람이 대화하고 있는 장소로 가장 적절한 곳을 고르시오.

① 커피숍
② 교문 앞
③ 수영장
④ 체육관
⑤ 버스 정류장

10 대화를 듣고, 여자가 원하는 것으로 가장 적절한 것을 고르시오.

① coffee
② spaghetti
③ pie
④ tea
⑤ ice cream

점수 /20

고난도

11 다음을 듣고, 'I'가 무엇인지 가장 적절한 것을 고르시오.

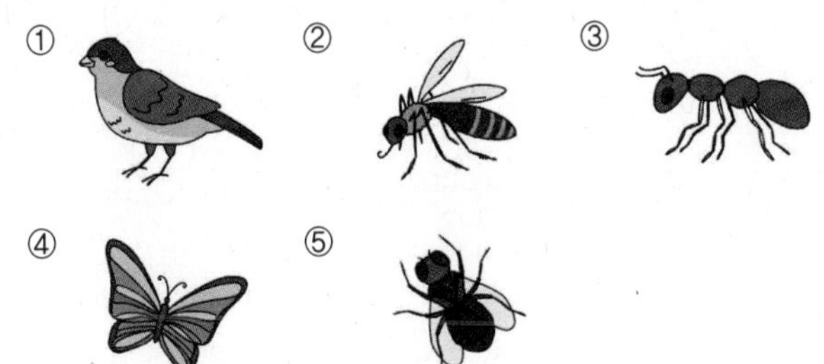

12 대화를 듣고, 두 사람의 관계로 가장 적절한 것을 고르시오.

① 손님 – 점원
② 아들 – 어머니
③ 직원 – 직장 상사
④ 학생 – 선생님
⑤ 남편 – 아내

13 대화를 듣고, 남자의 심정으로 가장 적절한 것을 고르시오.

① 외로움
② 슬픔
③ 행복함
④ 속상함
⑤ 자랑스러움

14 대화를 듣고, 남자가 가려고 하는 장소를 고르시오.

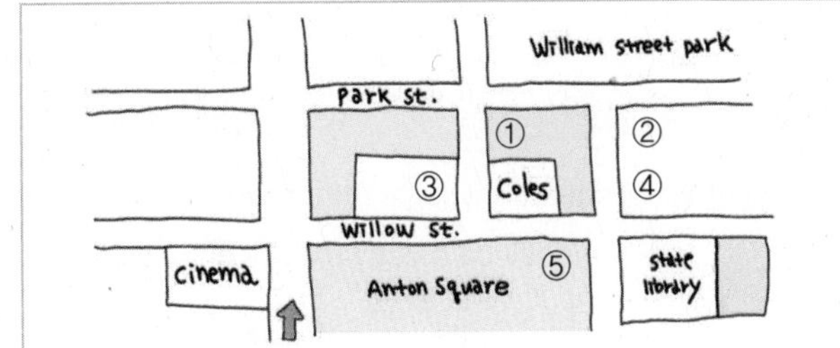

고난도

15 대화를 듣고, 남자가 Toronto에 머물 기간을 고르시오.

① one day
② two days
③ three days
④ four days
⑤ a week

16 다음을 듣고, 무엇에 관한 내용인지 가장 적절한 것을 고르시오.

① 반딧불이의 종류
② 반딧불이의 서식 조건
③ 반딧불이 이름의 유래
④ 반딧불이가 빛을 내는 이유
⑤ 반딧불이가 밝은 빛을 내는 시기

17 대화를 듣고, 여자가 Paul의 생일 파티에 갈 수 <u>없는</u> 이유로 가장 적절한 것을 고르시오.

① 몸이 아파서
② 엄마의 생신이어서
③ 여동생을 돌봐야 해서
④ 엄마의 병문안을 가야 해서
⑤ 친척집을 방문할 예정이어서

18 대화를 듣고, 여자가 남자에게 제안한 것으로 가장 적절한 것을 고르시오.

① 낮잠을 잘 것
② 집에 일찍 갈 것
③ 밤에 잠을 더 잘 것
④ 일찍 잠자리에 들 것
⑤ 더 좋은 침대를 살 것

[19~20] 대화를 듣고, 남자의 마지막 말에 이어질 여자의 응답으로 가장 적절한 것을 고르시오.

19 Woman: ______________________

① You should be more careful.
② Well, I'll go there this summer.
③ I'd like to go to a pop concert.
④ We're going to a movie tonight.
⑤ You'd better see a doctor right now.

고난도

20 Woman: ______________________

① Should I leave right now?
② I think you need some exercise.
③ Shall we drive to the department store?
④ How about going to the park for a walk?
⑤ Please put those bags around this corner.

다시 들으면서 듣기 만점에 도전하세요!
Dictation: 스크립트의 주요 부분을 다시 들으면서!
실전 ⊕: 세부 정보가 많은 스크립트를 다른 문제로 살살이!

01 그림 정보 파악 – 사물

save files, carry, small, connect 등을 통해 단서를 얻는다.

다음을 듣고, 'this'가 무엇인지 가장 적절한 것을 고르시오.

① ② ③ ④ ⑤

W This is a useful item when you use a computer. You can ________ ________ in it and ________ ________ ________ ________ ________ (파일을 저장하다 / 당신이 원하는 어느 곳이든 그것을 가지고 다니다). It's ________ ________ ________ ________ ________ ________ (당신의 주머니에 들어갈 만큼 작다). The files might be documents, video clips or MP3s. You can even put movies in it. Just connect this to any computer. You can access the files in it by clicking a folder.

02 그림 정보 파악 – 사물

대화를 듣고, 두 사람이 보고 있는 물건으로 가장 적절한 것을 고르시오.

① ② ③ ④ ⑤

M Are you going to buy it?
W Yes, ________ ________ ________ ________ ________ (나는 일어나기 위해 그것이 필요하다) in the morning.
M But don't you have a cell phone? Doesn't it have an alarm?
W It does, but I always turn off the alarm and go to sleep again.
M Do you mean you can't turn off this one?
W It's not easy. ________ ________ ________ ________ ________ (바퀴가 보이지)? After it rings, it ________ ________ (굴러다니다).

03 날씨 파악

오늘이 금요일이므로 내일은 주말이 된다.

다음을 듣고, 내일의 날씨로 가장 적절한 것을 고르시오.

① cloudy ② rain ③ nice, warm ④ snow ⑤

M Good morning. This is today's weather update. I'm your weather forecaster Steve Coyle. ________ ________ ________ (오늘은 금요일이다) and it'll be mostly cloudy but it won't be raining. ________ ________ ________ (주말에는), the weather will ________ ________ ________ ________ (날씨가 좋고 포근하다). On Monday, we are expecting rain but very little.

04 의도 추론

대화를 듣고, 남자의 마지막 말의 의도로 가장 적절한 것을 고르시오.

① 초대 ② 사과
③ 거절 ④ 칭찬
⑤ 요청

I'd really like to, but ~.은 '정말 그러고 싶지만, ~.'의 의미로, 상대방의 제안에 대해 거절할 때 사용하는 표현이다.

M What are you going to do this Saturday?

W I'm going to go shopping with my friend.

M Where are you going to go?

W To Dongdaemun. Do you ______ ______ ______ ______? (우리와 같이 가고 싶다)

M I'd really like to, but I ______ ______ ______ ______ on that day. (치과 진료 예약이 되어 있다)

05 내용 일치 파악

대화를 듣고, 남자에 대한 설명으로 일치하는 것을 고르시오.

① 팔이 부러졌다.
② 주말에 스키를 타러 갔다.
③ 스키를 타다가 부딪쳤다.
④ 집에 오는 길에 넘어졌다.
⑤ 다리에 붕대를 감고 있다.

That's too bad.는 '정말 안됐다.'는 의미로, 유감을 나타내는 표현이다.

W Jason, what happened to your leg? Why do you ______ ______ ______ ______? (깁스를 하다)

M I broke it.

W That's too bad. Did it happen yesterday?

M No, it was on Saturday.

W What happened? Did you go skiing?

M No. I ______ ______ ______ ______ on my way home. (얼음 위에서 넘어졌다)

06 어색한 대화 찾기

다음을 듣고, 두 사람의 대화가 어색한 것을 고르시오.

① ② ③ ④ ⑤

What does she(he) do?는 '그녀는(그는) 무엇을 하니?'라는 의미로, 직업을 묻는 표현이다.

의문사로 시작하는 의문문은 Yes / No로 답할 수 없음에 유의한다.

① **M** Did you like the movie?
W Yes, it was funny.

② **M** Is it 5 o'clock?
W Yes, it is.

③ **M** ______ ______ ______ ______? (뭘 먹을까)
W Yes, that's good.

④ **M** Where is the milk?
W It's ______ ______ ______. (냉장고 안에)

⑤ **M** What does she do?
W She's an English teacher.

07 숫자 파악 – 시각

대화를 듣고, 두 사람이 출발할 시각을 고르시오.

① 6:00
② 6:15 a quarter past six
③ 6:30
④ 6:45
⑤ 7:00

대화를 듣고, 음악회 시작 시간으로 가장 적절한 것을 고르시오.

① 6:00 ② 6:15
③ 6:30 ④ 6:45
⑤ 7:00

M Do you remember ________ ________ ________ ________ ________ tonight?
우리는 음악회에 갈 것이다

W Sure. When does the concert start?

M It begins at 7.

W Should we leave at 6:30? It will ________ ________ ________ ________ ________.
차로 15분 정도 걸리다

M That's too late. Before the concert, we have to eat something. Let's ________ ________ ________ ________ ________ ________.
6시 15분에 출발하다

W OK. Then we'll be able to have some snacks.

M All right. I'll pick you up at your house.

08 전화 목적 파악

Can you ~? 이후에 나오는 부분을 주의깊게 듣는다.

대화를 듣고, 여자가 전화를 건 목적으로 가장 적절한 것을 고르시오.

① 소풍을 같이 가려고
② 소풍 날짜를 물어보려고
③ 사진 촬영을 의뢰하려고
④ 이메일 주소를 확인하려고
⑤ 사진을 보내달라고 부탁하려고

[Telephone rings.]

W Hello, Nick. This is Sandy.

M Hi, Sandy. What's up?

W Well, I ________ ________ ________ ________ ________ ________ ________. I mean the pictures of our field trip.
나에게 사진을 보내달라고 부탁했다

M I sent them. I sent an e-mail with an attachment an hour ago.

W Oh, did you? But I didn't get it. ________ ________ ________ ________ one more time?
그것들을 보내 줄 수 있니

M OK. That's not difficult at all.

09 장소 추론

반복되는 어휘 waiting, bus 등에서 단서를 얻는다.

대화를 듣고, 두 사람이 대화하고 있는 장소로 가장 적절한 곳을 고르시오.

① 커피숍 ② 교문 앞
③ 수영장 ④ 체육관
⑤ 버스 정류장

M Hi, Miranda. Are you waiting for someone?

W Hi, Jack. ________ ________ ________ ________ ________ to the gym. I'm taking swimming lessons.
나는 버스를 기다리고 있다

M Wow. I'd like to go swimming, too. It's really hot.

W Where are you going?

M I'm going to my aunt's house. Oh, ________ ________ ________ ________. See you around.
버스가 온다

W See you. Bye.

10 특정 정보 파악

대화를 듣고, 여자가 원하는 것으로 가장 적절한 것을 고르시오.

① coffee ② spaghetti
③ pie ④ tea
⑤ ice cream

M Did you enjoy the dinner?

W Yes, I did. The spaghetti was great.

M I'm glad you enjoyed the meal. _________ _________ _________ _________ _________ _________? We have ice creams, pies and cakes.
후식은 무엇으로 하시겠어요

W I don't want dessert. _________ _________ _________ _________ _________?
차만 마셔도 될까요

M Of course. Do you need sugar or milk for your tea?

W With milk, please.

고난도

11 그림 "I" 파악(담화)

다음을 듣고, 'I'가 무엇인지 가장 적절한 것을 고르시오.

①

②

③

④

⑤

M I'm a kind of insect. I'm usually _________ _________ a fly or a mosquito. I have _________ _________ _________ _________, and they come with many different patterns. I fly from one flower to another flower. I eat nectar from those flowers. What am I?
~보다 큰 / 밝고 화려한 날개

12 관계 추론

대화를 듣고, 두 사람의 관계로 가장 적절한 것을 고르시오.

① 손님 – 점원
② 아들 – 어머니
③ 직원 – 직장 상사
④ 학생 – 선생님
⑤ 남편 – 아내

W Bill, _________ _________ _________ _________ _________ _________ for me?
이 쓰레기 좀 밖에 내다놓아 주겠니

M But _________ _________ _________ _________.
나는 학교에 늦었다

W It's only 8 o'clock and it won't take much time.

M All right.

W Don't forget to take your running shoes for _________ _________ _________. I washed them. They will be dry now.
네 체육 수업

M Oh, that's right. I almost forgot about them. Thank you.

➕ 대화를 듣고, 남자가 대화 후에 할 일로 가장 적절한 것을 고르시오.

① 운동화 빨기 ② 운동화 말리기
③ 시계 맞추기 ④ 아침 먹기
⑤ 쓰레기 내다버리기

13 심정 추론

대화를 듣고, 남자의 심정으로 가장 적절한 것을 고르시오.

① 외로움 ② 슬픔
③ 행복함 ④ 속상함
⑤ 자랑스러움

M Janet, can I borrow your math textbook?
W Sure, but what happened to your book?
M It's totally wet. Kelly ________ ________ ________ ________ (내 책상에 물을 엎질렀다) ________.
W Oh, no. Can you dry it?
M I don't think so. I guess I ________ ________ ________ ________ (새 것을 사야 한다) ________.
W Maybe Kelly will buy you another one.

14 그림 정보 파악 – 지도

turn right → one block → on your left로 이어지는 지시의 순서에 유의한다.

대화를 듣고, 남자가 가려고 하는 장소를 고르시오.

How can I get to ~?는 '제가 ~에 어떻게 갈 수 있나요?'라는 의미로, 길을 묻는 표현이다.

M Excuse me, ________ ________ ________ ________ (~에 어떻게 갈 수 있나요) the Saint George bus station?
W Walk up the street and ________ ________ ________ ________ (첫 번째 모퉁이에서 오른쪽으로 돌아라) ________. That's Willow Street. Walk down the street one block. The bus stop is ________ ________ ________ (당신의 왼쪽에) across Coles.
M Turn right on Willow Street and it's on the left across Coles.
W That's right.
M Thank you very much.

고난도

15 숫자 파악 – 날짜

캐나다에서 총 머무는 기간, Toronto와 Ottawa에서 각각 머무는 기간을 구분하여 듣는다.

대화를 듣고, 남자가 Toronto에 머물 기간을 고르시오.

① one day
② two days
③ three days
④ four days
⑤ a week

W ________ ________ ________ ________ (얼마나 머물 예정이니) in Canada?
M A week.
W Which cities are you going to visit?
M I have a business meeting ________ ________ ________ (Toronto에서 다음 주 월요일과 화요일에) ________ ________.
W What will you do after the meeting?
M I'll visit my friend in Ottawa and stay there for four days.
W Sounds great. Have a nice trip.

16 주제 파악

반복되는 어구 use light to ~를 주의 깊게 듣는다.

다음을 듣고, 무엇에 관한 내용인지 가장 적절한 것을 고르시오.

① 반딧불이의 종류
② 반딧불이의 서식 조건
③ 반딧불이 이름의 유래
④ 반딧불이가 빛을 내는 이유
⑤ 반딧불이가 밝은 빛을 내는 시기

W Fireflies get their names because they make light. Being able to light up has a few benefits for fireflies. Some fireflies use light to ________ ________ ________ (동물들을 겁 주어 떼어내다). Other fireflies use light to ________ ________ ________ ________ (다른 먹을 곤충들을 잡다). But most fireflies use light to ________ ________ ________ (진정한 짝을 찾다).

17 이유 파악

대화를 듣고, 여자가 Paul의 생일 파티에 갈 수 없는 이유로 가장 적절한 것을 고르시오.

① 몸이 아파서
② 엄마의 생신이어서
③ 여동생을 돌봐야 해서
④ 엄마의 병문안을 가야 해서
⑤ 친척집을 방문할 예정이어서

M I'll have a birthday party this Saturday.
W Really? Happy birthday, Paul.
M ______ ______ ______ ______ ______?
파티에 올 수 있니
W Thank you for inviting me, but my mom is in the hospital and I think I have to be home ______ ______ ______ ______ ______.
내 여동생을 돌보기 위해
M Oh, I didn't know that. I'm so sorry.
W That's all right. My mom will come home next week.

18 특정 정보 파악

you should ~ 이후에 나오는 부분을 주의깊게 듣는다.

대화를 듣고, 여자가 남자에게 제안한 것으로 가장 적절한 것을 고르시오.

① 낮잠을 잘 것
② 집에 일찍 갈 것
③ 밤에 잠을 더 잘 것
④ 일찍 잠자리에 들 것
⑤ 더 좋은 침대를 살 것

You should ~.는 충고나 조언을 나타내는 표현이다.

M I'm so tired.
W But it's only 3 o'clock.
M I know. I am always tired.
W Maybe you should ______ ______ ______.
낮잠을 자다
M But then I won't be able to sleep tonight.
W I think taking a nap ______ ______ ______ ______.
네 스트레스를 풀어 주는 데 도움을 주다
M Do you think so?
W Sure. But do not take a nap for ______ ______ ______ ______.
30분 이상
M OK. Wake me up in 30 minutes.

19 알맞은 응답 찾기

[19~20] 대화를 듣고, 남자의 마지막 말에 이어질 여자의 응답으로 가장 적절한 것을 고르시오.

Woman: ______________

① You should be more careful.
② Well, I'll go there this summer.
③ I'd like to go to a pop concert.
④ We're going to a movie tonight.
⑤ You'd better see a doctor right now.

M Where are you going this summer?
W I'm not sure. Do you ______ ______?
어떤 의견이라도 있다
M How about ______ ______ ______ ______?
제주도에 가는 것
W Jeju Island? Sounds great.
M I was there last summer.
W Really? How did you like it?
M ______ ______ ______.
환상적이었다
W ______________

고난도

20 알맞은 응답 찾기

호텔 프런트 데스크에서 가방을 맡기며 할 수 있는 대화를 생각해 본다.

Woman: ______________

① Should I leave right now?
② I think you need some exercise.
③ Shall we drive to the department store?
④ How about going to the park for a walk?
⑤ Please put those bags around this corner.

W Good afternoon. May I help you, sir?
M Yes. I'm going to Macy's Department Store before I ______ ______ ______.
이 호텔을 떠나다
W Then what can I help you with?
M Can you ______ ______ ______?
이 가방들을 봐 주다
W Sure. ______ ______ ______ do you have?
몇 개의 가방들
M Three.
W ______________

대화 내용 파악

무엇을 평가하는가?

일상생활이나 친숙한 일반적 주제에 관한 말이나 대화를 듣고 주제, 요지를 파악할 수 있는지를 평가한다.

어떻게 출제되는가?

- 대화를 듣고, 무엇에 관한 내용인지 가장 적절한 것을 고르시오.
- 대화를 듣고, 선생님의 무엇에 관한 내용인지 가장 적절한 것을 고르시오.

❶ 대화 초반에 주제나 소재가 되는 키워드 부분이 직접적으로 언급되므로 집중해서 듣는다.

[기출로 전략 확인]

대화를 듣고, 무엇에 관한 내용인지 가장 적절한 것을 고르시오. [2017 기출]

① 체육 대회 ② 합창 대회 ③ 봉사 활동
④ 영어 캠프 ⑤ 박물관 방문

W James, you look excited. What's new?
M Today my class will visit the Bike museum.
W Cool. What are you going to do there?
M We'll learn about the history of bikes.
W Will you do anything else?
M We'll also ride special bikes. It will be fun.

❶ 자전거 박물관을 방문하는 것에 관해 대화가 이어지고 있다.

여 James, 신이 나 보이는데. 무슨 일 있어?
남 오늘 우리 반이 자전거 박물관을 방문하거든.
여 좋겠다. 거기서 뭘 할 거야?
남 자전거의 역사에 대해 배울 거야.
여 다른 것도 해?
남 특별한 자전거도 탈 거야. 재미있을 거야.

대화 내용 파악 유형의 발문과 보기

대화를 듣고, 무엇에 관한 내용인지 가장 적절한 것을 고르시오. [2016 기출]

① 음악실 청소하기 ② 학용품 구입하기 ③ 컴퓨터 사용하기
④ 음악 숙제하기 ⑤ 책상 구입하기

만점 잡는 문장 **M** Nahee, we need to clean the music room now.

대화를 듣고, 무엇에 관한 내용인지 가장 적절한 것을 고르시오. [2016 기출]

① 학교 청소 ② 봉사 활동 ③ 장래 희망
④ 신체 검사 ⑤ 동물원 관람

만점 잡는 문장 **M** Hey, Jihye. What do you do for volunteer work?

대화 내용 파악에 쓰이는 표현

• 학교

What subject do you like the most? 가장 좋아하는 과목이 뭐니?

Your school sports day is next Monday, right? 너네 학교 운동회는 다음주 월요일이지?

Our homeroom teacher is going to get married this Saturday.
우리 담임 선생님이 이번 주 토요일에 결혼하셔.

We need to clean the music room now. 지금 음악실을 청소할 필요가 있어.

• 일상

I'm looking on the Internet for volunteer work to do. 인터넷으로 봉사 활동을 찾고 있어.

Do you have any plans for Chuseok? 추석에 뭐 할 거야?

What kind of movie do you want to see? 어떤 영화가 보고 싶어?

• 가족

Hi, how was your family trip last week? 안녕, 지난 주 가족 여행 어땠어?

I'm going to visit my grandparents with my family. 가족들과 조부모님 댁을 방문할 거야.

I ate seafood in Sokcho with my family. 가족들과 속초에서 해산물을 먹었어.

영어듣기능력평가 05 회

학년 반 번
이름

01 대화를 듣고, 여자가 가리키는 표지판으로 가장 적절한 것을 고르시오.

①
② 

③ 
④ 
⑤ 

02 대화를 듣고, 두 사람이 토요일에 하게 될 운동으로 가장 적절한 것을 고르시오.

① 
② 
③ 
④ 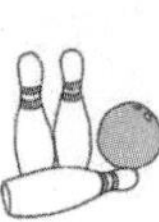
⑤ 

03 다음을 듣고, 부산의 내일 날씨로 가장 적절한 것을 고르시오.

① 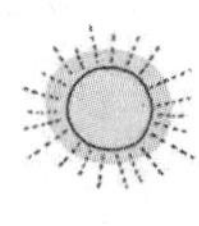
② 
③ 
④ 
⑤ 

04 대화를 듣고, 무엇에 관한 내용인지 가장 적절한 것을 고르시오.

① 가족 여행
② 새 학급 친구
③ 새 학기 계획
④ 이사 가는 친구
⑤ 새로 오신 선생님

05 대화를 듣고, 남자의 마지막 말의 의도로 가장 적절한 것을 고르시오.

① 동의 ② 거부
③ 격려 ④ 축하
⑤ 감사

06 대화를 듣고, 여자의 심정으로 가장 적절한 것을 고르시오.

① 화남 ② 흥분
③ 걱정 ④ 좌절
⑤ 슬픔

07 대화를 듣고, 남자가 기분이 나쁜 이유로 가장 적절한 것을 고르시오.

① 일자리를 구하지 못해서
② 카메라를 비싸게 구입해서
③ 디지털 카메라를 잃어버려서
④ 생물 시험 점수가 좋지 않아서
⑤ 여자가 자신에게 거짓말을 해서

08 대화를 듣고, 두 사람의 대화가 어색한 것을 고르시오.

① ② ③ ④ ⑤

09 대화를 듣고, 여자가 오늘 밤에 할 일로 가장 적절한 것을 고르시오.

① 아파트 청소하기
② 인터넷 게임 하기
③ 집에서 회사 일 하기
④ 청소 아주머니 알아보기
⑤ 남자를 집으로 초대하기

점수 /20

고난도

10 대화를 듣고, 두 사람이 만날 시각을 고르시오.

① 5시 30분 ② 6시
③ 6시 30분 ④ 7시
⑤ 7시 30분

11 다음을 듣고, 'this'가 가리키는 것으로 가장 적절한 것을 고르시오.

① 

③ 

12 대화를 듣고, 남자가 대화 직후에 할 일로 가장 적절한 것을 고르시오.

① 설거지하기 ② 요리 배우기
③ 커피 만들기 ④ 불고기 사러 가기
⑤ 텔레비전 시청하기

13 대화를 듣고, 여자가 가려고 하는 장소를 고르시오.

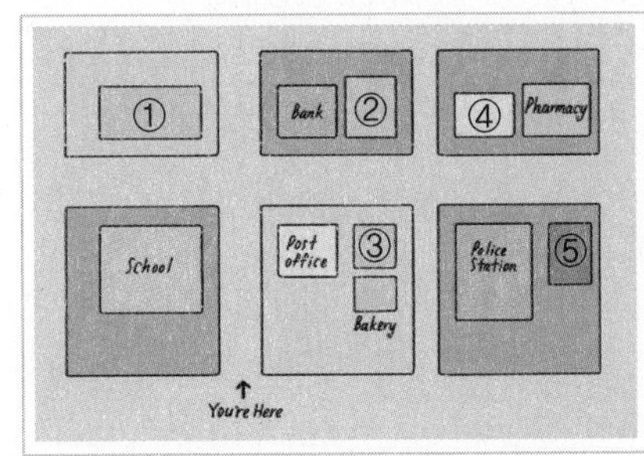

14 대화를 듣고, 남자의 장래 희망으로 가장 적절한 것을 고르시오.

① 선생님 ② 소설가
③ 신문 기자 ④ 패션 모델
⑤ 보석 디자이너

15 대화를 듣고, 두 사람이 대화하고 있는 장소로 가장 적절한 곳을 고르시오.

① 병원 ② 식당
③ 거실 ④ 공항
⑤ 기차역

고난도

16 대화를 듣고, 여자의 직업으로 가장 적절한 것을 고르시오.

① 시식코너 직원 ② 쇼핑몰 안내원
③ 옷수선점 직원 ④ 세탁소 직원
⑤ 옷가게 직원

17 대화를 듣고, 두 사람의 관계로 가장 적절한 것을 고르시오.

① 아버지 – 딸
② 남편 – 아내
③ 요리사 – 손님
④ 직장 상사 – 부하 직원
⑤ 비행기 조종사 – 승무원

18 대화를 듣고, 남자가 여자에게 부탁한 일로 가장 적절한 것을 고르시오.

① 창문 열어 주기
② 대신 운전해 주기
③ 현재 위치 알려 주기
④ 고속도로 요금 내 주기
⑤ 지도를 보고 방향 말해 주기

[19~20] 대화를 듣고, 남자의 마지막 말에 이어질 여자의 응답으로 가장 적절한 것을 고르시오.

19 Woman: ______________________

① I don't like mayonnaise, either.
② Sure! I like ham sandwiches a lot.
③ It's really delicious. You're a good cook.
④ Good! Here is $10 for the mayonnaise.
⑤ Wash your hands first before having dinner.

20 Woman: ______________________

① Okay, I'll buy the tickets for you.
② Then, where did you go last night?
③ I'm sorry, but I can't help you this time.
④ Then, let's see in front of the Hall at 6:30.
⑤ Really? But you like rock music, don't you?

다시 들으면서 듣기 만점에 도전하세요!
Dictation: 스크립트의 주요 부분을 다시 들으면서!
실전 ⊕: 세부 정보가 많은 스크립트를 다른 문제로 샅샅이!

01 그림 정보 파악 – 사물

swim, can't swim과 관계 있는 표지판을 고른다.

대화를 듣고, 여자가 가리키는 표지판으로 가장 적절한 것을 고르시오.

① ② ③ ④ ⑤

M Wow, this lake is very beautiful.
W Yeah, I think so, too.
M Hey, why don't we ________ ________ ________ ________ ? It'll be fun.
호수에서 수영하다
W John, look at the sign over there. It says we ________ ________ .
여기서는 수영을 할 수 없다
M Oh, I didn't see it.

02 그림 정보 파악 – 사물

대화를 듣고, 두 사람이 토요일에 하게 될 운동으로 가장 적절한 것을 고르시오.

① tennis ② soccer ③ baseball ④ bowling ⑤ volleyball

W Sam, ________ ________ ________ ________ with me this Sunday?
볼링 치러 갈래
M This Sunday? Sorry, I have something to do with my classmates.
W What are you going to do with them?
M We'll play basketball or soccer.
W Then, ________ ________ ________ ? If you're not busy, let's ________ ________ ________ .
토요일은 어때
그 날 볼링치러 가다
M Saturday? Okay, I'll go with you.

고난도

03 날씨 파악

'부산'에 대해 언급한 이후에 나오는 carry an umbrella, a heavy rain에서 단서를 얻는다.

다음을 듣고, 부산의 내일 날씨로 가장 적절한 것을 고르시오.

① clear, sunny ② cloudy ③ cold ④ rain ⑤

M Now take a look at the weather for tomorrow. Seoul and the Gyoung Ki area are going to have a clear and sunny Saturday. However, for the Chungcheong area, it will be cloudy and cold. If you are in Busan, please ________ ________ ________ .
우산을 챙기다
________ ________ ________ ________ from tonight until tomorrow.
많은 비가 내릴 것이다

⊕ 다음을 듣고, 토요일 서울과 경기 지역의 날씨로 가장 적절한 것을 고르시오.

① sunny ② cloudy
③ cold ④ rain
⑤ snowy

04 주제 파악

대화를 듣고, 무엇에 관한 내용인지 가장 적절한 것을 고르시오.

① 가족 여행
② 새 학급 친구
③ 새 학기 계획
④ 이사 가는 친구
⑤ 새로 오신 선생님

W What's up? You look sad.

M Did you hear Melanie is moving soon?

W No, I didn't. ________ ________ ________ ________?
그녀가 어디로 갈 거래

M Her family will go to America.

W When will they leave?

M In August. She said they'll move ________ ________ ________ ________ ________.
새 학기가 시작하기 전에

W That's too bad. I'll miss her.

05 의도 추론

대화를 듣고, 남자의 마지막 말의 의도로 가장 적절한 것을 고르시오.

① 동의 ② 거부
③ 격려 ④ 축하
⑤ 감사

W Hey, Jake. Are you going to the dance party?

M I don't know. I heard ________ ________ ________ ________ ________.
우리는 옷을 차려 입어야 한다

W Yes. Don't you have a suit?

M No. I have to buy one.

W It might be expensive, but ________ ________ ________ ________ ________.
한 번 살 가치는 있다

M You are right. I will need it, anyway.

06 심정 추론

I can't wait to ~.의 의미를 파악한다.

대화를 듣고, 여자의 심정으로 가장 적절한 것을 고르시오.

① 화남 ② 흥분
③ 걱정 ④ 좌절
⑤ 슬픔

I can't wait to ~.는 '몹시 ~하고 싶다.'는 의미로, 소망을 나타내는 표현이다.

W Great! My package finally arrived!

M Did it ________ ________ ________ ________ ________ ________ ________ ________?
여기 도착하는 데 오래 걸리다

W Yes, almost two months. I thought it would take one month.

M You waited for a long time.

W Yes. ________ ________ ________ ________ ________ ________.
나는 빨리 그것을 열어 보고 싶다

M Me too. I want to see it.

07 이유 파악

In fact, ~. 이후에 나오는 부분을 주의깊게 듣는다.

대화를 듣고, 남자가 기분이 나쁜 이유로 가장 적절한 것을 고르시오.

① 일자리를 구하지 못해서
② 카메라를 비싸게 구입해서
③ 디지털 카메라를 잃어버려서
④ 생물 시험 점수가 좋지 않아서
⑤ 여자가 자신에게 거짓말을 해서

W Peter, is there something wrong with you? You ________ ________ ________. (안 좋아 보이다)
M Do I? Nothing special.
W Hey, tell me. Did you get a bad score on the biology test?
M No. In fact, I ________ ________ ________ ________ in the afternoon. (내 디지털 카메라를 잃어버렸다)
W Really? You bought it just a week ago, didn't you?
M Yeah. I don't know ________ ________ ________ ________. (나는 왜 이렇게 부주의한지)

08 어색한 대화 찾기

다음을 듣고, 두 사람의 대화가 <u>어색한</u> 것을 고르시오.

① ② ③ ④ ⑤

① **M** Are you busy tomorrow?
W Yes, I am. I have to study all day for an English test.

② **M** Oh, the sky is ________ ________ ________ ________. (점점 더 어두워지고 있다)
W Right. It will rain soon.

③ **M** How about having seafood spaghetti for lunch?
W That's a good idea!

④ **M** Hey, where are you going now?
W To the post office.

⑤ **M** ________ ________ ________ ________ to London? (여행 어땠니)
W Sorry, I can't go with you this time.

09 할 일 파악

여자의 말 I should do that tonight.에서 that의 의미를 파악한다.

대화를 듣고, 여자가 오늘 밤에 할 일로 가장 적절한 것을 고르시오.

① 아파트 청소하기
② 인터넷 게임 하기
③ 집에서 회사 일 하기
④ 청소 아주머니 알아보기
⑤ 남자를 집으로 초대하기

+

대화를 듣고, 여자가 청소를 하지 못하는 이유로 가장 적절한 것을 고르시오.

① 적절한 도구가 없어서
② 집에 아무도 없어서
③ 일이 너무 바빠서
④ 이사온지 얼마 안 되어서
⑤ 치울 게 너무 많아서

W My apartment is ________ ________. (너무 지저분한)
M Why don't you clean it?
W I don't have time these days. I have extra work.
M You can ________ ________ ________ ________. (청소해 주는 아주머니를 찾다)
W Really? I should do that tonight.
M I can help you. I ________ ________ ________ ________ the other day. (웹사이트를 통해 한 명 찾았다)

고난도

10 숫자 파악 – 시각

뮤지컬 시작 시각(7 o'clock)과 만날 시각(one hour before)을 잘 듣고 계산한다.

대화를 듣고, 두 사람이 만날 시각을 고르시오.

① 5시 30분 ② 6시
③ 6시 30분 ④ 7시
⑤ 7시 30분

M Stella, what time does the musical start?

W At ________ ________ ________.
7시 정각

M Then, let's meet in front of the theater ________ ________ ________ the show starts.
1시간 전

W Don't you think it's too early?

M No. To have dinner, we need ________ ________ ________ ________.
30분 이상

W Maybe you're right. I see. See you later at the theater.

고난도

11 그림 "this" 파악(담화)

다음을 듣고, 'this'가 가리키는 것으로 가장 적절한 것을 고르시오.

① ② ③ ④ ⑤

M Many people use this ________ ________ ________. It has an electric motor, and it ________ ________ ________. Then, because the air moves in the room, you feel cooler. You can have this on the floor, on the wall, or even on the ceiling. What is this?
여름에 / 날개를 움직이다

12 할 일 파악

남자는 자신이 할 일을 Let me ~.를 사용하여 직접적으로 표현하고 있다.

대화를 듣고, 남자가 대화 직후에 할 일로 가장 적절한 것을 고르시오.

① 설거지하기
② 요리 배우기
③ 커피 만들기
④ 불고기 사러 가기
⑤ 텔레비전 시청하기

M Oh, I'm really full. I ________ ________ ________ ________.
더 이상 못 먹는다

W Me too. So, how was the *bulgogi*? Was it delicious?

M Yes, it was. I think you're a really good cook.

W My pleasure! I am glad you enjoyed the meal.

M ________ ________ ________ ________ ________. You just rest and watch TV.
내가 설거지를 할게

W Oh, thank you.

13 지도, 위치 파악

대화를 듣고, 여자가 가려고 하는 장소를 고르시오.

W Excuse me, is there a drugstore ________ ________?
이 근처에

M Hmm... let me think, yes! Go straight one block and turn right.

W Go straight and... Sorry?

M Turn right after walking one block from here, and walk about 20 meters.

W Okay, thanks, and?

M It'll be on your left side, ________ ________ ________ ________ ________.
경찰서 건너편에

14 특정 정보 파악

여자와 남자의 장래 희망을 구분하여 듣는다.

대화를 듣고, 남자의 장래 희망으로 가장 적절한 것을 고르시오.

① 선생님 teacher
② 소설가 novelist
③ 신문 기자
④ 패션 모델 fashion model
⑤ 보석 디자이너 jewelry designer

M Sara, what do you want to be in the future?

W Well... I want to become a fashion model or a jewelry designer.

M Wow, that's cool!

W What about you, Jason? Do you still want to be a teacher?

M No. I have a new dream. I ________ ________ ________ ________ ________.
소설가가 되고 싶다

W Oh, that's good. As you are ________ ________ ________, you'll become ________ ________ ________.
글을 잘 쓰는 / 훌륭한 작가

15 장소 추론

taking the train과 The train leaves에서 장소를 추론하는 단서를 얻는다.

대화를 듣고, 두 사람이 대화하고 있는 장소로 가장 적절한 곳을 고르시오.

① 병원 ② 식당
③ 거실 ④ 공항
⑤ 기차역

Why not?은 제안에 동의하는 표현이다.

W What time is it now?

M It's 5:40.

W Only 5:40? Oh, we still have to wait for one hour before ________ ________ ________.
기차를 타기

M Yeah, you're right. The train ________ ________ : ________.
6시 40분에 출발하다

W Hey, why don't we eat something? I feel a little bit hungry.

M Why not? Let's go downstairs. There are some restaurants there.

고난도

16 직업 파악

대화를 듣고, 여자의 직업으로 가장 적절한 것을 고르시오.

① 시식코너 직원 ② 쇼핑몰 안내원
③ 옷수선점 직원 ④ 세탁소 직원
⑤ 옷가게 직원

W Did you try them on? What do you think?

M I'm not sure. I think they're a little too tight.

W Would you like to ________ ________ ________?
더 큰 사이즈를 입다

M Yes, please.

W What size did you just try?

M Thirty. Actually, can I try both 31 and 32?

W Sure, ________ ________ ________. I will be right back.
잠시만 기다려라

17 실용문 정보 파악

핵심 어구 a day off, office 등을 통해 관계를 추론한다.

대화를 듣고, 두 사람의 관계로 가장 적절한 것을 고르시오.

① 아버지 – 딸
② 남편 – 아내
③ 요리사 – 손님
④ 직장 상사 – 부하 직원
⑤ 비행기 조종사 – 승무원

W Can I talk to you for a minute, Mr. Brown?

M Sure! What's up?

W Well... my parents are going to visit me tomorrow from England.

M Oh, I didn't know that your parents live there.

W They moved there last year. So, can I ________ ________ ________ ________ tomorrow and go to the airport to see them?
하루 휴가 내다

M Sure, you can. ________ ________ ________ ________ ________ tomorrow, just go to the airport.
사무실에 오는 대신에

W Thank you.

18 부탁 파악

Can you ~?와 Shall I~? 이후에 나오는 부분을 주의깊게 듣는다.

대화를 듣고, 남자가 여자에게 부탁한 일로 가장 적절한 것을 고르시오.

① 창문 열어 주기
② 대신 운전해 주기
③ 현재 위치 알려 주기
④ 고속도로 요금 내 주기
⑤ 지도를 보고 방향 말해 주기

W Could you drive today?
M Why? I thought you liked driving.
W Sometimes, but I don't know this area.
M OK, then. Can you ________ ________ ________. for me?
지도를 확인하다
W Sure. Shall I tell you ________ ________ ________ ________?
어느 길로 가야 하는지
M Yes, please. Only in the city, though.
W Do you know ________ ________ ________ ________ ________?
고속도로에서는 어디로 가야 하는지
M Yeah, I've been here before.

19 알맞은 응답 찾기

[19~20] 대화를 듣고, 남자의 마지막 말에 이어질 여자의 응답으로 가장 적절한 것을 고르시오.

Woman: ____________________

① I don't like mayonnaise, either.
② Sure! I like ham sandwiches a lot.
③ It's really delicious. You're a good cook.
④ Good! Here is $10 for the mayonnaise.
⑤ Wash your hands first before having dinner.

M Oh, I feel hungry. Do you have anything to eat?
W Just wait a minute. I'll make a sandwich for you.
M Thanks, Mom. If you need my help, please tell me.
W Then, can you go to the mart and ________ ________ ________ ________ ________?
마요네즈 한 통을 사다
M Sure! I can ________ ________ ________ ________ right away.
가게에 가다
W ____________________________________

20 알맞은 응답 찾기

함께 록 콘서트를 보러 가기 위해 만날 약속을 정하는 상황임을 파악한다.

Woman: ____________________

① Okay, I'll buy the tickets for you.
② Then, where did you go last night?
③ I'm sorry, but I can't help you this time.
④ Then, let's see in front of the Hall at 6:30.
⑤ Really? But you like rock music, don't you?

Don't mention it.은 '천만에.'라는 의미로, 감사에 대한 응답의 표현이며, You're welcome.과 바꿔 말할 수 있다.

M Alice, why don't we go to the Seven Star Concert Hall this evening?
W To the Seven Star Concert Hall?
M Yeah, I ________ ________ ________ for a rock concert.
무료 입장권이 있다
W Really? I like rock music a lot. Thank you, Andy.
M Don't mention it.
W ________ ________ ________ ________ ________?
콘서트가 몇 시에 시작하니
M At 7 o'clock.
W ____________________________________

영어듣기능력평가 06회

학년 반 번
이름

01 다음을 듣고, 'these'가 가리키는 것으로 가장 적절한 것을 고르시오.

① 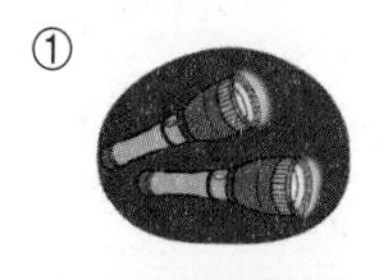
② 
③ 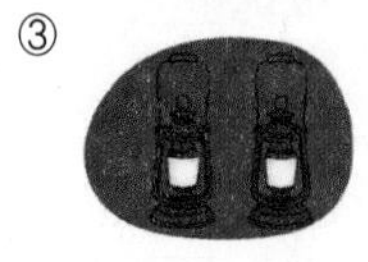
④ 
⑤ 

02 대화를 듣고, 여자가 그리게 될 대상을 고르시오.

① 
② 
③ 
④ 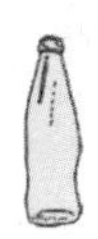
⑤ 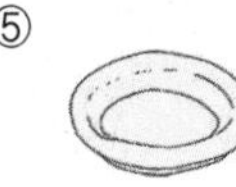

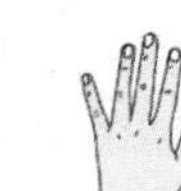

03 다음을 듣고, 내일 날씨로 가장 적절한 것을 고르시오.

① 
② 
③  
④  
⑤ 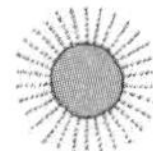

04 대화를 듣고, 남자가 할 일로 가장 적절한 것을 고르시오.

① 외식하러 가기
② 부모님 방문하기
③ 고기 주문하기
④ 파티에 참석하기
⑤ 파티 계획 세우기

05 다음을 듣고, 두 사람의 대화가 어색한 것을 고르시오.

① ② ③ ④ ⑤

고난도

06 대화를 듣고, 두 사람의 수업 시작 시각을 고르시오.

① 9:00
② 10:00
③ 10:10
④ 10:15
⑤ 10:45

07 대화를 듣고, 남자가 전화를 건 목적으로 가장 적절한 것을 고르시오.

① 수학 숙제에 대해 물어보려고
② 수학 문제의 해법을 알려 주려고
③ 학교에 결석한 이유를 말하려고
④ 숙제를 도와줄 것을 부탁하려고
⑤ 병원에 함께 가자고 제안하려고

08 대화를 듣고, 남자가 가려고 하는 장소를 고르시오.

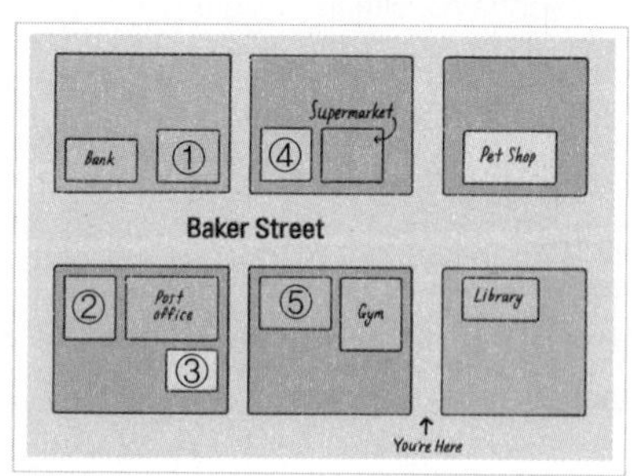

09 대화를 듣고, 남자가 전공하고 싶어 하는 분야로 가장 적절한 것을 고르시오.

① 수학
② 언어학
③ 역사학
④ 광고학
⑤ 컴퓨터 공학

10 대화를 듣고, 여자가 기뻐하는 이유로 가장 적절한 것을 고르시오.

① 복권에 당첨되어서
② 수학 점수를 잘 받아서
③ 독후감 대회에서 우승해서
④ 새로운 남자 친구가 생겨서
⑤ 갖고 싶은 책을 선물 받아서

점수 /20

11 다음을 듣고, Jack에 대해 언급되지 않은 것을 고르시오.

① 학년
② 동아리 가입 동기
③ 장래 희망
④ 좋아하는 운동
⑤ 좋아하는 TV 프로그램

12 대화를 듣고, 여자가 남자에게 제안한 것으로 가장 적절한 것을 고르시오.

① 샴푸 바꾸기
② 매일 머리 감기
③ 두피 크림 바르기
④ 샴푸의 양 줄이기
⑤ 머리 염색 그만하기

13 대화를 듣고, 여자의 마지막 말의 의도로 가장 적절한 것을 고르시오.

① 거절 ② 격려
③ 감사 ④ 주의
⑤ 동의

14 대화를 듣고, 체육대회가 열릴 날짜를 고르시오.

① May 5 ② May 12
③ May 17 ④ May 19
⑤ May 22

15 대화를 듣고, 두 사람이 대화하고 있는 장소로 가장 적절한 곳을 고르시오.

① hotel ② library
③ bookstore ④ classroom
⑤ post office

16 대화를 듣고, 여자의 심정으로 가장 적절한 것을 고르시오.

① excited ② bored
③ proud ④ interested
⑤ disappointe

17 대화를 듣고, 두 사람의 관계로 가장 적절한 것을 고르시오.

① 교사와 학생
② 의사와 환자
③ 점원과 고객
④ 어머니와 아들
⑤ 의사와 간호사

고난도
18 대화를 듣고, 복사에 필요한 종이의 수를 고르시오.

① 2 ② 5
③ 10 ④ 12
⑤ 20

[19~20] 대화를 듣고, 남자의 마지막 말에 이어질 여자의 응답으로 가장 적절한 것을 고르시오.

19 Woman: ______________________

① I had a good time in France.
② French is not easy for me, either.
③ Right. I can practice my French then.
④ Yes. I have to go shopping for the trip.
⑤ Why not? I want to take a trip together.

20 Woman: ______________________

① No. I am not good at vacuuming.
② Good. I want to buy the same one.
③ Yes. Mine got fine after vacuuming it out.
④ That's right. The computer will not working.
⑤ Yes. You need to take it to the repair shop.

영어듣기능력평가 06회 DICTATION

다시 들으면서 듣기 만점에 도전하세요!
Dictation: 스크립트의 주요 부분을 다시 들으면서!
실전 ⊕: 세부 정보가 많은 스크립트를 다른 문제로 샅샅이!

01 그림 "these" 파악(담화)

다음을 듣고, 'these'가 가리키는 것으로 가장 적절한 것을 고르시오.

① ② ③ ④ ⑤

M You can use one of these when the ________ ________ ________(전기가 나가다). It will give you some light in a dark room. Or, you can use these on your birthday. After your friends sing "Happy Birthday," you ________ ________ ________(소원을 빌다) and blow these out. What are these?

02 그림 정보 파악 – 사물

여자의 마지막 말 중 I will draw ~.에 주목하여 듣는다.

대화를 듣고, 여자가 그리게 될 대상을 고르시오.

① bicycle ② apple ③ hand ④ bottle ⑤

M What are you drawing for homework?
W I don't know. I was going to ________ ________ ________(자전거를 그리다) at first. But I changed my mind.
M Why?
W I thought it was too hard for me.
M Then, ________ ________ ________ ________ ________(사과나 손은 어때)?
W My friends are drawing them. So I will ________ ________ ________(병을 그리다).
M Sounds good.

고난도

03 날씨 파악

tomorrow 이후에 언급된 날씨 정보를 주의깊게 듣는다.

다음을 듣고, 내일 날씨로 가장 적절한 것을 고르시오.

① ② windy ③ ④ rain ⑤ nice

W Good evening. Here's the weather forecast. ________ ________(오늘은 날씨가 좋았다) enough to go out. But tomorrow will be a little different. ________ ________ ________ ________ ________(바람이 아주 많이 불 것이다) all day and you will feel very cold. But you don't have to take your umbrella with you when you go out. We will ________ ________(내일은 비가 오지 않다) ________.

04 할 일 파악

대화를 듣고, 남자가 할 일로 가장 적절한 것을 고르시오.

① 외식하러 가기
② 부모님 방문하기
③ 고기 주문하기
④ 파티에 참석하기
⑤ 파티 계획 세우기

Is there anything I can do for you?는 상대방에게 도와줄 일이 있는지 묻는 표현이다.

M Is there anything I can do for you, honey?
W Well, we ________ ________ ________ ________ online today.
(고기를 주문해야 한다)
M Why is that?
W My parents will visit us this Saturday. We're going to have a barbecue party.
M I see. How much meat should I order?
W ________ ________ ________, please.
(3킬로그램을 주문하라)
M Okay. I'll do it right away.

05 어색한 대화 찾기

다음을 듣고, 두 사람의 대화가 어색한 것을 고르시오.

① ② ③ ④ ⑤

What time do you have?는 현재 시각을 묻는 표현이다.

① W Would you tell me the way to the post office?
M Sure. Turn right and ________ ________ ________.
(그것은 당신의 왼편에 있다)
② W I ________ ________ ________ ________.
(바이올린 수업을 받고 싶다)
M Really? I just ________ ________ ________.
(이 바이올린을 샀다)
③ W Can I get you something to eat?
M Thank you. I'm so hungry.
④ W What time do you have?
M It's 9:30.
⑤ W I enjoyed the party. Thank you for inviting me.
M I am so happy to hear that.

고난도

06 숫자 파악 – 시각

현재 시각(10:10)과 수업까지 남은 시간(five minutes)을 잘 듣고 계산한다.

대화를 듣고, 두 사람의 수업 시작 시각을 고르시오.

① 9:00
② 10:00
③ 10:10
④ 10:15
⑤ 10:45

W Hurry up! We are late for the class. ________ ________ ________ : ________!
(벌써 10시 10분이다)
M Don't worry. We have time.
W Are you kidding? The class started at 10:00, didn't it?
M We still have ________ ________ ________.
(5분 남은)
W Are you sure?
M ________ ________ ________ because his 9 o'clock class ends at 10:10.
(그 후에 시작하다)
W I see. That gives us five minutes to get to class.
M Right. The class is a bit longer than ours.

07 전화 목적 파악

I'm calling ~. 이후에 나오는 부분을 주의깊게 듣는다.

대화를 듣고, 남자가 전화를 건 목적으로 가장 적절한 것을 고르시오.

① 수학 숙제에 대해 물어보려고
② 수학 문제의 해법을 알려 주려고
③ 학교에 결석한 이유를 말하려고
④ 숙제를 도와줄 것을 부탁하려고
⑤ 병원에 함께 가자고 제안하려고

[Telephone rings.]

W Hello.

M Hi! Jenny. It's me, Tom.

W Hi, Tom. Are you getting better? How's your cold?

M I'm feeling better. Thank you for asking. By the way, I'm calling to ________ ________ ________ ________ ________. (수학 숙제에 대해 물어보다)

W Let me tell you about it. The math teacher told us to ________ ________ ________ (문제들을 풀다) on page 16.

M Did he say just one page?

W Yes. We were so happy to hear that.

고난도

08 지도, 위치 파악

대화를 듣고, 남자가 가려고 하는 장소를 고르시오.

Bank ① ④ Supermarket Pet Shop
Baker Street
② Post office ③ ⑤ Gym Library
You're Here

W You look lost. Do you need any help?

M Oh, yes, please. I'm looking for White Lion.

W Oh, I know that restaurant. Go straight to Baker Street, and turn left ________ (모퉁이에서) ________ ________.

M White Lion is on Baker Street?

W Yes, it is. After you turn left, walk one more block. Then cross the street. It's ________ (큰 우체국 옆에) ________ ________ ________ ________ ________ and across from a bank.

M Thank you so much.

09 특정 정보 파악

남자가 과거에 전공하고 싶어 했던 것과 현재 전공하고 싶어 하는 것을 구분하여 듣는다.

대화를 듣고, 남자가 전공하고 싶어 하는 분야로 가장 적절한 것을 고르시오.

① 수학 math
② 언어학 language
③ 역사학 history
④ 광고학
⑤ 컴퓨터 공학 computer engineering

M Sarah, what do you want to study in the university?

W I want to study math. What about you?

M When I was young I wanted to ________ ________ ________ (역사학이나 언어학을 전공하다) ________. But later I ________ ________ ________ (내 마음을 바꾸었다).

W So what do you want to study?

M I want to ________ ________ ________ (컴퓨터 공학을 공부하다).

W Sounds interesting.

⊕ 대화를 듣고, 여자가 전공하고 싶어하는 분야로 가장 적절한 것을 고르시오

① 수학 ② 언어학 ③ 역사학
④ 광고학 ⑤ 컴퓨터 공학

10 이유 파악

대화를 듣고, 여자가 기뻐하는 이유로 가장 적절한 것을 고르시오.

① 복권에 당첨되어서
② 수학 점수를 잘 받아서
③ 독후감 대회에서 우승해서 win the first prize in the Book Report Contest
④ 새로운 남자 친구가 생겨서
⑤ 갖고 싶은 책을 선물 받아서

M You look so happy. Please tell me the reason. I want to share your happiness with you.

W Guess what, Henry.

M You got a good grade in math, or you got a new boyfriend?

W Well, no. It's more than that. Let me give you a hint. It's ________ (나의 작문에 관한) ________ ________.

M Did you ________ (우승하다) ________ ________ ________ in the Book Report Contest?

W Exactly! I'm so happy about that.

11 언급 및 비언급 파악

다음을 듣고, Jack에 대해 언급되지 않은 것을 고르시오.

① 학년 the first grade
② 동아리 가입 동기 to make good friends
③ 장래 희망 TV reporter
④ 좋아하는 운동 basketball
⑤ 좋아하는 TV 프로그램

M Nice to meet you all. My name is Jack Tyler. I'm in ______ ______ ______ of middle school. (1학년) I joined this biking club ______ ______ ______ ______. (좋은 친구들을 사귀기 위해) Someday I want to ______ ______ ______ ______. (TV 기자가 되다) I will interview famous people. I like to play basketball on weekends. I ______ ______ ______ ______ (농구를 하고 싶다) with you guys sometime in the future.

12 특정 정보 파악

제안의 표현인 how about ~? 이후에 나오는 부분을 주의깊게 듣는다.

대화를 듣고, 여자가 남자에게 제안한 것으로 가장 적절한 것을 고르시오.

① 샴푸 바꾸기
② 매일 머리 감기
③ 두피 크림 바르기
④ 샴푸의 양 줄이기
⑤ 머리 염색 그만하기

「stop A from B」는 'A가 B하지 못하게 하다'라는 의미로 stop 대신 keep, prevent 등을 쓸 수 있다.

M These days my hair is falling out. I don't know why.

W Do you ______ ______ ______ ______ ______? (매일 당신의 머리를 감다)

M Not every day, but once every two days.

W Then ______ ______ ______ ______ ______ into this one? (당신의 샴푸를 바꾸는 게 어떨까요)

M Would it help?

W Well, this shampoo stops your hair from falling out.

13 의도 추론

대화를 듣고, 여자의 마지막 말의 의도로 가장 적절한 것을 고르시오.

① 거절
② 격려
③ 감사
④ 주의
⑤ 동의

W What are you doing, Matt?

M I'm looking for my notebook. I think ______ ______. (나는 그것을 잃어버렸다)

W Is this your notebook?

M Oh! Yes. Where did you find it?

W In the classroom. You ______ ______ ______ yesterday. (그것을 거기에 놓고 갔다)

M Thank you, Mrs. Olsen.

W ______ ______ not to misplace your things. (주의해라)

14 숫자 파악 – 날짜

오늘의 날짜(May 12th)와 체육대회까지 남은 날짜(five days)를 잘 듣고 계산한다.

대화를 듣고, 여자의 마지막 말의 의도로 가장 적대화를 듣고, 체육대회가 열릴 날짜를 고르시오.

① May 5
② May 12
③ May 17
④ May 19
⑤ May 22

Same here.는 동의를 나타내는 표현이다.

M I can't wait for our school's sports day next week.

W Same here. ______ ______ ______ ______? (오늘이 며칠이지)

M ______ ______ ______. (5월 12일이다) We ______ ______ ______ ______ ______. (앞으로 5일 남았다)

W I feel excited.

M Me too. This is my first sports day in middle school.

W I'm sure we'll have a lot of fun on that day.

15 장소 추론

핵심어구 book, check out 등이 장소를 추론하는 단서이다.

대화를 듣고, 두 사람이 대화하고 있는 장소로 가장 적절한 곳을 고르시오.

① hotel 호텔
② library 도서관
③ bookstore 서점
④ classroom 교실
⑤ post office 우체국

⊕ 대화를 듣고, 남자가 책을 빌리지 못하는 이유로 가장 적절한 것을 고르시오.

① 자격이 되지 않아서
② 대여 불가한 책이라서
③ 구비되어 있지 않은 책이라서
④ 이미 대여중인 책이라서
⑤ 예약이 필요한 책이라서

W May I help you?

M Yes. I have a project and I ________ ________ ________ *The Family*.
책이 필요하다

W Well, let me check. *[Pause]* I'm sorry, but somebody has already ________ ________ ________ ________. You have to wait for a few days.
그 책을 대출했다

M A few days? Exactly how long do I have to wait for?

W It is going to come back next Monday. I mean, you have to wait for four days.

M I see.

16 심정 파악

대화를 듣고, 여자의 심정으로 가장 적절한 것을 고르시오.

① excited ② bored
③ proud ④ interested
⑤ disappointed

W I can't wait for Friday.

M Because of the field trip?

W Yes, I've always wanted to ________ ________ ________ ________!
새로 생긴 동물원에 가다

M Oh, didn't you hear? The school changed the field trip.

W ________ ________, what do you mean?
안 돼

M The weather forecast says it'll rain Friday, so we're going to the science museum instead.

W What? That sounds boring!

17 관계 추론

stomachache, medicine, headache 등의 어휘를 단서로 이용한다.

대화를 듣고, 두 사람의 관계로 가장 적절한 것을 고르시오.

① 교사와 학생
② 의사와 환자
③ 점원과 고객
④ 어머니와 아들
⑤ 의사와 간호사

How do you feel today?는 '오늘 기분이 어때요?'라는 의미로, 안부를 묻는 표현이다.

W Hello, Mr. Johnson. How do you feel today?

M A little better. But I ________ ________ ________ ________.
여전히 복통이 있다

W Did the medicine I gave you yesterday help you?

M Yes, I think so. I ________ ________ ________ ________ ________.
더 이상 두통은 없다

W In that case, keep taking it and see me tomorrow.

M Yes, I'll do that.

고난도

18 숫자 파악

2페이지 짜리 서류 10부를 양면 복사하는 상황임을 파악한다.

대화를 듣고, 복사에 필요한 종이의 수를 고르시오.

① 2　② 5
③ 10　④ 12
⑤ 20

M Can you make copies of this document?
W Sure. How many copies do you need?
M ________ ________. But it's only ________ ________ ________.
　10부　2페이지짜리
W Do you want ________ ________ ________ ________ ________?
　양면 복사
M Yes. Then we don't have to staple it.
W That's good. Then we will only need ________ ________ ________ ________.
　10장의 종이
M Yes, I'd like to save paper whenever possible.
W OK. They will be ready in about 5 minutes.

19 알맞은 응답 찾기

[19~20] 대화를 듣고, 남자의 마지막 말에 이어질 여자의 응답으로 가장 적절한 것을 고르시오.

Woman: ________________

① I had a good time in France.
② French is not easy for me, either.
③ Right. I can practice my French then.
④ Yes. I have to go shopping for the trip.
⑤ Why not? I want to take a trip together.

M Which language are you taking this semester?
W I'm thinking of taking French. Do you want to take it with me?
M I think it's too difficult for me.
W Actually my family is planning to ________ ________ ________ ________ this summer.
　프랑스로 여행을 가다
M Sounds nice. ________ ________ ________ you want to take French.
　그것이 이유이다
W ________________

20 알맞은 응답 찾기

Woman: ________________

① No. I am not good at vacuuming.
② Good. I want to buy the same one.
③ Yes. Mine got fine after vacuuming it out.
④ That's right. The computer will not working.
⑤ Yes. You need to take it to the repair shop.

W What's wrong with the computer?
M It doesn't start at all.
W Maybe it's because there is a lot of ________ ________ ________.
　컴퓨터 안에 있는 먼지
Before you take it to the repair shop, try to vacuum out all the dust in it.
M ________ ________ ________ ________ ________ ________?
　같은 경험을 해 보셨나요
W ________________

어색한 대화 찾기

무엇을 평가하는가?	일상생활이나 친숙한 일반적 주제에 관한 말이나 대화를 듣고 화자의 의도나 목적을 추론할 수 있는지를 평가한다.
어떻게 출제되는가?	• 대화를 듣고, 두 사람의 대화가 어색한 것을 고르시오.

❶ 의문사로 시작하는 의문문은 Yes/No의 답변을 취할 수 없고, 의문사가 답변의 단서가 되므로 집중하며 듣는다.

❷ 조동사, be동사, 일반동사 do로 시작하는 의문문은 Yes / No로 답변하는 경우가 많다.

[기출로 전략 확인]

대화를 듣고, 두 사람의 대화가 어색한 것을 고르시오. [2015 기출]

① ② ③ ④ ⑤

① **W** What time is it?
M It's ten to three.

② **W** Can I borrow your pen?
M I was there, too.

③ **W** I got a cold.
M Oh, that's too bad.

④ **W** Can I have some cookies?
M Sure. Help yourself.

⑤ **W** How can I get to the bus stop?
M Turn left at the corner.

❶ 'Can I borrow ~?'라는 허락을 구하는 질문에 허락의 'Yes'나 거절의 'No'가 아닌, 질문과 관계없는 대답을 하고 있다.

① **여** 지금 몇 시야?
남 2시 50분이야.

② **여** 펜 좀 빌릴 수 있을까?
남 나도 거기에 있었어.

③ **여** 나 감기 걸렸어.
남 이런, 안됐다.

④ **여** 쿠키 좀 먹어도 될까?
남 물론이야. 마음껏 먹어.

⑤ **여** 버스 정류장까지 어떻게 가야 하나요?
남 모퉁이에서 왼쪽으로 도세요.

어색한 대화 찾기 유형의 발문과 보기

다음을 듣고, 두 사람의 대화가 <u>어색한</u> 것을 고르시오. [2014 기출]

① ② ③ ④ ⑤

① **W** What time do you usually get up?
M It was last Saturday.

다음을 듣고, 두 사람의 대화가 <u>어색한</u> 것을 고르시오. [2014 기출]

① ② ③ ④ ⑤

① **M** I am sorry. It's my fault.
W My pleasure.

자연스러운 대화에 쓰이는 표현

- **질문(의문사)**

A Who's calling please? 전화 거신 분 누구시죠?
B This is Amy. 저 Amy인데요.

A What's your hobby? 너 취미가 뭐야?
B My hobby is swimming. 내 취미는 수영이야.

A How much is this hat? 이 모자 얼마인가요?
B It's $15. 15달러입니다.

- **질문(be동사 / 일반동사)**

A Aren't you hungry? 배고프지 않아?
B Not at all. I'm full. 전혀. 배불러.

A Do you have a red pen? 빨간 펜 있어?
B No, I don't have one. 아니. 빨간 펜 없어.

A Did you enjoy your meal? 식사는 맛있게 하셨나요?
B Yes, it was delicious. 네, 맛있었어요.

- **평서문**

A Thank you for helping me. 도와줘서 고마워요.
B It was my pleasure! 내가 좋아서 한 일이야!

A I don't feel well. 몸이 안 좋아.
B What's wrong? 무슨 일이야?

A You don't look so good. 안색이 안 좋아 보여.
B I have a headache. 나 두통이 있어.

영어듣기능력평가 07회

학년 반 번
이름

01 다음을 듣고, 'I'가 무엇인지 가장 적절한 것을 고르시오.

① ②  ③ 

④  ⑤ 

02 대화를 듣고, 여자가 생일 선물로 받은 것을 고르시오.

① 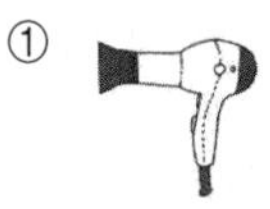 ②   ③  

④  ⑤ 

03 다음을 듣고, 오늘 오후의 날씨로 가장 적절한 것을 고르시오.

①  ② 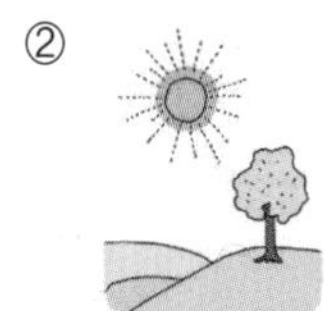 ③ 

④  ⑤ 

04 대화를 듣고, 남자가 토요일에 주로 하는 일로 가장 적절한 것을 고르시오.

① 축구하기 ② 교회 가기
③ 농구하기 ④ 컴퓨터 게임하기
⑤ 할머니 댁 방문하기

고난도

05 다음을 듣고, Eiffel Tower에 대한 설명으로 일치하는 것을 고르시오.

① 전 유럽의 상징물이다.
② 높이는 300미터를 넘지 않는다.
③ 100여 년 전에 만들어졌다.
④ 파리에서 가장 높은 탑이다.
⑤ 해마다 2만 명 이상이 방문한다.

06 대화를 듣고, 여자의 직업으로 가장 적절한 것을 고르시오.

① 화가 ② 편집자
③ 변호사 ④ 판매원
⑤ 광고주

07 다음을 듣고, 두 사람의 대화가 어색한 것을 고르시오.

① ② ③ ④ ⑤

08 대화를 듣고, 남자가 여자에게 부탁한 일로 가장 적절한 것을 고르시오.

① 파일 복구하기
② 보고서 작성하기
③ 컴퓨터 수리하기
④ 전자우편 확인하기
⑤ 전자우편으로 파일 보내기

09 대화를 듣고, 무엇에 관한 내용인지 가장 적절한 것을 고르시오.

① 자연 재해 ② 일기예보
③ 신문 기사 ④ 세계의 날씨
⑤ 환경 보호

10 다음을 듣고, 'these'가 가리키는 것으로 가장 적절한 것을 고르시오.

①  ② 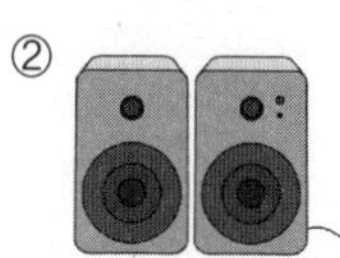 ③  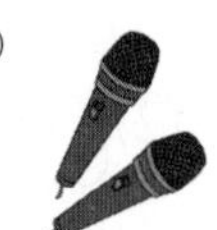

④ 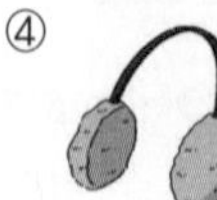 ⑤ 

점수 /20

11 대화를 듣고, 여자가 대화 직후에 할 일로 가장 적절한 것을 고르시오.

① 집에 가기 ② 전화하기
③ 교실 청소하기 ④ 책 반납하기
⑤ 피아노 연습하기

12 대화를 듣고, 남자의 마지막 말의 의도로 가장 적절한 것을 고르시오.

① 부정 ② 긍정
③ 동의 ④ 거절
⑤ 사과

13 대화를 듣고, 두 사람의 관계로 가장 적절한 것을 고르시오.

① 교사 – 학생
② 뉴스 리포터 – 시민
③ 면접관 – 면접 대기자
④ 라디오 진행자 – 청취자
⑤ 고객 센터 안내원 – 고객

14 대화를 듣고, 여자가 가려고 하는 장소를 고르시오.

Art museum	①	State library		Coffee Shop	②	Cinema
			Ann Street			
Church	③	Fire Station	↑	④	Police Station	⑤

고난도

15 대화를 듣고, 오늘 밤 불꽃놀이 쇼가 끝날 예상 시각을 고르시오.

① 10:00 ② 10:15
③ 10:30 ④ 10:45
⑤ 11:00

16 대화를 듣고, 여자의 심정으로 가장 적절한 것을 고르시오.

① 기쁨 ② 걱정됨
③ 만족스러움 ④ 외로움
⑤ 자랑스러움

17 대화를 듣고, 여자가 친구의 집까지 가는 교통 수단으로 가장 적절한 것을 고르시오.

① 도보 ② 버스
③ 택시 ④ 지하철
⑤ 승용차

18 대화를 듣고, 여자가 책을 빌릴 수 없는 이유로 가장 적절한 것을 고르시오.

① 원하는 책이 없어서
② 빌린 도서가 연체되어서
③ 대출 한도를 이미 채워서
④ 학생 도서관 카드를 잃어버려서
⑤ 도서관 컴퓨터가 작동되지 않아서

[19~20] 대화를 듣고, 남자의 마지막 말에 이어질 여자의 응답으로 가장 적절한 것을 고르시오.

19 Woman: ______________________

① No, thank you.
② No, on the 5th floor.
③ Yes, I'm coming home.
④ No, I don't like elevators.
⑤ Yes. I moved in last Saturday.

20 Woman: ______________________

① I like him a lot.
② I'm always busy.
③ It's a good job, I think.
④ I'd like to be a bank manager.
⑤ You have to wait for your turn.

영어듣기능력평가 07 회 DICTATION

다시 들으면서 듣기 만점에 도전하세요!
Dictation: 스크립트의 주요 부분을 다시 들으면서!
실전 ⊕: 세부 정보가 많은 스크립트를 다른 문제로 샅샅이!

01 그림 "I" 파악(담화)

다음을 듣고, 'I'가 무엇인지 가장 적절한 것을 고르시오.

① ② ③ ④ ⑤

M I am a bird, but I can't fly. ________ ________ ________, ________ (나는 것 대신) ________ (나는 수영을 할 수 있다) very well. I catch fish while I swim. When I lay an egg, I have to keep it warm. It's hard work for parents because I live in a cold place. You can see me standing on snow with thousands of my friends. I have ________ ________ ________ ________ ________ (검은색 등과 검은색 날개), but ________ ________ ________ ________ (나의 배는 흰색이다).

02 그림 정보 파악 – 사물

반복되는 어구 dry my hair에서 단서를 얻는다.

대화를 듣고, 여자가 생일 선물로 받은 것을 고르시오.

① ② ③ ④ ⑤

W Look, I got it from my sister for my birthday present.
M Do you use it every morning?
W Of course. You might not need it. You have short hair, so it dries quickly. But my hair is long. I need it to ________ ________ ________ (내 머리를 말리다) every morning.
M I sometimes ________ ________ ________ ________ ________ ________ (내 머리를 말리는 데 그것을 사용하다), too.

03 날씨 파악

in the afternoon이 포함된 날씨 정보를 주의깊게 듣는다.

다음을 듣고, 오늘 오후의 날씨로 가장 적절한 것을 고르시오.

① rain shower ② hot, sunny ③ ④ ⑤

M Good morning. This is Jim Kelly from the weather center. We are having hot dry summer days. Today, will be another ________ ________ ________ ________ (덥고 맑은 날) in the morning, but there is good news: ________ ________ ________ ________ ________ ________ (오후에 소나기). Let's hope it will cool us down in this hot dry weather. Thank you for listening.

04 특정 정보 파악

여자가 하는 일과 남자가 하는 일을 구분하여 듣는다.

대화를 듣고, 남자가 토요일에 주로 하는 일로 가장 적절한 것을 고르시오.

① 축구하기
② 교회 가기 go to church
③ 농구하기 basketball day
④ 컴퓨터 게임하기
⑤ 할머니 댁 방문하기 visits her

대화를 듣고, 여자가 토요일에 주로 하는 일로 가장 적절한 것을 고르시오.

① 축구하기 ② 교회 가기
③ 농구하기 ④ 컴퓨터 게임하기
⑤ 할머니 댁 방문하기

M ________ ________ ________ ________ on weekends? (너 주로 무엇을 하니?)
W My grandmother lives alone, so my family visits her on Saturdays.
M Wow. That's great. ________ ________ ________ ________. (토요일은 내가 농구하는 날이다) My friends and I usually ________ ________ ________ ________. (체육관에서 만나다)
W How about on Sunday?
M I go to church.

고난도

05 내용 일치 파악

다음을 듣고, Eiffel Tower에 대한 설명으로 일치하는 것을 고르시오.

① 전 유럽의 상징물이다.
② 높이는 300미터를 넘지 않는다.
③ 100여 년 전에 만들어졌다.
④ 파리에서 가장 높은 탑이다.
⑤ 해마다 2만 명 이상이 방문한다.

W The Eiffel Tower is a famous building. It is ________ ________ ________ ________ ________. (프랑스의 상징물) It is 324 meters tall. It was built in 1889, and it was the tallest building in Paris at that time. Today there are many buildings taller than the Eiffel, but it is still ________ ________ ________ ________. (파리에서 가장 높은 탑) Since the Eiffel Tower opened, ________ ________ ________ ________ ________ the landmark. (2억 명 이상의 방문객이 다녀갔다)

06 직업 추론

대화를 듣고, 여자의 직업으로 가장 적절한 것을 고르시오.

① 화가 ② 편집자
③ 변호사 ④ 판매원
⑤ 광고주

대화를 듣고, 남자가 전화를 건 목적으로 가장 적절한 것을 고르시오.

① 상품을 홍보하려고
② 약속을 변경하려고
③ 작업을 요청하려고
④ 물건을 소개하려고
⑤ 연락처를 물어보려고

[Cellphone rings.]
W Hello. This is Amanda.
M Hello. This is Jackson in A&T Co. I'd like to ask if you can ________ ________ ________ ________. (우리를 위해 그림을 그리다)
W Sure. What do you want to use it for?
M I need it ________ ________ ________ that will be in a magazine. (광고를 위해)
W What would you like to advertise?
M I want to advertise our new sneakers. We need ________ ________ ________ for them. (멋진 그림) I'll email you some details.
W Fine. I'll call you back after I review them.

07 어색한 대화 찾기

다음을 듣고, 두 사람의 대화가 어색한 것을 고르시오.

① ② ③ ④ ⑤

Here you go.는 '자, 여기 있어.'라는 의미로, 물건을 건넬 때 사용하는 표현이다.

① **W** Can I borrow your pen?
M Sure. Here you go.
② **W** How long is this desk?
M It is ________ ________ ________. (한 시간 이상)
③ **W** Where did you get that backpack?
M I bought it downtown.
④ **W** Do you think we should leave now?
M No, let's ________ ________ ________ ________. (Jenny가 오기를 기다리다)
⑤ **W** It's a nice day today, isn't it?
M Yes, it's ________ ________ ________. (따뜻하고 화창한)

08 부탁 파악

Can you ~? 이후에 나오는 부분을 주의깊게 듣는다.

대화를 듣고, 남자가 여자에게 부탁한 일로 가장 적절한 것을 고르시오.

① 파일 복구하기
② 보고서 작성하기
③ 컴퓨터 수리하기
④ 전자우편 확인하기
⑤ 전자우편으로 파일 보내기

email the file

Can you ~?는 상대방에게 부탁하거나 요청할 때 사용하는 표현으로 Could you ~?가 좀 더 공손한 표현이다.

[Telephone rings.]

W Hello.

M Helen, this is Dad. I need your help. Can you ________(컴퓨터를 켜다) ________ ________ ________?

W All right, Dad. I'm turning it on.

M Open the 'my document' folder. There is a powerpoint presentation file. The name of the file is "September presentation."

W Yes, I found it.

M Good. ________(그 파일을 전자우편으로 보내 주겠니) ________ ________ ________ to me?

W All right.

09 주제 파악

핵심 어구 the Earth, global warming, pollution, only one Earth, protect 등의 공통점을 파악한다.

대화를 듣고, 무엇에 관한 내용인지 가장 적절한 것을 고르시오.

① 자연 재해
② 일기예보
③ 신문 기사
④ 세계의 날씨
⑤ 환경 보호

M Do you know that ________(지구가 점점 더워지고 있다) ________ ________ ________ ________?

W I know. ________(지구 온난화) ________ is a real big issue these days.

M There are floods and droughts all over the world. I believe pollution is the reason for that.

W I agree with you. We should know that there is only one Earth and we ________(그것을 보호해야 한다) ________ ________ ________.

10 그림 "these" 파악(담화)

다음을 듣고, 'these'가 가리키는 것으로 가장 적절한 것을 고르시오.

① ② ③ ④ ⑤

M You use these to ________(음악을 듣다) ________ ________ or the radio. You put these on your head. If you use these, only you can ________(음악을 듣다) ________ ________. That is good because you won't disturb other people. But you have to be careful, because you can't hear other noises. What are these?

11 할 일 파악

대화를 듣고, 여자가 대화 직후에 할 일로 가장 적절한 것을 고르시오.

① 집에 가기
② 전화하기
③ 교실 청소하기
④ 책 반납하기
⑤ 피아노 연습하기

M Hey, Sara. What are you doing here? Can you help us and come to the school library?

W School library? For what?

M ________(우리는 도서관을 청소하고 있다) ________ ________ ________ today. Didn't you know that?

W Oh, no. I forgot that. Just wait a minute. ________(피아노 선생님께 전화할 것이다) ________ ________ ________ and tell her I'll be late for the lesson.

M All right. I'll see you at the library.

12 의도 추론

대화를 듣고, 남자의 마지막 말의 의도로 가장 적절한 것을 고르시오.

① 부정 ② 긍정
③ 동의 ④ 거절
⑤ 사과

No way.는 '말도 안 돼.'라는 의미로, 기막힘 · 놀람 등을 나타내는 표현이다.

[Cellphone rings.]

W Hello. This is Ann. Everybody there?

M Not quite.

W Hasn't Bob arrived there yet?

M No, ________ ________ ________ ________.
그는 항상 그렇듯이 늦고 있다

W I can't believe it! I was sure he would be there by now.

M It is not surprising, though. He's late every day.

W But he promised me that he ________ ________ ________ ________ ________.
오늘은 제 시간에 올 것이다

M No way.

13 관계 추론

반복되는 어구 radio quiz show, calling 등에서 대화의 상황을 파악한다.

대화를 듣고, 두 사람의 관계로 가장 적절한 것을 고르시오.

① 교사 – 학생
② 뉴스 리포터 – 시민
③ 면접관 – 면접 대기자
④ 라디오 진행자 – 청취자
⑤ 고객 센터 안내원 – 고객

[Telephone rings.]

M Hello.

W Hello, this is the HBS ________ ________ ________, "Quiz Quiz." Who are you and where are you calling from?
라디오 퀴즈 쇼

M I'm Juwon from Gwangju.

W ________ ________ and nice to meet you, Juwon. ________ ________. We are talking to another person for today's show. Juwon, are you ready to meet your partner?
전화 주셔서 감사합니다 / 끊지 말고 기다리세요

M Yes, I am.

14 그림 정보 파악 – 지도

across from(~의 건너편), between A and B(A와 B 사이에) 등의 위치를 나타내는 표현에 주목한다.

대화를 듣고, 여자가 가려고 하는 장소를 고르시오.

W Excuse me, where is the City Information Center?

M Go straight. You will meet Ann Street.

W Go to the Ann Street.

M And ________ ________. You can see the Information Center ________ ________. It's ________ ________ ________ ________ ________, ________ ________ ________ ________ ________.
우회전하라 / 당시의 왼편에 / 경찰서 건너편에 / 커피숍과 영화관 사이에

W Thank you.

고난도

15 숫자 파악 – 시각

불꽃놀이 쇼가 계속되거나 중단 혹은 취소될 조건을 확인하며 듣는다.

대화를 듣고, 오늘 밤 불꽃놀이 쇼가 끝날 예상 시각을 고르시오.

① 10:00 ② 10:15
③ 10:30 ④ 10:45
⑤ 11:00

It depends.는 '그것은 때와 형편에 달려 있다.', '사정 나름이다.'라는 의미이다.

W When will the fireworks show start?
M It should begin at 10 o'clock.
W How long will it last?
M It's _____ _____ _____ _____ _____. (보통은 30분 정도)
W So it will _____ _____ _____ _____ : _____? (10시 30분에 끝나다)
M Yes, that's how it's scheduled as long as the weather is nice this evening.
W It looks like _____ _____ _____ _____ _____, but what happens if the weather is bad? (오늘 밤에는 하늘이 맑을 것이다)
M It depends. They might cancel the show or finish it early.

16 심정 추론

대화를 듣고, 여자의 심정으로 가장 적절한 것을 고르시오.

① 기쁨 ② 걱정됨
③ 만족스러움 ④ 외로움
⑤ 자랑스러움

What should I do?는 고민이나 걱정이 있을 때 조언을 구하는 표현이다.

W Paul, please come here and help me.
M What's the matter?
W The computer monitor suddenly _____ _____. (까맣게 되었다)
M Push the reset button.
W No way. I'm working on an important file. If I push the button, I'll _____ _____. (그 파일을 잃어버리다)
M Do you mean you didn't save it?
W I didn't. Oh, please, _____ _____ _____ _____? (어떻게 해야 하죠)

17 특정 정보 파악

driving과 subway 중에서 여자가 마지막에 선택한 교통 수단이 무엇인지에 집중하며 듣는다.

대화를 듣고, 여자가 친구의 집까지 가는 교통 수단으로 가장 적절한 것을 고르시오.

① 도보 ② 버스
③ 택시 ④ 지하철
⑤ 승용차

How are you coming?에서 How는 교통수단을 묻는 의문사이다.

[Cellphone rings.]
W Hi, Steve. I'm leaving for your house. Can you tell me your address?
M How are you coming?
W _____ _____. I have a GPS car navigation system. (난 운전하고 갈 것이다)
M Well, I don't think you can come in time for the party if you drive.
W Why not? Because of the traffic?
M That's right. _____ _____ _____ _____ _____ _____? It'll only take 40 minutes. (지하철을 타는 게 어때)
W All right. I don't want to be late. Thanks for your advice.

18 이유 파악

대화를 듣고, 여자가 책을 빌릴 수 없는 이유로 가장 적절한 것을 고르시오.

① 원하는 책이 없어서
② 빌린 도서가 연체되어서
③ 대출 한도를 이미 채워서
④ 학생 도서관 카드를 잃어버려서
⑤ 도서관 컴퓨터가 작동되지 않아서

W Good afternoon, I'd like to borrow this book.
M Can I see your student library card?
W Here it is.
M Oh, you ________ ________ ________ ________ ________. (이미 3권을 빌렸다)
W Have I?
M Yes. Students ________ ________ ________ ________ ________ ________ at a time. (3권 이상 빌릴 수 없다) You have to return one of the books you've borrowed.

19 알맞은 응답 찾기

[19~20] 대화를 듣고, 남자의 마지막 말에 이어질 여자의 응답으로 가장 적절한 것을 고르시오.

Woman: ____________________

① No, thank you.
② No, on the 5th floor.
③ Yes, I'm coming home.
④ No, I don't like elevators.
⑤ Yes. I moved in last Saturday.

W Hold the elevator, please!
M No problem.
W Thank you.
M ________ ________ ________ ________ ________ ________? (몇 층에 가시죠)
W Oh, the 5th please.
M ________ ________ ________ ________? (여기에 사시나요)
W ____________________

20 알맞은 응답 찾기

Woman: ____________________

① I like him a lot.
② I'm always busy.
③ It's a good job, I think.
④ I'd like to be a bank manager.
⑤ You have to wait for your turn.

It's been a long time!은 오랜만에 만났을 때 하는 인사 표현으로, 간단하게 Long time no see.라고 말할 수 있다.

W Hi, Arnold. It's been a long time!
M It sure has. How are you doing?
W I'm doing fine. I'm ________ ________ ________ ________. (은행에서 근무하고 있다)
M Great. ________ ________ ________ ________? (그 일이 마음에 드니)
W ____________________

영어듣기능력평가 08회

학년 반 번
이름

01 다음을 듣고, 'this'가 무엇인지 가장 적절한 것을 고르시오.

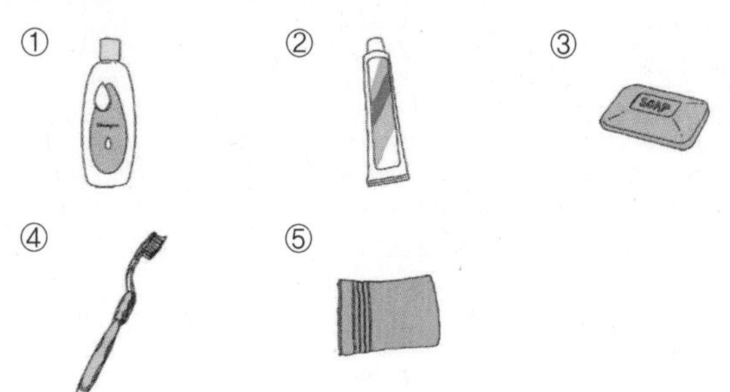

02 대화를 듣고, 가방이 있는 곳을 고르시오.

03 다음을 듣고, Washington의 내일 날씨로 가장 적절한 것을 고르시오.

04 다음을 듣고, 'I'가 무엇인지 가장 적절한 것을 고르시오.

고난도

05 대화를 듣고, 남자가 디즈니랜드에 가는 데 걸리는 시간을 고르시오.

① 20분　② 30분
③ 1시간 30분　④ 1시간 50분
⑤ 2시간 30분

06 대화를 듣고, 남자가 여자에게 부탁한 일로 가장 적절한 것을 고르시오.

① 책을 빌려 줄 것
② 책을 사다 줄 것
③ 같이 서점에 가 줄 것
④ 서점에 가는 길을 알려 줄 것
⑤ 인터넷으로 책을 주문해 줄 것

07 대화를 듣고, 여자의 심정으로 가장 적절한 것을 고르시오.

① 감동스러운　② 걱정스러운
③ 초조한　④ 부끄러운
⑤ 설레는

08 다음을 듣고, 두 사람의 대화가 어색한 것을 고르시오.

①　②　③　④　⑤

09 대화를 듣고, 두 사람이 대화하고 있는 장소로 가장 적절한 곳을 고르시오.

① 호수　② 해변
③ 계곡　④ 수영장
⑤ 목욕탕

10 대화를 듣고, 여자가 기분이 나쁜 이유로 가장 적절한 것을 고르시오.

① 지갑을 잃어버려서
② 쇼핑몰이 문을 닫아서
③ 친구와 말다툼을 해서
④ 쇼핑몰 직원이 불친절해서
⑤ 물건을 비싼 가격에 구입해서

점수 /20

11 대화를 듣고, 남자의 마지막 말의 의도로 가장 적절한 것을 고르시오.

① 수락 ② 위로
③ 불평 ④ 감사
⑤ 충고

12 다음을 듣고, 여자에 대해 언급되지 않은 것을 고르시오.

① 국적 ② 나이
③ 현재 사는 곳 ④ 장래 희망
⑤ 취미

13 대화를 듣고, 남자가 전화를 건 목적으로 가장 적절한 것을 고르시오.

① 자동차를 빌리려고
② 병문안을 같이 가려고
③ 자동차 사고를 알리려고
④ 저녁 식사를 함께 하려고
⑤ 병원의 위치를 물어보려고

14 대화를 듣고, 여자의 장래 희망으로 가장 적절한 것을 고르시오.

① 아나운서 ② 의사
③ 기자 ④ 간호사
⑤ 관광 안내원

15 대화를 듣고, 여자가 남자에게 충고한 것으로 가장 적절한 것을 고르시오.

① 긍정적으로 생각하라.
② 규칙적인 생활을 하라.
③ 음식을 적당히 먹어라.
④ 매일 아침 조깅을 하라.
⑤ 일찍 자고 일찍 일어나라.

16 대화를 듣고, 여자가 남자의 제안을 거절한 이유로 가장 적절한 것을 고르시오.

① 뮤지컬이 재미 없어서
② 친구와 약속이 있어서
③ 사무실에 출근해야 해서
④ 할머니를 찾아 뵈어야 해서
⑤ 입장권 가격이 너무 비싸서

고난도

17 다음을 듣고, T-Rex에 대한 설명으로 일치하는 것을 고르시오.

① 과학자들이 2005년에 그들의 혈액 세포를 발견했다.
② 그들의 뼈에서 공룡 DNA를 발견했다.
③ 그들과 비슷한 동물은 현재 존재하지 않는다.
④ 그들과 가장 유사한 동물은 악어와 도마뱀이다.
⑤ 그들의 주요 먹이는 닭이다.

18 다음을 듣고, 무엇에 관한 안내인지 가장 적절한 것을 고르시오.

① 한국의 전통 가옥
② 한국어 학원 광고
③ 한국인의 예의 범절
④ 한국어 말하기 대회
⑤ 한국 생활의 어려움

[19~20] 대화를 듣고, 여자의 마지막 말에 이어질 남자의 응답으로 가장 적절한 것을 고르시오.

19 Man: ______________________

① Thank you very much, Sally.
② Me neither. I don't like climbing.
③ I'm sorry, but I can't go with you.
④ Really? When did you go to Seoul?
⑤ Wow! You'll have a great time there.

20 Man: ______________________

① Sorry, I lost your tennis ball.
② Which sport do you like most?
③ Okay, I'll buy this tennis racket.
④ Yeah, I like tennis more than soccer.
⑤ How about this Saturday afternoon?

영어듣기능력평가 08회 DICTATION

다시 들으면서 듣기 만점에 도전하세요!
Dictation: 스크립트의 주요 부분을 다시 들으면서!
실전 ⊕: 세부 정보가 많은 스크립트를 다른 문제로 샅샅이!

01 그림 "this" 파악 (담화)

사물에 대한 설명은 주로 동사로 용도를, 명사로 모양을, 형용사로 성질을 표현한다.

다음을 듣고, 'this'가 무엇인지 가장 적절한 것을 고르시오.

① ② ③ ④ ⑤

M We can usually see this in the bathroom of almost every house, apartment, or building. Its shape is ________ ________ ________ (둥글거나 직사각형), and it is a little bit hard. However, once you put water on this, it ________ ________ (부드러워지다). You can use this when you ________ ________ ________ (당신의 몸을 씻다); especially your face and hands.

02 그림 정보 파악 – 위치

대화를 듣고, 가방이 있는 곳을 고르시오.

① ② ③ ④ ⑤

M What's wrong? What are you looking for?
W I forgot my bag. Can you go back and get for me?
M Did you leave it on the chair?
W No, it's ________ ________ ________ ________ (탁자 위에 있다).
M Is it beside the flower vase or the lamp?
W I think it's ________ ________ ________ ________ ________ ________ (꽃병과 전등 사이에).
M OK. I'll be back with it in a few minutes.

03 날씨 파악

Washington이 언급된 부분을 주의 깊게 듣는다.

다음을 듣고, Washington의 내일 날씨로 가장 적절한 것을 고르시오.

① sunny
②
③ windy
④
⑤

W Now, let's move on to ________ ________ (내일 날씨) in East area. Boston will be mostly sunny. However, in New York it'll rain with strong winds. And, it'll ________ ________ (바람이 많이 불다) in the Washington area. Same story for Philadelphia. Finally, Delaware will have partly cloudy skies. That's all for today's weather forecast.

⊕ 다음을 듣고, Philadelphia의 내일 날씨로 가장 적절한 것을 고르시오.

① sunny ② clilly
③ windy ④ snowy
⑤ rainy

04 그림 "I" 파악 (담화)

다음을 듣고, 'I'가 무엇인지 가장 적절한 것을 고르시오.

① ② ③ ④ ⑤

M I'm the biggest among all the land mammals. My favorite food is a banana. I can peel my own bananas, because I'm ________ ________. I have a special trunk. I can ________ ________ ________ to drink, smell, pick up food, and touch things. What am I?

(매우 영리한 / 코를 이용하다)

고난도

05 숫자 파악 – 시각

대화를 듣고, 남자가 디즈니랜드에 가는 데 걸리는 시간을 고르시오.

① 20분
② 30분
③ 1시간 30분
④ 1시간 50분
⑤ 2시간 30분

M Excuse me, ________ ________ ________ ________ ________ from here to the Express Way? (얼마나 걸리나요)

W To the Express Way? It'll take ________ ________ ________. (약 20분)

M Then, from the Express Way, how long does it take to Disney Land?

W ________ ________ ________ ________ ________. It's not that far. (약 한 시간 반)

M I see. Thank you very much.

06 부탁 파악

대화를 듣고, 남자가 여자에게 부탁한 일로 가장 적절한 것을 고르시오.

① 책을 빌려 줄 것
② 책을 사다 줄 것
③ 같이 서점에 가 줄 것
④ 서점에 가는 길을 알려 줄 것
⑤ 인터넷으로 책을 주문해 줄 것

M Wow! I can't believe you have this book. Where did you get it?

W I bought it online. Why?

M It was a bestseller for 237 weeks in Britain. I wanted to read it, but it's ________ ________ ________ at bookstores. (전부 품절인)

W I believe it. I thought it was really good.

M If you're done, ________ ________ ________ ________? (내가 그것을 읽어도 돼니)

W Sure. ________ ________ ________ ________ now. (그것을 빌려도 돼)

07 심정 파악

대화를 듣고, 여자의 심정으로 가장 적절한 것을 고르시오.

① 감동스러운 ② 걱정스러운
③ 초조한 ④ 부끄러운
⑤ 설레는

M Mom, I'm home!

W You're a little late. I was wondering where you were.

M Sorry, Mom. I'm late because I bought this for you ________ ________ ________ ________. (집에 오는 길에)

W What is this?

M Tomorrow's your birthday!

W Wow, thank you, son. I thought you forgot.

M I could never ________ ________ ________. I hope you like it. (네 생일을 잊다)

08 어색한 대화 찾기

다음을 듣고, 두 사람의 대화가 어색한 것을 고르시오.

① ② ③ ④ ⑤

What time shall we meet?은 시간 약속을 할 때 사용하는 표현이다.

① M ________ ________ ________ ________, cats or dogs?
어느 것을 더 좋아하세요

W I like dogs more than cats.

② M May I speak to Jennifer?

W This is Jennifer. Who is speaking?

③ M Why don't you have one more sandwich?

W No, thanks. I'm really full.

④ M Will you go bowling with me tomorrow?

W That sounds interesting. What time shall we meet?

⑤ M ________ ________ ________ your digital camera?
나에게 ~을 빌려 줄래

W Oh, ________ ________ ________ ________. Where did you take it?
이 사진은 정말 멋지다

고난도

09 장소 추론

핵심 어구 sand, sun tanning, salt water 등에서 단서를 얻는다.

대화를 듣고, 두 사람이 대화하고 있는 장소로 가장 적절한 곳을 고르시오.

① 호수 ② 해변
③ 계곡 ④ 수영장
⑤ 목욕탕

W It's so hot today. There are so many people here.

M It's always really crowded on days like today.

W I can see why. I like swimming in hot weather.

M There are a lot of ________ ________ ________ ________ ________, too.
모래에 앉아 있는 사람

W I guess they ________ ________ ________.
선탠을 좋아하다

M Not me. I ________ ________ ________ ________ ________.
시원한 바닷물이 더 좋다

10 이유 파악

기분이 나쁜 이유를 직접적으로 언급하는 부분을 주의깊게 듣는다.

대화를 듣고, 여자가 기분이 나쁜 이유로 가장 적절한 것을 고르시오.

① 지갑을 잃어버려서
② 쇼핑몰이 문을 닫아서
③ 친구와 말다툼을 해서
④ 쇼핑몰 직원이 불친절해서
⑤ 물건을 비싼 가격에 구입해서

M Lucy, did you go to the ABC Shopping Mall in the afternoon?

W Yes, I did. But I ________ ________ ________.
아무 것도 못 샀다

M Why? Was the shopping mall closed today?

W No. I ________ ________ ________ on the way to the mall. I feel so bad now.
내 지갑을 잃어버렸다

M I'm sorry to hear that.

11 의도 추론

상대방이 부탁(Can you ~?)했을 때 수락(If you want ~.) 또는 거절(I'm sorry ~.)로 응답할 수 있다.

대화를 듣고, 남자의 마지막 말의 의도로 가장 적절한 것을 고르시오.

① 수락 ② 위로
③ 불평 ④ 감사
⑤ 충고

W Oh, you skate very well. When did you learn to skate?

M When I was in elementary school. I took lessons for more than three years.

W Wow, you're great! Hey, if you don't mind, ________ ________ ________ ________ ________ ________? I'd like to skate as well as you do. (나에게 스케이트 타는 법 좀 가르쳐 줄래)

M Um... ________ ________ ________, I'll teach you. (네가 원하면)

12 언급 및 비언급 파악

다음을 듣고, 여자에 대해 언급되지 <u>않은</u> 것을 고르시오.

① 국적 Brazil
② 나이 14 years old
③ 현재 사는 곳 Rio de Janeiro
④ 장래 희망
⑤ 취미 playing and watching soccer

I'd like to introduce myself (to you).는 상대방에게 자신을 소개할 때 사용하는 표현이다.

W Hi, I'd like to introduce myself to you. ________ ________ ________ and I'm ________ ________ ________ now. I was born in Sao Paulo and my family moved to Rio De Janeiro when I was five. Since then, we ________ ________ ________ in Rio De Janeiro. Like any other Brazilian girl, my hobby is ________ ________ ________. I'm really happy to meet all of you. (나는 브라질 출신이다 / 14살 / 여기에서 계속 살고 있다 / 축구를 하고 보는 것)

13 전화 목적 파악

why don't we ~? 이후에 나오는 부분에서 전화를 건 목적을 알 수 있다.

대화를 듣고, 남자가 전화를 건 목적으로 가장 적절한 것을 고르시오.

① 자동차를 빌리려고
② 병문안을 같이 가려고
③ 자동차 사고를 알리려고
④ 저녁 식사를 함께 하려고
⑤ 병원의 위치를 물어보려고

[Cellphone rings.]

W Hello? Sally speaking.

M Hi, Sally. It's me, Tom. Did you know Issac ________ ________ ________ now? (입원해 있다)

W Yeah, I heard that he got in a car accident.

M That's right. He is in Saint Maria Hospital. Sally, ________ ________ ________ ________ him this evening? (병문안 가는 게 어때)

W Okay, let's go together.

14 특정 정보 파악

여자의 말 중 I want to be ~. 이후에 나오는 부분을 주의깊게 듣는다.

대화를 듣고, 여자의 장래 희망으로 가장 적절한 것을 고르시오.

① 아나운서 announcer
② 의사 doctor
③ 기자 reporter
④ 간호사 nurse
⑤ 관광 안내원 tour guide

W David, did you ever think about what you want to be?

M Sure! I want to be an announcer or a reporter. What about you, Jessica?

W Well... about a month ago, I wanted to ________ ________ ________ ________ ________. But I ________ ________ ________ ________. (간호사나 의사가 되다 / 새로운 꿈이 생기다)

M Really? What's your new dream?

W I want to be ________ ________ ________. I want to travel all around the world. (관광 안내원)

15 특정 정보 파악

대화를 듣고, 여자가 남자에게 충고한 것으로 가장 적절한 것을 고르시오.

① 긍정적으로 생각하라.
② 규칙적인 생활을 하라.
③ 음식을 적당히 먹어라.
④ 매일 아침 조깅을 하라.
⑤ 일찍 자고 일찍 일어나라.

Thank you for ~.는 감사를 나타내는 표현으로, for 뒤에 감사하는 이유를 덧붙여 말한다.

why don't you ~? 이후에 나오는 부분을 주의깊게 듣는다.

M Cathy, you look always healthy.

W Do I? Thank you for saying so.

M If you have a secret way to ________ ________, please let me know it. (건강을 유지하다) I want to be as healthy as you are.

W Well... then, ________ ________ ________ ________ every morning? You'll be healthy. (조깅을 하는 게 어때)

M I see. Thank you for the tip.

16 이유 파악

대화를 듣고, 여자가 남자의 제안을 거절한 이유로 가장 적절한 것을 고르시오.

① 뮤지컬이 재미 없어서
② 친구와 약속이 있어서
③ 사무실에 출근해야 해서
④ 할머니를 찾아 뵈어야 해서
⑤ 입장권 가격이 너무 비싸서

➕ 대화를 듣고, 대화 후에 남자가 할 일로 가장 적절한 것을 고르시오.

① 입장권 구입하기
② 예약시간 변경하기
③ 입장권 환불하기
④ 다른 친구에게 연락하기
⑤ 비행기표 구입하기

거절의 말(Oh, no!) 이후에 이어지는 이유에 주목한다.

M Alice, you said you wanted to see the musical, *Happy House,* didn't you?

W Yeah, I really want to see it.

M Good! Then, let's ________ ________ ________ ________. I have free tickets for this Friday. (그 뮤지컬을 보러 가다)

W This Friday? Oh, no! I ________ ________ ________ ________ ________ in Florida on that day. Can you get tickets for Sunday? (할머니 댁을 방문해야 한다)

M No. Well... I have to ________ ________ ________ to go with me. (다른 친구에게 물어보다)

고난도

17 내용 일치 파악

다음을 듣고, T-Rex에 대한 설명으로 일치하는 것을 고르시오.

① 과학자들이 2005년에 그들의 혈액 세포를 발견했다.
② 그들의 뼈에서 공룡 DNA를 발견했다.
③ 그들과 비슷한 동물은 현재 존재하지 않는다.
④ 그들과 가장 유사한 동물은 악어와 도마뱀이다.
⑤ 그들의 주요 먹이는 닭이다.

W A group of scientists made an exciting discovery in a T-Rex bone in 2005. They found ________ ________ ________! (약간의 혈액 세포) There was no DNA, but there was ________ ________. (약간의 단백질) Scientists used the protein to see which animals today are similar to the dinosaur. Can you guess the closest relative? Maybe you think ________ ________ ________ ________, (악어나 거대한 도마뱀) but it is chickens! Think about that next time you eat chicken.

18 주제 파악

learning Korean, studying Korean, learn Korean 등의 어구에서 단서를 얻는다.

다음을 듣고, 무엇에 관한 안내인지 가장 적절한 것을 고르시오.

① 한국의 전통 가옥
② 한국어 학원 광고
③ 한국인의 예의 범절
④ 한국어 말하기 대회
⑤ 한국 생활의 어려움

M Are you interested in ________ ________ (한국어 배우기)? Are you thinking about studying Korean? Then, ________ ________ ________ ________ (우리 한국어 학원을 방문하라) right now! We're waiting for you. We have lots of good teachers and all of them are from Korea. Once you ________ ________ ________ (여기서 한국어를 배우다) from us, you'll be a good Korean speaker soon.

19 알맞은 응답 찾기

해변에서 수영하고 한라산에도 오르겠다는 여자의 말에 대한 남자의 응답을 생각해 본다.

[19~20] 대화를 듣고, 여자의 마지막 말에 이어질 남자의 응답으로 가장 적절한 것을 고르시오.

Man: ________________

① Thank you very much, Sally.
② Me neither. I don't like climbing.
③ I'm sorry, but I can't go with you.
④ Really? When did you go to Seoul?
⑤ Wow! You'll have a great time there.

M Sally, when are you going to Jeju Island?
W This Sunday. ________ ________ ________ ________ (나는 너무 흥분된다) now.
M Yeah, you look very happy now. What are you going to do there?
W I will swim at the beach. And I'll ________ ________ ________ ________ (한라산에 오르다).
M ________________________________

20 알맞은 응답 찾기

Man: ________________

① Sorry, I lost your tennis ball.
② Which sport do you like most?
③ Okay, I'll buy this tennis racket.
④ Yeah, I like tennis more than soccer.
⑤ How about this Saturday afternoon?

M Cindy, do you like playing tennis?
W Yes, I do. Tennis is one of my favorite sports. You know, I once won a tennis contest.
M Really? When?
W When I was an elementary school student.
M Oh, I didn't know that. Then, how about ________ ________ ________ ________ (나와 테니스를 치는 것)?
W That's a great idea. ________ ________ ________ ________ ________ (언제 ~하고 싶니) play?
M ________________________________

이유 • 의도 파악

무엇을 평가하는가?	일상생활이나 친숙한 일반적 주제에 관한 말이나 대화를 듣고 화자의 의도나 사건의 원인과 결과를 추론할 수 있는지를 평가한다.
어떻게 출제되는가?	• 대화를 듣고, 남자가 여자를 도와줄 수 없는 이유로 가장 적절한 것을 고르시오. • 대화를 듣고, 남자가 밤에 잠을 늦게 잔 이유로 가장 적절한 것을 고르시오. • 대화를 듣고, 남자의 마지막 말의 의도로 가장 적절한 것을 고르시오.

key solution

❶ 이유를 묻는 경우, 이유를 직접적으로 물어보는 경우가 많으므로 답변에 집중한다.

❷ 의도를 묻는 경우, 전체적인 상황을 인지하고 마지막 말의 원인을 정확하게 파악한다.

[기출로 전략 확인]

대화를 듣고, 남자가 공원에서 자전거를 탈 수 없는 이유로 가장 적절한 것을 고르시오.

[2017 기출]

① 자전거가 고장 나서
② 다리를 다쳐서
③ 자전거 도로가 아니어서
④ 공사 중이어서
⑤ 축제 기간 중이어서

W Excuse me. You can't ride your bike in the park today.
M Really? Why not?
W We are having a Kimchi festival here.
M Oh, sorry! That's why there are so many people.
W That's right. The festival will be held until this Friday.
M Oh, I see. I should find another place then.

여 실례합니다. 오늘 공원에서 자전거를 탈 수 없습니다.
남 정말이요? 왜 안되나요?
여 여기서 김치 축제가 열릴 예정입니다.
남 아, 죄송해요! 그래서 사람이 이렇게 많았군요.
여 맞아요. 축제는 이번 주 금요일까지 열립니다.
남 아, 알겠습니다. 그럼 다른 장소를 찾아봐야겠네요.

❷ 자전거를 타면 안되는 이유를 남자가 직접적으로 물어보고 그에 대한 답변으로 김치 축제를 언급하고 있다.

이유 • 의도 파악 유형의 발문과 보기

대화를 듣고, 남자가 여자를 도와줄 수 없는 이유로 가장 적절한 것을 고르시오. [2018 기출]

① 집에 가야하기 때문에
② 시험을 봐야하기 때문에
③ 청소를 해야 하기 때문에
④ 우체국에 가야하기 때문에
⑤ 동아리 모임이 있기 때문에

만점 잡는 문장 **W** Could you help me with my math homework at lunch time?
M I'd love to, but I can't. I have a club meeting in the art room then.

대화를 듣고, 남자의 마지막 말의 의도로 가장 적절한 것을 고르시오. [2017 기출]

① 제안
② 의심
③ 거절
④ 부정
⑤ 허락

만점 잡는 문장 **W** W He won the first prize at the dance contest.
M Why don't we invite him to our school festival?

이유 • 의도 파악 파악하기에 쓰이는 표현

• 이유

A You look tired. What did you do last night? 피곤해 보인다. 어젯밤에 뭐 했니?
B I watched a soccer match on TV until 2 a.m. 새벽 2시까지 TV로 축구경기를 봤어.

A Why did you join the music club? 음악 클럽에 왜 가입 했니?
B Because I wanted to learn many songs. 많은 노래를 배우고 싶었기 때문이야.

My cats were sick and I had to take care of them all weekend. 고양이가 아파서 주말 내내 돌봐야 했어.

• 의도(승낙)

A Can I borrow your badminton racket? 배드민턴 라켓 좀 빌릴 수 있을까?
B No problem. 물론이지.

(거절)

A Do you want to see the concert with me? 나랑 같이 콘서트 보러 갈래?
B I'm sorry, but I can't. I don't feel well today. 미안하지만 안 되겠어. 오늘 몸이 안 좋아.

(제안)

A There are so many things to do. 할 일이 너무 많아.
B I think you should get some rest. 넌 좀 쉬어야 해.

영어듣기능력평가 09회

학년 반 번
이름

01 대화를 듣고, 여자의 집을 고르시오.

02 대화를 듣고, 여자가 취할 자세를 고르시오.

03 다음을 듣고, 오늘 오후의 날씨로 가장 적절한 것을 고르시오.

고난도

04 다음을 듣고, 무엇에 관한 내용인지 가장 적절한 것을 고르시오.

① 의학 실험의 유형
② 의사가 되는 방법
③ 병원 내 다양한 직업들
④ 병원에서 가장 힘든 일
⑤ 병원에서의 일들이 힘든 이유

05 대화를 듣고, 여자가 가입할 동아리로 가장 적절한 것을 고르시오.

① 춤 동아리 ② 여행 동아리
③ 영화 동아리 ④ 테니스 동아리
⑤ 유적 답사 동아리

06 다음을 듣고, 두 사람의 대화가 어색한 것을 고르시오.

① ② ③ ④ ⑤

07 대화를 듣고, Mr. Kim이 도착할 시각을 고르시오.

① 1시 30분 ② 2시
③ 2시 30분 ④ 3시
⑤ 3시 30분

08 대화를 듣고, 남자가 전화를 건 목적으로 가장 적절한 것을 고르시오.

① 안부를 물어보려고
② 수학 책을 빌리려고
③ 수학 문제를 풀어달라고
④ 수학 숙제를 알려 주려고
⑤ 이삿짐 옮기는 것을 도와달라고

09 대화를 듣고, 두 사람이 대화하고 있는 장소로 가장 적절한 곳을 고르시오.

① 방송국 ② 음식점
③ 야구장 ④ 도서관
⑤ 극장

10 대화를 듣고, 남자의 과학 프로젝트로 가장 적절한 것을 고르시오.

① 로켓 ② 로봇
③ 전기 ④ 인터넷
⑤ 태양 에너지

점수 /20

11 다음을 듣고, 'this'가 가리키는 것으로 가장 적절한 것을 고르시오.

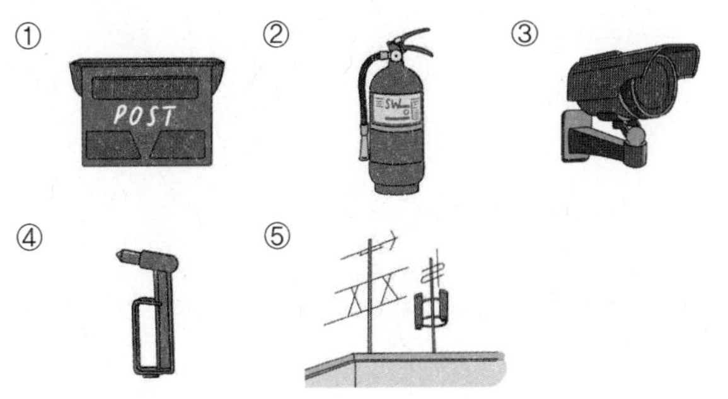

12 대화를 듣고, 두 사람의 관계로 가장 적절한 것을 고르시오.

① 사장 – 비서　② 아버지 – 딸
③ 교사 – 학생　④ 교사 – 학부모
⑤ 점원 – 손님

13 대화를 듣고, 남자의 심정으로 가장 적절한 것을 고르시오.

① 슬픔　② 감사
③ 기쁨　④ 화남
⑤ 미안함

14 대화를 듣고, 여자가 가려고 하는 장소를 고르시오.

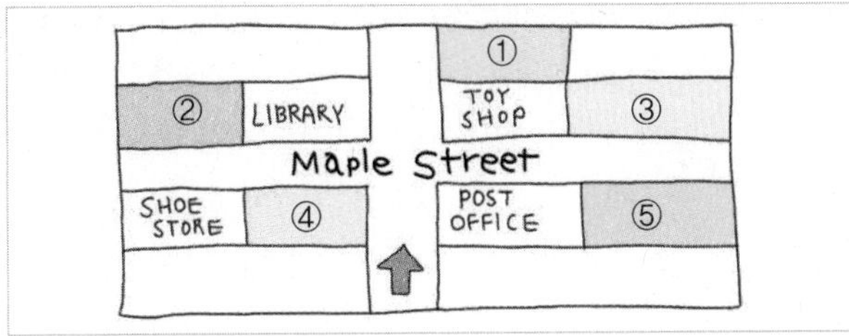

15 대화를 듣고, 여자가 할머니 댁에 머물 기간을 고르시오.

① three days　② five days
③ six days　④ seven days
⑤ ten days

고난도

16 대화를 듣고, 대화의 내용과 일치하는 것을 고르시오.

① 여자는 더워서 에어컨을 켰다.
② 남자는 방 안이 답답하다고 생각한다.
③ 여자는 방 안이 너무 춥다고 생각한다.
④ 여자는 창문을 열고 선풍기를 켰다.
⑤ 남자는 더울 때 에어컨 켜는 것을 좋아한다.

17 대화를 듣고, 여자가 약속 시간에 늦은 이유로 가장 적절한 것을 고르시오.

① 늦잠을 자서
② 시계가 고장 나서
③ 공연 시간을 잘못 알아서
④ 공연 입장권을 잃어버려서
⑤ 저녁 식사 준비를 해야 해서

18 대화를 듣고, 여자가 남자에게 제안한 것으로 가장 적절한 것을 고르시오.

① 새로운 넥타이를 살 것
② 더러운 넥타이를 벗을 것
③ 세탁소에 넥타이를 맡길 것
④ 여분의 넥타이를 빌려 줄 것
⑤ 다른 사람의 넥타이를 빌릴 것

[19~20] 대화를 듣고, 남자의 마지막 말에 이어질 여자의 응답으로 가장 적절한 것을 고르시오.

19 Woman: ______________________

① Thank you.
② Sorry. I can't.
③ You're welcome.
④ I will write it down.
⑤ It's too hard for me.

20 Woman: ______________________

① You're good at painting.
② Thank you for helping me.
③ I'll teach you how to paint.
④ Of course. I bought them, too.
⑤ This paintbrush is very expensive.

다시 들으면서 듣기 만점에 도전하세요!
Dictation: 스크립트의 주요 부분을 다시 들으면서!
실전 ⊕: 세부 정보가 많은 스크립트를 다른 문제로 살살이!

01 그림 정보 파악 – 사물

대화를 듣고, 여자의 집을 고르시오.

① ② ③ ④ ⑤

W This is my new house. What do you think?
M It's quite big.
W It's ________ ________ ________. (2층 집)
M I see. Each floor ________ ________ ________ ________. (2개의 창문만 있다)
W Yes, it isn't many, but it's enough for me. I can open the windows and take a deep breath of fresh air every morning.
M I like it. I think it's a lovely house.

02 그림 정보 파악 – 인물

raise one hand, stand beside the chair, look at your hand가 지시하는 동작을 머릿속으로 그려본다.

대화를 듣고, 여자가 취할 자세를 고르시오.

① ② ③ ④ ⑤

M Hey, would you ________ ________ ________? (한 손을 들다)
W Like this? Should I ________ ________ ________ ________ or sit on the chair? (의자 옆에 서 있다)
M Stand for a moment, please. And would you ________ ________ ________ ________ in the air? (당신의 손을 보다)
W OK. Like this?
M Yes. Now I'm going to take a picture of you.

고난도

03 날씨 파악

In the afternoon 이후에 언급된 날씨 정보를 주의깊게 듣는다.

다음을 듣고, 오늘 오후의 날씨로 가장 적절한 것을 고르시오.

① fog ② wind, rain ③ ④ ⑤

M Good morning, everyone. This morning we have thick fog around the Seoul area. But the fog will go away around noon. In the afternoon, we'll ________ ________ ________ ________ ________ (약간의 바람이 불다) and ________ (비가 오다) and it'll be colder than it is now. So ________ ________ ________ (우산을 가져가라) with you and be sure to wear your coat.

고난도

04 주제 파악

다양한 직업군과 관련된 표현을 주의깊게 듣는다.

다음을 듣고, 무엇에 관한 내용인지 가장 적절한 것을 고르시오.

① 의학 실험의 유형
② 의사가 되는 방법
③ 병원 내 다양한 직업들
④ 병원에서 가장 힘든 일
⑤ 병원에서의 일들이 힘든 이유

W When people think of hospital jobs, they think of doctors and nurses. But there are many other jobs in the hospital. There are people ________ ________ ________. (실험실에서 일하는) They do blood tests and X-rays. Some people take care of medicine. ________ ________ ________ and sell over-the-counter drugs. (약사들은 처방전이 필요한 약을 조제한다) And there are many who ________ ________ ________ (사무 일을 하다), or ________ ________ (청소 일을 하다). These are all important jobs.

05 특정 정보 파악

I'll choose ~. 이후에 나오는 부분을 통해 여자가 최종적으로 선택한 동아리를 파악한다.

대화를 듣고, 여자가 가입할 동아리로 가장 적절한 것을 고르시오.

① 춤 동아리 dance club
② 여행 동아리 travel club
③ 영화 동아리
④ 테니스 동아리 tennis club
⑤ 유적 답사 동아리

I'm going to ~.는 '나는 ~할 것이다.'라는 의미로, 미래의 계획을 나타내는 표현이다.

W Did you choose ________ ________ ________ ________? (가입할 동아리)
M Yes. I'm going to join the tennis club. How about you?
W Well, I'm thinking of joining the travel club, but I also want to join the dance club.
M But you always said ________ ________ ________ ________ ________ all over the country. (너는 여행하고 싶어 하다)
W Right. Hmm.... I'll ________ ________ ________. (여행 동아리를 선택하다)

06 어색한 대화 찾기

다음을 듣고, 두 사람의 대화가 어색한 것을 고르시오.

① ② ③ ④ ⑤

by car: 차로
by train: 기차로
by plane: 비행기로
by subway: 지하철로
on foot: 도보로

① **M** How was your day, honey?
W It was great as usual.
② **M** Can I have your name?
W My name is Kim Bora.
③ **M** Why don't we ________ ________ ________ ________ tonight? (영화 보러 가다)
W Sorry. I'm busy tonight.
④ **M** Are you ________ ________ ________? (그곳에 차로 갈 예정이다)
W I ________ ________ ________ ________ yesterday. (새 차를 샀다)
⑤ **M** Would you give me two tickets for the 3 o'clock show?
W The tickets are all sold out.

07 숫자 파악 – 시각

현재 시각(2 o'clock)과 남은 시각(thirty minutes left)을 잘 듣고 계산한다.

대화를 듣고, Mr. Kim이 도착할 시각을 고르시오.

① 1시 30분 ② 2시
③ 2시 30분 ④ 3시
⑤ 3시 30분

대화를 듣고, Mr. Kim이 원래 오기로 했던 시간을 고르시오.

① 1시 30분 ② 2시
③ 2시 30분 ④ 3시
⑤ 3시 30분

W Did Mr. Kim arrive yet?

M Not yet. He just called me. He said that he would ________ ________ ________ ________. (30분 늦다)

W Really? What time is it now?

M ________ ________ ________. (2시다)

W Then, we have ________ ________ ________ until he comes. (30분 남은)

M Yes.

08 전화 목적 파악

Would you ~? 이후에 나오는 부분을 주의깊게 듣는다.

대화를 듣고, 남자가 전화를 건 목적으로 가장 적절한 것을 고르시오.

① 안부를 물어보려고
② 수학 책을 빌리려고
③ 수학 문제를 풀어달라고
④ 수학 숙제를 알려 주려고
⑤ 이삿짐 옮기는 것을 도와달라고

Would you come to my place?는 '우리 집에 올래?'라는 의미로, 부탁이나 초대의 표현이다.

[Telephone rings.]

M Hello, may I speak to Jenny, please?

W Speaking.

M This is Brooks. Do you ________ ________ ________ ________ ________ now? (나를 도와줄 시간이 좀 있다)

W Yes, I do.

M Would you come to my place and ________ ________ ________ ________? I can't solve some math problems. (수학을 도와주다)

W OK. I'll be there soon.

09 장소 추론

핵심 어구 see the actor, The movie's going to start 등을 통해 장소를 추론해 본다.

대화를 듣고, 두 사람이 대화하고 있는 장소로 가장 적절한 것을 고르시오.

① 방송국 ② 음식점
③ 야구장 ④ 도서관
⑤ 극장

W I can't wait to ________ ________ ________. He's so handsome. (그 배우를 보다)

M You're always saying that.

W Sorry. We should have gotten ________ ________ ________ ________ before sitting down. (약간의 팝콘과 콜라)

M You're right. But I'll go and get them.

W Thanks. Hurry back. ________ ________ ________ ________ ________ in a few minutes. (영화가 시작할 예정이다)

10 특정 정보 파악

대화를 듣고, 남자의 과학 프로젝트로 가장 적절한 것을 고르시오.

① 로켓 ② 로봇
③ 전기 ④ 인터넷
⑤ 태양 에너지

대화를 듣고, 여자가 할 일로 가장 적절한 것을 고르시오.

① 축소 모형 만들기
② 과학 프로젝트 주제 정하기
③ 인터넷으로 정보 찾기
④ 남자의 프로젝트 도와주기
⑤ 과학 선생님과 상담하기

W What do you have there?

M It's my science project. I'm building a model.

W What kind of a model is it?

M I'm trying to ________ ________ ________ ________. What are you doing? (축소 모형 로켓을 만들다)

W I might do a project about ________ ________. (전기를 만드는 것)

M That could be fun. It sounds like you have some research to do.

W That's right. I'll start ________ ________ ________ ________. (인터넷에서 정보 찾는 것)

11 그림 "this" 파악 (담화)

다음을 듣고, 'this'가 가리키는 것으로 가장 적절한 것을 고르시오.

① ② ③ ④ ⑤

POST

M You can find this in any ________ ________ or on a bus or a train. In fact, the law requires that every building should have this. If there is a fire, you can use this to ________ ________ ________ ________. What is this?

(공공장소 / 불을 끄다)

12 관계 추론

대화를 듣고, 두 사람의 관계로 가장 적절한 것을 고르시오.

① 사장 – 비서 ② 아버지 – 딸
③ 교사 – 학생 ④ 교사 – 학부모
⑤ 점원 – 손님

반복되는 어휘 lesson, class 등에서 단서를 얻는다.

M Christine, can you ________ ________ ________? (내 수업을 이해하다)
W It's a little hard for me, but I think I can do it.
M I'm happy to hear that. If you don't give up, you can ________ ________ ________. (좋은 성적을 받다)
W I'm trying. Nowadays, I am trying hard to ________ ________ ________ in your class. (필기를 잘 하다)
M That's a good way to follow the class.

13 심정 추론

대화를 듣고, 남자의 심정으로 가장 적절한 것을 고르시오.

① 슬픔 ② 감사
③ 기쁨 ④ 화남
⑤ 미안함

What can I help you with?는 점원이 손님에게 무엇을 도와줄지 묻는 표현이다.

감정을 나타내는 표현(feel terrible)을 주의깊게 듣는다.

M Excuse me.
W Yes. What can I help you with?
M There is ________ ________ ________ ________ ________. (수프에 머리카락)
W Oh, really? I'm so sorry. Let me bring you another bowl of soup.
M You don't have to do that. I don't want to eat anything here.
I ________________. (기분이 아주 안 좋다)
W I'm really sorry, sir.

14 그림 정보 파악 – 지도

대화를 듣고, 여자가 가려고 하는 장소를 고르시오.

Would you tell me where ~ is?는 길을 물을 때 사용하는 표현으로, How do(can) I get to ~?로 바꿔 말할 수 있다.

마지막 남자의 말 next to the library가 중요한 단서가 된다.

W Excuse me. Would you tell me where Wilson Bank is?
M ________ ________ ________ ________. And turn left at Maple Street. (한 블록 직진하라)
W ________ ________ at Maple Street? (좌회전하라)
M That's right. And you will see the library on your right.
W The library on my right? Is it across from the library?
M No, the bank is right ________ ________ ________ ________. (도서관 옆에)
W Now I see. Thank you very much.

15 숫자 파악 – 날짜

할머니 댁으로 떠나는 요일과 어떤 요일까지 머무를 것인지를 주의깊게 듣는다.

대화를 듣고, 여자가 할머니 댁에 머물 기간을 고르시오.

① three days
② five days
③ six days
④ seven days
⑤ ten days

M When are you leaving for your grandmother's house?

W I'm ______ ______.
다음 주 월요일에 떠나다

M When will you come back?

W I'm ______ ______ ______ of the same week.
금요일까지 그곳에서 머물다

M I see. I hope you have a good time there.

W Thanks.

고난도

16 내용 일치 파악

대화를 듣고, 대화의 내용과 일치하는 것을 고르시오.

① 여자는 더워서 에어컨을 켰다.
② 남자는 방 안이 답답하다고 생각한다.
③ 여자는 방 안이 너무 춥다고 생각한다.
④ 여자는 창문을 열고 선풍기를 켰다.
⑤ 남자는 더울 때 에어컨 켜는 것을 좋아한다.

M Why did you open the window?

W I wanted to get some fresh air. It's ______ ______ ______.
이 안은 답답한

M Just turn on the air conditioner.

W But I don't like air conditioning. It's too cold.

M On a hot day, I think ______ ______ ______.
에어컨을 켜는 것이 최고이다

W I ______ ______ ______ ______ ______ and use a fan.
창문을 여는 것을 더 좋아하다

M Alright. It's not too hot anyway.

17 이유 파악

Sorry. 뒤에 이어지는 이유 부분을 집중해서 듣는다.

대화를 듣고, 여자가 약속 시간에 늦은 이유로 가장 적절한 것을 고르시오.

① 늦잠을 자서
② 시계가 고장 나서
③ 공연 시간을 잘못 알아서
④ 공연 입장권을 잃어버려서
⑤ 저녁 식사 준비를 해야 해서

M Jane! Was there a problem? You're thirty minutes late.

W Sorry. I thought ______ ______ ______ ______ ______ ______.
뮤지컬이 6시에 시작할 것이다

M No, it starts at five.

W ______ ______ ______. I'm terribly sorry. I'll buy you dinner tonight.
내 실수다

M Anyway let's go into the theater. The musical will start soon.

18 특정 정보 파악

대화를 듣고, 여자가 남자에게 제안한 것으로 가장 적절한 것을 고르시오.

① 새로운 넥타이를 살 것
② 더러운 넥타이를 벗을 것
③ 세탁소에 넥타이를 맡길 것
④ 여분의 넥타이를 빌려 줄 것
⑤ 다른 사람의 넥타이를 빌릴 것

M I have an important meeting at 2, but ________ ________ ________ (내 넥타이에 얼룩이 졌다) ________ ________ ________.
W Do you have an extra tie?
M No, I didn't bring one.
W What are you going to do? Are you going to take it to the cleaner?
M Not really. Maybe I should go and buy a new tie.
W You don't have enough time. Is there someone you could ________ (넥타이를 빌리다) ________ ________?
M That's a good idea. Who's here today?
W I'll ask Tim. He always wears a tie.

19 알맞은 응답 찾기

[19~20] 대화를 듣고, 남자의 마지막 말에 이어질 여자의 응답으로 가장 적절한 것을 고르시오.

Woman: ________________

① Thank you.
② Sorry, I can't.
③ You're welcome.
④ I will write it down.
⑤ It's too hard for me.

Is there anything I can help you with?는 상대방에게 도와줄 일이 있는지 묻는 표현이다.

남자가 여자의 부탁을 수락하는 상황임을 파악한다.

W Tony. Would you come here for a minute?
M Is there anything I can help you with, Mom?
W Yes. Would you ________ (쓰레기 봉투를 내다놓다) ________ ________ ________ to the front of the house?
M That's no problem. I'll ________ (바로 그 일을 하다) ________ ________ ________.
W ________________________________

20 알맞은 응답 찾기

Woman: ________________

① You're good at painting.
② Thank you for helping me.
③ I'll teach you how to paint.
④ Of course. I bought them, too.
⑤ This paintbrush is very expensive.

W Honey, what are you doing this Saturday?
M I have nothing to do.
W We have to ________ (현관문에 페인트칠을 하다) ________ ________. It looks too old. So I already bought some paint.
M You're so diligent. And ________ (페인트 붓은요) ________ ________?
W ________________________________

영어듣기능력평가 10회

학년 반 번
이름

01 다음을 듣고, 그림을 바르게 설명한 것을 고르시오.

① ② ③ ④ ⑤

02 대화를 듣고, 남자가 기르고 있는 애완동물을 고르시오.

① 
② 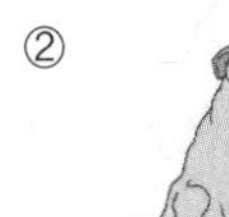
③  
④ 
⑤  

03 다음을 듣고, 포항의 오늘 오후의 날씨로 가장 적절한 것을 고르시오.

① 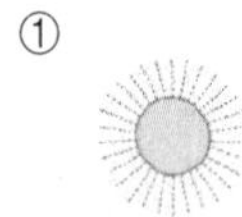
② 
③  
④ 
⑤ 

04 대화를 듣고, 두 사람이 이용할 교통 수단으로 가장 적절한 것을 고르시오.

① 지하철 ② 버스
③ 승용차 ④ 자전거
⑤ 택시

05 대화를 듣고, 여자의 마지막 말의 의도로 가장 적절한 것을 고르시오.

① 격려 ② 초대
③ 칭찬 ④ 확인
⑤ 비난

06 대화를 듣고, 여자의 심정으로 가장 적절한 것을 고르시오.

① bored ② happy
③ surprised ④ angry
⑤ worried

07 대화를 듣고, 남자가 여자를 도와줄 수 없는 이유로 가장 적절한 것을 고르시오.

① 손을 다쳐서
② 차가 고장나서
③ 가구가 너무 무거워서
④ 손과 옷이 너무 더러워서
⑤ 집에서 멀리 떨어져 있어서

08 다음을 듣고, 'this'가 가리키는 것으로 가장 적절한 것을 고르시오.

① 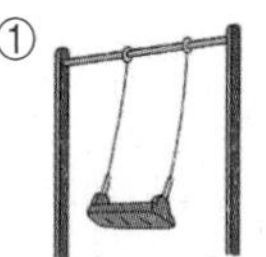 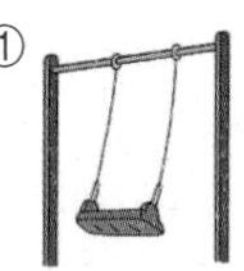
② 
③ 
④ 
⑤ 

09 대화를 듣고, 무엇에 관한 내용인지 가장 적절한 것을 고르시오.

① 왕가에 관한 다큐멘터리
② 여자가 좋아하는 역사 채널
③ 최근에 감명 깊게 본 TV 프로그램
④ 두 사람이 좋아하는 다큐멘터리의 종류
⑤ 두 사람이 오늘 저녁에 함께 볼 다큐멘터리

점수 /20

고난도
10 대화를 듣고, 여자가 집으로 출발할 시각을 고르시오.

① 6:30 ② 7:00
③ 7:30 ④ 8:00
⑤ 8:30

고난도
11 대화를 듣고, 여자가 거스름돈으로 받은 금액을 고르시오.

① 1,500원 ② 2,500원
③ 3,500원 ④ 4,000원
⑤ 5,000원

12 대화를 듣고, 남자가 찾고 있는 밀가루의 위치로 가장 적절한 것을 고르시오.

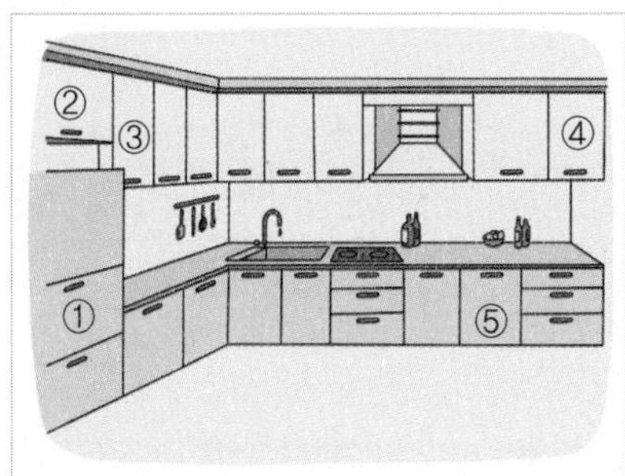

고난도
13 다음을 듣고, 식물원 관람에 대한 설명으로 일치하지 않는 것을 고르시오.

① 2시간 머물 예정이다.
② 12시까지 돌아와야 한다.
③ 입장권은 각자 사야 한다.
④ 실내에서 음식을 먹을 수 없다.
⑤ 물병을 가지고 들어갈 수 있다.

14 대화를 듣고, 남자 아버지의 직업으로 가장 적절한 것을 고르시오.

① 교수 ② 의사
③ 연구원 ④ 영화 감독
⑤ 영화 배우

15 대화를 듣고, 두 사람이 대화하고 있는 장소로 가장 적절한 곳을 고르시오.

① 공항 ② 호텔
③ 식당 ④ 여행사
⑤ 백화점

16 대화를 듣고, 여자가 남자에게 부탁한 일로 가장 적절한 것을 고르시오.

① 쇼핑 함께 가기
② 재미있는 일 하기
③ 자동차 태워 주기
④ 자동차 빌려 주기
⑤ 집들이 선물 사다 주기

17 대화를 듣고, 두 사람의 관계로 가장 적절한 것을 고르시오.

① 약사 – 환자 ② 간호사 – 환자
③ 의사 – 간호사 ④ 식당 종업원 – 손님
⑤ 유치원 교사 – 학부모

18 대화를 듣고, 남자가 여자에게 제안한 것으로 가장 적절한 것을 고르시오.

① 도움 청하기
② 쓰레기 청소하기
③ 높은 울타리 치기
④ 이웃과 말해 보기
⑤ 경찰에게 신고하기

[19~20] 대화를 듣고, 여자의 마지막 말에 이어질 남자의 응답으로 가장 적절한 것을 고르시오.

19 Man: ______________________

① I don't want to be late.
② I have to be there before 6.
③ All our friends will come, too.
④ Can you give my present to Greg?
⑤ I have to go to my aunt's wedding.

20 Man: ______________________

① No. My brother doesn't like me.
② Yes. I like my older brother a lot.
③ No. I'm the only child in my family.
④ Yes. I want to have an older brother.
⑤ No. I don't know anybody in this club.

영어듣기능력평가 10회 DICTATION

다시 들으면서 듣기 만점에 도전하세요!
Dictation: 스크립트의 주요 부분을 다시 들으면서!
실전 ⊕: 세부 정보가 많은 스크립트를 다른 문제로 살살이!

01 그림 정보 파악 – 토익형

행동을 묘사하고 있는 동사에 집중하여 듣는다.

다음을 듣고, 그림을 바르게 설명한 것을 고르시오.

① ② ③ ④ ⑤

W ① She is ______ ______ ______. (나무를 심고 있다)
② She is ______ ______ ______. (식물에 물을 주고 있다)
③ She is buying some flowers.
④ She is picking flowers.
⑤ She is carrying a flowerpot.

02 그림 정보 파악 – 사물

대화를 듣고, 남자가 기르고 있는 애완동물을 고르시오.

①　②　③　④　⑤

W Look at ______ ______. I'd like to have one. (귀여운 아기고양이들)
M Ask your mom to have a pet.
W She doesn't like cats, dogs and hamsters.
M My mom didn't like pets, either. But she likes Ming Ming now.
W When did you get her?
M A year before. She was ______ ______ ______ ______ then. (아주 작은 강아지)

03 날씨 파악

'포항'이 언급되는 부분을 주의깊게 듣는다.

다음을 듣고, 포항의 오늘 오후의 날씨로 가장 적절한 것을 고르시오.

①　②　③　④ snow　⑤

W Good morning. This is Kim Jisu from HBS weather center. It is cloudy ______ ______ ______ ______. (한반도 전체) In Seoul and Incheon, we are expecting rain soon. However, in the southeastern part of the country in Pohang and Daegu, it will start ______ ______ ______ ______ ______. (오후 늦게 눈이 내리는 것) It will be the first snow this year. It will also snow in Jeju.

04 특정 정보 파악

Why don't we ~? 이후에 나오는 부분을 주의깊게 듣는다.

대화를 듣고, 두 사람이 이용할 교통 수단으로 가장 적절한 것을 고르시오.

① 지하철 ② 버스
③ 승용차 ④ 자전거
⑤ 택시

M Where is the meeting place?

W In front of Mega World ticket booth.

M Can we ________ ________ ________? (지하철을 타다)

W It's not very far from here. ________ ________ ________ ________ ________? (택시를 타는 게 어때)

M Isn't it too expensive?

W It won't be that expensive if we pay together.

M Good idea.

05 의도 추론

대화를 듣고, 여자의 마지막 말의 의도로 가장 적절한 것을 고르시오.

① 격려 ② 초대
③ 칭찬 ④ 확인
⑤ 비난

Go for it!은 '힘 내!'라는 의미로, 상대방을 격려하는 표현이다.

W You are the next speaker, Larry. Are you ready?

M I am really nervous. I think I will forget everything as soon as I stand on the stage.

W You can't forget it because ________ ________ ________ ________. (넌 연습을 아주 많이 했다) Look at people's eyes and speak clearly. Don't talk fast.

M Okay.

W I know ________ ________ ________ ________ ________ ________, Larry. (넌 아주 잘 할 것이다) Go for it!

06 심정 추론

What if ~?의 표현을 통해 여자의 심경을 추론할 수 있다.

대화를 듣고, 여자의 심정으로 가장 적절한 것을 고르시오.

① bored 지루한
② happy 기쁜
③ surprised 놀란
④ angry 화가 난
⑤ worried 걱정스러운

What if ~?는 '~라면 어쩌죠?'라는 의미로, 가정을 나타내는 표현이다.

W Mr. Gang, I think I have to go home now.

M What's the problem, Nara?

W I think ________ ________ ________ ________. (나는 열이 있다) I feel cold now.

M Oh, I see. I'll call your mom. Go straight home.

W Mr. Gang, ________ ________ ________ ________? (만약 신종플루면 어쩌죠)

M ________ ________ ________ (괜찮을 것이다) if you take medicine. Take good care of yourself.

W Yes, I will.

07 이유 파악

거절의 말 I can't. 뒤에 이어지는 이유 부분을 집중해서 듣는다.

대화를 듣고, 남자가 여자를 도와줄 수 <u>없는</u> 이유로 가장 적절한 것을 고르시오.

① 손을 다쳐서
② 차가 고장나서
③ 가구가 너무 무거워서
④ 손과 옷이 너무 더러워서
⑤ 집에서 멀리 떨어져 있어서

W Ryan! Where are you?

M ________ ________ ________ (나는 자동차를 고치고 있다) in the garage.

W Can you come and carry this? It's too heavy.

M Oh, I can't. ________ ________ ________ ________ ________ ________ (내 손과 옷이 정말 더럽다) now. I can't come inside the house right now.

W When do you think you can finish it?

M Well, it won't take long.

08 그림 "this" 파악 (담화)

다음을 듣고, 'this'가 가리키는 것으로 가장 적절한 것을 고르시오.

① ② ③ ④ ⑤

M You can see this in playgrounds, parks, or schools. First, you ________ ________ ________ (계단을 오르다), and sit down at the top. Then, you slide all the way down. It is fun, because you can ________ ________ ________ (빠르게 내려가다). What is this?

09 주제 파악

대화를 듣고, 무엇에 관한 내용인지 가장 적절한 것을 고르시오.

① 왕가에 관한 다큐멘터리
② 여자가 좋아하는 역사 채널
③ 최근에 감명 깊게 본 TV 프로그램
④ 두 사람이 좋아하는 다큐멘터리의 종류
⑤ 두 사람이 오늘 저녁에 함께 볼 다큐멘터리

⊕ 대화를 듣고, 대화 후에 여자가 할 일로 가장 적절한 것을 고르시오.

① 역사에 대한 다큐멘터리 시청하기
② 동물에 대한 다큐멘터리 시청하기
③ 자연 프로그램 추천해주기
④ 역사 프로그램 추천해주기
⑤ 남자와 만날 약속 시간 정하기

W Do you like watching documentaries on TV?
M Yes, I ________ ________ ________ (자연 프로그램을 좋아하다). I enjoy watching what animals do.
W I like those, but I ________ ________ ________ (역사 프로그램이 더 좋다).
M History shows about wars are interesting.
W I'd rather watch shows about kings and queens.
M I know you watch the history channel a lot. Can you recommend one?
W Sure.

고난도

10 숫자 파악 – 시각

대화를 듣고, 여자가 집으로 출발할 시각을 고르시오.

① 6:30 ② 7:00
③ 7:30 ④ 8:00
⑤ 8:30

M Jenny, your cell phone has a message.
W Oh, thank you.
M What does it say?
W It's my mother. She said I have to ________ ________ ________ ________ ________ ________ (8시 전에 집으로 오다).
M What time is it now?
W ________ ________ ________ (7시다). I have to ________ ________ ________ ________ (30분 후에 출발하다).
M Okay. Let's practice just two more times and finish today's practice.

고난도

11 숫자 파악 – 금액

구입한 물건과 각각의 가격을 잘 듣고 계산한다.

대화를 듣고, 여자가 거스름돈으로 받은 금액을 고르시오.

① 1,500원 ② 2,500원
③ 3,500원 ④ 4,000원
⑤ 5,000원

M May I help you?
W Yes, I'd like to buy a pack of A4 copy paper.
M It's ________ ________. (2,500원)
W And this wrapping paper, too.
M It's ________ ________. (1,000원)
W Here's ________ ________. (5,000원)
M And here is your change. Thank you.

12 위치 파악

대화를 듣고, 남자가 찾고 있는 밀가루의 위치로 가장 적절한 것을 고르시오.

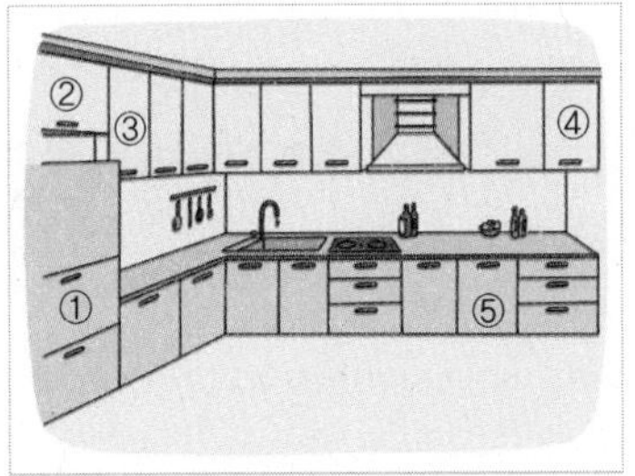

M Do we have any flour?
W I think I put it in the fridge. Check the middle part.
M I checked there already, but it wasn't there.
W Really? Hmm, what about the cupboard right ________ ________ ________? (냉장고 위에)
M Let me check. *[pause]* It's not here, either.
W Then it must be in one of the other upper cupboards.
M Yes, I found it. It was in the cupboard ________ ________ ________ ________. (맨 오른쪽에)

고난도

13 내용 일치 파악

다음을 듣고, 식물원 관람에 대한 설명으로 일치하지 않는 것을 고르시오.

① 2시간 머물 예정이다.
② 12시까지 돌아와야 한다.
③ 입장권은 각자 사야 한다.
④ 실내에서 음식을 먹을 수 없다.
⑤ 물병을 가지고 들어갈 수 있다.

W This is your tour guide, Jane. We are arriving in front of the Botanical Gardens. We are ________ ________ ________ ________ (이곳에 2시간 동안 머물다). It's 10 o'clock now, so you have to ________ ________ ________ ________ ________ ________ ________ ________ (12시까지 버스로 돌아오다). When you get off the bus, I'll give you a ticket for the Botanical Gardens. You ________ ________ ________ (음식물을 가지고 들어갈 수 없다) in the Gardens, but ________ ________ ________ ________ (물병은 괜찮다).

14 직업 추론

남자 아버지의 직업에 대한 언급은 마지막 부분에 처음 나오며, 간접적으로 언급되는 것에 주의한다.

대화를 듣고, 남자 아버지의 직업으로 가장 적절한 것을 고르시오.

① 교수 ② 의사
③ 연구원 ④ 영화 감독
⑤ 영화 배우

What kind of job do you want to have?는 장래에 갖고 싶은 직업을 묻는 표현으로, What do you want to be?로 바꿔 말할 수 있다.

➕ 대화를 듣고, 남자가 현재 원하는 장래 희망으로 가장 적절한 것을 고르시오.

① 교수 ② 의사
③ 연구원 ④ 영화 감독
⑤ 영화 배우

W George, what kind of job do you want to have?
M I'd like to be an actor.
W I believe you will ________ ________ ________ ________. (훌륭한 배우가 되다)
M My father doesn't think so. He wants me to ________ ________ ________. (의사가 되다)
W ________ ________ ________? (그분처럼)
M That's right. But I don't have any interest in medicine.

15 장소 추론

대화를 듣고, 두 사람이 대화하고 있는 장소로 가장 적절한 곳을 고르시오.

① 공항 ② 호텔
③ 식당 ④ 여행사
⑤ 백화점

single room: 1인용 침실
double room: 2인용 침실
twin room: 1인용 침대가 2개 있는 방

W Good afternoon, sir. How may I help you?
M Good afternoon. I would like to check in.
W Sure. Do you have a reservation?
M Yes, under Ben Johnson.
W I have it here, Mr. Johnson. ________ ________(1인실), ________ ________ ________(3일 동안)?
M Yes, that's correct.
W OK, ________ ________ ________ ________(여기 키 카드가 있다). It's ________ ________(731호실).
M Thank you.

16 부탁 파악

대화를 듣고, 여자가 남자에게 부탁한 일로 가장 적절한 것을 고르시오.

① 쇼핑 함께 가기
② 재미있는 일 하기
③ 자동차 태워 주기
④ 자동차 빌려 주기
⑤ 집들이 선물 사다 주기

Do you want me to ~? 이후에 나오는 부분을 주의깊게 듣는다.

W Do you have some free time tomorrow?
M Sure. What do you have in mind?
W Actually, I need your help.
M What do you want me to do?
W I have to go shopping for ________ ________ ________ ________(내 여동생의 집들이). But my car is in for repair.
M Do you ________ ________ ________ ________(내가 차로 태워다 주기를 원하다) to the department store?
W That would be great.
M No problem.
W Thanks a lot. I'll see you tomorrow morning.

17 관계 추론

대화를 듣고, 두 사람의 관계로 가장 적절한 것을 고르시오.

① 약사 – 환자
② 간호사 – 환자
③ 의사 – 간호사
④ 식당 종업원 – 손님
⑤ 유치원 교사 – 학부모

Can I have your prescription?은 약사가 환자에게 처방전을 달라고 요청할 때 사용하는 표현이다.

약 복용법에 대해 자세히 설명하는 내용을 통해 두 사람의 관계를 추론할 수 있다.

W Good afternoon. ________ ________ ________ ________ ________(처방전을 주시겠어요)?
M Here it is.
W Thank you. Just wait for a moment while ________ ________ ________ ________ ________(당신의 약이 준비되다).
M I'd like to buy this band-aid, too.
W OK. ________ ________ ________(제가 말씀드릴게요) you about your medicine. Take this pink syrup four times a day. Take these pills three times a day after a meal. It's 4,500 won including the band-aid.
M Here you are.

18 특정 정보 파악

you should ~. 이후에 제안하는 내용이 언급되어 있다.

대화를 듣고, 남자가 여자에게 제안한 것으로 가장 적절한 것을 고르시오.

① 도움 청하기
② 쓰레기 청소하기
③ 높은 울타리 치기
④ 이웃과 말해 보기
⑤ 경찰에게 신고하기

W I'm having a problem with my neighbor.
M Why? What is he doing to you?
W Things from his home ______ ______ ______ ______ ______.
계속 내 잔디밭으로 불어 넘어오다
M You mean garbage? Maybe you should ______ ______ ______ ______ ______.
그와 그것에 대해 이야기 해 보다
W I thought a fence would help.
M It might not. Anyway, he may not even know there is a problem.
W I guess you're right. But I'm just a little shy.
M I know you are, but you should ______ ______ ______ ______.
그가 그것을 알게 하다

19 알맞은 응답 찾기

Why not?은 남자가 파티에 오지 못하는 이유를 묻는 말임에 유의한다.

[19~20] 대화를 듣고, 여자의 마지막 말에 이어질 남자의 응답으로 가장 적절한 것을 고르시오.

Man: ______________

① I don't want to be late.
② I have to be there before 6.
③ All our friends will come, too.
④ Can you give my present to Greg?
⑤ I have to go to my aunt's wedding.

[Telephone rings.]
W Hello.
M Hello, Maggie. This is Thomas. Are you going to Greg's birthday party today?
W Yes. I thought you were coming, too.
M Actually, I called you because of that. I ______ ______ ______ ______ ______.
그 파티에 갈 수 없다
W ______ ______?
왜 못 오는데
M ______________

20 알맞은 응답 찾기

Man: ______________

① No. My brother doesn't like me.
② Yes. I like my older brother a lot.
③ No. I'm the only child in my family.
④ Yes. I want to have an older brother.
⑤ No. I don't know anybody in this club.

M Excuse me. Can I come in?
W Of course. Welcome to the newspaper club.
M ______ ______ ______ ______ ______ ______.
나는 이 동아리에 가입하고 싶다
W That's great. What's your name?
M I'm Lee Hun in 1st grade.
W Nice to meet you, Hun. You look like someone in the second grade. Do you ______ ______ ______ ______ ______?
형이나 누나가 있다
M ______________

장소 • 관계 • 직업 • 심정 파악

무엇을 평가하는가?	일상생활이나 친숙한 일반적 주제에 관한 말이나 대화를 듣고 상황 및 화자 간의 관계, 그리고 화자의 심정이나 태도를 추론할 수 있는지를 평가한다.
어떻게 출제되는가?	• 대화를 듣고, 두 사람이 대화하는 장소로 가장 적절한 곳을 고르시오. • 대화를 듣고, 두 사람의 관계로 가장 적절한 것을 고르시오. • 대화를 듣고, 여자가 언급한 엄마의 직업으로 가장 적절한 것을 고르시오. • 대화를 듣고, 남자의 심정으로 가장 적절한 것을 고르시오.

❶ 장소, 관계, 직업을 묻는 경우, 대화의 주제나 소재가 중요한 역할을 하므로 주의하며 듣는다.

❷ 심정을 묻는 경우, 화자의 어조와 전체적인 상황을 동시에 파악한다.

[기출로 전략 확인]

대화를 듣고, 남자의 직업으로 가장 적절한 것을 고르시오. [2018 기출]

① 화가　② 식당 점원　③ 방송 작가
④ 버스 기사　⑤ 안과 의사

M Good evening, ma'am. How did you like your steak?
W It was delicious, thank you.
M Great. Would you like some dessert?
W Yes. Could you show me the menu?
M Certainly. Here you are.
W Um... I'll have the chocolate cake, please.
M Sure. I'll bring it now.

❶ 남자가 여자에게 음식 맛을 물어보고, 후식을 권유하고, 여자가 주문한 메뉴를 준비하려는 모습으로 남자의 직업을 유추할 수 있다.

남 안녕하세요. 스테이크는 마음에 드셨나요?
여 맛있었어요, 감사합니다.
남 잘됐군요. 후식을 드시겠습니까?
여 네. 메뉴 좀 볼 수 있을까요?
남 물론이죠. 여기 있습니다.
여 음... 초콜릿 케이크 부탁해요.
남 네. 지금 가져다 드리겠습니다.

장소 • 관계 파악 유형의 발문과 보기

대화를 듣고, 두 사람이 대화하는 장소로 가장 적절한 곳을 고르시오. [2016 기출]

① 식당 ② 영화관 ③ 가구점
④ 음악실 ⑤ 도서관

만점 잡는 문장 **W** Hi. I'm looking for a dinner table for four people.
M These are all four-person dinner tables.

대화를 듣고, 두 사람의 관계로 가장 적절한 것을 고르시오. [2017 기출]

① 의사 – 환자 ② 교사 – 학생 ③ 요리사 – 손님
④ 버스 운전기사 – 승객 ⑤ 자동차 정비사 – 고객

만점 잡는 문장 **M** Well, there is a small hole in the tire.
W How long will it take to fix the tire?
M It'll take about one hour.

장소 • 관계 • 직업 • 심정 파악하기에 쓰이는 어휘 및 표현

• 장소(세탁소)

A Can you dry-clean this jacket for me? 이 재킷을 드라이크리닝 해 주시겠어요?
B Sure. Anything else? 물론이죠. 다른 건 없나요?

• 관계(사진사 – 손님)

A Hi. I'm here to pick up my passport pictures. My name is Kim Bora.
안녕하세요 여권용 사진을 찾으러 왔어요. 이름은 김보라입니다.
B Kim Bora... Um... Let me see. Oh! Here you are. 김보라... 음... 봅시다... 아! 여기 있네요.

• 직업(열차 매표원)

A I want to buy a train ticket to New York. When is the next train?
뉴욕 행 열차표를 사고 싶습니다. 다음 열차 시간이 언제지요?
B Let me check. The next train for New York leaves in 20 minutes.
봐 볼게요. 뉴욕 행 다음 열차는 20분 후에 있습니다.

(작가)

A Could you tell me about your book? 당신 책에 대해 말해 주시겠어요?
B Sure. It's a love story about my husband and me. 물론이죠. 그것은 남편과 저의 사랑 이야기 입니다.

• 심정

excited 신난	happy 행복한	proud 자랑스러운	glad 기쁜
upset 속상한	sad 슬픈	worried 걱정하는	angry 화가 난
shy 수줍은	nervous 초조한	relaxed 느긋한	bored 지루해 하는

영어듣기능력평가 11회

학년 반 번
이름

01 대화를 듣고, 'this'가 무엇인지 가장 적절한 것을 고르시오.

02 대화를 듣고, 남자가 사려고 하는 신발을 고르시오.

03 다음을 듣고, 대전의 토요일 날씨로 가장 적절한 것을 고르시오.

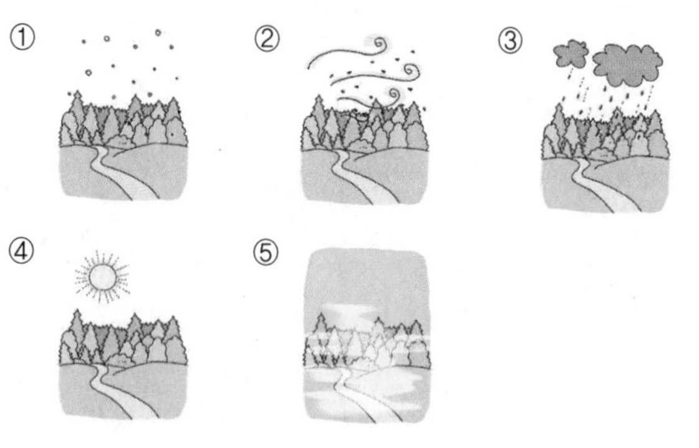

04 대화를 듣고, 여자가 남자에게 부탁한 일로 가장 적절한 것을 고르시오.

① 서점에 다녀올 것
② 우유를 사다 줄 것
③ 3달러를 빌려 줄 것
④ 식탁을 정리해 줄 것
⑤ 스포츠 잡지를 사다 줄 것

05 다음을 듣고, 두 사람의 대화가 <u>어색한</u> 것을 고르시오.

① ② ③ ④ ⑤

고난도

06 대화를 듣고, 남자가 예약한 항공편의 출발 요일과 시각을 고르시오.

① Saturday – 10:00
② Saturday – 5:20
③ Sunday – 10:00
④ Sunday – 5:20
⑤ Sunday – 7:00

07 대화를 듣고, 남자가 전화를 건 목적으로 가장 적절한 것을 고르시오.

① 분실물을 신고하려고
② 호텔 예약을 취소하려고
③ 호텔의 위치를 물어보려고
④ 직원 채용에 대해 알아보려고
⑤ 불친절한 서비스에 대해 항의하려고

08 대화를 듣고, 남자가 지불할 금액을 고르시오.

① $3
② $5
③ $8
④ $15
⑤ $25

09 대화를 듣고, 두 사람이 방과 후에 만나려는 이유로 가장 적절한 것을 고르시오.

① 선물을 사기 위해
② 요리를 하기 위해
③ 컴퓨터를 배우기 위해
④ 역사 시험을 준비하기 위해
⑤ 발표 준비를 같이 하기 위해

10 대화를 듣고, 남자가 기분이 좋은 이유로 가장 적절한 것을 고르시오.

① 오래된 친구를 만나서
② 시간제 일자리를 구해서
③ 한국인 친구를 사귀어서
④ 한국 음식을 먹게 되어서
⑤ 시험에서 좋은 성적을 받아서

점수 /20

11 다음을 듣고, 'I'가 무엇인지 가장 적절한 것을 고르시오.

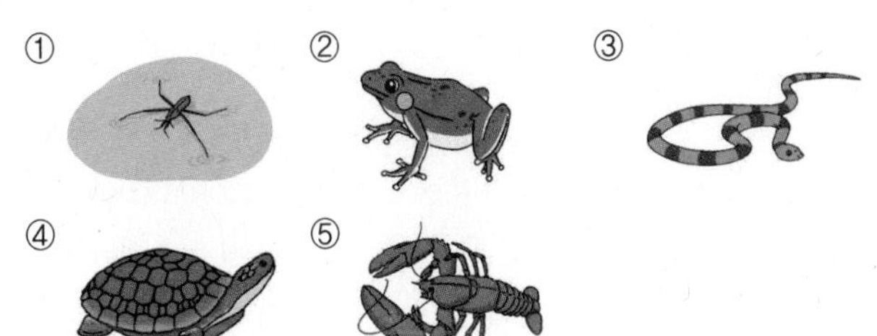

12 대화를 듣고, 남자가 여자에게 충고한 것으로 가장 적절한 것을 고르시오.

① 단 것을 먹지 마라.
② 치아에 좋은 음식을 먹어라.
③ 충치 치료를 지금 바로 하라.
④ 식사 후에는 꼭 양치질을 하라.
⑤ 정기적으로 치아 검진을 받아라.

13 대화를 듣고, 두 사람의 관계로 가장 적절한 것을 고르시오.

① 은행원 – 고객
② 변호사 – 의뢰인
③ 극장 매표원 – 손님
④ 도서관 사서 – 학생
⑤ 비행기 승무원 – 탑승객

고난도

14 대화를 듣고, 여자가 한국에 머물 기간을 고르시오.

① 5일 ② 7일
③ 12일 ④ 15일
⑤ 21일

15 대화를 듣고, 두 사람이 대화하고 있는 장소로 가장 적절한 곳을 고르시오.

① 극장 ② 학교
③ 예식장 ④ 콘서트 홀
⑤ 편의점

고난도

16 대화를 듣고, 여자가 남자의 제안을 거절한 이유로 가장 적절한 것을 고르시오.

① 낚시하는 법을 몰라서
② 학교 숙제를 해야 해서
③ Robin과 약속이 있어서
④ 자원봉사 활동을 해야 해서
⑤ 부모님이 허락하지 않으셔서

17 대화를 듣고, 무엇에 관한 내용인지 가장 적절한 것을 고르시오.

① 과학 발표 주제 ② 과학 발표 일정
③ 과학 성적 ④ 전류의 특성
⑤ 과학선생님 성격

18 대화를 듣고, 여자의 직업으로 가장 적절한 것을 고르시오.

① 서점 직원 ② 도서관 사서
③ 상담 교사 ④ 관광 안내원
⑤ 우체국 직원

[19~20] 대화를 듣고, 여자의 마지막 말에 이어질 남자의 응답으로 가장 적절한 것을 고르시오.

19 Man: ______________________

① Yeah, I didn't have breakfast.
② Okay, I'll order chicken curry.
③ That's good! I like both food.
④ Right. This restaurant is famous.
⑤ Please help yourself. It's all for you.

20 Man: ______________________

① Don't worry. I'll lend you $25.
② You're too young to see the movie.
③ No, I don't want to see *Harry Potter*.
④ Okay, let's see the movie tomorrow.
⑤ Here are the tickets. Enjoy your movie.

영어듣기능력평가 11 회 DICTATION

다시 들으면서 듣기 만점에 도전하세요!
Dictation: 스크립트의 주요 부분을 다시 들으면서!
실전 ⊕: 세부 정보가 많은 스크립트를 다른 문제로 살살이!

01 그림 "this" 파악 (담화)

대화를 듣고, 'this'가 무엇인지 가장 적절한 것을 고르시오.

① climbing
② hang gliding
③ scuba diving
④
⑤

핵심 어구 climb up, reach the top of the mountain 등을 주의깊게 듣는다.

W This is one of our favorite outdoor activities. Unlike other activities such as hang gliding or scuba diving, this doesn't need anything special. For this you need only a pair of good shoes and your health. When you do this, you ________ ________ ________ ________(등산을 하다). When you ________ ________ ________ ________ ________(산의 정상에 오르다), you will feel refreshed.

02 그림 정보 파악 – 사물

대화를 듣고, 남자가 사려고 하는 신발을 고르시오.

①
②
③
④
⑤

W Can I help you?
M Well, I need sandals for a trip. I'm planning to go to the beach.
W What about these? I think these are ________ ________ ________(샌들보다 더 좋다) for your trip.
M They look like sneakers.
W They're not. We call them water shoes. You can ________ ________ ________(그것을 물 속에서 사용하다), and they dry really quickly.
M Can I wear them out of water?
W Of course. They cover your feet well and ________ ________ ________ ________(그것은 걷기에도 좋다) in mountains.
M Okay, I'll take them.

고난도

03 날씨 파악

다음을 듣고, 대전의 토요일 날씨로 가장 적절한 것을 고르시오.

① snow
②
③ rain
④ sunny
⑤

'대전'이 언급된 부분을 주의깊게 듣는다.

W Taking a look at ________ ________ ________ ________(토요일 날씨), we'll have clear and sunny skies in the Seoul area. It will be sunny also in Daegu and Gwangju. However, in Daejeon, there will be ________ ________ ________ ________(눈이 올 확률이 높은). In the Busan area, it'll be partly cloudy in the morning and it will snow or rain in the evening. That's all. I'm Jina Shin. Thank you.

04 부탁 파악

대화를 듣고, 여자가 남자에게 부탁한 일로 가장 적절한 것을 고르시오.

① 서점에 다녀올 것
② 우유를 사다 줄 것 buy some milk
③ 3달러를 빌려 줄 것
④ 식탁을 정리해 줄 것
⑤ 스포츠 잡지를 사다 줄 것
buy a sports magazine

대화를 듣고, 남자의 아버지가 남자에게 부탁한 일로 가장 적절한 것을 고르시오.

① 서점에 다녀올 것
② 우유를 사다 줄 것
③ 3달러를 빌려 줄 것
④ 식탁을 정리해 줄 것
⑤ 스포츠 잡지를 사다 줄 것

아빠와 엄마가 각자 아들에게 부탁한 것을 구분하여 듣는다.

W Where are you going, David? Lunch will be ready soon.
M I'm going to the bookstore. Dad asked me to buy a sports magazine.
W Really? Then can you ______ ______ ______ (우유를 좀 사다) at the mart next to the bookstore?
M Sure, no problem.
W Thank you. Here is ______ ______ ______ ______ (우유 값 3달러).

05 어색한 대화 찾기

다음을 듣고, 두 사람의 대화가 어색한 것을 고르시오.

① ② ③ ④ ⑤

① **W** Did you ever ______ ______ (김치를 먹어 보다)?
M Yes, of course. It was spicy but good.
② **W** I'd like to stay at your hotel.
M How many days are you going to stay?
③ **W** Can I ______ ______ ______ ______ (네 휴대전화를 사용하다)?
M I'm sorry, but I ______ ______ ______ ______ ______ (그의 전화번호를 모르다).
④ **W** Can you speak Korean?
M A little bit. I learned Korean last winter.
⑤ **W** The sky is so dark. It will rain soon.
M I think so. We have to get an umbrella.

고난도

06 숫자 파악 – 날짜, 시각

대화를 듣고, 남자가 예약한 항공편의 출발 요일과 시각을 고르시오.

① Saturday – 10:00
② Saturday – 5:20
③ Sunday – 10:00
④ Sunday – 5:20
⑤ Sunday – 7:00

「One ~, and the other ...」는 두 대상을 설명할 때 사용하는 표현으로, '하나는 ~, 나머지 하나는 …'라고 해석한다.

두 가지 항공편이 언급되고 그 중 하나를 선택하는 상황이므로, 요일과 시각을 메모하면서 듣는다.

M Excuse me, I'd like to book a ticket to London for this Saturday.
W I'm sorry, but there are ______ ______ ______ (토요일에는 항공편이 없는).
M How about Sunday?
W Let me check. We have two flights. One ______ ______ ______ ______ ______ (오전 10시에 출발하다), and the other departs at 5:20 in the afternoon.
M Then, I'll ______ ______ ______ ______ (오전 항공편을 예약하다).
W Fine.

07 전화 목적

I'd like to ~. 이후에 나오는 부분을 주의깊게 듣는다.

대화를 듣고, 남자가 전화를 건 목적으로 가장 적절한 것을 고르시오.

① 분실물을 신고하려고
② 호텔 예약을 취소하려고
③ 호텔의 위치를 물어보려고
④ 직원 채용에 대해 알아보려고
⑤ 불친절한 서비스에 대해 항의하려고

[Telephone rings.]

W Rainbow Hotel. How can I help you?

M Hi, I booked your hotel through the Internet. ________ ________ ________ is 2024. (내 예약 번호)

W Wait a minute, please. Yes, you booked a single room for three nights.

M That's right. But, I'd like to ________ ________ ________. (내 예약을 취소하다)

W No problem. ________ ________ ________ your reservation. (내가 취소하게 하다)

08 숫자 파악 – 금액

한 벌당 가격($3)과 주문한 개수(5 shirts)를 잘 듣고 계산한다.

대화를 듣고, 남자가 지불할 금액을 고르시오.

① $3 ② $5
③ $8 ④ $15
⑤ $25

M Excuse me, I'd like to ________ ________ ________ ________ ________. (이 드레스 셔츠들을 드라이 클리닝하다)

W It costs ________ ________ ________. How many shirts do you have? (셔츠 한 벌당 3달러)

M I have ________ ________. Can I pay when I get them back? (셔츠 다섯 벌)

W Yes, you can. Please let me know your name or phone number.

M My name is Bob Morgan.

09 이유 파악

대화를 듣고, 두 사람이 방과 후에 만나려는 이유로 가장 적절한 것을 고르시오.

① 선물을 사기 위해
② 요리를 하기 위해
③ 컴퓨터를 배우기 위해
④ 역사 시험을 준비하기 위해
⑤ 발표 준비를 같이 하기 위해

W Roger, can you meet me after school?

M All right. Do you want to talk about ________ ________ ________ ________ ________? (역사 수업 발표)

W That's right. You and I are a team for that.

M I'm happy to ________ ________ ________ ________ ________. You are a queen of history. (너와 한 팀이 되다)

W I'm glad to work with you, too. I heard you are really good at making presentation slides. I need to learn from you.

M Okay. See you after school.

10 이유 파악

핵심 어구 got a part-time job, start to work 등에서 단서를 얻는다.

대화를 듣고, 남자가 기분이 좋은 이유로 가장 적절한 것을 고르시오.

① 오래된 친구를 만나서
② 시간제 일자리를 구해서
got a part-time job
③ 한국인 친구를 사귀어서
④ 한국 음식을 먹게 되어서
⑤ 시험에서 좋은 성적을 받아서 물을 사기 위해

W Hi, Peter!

M Hi, Susan! Nice to see you!

W Oh, you look quite good. Did you get an A^+ on the test?

M Well... don't be surprised. I finally ________ ________ ________. (시간제 일자리를 구했다)

W Really? Congratulations, Peter. Where are you going to work?

M At a Korean restaurant on Oxford Street. I ________ ________ ________ next Monday. (일을 시작하다)

11 그림 "I" 파악 (담화)

다음을 듣고, 'I'가 무엇인지 가장 적절한 것을 고르시오.

① ② ③ ④ ⑤

M You can find me near water like ponds and streams. You can see me the most in summer. I have ________ ________ ________ ________ ________. I can jump far because I have long back legs. But my front legs are short. I ________ ________ and mosquitos. What am I?

부드러운 피부와 큰 눈 / 파리를 먹다

12 특정 정보 파악

you should ~. 이후에 나오는 부분을 주의깊게 듣는다.

대화를 듣고, 남자가 여자에게 충고한 것으로 가장 적절한 것을 고르시오.

① 단 것을 먹지 마라.
② 치아에 좋은 음식을 먹어라.
③ 충치 치료를 지금 바로 하라.
④ 식사 후에는 꼭 양치질을 하라.
⑤ 정기적으로 치아 검진을 받아라.

You don't have to ~.는 '~할 필요가 없다.'는 의미로, 불필요를 나타내는 표현이다.

M Please open your mouth and say "Ah...."
W Ah....
M Okay, that's all. Fortunately, you don't have to have any teeth pulled out.
W Whew... what a relief!
M But ________ ________ ________ ________ after every meal. Otherwise, you'll be in a big trouble.

당신은 양치질을 해야 한다

W I see. I'll ________ ________ ________.

당신의 충고를 따르다

⊕ 대화를 듣고, 두 사람의 관계로 가장 적절한 것을 고르시오.

① 미용실 직원 – 손님
② 소아과 의사 – 보호자
③ 약사 – 손님
④ 치과 의사 – 환자
⑤ 식당 종업원 – 손님

13 관계 추론

대화를 듣고, 두 사람의 관계로 가장 적절한 것을 고르시오.

① 은행원 – 고객
② 변호사 – 의뢰인
③ 극장 매표원 – 손님
④ 도서관 사서 – 학생
⑤ 비행기 승무원 – 탑승객

W May I help you?
M I'd like to get the ticket. I ________ ________ ________.

인터넷에서 그것을 예매했다

W Can I have your name, sir?
M My name's Paul Kim.
W We have you here. Did you ________ ________ ________ for the 7 o'clock play?

2장의 표를 예매하다

M That's right.
W Well, here's your ticket. ________ ________.

연극 즐겁게 관람하세요

M Thanks.

고난도

14 숫자 파악 – 날짜

서울과 대전에서 각각 머무는 기간을 잘 듣고 계산한다.

대화를 듣고, 여자가 한국에 머물 기간을 고르시오.

① 5일 ② 7일
③ 12일 ④ 15일
⑤ 21일

M I heard that you're going on a business trip to Korea.
W Yeah, I'll leave for Korea this Friday.
M How long are you going to stay there?
W Well... I'll ______ ______ ______ ______ ______ (서울에서 일주일 머물다). And then, I have to go to Daejeon. I'm going to ______ ______ ______ ______ (그곳에서 5일 동안 머물다).
M Then, you will come back here, won't you?
W Yeah, that's right.

15 장소 추론

핵심 어휘 movie, tickets, popcorn, drinks 등에서 단서를 얻는다.

대화를 듣고, 두 사람이 대화하고 있는 장소로 가장 적절한 곳을 고르시오.

① 극장 ② 학교
③ 예식장 ④ 콘서트 홀
⑤ 편의점

W David, look at all those people! It's really crowded.
M It's Saturday night. Everyone wants to enjoy their time just like us.
W So, did you ______ ______ ______ ______ (어떤 영화를 볼지 결정하다)?
M Yes, I did. What about *Avatar*?
W That's what I want to see, too. Okay, I'll ______ ______ ______ ______ (가서 표를 사 오다) now. You ______ ______ ______ ______ (팝콘과 음료수를 좀 사다) over there.
M Good! I'll get soda and popcorn.

고난도

16 이유 파악

거절의 말 I'd love to ~, but I can't. 뒤에 이유가 나오므로 그 부분에 집중한다.

대화를 듣고, 여자가 남자의 제안을 거절한 이유로 가장 적절한 것을 고르시오.

① 낚시하는 법을 몰라서
② 학교 숙제를 해야 해서
③ Robin과 약속이 있어서
④ 자원봉사 활동을 해야 해서
⑤ 부모님이 허락하지 않으셔서

W Robert, you look excited. Is there something interesting?
M Yes, there is. Tomorrow, I'm going to ______ ______ (낚시하러 가다) in the Colorado River with Robin and Lucy.
W Go fishing in the Colorado River? Sounds exciting.
M Hey, Susan, ______ ______ ______ ______ (우리와 함께 하는 게 어때)? If you do, we'll have much more fun.
W I'd love to join you, but I can't. I have to ______ ______ ______ (자원봉사 활동을 하다) at an orphanage tomorrow.
M Do you? Oh, I didn't know you did such good things.

17 주제, 소재 파악

대화를 듣고, 무엇에 관한 내용인지 가장 적절한 것을 고르시오.

① 과학 발표 주제 ② 과학 발표 일정
③ 과학 성적 ④ 전류의 특성
⑤ 과학선생님 성격

M Suyeon, what's wrong? You look worried.

W I might have to ________ ________ ________ of my presentation. (주제를 바꾸다)

M You mean for the science class?

W Yes, I was going to do it on electric current, but it's not going well.

M Have you talked to Mr. Brown about it?

W Not yet, I'm afraid ________ ________ ________ ________. (그가 화를 낼 것이다)

M No, he is always happy to help us.

18 직업 추론

대화가 이루어지는 장소를 파악하여 여자의 직업을 추론해 본다.

대화를 듣고, 여자의 직업으로 가장 적절한 것을 고르시오.

① 서점 직원 ② 도서관 사서
③ 상담 교사 ④ 관광 안내원
⑤ 우체국 직원

W Good afternoon. How can I help you?

M ________ ________ ________ ________ ________ ________ to Britain. (나는 이 상자를 보내고 싶다)

W Okay. What do you have inside?

M It's a book.

W Would you ________ ________ ________ ________ ________ there? (저울 위에 그것을 올려 놓다)

M All right. How long will it take to get there?

W It'll take a week. It's 6,000 won.

M Here it is.

19 알맞은 응답 찾기

[19~20] 대화를 듣고, 여자의 마지막 말에 이어질 남자의 응답으로 가장 적절한 것을 고르시오.

Man: ________________

① Yeah, I didn't have breakfast.
② Okay, I'll order chicken curry.
③ That's good! I like both food.
④ Right. This restaurant is famous.
⑤ Please help yourself. It's all for you.

W Did you clean your room, Daniel?

M No, I didn't. I was busy because of my homework.

W Then when will you clean your room?

M I'll do it right after I have dinner. By the way, ________ ________ ________ this evening? (저녁 식사는 뭐예요)

W I'm going to ________ ________ ________ ________ ________ ________. (치킨 카레와 토마토 샐러드를 만들다)

M ________________

20 알맞은 응답 찾기

마지막에 여자가 어떤 목적으로 돈을 지불하는지를 파악한다.

Man: ________________

① Don't worry. I'll lend you $25.
② You're too young to see the movie.
③ No, I don't want to see Harry Potter.
④ Okay, let's see the movie tomorrow.
⑤ Here are the tickets. Enjoy your movie.

How would you like to pay?는 돈의 지불 방법을 묻는 표현이다.

W Excuse me, I'd like to ________ ________ ________ ________ ________, *King Kong*. (영화표를 사다)

M I see. What time do you want to see it?

W At 5:30. I need two tickets. How much is it altogether?

M It's $25. How would you like to pay?

W I'll ________ ________ ________. Here is $25. (현금으로 지불하다)

M ________________

영어듣기능력평가 12회

학년 반 번
이름

01 대화를 듣고, 여자가 친구에게 줄 생일 선물을 고르시오.

①  ②  ③ 

④ 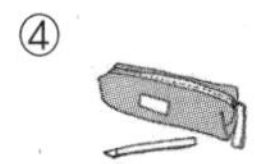 ⑤ 

02 다음을 듣고, 들려주는 내용과 일치하지 않는 것을 고르시오.

03 다음을 듣고, 이번 주말의 날씨로 가장 적절한 것을 고르시오.

04 다음을 듣고, 'this'가 가리키는 것으로 가장 적절한 것을 고르시오.

05 다음을 듣고, 남자에 대해 언급되지 않은 것을 고르시오.

① 이름 ② 캠프 참여 경험
③ 봉사 활동 경험 ④ 자신의 장점
⑤ 장래 희망

06 대화를 듣고, 여자의 직업으로 가장 적절한 것을 고르시오.

① 버스 기사 ② 상점 직원
③ 호텔 매니저 ④ 관광 안내원
⑤ 극장 매표원

07 다음을 듣고, 두 사람의 대화가 어색한 것을 고르시오.

① ② ③ ④ ⑤

08 대화를 듣고, 여자가 남자에게 부탁한 일로 가장 적절한 것을 고르시오.

① 여행사를 소개해 줄 것
② 여행지를 추천해 줄 것
③ 여행 시 주의사항을 안내해 줄 것
④ 안내원에게 여행 일정을 물어볼 것
⑤ 안내원의 이메일 주소를 알려 줄 것

09 대화를 듣고, 무엇에 관한 내용인지 가장 적절한 것을 고르시오.

① 영어 듣기 평가 ② 영단어 학습법
③ 도서 대출 절차 ④ 영어 쓰기 평가
⑤ 효과적인 사전 사용법

10 대화를 듣고, 남자가 가려고 하는 장소를 고르시오.

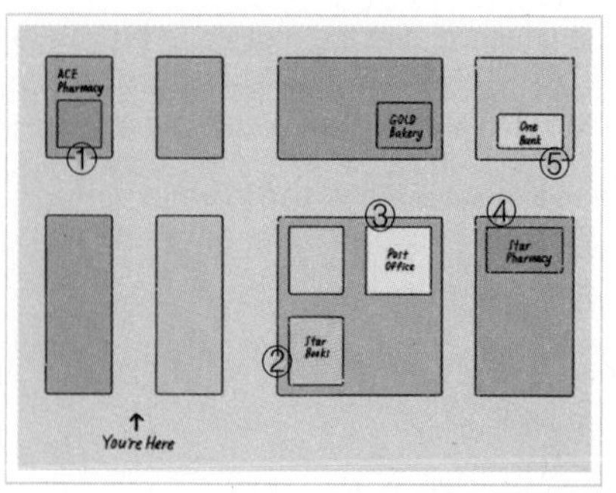

점수 /20

11 대화를 듣고, 남자가 할 일로 가장 적절한 것을 고르시오.

① 안장 높이기
② 커피 사 오기
③ 점심 준비하기
④ 자전거 빌려 주기
⑤ 체인에 기름칠 하기

12 대화를 듣고, 남자의 마지막 말의 의도로 가장 적절한 것을 고르시오.

① 격려
② 후회
③ 축하
④ 놀람
⑤ 실망

13 대화를 듣고, 남자가 테니스를 칠 수 <u>없는</u> 이유로 가장 적절한 것을 고르시오.

① 숙제를 해야 해서
② 할머니를 간호해야 해서
③ 토요일에 선약이 있어서
④ 친구의 병문안을 가야 해서
⑤ 친구의 숙제를 도와주어야 해서

14 대화를 듣고, 여자가 가려고 하는 장소를 고르시오.

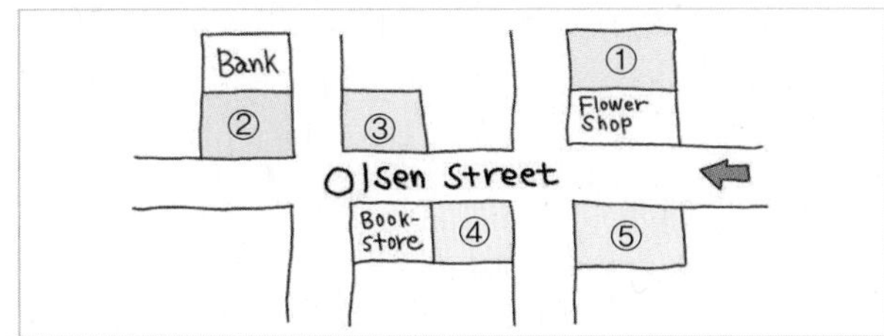

고난도

15 대화를 듣고, 현재 시각을 고르시오.

① 2:00
② 3:00
③ 4:00
④ 5:00
⑤ 6:00

16 대화를 듣고, 여자의 심정으로 가장 적절한 것을 고르시오.

① 걱정됨
② 놀람
③ 미안함
④ 당황함
⑤ 만족스러움

고난도

17 다음을 듣고, London에 대한 설명으로 일치하지 <u>않는</u> 것을 고르시오.

① 영국의 수도이다.
② 다양한 언어가 사용된다.
③ 비가 많이 온다.
④ 3번의 올림픽을 개최했다.
⑤ 세계에서 가장 오래된 2층 버스가 있다.

18 대화를 듣고, 두 사람의 관계로 가장 적절한 것을 고르시오.

① 배우 – 팬
② 아버지 – 딸
③ 가수 – 매니저
④ 음악 교사 – 학생
⑤ 쇼 진행자 – 초대 손님

[19~20] 대화를 듣고, 남자의 마지막 말에 이어질 여자의 응답으로 가장 적절한 것을 고르시오.

19 Woman: ______________________

① No, I'll turn it off.
② You can turn it on.
③ The radio is my good friend.
④ I usually turn off the radio when I drive.
⑤ Yes, I think I should turn the volume up.

20 Woman: ______________________

① Now it's your turn.
② I don't like this game.
③ OK. I'm ready to play.
④ Great. I'll go out soon.
⑤ Don't worry. I'll wait for you.

영어듣기능력평가 12회 DICTATION

다시 들으면서 듣기 만점에 도전하세요!
Dictation: 스크립트의 주요 부분을 다시 들으면서!
실전 ⊕: 세부 정보가 많은 스크립트를 다른 문제로 살살이!

01 그림 정보 파악 – 사물

대화를 듣고, 여자가 친구에게 줄 생일 선물을 고르시오.

① key chain ② teddy bear ③ picture frame ④ ⑤

What do you think of(about) ~?는 상대방의 의견을 묻는 표현이다.

M What are you buying Mary for her birthday? I'm going to _____ _____ _____ _____. (그녀에게 열쇠 고리를 사 주다)

W Well, I didn't decide yet. What do you think of a teddy bear?

M I don't think it's a good idea. She's a middle school student.

W Then, _____ _____ _____ _____ _____? (사진 액자는 어때)

M That's better.

W Then, I'll get one for her.

02 그림 정보 파악 – 위치

다음을 듣고, 들려 주는 내용과 일치하지 않는 것을 고르시오.

① ② ③ ④ ⑤

M This is the living room of my house. There is a big sofa in the middle of the room. A coffee table is in front of the sofa. I usually read newspapers there. Can you see _____ _____ _____ _____ _____? (소파 위에 신문) My mom will not be happy with that. I have to _____ _____ _____ _____ _____. (지금 당장 그것을 치우다) I have a plant. It's next to the sofa. Behind the sofa, there is a three-tiered bookshelf. It's a small living room, but I like to be here.

03 날씨 파악

this weekend 이후에 나오는 부분을 주의 깊게 듣는다.

다음을 듣고, 이번 주말의 날씨로 가장 적절한 것을 고르시오.

① ② ③ snow ④ wind ⑤

W We are going to have a snowstorm next Monday. It will bring us a lot of snow. I'm afraid we'll have a hard time cleaning up the snow. The snow will continue until next Wednesday. However, this weekend we'll _____ _____ _____ _____ _____ _____. (약간의 바람만 불다) The weather will be _____ _____ _____ _____. (야외 활동을 하기에 충분히 좋은)

04 그림 "this" 파악 (담화)

다음을 듣고, 'this'가 가리키는 것으로 가장 적절한 것을 고르시오.

①

②

③

④

⑤

M You can use this when you clean your house. It's a kind of electric machine. You hold this with your hand, ________ ________ ________ ________ (스위치를 켜다), and move it around on the floor. Then, this ________ ________ ________ ________ (모든 먼지를 빨아들이다) and dirt from the floor. What is this?

05 언급 및 비언급 파악

다음을 듣고, 남자에 대해 언급되지 않은 것을 고르시오.

① 이름 Jason Lee
② 캠프 참여 경험 my first time
③ 봉사 활동 경험
④ 자신의 장점 listening to others
⑤ 장래 희망 counselor

M Good afternoon. My name is Jason Lee. This is ________ ________ ________ ________ ________ ________ (이번 캠프에는 처음), but I want to be close to you guys during this camp. ________ ________ ________ ________ (나는 잘 경청한다) to others, so tell me all the troubles you have. In the future, I want to ________ ________ ________ (상담가가 되다) for young people.

06 직업 추론

관광지에서 안내원과 관광객들이 나누는 대화임을 파악한다.

대화를 듣고, 여자의 직업으로 가장 적절한 것을 고르시오.

① 버스 기사
② 상점 직원
③ 호텔 매니저
④ 관광 안내원
⑤ 극장 매표원

W Would you hurry and ________ ________ ________ ________ (버스에 탑승하다), please? The bus driver is waiting.

M What's ________ ________ ________ ________ ________ (구경할 다음 장소)?

W We're going to see Tora Castle. That's the most famous place in this area.

M Really? Why is it famous?

W When the bus starts going, I will ________ ________ ________ ________ (모두에게 역사를 설명하다) of the castle.

M OK. Thank you. I'm really enjoying this tour.

07 어색한 대화 찾기

다음을 듣고, 두 사람의 대화가 <u>어색한</u> 것을 고르시오.

① ② ③ ④ ⑤

How's the weather?는 날씨를 묻는 표현으로, What's the weather like?로 바꿔 말할 수 있다.

① **W** What does your mother do?
M She's working for a food company.

② **W** How's the weather today?
M It's partly cloudy.

③ **W** What's wrong with you?
M I have a little bit of a headache.

④ **W** ________ ________ ________ ________ ________? (너는 누구를 기다리고 있니)
M He will ________ ________ ________. (곧 돌아오다)

⑤ **W** Do you want to go out for dinner?
M Yes. I really want to go out.

08 부탁 파악

Would you ~? 이후에 나오는 부분을 주의깊게 듣는다.

대화를 듣고, 여자가 남자에게 부탁한 일로 가장 적절한 것을 고르시오.

① 여행사를 소개해 줄 것
② 여행지를 추천해 줄 것
③ 여행 시 주의사항을 안내해 줄 것
④ 안내원에게 여행 일정을 물어볼 것
⑤ 안내원의 이메일 주소를 알려 줄 것

Why not?은 동의 또는 수락을 나타내는 표현이다.

W How was your trip to Europe?
M We had a good time there. Especially ________ ________ ________ ________. (우리 안내원이 좋았다) She guided us to many wonderful places.
W Sounds great. Would you ________ ________ ________ ________ ________? (나에게 그녀의 이메일 주소를 알려 주다)
M Why not? Are you going there?
W Yes, in a few weeks.
M Great. I'm sure she'll do a great job for you, too.

09 주제 파악

반복되는 어휘 English, essay, writing 등에서 단서를 얻는다.

대화를 듣고, 무엇에 관한 내용인지 가장 적절한 것을 고르시오.

① 영어 듣기 평가
② 영단어 학습법
③ 도서 대출 절차
④ 영어 쓰기 평가
⑤ 효과적인 사전 사용법

+ 대화를 듣고, 남자가 여자에게 부탁한 일로 가장 적절한 것을 고르시오.

① 영어단어 같이 외우기
② 사전 빌려주기
③ 에세이 같이 쓰기
④ 사전 반납하기
⑤ 도서관 같이 가기

M Mina, are you studying English even during a break?
W I'm memorizing English words for ________ ________ ________. (내 에세이 쓰기)
M Do you mean ________ ________ ________ ________ ________ ________? (영어 시간의 쓰기 평가) Can't we use a dictionary?
W Yes, You can use a dictionary if you want, but it would be much easier if I know all the words I'm going to use in the essay, wouldn't it?
M It makes sense. Can I borrow your dictionary?
W Sure, but it's not mine. I borrowed it from the library.
M Okay. I'll return it after I use it. Thanks.

10 지도, 위치 파악

대화를 듣고, 남자가 가려고 하는 장소를 고르시오.

ACE Pharmacy ①
GOLD Bakery
One Bank ⑤
③ Post Office
④ Star Pharmacy
② Star Books
You're Here

M Excuse me. How can I get to the train station?

W Oh, you have to ________ ________ ________.
버스를 타다

M Where should I take the bus?

W Go straight one block and turn right.

M One block and turn right.

W Yes, then walk two more blocks.

M Should I ________ ________ ________?
교차로를 건너다

W Yes, then you can take the bus in front of Star Pharmacy.

11 할 일 파악

의지를 나타내는 표현인 I think ~., Let me ~. 이후에 나오는 부분을 주의깊게 듣는다.

대화를 듣고, 남자가 할 일로 가장 적절한 것을 고르시오.

① 안장 높이기
② 커피 사 오기
③ 점심 준비하기
④ 자전거 빌려 주기
⑤ 체인에 기름칠 하기

M Is that your bicycle?

W Yes, but I haven't ridden it for a few months. I'm afraid it's not working well.

M Then, let me check it. I think ________ ________ ________ ________.
체인에 기름칠이 좀 필요하다

W Oh, really? Then I can ride it more easily, right?

M It will help. Let me ________ ________ ________ ________ for you.
체인에 기름칠을 하다

W While you're doing that, I'll get a cup of coffee for you.

➕ 대화를 듣고, 여자가 대화 직후에 할 일로 가장 적절한 것을 고르시오.

① 안장 높이기
② 커피 사 오기
③ 점심 준비하기
④ 자전거 빌려 주기
⑤ 체인에 기름칠 하기

12 의도 추론

대화를 듣고, 남자의 마지막 말의 의도로 가장 적절한 것을 고르시오.

① 격려 ② 후회
③ 축하 ④ 놀람
⑤ 실망

W Oh, Tom. I heard you ________ ________ ________. What happened?
다리가 부러졌다

M Well, I tried to jump over the fence around the parking lot, but wasn't successful.

W I saw some boys sometimes ________ ________ ________. I always thought it was dangerous.
그것을 뛰어넘다

M You're right. I learned the lesson the hard way. ________ ________ ________ ________.
다시는 그러지 않겠다

13 이유 파악

제안을 거절한 뒤 I have to ~. 뒤에 거절한 이유가 제시되므로 이 부분을 주의 깊게 듣는다.

대화를 듣고, 남자가 테니스를 칠 수 없는 이유로 가장 적절한 것을 고르시오.

① 숙제를 해야 해서
② 할머니를 간호해야 해서
take care of her
③ 토요일에 선약이 있어서
④ 친구의 병문안을 가야 해서
⑤ 친구의 숙제를 도와주어야 해서

W Jack, how about playing tennis this Saturday?

M I'd like to do that, but I can't.

W Why is that? Do you have homework to do?

M No, ________ ________ ________ ________. I have to ________ ________ ________ ________.
할머니가 병원에 있다 / 그녀를 간호하다

W Sorry to hear that.

14 그림 정보 파악 – 지도

two blocks → across from the bookstore → on your right로 이어지는 지시의 순서를 주의깊게 듣는다.

대화를 듣고, 여자가 가려고 하는 장소를 고르시오.

Bank
②
③
①
Flower Shop
Olsen Street
Book-store
④
⑤

W Excuse me, where is Kim's Company?

M Go straight for ________ ________ ________ ________ ________. You'll see the bookstore on your left.
(Olsen 거리를 따라 두 블록)

W Two blocks and the bookstore is on my left, right?

M Yes. Kim's Company is right ________ ________ ________ ________. So the building is ________ ________ ________.
(서점 건너편 / 당신의 오른편에)

W Now I see. Thank you very much.

고난도

15 숫자 파악 – 시각

Randy가 도착할 시각(at six)과 몇 시간 남았는지를(two hours left) 잘 듣고 계산한다.

대화를 듣고, 현재 시각을 고르시오.

① 2:00 ② 3:00
③ 4:00 ④ 5:00
⑤ 6:00

W When will Randy's plane arrive?

M He said it would ________ ________ ________.
(6시에 도착하다)

W Then, we have ________ ________ ________.
(2시간 남은)

M Yes. We're leaving for the airport at five. I can't wait to see Randy.

W Me too. I haven't seen him for two years.

16 심정 추론

대화를 듣고, 여자의 심정으로 가장 적절한 것을 고르시오.

① 걱정됨 ② 놀람
③ 미안함 ④ 당황함
⑤ 만족스러움

W Paul, what do you have in your hand?

M It's ________ ________ ________ ________ ________. I did it in English class.
(내가 만든 그림책)

W Great. Let me see it. Did you ________ ________ ________, too?
(이야기를 쓰다)

M Yes, but it is not very good. You know, I'm not an artistic person.

W I think the pictures are nice. Believe your mom, honey. You ________ ________ ________ ________.
(아주 잘 했다)

고난도

17 내용 일치 파악

다음을 듣고, London에 대한 설명으로 일치하지 않는 것을 고르시오.

① 영국의 수도이다.
② 다양한 언어가 사용된다.
③ 비가 많이 온다.
④ 3번의 올림픽을 개최했다.
⑤ 세계에서 가장 오래된 2층 버스가 있다.

W London is ________ ________ ________ (수도) of the United Kingdom. People from around the world come to London to travel, to study or to live. It is said that ________ ________ ________ ________ (300개 이상의 언어들) are spoken in London. London is known as a rainy city. It rains a lot in summer and it rains a lot even in winter. The city hosted the Olympic Games three times. The latest one was in 2012. The city has a subway system. It is called London Underground. It is ________ ________ ________ ________ (가장 오래된 지하철 시스템) in the world.

18 관계 추론

대화를 듣고, 두 사람의 관계로 가장 적절한 것을 고르시오.

① 배우 – 팬
② 아버지 – 딸
③ 가수 – 매니저
④ 음악 교사 – 학생
⑤ 쇼 진행자 – 초대 손님

W How was my singing? Was I good?
M You sounded a little tired.
W Actually, I'm very tired. ________ ________ ________ (오늘 일정이 끝났나요) now?
M No, you have to ________ ________ ________ ________ ________ (Mr. Larry 쇼에 가다) to sing a song there.
W Is that my last appointment today?
M Yes, but tomorrow is busy too. Sorry about that.

19 알맞은 응답 찾기

Would you mind ~?에 대한 대답 방법을 익혀 둔다.

[19~20] 대화를 듣고, 남자의 마지막 말에 이어질 여자의 응답으로 가장 적절한 것을 고르시오.

Woman: ____________________

① No, I'll turn it off.
② You can turn it on.
③ The radio is my good friend.
④ I usually turn off the radio when I drive.
⑤ Yes, I think I should turn the volume up.

Would you mind ~?에 대해 요청을 수락할 때는 부정으로, 거절할 때는 긍정으로 한다.

M Thank you for ________ ________ ________ ________ (나를 태워 주는 것) home.
W My pleasure.
M How long have you lived in this town?
W For more than 10 years.
M It's hard to talk. Would you ________ ________ ________ ________ (라디오 끄는 것을 꺼리다)?
W ____________________

20 알맞은 응답 찾기

Woman: ____________________

① Now it's your turn.
② I don't like this game.
③ OK. I'm ready to play.
④ Great. I'll go out soon.
⑤ Don't worry. I'll wait for you.

W Do you know how to ________ ________ ________ ________ (이 카드 게임을 하다)?
M Yeah, actually, it's one of my favorite games.
W Sounds great! We're going to have a wonderful time this evening.
M I think so. ________ ________ ________ (시작하자) right away.
W ____________________

적절한 응답

무엇을 평가하는가?	일상생활이나 친숙한 일반적 주제에 관한 말이나 대화를 듣고 주제, 요지를 파악할 수 있는지를 평가한다.
어떻게 출제되는가?	• 대화를 듣고, 무엇에 관한 내용인지 가장 적절한 것을 고르시오. • 대화를 듣고, 선생님의 무엇에 관한 내용인지 가장 적절한 것을 고르시오.

❶ 적절한 응답을 고르는 경우, 전반적인 내용을 이해하면서 마지막 말에 집중한다.

[기출로 전략 확인]

대화를 듣고, 남자의 마지막 말에 이어질 여자의 응답으로 가장 적절한 것을 고르시오.

[2018 기출]

Woman: ______________________________

① Nice to meet you.
② I'd love to, but I can't.
③ No, I don't have one.
④ Thank you for your advice.
⑤ Oh, I'm sorry to hear that.

W Hi, Dave. What are you doing here?
M I'm waiting for the bus to go home.
W But you left school early. Why are you still here?
M The bus didn't come yet.
W Really? Why don't you just walk home?
M I want to, but I hurt my foot yesterday.

❶ 어제 다리를 다쳤다고 말하고 있으므로, 위로나 동정의 답변이 올 수 있다.

여 안녕, Dave. 여기서 뭐해?
남 집에 가려고 버스 기다리고 있어.
여 하지만 일찍 학교에서 나갔잖아. 왜 아직도 여기에 있어?
남 버스가 아직 안 왔어.
여 진짜? 그냥 집에 걸어가는 게 어때?
남 그러고 싶은데 어제 발을 다쳤어.

적절한 응답의 발문과 보기

대화를 듣고, 남자의 마지막 말에 이어질 여자의 말로 가장 적절한 것을 고르시오. [2018 기출]

Woman: ______________________

① I'm 14 years old.
② I'll go there by train.
③ I'm doing my homework.
④ I had some delicious seafood.
⑤ I'll join the swimming camp.

만점 잡는 문장 **M** We'll visit Ulleungdo.
W Oh, I went there last year.
M Really? What did you do in Ulleungdo?

대화를 듣고, 여자의 마지막 말에 이어질 남자의 응답으로 가장 적절한 것을 고르시오. [2017 기출]

Man: ______________________

① Yes, I like dancing too.
② No, I can't dance very well.
③ I'm not interested in dancing.
④ I practiced at a dance school.
⑤ I want to join the dance contest.

만점 잡는 문장 **M** I practiced B-boy dancing.
W Really? Where did you practice?

적절한 응답에 쓰이는 어휘 및 표현

- **감사/동의/축하**

Thank you for your advice. 충고 고마워
Sure. Why not? 물론이야.
You did a good job! 아주 잘했어!
That's a good idea. 좋은 생각이야.
Congratulations! 축하해!
That's fantastic! 환상적이다!

- **거절/불만**

I'd love to, but I can't. 나도 그러고 싶은데 할 수 없어.
It's not fair. 불공평해.
Sorry, I can't have dinner with you. 미안, 너랑 저녁을 먹을 수 없어.
I don't think it is a good idea. 그건 좋은 생각이 아닌 거 같아.

- **위로/격려/제안**

Oh, I'm sorry to hear that. 그 말을 들으니 안됐다.
Don't worry about it. 걱정하지 마.
That's too bad. 참 안됐다.
Let me help you. 내가 도와줄게.

영어듣기능력평가 13회

학년 반 번
이름

01 다음을 듣고, 'I'가 무엇인지 가장 적절한 것을 고르시오.

02 대화를 듣고, 휴대전화가 있는 곳을 고르시오.

03 다음을 듣고, 내일 오전의 날씨로 가장 적절한 것을 고르시오.

04 다음을 듣고, 민주가 지난 토요일에 한 일로 언급되지 않은 것을 고르시오.

① 서점 가기 ② TV 보기
③ 숙제하기 ④ 엄마 도와드리기
⑤ 식탁 차리기

05 대화를 듣고, 남자가 대화 직후에 할 일로 가장 적절한 것을 고르시오.

① 집에 돌아 가기 ② 식당을 찾아가기
③ 식당에 전화하기 ④ 딸 핸드폰에 전화하기
⑤ 딸 핸드폰 찾으러 가기

고난도

06 다음을 듣고, School Soccer Tourrament에 대한 설명으로 일치하지 않는 것을 고르시오.

① 다음 주 월요일에 시작된다.
② 팀에 2명의 여학생이 포함되어야 한다.
③ 담임선생님도 선수가 될 수 있다.
④ 경기는 매일 방과 후에 시작된다.
⑤ 결승전은 학교 체육대회 날에 열린다.

07 대화를 듣고, 두 사람이 내일 만나기로 한 시각을 고르시오.

① 7:30 ② 8:00
③ 8:30 ④ 9:00
⑤ 9:30

08 다음을 듣고, 두 사람의 대화가 어색한 것을 고르시오.

① ② ③ ④ ⑤

09 대화를 듣고, 남자의 직업으로 가장 적절한 것을 고르시오.

① 부동산 중개인 ② 건축가
③ 인테리어디자이너 ④ 건물 경비
⑤ 청소업체 직원

10 대화를 듣고, Fred가 역사 과목을 좋아하는 이유로 가장 적절한 것을 고르시오.

① 숙제가 많지 않아서
② 여자 친구가 있어서
③ 역사에 흥미가 있어서
④ 역사 선생님이 되고 싶어서
⑤ 선생님의 수업이 재미있어서

점수 /20

11 대화를 듣고, 남자의 마지막 말의 의도로 가장 적절한 것을 고르시오.

① 칭찬 ② 감사
③ 놀람 ④ 기대
⑤ 위로

12 대화를 듣고, 여자가 도서관까지 가는 교통 수단으로 가장 적절한 것을 고르시오.

① 버스 ② 지하철
③ 택시 ④ 도보
⑤ 자전거

13 대화를 듣고, 두 사람의 관계로 가장 적절한 것을 고르시오.

① 사진작가 – 모델 ② 관광객 – 관광객
③ 택시 기사 – 손님 ④ 관광 안내원 – 관광객
⑤ 공원 매표원 – 방문객

14 대화를 듣고, 남자가 전화를 건 목적으로 가장 적절한 것을 고르시오.

① 안부를 전하려고
② 숙제를 알려 주려고
③ 드라마를 같이 보려고
④ 생일 파티에 초대하려고
⑤ 친구의 전화번호를 물어보려고

15 대화를 듣고, 여자의 장래 희망으로 가장 적절한 것을 고르시오.

① 약사 ② 의사
③ 간호사 ④ 제약 연구원
⑤ 재활 치료사

고난도

16 대화를 듣고, 남자가 주장하는 바로 가장 적절한 것을 고르시오.

① 서둘러 짐을 싸야 한다.
② 아침 일찍 출발해야 한다.
③ 반드시 아침 식사를 해야 한다.
④ 자명종을 맞춰 놓고 자야 한다.
⑤ 비행기 출발 시간을 확인해야 한다.

17 다음을 듣고, 무엇에 관한 안내인지 가장 적절한 것을 고르시오.

① 상품 광고 ② 쇼핑몰 홍보
③ 미아 찾기 ④ 백화점 이용 방법
⑤ AS 센터 위치

18 다음을 듣고, 딸에 대한 여자의 심정으로 가장 적절한 것을 고르시오.

① 걱정됨 ② 미안함
③ 부러움 ④ 자랑스러움
⑤ 측은함

[19~20] 대화를 듣고, 여자의 마지막 말에 이어질 남자의 응답으로 가장 적절한 것을 고르시오.

19 Man: ______________________

① I'm not a good photographer.
② Please wait until I say "Now."
③ No, you don't have to be sorry.
④ Be careful. It's an expensive camera.
⑤ Push the button until you hear the 'click.'

고난도

20 Man: ______________________

① It is a shiny black one.
② I listen to music with it.
③ I have it since I was 7th grade.
④ I'm sure I put it on my desk before breakfast.
⑤ It was my birthday present from Aunt Margaret.

영어듣기능력평가 13 회 DICTATION

다시 들으면서 듣기 만점에 도전하세요!
Dictation: 스크립트의 주요 부분을 다시 들으면서!
실전 ⊕: 세부 정보가 많은 스크립트를 다른 문제로 샅샅이!

01 그림 "I" 파악 (담화)

다음을 듣고, 'I'가 무엇인지 가장 적절한 것을 고르시오.

① ② ③ ④ ⑤

M I live in Australia. I can jump fast with my back legs. I have a ________, ________ ________ (길고 강한 꼬리). It helps me balance when I jump. When I was a little baby, my mother carried me ________ ________ ________ (주머니 안에) of her stomach. What am I?

02 그림 정보 파악 – 위치

대화를 듣고, 휴대전화가 있는 곳을 고르시오.

① ② ③ ④ ⑤

M Mom, I left my cell phone on the sofa. Can you get it for me?
W Well, it ________ ________ ________ ________ (소파 위에 없다).
M Then it may be on the table in the kitchen.
W No, it isn't there. Wait. Let me call your phone.
M I can hear the cell phone ringing. It's ________ ________ ________ ________ (커피 탁자 위에) in front of the TV.

고난도

03 날씨 파악

tomorrow morning이 언급된 부분의 날씨 정보를 주의깊게 듣는다.

다음을 듣고, 내일 오전의 날씨로 가장 적절한 것을 고르시오.

① sunny ② ③ ④ rain ⑤ foggy

W Good afternoon. This is Lee Yunjin with the weather update. ________ ________ ________ (비가 그칠 것이다) soon and we'll be able to see the full moon at night. Temperatures will go up to 25 degrees. ________ ________ ________ (안개가 낄 것이다) throughout the country tomorrow morning. In the afternoon, it will be sunny and nice.

04 언급 및 비언급 파악

언급은 되었지만 하지 못한 일을 파악한다.

다음을 듣고, 민주가 지난 토요일에 한 일로 언급되지 않은 것을 고르시오.

① 서점 가기 go to a bookstore
② TV 보기 watched TV
③ 숙제하기 did her homework
④ 엄마 도와드리기 helped her mom
⑤ 식탁 차리기 set the table

대화를 듣고, 민주가 현아와 함께 한 일로 가장 적절한 것을 고르시오.

① 학교 가기 ② 서점 가기
③ 병원 가기 ④ 숙제 하기
⑤ 식탁 차리기

M Last Saturday, there was no class at school. Minju wanted to go to a bookstore with her best friend, Hyuna, but Hyuna got a cold. She had to stay at home. Minju visited her sick friend and they ________ ________ ________ ________ ________ together. (병원에 갔다) They ________ ________ (TV를 보았다) at Hyuna's house. In the afternoon, Minju came home and ________ ________ ________ (숙제를 했다). She helped her mom cook dinner and ________ ________ ________ (식탁을 차리다).

05 할 일 파악

대화를 듣고, 남자가 대화 직후에 할 일로 가장 적절한 것을 고르시오.

① 집에 돌아 가기
② 식당을 찾아가기
③ 식당에 전화하기
④ 딸 핸드폰에 전화하기
⑤ 딸 핸드폰 찾으러 가기

G Oh, no, I left my cell phone at home.
M Again? I can't believe it.
G Sorry, but can I go back and get it?
M But we'll ________ ________ ________ ________ ________ (예약 시간에 늦다).
G I'm really sorry. Could you call the restaurant, and tell them we will be a little late?
M Okay. I guess I'll have to.
G Thank you, Dad! I'll ________ ________ ________ (금방 돌아오다).

고난도

06 내용 일치 파악

다음을 듣고, School Soccer Tournament에 대한 설명으로 일치하지 않는 것을 고르 시오.

① 다음 주 월요일에 시작된다.
② 팀에 2명의 여학생이 포함되어야 한다.
③ 담임선생님도 선수가 될 수 있다.
④ 경기는 매일 방과 후에 시작된다.
⑤ 결승전은 학교 체육대회 날에 열린다.

W School Soccer Tournament starts next Monday. Each class must select 11 players and ________ ________ ________ ________ (적어도 그들 중 2명) must be girls. The homeroom teacher can play in a team. Games will ________ ________ ________ ________ ________ ________ (매일 아침 8시에 시작되다). The final match will be on school sports day. We hope everybody enjoys the games.

07 숫자 파악 – 시각

문제에서 요구하는 시각을 가려 듣는다.

대화를 듣고, 두 사람이 내일 만나기로 한 시각을 고르시오.

① 7:30 ② 8:00
③ 8:30 ④ 9:00
⑤ 9:30

M How about going to the City Swimming Pool tomorrow?

W Sounds good. They say tomorrow will be a really hot day.

M Let's go early before a lot of people come.

W Great. What time can you make it?

M Can you come at 8 o'clock?

W The swimming pool ________ ________ ________ ________ ________ ________.
9시에 열고 7시에 닫는다

M Then ________, ________ ________ ________ ________ : ________. It will be really hot after nine.
8시 30분에 만나자

W All right.

08 어색한 대화 찾기

다음을 듣고, 두 사람의 대화가 어색한 것을 고르시오.

① ② ③ ④ ⑤

Can I take your order?는 '주문하시겠어요?'라는 의미로, 음식을 주문 받을 때 사용하는 표현이다.

① **M** Please ________ ________ ________.
앉으세요
W Thank you.

② **M** Can I take your order?
W You ________ ________ ________ ________ ________ here.
줄을 서야 한다

③ **M** Can I help you?
W Yes, I'm looking for snow boots.

④ **M** Where is the nearest bus stop?
W It's just around the corner.

⑤ **M** What season do you like most?
W I like summer because I can swim.

09 직업 파악

대화를 듣고, 남자의 직업으로 가장 적절한 것을 고르시오.

① 부동산 중개인
② 건축가
③ 인테리어디자이너
④ 건물 경비
⑤ 청소업체

M So... what do you think of this apartment?

W It's really ________ ________ ________. How much is it?
깨끗하고 좋은

M It's $800 a month.

W Wow, the rent is ________ ________ ________. Do you have any cheaper place?
나에게는 너무 비싼

M Yes, I do have one. Do you want to go and have a look?

W Yes, please. How far is it from here?

⊕ 대화를 듣고, 두 사람이 대화하는 장소로 가장 적절한 것을 고르시오.

① 우체국
② 병원
③ 아파트
④ 부동산
⑤ 학교

10 이유 파악

이유를 묻는 문제이므로 because of(~ 때문에) 이후에 나오는 부분을 집중하여 듣는다.

대화를 듣고, Fred가 역사 과목을 좋아하는 이유로 가장 적절한 것을 고르시오.

① 숙제가 많지 않아서
② 여자 친구가 있어서
③ 역사에 흥미가 있어서
④ 역사 선생님이 되고 싶어서
⑤ 선생님의 수업이 재미있어서

M I need to go to history class now. I have a couple of things to ask before the class starts.

W Wow, Fred. I didn't know you liked history so much. Do you have a girl friend in the class?

M No. It's ________ ________ ________ ________ (선생님 때문에). Mr. Miller ________ ________ ________ ________ (수업을 정말 재미있게 하신다).

W You're right. I enjoy listening to his storytelling about historical events.

M I have to go. See you in the class.

11 의도 추론

looking forward to, can't wait가 의미하는 바를 파악한다.

화를 듣고, 남자의 마지막 말의 의도로 가장 적절한 것을 고르시오.

① 칭찬 ② 감사
③ 놀람 ④ 기대
⑤ 위로

M You look tired.

W Yes, I am. The final exam's starting next week.

M I'm tired, too. I had to ________ ________ ________ ________ (보고서 작성을 끝내다) last night.

W On the other hand, it means the summer vacation is ________ ________ ________ ________ (바로 코앞에 다가온).

M Oh, you're right. I'm really ________ ________ ________ ________ (그것을 손꼽아 기다리고 있다). I can't wait.

12 특정 정보 파악

최종적으로 여자가 이용하기로 결정한 교통 수단을 주의깊게 듣는다.

대화를 듣고, 여자가 도서관까지 가는 교통 수단으로 가장 적절한 것을 고르시오.

① 버스 bus
② 지하철 subway
③ 택시 taxi
④ 도보
⑤ 자전거

M Where are you going?

W I'm going to Thomson Library.

M How are you going there?

W Which way is better, bus or subway?

M You'd better take the subway. But if you are in a hurry, ________ ________ ________ (택시를 타다).

W Well, I am not in a hurry. So I'll ________ ________ ________ (지하철을 타다).

13 관계 추론

대화를 듣고, 두 사람의 관계로 가장 적절한 것을 고르시오.

① 사진작가 – 모델
② 관광객 – 관광객
③ 택시 기사 – 손님
④ 관광 안내원 – 관광객
⑤ 공원 매표원 – 방문객

W Excuse me, sir. Would you ________ ________ ________ ________ ________ (내 사진을 찍어 주다)? This place is very beautiful.

M Sure. This is my first time in ________ ________ ________ ________ (이렇게 아름다운 곳). Anyway, do you want to have the whole building in your picture?

W Yes, please. You can press this button.

M Okay. On the count of three. One, two, three.

W Oh, thank you very much.

M You're welcome.

14 전화 목적 파악

I called you ~. 이후에 나오는 부분을 주의깊게 듣는다.

대화를 듣고, 남자가 전화를 건 목적으로 가장 적절한 것을 고르시오.

① 안부를 전하려고
② 숙제를 알려 주려고
③ 드라마를 같이 보려고
④ 생일 파티에 초대하려고
⑤ 친구의 전화번호를 물어보려고

[Telephone rings.]

W Hello.

M Hello, Helen. This is Charley.

W Hi, Charley. You called me at a bad time.

M Oh, I'm sorry. What are you doing?

W I'm ________ ________ ________, *Ghost*. Aren't you watching it?
드라마를 보고 있다

M No, I'm doing my homework. Helen, do you have James's phone number? I called you ________ ________ ________ ________.
그의 전화번호를 물어보려고

W Well, I think I have it on my phone. Wait. I'll look for it.

M Thanks.

15 특정 정보 파악

대화를 듣고, 여자의 장래 희망으로 가장 적절한 것을 고르시오.

① 약사 ② 의사
③ 간호사 ④ 제약 연구원
⑤ 재활 치료사

What are you interested in?은 '너는 무엇에 관심이 있니?'라는 의미로, 관심 있는 분야를 묻는 표현이다.

M Mary, what ________ ________ ________ ________?
관심이 있니

W There are so many sick people in the hospital. I'd like to ________ ________ ________.
아픈 사람들을 돕다

M Do you want to be a doctor?

W No, I want to take care of sick people, give medicine and ________ ________ ________ ________ ________.
수술실에서 의사들을 돕다

M Then this would be a nice job for you.

고난도

16 특정 정보 파악

대화를 듣고, 남자가 주장하는 바로 가장 적절한 것을 고르시오.

① 서둘러 짐을 싸야 한다.
② 아침 일찍 출발해야 한다.
③ 반드시 아침 식사를 해야 한다.
④ 자명종을 맞춰 놓고 자야 한다.
⑤ 비행기 출발 시간을 확인해야 한다.

W Did you finish packing for the trip?

M It's almost done. When are we going to leave tomorrow?

W We have to arrive at the airport before 9 o'clock.

M Then we have to ________ ________ ________ ________.
6시경에 출발하다

W Isn't it too early? We need to eat breakfast, too. How about 7 o'clock?

M I think we can have breakfast at the airport. I ________ ________ ________ ________ ________.
늦고 싶지 않다

W All right. I'll set the alarm at 5 o'clock.

17 주제 파악

다음을 듣고, 무엇에 관한 안내인지 가장 적절한 것을 고르시오.

① 상품 광고
② 쇼핑몰 홍보
③ 미아 찾기
④ 백화점 이용 방법
⑤ AS 센터 위치

Thank you for your cooperation.은 협조에 감사함을 표할 때 사용하는 표현이다.

W Welcome to Korea Department Store. For your safety, inline skates and roller shoes ________ ________ ________ ________ in the shopping mall. Also on the 2nd floor where food corners are located, ________ ________ ________ ________. It's for everybody's comfortable shopping. Thank you for your cooperation.

(어느 곳에서도 허용되지 않는다 / 애완동물은 출입할 수 없다)

18 심정 추론

다음을 듣고, 딸에 대한 여자의 심정으로 가장 적절한 것을 고르시오.

① 걱정됨
② 미안함
③ 부러움
④ 자랑스러움
⑤ 측은함

내용의 반전이 일어나는 부분(However)을 중심으로 과거와 현재의 상황을 파악한다.

W I have a beautiful daughter. Five years ago, she was sick and in the hospital for three months. She ________ ________ ________. After she came home, she started to learn swimming for her health. At first, she could swim only 10 minutes. However, she ________ ________ ________. She went to the swimming pool three times a week for 5 years. Now she ________ ________ ________ ________. She is on the swimming team in her school.

(매우 약했다 / 포기하지 않았다 / 훌륭한 수영 선수이다)

19 알맞은 응답 찾기

[19~20] 대화를 듣고, 여자의 마지막 말에 이어질 남자의 응답으로 가장 적절한 것을 고르시오.

Man: ____________________

① I'm not a good photographer.
② Please wait until I say "Now."
③ No, you don't have to be sorry.
④ Be careful. It's an expensive camera.
⑤ Push the button until you hear the 'click.'

Pardon? / Sorry? / Excuse me? 등은 상대방의 말을 못 알아들었을 때 되묻는 표현이다.

M Excuse me. ________ ________ ________ ________ ________ for me? (사진 좀 찍어 주시겠어요)
W Sure.
M Thank you.
W Which button do I have to push?
M Push the big round button. ________ ________ until you hear the 'click' sound. (그것을 눌러라)
W ________? (뭐라고 하셨죠)
M ____________________

고난도

20 알맞은 응답 찾기

Man: ____________________

① It is a shiny black one.
② I listen to music with it.
③ I have it since I was 7th grade.
④ I'm sure I put it on my desk before breakfast.
⑤ It was my birthday present from Aunt Margaret.

M Mom, did you see my MP3 player?
W I think I ________ ________ ________ ________ ________ this morning. (책상 위에서 그것을 보았다)
M It's not there.
W Did you check your bag?
M I did. I checked the pockets of my jacket, too.
W Well, ________ ________ ________ ________ ________ you saw it? (언제가 마지막이니)
M ____________________

영어듣기능력평가 14회

학년 반 번
이름

01 다음을 듣고, 그림을 바르게 설명한 것을 고르시오.

① ② ③ ④ ⑤

02 대화를 듣고, 여자가 가리키는 표지판으로 가장 적절한 것을 고르시오.

①  ②  ③ 
④  ⑤ 

03 다음을 듣고, Singapore의 내일 날씨로 가장 적절한 것을 고르시오.

① 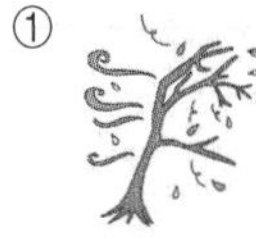 ②  ③ 
④  ⑤ 

04 대화를 듣고, 여자가 대화 직후에 할 일로 가장 적절한 것을 고르시오.

① 우산 가져오기
② 식당 예약하기
③ 음식 주문하기
④ 음식 요리하기
⑤ Alex 거리 청소하기

05 다음을 듣고, 'this'가 가리키는 것으로 가장 적절한 것을 고르시오.

①  ② ③ 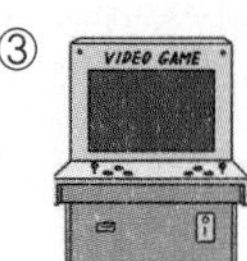

④ 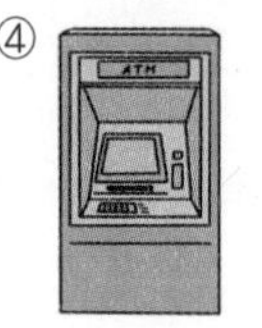

⑤ 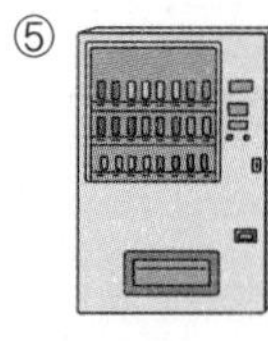

06 다음을 듣고, 두 사람의 대화가 어색한 것을 고르시오.

① ② ③ ④ ⑤

고난도

07 대화를 듣고, 남자가 한국에 머문 기간을 고르시오.

① 3일 ② 5일
③ 6일 ④ 8일
⑤ 11일

08 대화를 듣고, 남자가 전화를 건 목적으로 가장 적절한 것을 고르시오.

① 텐트를 빌리려고
② 여자를 도와주려고
③ 캠핑을 제안하려고
④ 주말 계획을 물어보려고
⑤ 캠핑 장소를 알려 주려고

09 대화를 듣고, 두 사람이 대화하고 있는 장소로 가장 적절한 곳을 고르시오.

① 병원 ② 집
③ 운동장 ④ 식당
⑤ 스케이트장

10 대화를 듣고, 무엇에 관한 내용인지 가장 적절한 것을 고르시오.

① 방학 계획 ② 새학기 계획
③ 방학 숙제 ④ 과제 제출 방법
⑤ 시간 활용

점수 /20

고난도

11 대화를 듣고, 여자가 탈 기차의 요일과 시각을 고르시오.

① 금요일 – 오전 9시
② 토요일 – 오전 9시
③ 토요일 – 오후 2시 30분
④ 일요일 – 오후 2시 30분
⑤ 일요일 – 저녁 6시

12 대화를 듣고, 현재 여자가 있는 장소를 고르시오.

13 대화를 듣고, 남자가 여자에게 불평하는 이유로 가장 적절한 것을 고르시오.

① 전화 통화를 너무 오래 해서
② 약속 시간에 항상 늦게 와서
③ 휴대전화 벨소리가 너무 커서
④ 휴대전화를 너무 자주 확인해서
⑤ 남자의 휴대전화를 잃어버려서

14 대화를 듣고, 두 사람의 관계로 가장 적절한 것을 고르시오.

① 의사 – 환자
② 교사 – 학생
③ 어머니 – 아들
④ 사장 – 종업원
⑤ 수의사 – 애완동물 주인

15 대화를 듣고, 남자의 마지막 말의 의도로 가장 적절한 것을 고르시오.

① 승낙　② 거절
③ 감사　④ 부정
⑤ 부탁

16 대화를 듣고, 남자가 기분이 좋은 이유로 가장 적절한 것을 고르시오.

① 보고 싶은 영화를 봐서
② 형이 찾아오기로 해서
③ 전화기를 새로 구입해서
④ San Diego로 이사를 가서
⑤ 금요일이 자신의 생일이어서

17 대화를 듣고, 여자가 남자에게 제안한 것으로 가장 적절한 것을 고르시오.

① 땀 흘리지 않기
② 따뜻하게 옷 입기
③ 더운물로 샤워하기
④ 따뜻한 음료 마시기
⑤ 방안 적정 온도 유지하기

18 다음을 듣고, Robert에 대해 언급되지 않은 것을 고르시오.

① 직업　② 나이
③ 가족　④ 좋아하는 음식
⑤ 취미

[19~20] 대화를 듣고, 여자의 마지막 말에 이어질 남자의 응답으로 가장 적절한 것을 고르시오.

19 Man: ______________________

① Okay, I'll lend mine to you.
② But I don't know how to use it.
③ Don't worry. I'll take a picture of you.
④ Where did you put your digital camera?
⑤ Excuse me, how much is this digital camera?

20 Man: ______________________

① Sure! You'd better see it, too.
② Good! I'll buy your ticket, too.
③ Right, I want to be a movie star.
④ No, I didn't. I didn't have lunch.
⑤ Why don't we go shopping tomorrow?

영어듣기능력평가 14회 DICTATION

다시 들으면서 듣기 만점에 도전하세요!
Dictation: 스크립트의 주요 부분을 다시 들으면서!
실전 ⊕: 세부 정보가 많은 스크립트를 다른 문제로 살살이!

01 그림 정보 파악 – 토익형

다음을 듣고, 그림을 바르게 설명한 것을 고르시오.

① ② ③ ④ ⑤

M ① He is __________ __________ with his friend. (눈사람을 만들고 있다)
② He is walking on the beach with his mom.
③ He is going to school in the morning.
④ He is __________ __________. (양치질을 하고 있다)
⑤ He is watching a movie with his brother.

02 그림 정보 파악 – 사물

핵심 어구 take a picture, can't take a picture, no picture taking 등에서 단서를 얻는다.

대화를 듣고, 여자가 가리키는 표지판으로 가장 적절한 것을 고르시오.

① 
② 
③ 
④ 
⑤ 

M Alice, can you take a picture of me __________ __________ __________ __________ __________? (조각상 앞에서)
W Hey, you can't take a picture here.
M Why not?
W Look at the sign over there! The sign says __________ __________ __________. (여기서 사진을 찍을 수 없다)
M Oops. I didn't see it. Thank you for telling me.

고난도

03 날씨 파악

Singapore이 언급되는 부분을 주의깊게 듣는다.

다음을 듣고, Singapore의 내일 날씨로 가장 적절한 것을 고르시오.

① 
wind, windy

② 
showers

③ 

④ 

⑤ 
snow

W Let's move on to other parts of Asia for tomorrow's weather. Beijing is mainly cloudy and it will be __________ __________ __________ __________ __________. (강한 바람과 함께 훨씬 더 추운) Tokyo's looking at some clouds and a high of 13. And there's a 40% chance of thunderstorms expected in Bangkok, and __________ __________ __________ __________ __________ in Singapore. (소나기가 올 확률이 아주 높음) Taipei continues to be windy with a few snow in the evening.

04 할 일 파악

I'll ~. 이후에 나오는 부분을 주의깊게 듣는다.

대화를 듣고, 여자가 대화 직후에 할 일로 가장 적절한 것을 고르시오.

① 우산 가져오기 bring an umbrella
② 식당 예약하기
③ 음식 주문하기
④ 음식 요리하기
⑤ Alex 거리 청소하기

Do you have anything special ~?은 특별히 무언가 하고 싶은 것이 있는지 묻는 표현이다.

W It's 6 o'clock. How about having dinner together?

M Sounds good! Do you have anything special to eat?

W Well... what about Italian food? There is a good Italian restaurant on Alex Street.

M Good! But the sky is so dark. ________ ________ ________, I think. (곧 비가 내릴 것이다)

W Yeah, that's right. Just wait a minute here. I'll ________ ________ ________. (우산을 가져오다)

05 그림 "this" 파악 (담화)

다음을 듣고, 'this'가 가리키는 것으로 가장 적절한 것을 고르시오.

① ② ③ ④ ⑤

M You can use this to buy various products. For example, you can buy snacks, beverages, tickets, and so on. To use this, you put money in first. Next you simply ________ (버튼을 누르다) ________ ________ to choose your item. Then, the ________ (물건이 나오다) ________ ________. What is this?

06 어색한 대화 찾기

다음을 듣고, 두 사람의 대화가 어색한 것을 고르시오.

① ② ③ ④ ⑤

What made ~?는 '왜 ~?'라는 의미로, 이유를 묻는 표현이다.

① **W** What did you do last weekend?
M I went fishing on Saturday with my family.

② **W** John, you look excited. ________ ________ ________ you? (~에게 무슨 일 있었니)
M I got A+ on the math test!

③ **W** ________ ________ ________ ________ my new hair style? (~에 대해 어떻게 생각하니)
M I see. ________ ________ ________ tomorrow. (내가 너와 함께 가겠다)

④ **W** Have a seat, please. What made you come here?
M I think I have a cold.

⑤ **W** Did you finish your biology report?
M Sure, I did. I finished it last night.

고난도

07 숫자 파악 – 날짜

서울에 머문 기간과 대전에 머문 기간을 잘 듣고 계산한다.

대화를 듣고, 남자가 한국에 머문 기간을 고르시오.

① 3일 ② 5일
③ 6일 ④ 8일
⑤ 11일

W Sam, when did you come back from your trip to Korea?

M Last weekend. It was a really wonderful trip.

W Was it? So did you visit Seoul?

M Of course, I did. I ___ ___ ___ ___ ___ (그곳에서 5일 동안 머물렀다). And I also ___ ___ ___ ___ ___ (3일 동안 대전을 방문했다).

W How about Busan? You wanted to stay there for about three days.

M It was canceled. After Daejeon, I just came back home.

고난도

08 전화 목적 파악

can I ~? 이후에 나오는 부분을 주의 깊게 듣는다.

대화를 듣고, 남자가 전화를 건 목적으로 가장 적절한 것을 고르시오.

① 텐트를 빌리려고 borrow your tent
② 여자를 도와주려고
③ 캠핑을 제안하려고
④ 주말 계획을 물어보려고
⑤ 캠핑 장소를 알려 주려고

That's why ~.는 '그래서 ~이다.'라는 의미로, 결과나 결론을 말할 때 사용하는 표현이다.

[Cellphone rings.]

W Hello? Cindy speaking!

M Hi, Cindy. It's me, Brad.

W Hi, Brad. I heard that you're going camping with your brother during this weekend.

M Right. And ___ ___ ___ ___ (그래서 내가 전화한 것이다) you. Cindy, if you don't mind, can I ___ ___ ___ (너의 텐트를 빌리다)?

W Sure, no problem. I'll lend it to you.

09 장소 추론

핵심 어구 a bad cold, temperature, medicine 등에서 단서를 얻는다.

대화를 듣고, 두 사람이 대화하고 있는 장소로 가장 적절한 곳을 고르시오.

① 병원 ② 집
③ 운동장 ④ 식당
⑤ 스케이트장

+ 대화를 듣고, 두 사람의 관계로 가장 적절한 것을 고르시오.

① 의사 – 환자 ② 약사 – 손님
③ 교사 – 학생 ④ 교사 – 학부모
⑤ 의사 – 간호사

W Hi, have a seat please. What seems to be the problem?

M I think I ___ ___ ___ ___ (심한 감기에 걸리다). I have a runny nose and a fever.

W Let me ___ ___ ___ (당신의 체온을 재 보다). Wait a minute.... Well... you are 37.2 degrees.

M Is it serious?

W Well... it's not that serious. ___ ___ (약을 복용하다) and have a good rest, and then you'll ___ ___ (더 좋아지다).

10 주제, 소재 파악

대화를 듣고, 무엇에 관한 내용인지 가장 적절한 것을 고르시오.

① 방학 계획 ② 새학기 계획
③ 방학 숙제 ④ 과제 제출 방법
⑤ 시간 활용

M Oh, no. Is today already the 22nd?

W Yes, it is. Why?

M The vacation is almost over! I haven't finished my homework.

W But there are still ________ ________ ________. (5일 남다)

M Yeah, but actually I haven't even started it.

W Really? What did you do all this time?

M I don't know. ________ (시간이 흘렀다) just ________. Can you help me with it, please?

고난도

11 숫자 파악 – 날짜, 시각

요일과 시각을 각각 구분하여 메모하고, 구매 의사를 밝히는 부분(I'll buy ~.)에 집중한다.

대화를 듣고, 여자가 탈 기차의 요일과 시각을 고르시오.

① 금요일 – 오전 9시
② 토요일 – 오전 9시
③ 토요일 – 오후 2시 30분
④ 일요일 – 오후 2시 30분
⑤ 일요일 – 저녁 6시

「One ~, another …, and the other ~.」는 세 개의 대상을 설명할 때 사용하는 표현으로, '하나는 ~, 다른 하나는 …, 나머지 하나는 ~'이라고 해석한다.

W Hi, I'd like to go to Detroit this Friday. Are there any tickets left?

M On this Friday? Sorry, we don't have any tickets. Instead, we have tickets on Saturday and Sunday.

W Then, I'll ________ ________ ________ ________ (토요일 표를 사다). What time does the train leave?

M There are three trains on Saturday. One is 9:00 in the morning, another is 2:30 in the afternoon, and the other is 6:00 in the evening.

W Um... I'll ________ ________ ________ ________ (가장 이른 것을 사다). How much is it?

M It's $80.

12 그림 정보 파악 – 위치

남자가 있는 장소, 여자가 있는 장소, 두 사람이 만날 장소를 구분하여 듣는다.

대화를 듣고, 현재 여자가 있는 장소를 고르시오.

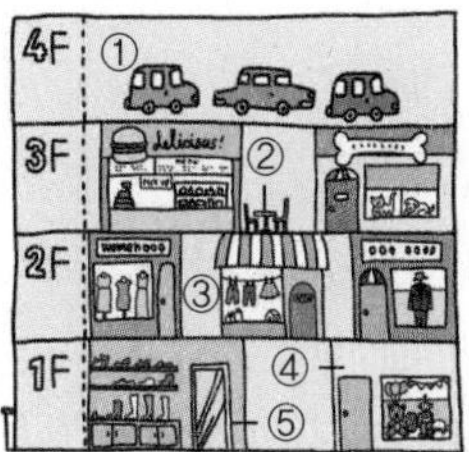

Where can we meet?은 만날 장소를 묻는 표현이다.

➕ 대화를 듣고, 두 사람이 만나기로 한 장소를 고르시오.

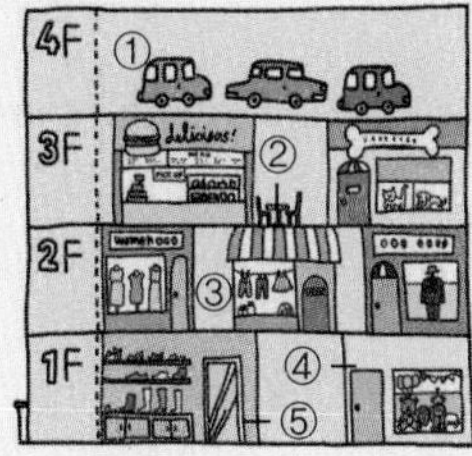

[Cellphone rings.]

M Hello, Laura. I'm in the building now.

W Oh, Jack. Where did you park your car?

M The parking area on the 4th floor. Where are you now?

W I'm ________ ________ ________ ________ ________ ________ ________ (재킷을 보느라 2층에) for me.

M Okay, where can we meet?

W Let's meet at the snack corner ________ ________ ________ ________ (3층의). We can eat something there.

M All right. I'll be there right away.

13 이유 파악

대화를 듣고, 남자가 여자에게 불평하는 이유로 가장 적절한 것을 고르시오.

① 전화 통화를 너무 오래 해서
② 약속 시간에 항상 늦게 와서
③ 휴대전화 벨소리가 너무 커서
④ 휴대전화를 너무 자주 확인해서
⑤ 남자의 휴대전화를 잃어버려서

M Oh, Mina, would you stop doing that?
W Stop doing what?
M You're ________ ________ ________ ________ ________. (네 휴대전화를 2분마다 확인하고 있다)
W I am not.
M You are. You keep looking at it and touching it. It's ________ ________ ________ ________. (너와 이야기 하기가 힘든)
W Oh, I'm sorry. I'll put it in my bag.

14 관계 추론

대화가 이루어지는 장소를 파악하여 두 사람의 관계를 추론해 본다.

대화를 듣고, 두 사람의 관계로 가장 적절한 것을 고르시오.

① 의사 – 환자
② 교사 – 학생
③ 어머니 – 아들
④ 사장 – 종업원
⑤ 수의사 – 애완동물 주인

[Someone knocks the door.]
W The door is open. Please come in.
M Hi!
W Hi, have a seat, please. So ________ ________ ________ ________? (당신의 애완동물에게 무슨 문제가 있나요)
M My pet dog has a fever. And she hasn't eaten anything since last night.
W Well... I think she has a cold now. Let me ________ ________ ________ first. Can you hold on her for a moment? (그녀의 체온을 재 보다)
M Yes, I can.

15 마지막 말 의도 파악

대화를 듣고, 남자의 마지막 말의 의도로 가장 적절한 것을 고르시오.

① 승낙 ② 거절
③ 감사 ④ 부정
⑤ 부탁

M Mmm... Your pie was so good. What did you make it with?
W I put chicken, green onions, bell peppers, and some spices. Did you like it?
M Yes, it was ________ ________. Thank you again for inviting me. (정말 맛있는)
W You're welcome. Thank you for coming. Would you like some more?
M I would love to, but ________ ________ now. (배가 부르다)

16 이유 파악

대화를 듣고, 남자가 기분이 좋은 이유로 가장 적절한 것을 고르시오.

① 보고 싶은 영화를 봐서
② 형이 찾아오기로 해서
③ 전화기를 새로 구입해서
④ San Diego로 이사를 가서
⑤ 금요일이 자신의 생일이어서

W Albert, you look happy. Did something good happen?
M Yeah, something did. You know, I ________ ________ ________ ________ ________ ________ a minute ago. (내 형한테 전화를 받았다)
W You mean, your older brother, Jason in San Diego?
M That's right. ________ ________ ________ to see me this Friday. (그가 여기 올 것이다)
W Wow, you must be very happy.

17 특정 정보 파악

대화를 듣고, 여자가 남자에게 제안한 것으로 가장 적절한 것을 고르시오.

① 땀 흘리지 않기
② 따뜻하게 옷 입기
③ 더운물로 샤워하기
④ 따뜻한 음료 마시기
⑤ 방안 적정 온도 유지하기

you should ~. 이후에 나오는 부분을 주의깊게 듣는다.

W Rodger, are you feeling all right?

M I don't feel very well. I ________ ________ ________ ________. It hurts every time I swallow something.
목이 아프다

W I think you should ________ ________ ________ ________.
따뜻한 차를 좀 마시다

M Does it help?

W Of course. Haven't you heard that ________ ________ ________ ________ ________ ________?
감기는 따뜻한 음료를 싫어한다

M I haven't, but it seems to be a good idea.

18 언급 및 비언급 파악

다음을 듣고, Robert에 대해 언급되지 않은 것을 고르시오.

① 직업 teacher
② 나이 46 years old
③ 가족 wife, son
④ 좋아하는 음식
⑤ 취미 reading

M Hi, students. I'm ________ ________ ________, Robert Jackson. I'm 46 years old and I have a wife and a 14-year-old son like you.
여러분의 담임선생님
I graduated from this middle school. So, I'm your senior. ________ ________ ________ ________, especially detective stories. I have read more than 100 detective stories. So if you want to read one, please tell me. I'll lend them to you.
내 취미는 독서이다

19 알맞은 응답 찾기

[19~20] 대화를 듣고, 여자의 마지막 말에 이어질 남자의 응답으로 가장 적절한 것을 고르시오.

Man: ____________________

① Okay, I'll lend mine to you.
② But I don't know how to use it.
③ Don't worry. I'll take a picture of you.
④ Where did you put your digital camera?
⑤ Excuse me, how much is this digital camera?

Can I ask you a favor?는 상대방에게 부탁할 때 사용하는 표현이다.

W Kevin, can I ask you a favor?

M Sure! What is it?

W You have a digital camera, don't you?

M Yes, I do. Ah, do you want to ________ ________ ________ ________?
내 디지털 카메라를 사용하다

W That's right. I'm going to take a trip to Grand Canyon tomorrow. But ________ ________ ________ ________ at the moment.
내 디지털 카메라가 고장 났다

M ____________________

20 알맞은 응답 찾기

Man: ____________________

① Sure! You'd better see it, too.
② Good! I'll buy your ticket, too.
③ Right, I want to be a movie star.
④ No, I didn't. I didn't have lunch.
⑤ Why don't we go shopping tomorrow?

W Ralph, I called you this afternoon. But you didn't answer.

M I'm sorry. Maybe you called me ________ ________ ________ ________ ________.
내가 영화를 보고있는 동안에

W Watching a movie? What did you see?

M I saw *Spider Man 3*. I saw it with my family.

W Oh, I heard that it was an interesting movie. ________ ________ ________ ________?
재미있었니

M ____________________

위치 • 언급 유무 파악

무엇을 평가하는가?	일상생활이나 친숙한 일반적 주제에 관한 위치 또는 도표에 관한 말이나 대화를 듣고 세부 정보를 파악할 수 있는지를 평가한다.
어떻게 출제되는가?	• 대화를 듣고, 여자가 가려고 하는 장소를 고르시오. • 다음을 듣고, 남자가 동아리 활동에 대해 언급하지 않은 것을 고르시오.

❶ 위치를 묻는 경우, 지도를 보고 건물의 위치나 거리의 이름 등을 파악한다.

❷ 출발점에서 방향이나 위치를 나타내는 표현을 따라 가며 최종 목적지를 찾는다.

❸ 언급 유무를 묻는 경우, 주의해서 들어야 할 내용을 파악 한 후 선택지를 지워가며 정답을 찾는다.

[기출로 전략 확인]

대화를 듣고, 남자의 마지막 말에 이어질 여자의 응답으로 가장 적절한 것을 고르시오.

[2018 기출]

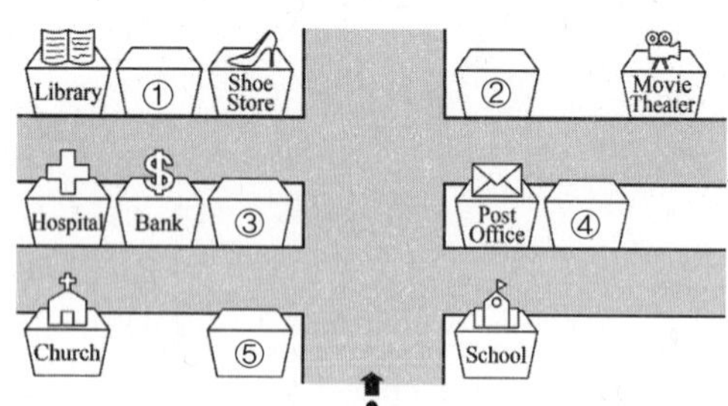

W Hi, Daniel. What's wrong?
M My cell phone is broken.
W Really? I know a good service center.
M Great! How can I get there?
W Go straight two blocks and turn left.
M Okay.
W It'll be on your right between the library and the shoe store.
M Oh, I see. Thanks.

❷ 'go straight', 'turn left', 'on your right', 'between'등 방향이나 위치를 나타내는 표현을 따라 간다.

여 안녕 Daniel. 무슨 일이야?
남 휴대전화가 망가졌어.
여 진짜? 나 괜찮은 서비스 센터를 알고있어.
남 잘됐다! 어떻게 가야 해?
여 두 블록을 쭉 가서 왼쪽으로 돌아.
남 알겠어.
여 네 오른쪽으로 도서관과 신발가게 사이에 있어.
남 아, 알겠어. 고마워.

위치 • 언급 유무 파악 유형의 발문과 보기

대화를 듣고, 여자가 찾고 있는 휴대전화의 위치로 가장 적절한 것을 고르시오. [2017 기출]

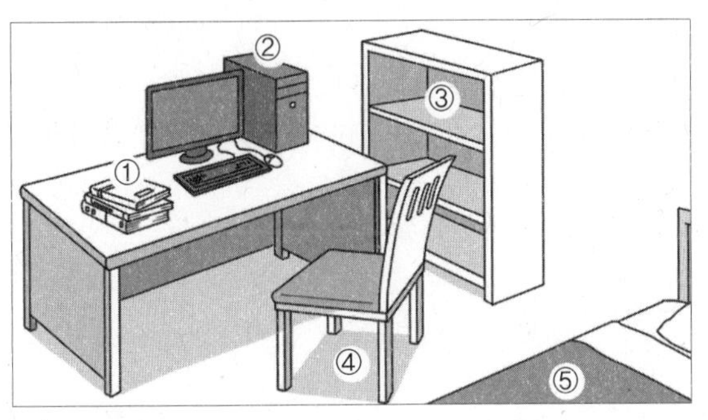

오답 찍는 문장 **M** I think I saw it next to the computer this morning.

⋮

만점 잡는 문장 **W** Oh... It's under the chair.

다음을 듣고, 여자가 친구에 대해 언급하지 않은 것을 고르시 오. [2018 기출]

① 학교 ② 외모 ③ 취미 ④ 생일 ⑤ 성격

만점 잡는 문장 ① She goes to Brown Middle School.
② She has long curly hair.
③ Her hobby is making things with paper.
④ She is kind, so many people like her.

위치 • 언급 유무 파악에 쓰이는 어휘 및 표현

• 위치

next to ~ 옆에	in front of ~ 앞에	along ~을 따라서	behind ~ 뒤에
on ~ 위에	under ~ 아래에	beside ~ 옆에	near ~ 근처에
across ~을 가로질러	go straight 직진하다	between A and B A와 B 사이에	bored 지루해 하는
opposite ~의 맞은 편에	turn right 우회전하다	turn left 좌회전하다	

• 언급 유무

(출신) My hometown is Incheon, Korea. 내 고향은 한국에 있는 인천이야.
(장래 희망) I want to be a famous figure skater. 나는 유명한 피겨 스케이팅 선수가 되고 싶어.
(취미) My hobby is taking pictures. 내 취미는 사진을 찍는 거야.
(색상) The shoes come in blue and pink. 신발 색상은 파란색과 분홍색이 있습니다.
(할인율/가격) Buy now and get 20% off. So, they're only $24.
지금 사면 20%할인이 되어 단돈 24달러 입니다.

영어듣기능력평가 15회

학년　　반　　번
이름

01 대화를 듣고, 여자가 그린 생일 초대 카드의 앞면을 고르시오.

① 

② 

③ 

④ 

⑤ 

02 다음을 듣고, 여자가 바꾸려고 하는 것이 <u>아닌</u> 것을 고르시오.

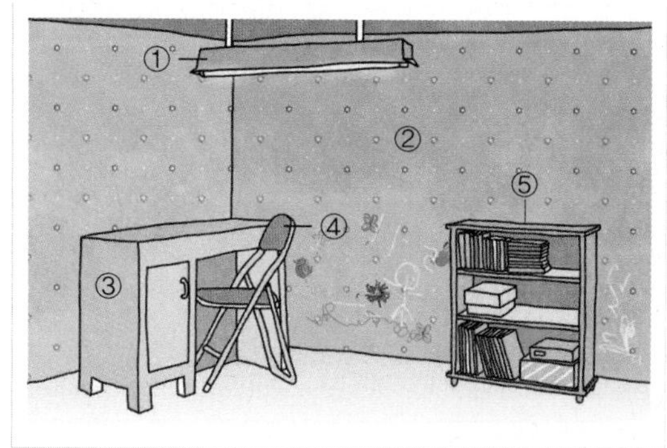

03 다음을 듣고, 서울의 내일 오후 날씨로 가장 적절한 것을 고르시오.

04 대화를 듣고, 남자가 수집하는 것으로 가장 적절한 것을 고르시오.

① 동전　② 숟가락
③ 인형　④ 우표
⑤ 우편엽서

05 대화를 듣고, 남자의 마지막 말의 의도로 가장 적절한 것을 고르시오.

① 제안　② 거절
③ 칭찬　④ 사과
⑤ 감사

06 대화를 듣고, 남자의 심정으로 가장 적절한 것을 고르시오.

① angry　② bored
③ happy　④ surprised
⑤ disappointed

07 대화를 듣고, 여자가 동아리 모임에 참석하지 <u>못하는</u> 이유로 가장 적절한 것을 고르시오.

① 여행을 가야 해서
② 아르바이트를 해야 해서
③ 자원봉사 활동을 해야 해서
④ 병원 진료가 예약되어 있어서
⑤ 부모님과 체험 학습을 가야 해서

08 다음을 듣고, 두 사람의 대화가 <u>어색한</u> 것을 고르시오.

①　②　③　④　⑤

09 대화를 듣고, 남자가 이용할 교통 수단으로 가장 적절한 것을 고르시오.

① airplane　② ship
③ car　④ bus
⑤ train

10 대화를 듣고, 여자가 타고 갈 기차의 출발 시각을 고르시오.

① 1시　② 2시
③ 2시 30분　④ 3시
⑤ 3시 30분

점수 /20

11 다음을 듣고, 'this'가 가리키는 것으로 가장 적절한 것을 고르시오.

① 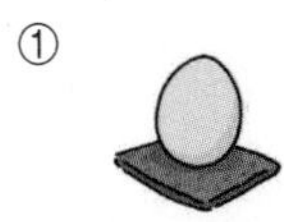
② 
③ 

④ 
⑤ 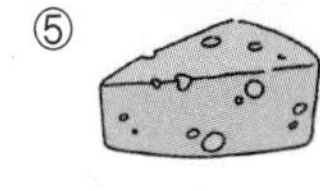

고난도
12 다음 표를 보면서 대화를 듣고, 대화의 내용과 일치하지 않는 것을 고르시오.

From:	① Mr. Lee
	② Yukee Company
To:	③ Mr. Kinsley
Message:	④ Call him at 555-6236
	⑤ Mr. Lee wants to have a return call around five.

고난도
13 다음을 듣고, Children's Basketball Day에 대한 설명으로 일치하지 않는 것을 고르시오.

① 이번 주 토요일에 열린다.
② Clinton 공원에서 열린다.
③ 오후 2시에 끝난다.
④ 무료 행사이다.
⑤ 농구를 할 수 있다.

14 대화를 듣고, 남자의 직업으로 가장 적절한 것을 고르시오.

① 기자 ② 요리사
③ 사진작가 ④ 카메라맨
⑤ 잡지 편집장

15 대화를 듣고, 두 사람이 대화하고 있는 장소로 가장 적절한 곳을 고르시오.

① kitchen ② restaurant
③ post office ④ grocery store
⑤ department store

16 다음을 듣고, 표를 잘못 설명한 것을 고르시오.

Music Class

	Violin Class A	Violin Class B	Violin Class C
Time	9:00~10:30	11:00~12:30	10:00~11:30
Room Number	201	201	202
Instructor	Ron	Ron	Sam

① ② ③ ④ ⑤

17 대화를 듣고, 두 사람의 관계로 가장 적절한 것을 고르시오.

① 아버지 – 딸
② 남편 – 아내
③ 교사 – 학생
④ 교장 – 학부모
⑤ 버스 기사 – 승객

18 대화를 듣고, Brad가 이번 주 토요일에 할 일로 가장 적절한 것을 고르시오.

① 독서하기
② 서점에 가기
③ 사촌 집 방문하기
④ 친구의 독후감 숙제 도와주기
⑤ 사촌에게 도시 구경 시켜 주기

[19~20] 대화를 듣고, 남자의 마지막 말에 이어질 여자의 응답으로 가장 적절한 것을 고르시오.

고난도
19 Woman: ______________________

① Suit yourself.
② That's the spirit.
③ I'm ashamed of it.
④ It serves you right.
⑤ You did a good job.

20 Woman: ______________________

① Thank you for saying so.
② Right. I'm not going there.
③ Sure. I make mistakes, too.
④ Yes. The interview was easy.
⑤ No. I'm not good at interview.

영어듣기능력평가 15회 DICTATION

다시 들으면서 듣기 만점에 도전하세요!
Dictation: 스크립트의 주요 부분을 다시 들으면서!
실전 ⊕: 세부 정보가 많은 스크립트를 다른 문제로 샅샅이!

01 그림 정보 파악 – 사물

얼굴과 Happy Birthday!라는 어구의 위치와 관련된 표현을 주의깊게 듣는다.

대화를 듣고, 여자가 그린 생일 초대 카드의 앞면을 고르시오.

① ②

③  ④ 

⑤ 

I hope ~.는 '나는 ~을 바란다.'는 의미로, 소망을 말하는 표현이다.

M Oh, you're making the invitation card for your birthday.
W Yes, dad. I __________ __________ __________ __________ __________ (내 얼굴을 가운데에 넣다). I have a big smile.
M Yes. I can see your teeth. You look good.
W Thanks. __________ __________ __________ (내 얼굴 아래에), I wrote the words, "Happy Birthday."
M Good. I hope you have a great birthday party.

02 그림 정보 파악 – 위치

다음을 듣고, 여자가 바꾸려고 하는 것이 아닌 것을 고르시오.

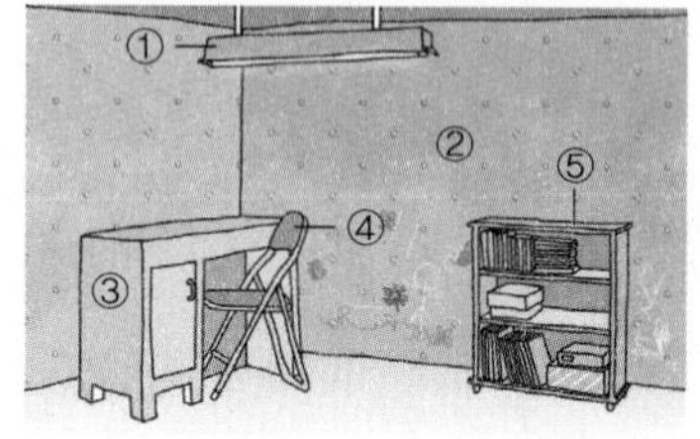

W This is my room. Everything in this room is too old. The light is not bright enough. The wallpaper is dark and dirty. I'd like to change them. The bookshelf is too small. I need a bigger one. I think I need a new desk, too. I want to put my desktop computer on the desk. __________ __________ __________ __________ __________ (의자는 생일 선물이었다) from my parents. __________ __________ __________ (나는 그것이 좋다).

03 날씨 파악

내일 오전 날씨와 오후 날씨를 구분하여 듣는다.

다음을 듣고, 서울의 내일 오후 날씨로 가장 적절한 것을 고르시오.

①   ②

rain

③  ④ 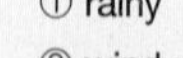

wind

⑤ 

M Good evening. This is Matt Kim. For Seoul's weather tomorrow, tomorrow will __________ __________ __________ __________ __________ __________ (약간의 비로 시작하다), so don't forget to take your umbrella with you. In the afternoon, the rain will stop but we will __________ __________ __________ __________ (강한 바람이 불다) all afternoon.

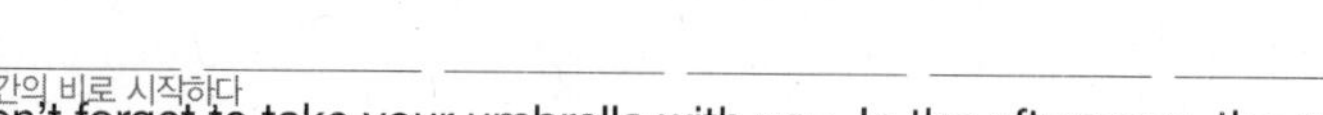

⊕ **다음을 듣고, 서울의 내일 오전 날씨로 가장 적절한 것을 고르시오.**

① rainy ② snowy
③ windy ④ sunny
⑤ cloudy

04 특정 정보 파악

어떤 것을 수집하느냐는 여자의 질문에 대한 남자의 대답을 주의깊게 듣는다.

대화를 듣고, 남자가 수집하는 것으로 가장 적절한 것을 것을 고르시오.

① 동전 coins
② 숟가락 spoons
③ 인형
④ 우표 stamps
⑤ 우편엽서 postcards

M What are all these things? There are coins, spoons, and postcards.

W I got those things when I __________ __________ __________ __________.
전 세계를 여행했다

M Wow.

W Do you collect anything?

M I __________ __________. That's my hobby.
우표를 모으다

W That's a good hobby.

05 의도 추론

요청(Can I ~?)에 대해 수락하는지 거절하는지에 주목하여 듣는다.

대화를 듣고, 남자의 마지막 말의 의도로 가장 적절한 것을 고르시오.

① 제안 ② 거절
③ 칭찬 ④ 사과
⑤ 감사

W Dad, can I ask you a favor?

M What is it?

W I want to have a pet dog.

M But you have __________ __________ __________ __________. I don't think having a pet dog is a good idea.
털에 대한 알레르기

W Then can I have Chihuahua? It has short fur.

M I'm sorry, but I __________ __________ __________ __________ __________ __________.
네가 아픈 것을 원하지 않는다

06 심정 추론

대화를 듣고, 남자의 심정으로 가장 적절한 것을 고르시오.

① angry 화가 난
② bored 지루한
③ happy 행복한
④ surprised 놀란
⑤ disappointed 실망한

W How was your dance contest?

M I don't want to talk about it.

W Why? Did you make some mistakes?

M You know, I prepared for the contest so hard. But I __________ __________ __________ __________ well.
내 몸을 움직일 수 없었다

W __________ __________ __________.
정말 안됐다

M I don't know why I did that.

고난도

07 이유 파악

거절의 말 뒤에 이유를 말하는 부분을 주의 깊게 듣는다.

대화를 듣고, 여자가 동아리 모임에 참석하지 못하는 이유로 가장 적절한 것을 고르시오.

① 여행을 가야 해서
② 아르바이트를 해야 해서
③ 자원봉사 활동을 해야 해서
④ 병원 진료가 예약되어 있어서
⑤ 부모님과 체험 학습을 가야 해서

M Sojin, are you coming to the club meeting?

W Sorry, I can't. I have to ________ ________ ________ ________ ________. (이주민 노동자 센터에 가다)

M What's the migrant worker center?

W It's a center for the workers from other countries.

M Why are you going there?

W I ________ ________ ________ ________ ________ take care of the workers. (의사와 간호사를 도와주려고 지원했다)

08 어색한 대화 찾기

다음을 듣고, 두 사람의 대화가 어색한 것을 고르시오.

① ② ③ ④ ⑤

「call A B」는 'A를 B라고 부르다'라는 의미이다.

① **M** How much does this basket cost?
W It costs two dollars.

② **M** ________ ________ ________ ________ ________? (주문하시겠어요)
W Would you recommend something?

③ **M** ________ ________ ________ ________ ________ Green Bank is? (어디에 ~이 있는지 알려 주시겠어요)
W ________ ________ ________ ________ on foot. (15분 걸리다)

④ **M** You don't look good today.
W I think I have a cold.

⑤ **M** What can I call you?
W You can call me Jennifer.

09 특정 정보 파악

We're going ~. 이후에 나오는 부분을 주의깊게 듣는다.

대화를 듣고, 남자가 이용할 교통 수단으로 가장 적절한 것을 고르시오.

① airplane 비행기
② ship 배
③ car 자동차
④ bus 버스
⑤ train 기차

W Chulsu, what are you doing this weekend?

M My parents and I are going to my grandmother's house.

W Where does she live?

M She lives on Jeju Island. We're ________ ________ ________ ________. (배로 그곳에 갈 것이다)

W Not by plane?

M Yes. I think ________ ________ ________ will be fun even though it takes a long time. (배를 타는 것)

10 숫자 파악 – 시각

대화를 듣고, 여자가 타고 갈 기차의 출발 시각을 고르시오.

① 1시 ② 2시
③ 2시 30분 ④ 3시
⑤ 3시 30분

여자가 잘못 알고 있었던 시각이 언급될 때 혼동하지 않도록 주의한다.

[Telephone rings.]

M Hello?

W Hello? This is Sumi. You're Minsu, right?

M Yes. Are you calling ________ ________ ________? (기차에서)

W No. I thought the train ________ ________ ________ ________, but I was wrong. (2시에 출발할 것이다)

M Then what time does your train leave?

W They say ________ ________ ________ ________. (3시에 출발하다)

11 그림 "this" 파악 (담화)

다음을 듣고, 'this'가 가리키는 것으로 가장 적절한 것을 고르시오.

① ② ③ ④ ⑤

M You can buy this in a grocery store. And you should ________ this ________ ________ ________ ________. (시원한 곳에 보관하다) You can cook this, and use it in many different dishes. You can boil or fry it. And you can mix it with other ingredients. If you fry this, you should ________ ________ ________ first. What is this? (껍질을 깨다)

12 실용문 정보 파악

다음 표를 보면서 대화를 듣고, 대화의 내용과 일치하지 않는 것을 고르시오.

From:	① Mr. Lee
	② Yukee Company
To:	③ Mr. Kinsley
Message:	④ Call him at 555-6236
	⑤ Mr. Lee wants to have a return call around five.

May I speak to ~?는 통화할 상대를 바꿔달라고 부탁하는 표현이다.

[Telephone rings.]

W Hello, Nori Communication.

M Hello? This is Mr. Lee from Yukee Company. May I speak to Mr. Kinsley?

W He just went out and he'll be back at three.

M Would you tell me his cell phone number?

W Sorry, I can't. But I can leave him a message.

M OK. Then, ask him to ________ ________ ________ ________-________. (555-6236번으로 나에게 전화해라)

W What time should he call you back?

M ________ ________ ________. (4시경)

고난도

13 내용 일치 파악

다음을 듣고, Children's Basketball Day에 대한 설명으로 일치하지 않는 것을 고르시오.

① 이번 주 토요일에 열린다.
② Clinton 공원에서 열린다.
③ 오후 2시에 끝난다.
④ 무료 행사이다.
⑤ 농구를 할 수 있다.

W This Saturday , we're having a Children's Basketball Day at Clinton park. The event will begin at nine in the morning and ________ ________ ________ in the afternoon. (3시에 끝나다) ________ ________ ________ ________ for all children. This will be a good (이 행사는 무료이다) opportunity for the children to play basketball with each other.

14 직업 추론

핵심 어휘 camera, picture 등을 단서로 이용한다.

대화를 듣고, 남자의 직업으로 가장 적절한 것을 고르시오.

① 기자　② 요리사
③ 사진작가　④ 카메라맨
⑤ 잡지 편집장

W Your bag looks heavy. What do you have in there?

M It's ________ ________ ________ ________. They are heavy. (내 카메라와 렌즈들)

W Are you a camera man for news reports?

M No, I ________ ________ ________ ________ ________ ________. (잡지용 음식 사진을 찍다)
I work with many cooks. When a cook makes a dish, I take the picture of it.

W Wow, do you get to taste the food?

M Sometimes.

15 장소 추론

두 사람이 현재 있는 장소와 남자가 앞으로 가게 될 장소를 혼동하지 않도록 주의한다.

대화를 듣고, 두 사람이 대화하고 있는 장소로 가장 적절한 곳을 고르시오.

① kitchen 부엌
② restaurant 식당
③ post office 우체국
④ grocery store 식료품점
⑤ department store 백화점

대화를 듣고, 남자가 대화 후에 할 일로 가장 적절한 것을 고르시오.

① 우체국 가기　② 편지 쓰기
③ 숟가락 건네주기　④ 요리하기
⑤ 수프 먹어보기

W Tommy, are you going out?

M Yes. I'm going to the post office. I have to ________ ________ ________. (이 편지를 부치다)

W Before you go out, would you ________ ________ ________? I made it. Have a seat at the dinner table. (이 수프를 먹어 보다)

M Thanks, Mom. Would you ________ ________ ________ ________? (숟가락을 나에게 주다)

W Oh, I forgot. Here it is.

16 실용문 정보 파악

다음을 듣고, 표를 잘못 설명한 것을 고르시오.

Music Class

	Violin Class A	Violin Class B	Violin Class C
Time	9:00~10:30	11:00~12:30	10:00~11:30
Room Number	201	201	202
	Ron	Ron	Sam

①　②　③　④　⑤

M ① Violin Class A ________ ________ ________. (9시에 시작하다)
② Violin Class B begins at eleven.
③ Violin Class C begins ________ ________ ________ than Violin Class A. (한 시간 늦게)
④ Ron teaches Violin Class A and C.
⑤ Sam ________ ________ ________ in room number 202. (자신의 수업을 가르치다)

17 관계 추론

대화를 듣고, 두 사람의 관계로 가장 적절한 것을 고르시오.

① 아버지 – 딸
② 남편 – 아내
③ 교사 – 학생
④ 교장 – 학부모
⑤ 버스 기사 – 승객

두 사람이 공통적으로 말하고 있는 Barry가 누구인지 파악한다.

W John, it's ______ ______ ______ ______ Barry. (태우러 갈 시간)
M OK. I'm ready. What time does his school finish?
W It finishes at two. ______ ______ ______ ______ ______ these days. (우리 Barry가 잘 하고 있다)
M Really?
W Yes. He began to be interested in studying.
M I'm so happy to hear that. And I'm ______ ______ ______ ______. (우리 아들이 자랑스러운)
W Me too.

18 할 일 파악

대화를 듣고, Brad가 이번 주 토요일에 할 일로 가장 적절한 것을 고르시오.

① 독서하기
② 서점에 가기
③ 사촌 집 방문하기
④ 친구의 독후감 숙제 도와주기
⑤ 사촌에게 도시 구경 시켜 주기

남자가 사촌을 위해 할 일이 무엇인지에 집중하며 듣는다.

W Brad, would you help me with my book report this Saturday?
M Sorry, I can't. I ______ ______ ______ ______ on Saturday. (해야 할 일이 있다)
W Are you going somewhere?
M No, but I have to ______ ______ ______ ______ ______ ______. (내 사촌에게 도시 구경을 시켜 주다) He's coming on Friday.
W It'll be fun to ______ ______ ______ around the city. (네 사촌을 안내해 주다)
M That's right.

고난도

19 알맞은 응답 찾기

[19~20] 대화를 듣고, 남자의 마지막 말에 이어질 여자의 응답으로 가장 적절한 것을 고르시오.

Woman: ______________

① Suit yourself.
② That's the spirit.
③ I'm ashamed of it.
④ It serves you right.
⑤ You did a good job.

Practice will make perfect.는 '연습이 완벽함을 만들 것이다.'는 의미로, 연습의 중요성을 나타내는 속담이다.

M Mrs. Evans, can James and I ______ ______ ______ ______ after school today? (체육관에 남다)
W What are you guys going to do?
M James will help me ______ ______ ______. (배구 서브 연습을 하다)
W Hmm, are you practicing for the match?
M Well, you know, I made several service mistakes during the last games. I can't do that anymore. I believe ______ ______ ______ ______. (연습이 완벽함을 만들 것이다)
W ______________

20 알맞은 응답 찾기

Woman: ______________

① Thank you for saying so.
② Right. I'm not going there.
③ Sure. I make mistakes, too.
④ Yes. The interview was easy.
⑤ No. I'm not good at interview.

I'm afraid ~.는 '(유감이지만) ~인 것 같다.'라는 의미로, 유감 · 안타까움을 나타낼 때 사용하는 표현이다.

W How was your interview?
M I'm afraid I ______ ______ ______ ______ ______. I was so nervous. (실수를 많이 했다)
W You prepared for the interview a lot.
M Right. But I didn't know what to say at that time.
W Don't worry. ______ ______ ______. (모두가 실수를 한다)
M ______ ______ ______ ______? (정말 그렇게 생각하니)
W ______________

영어듣기능력평가 16회

학년 반 번
이름

01 다음을 듣고, 'it'이 무엇인지 가장 적절한 것을 고르시오.

① 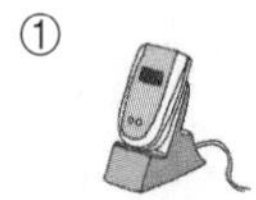
②
③ 
④ 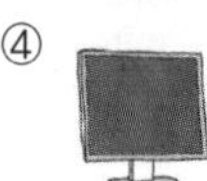
⑤ 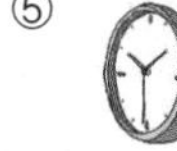

고난도

02 대화를 듣고, 대화의 내용과 일치하지 <u>않는</u> 것을 고르시오.

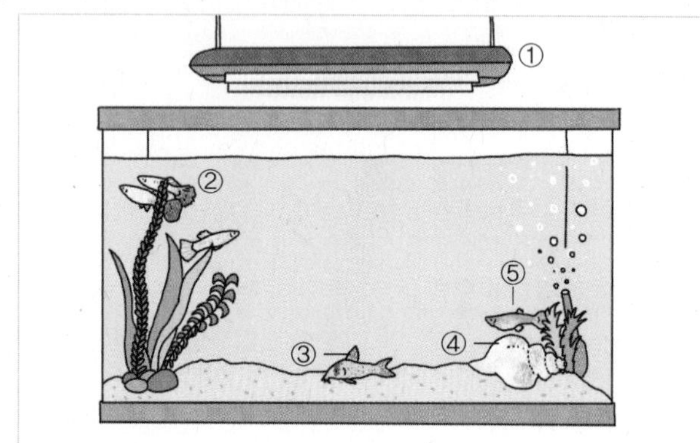

03 다음을 듣고, 다음 주 월요일 날씨로 가장 적절한 것을 고르시오.

① 
② 
③ 
④ 
⑤ 

04 대화를 듣고, 남자가 내일 할 일로 가장 적절한 것을 고르시오.

① 쇼핑하기
② 농구 시합하기
③ 영화 관람하기
④ 컴퓨터 게임하기
⑤ 영어 시험 보기

05 다음을 듣고, 두 사람의 대화가 <u>어색한</u> 것을 고르시오.

① ② ③ ④ ⑤

06 대화를 듣고, 여자가 타고 갈 기차의 출발 시각을 고르시오.

① 2:00
② 2:30
③ 3:00
④ 3:20
⑤ 3:30

07 대화를 듣고, 남자가 오늘 저녁에 할 일로 가장 적절한 것을 고르시오.

① 병문안 가기
② 병원 예약하기
③ 아버지 간호하기
④ 여자의 집 방문하기
⑤ 검사 결과 확인하기

08 다음을 듣고, 'I'가 무엇인지 가장 적절한 것을 고르시오.

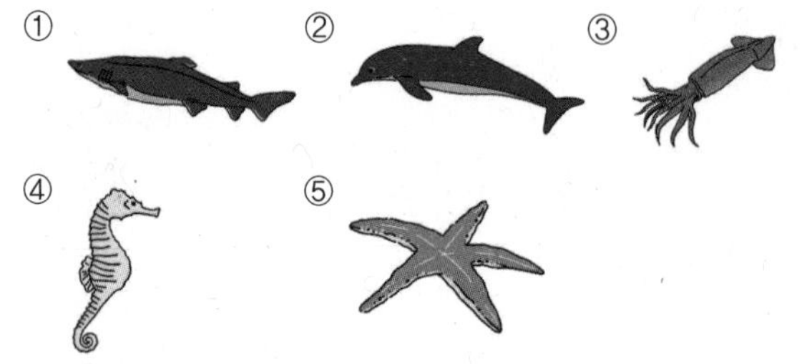

09 대화를 듣고, 남자의 장래 희망으로 가장 적절한 것을 고르시오.

① hotel chef
② talk show host
③ TV producer
④ hotel manager
⑤ news reporter

10 다음을 듣고, Mrs. Jones에 대해 언급되지 <u>않은</u> 것을 고르시오.

① 이름
② 가르치는 과목
③ 수업하는 요일
④ 사는 곳
⑤ 좋아하는 운동

점수 /20

고난도

11 대화를 듣고, 여자가 기분이 나쁜 이유로 가장 적절한 것을 고르시오.

① 동아리 친구와 다투어서
② 밴드 동아리 가입이 취소되어서
③ 밴드 동아리 공연이 연기되어서
④ 부모님이 밴드 동아리 가입을 허락하지 않으셔서
⑤ 밴드 동아리 연습이 취소된 것을 알려 주지 않아서

12 대화를 듣고, 여자가 남자에게 충고한 것으로 가장 적절한 것을 고르시오.

① 일찍 일어나기
② 자기 전에 머리 감기
③ 입 가리고 재채기하기
④ 따뜻한 옷 입고 다니기
⑤ 머리를 말린 후에 외출하기

13 다음을 듣고, 무엇에 관한 내용인지 가장 적절한 것을 고르시오.

① 관광지 홍보
② 캠프 여행 소개
③ 여행 일정 안내
④ 여름 야외 활동
⑤ 학급 야영 계획

14 대화를 듣고, 방학이 시작되는 날짜를 고르시오.

① July 9
② July 12
③ July 10
④ July 18
⑤ July 19

15 대화를 듣고, Fine Repair의 위치로 가장 알맞은 곳을 고르시오.

16 대화를 듣고, 여자가 남자의 요청을 거절한 이유로 가장 적절한 것을 고르시오.

① 동전이 없어서
② 배터리가 없어서
③ 시간이 부족해서
④ 휴대전화가 없어서
⑤ 휴대전화가 고장 나서

17 대화를 듣고, 여자의 심정으로 가장 적절한 것을 고르시오.

① satisfied
② hopeful
③ shy
④ worried
⑤ bored

18 대화를 듣고, 여자가 제안한 것으로 가장 적절한 것을 고르시오.

① 장화 구입하기
② 우산 잘 펴서 말리기
③ 신발 젖지 않게 하기
④ 우산 잃어버리지 않기
⑤ 남자용 우비 구입하기

[19~20] 대화를 듣고, 남자의 마지막 말에 이어질 여자의 응답으로 가장 적절한 것을 고르시오.

19 Woman: ____________________

① I will keep dieting.
② Because I have to.
③ I will keep that in mind.
④ I run in the park every evening.
⑤ Losing weight is not easy at all.

20 Woman: ____________________

① I hope you can make it.
② I'm thinking of a drama club.
③ Dancing club is very popular.
④ I'll do my best for the audition.
⑤ I need to practice for the audition.

영어듣기능력평가 16회 DICTATION

다시 들으면서 듣기 만점에 도전하세요!
Dictation: 스크립트의 주요 부분을 다시 들으면서!
실전 ⊕: 세부 정보가 많은 스크립트를 다른 문제로 살살이!

01 그림 정보 파악 – 사물

장소(on the wall, on your desk), 용도(tells you days and dates)에 관한 언급을 종합해 본다.

다음을 듣고, 'it'이 무엇인지 가장 적절한 것을 고르시오.

①  ②  ③  ④  ⑤

W You can put it ________ ________ ________ (벽에) or ________ ________ ________ (책상 위에). There are numbers on it. It ________ ________ ________ ________ ________ (당신에게 날짜와 요일을 알려 주다). It shows holidays, too. You can circle important days. When you look at this, you will not forget what you should do that day.

고난도

02 그림 정보 파악 – 사물

대화를 듣고, 대화의 내용과 일치하지 않는 것을 고르시오.

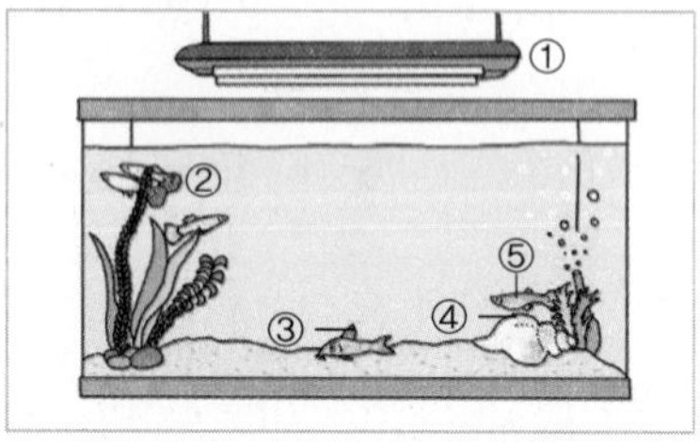

① ② ③ ④ ⑤

W You've got a new fish tank! Are they guppies?
M Yes. Four guppies and one algae eater. They say algae eater ________ ________ ________ ________ ________ ________ (어항 바닥에 살다) and cleans the water.
W Some are hiding ________ ________ ________ ________ (수초 뒤에).
M One is here. ________ ________ ________ (조개 껍질 옆에).
W Did you pick the shell from the beach?
M No, I bought one. I bought the light, too. I didn't know I need a light for the fish.
W It seems to make the fish tank more beautiful.

03 날씨 파악

on Monday가 언급되는 부분을 주의깊게 듣는다.

다음을 듣고, 다음 주 월요일 날씨로 가장 적절한 것을 고르시오.

①  ②  ③  nice, warm ④  rain ⑤

M This is today's weather update. Are you enjoying the nice warm weather today? The temperature is higher than average this week. We are going to have this warm weather until the weekend. On Sunday night, however, ________ ________ ________ ________ (기온이 떨어질 것이다) and ________ ________ ________ (비가 올 것이다) through the whole country on Monday.

⊕ 다음을 듣고, 오늘의 날씨로 가장 적절한 것을 고르시오.

① cloudy ② snowy
③ sunny ④ rainy
⑤ windy

04 할 일 파악

오늘 할 일(go shopping)과 내일 하기로 약속한 일(play computer games)을 구분하여 듣는다.

대화를 듣고, 남자가 내일 할 일로 가장 적절한 것을 고르시오.

① 쇼핑하기 go shopping
② 농구 시합하기
③ 영화 관람하기
④ 컴퓨터 게임하기 play computer games
⑤ 영어 시험 보기

M How was your English test?

W It wasn't that hard. I think I did quite well.

M That's good. Can we ________ ________ ________ together? You know, the test is finished. (컴퓨터 게임을 하다)

W Oh, ________ ________ ________ ________? I have to go shopping with my mom now. (내일 하면 어떨까)

M All right. Let's do it tomorrow afternoon. I'll send you a text message.

+ 대화를 듣고, 여자가 오늘 할 일로 가장 적절한 것을 고르시오.

① 쇼핑하기 ② 농구 시합하기
③ 영화 관람하기 ④ 컴퓨터 게임하기
⑤ 영어 시험 보기

05 어색한 대화 찾기

다음을 듣고, 두 사람의 대화가 어색한 것을 고르시오.

① ② ③ ④ ⑤

Are we there yet?은 '다 왔나요?'라는 의미로, 도착 여부를 묻는 표현이다.

① M ________ ________ ________ ________? (다 왔나요)
W Not yet, honey.

② M How much did you pay for it?
W It was 25 dollars.

③ M Do you mind ________ ________ ________ ________? (소리를 줄이는 것)
W That's not mine but ________ ________ ________ ________. (내가 그것을 켤 것이다)

④ M Who's the man over there?
W He's our new English teacher.

⑤ M What sport do you like best?
W I'm a big fan of baseball.

06 숫자 파악 – 시각

문제에서 요구하는 시각이 무엇인지에 초점을 맞춰 숫자에 집중하며 듣는다.

대화를 듣고, 여자가 타고 갈 기차의 출발 시각을 고르시오.

① 2:00 ② 2:30
③ 3:00 ④ 3:20
⑤ 3:30

W How long will it take to get to Seoul Station?

M ________ ________ ________. But you know, taxi drivers can't tell time on Saturday afternoon. Look at the traffic! (20분쯤)

W Oh, I have to be there by three. My train will ________ ________ ________. (3시 20분에 출발하다)

M It's two thirty now. I think we can make it.

07 할 일 파악

문제에서 요구하는 시각이 무엇인지에 초점을 맞춰 숫자에 집중하며 듣는다.

대화를 듣고, 남자가 오늘 저녁에 할 일로 가장 적절한 것을 고르시오.

① 병문안 가기
② 병원 예약하기
③ 아버지 간호하기
④ 여자의 집 방문하기
⑤ 검사 결과 확인하기

M Sarah, how's your father doing?

W He's getting better. He'll come home next Monday.

M That's great. ________ ________ ________ ________? (오늘 그분을 문병해도 될까)

W Of course. He'll be happy to see you.

M What time is good?

W Can you come before 8 o'clock?

M All right. ________ ________ ________ ________. (6시쯤에 갈 것이다)

08 그림 "I" 파악 (담화)

다음을 듣고, 'I'가 무엇인지 가장 적절한 것을 고르시오.

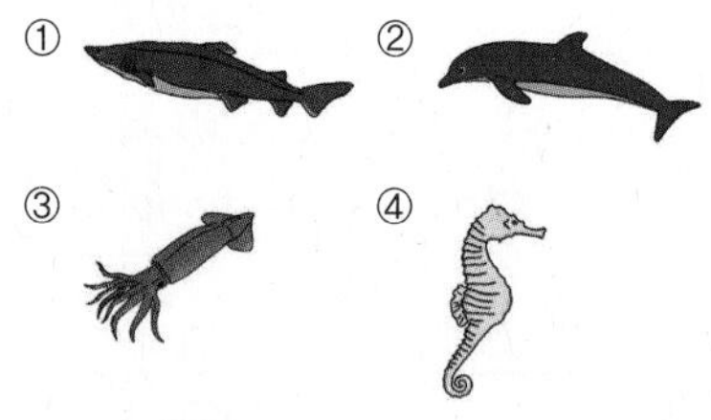

①
②
③
④
⑤

M I look like a big fish, but actually I'm not a fish. I live in the sea, but I'm a mammal, ________ ________(사람과 같은). I live all around the world. But you can also see me in some aquariums. I ________ ________ ________ ________(흥미로운 쇼를 하다) there. What am I?

09 특정 정보 파악

남자가 원하는 직업과 여자가 원하는 직업을 구분하여 듣는다.

대화를 듣고, 남자의 장래 희망으로 가장 적절한 것을 고르시오.

① hotel chef 호텔 주방장
② talk show host 토크 쇼 진행자
③ TV producer TV 프로듀서
④ hotel manager 호텔 매니저
⑤ news reporter 뉴스 기자

M I think you're interested in cooking.

W I am. I'd like to ________ ________ ________ ________(호텔 주방장이 되다).

M I think you'll make a good chef.

W I know what you are going to be. Don't you want to be a TV producer?

M Well, actually I want to ________ ________ ________ ________ ________(토크 쇼 진행자가 되다).

W A talk show host like Oprah Winfrey?

M That's right.

10 언급 및 비언급 파악

다음을 듣고, Mrs. Jones에 대해 언급되지 않은 것을 고르시오.

① 이름 Mrs. Jones
② 가르치는 과목 English
③ 수업하는 요일 every Wednesday
④ 사는 곳
⑤ 좋아하는 운동 racquetball, tennis

W Nice to meet you, everyone. I'm Mrs. Jones, ________ ________ ________(여러분의 영어회화 선생님). You will have English class with me ________ ________(매주 수요일). My first name is Gloria but I want you to call me Mrs. Jones. I ________ ________ ________(~하는 것을 좋아하다) racquetball and tennis.

11 이유 파악

「should have p.p.」가 사용된 부분의 의미를 파악한다.

대화를 듣고, 여자가 기분이 나쁜 이유로 가장 적절한 것을 고르시오.

① 동아리 친구와 다투어서
② 밴드 동아리 가입이 취소되어서
③ 밴드 동아리 공연이 연기되어서
④ 부모님이 밴드 동아리 가입을 허락하지 않으셔서
⑤ 밴드 동아리 연습이 취소된 것을 알려 주지 않아서

This is not right.는 '이것은 옳지 않다.'는 의미로, 부당함을 나타낼 때 사용하는 표현이다.

M Where are you going, Mary?
W To the clubroom. Our band practices every Friday and Saturday, you know.
M Well, Mary. I've just met Zoe and she said ________ ________ ________ ________ today. (연습이 없었다)
W Did she? But ________ ________ ________ ________ ________. (아무도 그것에 대해 내게 말해 주지 않았다)
M Didn't you get the text message?
W No, I didn't. This is not right. Somebody should have told me about it.
M I agree.

12 특정 정보 파악

충고의 내용이 직접적으로 드러나지 않으므로 여자의 마지막 말의 의미를 정확히 파악한다.

대화를 듣고, 여자가 남자에게 충고한 것으로 가장 적절한 것을 고르시오.

① 일찍 일어나기
② 자기 전에 머리 감기
③ 입 가리고 재채기하기
④ 따뜻한 옷 입고 다니기
⑤ 머리를 말린 후에 외출하기

(God) Bless you.는 재채기를 한 사람에게 '몸조심 하세요.' 또는 '저런.'의 의미로 사용하는 표현이다.

M A-choo!
W Bless you. Brian, look at you! ________ ________ ________ ________ ________. (네 머리카락이 아직도 젖어 있다)
M Because I washed it just before I came out.
W You might get a bad cold.
M You're right. Oh, my hair is frozen.
W That's why you keep sneezing.
M I didn't have time to ________ ________. (그것을 말리다)
W It won't take much time if you ________ ________ ________ ________. (헤어 드라이어를 사용하다)

13

다음을 듣고, 무엇에 관한 내용인지 가장 적절한 것을 고르시오.

① 관광지 홍보
② 캠프 여행 소개
③ 여행 일정 안내
④ 여름 야외 활동
⑤ 학급 야영 계획

M Last week, my class ________ ________ ________ ________ ________ ________. (3일간의 캠프 여행을 갔다) First day, we ________ ________ (래프팅을 즐겼다) in Dong-Gang River. We got all wet on the rafts. It was exciting. The second day, we visited a famous cave. It was hot outside, but inside the cave, it was cool. We visited the beach and played there ________ ________ ________ ________ ________ (집으로 출발하기 전에). It was a great trip.

14 숫자 파악 – 날짜

대화를 듣고, 방학이 시작되는 날짜를 고르시오.

① July 9 ② July 12
③ July 10 ④ July 18
⑤ July 19

Summer vacation is just around the corner.는 '여름 방학이 임박했다.'는 의미로, just around the corner는 '바로 근처에, 임박한'이라는 의미이다.

M Summer vacation is just around the corner.
W I know. But I should come to school anyway during the vacation.
M Do you have summer school classes?
W I do. ________ ________ ________ ________. (7월 19일에 수업이 시작한다)
M That's the first day of vacation. Doesn't ________ ________ ________ ________ ________? (우리 방학이 19일에 시작하다)
W You're right.
M Oh, that's too bad. It's not a vacation for you at all.

15 지도, 위치 파악

대화를 듣고, Fine Repair의 위치로 가장 알맞은 곳을 고르시오.

W Tom, my cell phone's broken. Do you know a good repair shop near here?
M Sure, I know one. It's called Fine Repair.
W Can you tell me where it is?
M Go straight to Green Street, and turn right.
W Turn right? Okay.
M Walk one more block, then you will see Smile Bank. ________ ________ straight, and it's just ________ ________ ________. (계속 걸어라 / 은행을 지나서)
W Thanks!

16 이유 파악

I'm sorry라는 거절의 말 뒤에 이어지는 이유를 집중하여 듣는다.

대화를 듣고, 여자가 남자의 요청을 거절한 이유로 가장 적절한 것을 고르시오.

① 동전이 없어서
② 배터리가 없어서
③ 시간이 부족해서
④ 휴대전화가 없어서
⑤ 휴대전화가 고장 나서

My cell phone is dead.는 '내 휴대전화가 작동하지 않아.'라는 의미로, 여기서 dead는 기계 등이 작동을 멈추고 반응하지 않을 때 사용하는 표현이다.

M Oh, this is bad. ________ ________ ________ ________. (내 휴대전화가 작동하지 않는다)
W It looks like the battery ran out.
M Can I use your cell phone, Yolanda? I'll send just one text message.
W I'm sorry, Mark. I ________ ________ ________ ________ ________. Why don't we use the pay phone over there? (휴대전화가 없다)

17 심정 파악

대화를 듣고, 여자의 심정으로 가장 적절한 것을 고르시오.

① satisfied ② hopeful
③ shy ④ worried
⑤ bored

M That was a really good meal. So, shall we go?
W Oh, no, wait. Where is my wallet?
M Your wallet?
W Yes, I can't ________ ________ ________ in my purse. I don't know where it is. (지갑을 찾다)
M Maybe you left it at home?
W No, I used it to pay for the bus when I came here.
M Oh, no. Maybe you should ________ ________ ________. (화장실을 확인하다)

18 특정 정보 파악

대화를 듣고, 여자가 제안한 것으로 가장 적절한 것을 고르시오.

① 장화 구입하기
② 우산 잘 펴서 말리기
③ 신발 젖지 않게 하기
④ 우산 잃어버리지 않기
⑤ 남자용 우비 구입하기

you can ~. 이후에 나오는 부분을 주의깊게 듣는다.

W It's raining outside. ______ ______ ______.
우산을 가져가라

M Oh, I hate rainy days. I don't like it when ______ ______ ______ ______ ______.
신발이 완전히 젖어버리다

W If you don't like wet shoes on a rainy day, you can ______ ______ ______ ______ ______.
장화를 한 켤레 사다

M Aren't they for girls?

W I don't think so. I saw a lot of rain boots for boys.

M Okay, Mom.

19 알맞은 응답 찾기

[19~20] 대화를 듣고, 남자의 마지막 말에 이어질 여자의 응답으로 가장 적절한 것을 고르시오.

Woman: ______________________

① I will keep dieting.
② Because I have to.
③ I will keep that in mind.
④ I run in the park every evening.
⑤ Losing weight is not easy at all.

핵심 어구 on a diet, lose weight 등을 통해 어울리는 말을 파악한다.

M Have some French fries. Aren't you eating?

W No, thank you. ______ ______ ______ ______.
나는 다이어트 중이다

M Why are you on a diet?

W Well, I'd like to ______ ______ ______.
몸무게를 좀 줄이다

M Oh, would you? What else do you do to lose weight?

W ______________________

20 알맞은 응답 찾기

Woman: ______________________

① I hope you can make it.
② I'm thinking of a drama club.
③ Dancing club is very popular.
④ I'll do my best for the audition.
⑤ I need to practice for the audition.

M What club are you interested in?

W Well, I'm thinking of ______ ______ ______ ______.
춤 동아리에 가입하는 것

M All the girls seem to try to get into the dancing club.

W You're right. That's why there will be an audition.

M ______ ______ ______ ______ ______ ______ ______ if you can't get in the dancing club?
어느 동아리에 가입할 거니

W ______________________

특정 정보 파악

무엇을 평가하는가?

일상생활 관련 대상이나 친숙한 일반적 주제에 관한 말이나 대화를 듣고 세부 정보를 파악할 수 있는지를 평가한다.

어떻게 출제되는가?

• 대화를 듣고, 두 사람이 만날 시각을 고르시오.
• 대화를 듣고, 두 사람이 함께 이용할 교통수단으로 가장 적절한 것을 고르시오.
• 대화를 듣고, 남자의 장래 희망으로 가장 적절한 것을 고르시오.

❶ 지시문을 보고 어떤 정보를 찾아야 하는지 파악 한 후, 특정 정보에 주의하며 듣는다.
❷ 전체적인 상황보다는 시각, 교통수단, 장래 희망 등 특정 정보를 듣는데 집중한다.

[기출로 전략 확인]

대화를 듣고, 남자의 장래 희망으로 가장 적절한 것을 고르시오. [2017 기출]

① 사진 작가 ② 치과 의사 ③ 한식 요리사
④ 피아니스트 ⑤ 테니스 선수

❶ 남자의 장래 희망으로 상대방의 장래 희망과 헷갈리지 않도록 주의한다.

W Stuart, you look a little tired.
M Yeah. I practiced tennis for 4 hours yesterday.
W Wasn't it hard?
M It was not easy, but I love tennis.
W Oh, I didn't know that.
M I actually want to become a famous tennis player.
W I hope your dream comes true.

❷ 'I want to become ~ 직업.'표현을 통해 남자의 장래 희망을 알 수 있다.

여 Stuart, 좀 지쳐 보이는구나.
남 응. 어제 4시간동안 테니스 연습을 했거든.
여 힘들지 않았니?
남 쉽지 않았지만 난 테니스를 좋아하니까.
여 아, 몰랐어.
남 사실 유명한 테니스 선수가 되고 싶어.
여 네 꿈이 이루어졌으면 좋겠다.

특정 정보 파악 유형의 발문과 보기

대화를 듣고, 남자가 이용할 교통수단으로 가장 적절한 것을 고르시오. [2018 기출]

① 배 ② 자동차 ③ 비행기
④ 지하철 ⑤ 고속열차

만점 잡는 문장 **M** I'll walk there. It's not far.
W But it's raining outside. I'll take you by car.
M Thanks. That will be great.

대화를 듣고, 요가 수업이 시작되는 시각을 고르시오. [2017 기출]

① 3 : 30 p.m. ② 4 : 00 p.m. ③ 4 : 30 p.m.
④ 5 : 00 p.m. ⑤ 5 : 30 p.m.

만점 잡는 문장 **M** Thanks. When does the yoga class start?
W It begins at 4:30 p.m. every Friday.

특정 정보 파악하기에 쓰이는 표현

• 시각

Let's meet in front of the stadium at 6:30. 경기장 앞에서 6시 30분에 만나자.
How about meeting at 12:30? 12시 30분에 만나는 거 어때?
Let's make it at four o'clock this afternoon. 오늘 오후 4시에 만나자.
We have to be at the concert hall by 6:30. 콘서트 홀에 6시 30분까지는 가야해.

• 교통수단

I'm going to ride my bicycle. 난 자전거를 탈 거야.
Let's take the subway. 지하철 타자.
I will walk there after my piano lesson. 피아노 수업이 끝나고 거기에 걸어 갈 거야.
My mom said she would take me there by car. 엄마가 거기까지 차로 태워 준다고 했어.
I usually take a bus, but I think I have to take a taxi today.
보통 버스를 타는데 오늘은 택시를 타야 할 거 같아.

• 장래 희망

A You should be a cook. 넌 요리사가 되어야 해.
B That's my dream job! 그게 나의 꿈의 직업이야!

I love all animals. So I want to be an animal doctor. 나는 동물들을 좋아해서 수의사가 되고 싶어.
I want to become a singer when I grow up. 나는 커서 가수가 되고 싶어.

영어듣기능력평가 17회

학년 반 번
이름

01 다음을 듣고, 'this'가 가리키는 것으로 가장 적절한 것을 고르시오

① 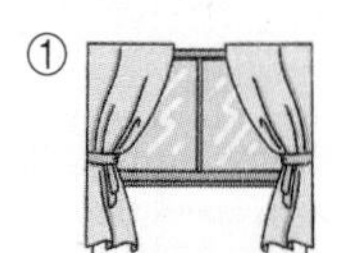
② 
③ 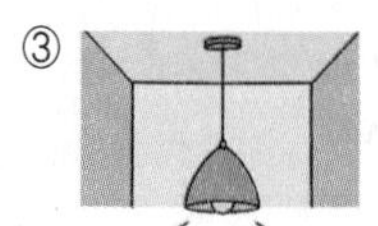
④ 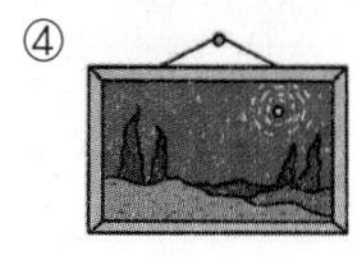
⑤ 

02 대화를 듣고, 여자가 기념품으로 구입한 것을 고르시오.

① 
② 

③ 

④ 
⑤ 

03 다음을 듣고, 서울의 내일 날씨로 가장 적절한 것을 고르시오.

① 

② 
③ 

④ 

⑤ 

04 대화를 듣고, 남자가 저녁에 배우는 것으로 가장 적절한 것을 고르시오.

① 인물 사진 ② 영어 회화
③ 세계 요리 ④ 사교 댄스
⑤ 기초 수채화

05 다음을 듣고, 모임에 대해 언급되지 않은 것을 고르시오.

① 장소 ② 시작 시각
③ 끝나는 시각 ④ 주제
⑤ 준비물

06 대화를 듣고, 남자의 직업으로 가장 적절한 것을 고르시오.

① 경찰관 ② 서점 직원
③ 역사 교사 ④ 도서관 사서
⑤ 가구 판매점 주인

07 다음을 듣고, 두 사람의 대화가 어색한 것을 고르시오.

① ② ③ ④ ⑤

08 대화를 듣고, 남자가 여자에게 부탁한 일로 가장 적절한 것을 고르시오.

① 집안 청소하기
② 고양이 돌봐 주기
③ 고양이 분양해 주기
④ 고양이 먹이 구입하기
⑤ 가족 여행에 참석하기

09 대화를 듣고, 무엇에 관한 내용인지 가장 적절한 것을 고르시오.

① 여행 계획 ② 지도 구입
③ 취미 활동 ④ 가족 모임
⑤ 환경 보호

고난도

10 대화를 듣고, 두 사람이 만들 티셔츠의 개수를 고르시오.

① 500 ② 520
③ 600 ④ 620
⑤ 700

점수 /20

11 대화를 듣고, 두 사람이 할 일로 가장 적절한 것을 고르시오.

① 산책하기
② 숙제하기
③ 독서하기
④ 서점 가기
⑤ 자동차 수리하기

12 대화를 듣고, 남자의 마지막 말의 의도로 가장 적절한 것을 고르시오.

① 칭찬 ② 충고
③ 감사 ④ 사과
⑤ 허락

13 대화를 듣고, 여자가 고마워하는 이유로 가장 적절한 것을 고르시오.

① 음악 숙제를 알려 주어서
② 노래 파일을 선물로 주어서
③ 컴퓨터로 노래를 들려 주어서
④ 컴퓨터로 영화를 보여 주어서
⑤ 노래 다운로드 하는 것을 도와주어서

14 대화를 듣고, 남자가 가려고 하는 장소를 고르시오.

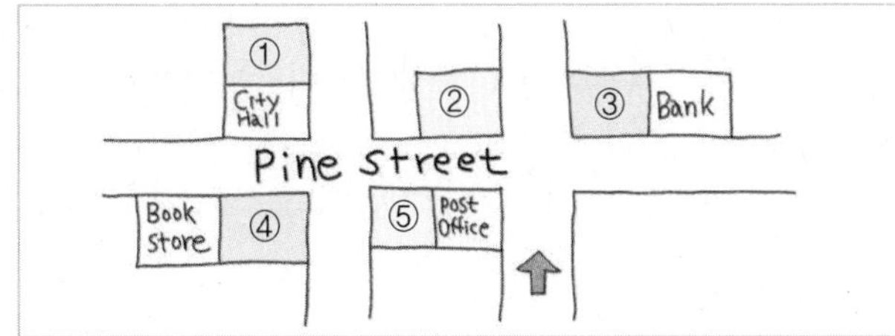

고난도

15 대화를 듣고, 두 사람이 집을 나서는 시각을 고르시오.

① 4:00 ② 4:30
③ 5:00 ④ 5:30
⑤ 6:00

16 대화를 듣고, 여자의 심정으로 가장 적절한 것을 고르시오.

① 기쁨 ② 미안함
③ 부러움 ④ 외로움
⑤ 당황스러움

고난도

17 대화를 듣고, 여자가 제안한 것으로 가장 적절한 것을 고르시오.

① 메모리 정리하기
② 바이러스 체크하기
③ 새 컴퓨터 구입하기
④ 컴퓨터 껐다가 다시 켜기
⑤ 컴퓨터 전원을 끈 상태로 잠시 두기

18 대화를 듣고, 두 사람의 관계로 가장 적절한 것을 고르시오.

① 의사 – 환자 ② 교사 – 학생
③ 아버지 – 딸 ④ 사장 – 종업원
⑤ 가게 점원 – 손님

[19~20] 대화를 듣고, 여자의 마지막 말에 이어질 남자의 응답으로 가장 적절한 것을 고르시오.

19 Man: ______________________

① I'm happy to have the interview.
② I don't think we need new members.
③ Because we really need new members.
④ I have a dental appointment on that day.
⑤ Because you are the club president this year.

20 Man: ______________________

① OK. Then I'll treat next time.
② That's right. The food here is good.
③ Would you tell me how much it is?
④ What's the problem with the food?
⑤ I'm sure. This is my first time here.

영어듣기능력평가 17회 DICTATION

다시 들으면서 듣기 만점에 도전하세요!
Dictation: 스크립트의 주요 부분을 다시 들으면서!
실전 ⊕: 세부 정보가 많은 스크립트를 다른 문제로 샅샅이!

01 그림 "this" 파악 (담화)

다음을 듣고, 'this'가 가리키는 것으로 가장 적절한 것을 고르시오.

① ② ③ ④ ⑤

M You can see this in many rooms. People use this to ________ ________ ________ (햇빛을 막다) in hot weather, or to keep the room warm in cold weather. Sometimes, people use it to decorate a room. The room can look cozier and nicer with this. This is usually ________ ________ ________ (천으로 만든). What is this?

02 그림 정보 파악 – 사물

남자가 구입한 것(T-shirts and postcards)과 여자가 구입한 것(a small lady doll)을 구분하여 듣는다.

대화를 듣고, 여자가 기념품으로 구입한 것을 고르시오.

① T-shirt ② postcard ③ ④ ⑤ doll

W Tomorrow we're leaving for home at last.
M Right. I miss my family.
W Me too. By the way, did you buy anything for your family?
M Yes. I ________ ________ ________ (티셔츠와 우편엽서를 샀다). How about you?
W I ________ ________ ________ ________ (작은 여자 인형을 샀다) for my sister. Here it is.
M She's so pretty.

03 날씨 파악

tomorrow가 언급되는 부분을 주의깊게 듣는다.

다음을 듣고, 서울의 내일 날씨로 가장 적절한 것을 고르시오.

① pleasant ② rainy, rainfall ③ ④ ⑤

M The rain will start this afternoon and continue until around midnight. Rainfall will be from between 1 and 2 inches across parts of Seoul area. However, Seoul will experience ________ ________ ________ ________ (내일은 6월의 쾌청한 날). You can ________ ________ ________ ________ ________ (많은 햇빛을 즐기다), a good day for a picnic.

04 특정 정보 파악

I'm learning ~. 이후에 나오는 부분을 주의깊게 듣는다.

대화를 듣고, 남자가 저녁에 배우는 것으로 가장 적절한 것을 고르시오.

① 인물 사진 ② 영어 회화
③ 세계 요리 ④ 사교 댄스
⑤ 기초 수채화

W Ryan, do you have time tomorrow evening?

M Well, I have to ________ ________ ________ ________ ________ at the cultural center. (저녁 수업에 가다)

W What class are you taking? A drawing class?

M No. I'm ________ ________ ________ ________ Italian food. (요리하는 방법을 배우고 있다)

W Sounds interesting.

05 언급 및 비언급 파악

다음을 듣고, 모임에 대해 언급되지 않은 것을 고르시오.

① 장소 Wilmar center
② 시작 시각 5 PM
③ 끝나는 시각 7 PM
④ 주제 how to prepare for the field trip
⑤ 준비물

W Let me tell you about our next meeting. We'll have the meeting ________ ________ ________, room number 201 next Wednesday 5 PM. ________ ________ ________ at 7 PM. ________ ________ ________ ________ ________ is about how to prepare for the field trip. I hope every member will come to the meeting. (Wilmar 센터에서) (그것은 끝날 것이다)

06 직업 추론

핵심 어구 book, check out을 통해 대화 장소와 인물의 직업을 추론해 본다.

대화를 듣고, 남자의 직업으로 가장 적절한 것을 고르시오.

① 경찰관
② 서점 직원
③ 역사 교사
④ 도서관 사서
⑤ 가구 판매점 주인

W Excuse me, sir.

M Yes. What can I help you with?

W Would you ________ ________ ________ ________ ________? I need it for my history class. (내가 이 책을 찾는 것을 도와주다)

M Let me see. You're lucky. Nobody has ________ ________ ________ yet. Go down the aisle and it's on the last shelf. (그 책을 대출해 갔다)

W Thank you for your help.

07 어색한 대화 찾기

물건을 빌려달라는 요청에 어울리는 응답이 무엇일지 생각해 본다.

다음을 듣고, 두 사람의 대화가 어색한 것을 고르시오.

① ② ③ ④ ⑤

You'd better ~.는 '~하는 게 좋겠다.'라는 의미로, 충고나 조언을 할 때 사용하는 표현이며, I think you should ~.로 바꿔 말할 수 있다.

① **M** How old is your younger sister?
W She's eleven years old.

② **M** What can I do for you?
W ________ ________ ________ over there, please. (이 짐을 옮기다)

③ **M** I have a little bit of a fever.
W You'd better go see a doctor.

④ **M** I can't solve this math problem.
W Let me help you with it.

⑤ **M** Can I ________ ________ ________? (네 연필을 빌리다)
W ________ ________ ________ ________. (나를 도와줘서 고맙다)

08 부탁 파악

대화를 듣고, 남자가 여자에게 부탁한 일로 가장 적절한 것을 고르시오.

① 집안 청소하기
② 고양이 돌봐 주기 take care of our cat
③ 고양이 분양해 주기
④ 고양이 먹이 구입하기
⑤ 가족 여행에 참석하기

Would you ~? 이후에 나오는 부분을 주의깊게 듣는다.

W Hi, Mr. Jackson. What can I do for you?

M Well, my family is taking a trip. We'll be back on next Monday. So would you ________ ________ ________ ________ ________ while we're gone?
우리 고양이를 돌봐 주다

W That's no problem. ________ ________ ________.
나는 고양이를 정말 좋아한다

M Thank you for your help.

W I hope you and your family have a good trip.

09 주제 파악

대화를 듣고, 무엇에 관한 내용인지 가장 적절한 것을 고르시오.

① 여행 계획 ② 지도 구입
③ 취미 활동 ④ 가족 모임
⑤ 환경 보호

「It'll take about + 시간」은 '~하는 데 약 …시간이 걸리다.'의 의미로, 소요 시간을 말할 때 사용하는 표현이다.

W Honey, ________ ________ ________ ________ ________ ________ first?
어디를 방문하고 싶나요

M Well, how about the palace near the train station?

W That would be nice. Let me see the map. Hmm... the palace is not far from the Natural History Museum.

M You're right. We can ________ ________ ________ ________ ________ ________. I've always wanted to visit there.
오후 내내 박물관에서 보내다

W Do we have to ________ ________ ________ for the night?
호텔을 예약하다

M Actually I already booked a hotel. It'll take about 30 minutes from the museum.

W That's great. I'm so excited.

고난도

10 숫자 파악

대화를 듣고, 두 사람이 만들 티셔츠의 개수를 고르시오.

① 500 ② 520
③ 600 ④ 620
⑤ 700

처음에 언급된 개수(500)와 두 번 추가되는 숫자들(20, 100)을 유의하여 듣는다.

M Sophie, how many T-shirts do we have to make for the festival?

W Well, we'll give one to every student in the school. So I think ________ ________ ________.
500장이 좋을 것이다

M But you missed our teachers. ________ ________ ________.
20명의 선생님들이 계시다

W You're right. Is that all?

M Well, I want to ________ ________ ________ to sell to our guests.
100장을 더 만들다

W That's a great idea.

11 할 일 파악

대화를 듣고, 두 사람이 할 일로 가장 적절한 것을 고르시오.

① 산책하기
② 숙제하기
③ 독서하기
④ 서점 가기
⑤ 자동차 수리하기

W It's nice weather! Let's take a walk, Tom.

M I want to, but I have to ________ ________ ________ ________.
책을 사러 가다

W Really? Can I come along? I need to ________ ________ ________ ________.
새로운 소설책을 사다

M Why not?

W I can ________ ________ ________ ________ ________ ________ ________.
서점까지 너를 태워 주다

M That's good.

12 의도 추론

대화를 듣고, 남자의 마지막 말의 의도로 가장 적절한 것을 고르시오.

① 칭찬 ② 충고
③ 감사 ④ 사과
⑤ 허락

I have something to say to you.는 '너에게 할 말이 있어.', '드릴 말씀이 있어요.'라는 의미로, 상대방에게 말을 건넬 때 사용하는 표현이다.

W Dad, I have something to say to you.
M What is it?
W I want to ________ ________ with my friends next week.
캠핑하러 가다
M How many nights will you go for?
W Just one night. And we go with our teacher, Miss Kim.
M Then ________ ________ ________ ________.
너는 그곳에 가도 좋다

13 이유 파악

여자가 하려고 하는 것이 무엇인지 파악한다.

대화를 듣고, 여자가 고마워하는 이유로 가장 적절한 것을 고르시오.

① 음악 숙제를 알려 주어서
② 노래 파일을 선물로 주어서
③ 컴퓨터로 노래를 들려 주어서
④ 컴퓨터로 영화를 보여 주어서
⑤ 노래 다운로드 하는 것을 도와주어서

M What are you doing on the Internet?
W I'm trying to ________ ________ ________ ________, but it's not doing well.
내가 가장 좋아하는 노래를 다운로드 하다
M Then, ________ ________ ________ ________.
내가 너를 도와주겠다
W Thanks. This is my first time to download.
M I'll show you ________ ________ ________ ________. Next time it will be easy for you.
그것을 하는 방법
W You're so kind.

14 그림 정보 파악 – 지도

go straight → turn left → next to the post office로 이어지는 지시의 순서에 유의한다.

대화를 듣고, 남자가 가려고 하는 장소를 고르시오.

M Excuse me, where is the flower shop?
W Go straight and ________ ________ at Pine Street.
좌회전하다
M Turn left at Pine Street?
W Yes. And then ________ ________ ________ ________. It's on the left corner ________ ________ ________ ________ ________.
한 블록 직진하다
우체국 옆에
M One block and it's ________ ________ ________ ________?
왼쪽 모퉁이에
W That's right.

고난도

15 숫자 파악 – 시각

수업이 끝나는 시각(5:30)과 집에서 출발하는 시각(thirty minutes before)을 잘 듣고 계산한다.

대화를 듣고, 두 사람이 집을 나서는 시각을 고르시오.

① 4:00 ② 4:30
③ 5:00 ④ 5:30
⑤ 6:00

M Let's go pick up Tommy, honey.

W We don't have to leave now. His __________ __________ __________ __________ (수영 수업은 5시 30분에 끝난다) __________ : __________.

M Really? I thought his class would finish at 4:00.

W His class schedule was changed.

M I didn't know that.

W We can leave home __________ __________ __________ __________ (그의 수업이 끝나기 30분 전에) __________.

M I see.

16 심정 추론

대화를 듣고, 여자의 심정으로 가장 적절한 것을 고르시오.

① 기쁨 ② 미안함
③ 부러움 ④ 외로움
⑤ 당황스러움

M Did you bring my book?

W Yes. Let me take it out of my bag.

M That's my sister's book and I promised to __________ __________ __________ (그것을 그녀에게 돌려주다) __________ today.

W Well, I __________ __________ __________ __________ (그 책을 찾을 수가 없다). I thought it was in my bag.

M Could you double check in your bag?

고난도

17 특정 정보 파악

Why don't you ~? 이후에 나오는 부분을 주의 깊게 듣는다.

대화를 듣고, 여자가 제안한 것으로 가장 적절한 것을 고르시오.

① 메모리 정리하기
② 바이러스 체크하기
③ 새 컴퓨터 구입하기
④ 컴퓨터 껐다가 다시 켜기
⑤ 컴퓨터 전원을 끈 상태로 잠시 두기

What don't you ~?는 '~하는 게 어때?'라는 의미로, 제안을 나타내는 표현이다.

M I have to finish this report today and the computer isn't working well.

W Oh, what can be the problem?

M I think I need a new computer. This one's too old.

W It can't be. We bought it only last year.

M I checked for viruses and it doesn't have any. I __________ __________ (여러 번 그것을 재 작동시켰다) __________, but it is still acting strange.

W Why don't you just __________ __________ __________ __________ (전원을 끄고 좀 기다려 보다) __________ __________? That computer might have been on for too long.

➕ 대화를 듣고, 처음에 남자가 제안한 일로 가장 적절한 것을 고르시오.

① 메모리 정리하기
② 바이러스 체크하기
③ 새 컴퓨터 구입하기
④ 컴퓨터 껐다가 다시 켜기
⑤ 컴퓨터 전원을 끈 상태로 잠시 두기

18 관계 추론

여자가 남자에게 감사해하는 이유가 무엇인지 파악한다.

대화를 듣고, 두 사람의 관계로 가장 적절한 것을 고르시오.

① 의사 – 환자
② 교사 – 학생
③ 아버지 – 딸
④ 사장 – 종업원
⑤ 가게 점원 – 손님

대화를 듣고, 여자가 남자에게 고마워하는 이유로 가장 적절한 것을 고르시오.

① 항상 최선을 다해주어서
② 학생들과 친하게 지내주어서
③ 좋은 말을 많이 해주어서
④ 직업을 구하는데 도움을 주어서
⑤ 좋은 선물을 주어서

W Mr. Brown, I'd like to thank you.

M Thank me for what?

W You always ________ ________ ________ ________ ________ ________. (당신의 학생들을 위해 최선을 다했다)

M That's my job. Thank you anyway for saying so. And you were also ________ ________ ________. (좋은 학생)

W Thanks. Here is a small present for you.

19 알맞은 응답 찾기

못 오는 이유를 묻는 질문 다음에 이어질 말을 생각해 본다.

[19~20] 대화를 듣고, 여자의 마지막 말에 이어질 남자의 응답으로 가장 적절한 것을 고르시오.

Man: ____________________

① I'm happy to have the interview.
② I don't think we need new members.
③ Because we really need new members.
④ I have a dental appointment on that day.
⑤ Because you are the club president this year.

Why's that?은 '그건 왜지?'라는 의미로, 이유를 묻는 표현이다.

W Fred, we're ________ ________ ________ ________ ________ ________ of the club. (새내기 회원을 뽑는 인터뷰를 할 것이다)

M Interviews for the new members?

W Yes, twenty freshmen are expected to come for the interview.

M Wow. I didn't know that our club is that popular. When is the interview?

W It's the day after tomorrow.

M On Thursday? Oh, sorry, Jenny. I'm afraid ________ ________ ________. (나는 갈 수 없다)

W ________ ________? (그건 왜지)

M ____________________

20 알맞은 응답 찾기

Man: ____________________

① OK. Then I'll treat next time.
② That's right. The food here is good.
③ Would you tell me how much it is?
④ What's the problem with the food?
⑤ I'm sure. This is my first time here.

W John, ________ ________ ________ ________ ________ today's dinner. (내가 ~을 사고 싶다)

M No, you don't have to do that.

W I really want to pay for it. You helped me with a lot of things for the week.

M ________ ________ ________? (진심이에요)

W Yes, I really ________ ________ ________ ________. (그렇게 하고 싶다)

M ____________________

영어듣기능력평가 18회

학년 반 번
이름

01 다음을 듣고, 'this'가 무엇인지 가장 적절한 것을 고르시오.

02 대화를 듣고, 지갑이 있는 곳을 고르시오.

03 다음을 듣고, 내일 날씨로 가장 적절한 것을 고르시오.

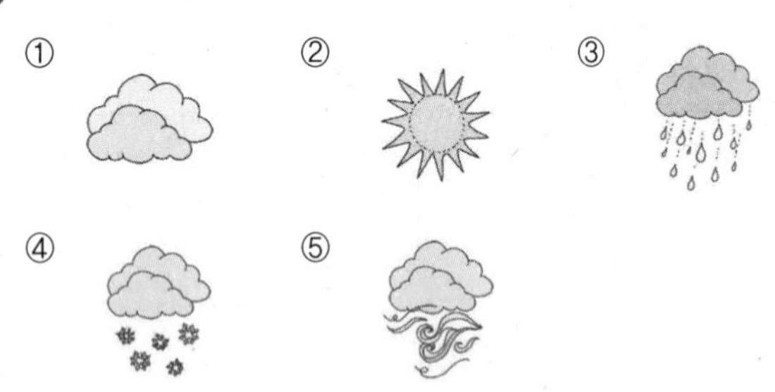

04 대화를 듣고, 남자의 아버지가 방문하기로 한 날짜를 고르시오.

① 10월 3일　② 10월 12일
③ 10월 17일　④ 10월 22일
⑤ 10월 24일

05 다음을 듣고, 'I'가 무엇인지 가장 적절한 것을 고르시오.

고난도

06 대화를 듣고, 이어지는 질문에 알맞은 응답을 고르시오.

① April 2　② April 18
③ April 20　④ April 22
⑤ April 24

07 대화를 듣고, 남자의 장래 희망으로 가장 적절한 것을 고르시오.

① 가수　② 교수
③ 변호사　④ 영화 배우
⑤ 뮤지컬 배우

08 다음을 듣고, 두 사람의 대화가 어색한 것을 고르시오.

①　②　③　④　⑤

09 대화를 듣고, 두 사람이 대화하고 있는 장소로 가장 적절한 곳을 고르시오.

① 약국　② 공원
③ 거실　④ 응급실
⑤ 동물 병원

10 대화를 듣고, 남자가 서점에 간 이유로 가장 적절한 것을 고르시오.

① 물건을 찾으려고
② 책을 구입하려고
③ 영수증을 받으려고
④ 중고 서적을 팔려고
⑤ 구입한 책을 교환하려고

점수 /20

11 대화를 듣고, 여자가 남자에게 부탁한 일로 가장 적절한 것을 고르시오.

① 서둘러서 집에 와 줄 것
② 세탁물을 세탁소에 맡겨 줄 것
③ 세탁기를 돌려 빨래를 해 줄 것
④ 세탁소 영업 시간을 알아봐 줄 것
⑤ 세탁소에서 세탁물을 찾아와 줄 것

12 다음을 듣고, Jennifer에 대해 언급되지 않은 것을 고르시오.

① 나이
② 전에 살던 지역
③ 좋아하는 과목
④ 취미
⑤ 가족

13 대화를 듣고, 남자가 전화를 건 목적으로 가장 적절한 것을 고르시오.

① 같이 공부하려고
② 함께 여행을 가려고
③ 디지털 카메라를 빌리려고
④ 공원에 가는 길을 물어보려고
⑤ Robert의 생일 선물을 함께 사려고

14 대화를 듣고, 두 사람이 만나기로 한 시각을 고르시오.

① 5시
② 5시 30분
③ 6시
④ 6시 30분
⑤ 7시

15 대화를 듣고, 여자가 대화 직후에 할 일로 가장 적절한 것을 고르시오.

① 스케줄 확인하기
② 병원 예약하기
③ 축구경기 보러 가기
④ 문병 가기
⑤ 친구의 안부 묻기

16 다음을 듣고, 무엇에 관한 내용인지 가장 적절한 것을 고르시오.

① 진로 선택 요령
② 공부 잘 하는 비결
③ 학생 생활 지도 안내
④ 겨울 방학 일정 소개
⑤ 신규 교사 환영 인사

고난도

17 다음을 듣고, 말하고 있는 사람의 직업으로 가장 적절한 것을 고르시오.

① 기자
② 뉴스 앵커
③ 수의사
④ 환경 운동가
⑤ 동물원 사육사

18 대화를 듣고, 남자가 여자에게 제안한 것으로 가장 적절한 것을 고르시오.

① 스노클링 해 보기
② 일주일 이상 머물기
③ 겨울 스포츠 즐기기
④ 전통 음식을 먹어 보기
⑤ 스쿠버 다이빙 배우기

[19~20] 대화를 듣고, 여자의 마지막 말에 이어질 남자의 응답으로 가장 적절한 것을 고르시오.

19 Man: ______________________

① Then, I'll find another hotel.
② Why do you like this hotel?
③ Good. Let's stay at this hotel.
④ Can I stay at your hotel today?
⑤ No, I don't want to work at this hotel.

20 Man: ______________________

① Sorry, I can't lend you $10.
② Okay, I'll order the beef steak.
③ No problem. I'll pay for lunch.
④ Thanks to you, I had a good meal.
⑤ Oh, I'll visit the restaurant right now.

영어듣기능력평가 18회 DICTATION

다시 들으면서 듣기 만점에 도전하세요!
Dictation: 스크립트의 주요 부분을 다시 들으면서!
실전 ⊕: 세부 정보가 많은 스크립트를 다른 문제로 샅샅이!

01 그림 "this" 파악 (담화)

반복되는 어휘 water를 단서로 이용한다.

다음을 듣고, 'this'가 무엇인지 가장 적절한 것을 고르시오.

① ② ③ ④ ⑤

M This is a kind of electronic machine. You can use this ________ ________ ________ (물을 마실 때). People think that tap water is not good enough to drink. So they use this machine to ________ ________ ________ ________ (수돗물을 더 좋게 만들다). You can ________ ________ ________ ________ ________ ________ ________ (차가운 물과 뜨거운 물 모두를 얻는다) from this. As this is an electronic machine, you can not use this without electricity.

02 그림 정보 파악 – 위치

대화를 듣고, 지갑이 있는 곳을 고르시오.

① ② ③ ④ ⑤

M Honey, did you see my wallet? I can't find it.
W Didn't you put it next to the computer?
M No, it wasn't there.
W Did you ________ ________ ________ ________ (바지나 재킷을 확인하다)?
M I already did. But....
W How about under the bed or in your drawer of the desk?
M Oh, I got it. I ________ ________ ________ ________ (그것을 서랍 속에서 찾았다). Thank you, honey.

03 날씨 파악

시간 순서(this morning, this afternoon, tomorrow)에 따라 나오는 정보 중 내일 날씨에 집중한다.

다음을 듣고, 내일 날씨로 가장 적절한 것을 고르시오.

① ② warmer, sunnier, nice ③ showers ④ ⑤

W Taking a look at the weather now. We have cloudy skies this morning with a 50% ________ ________ ________ ________ ________ (오늘 오후에 소나기 올 가능성). High temperatures today will reach up to 11 degrees. Lows tonight will drop to around zero. However, ________ ________ ________ ________ ________ ________ (내일은 더 따뜻하고 더 화창). You can enjoy outdoor activities in the nice weather. The current temperature in Seoul is 5 degrees.

04 숫자 파악 – 날짜

원래 예정된 방문 날짜에서 며칠을 연기했는지를 파악한다.

대화를 듣고, 남자의 아버지가 방문하기로 한 날짜를 고르시오.

① 10월 3일 ② 10월 12일
③ 10월 17일 ④ 10월 22일
⑤ 10월 24일

W Your dad is ________ ________ ________ ________ ________, right?
10월 17일에 우리를 방문하다

M He planned to, but I just got a call from him and he said he got something to do for his company suddenly.

W So does he want to ________ ________ ________ from October 17th? By how much? A week?
날짜를 연기하다

M Well, he said that five days would be enough for him to finish his work.

W You mean, he'll ________ ________ ________ ________.
10월 22일에 우리를 방문하다

M Yes.

05 그림 "I" 파악 (담화)

다음을 듣고, 'I'가 무엇인지 가장 적절한 것을 고르시오.

① ② ③ ④ ⑤

M I have ________ ________ ________ ________ ________. People usually think I'm yellow, but I can be a different color. I like eating worms, bugs, seeds, and grains. I ________ ________ ________ ________, and it takes 21 days for me to hatch. What am I?
두 다리와 하나의 부리 / 알에서 나오다

고난도

06 특정 정보 파악

대화를 듣고, 이어지는 질문에 알맞은 응답을 고르시오.

① April 2 ② April 18
③ April 20 ④ April 22
⑤ April 24

W Albert, do you know when your mother's birthday is?

M Of course, ________ ________ ________.
4월 20일이다

W Then, what about your father's birthday? Do you remember it, too?

M Yes, of course. ________ ________ ________ is just ________ ________ ________ my mother's birthday.
나의 아버지의 생신 / ~보다 이틀 늦은

W Really? Oh, that's easy to remember.

07 특정 정보 파악

대화를 듣고, 남자의 장래 희망으로 가장 적절한 것을 고르시오.

① 가수 singer
② 교수 professor
③ 변호사 lawyer
④ 영화 배우
⑤ 뮤지컬 배우

It's because of ~.는 '그것은 ~ 때문이다.'라는 의미로, 이유를 말할 때 사용하는 표현이다.

장래 희망(I want to be ~)을 나타내는 부분과 좋아하는 것(I really like ~)을 말하는 부분에 집중한다.

W Ted, you don't look good. What's wrong with you?

M It's because of my parents. They want me to become a lawyer or a professor.

W Really? But you already have your own dream, don't you?

M You're right. I ______ ______ ______ ______ ______. (가수가 되고 싶다)
I really ______ ______ ______ ______. (노래하고 춤 추는 것을 좋아하다)

W Don't worry about it too much. Someday your parents will understand you.

08 어색한 대화 찾기

다음을 듣고, 두 사람의 대화가 어색한 것을 고르시오.

① ② ③ ④ ⑤

① **W** If you don't use the computer, why don't you turn it off?
M OK. I'll turn it off right now.

② **W** Did you buy a birthday present for Jessica?
M No, I didn't. What about you?

③ **W** ______ ______ ______ ______ ______ ______ ______ (~에 가는 길을 알려 주시겠어요?)
the Green Department Store?
M No. I ______ ______ ______ ______ ______. (그곳에서 일하고 싶지 않다)

④ **W** Oh, I feel hungry. Is there something to eat?
M There is some pizza on the kitchen table.

⑤ **W** I'd like to borrow these two books.
M Can I see your library card, please?

09 장소 추론

대화를 듣고, 두 사람이 대화하고 있는 장소로 가장 적절한 곳을 고르시오.

① 약국 ② 공원
③ 거실 ④ 응급실
⑤ 동물 병원

What seems to be the problem?은 병원 등에서 상대방에게 아픈 곳을 묻는 표현이다.

➕ 대화를 듣고, 여자의 직업으로 가장 적절한 것을 고르시오.

① 소아과 의사 ② 미용사
③ 경찰 ④ 환경미화원
⑤ 수의사

두 사람이 공통적으로 말하고 있는 Bella가 누구인지 파악한다.

W What seems to be the problem with Bella?

M She doesn't eat. She hasn't eaten for the whole day.

W Let me ______ ______ ______ ______ (눈과 이빨을 확인하다). Hmm... her eyes are okay and her teeth seem to be okay, too. Maybe she just ate something bad.

M She might have eaten something from the garbage or from the ground while I was walking her in the park.

W ______ ______ ______ ______ (걔들이 원래 그렇다). She will be okay in a couple of days but I think she needs to ______ ______ ______ ______ (병원에 있다) tonight.

M Okay. I'll come again tomorrow .

10 이유 파악

남자가 영수증을 보여 주는 이유는 교환(exchange) 또는 환불(refund)일 가능성이 높다.

대화를 듣고, 남자가 서점에 간 이유로 가장 적절한 것을 고르시오.

① 물건을 찾으려고
② 책을 구입하려고
③ 영수증을 받으려고
④ 중고 서적을 팔려고
⑤ 구입한 책을 교환하려고

M Hi, I bought these two books yesterday. __________ __________ __________. (영수증 여기 있어요)

W Yeah, I remember you. You bought them for your daughter.

M That's right. But my daughter __________ __________ __________. (이미 그것을 읽었다) So, can I __________ __________ __________ __________ another book? (이 책을 ~로 교환하다)

W Yes, you can. How about this one? Young girls think it's interesting.

11 부탁 파악

Can you ~? 이후에 나오는 부분을 주의깊게 듣는다.

대화를 듣고, 여자가 남자에게 부탁한 일로 가장 적절한 것을 고르시오.

① 서둘러서 집에 와 줄 것
② 세탁물을 세탁소에 맡겨 줄 것
③ 세탁기를 돌려 빨래를 해 줄 것
④ 세탁소 영업 시간을 알아봐 줄 것
⑤ 세탁소에서 세탁물을 찾아와 줄 것

[Cellphone rings.]

M Hello.

W Hello, honey. Are you coming home now?

M I need to talk with my boss a little bit, but I'm coming home soon.

W That's good. Can you __________ __________ __________ __________ __________ (세탁소에 들르다) on your way home? I got the message that our clothes were ready last week, but I didn't have time to pick them up.

M Okay. What do I have to pick up?

W Your suits, my winter coat and my pants.

M All right. __________ __________ __________. (내가 그것들을 가져가겠다)

W Thanks, honey.

12 언급 및 비언급 파악

다음을 듣고, Jennifer에 대해 언급되지 않은 것을 고르시오.

① 나이 14 years old
② 전에 살던 지역 Seattle
③ 좋아하는 과목 history
④ 취미 playing the violin
⑤ 가족

W Hi, nice to meet you. My name is Jennifer Johnson and I'm 14 years old. I __________ __________ (이곳으로 이사 왔다) last weekend from Seattle. __________ __________ __________ __________ (내가 가장 좋아하는 과목은 ~이다) history and __________ __________ __________ (내 취미는 ~이다) playing the violin. I belonged to a violin club at my previous school. I hope to have a good time with all of you. Thank you.

13 전화 목적 파악

Will you join us? 뒤에 이어지는 말을 주의깊게 듣는다.

대화를 듣고, 남자가 전화를 건 목적으로 가장 적절한 것을 고르시오.

① 같이 공부하려고
② 함께 여행을 가려고
③ 디지털 카메라를 빌리려고
④ 공원에 가는 길을 물어보려고
⑤ Robert의 생일 선물을 함께 사려고

[Cellphone rings.]

W Carol speaking.

M Hi, Carol. This is John. __________ __________ __________ __________ __________ (무슨 계획 있니) this weekend?

W This weekend? No, nothing special. Why?

M Then, __________ __________ __________ __________ (우리와 함께 할래)? Robert, Susan, Jessica, and I are going to __________ __________ __________ (여행을 가다) to the Redwood National Park.

W Really? That sounds interesting. Okay, I'll join you.

14 숫자 파악 – 시각

연급되는 여러 가지 시각 중 문제가 요구하는 것을 정확히 듣는다.

대화를 듣고, 두 사람이 만나기로 한 시각을 고르시오.

① 5시 ② 5시 30분
③ 6시 ④ 6시 30분
⑤ 7시

Let's make it ~.은 시간 약속을 정할 때 사용하는 표현이다.

대화를 듣고, 남자가 오늘 일을 끝마칠 시간으로 가장 적절한 것을 고르시오.

① 5시 ② 5시 30분
③ 6시 ④ 6시 30분
⑤ 7시

W Randy, can we go to a movie tonight?

M Sounds great. I've wanted to watch the newly released 3D movie.

W What time do you finish work today?

M Today, I can leave no later than 6.

W All right. I'll _____ _____ _____ _____ _____ _____ _____ (8시 영화표를 사 놓다) so that we can have dinner before the movie.

M Perfect. There's a spaghetti house just across from the movie theater.

W Can we meet there at 7 o'clock, then?

M _____ _____ _____ _____ _____ : _____. (6시 30분으로 하자)

W Okay. Don't make me wait for you.

고난도

15 할 일 파악

대화를 듣고, 여자가 대화 직후에 할 일로 가장 적절한 것을 고르시오.

① 스케줄 확인하기
② 병원 예약하기
③ 축구경기 보러 가기
④ 문병 가기
⑤ 친구의 안부 묻기

W Hi, Jack. Where are you going?

M I'm going to the hospital to visit Younghun.

W Is he in the hospital? Why?

M You didn't know? He _____ _____ (다치다) while playing soccer.

W No way. That's too bad.

M Yeah, he has to stay there for two weeks. _____ _____ _____ (~할래?) _____ come with me?

W Sure, I'd love to. I'm free now anyway.

16 주제 파악

Here are ~.를 통해 주제를 제시하고, 그 주제에 맞는 비결을 나열하는 형태의 담화이다.

다음을 듣고, 무엇에 관한 내용인지 가장 적절한 것을 고르시오.

① 진로 선택 요령
② 공부 잘 하는 비결
③ 학생 생활 지도 안내
④ 겨울 방학 일정 소개
⑤ 신규 교사 환영 인사

M Almost every student wants good grades. But only some students study well and get good grades. Here are some simple basic _____ _____ _____ _____ (공부를 잘 하는 비결). First, you have to _____ _____ (규칙적으로 공부하다). Try to study even at least 30 minutes every day. Second, _____ _____ _____ (집중하라) while you're studying. Third, _____ _____ _____ _____ (선생님 말씀에 귀를 기울여라) in the classroom. If you keep these simple rules, you'll be a good student before long.

고난도

17 직업 추론

반복되는 어휘 zoo, animals 등에서 단서를 얻는다.

다음을 듣고, 말하고 있는 사람의 직업으로 가장 적절한 것을 고르시오.

① 기자 ② 뉴스 앵커
③ 수의사 ④ 환경 운동가
⑤ 동물원 사육사

W Welcome to the Children's Zoo. For _____ _____ _____ _____ (동물들의 안전) _____ in the zoo, we ask for your cooperation. Please don't feed the animals. Animals in the zoo _____ _____ _____ _____ _____ (우리에 의해 규칙적으로 먹이를 얻는다). Because of the food people give them, animals may become seriously ill or even die. Parents, please don't let your children give anything to the animals. Thank you for your help and enjoy your visit.

18 특정 정보 파악

대화를 듣고, 남자가 여자에게 제안한 것으로 가장 적절한 것을 고르시오.

① 스노클링 해 보기
② 일주일 이상 머물기
③ 겨울 스포츠 즐기기
④ 전통 음식 먹어 보기
⑤ 스쿠버 다이빙 배우기

W I'm planning to go to Australia next month. I'm really looking forward to it. I'll enjoy summer there.

M I think ______ ______ ______ ______. The city is famous for them.
(넌 해양 스포츠를 해 볼 수 있다)

W Such as scuba diving? I'm staying there for four days only. Do you think I can learn it in a day or two?

M ______ ______ ______? It doesn't need any special trainings.
(스노클링은 어때)

W That sounds interesting.

M You'll be able to ______ ______ ______ ______ ______.
(아름다운 열대 해양 생물을 즐기다)

19 알맞은 응답 찾기

[19~20] 대화를 듣고, 여자의 마지막 말에 이어질 남자의 응답으로 가장 적절한 것을 고르시오.

Man: ____________________

① Then, I'll find another hotel.
② Why do you like this hotel?
③ Good. Let's stay at this hotel.
④ Can I stay at your hotel today?
⑤ No, I don't want to work at the hotel.

M What do you think about this hotel?

W It's nice. But I think $200 a day is ______ ______ ______.
(우리에게는 너무 비싼)

M But you want to stay at a hotel near the beach, don't you?

W Well... that's true. But I ______ ______ ______ ______ $200 for just one day.
(쓰고 싶지 않다)

M ____________________

20 알맞은 응답 찾기

Man: ____________________

① Sorry, I can't lend you $10.
② Okay, I'll order the beef steak.
③ No problem. I'll pay for lunch.
④ Thanks to you, I had a good meal.
⑤ Oh, I'll visit the restaurant right now

That's really good money.는 '정말로 높은 봉급이다.'라는 의미이다.

W James, I have a good news for you. An Italian restaurant needs a waiter. I think ______ ______ ______ ______.
(너에게 딱 맞다)

M Really? Where is it? I can't work at a restaurant far from school.

W Don't worry. It's very ______ ______ ______. It's only a 5 minute walk.
(학교에서 가까운)

M That's good. How much do they pay per hour?

W It's $10 an hour. You know, that's ______ ______ ______.
(정말로 좋은 벌이)

M ____________________

할 일 • 부탁한 일 • 제안한 일 파악

무엇을 평가하는가?	일상생활이나 친숙한 일반적 주제에 관한 말이나 대화를 듣고 일이나 사건의 순서, 전후 관계를 추론할 수 있는지를 평가한다.
어떻게 출제되는가?	• 대화를 듣고, 남자가 대화 직후 할 일로 가장 적절한 것을 고르시오. • 대화를 듣고, 남자가 여자에게 부탁한 일로 가장 적절한 것을 고르시오. • 대화를 듣고, 여자가 남자에게 제안한 것으로 가장 적절한 것을 고르시오.

❶ 부탁한 일은 'Can you ~?', 'Could you ~?', 'Would you ~?' 같이 직접적인 표현을 사용하는 경우가 많다.

❷ 제안한 일은 'Why don't you ~?', 'What[How] about ~?', 'Let's ~.' 같은 표현을 사용한다.

[기출로 전략 확인]

대화를 듣고, 여자가 남자에게 제안한 것으로 가장 적절한 것을 고르시오. [2018 기출]

① 과학 실험하기
② 축제 참가하기
③ 배드민턴 연습하기
④ 미술 작품 감상하기
⑤ 댄스 동아리 가입하기

M Wow! Mina, you're really good at dancing.
W Thank you for saying so.
M Where did you learn to dance?
W I joined a dancing club last year.
M Cool! I want to learn to dance, too.
W Then why don't you join our club?

❷ 여자가 'Why don't you ~?' 표현을 사용한 것을 듣고, 이 문장에서 남자에게 제안하는 내용이 나올 것임을 예상한다.

남 와! Mina, 너 춤 정말 잘 춘다.
여 칭찬해줘서 고마워.
남 춤 추는 건 어디서 배웠어?
여 작년에 댄스 동아리에 가입했어.
남 멋지다! 나도 춤 추는 걸 배우고 싶어.
여 그럼 우리 동아리에 가입하는 거 어때?

할 일 • 부탁한 일 파악 유형의 발문과 보기

대화를 듣고, 남자가 대화 직후에 할 일로 가장 적절한 것을 고르시오. [2018 기출]

① 진로 상담하기 ② 병원 진료받기
③ 자켓 구입하기 ④ 식당으로 돌아가기
⑤ 분리수거 도와주기

만점 잡는 문장 **M** Wait here, and I'll go back to the restaurant right now.

대화를 듣고, 남자가 여자에게 부탁한 일로 가장 적절한 것을 고르시오. 2018 기출 [2018 기출]

① 꽃 사오기 ② 풍선 장식하기 ③ 케이크 가져오기
④ 음료수 준비하기 ⑤ 축하 노래 부르기

오답 찍는 문장 **M** Ben will bring a cake and I'll get some drinks.
W Then what do I need to bring?
만점 잡는 문장 **M** Can you buy some flowers for her?

할 일 • 부탁한일 • 제안한 일 파악하기에 쓰이는 표현

• 할 일

A Why don't you find it on the Internet? 인터넷으로 찾아보는 거 어때?
B Okay, I will do that right now. 그래. 지금 바로 찾아봐야겠다.

A You should hurry up. The sale ends today. 서둘러야 해. 세일이 오늘 끝나.
B Really? I'll go there now. 진짜? 지금 가야겠다.

A Just get the milk. I'll wait for you at the counter. 우유를 갖고 와. 계산대에서 기다릴게.
B Okay. 알겠어.

• 부탁한 일

Can you lend Korean history books to me? 한국 역사책을 빌려줄 수 있니?
Could you bring my English book to school, please? 학교에 내 영어책 좀 가져다 줄 수 있어요?
Would you please wash my school uniform shirt? 내 교복 셔츠 좀 빨아줄 수 있어요?

• 제안한 일

Let's make cookies together after school. 방과 후에 같이 쿠키를 만들자.
Why don't you tell your homeroom teacher? 담임 선생님한테 말하는 거 어때?
What about joining the dance club? 댄스 동아리에 가입하는 거 어때?
How about using the Internet? 인터넷을 이용하는 거 어때?

영어듣기능력평가 19회

학년 반 번
이름

01 다음을 듣고, 'I'가 무엇인지 가장 적절한 것을 고르시오.

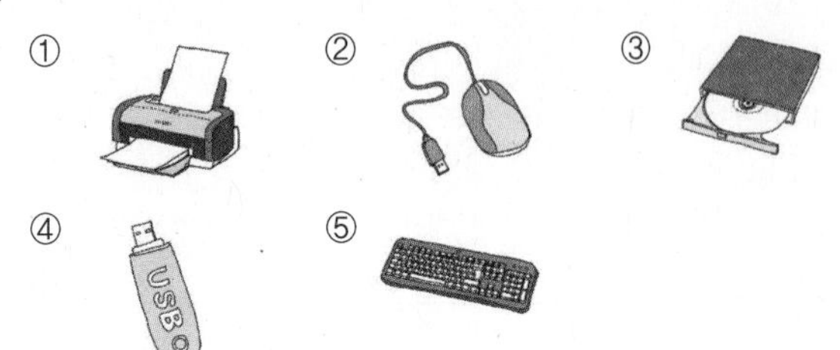

02 대화를 듣고, 두 사람이 내일 하게 될 운동으로 가장 적절한 것을 고르시오.

03 다음을 듣고, 서울의 오늘 날씨로 가장 적절한 것을 것을 고르시오.

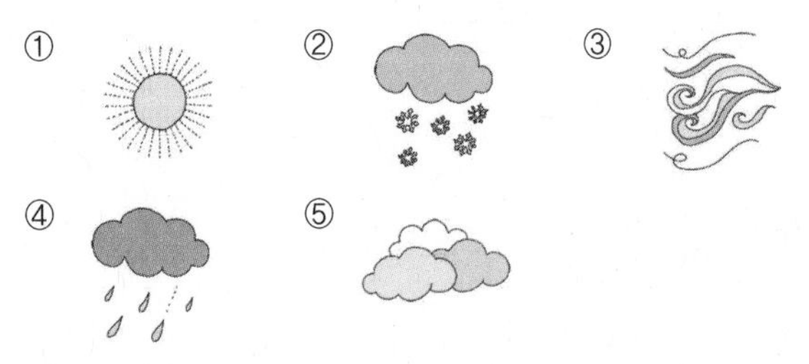

04 대화를 듣고, 두 사람이 오늘 오후에 할 일로 가장 적절한 것을 고르시오.

① 책 읽기
② 책 빌리기
③ 서점 가기
④ 독후감 작성하기
⑤ 친구 병문안 가기

05 다음을 듣고, 두 사람의 대화가 어색한 것을 고르시오.

① ② ③ ④ ⑤

고난도

06 대화를 듣고, 두 사람이 만날 시각을 고르시오.

① 2:30 ② 3:00
③ 4:00 ④ 4:30
⑤ 5:00

07 대화를 듣고, 남자가 전화를 건 목적으로 가장 적절한 것을 고르시오.

① 병원 예약을 하려고
② 건강에 관한 상담을 하려고
③ 학교에 결석한다는 것을 알리려고
④ 학부모와 상담 시간 약속을 하려고
⑤ 학생이 학교에 오지 않은 이유를 확인하려고

08 다음을 듣고, 'this'가 가리키는 것으로 가장 적절한 것을 고르시오.

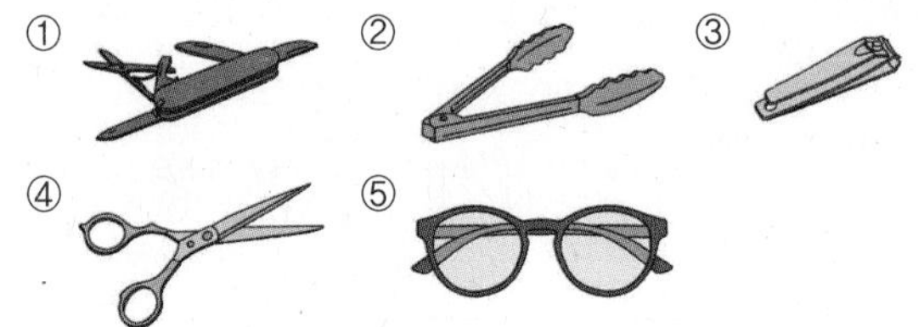

09 대화를 듣고, 남자가 이용하려는 교통 수단으로 가장 적절한 것을 고르시오.

① 배 ② 버스
③ 기차 ④ 비행기
⑤ 자동차

10 대화를 듣고, 남자가 기뻐하는 이유로 가장 적절한 것을 고르시오.

① 시합에서 이겨서
② 체중 감량에 성공해서
③ 여자에게 칭찬을 받아서
④ 자신에게 맞는 헬스클럽을 찾아서
⑤ 효과적인 식이요법을 알게 되어서

점수 /20

11 다음을 듣고, Green Concert에 대해 언급되지 않은 것을 고르시오.

① 장소 ② 시간
③ 개최 이유 ④ 입장료
⑤ 출연진

12 대화를 듣고, 여자가 남자에게 제안한 것으로 가장 적절한 것을 고르시오.

① 가방을 주기적으로 세탁할 것
② 가방을 깨끗한 곳에 보관할 것
③ 가방에 책을 너무 많이 넣지 말 것
④ 알코올을 너무 자주 사용하지 말 것
⑤ 수건에 알코올을 묻혀 가방을 닦을 것

고난도

13 다음을 듣고, Spring Book Festival에 대한 설명으로 일치하지 않는 것을 고르시오.

① 금요일에 있을 예정이다.
② 학교에 자신이 좋아하는 책을 들고 온다.
③ 오전에는 책을 읽고 독후감을 쓴다.
④ 좋아하는 책을 친구들에게 소개하는 시간이 있다.
⑤ 연극반 학생들이 연극을 공연할 것이다.

14 대화를 듣고, 여자가 가려고 하는 장소를 고르시오.

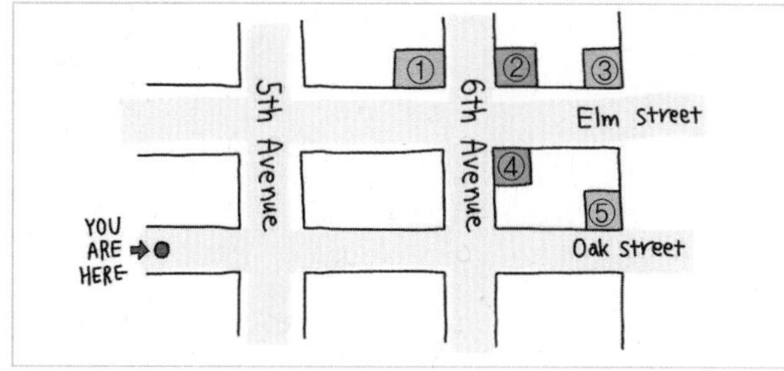

15 대화를 듣고, 두 사람이 대화하고 있는 장소로 가장 적절한 곳을 고르시오.

① 영화관 ② 옷가게
③ 미술 학원 ④ 미술관
⑤ 패션쇼장

16 대화를 듣고, 남자가 가려고 하는 장소를 고르시오.

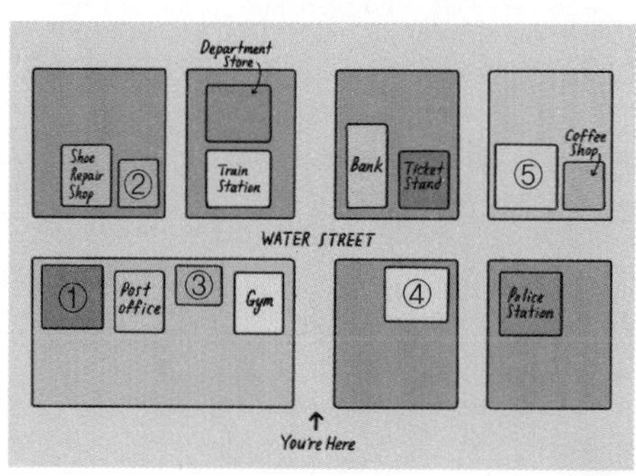

17 대화를 듣고, 남자가 우울해하는 이유로 가장 적절한 것을 고르시오.

① 축구 경기가 취소되어서
② 연습에 참가할 수 없어서
③ 자신의 팀이 경기에 져서
④ 축구팀에 선발되지 않아서
⑤ 자신의 팀의 골대에 골을 넣어서

18 대화를 듣고, 무엇에 관한 내용인지 가장 적절한 것을 고르시오.

① 박물관 관람하기 ② 특산물 쇼핑하기
③ 시장 구경하기 ④ 여행지 선정하기
⑤ 여행 일정짜기

[19~20] 대화를 듣고, 남자의 마지막 말에 이어질 여자의 응답으로 가장 적절한 것을 고르시오.

19 Woman: ____________________

① I'm happy with my style.
② My hairdresser is so nice.
③ Unfortunately I fell asleep.
④ I like brown more than red.
⑤ I was looking into the mirror.

20 Woman: ____________________

① I just turned on the computer.
② I have to say this. You really did a good job.
③ All right. You have to finish the homework after the game.
④ You're right. I need to go to my room for the homework.
⑤ I'm so sorry. We don't have enough time to play together.

영어듣기능력평가 19회 DICTATION

다시 들으면서 듣기 만점에 도전하세요!
Dictation: 스크립트의 주요 부분을 다시 들으면서!
실전 ⊕: 세부 정보가 많은 스크립트를 다른 문제로 샅샅이!

01 그림 "I" 파악 (담화)

컴퓨터의 친구로 동물처럼 생긴 것이 무엇인지 생각해 본다.

다음을 듣고, 'I'가 무엇인지 가장 적절한 것을 고르시오.

① ② ③ ④ ⑤

M I am a computer's friend. Whenever I ______ ______ ______ (패드 위에서 움직이다), an arrow on the screen moves along too. ______ ______ ______ (나를 두 번 빠르게 클릭하라) with the arrow on an icon on the screen. You can open a program by doing that. I am called as the name of an animal because I ______ ______ ______ (그 동물처럼 생기다) ______.

02 그림 정보 파악 – 사물

I want to ~. 이후에 나오는 부분을 주의깊게 듣는다.

대화를 듣고, 두 사람이 내일 하게 될 운동으로 가장 적절한 것을 고르시오.

① swimming ② tennis ③ table tennis ④ badminton ⑤ soccer

W Peter, why don't we play tennis tomorrow?
M Well... I played tennis yesterday. What about swimming?
W The weather is ______ ______ ______ ______ (수영하기에는 너무 추운), I think.
M Then, what do you want to do?
W How about ______ ______ ______ (실내 운동) such as table tennis or badminton?
M I don't know how to play table tennis. So, I ______ ______ ______ (배드민턴을 치고 싶다) ______.
W Okay! I'll follow you.

03 날씨 파악

Today in Seoul이 언급된 부분을 주의깊게 듣는다.

다음을 듣고, 서울의 오늘 날씨로 가장 적절한 것을 고르시오.

① ② snow ③ ④ rain ⑤ cloudy

W Good morning. Here's the weather forecast for tomorrow. Yesterday we had much snow all over the country. Fortunately the snow has stopped today. ______ ______ (더 이상의 눈이 오지 않을 것으로 예상된다) ______ ______ ______. Today in Seoul we'll have ______ ______ (부분적으로 흐린 하늘) ______, and in Busan we'll have a little bit of rain. For Busan citizens, be sure to take an umbrella with you.

04 할 일 파악

대화를 듣고, 두 사람이 오늘 오후에 할 일로 가장 적절한 것을 고르시오.

① 책 읽기
② 책 빌리기
③ 서점 가기
④ 독후감 작성하기
⑤ 친구 병문안 가기

남자가 하고자 하는 일이 무엇인지에 초점을 맞추어 듣는다.

W What are you going to do this afternoon?

M I'm going to ________ ________ ________ (책을 사다) about dieting ________ ________ ________ (서점에서). How about you?

W Actually, I just called one of my friends to meet her, but she said she has to go for a job interview.

M Then, why don't you ________ ________ ________ (나와 함께 가다)?

W Sounds great.

05 어색한 대화 찾기

다음을 듣고, 두 사람의 대화가 어색한 것을 고르시오.

① ② ③ ④ ⑤

Can you ~? / Could you ~?는 상대방에게 부탁하거나 요청할 때 사용하는 표현이다.

① W What a lovely day!
M How about going on a picnic?

② W How about playing tennis this afternoon?
M I'd love to, but it looks like rain.

③ W ________ ________ ________ ________ ________ (그 영화가 언제 시작하죠)?
M I think it was ________ ________ ________ ________ (아주 슬픈 영화).

④ W What can I do for you, sir?
M Can you ________ ________ ________ (샴푸를 추천해 주다) for dry hair?

⑤ W Could you turn down your TV?
M I'll turn it down right away.

고난도

06 숫자 파악 – 시각

대화를 듣고, 두 사람이 만날 시각을 고르시오.

① 2:30 ② 3:00
③ 4:00 ④ 4:30
⑤ 5:00

대화를 듣고, 여자의 학교 수업이 끝나는 시간을 고르시오.

① 2:30 ② 3:00
③ 4:00 ④ 4:30
⑤ 5:00

동아리 모임이 끝나는 시각(four o'clock)과 얼마 후에 만나기로 하는지(thirty minutes after)를 주의깊게 듣는다.

M Jane, how about meeting at two in front of your school?

W Well, let me check my schedule. My last class ends at 2:30, but I have a club meeting after class.

M When does the meeting finish? We have to arrive at Grandma's house by five.

W It will be ________ ________ ________ ________ (4시에 끝나다).

M Then let me give you thirty minutes more just in case.

W Okay, Dad. I'll meet you ________ ________ ________ ________ ________ (동아리 모임 끝나고 30분 뒤에).

07 전화 목적 파악

I'm calling to ~. 이후에 나오는 부분을 주의깊게 듣는다.

대화를 듣고, 남자가 전화를 건 목적으로 가장 적절한 것을 고르시오.

① 병원 예약을 하려고
② 건강에 관한 상담을 하려고
③ 학교에 결석한다는 것을 알리려고
④ 학부모와 상담 시간 약속을 하려고
⑤ 학생이 학교에 오지 않은 이유를 확인하려고

대화를 듣고, 두 사람의 관계로 가장 적절한 것을 고르시오.

① 교사 – 학생 ② 교사 – 학부모
③ 의사 – 환자 ④ 의사 – 보호자
⑤ 병원 접수 담당자 – 환자

[Telephone rings.]

M Hi, Mrs. Schoolings. This is Tim Lopez. I'm calling to inform you that ________ ________ ________ ________ ________ ________ today.
당신의 딸 Lynda가 학교에 오지 않았다

W Good afternoon, Mr. Lopez. Lynda couldn't come to school today. She has a fever.

M Oh, have you taken her to see the doctor?

W She has an appointment with the doctor at 2.

M Oh, I see. I hope ________ ________ ________.
그녀가 곧 회복될 것이다

W I'm sorry for not calling you first.

M That's okay. I hope ________ ________ ________ ________. Good bye, Mrs. Schoolings.
나는 내일 그녀를 볼 수 있다

W Thank you for calling, Mr. Lopez.

08 그림 "this" 파악 (담화)

다음을 듣고, 'this'가 가리키는 것으로 가장 적절한 것을 고르시오.

① ② ③ ④ ⑤

M This is a tool we use a lot in our daily lives. This has two parts. One part works as a handle, and the other part has two ________ ________. These blades are screwed together, and ________ ________ like paper or cloth. What is this?
날카로운 금속 칼날
얇은 것들을 자르다

09 특정 정보 파악

대화를 듣고, 남자가 이용하려는 교통 수단으로 가장 적절한 것을 고르시오.

① 배
② 버스 by bus
③ 기차 by train
④ 비행기 by plane
⑤ 자동차 by car

Thanksgiving Day: 추수감사절, 추석
New Year's Day : 설날
Arbor Day : 식목일
Children's Day : 어린이날
Parents' Day : 어버이날

W Thanksgiving Day is just one week away from now.

M Yes. I'm looking forward to seeing my family.

W So how are you going home? By bus or by train?

M Well, at first I was thinking of going by car, but I thought it would be tiring to drive. So I ________ ________ ________ ________ ________.
버스를 타기로 결심했다

W But I think the plane is better than the bus.

M I think so, but ________ ________ ________ ________ ________ ________ from my house. The bus stops near my house and it's easy for my dad to pick me up.
공항이 좀 멀다

W I see.

10 이유 파악

이유를 묻는 말인 what made ~. 이후에 나오는 대답을 주의깊게 듣는다.

대화를 듣고, 남자가 기뻐하는 이유로 가장 적절한 것을 고르시오.

① 시합에서 이겨서
② 체중 감량에 성공해서
③ 여자에게 칭찬을 받아서
④ 자신에게 맞는 헬스클럽을 찾아서
⑤ 효과적인 식이요법을 알게 되어서

W You look happy today, Kevin.
M Do I look happy? I have a good reason for that.
W Tell me what made you so happy.
M Well, I __________ __________ and found out that I __________ (내 몸무게를 재어 보았다) (5킬로그램을 뺐다) __________ at last.
W Congratulations. You __________ __________ __________ (식이요법에 성공했다). I envy you. You have a strong will.
M Thank you for saying so.

11 언급 및 비언급 파악

다음을 듣고, Green Concert에 대해 언급되지 않은 것을 고르시오.

① 장소 Baron High School gym
② 시간 six o'clock
③ 개최 이유 for the benefit of poor people
④ 입장료
⑤ 출연진 John Doran, Baron, Baron High School orchestra

W Hello, everyone. Today I'd like to make an announcement about the Green Concert. First I'd like to thank you for buying tickets. The concert will be __________ (Baron 고등학교 체육관에서) __________ __________ __________ __________ at six o'clock on the evening of __________ __________ (4월 16일). The concert is __________ __________ __________ __________ (가난한 사람들을 위한) __________ __________ in the neighborhood. For the concert, we invited singer John Doran and the Baron High School orchestra. I am sure you will have fun.

12 특정 정보 파악

남자의 말 What should I do?가 조언을 요청하는 표현임을 파악한다.

대화를 듣고, 여자가 남자에게 제안한 것으로 가장 적절한 것을 고르시오.

① 가방을 주기적으로 세탁할 것
② 가방을 깨끗한 곳에 보관할 것
③ 가방에 책을 너무 많이 넣지 말 것
④ 알코올을 너무 자주 사용하지 말 것
⑤ 수건에 알코올을 묻혀 가방을 닦을 것

W What are you doing, Jack?
M My bag got dirty and I'm trying to clean it up with this towel.
W Let me see. I'm afraid you won't get it cleaned with only a towel.
M Then what should I do?
W __________ __________ __________ __________ __________ (수건에 알코올을 묻혀라) and __________ (네 가방을 문질러라) __________ __________ with it. That will really work.
M Thanks for the tip. I'll try it right away.

고난도

13 내용 일치 파악

다음을 듣고, Spring Book Festival에 대한 설명으로 일치하지 않는 것을 고르시오.

① 금요일에 있을 예정이다.
② 학교에 자신이 좋아하는 책을 들고 온다.
③ 오전에는 책을 읽고 독후감을 쓴다.
④ 좋아하는 책을 친구들에게 소개하는 시간이 있다.
⑤ 연극반 학생들이 연극을 공연할 것이다.

M We're having the Spring Book Festival this coming Friday. Students are coming to school with their favorite books. In the morning, we are going to __________ __________ __________ __________ (광고하기 위한 포스터를 만들다) their chosen books. After that, students will be asked to __________ __________ __________ (자신이 가장 좋아하는 책을 소개하다) to their classmates with the poster. After lunch, all students are coming to the auditorium to watch a play. The drama club prepared a wonderful play for the festival. I hope all of you enjoy the wonderful book festival.

14 그림 정보 파악 – 지도

대화를 듣고, 여자가 가려고 하는 장소를 고르시오.

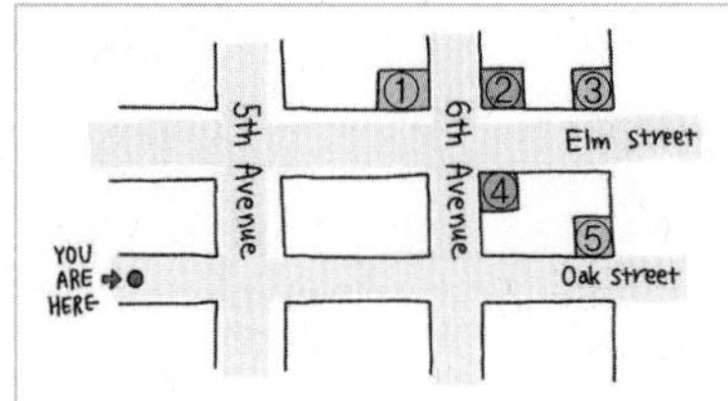

W Excuse me but can you show me how to get to the Modern theater?

M Modern theater? That's just a 10 minute walk from here. You are on the Oak Street. Walk two blocks down the street and __________ __________ __________ __________ __________.
6번가에서 좌회전하다

W Okay, walk two blocks and turn left.

M Just walk another block along the 6th Avenue and turn left. You will find the building __________ __________ __________.
당신의 오른편에

W Thank you very much.

M My pleasure.

15 장소 추론

대화를 듣고, 두 사람이 대화하고 있는 장소로 가장 적절한 곳을 고르시오.

① 영화관 ② 옷가게
③ 미술 학원 ④ 미술관
⑤ 패션쇼장

핵심 어휘 color, painter, work, paintings 등과 관련된 장소를 추론해 본다.

W What do you think about this one? I really like the color.

M Do you know about the painter? It must have taken a long time to complete the work.

W Can I take a picture of this?

M You can, but __________ __________ __________ __________. The sudden bright light __________ __________ __________ __________ __________.
플래시를 사용하지 마라 / 그림에 좋지 않다

W Okay. Can you hold my coffee while I take a picture?

M Actually, __________ __________ __________ __________ __________ here. Please remember that next time.
음식과 음료수는 허용되지 않는다

W Oh, I'm sorry.

16 지도 위치 파악

대화를 듣고, 남자가 가려고 하는 장소를 고르시오.

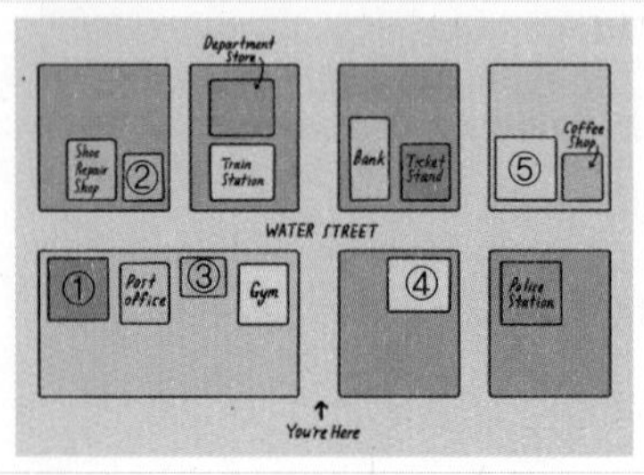

M Hi, Marie! Where did you __________ __________ __________? They're very nice.
그 운동화를 사다

W Thanks. They're from XYZ Shoe Store.

M Where is that?

W You know Water Street, right? Go straight to there, and turn left.

M Okay, turn left on Water Street, and then?

W Walk until you see the post office on your left. It's just __________ __________ it.
~의 맞은 편에

M Thanks! I'll go check right now.

17 이유 파악

대화를 듣고, 남자가 우울해하는 이유로 가장 적절한 것을 고르시오.

① 축구 경기가 취소되어서
② 연습에 참가할 수 없어서
③ 자신의 팀이 경기에 져서
④ 축구팀에 선발되지 않아서
⑤ 자신의 팀의 골대에 골을 넣어서

남자의 mistake가 무엇인지 파악한다.

W What's wrong with you, Tom? You look so sad. You were so happy to join the team finally. What's wrong?

M I ________ ________ ________ ________ during practice.
큰 실수를 했다

W Tell me what happened.

M Our team had its first soccer practice today. I ________ ________ ________ ________ ________ ________ ________ by mistake. Can you believe it?
우리 팀의 골대로 공을 차 넣었다

W Anybody can make a mistake. They'll see soon that you are a good player.

18 주제, 소재 파악

대화를 듣고, 무엇에 관한 내용인지 가장 적절한 것을 고르시오.

① 박물관 관람하기 ② 특산물 쇼핑하기
③ 시장 구경하기 ④ 여행지 선정하기
⑤ 여행 일정짜기

W I'd like to ________ ________ ________ when we're there.
박물관에 방문하다

M Can we do that on the second day? I want to rest first.

W But I want to ________ ________ ________ ________ on the second day.
지역 시장을 확인하다

M We can go to the museum in the morning and the market in the afternoon.

W I guess that could work.

M What about on our third day? Do you have any ideas?

19 알맞은 응답 찾기

[19~20] 대화를 듣고, 남자의 마지막 말에 이어질 여자의 응답으로 가장 적절한 것을 고르시오.

Woman: ________________

① I'm happy with my style.
② My hairdresser is so nice.
③ Unfortunately I fell asleep.
④ I like brown more than red.
⑤ I was looking into the mirror.

M Why are you looking so unhappy?

W It's about my hair. I wanted it to be dyed brown.

M But ________ ________ ________ now.
네 머리는 빨간색이다

W Well, I asked my hairdresser to ________ ________ ________.
갈색으로 염색하다

M You mean, he made a mistake, right?

W Yes. What am I supposed to do now?

M ________ ________ ________ while he was dying it red?
너는 무엇을 하고 있었니

W ________________

20 알맞은 응답 찾기

Woman: ________________

① I just turned on the computer.
② I have to say this. You really did a good job.
③ All right. You have to finish the homework after the game.
④ You're right. I need to go to my room for the homework.
⑤ I'm so sorry. We don't have enough time to play together.

W You're playing the computer game again.

M I just started. I studied for two hours. Please believe me, Mom.

W Okay. I believe you this time. And ________ ________ ________ ________ ________?
네 숙제는 끝냈니

M Not yet, but I did half of it. Please ________ ________ ________ ________ ________.
나에게 30분만 주다

W ________________

영어듣기능력평가 20회

학년 반 번
이름

01 다음을 듣고, 'this'가 무엇인지 가장 적절한 것을 고르시오.

①  ②  ③ 

④  ⑤ 

02 다음을 듣고, 그림과 어울리지 않는 말을 고르시오.

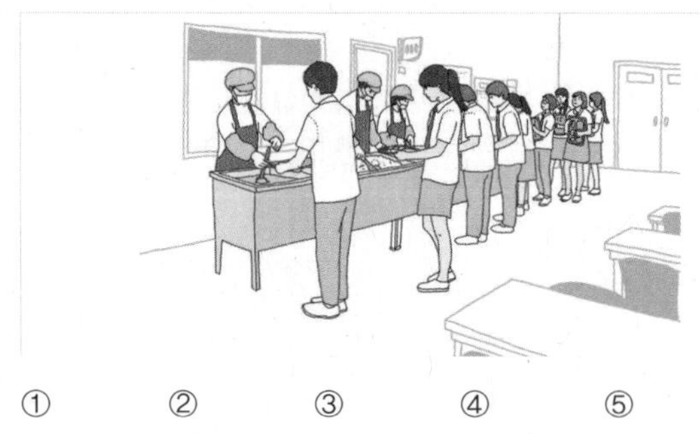

① ② ③ ④ ⑤

03 다음을 듣고, 그림을 잘못 설명한 것을 고르시오.

① ② ③ ④ ⑤

04 다음을 듣고, 'this'가 가리키는 것으로 가장 적절한 것을 고르시오

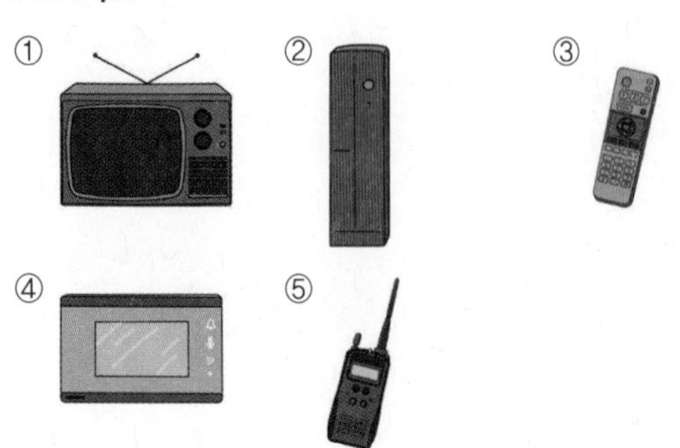

고난도

05 대화를 듣고, 두 사람이 사기로 한 양말의 개수와 가격을 고르시오.

① 3켤레 – $10 ② 6켤레 – $18
③ 6켤레 – $19 ④ 9켤레 – $27
⑤ 9켤레 – $28

06 다음을 듣고, 두 사람의 대화가 어색한 것을 고르시오.

① ② ③ ④ ⑤

07 대화를 듣고, 남자가 여자에게 부탁한 일로 가장 적절한 것을 고르시오.

① 방 청소를 해 줄 것
② 설거지를 함께 할 것
③ 책상 정리를 해 줄 것
④ 새 휴대전화를 사 줄 것
⑤ 역사 보고서를 가져다줄 것

고난도

08 대화를 듣고, 여자가 목표로 하는 달리기 기록을 고르시오.

① 4분 7초 ② 4분 17초
③ 4분 27초 ④ 4분 37초
⑤ 4분 47초

09 대화를 듣고, 여자가 기분이 나쁜 이유로 가장 적절한 것을 고르시오.

① 친구와 사이가 좋지 않아서
② 동생이 병원에 입원해 있어서
③ MP3 플레이어가 고장이 나서
④ 동생이 자신의 물건을 잃어버려서
⑤ 디지털 카메라를 비싸게 구입해서

10 대화를 듣고, 여자가 남자를 위해 할 일로 가장 적절한 것을 고르시오.

① 세차 도와주기 ② 샌드위치 만들어 주기
③ 토마토 가져다주기 ④ 오렌지 주스 사다 주기
⑤ 상한 우유 버리기

점수 /20

11 대화를 듣고, 남자가 겨울 방학에 할 일로 가장 적절한 것을 고르시오.

① 수영 배우기
② 한국어 공부하기
③ 일해서 돈 모으기
④ 한국으로 여행 가기
⑤ 스쿠버 다이빙 배우기

고난도

12 대화를 듣고, 대화의 내용과 일치하는 것을 고르시오.

① 여자는 병원에서 일하고 있다.
② 여자는 정기적인 자원봉사 활동을 하고 있다.
③ 남자는 일요일에 야구 연습이 있다.
④ 남자는 토요일에 '깨끗한 강 만들기' 캠페인에 참여할 예정이다.
⑤ 여자는 남자의 일정에 맞는 자원봉사 활동을 찾아 주고 있다.

13 대화를 듣고, 여자가 중국으로 출장 가는 날짜를 고르시오.

① June 11 ② June 13
③ June 15 ④ July 13
⑤ July 15

14 대화를 듣고, 두 사람이 대화하고 있는 장소로 가장 적절한 곳을 고르시오.

① 학교 ② 병원
③ 운동장 ④ 어학원
⑤ 스포츠 센터

15 대화를 듣고, 여자의 마지막 말의 의도로 가장 적절한 것을 고르시오.

① 칭찬 ② 감사
③ 거절 ④ 충고
⑤ 후회

16 대화를 듣고, 여자가 남자에게 부탁한 일로 가장 적절한 것을 고르시오.

① 부엌을 청소해 줄 것
② 소 먹이를 사다 줄 것
③ 자동차를 수리해 줄 것
④ 울타리를 페인트칠 할 것
⑤ 저녁 식사를 준비해 줄 것

17 대화를 듣고, Green Hotel의 위치로 가장 알맞은 장소를 고르시오.

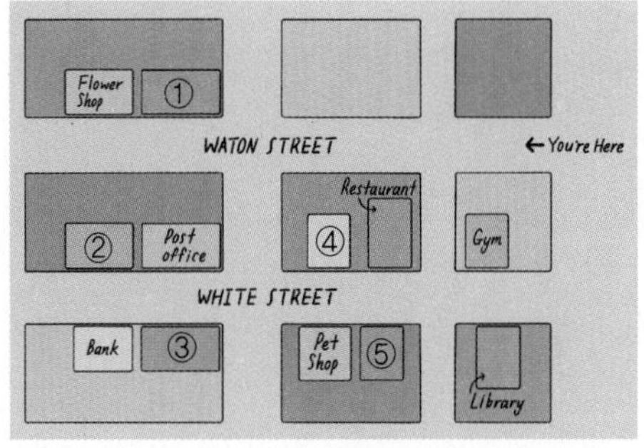

18 대화를 듣고, 남자의 심정으로 가장 적절한 것을 고르시오.

① excited ② worried
③ disappointed ④ tired
⑤ proud

[19~20] 대화를 듣고, 남자의 마지막 말에 이어질 여자의 응답으로 가장 적절한 것을 고르시오.

19 Woman: ______________________

① I see. I'll help you right now.
② No thanks. I have a good bike.
③ Don't worry. It's not your fault.
④ Right. I lost my bicycle yesterday.
⑤ Okay. I'll go to the shop tomorrow.

20 Woman: ______________________

① You can use my baseball glove.
② I will! Kevin will like our presents.
③ Because of you, I finished my job.
④ I went to the soccer stadium last night.
⑤ No. I don't like both baseball and soccer.

다시 들으면서 듣기 만점에 도전하세요!
Dictation: 스크립트의 주요 부분을 다시 들으면서!
실전 ⊕: 세부 정보가 많은 스크립트를 다른 문제로 샅샅이!

고난도

01 그림 "this" 파악(담화)

사물의 기능(keep food fresh, make ice), 설치 장소(in the kitchen) 등의 특징을 단서로 이용한다.

다음을 듣고, 'this'가 무엇인지 가장 적절한 것을 고르시오.

① ② ③ ④ ⑤

M You can easily see this _________ _________ _________ (부엌에서) of your house. This is _________ _________ _________ (전자 제품). When you want to _________ _________ _________ (음식을 신선하게 보관하다), you put it in this. Also, when you want to _________ _________ (얼음을 만들다), you can use this. If you put water in this, the water turns into ice. In modern life, many people say that we can't live without this.

02 그림 정보 파악 – 토익형

다음을 듣고, 그림과 어울리지 않는 말을 고르시오.

① ② ③ ④ ⑤

W ① _________ _________ _________ (나는 줄 서 있다). Stand behind me.
② Wait for your turn. Don't _________ _________ _________ (새치기 하다).
③ Do not _________ _________ _________ _________ _________ (복도에서 뛰다). Safety first.
④ Can I have more of the soup?
⑤ What's for lunch today?

고난도

03 날씨 파악

다음을 듣고, 그림을 잘못 설명한 것을 고르시오.

	MON	TUE	WED	THU	FRI	SAT	SUN
7 DAY FORECAST	21	21	21	21	20	20	22
	31	32	31	31	31	31	33

① ② ③ ④ ⑤

M ① It will be raining on Monday, Tuesday and Thursday.
② The temperature will be _________ _________ (가장 높은) on Tuesday.
③ On Wednesday, it's not going to rain.
④ It will be rainy on Saturday morning, but _________ _________ _________ _________ (그 비는 곧 그칠 것이다).
⑤ On the weekend, the weather will be okay for _________ _________ (야외 활동).

04 그림 "this" 파악(담화)

다음을 듣고, 'this'가 가리키는 것으로 가장 적절한 것을 고르시오.

① ② ③ ④ ⑤

M You might ________ this ________ ________ ________ at home. You can control other devices with this. By pressing buttons on this, you can ________ the devices ________ ________ ________. You can also control the volume or change the channels with this. What is this?

거의 매일 사용하다 / 켜거나 끄다

고난도

05 숫자 파악

대화를 듣고, 두 사람이 사기로 한 양말의 개수와 가격을 고르시오.

① 3켤레 – $10
② 6켤레 – $18
③ 6켤레 – $19
④ 9켤레 – $27
⑤ 9켤레 – $28

bundle sale: 묶음 할인 판매
clearance sale: 재고품 정리 특매
winter sale: 겨울 용품 특매
garage sale: 중고 가구 염가 판매

W Honey, we need to buy some winter socks.
M Clothes sections are over there. Oh, look at this. They're having a bundle sale.
W Hmm... $10 for three pairs of socks. That's not bad.
M If we buy six pairs, it would be $19. Look at the prices.
W Is it going to be cheaper if we buy more?
M I think so. ________ ________ ________ ________ and $37 for twelve pairs.
9켤레에 28달러
W ________ ________ ________ ________ ________. Did you say $27?
9켤레면 충분할 것이다
M No, that would be $28.

06 어색한 대화 찾기

다음을 듣고, 두 사람의 대화가 어색한 것을 고르시오.

① ② ③ ④ ⑤

① **M** When did you see the concert?
W Last weekend. It was really good.

② **M** What do you want to be ________ ________ ________?
장래에
W A math teacher. I want to ________ ________ ________ ________.
수학 선생님이 되다

③ **M** Which do you like better, classical or rock music?
W Well... I like rock music more than classical music.

④ **M** ________ ________ ________ do you read a month?
몇 권의 책
W Yeah, I ________ ________ ________ most.
시 읽는 것을 좋아하다

⑤ **M** Is this your MP3 player?
W Yeah, I bought it last weekend.

07 부탁 파악

Can you ~? 이후에 나오는 부분을 주의 깊게 듣는다.

대화를 듣고, 남자가 여자에게 부탁한 일로 가장 적절한 것을 고르시오.

① 방 청소를 해 줄 것
② 설거지를 함께 할 것
③ 책상 정리를 해 줄 것
④ 새 휴대전화를 사 줄 것
⑤ 역사 보고서를 가져다줄 것

[Cellphone rings.]

W Hello, Linda speaking!

M Mom, it's me, Kevin! Where are you now?

W At home. I'm washing the dishes now. Why?

M Mom, I'm sorry, but I ________ ________ ________ ________ at home. (역사 두고 왔다)

W You should be more careful. Where is the report?

M It's on my desk in my room. ________ ________ ________ to me now? (그것을 가져다주시겠어요)

W Yes, I can. I'll go to your school right now.

고난도

08 숫자 파악 – 시각

대화를 듣고, 여자가 목표로 하는 달리기 기록을 고르시오.

① 4분 7초 ② 4분 17초
③ 4분 27초 ④ 4분 37초
⑤ 4분 47초

W Mr. Jackson, what was my time today?

M ________ ________ ________ ________. (4분 37초)

W Really? Oh, that's great. I ran about 20 seconds faster than last month.

M That's right. But to become the champion, ________ ________ ________ ________. (너는 훨씬 더 빨리 달려야 한다)

W How fast do I have to run to win the gold medal?

M Well.... As you know, your today's record is 4 minutes 37 seconds. I think you must be ________ ________ ________ ________ ________ ________. (이 기록보다 10초 더 빠른)

W 10 seconds! Okay, I see. I'll do my best to run that fast!

09 이유 파악

이유를 묻는 말 Why? 뒤의 여자의 대답에 주목하여 듣는다.

대화를 듣고, 여자가 기분이 나쁜 이유로 가장 적절한 것을 고르시오.

① 친구와 사이가 좋지 않아서
② 동생이 병원에 입원해 있어서
③ MP3 플레이어가 고장이 나서
④ 동생이 자신의 물건을 잃어버려서
⑤ 디지털 카메라를 비싸게 구입해서

M Alice, you don't look good. What's wrong with you?

W ________ ________ ________ ________ ________, Jane. (그것은 내 여동생 때문이다)

M Your sister, Jane? Why? Tell me in more detail.

W She ________ ________ ________ ________. (내 MP3 플레이어를 잃어버렸다)

M Again? She lost your digital camera last month, didn't she?

W Yeah, that's right. She's really careless.

10 할 일 파악

대화를 듣고, 여자가 남자를 위해 할 일로 가장 적절한 것을 고르시오.

① 세차 도와주기
② 샌드위치 만들어 주기
③ 토마토 가져다주기
④ 오렌지 주스 사다 주기
⑤ 상한 우유 버리기

W It's already 4:30. Don't you feel hungry?

M Yes, a little bit.

W Then, I'll ________ ________ ________ ________. What about a tomato sandwich? (너에게 샌드위치를 만들어 주다)

M OK. That's fine. Ah, can you also bring me a glass of orange juice?

W Sorry, we don't have any orange juice. ________ ________ ________? (우유는 어때)

M Sure, no problem.

11 할 일 파악

대화를 듣고, 남자가 겨울 방학에 할 일로 가장 적절한 것을 고르시오.

① 수영 배우기
② 한국어 공부하기
③ 일해서 돈 모으기
④ 한국으로 여행 가기
⑤ 스쿠버 다이빙 배우기

대화를 듣고, 여자가 겨울 방학에 할 일로 가장 적절한 것을 고르시오.

① 수영 배우기
② 한국어 공부하기
③ 일해서 돈 모으기
④ 한국으로 여행 가기
⑤ 스쿠버 다이빙 배우기

마음이 바뀐 부분을 주의깊게 듣는다.

W Oh, the winter vacation is coming soon.
M Yeah, that's right. So, will you really learn swimming during the vacation?
W Yes, I will. What about you, Pedro? Are you going to learn scuba diving?
M No, I ________ ________ ________. (마음이 바뀌었다)
W Then, what are you going to do this vacation?
M Well... I'll ________ ________ ________ (일자리를 구하다) and ________ ________ ________. (돈을 좀 모으다)
W What do you want to save money for?
M I'm going to take a trip to Korea next summer vacation!

고난도

12 내용 일치 파악

대화를 듣고, 대화의 내용과 일치하는 것을 고르시오.

① 여자는 병원에서 일하고 있다.
② 여자는 정기적인 자원봉사 활동을 하고 있다.
③ 남자는 일요일에 야구 연습이 있다.
④ 남자는 토요일에 '깨끗한 강 만들기' 캠페인에 참여할 예정이다.
⑤ 여자는 남자의 일정에 맞는 자원봉사 활동을 찾아 주고 있다.

대화를 듣고, 무엇에 관한 내용인지 가장 적절한 것을 고르시오.

① 주말 정기 모임 ② 캠페인 참여
③ 야구 연습 일정 ④ 자원봉사 활동
⑤ 병원 예약

W So, did you say you ________ ________ ________ ________? (정기적인 자원봉사 활동을 원하다)
M Yes, Mrs. Hong. I'd like to find volunteer work that I can do regularly.
W There is Clean River campaign on every Saturday morning. How about that?
M Oh, no. I have baseball practice every Saturday morning.
W Do you? Then, how about Sunday afternoon?
M What kind of work is it?
W You can help doctors and nurses ________ ________ ________ ________ ________ ________. (병원에서 외국인 근로자들을 치료하는) It opens only on Sunday afternoon.
M That would be very good for me. Thank you.

13 숫자 파악 – 날짜

대화를 듣고, 여자가 중국으로 출장 가는 날짜를 고르시오.

① June 11 ② June 13
③ June 15 ④ July 13
⑤ July 15

What do you mean ~?은 '~이 무슨 말이니?'라는 의미로, 상대방의 말을 이해하지 못했을 때 그 의미를 묻는 표현이다.

처음에 가려고 했던 날짜(July 13th)와 변경된 날짜(15th)를 구분해서 듣는다.

M I heard that you will go on a business trip to China ________ ________ ________. (7월 13일에) Is it true?
W Half right, half wrong.
M What do you mean by that?
W Well... I'll leave for China, but ________ ________ ________ ________. (13일은 아니다)
M Then, when are you leaving?
W ________ ________ ________ ________. (15일에) There were no airline tickets on the 13th.

14 장소 추론

대화를 듣고, 두 사람이 대화하고 있는 장소로 가장 적절한 곳을 고르시오.

① 학교 ② 병원
③ 운동장 ④ 어학원
⑤ 스포츠 센터

What a surprise to see you here!는 '너를 이곳에서 만나다니!'라는 의미로, 뜻밖의 사람을 우연히 만났을 때 사용하는 표현이다.

W Hi, George. What a surprise to see you here!

M It is. I didn't expect to see someone I know here.

W Are you here for ________ ________ ________? (수영 수업)

M No, I'm taking ________ ________ ________. How about you? (배드민턴 수업)

W I'm taking ________ ________ ________. The doctor recommended me to do yoga regularly. (요가 수업)

M Good for you. So, ________ ________ ________ ________? (수업은 끝났니)

W Yes. The class ended at 7:30.

M Mine begins at 8. Would you like something to drink? I have a little bit of time before the class.

W Great.

15 의도 추론

여자의 마지막 말 중 should have learned에 담긴 의미를 파악한다.

대화를 듣고, 여자의 마지막 말의 의도로 가장 적절한 것을 고르시오.

① 칭찬 ② 감사
③ 거절 ④ 충고
⑤ 후회

M Oh, is this trophy yours?

W No, it is Angela's, my sister. She won it in a tennis competition last year.

M Is your sister ________ ________ ________ ________? (훌륭한 테니스 선수)

W Yes, she is. She is really good at playing tennis.

M Sounds good! When did she learn to play tennis?

W When she was an elementary school student.

M What about you? Can you also play tennis well?

W No, I can't. ________ ________ ________ ________ to play it when I was little like my sister. (나는 배웠어야 했다)

16 부탁 파악

부탁하는 말 Can you ~?의 앞뒤 내용을 주의깊게 듣는다.

대화를 듣고, 여자가 남자에게 부탁한 일로 가장 적절한 것을 고르시오.

① 부엌을 청소해 줄 것
② 소 먹이를 사다 줄 것
③ 자동차를 수리해 줄 것
④ 울타리를 페인트칠 할 것
⑤ 저녁 식사를 준비해 줄 것

W Sam, can I talk to you for a minute?

M Sure! What is it?

W Well, a part of the fence around the farm is broken. Do you know that?

M Yeah, I saw it. I'll take care of it tomorrow.

W Good! Ah, we ________ ________ ________ ________ ________. Can you buy some this afternoon? (소 먹이가 더 필요하다)

M I see. After lunch, ________ ________ ________ ________. (좀 사러 갈 것이다)

W Thank you. The car keys are on the table in the kitchen.

17 지도, 위치 파악

대화를 듣고, Green Hotel의 위치로 가장 알맞은 장소를 고르시오.

W Excuse me, I'm looking for Green Hotel. Is it around here?

M Yes, it's on White Street.

W Where is that?

M Go straight two blocks and turn left.

W Turn left?

M Yes, and ________ ________ ________ ________ (조금 걷다), then you will see White Street. Then turn right, and the hotel is ________ ________ ________ (바로 ~옆에) the post office.

W Do I have to cross the street?

M No, you don't have to.

18 심정 파악

대화를 듣고, 남자의 심정으로 가장 적절한 것을 고르시오.

① excited ② worried
③ disappointed ④ tired
⑤ proud

W Where are you going, Hyunsu?

M Hi, Maya! I'm going home.

W Home? But you have club activities on Thursdays, don't you?

M Yes, but my grandparents are coming home today. I want to ________________ ________ ________ (가서 그들을 기다리다).

W Where are they coming from?

M They live in Canada, and they always ________________ ________ (좋은 선물을 가져오다) for me.

W Ah, now I see why you are skipping your club activities.

19 알맞은 응답 찾기

[19~20] 대화를 듣고, 남자의 마지막 말에 이어질 여자의 응답으로 가장 적절한 것을 고르시오.

Woman: ______________________

① I see. I'll help you right now.
② No thanks. I have a good bike.
③ Don't worry. It's not your fault.
④ Right. I lost my bicycle yesterday.
⑤ Okay. I'll go to the shop tomorrow.

one of the newest ones on the market은 '시중에 판매되는 가장 최신형 자전거 중 하나'라는 의미로 최상급을 나타내는 표현이다.

W Daniel, you have a new bicycle. When did you buy it?

M Two days ago. You know, it's one of the newest ones on the market.

W Wow, it looks very good. ________ ________ ________ ________ ________ (얼마를 지불했니) for it?

M Don't be surprised! It's only $80.

W Only $80? That's great! ________ ________ ________ ________ ________ (나는 하나 사고 싶다) as well. Where did you buy it?

M At the ABC Bike Shop. It's on Lake Street.

W ______________________

20 알맞은 응답 찾기

Woman: ______________________

① You can use my baseball glove.
② I will! Kevin will like our presents.
③ Because of you, I finished my job.
④ I went to the soccer stadium last night.
⑤ No. I don't like both baseball and soccer.

M Oh, this Saturday is ________ ________ (Kevin의 생일).

W Yeah, that's right. What should we buy our son?

M He likes sports a lot. How about a baseball glove or a soccer ball?

W That's a good idea. Then, let's ________ ________ ________ ________ (그것들 둘 다 사 주다) for him!

M Buy both of them? Well... aren't they too expensive?

W No, I know where we can buy them cheaply.

M I see. Then ________ ________ ________ ________ ________ (꼭 그것들을 사 와라) tomorrow.

W ______________________

고난도 영어듣기능력평가

학년 반 번
이름

01 다음을 듣고, 'this'가 가리키는 것으로 가장 적절한 것을 고르시오.

02 대화를 듣고, 무엇에 관한 내용인지 가장 적절한 것을 고르시오.

① 노트북 교환 ② 서비스센터 위치
③ 노트북 수리 ④ 올바른 노트북 사용법
⑤ 가전제품 구입

03 다음을 듣고, 내일 뉴욕의 날씨로 가장 적절한 것을 고르시오.

04 대화를 듣고, 남자의 마지막 말의 의도로 가장 적절한 것을 고르시오.

① 승낙 ② 거절
③ 의심 ④ 사과
⑤ 제안

05 다음을 듣고, 여자가 사촌에 대해 언급하지 않은 것을 고르시오.

① 사는 곳 ② 성격
③ 외모 ④ 생일
⑤ 취미

06 대화를 듣고, 두 사람이 만날 시각을 고르시오.

① 2 p.m. ② 3 p.m.
③ 4 p.m. ④ 5 p.m.
⑤ 6 p.m

07 대화를 듣고, 남자의 장래 희망으로 가장 적절한 것을 고르시오.

① 김치 연구가 ② 유명 요리사
③ TV 쇼 진행자 ④ 연예인
⑤ 식당 운영자

08 대화를 듣고, 여자의 심정으로 가장 적절한 것을 고르시오.

① relaxed ② sad
③ disappointed ④ frightened
⑤ shy

09 대화를 듣고, 두 사람이 대화하는 장소로 가장 적절한 곳을 고르시오.

① 기차역 ② 영화관
③ 호텔 ④ 부동산 중개사무소
⑤ 관광안내소

10 대화를 듣고, 여자의 무엇에 관한 내용인지 가장 적절한 것을 고르시오.

① 건강 ② 동생
③ 어머니 ④ 장래희망
⑤ 반려동물

점수 /20

11 대화를 듣고, 아빠가 출장에서 돌아오는 요일을 고르시오.

① 화요일 ② 수요일
③ 월요일 ④ 토요일
⑤ 일요일

12 대화를 듣고, 여자가 내일 남자를 만날 수 없는 이유로 가장 적절한 것을 고르시오.

① 미리 통보를 받지 못해서
② 날짜를 잘못 알고 있어서
③ 축구 경기 구경을 가야 해서
④ 연극 관람을 가기로 해서
⑤ 연극 연습에 참가해야 해서

13 대화를 듣고, 두 사람의 관계로 가장 적절한 것을 고르시오.

① 교사 – 학생 ② 교사 – 학부모
③ 부모 – 자녀 ④ 가게 점원 – 손님
⑤ 변호사 – 고객

14 대화를 듣고, 여자가 가려고 하는 장소를 고르시오.

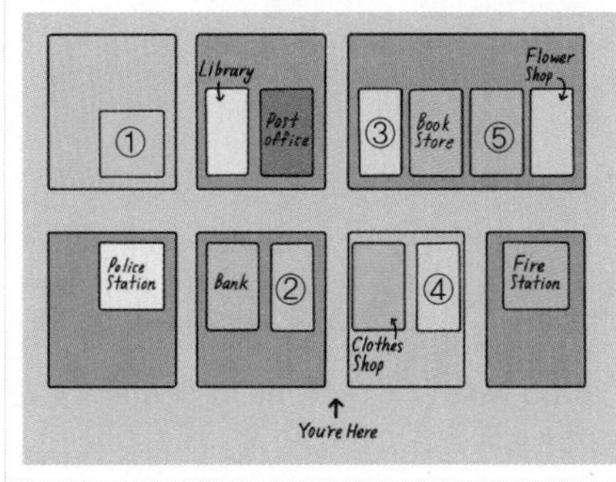

15 대화를 듣고, 여자가 남자에게 부탁한 일로 가장 적절한 것을 고르시오.

① 숙제 마저 끝내기 ② 바깥 활동하기
③ 쓰레기 버리기 ④ 재활용품 모으기
⑤ 집안 청소하기

16 대화를 듣고, 여자가 남자에게 제안한 것으로 가장 적절한 것을 고르시오.

① 세차 도와주기 ② 아버지에게 부탁하기
③ 자전거 타러 가기 ④ 공원에 소풍가기
⑤ 자전거 타는 법 가르쳐주기

17 대화를 듣고, 여자가 대화 직후에 할 일로 가장 적절한 것을 고르시오.

① 시험 공부하기 ② 공책 가지러 가기
③ 수업내용 가르쳐주기 ④ 복사하러 가기
⑤ 남자 기다리기

18 대화를 듣고, 여자의 직업으로 가장 적절한 것을 고르시오.

① 우체국 직원 ② 집배원
③ 항공사 직원 ④ 공항 체크인 직원
⑤ 호텔 직원

[19~20] 대화를 듣고, 여자의 마지막 말에 이어질 남자의 응답으로 가장 적절한 것을 고르시오.

19 Man: ____________________

① It was really nice.
② I didn't go there.
③ Let's go together.
④ I will visit next week.
⑤ That's a great idea.

20 Man: ____________________

① I'm going there this week.
② Sure, I'd like to see that movie.
③ No, I don't want to go alone.
④ Oh, that's too bad.
⑤ Sure, that'd be great.

고난도 영어듣기능력평가 DICTATION

다시 들으면서 듣기 만점에 도전하세요!
Dictation: 스크립트의 주요 부분을 다시 들으면서!
실전 ⊕: 세부 정보가 많은 스크립트를 다른 문제로 샅샅이!

01 그림 "this" 파악(담화)

사물의 모양, 재질, 용도를 보고 답을 찾는다.

다음을 듣고, 'this'가 가리키는 것으로 가장 적절한 것을 고르시오.

① ② ③ ④ ⑤

M You can see this in a kitchen. Usually, this looks like a large big spoon with a long handle and a deep bowl. This can be ________ ________ ________(금속으로 만든), wood, or plastic. You use this when you serve ________ ________ ________ ________(액체 형태의 음식), such as soup or sauce. What is this?

02 주제, 소재 파악

대화를 듣고, 무엇에 관한 내용인지 가장 적절한 것을 고르시오.

① 노트북 교환
② 서비스센터 위치
③ 노트북 수리
④ 올바른 노트북 사용법
⑤ 가전제품 구입

W Hey, Nick, do you know a good electronics service center?
M What's the problem?
W My laptop ________ ________(망가졌다). There is no sound at all.
M Did you look into the sound control panel?
W Yes, but it didn't work.
M How about the sound driver? You can turn it off and on.
W Really? Let me try. [pause] Oh, wow, it's working again. Thanks!
M ________ ________(천만에).

03 날씨 파악

다른 나라의 날씨와 헷갈리지 않도록 집중하며 듣는다.

다음을 듣고, 내일 뉴욕의 날씨로 가장 적절한 것을 고르시오.

① ② ③ ④ ⑤

W Good morning! Here is tomorrow's world weather forecast. In Seoul, it will be cloudy but warm. In Tokyo, it'll ________ ________ ________(비가 내리기 시작하다) in the afternoon. In New York, it'll be sunny and mild. London will have some rain, and Paris will be cloudy and windy. Sydney will ________ ________ ________ ________ ________(눈이 오고 춥다).

04 마지막 말 의도 파악

대화를 듣고, 남자의 마지막 말의 의도로 가장 적절한 것을 고르시오.

① 승낙 ② 거절
③ 의심 ④ 사과
⑤ 제안

대화를 듣고, 남자가 레스토랑을 예약한 시간을 고르시오.

① 6:00 ② 6:30
③ 7:00 ④ 7:30
⑤ 8:00

[Phone rings.]

W Restaurant Ciel. How may I help you?

M Hi, could I ________ ________ ________ for tomorrow? (예약하다)

W Certainly. For what time, and how many people, sir?

M For four people. Will 6:30 be okay?

W I'm really sorry, sir, but I'm afraid we're ________ ________ (이미 예약이 가득 찬) at that time. What about 8 o'clock?

M Hmm.... it's a bit late, but I guess I can't help.

05 언급 유무 파악(담화)

다음을 듣고, 여자가 사촌에 대해 언급하지 않은 것을 고르시오.

① 사는 곳 ② 성격
③ 외모 ④ 생일
⑤ 취미

언급된 사항을 보기에서 지워가며 답을 찾는다.

W I'd like to ________ ________ ________ (내 사촌을 소개하다) Ann. She lives in Los Angeles, California. She is one year older than me. Her mother is my mother's younger sister. I like Ann because she's very ________ ________ ________ (다정하고 활발한). She's tall, and she has short brown hair. She likes to play beach volleyball with her friends.

06 숫자 파악 – 시각

대화를 듣고, 두 사람이 만날 시각을 고르시오.

① 2 p.m. ② 3 p.m.
③ 4 p.m. ④ 5 p.m.
⑤ 6 p.m.

최종 합의한 시간이 언급되기 전까지 섣부르게 답을 체크하지 않는다.

M Hi, Chris. Do you still want to ________ ________ (볼링 치러 가다) on Sunday?

W Sure, why not? What time would you like to go?

M What about six?

W Isn't it too late? We have school on Monday, you know.

M Okay, then what about two?

W It's too early. I usually finish my lunch at two.

M Then at three or four? I'm okay either way.

W Three sounds good. ________ ________ ________ (그때 보자)!

07 특정 정보 파악 – 장래 희망

여자의 장래 희망과 헷갈리지 않도록 주의한다.

대화를 듣고, 남자의 장래 희망으로 가장 적절한 것을 고르시오.

① 김치 연구가 ② 유명 요리사
③ TV 쇼 진행자 ④ 연예인
⑤ 식당 운영자

W Hi, Tony, did you have a good weekend?

M Yes, I helped my mom make kimchi, and it was fun!

W I didn't know you ________ ________ ________ ________ cooking. (~에 흥미를 가지다)

M Yes, I want to be a famous chef one day.

W Really? I want to be a TV show host. Maybe, I'll invite you to my show.

M Sounds great. I hope our ________ ________ ________. (꿈이 이루어지다)

08 심정 파악

대화를 듣고, 여자의 심정으로 가장 적절한 것을 고르시오.

① relaxed ② sad
③ disappointed ④ frightened
⑤ shy

M Look over there! Isn't that David Shaw?

W What? Are you serious? It can't be!

M Yes, I'm sure it's him. ________ ________ ________ go say hi? You're a fan, right? (하는 게 어때?)

W Yeah, but I'm afraid he'll run away.

M Come on. A chance like this doesn't come often.

W I'd like to, but.... I'm not ready.

M Who knows? Maybe you could ________ ________ ________ with him. (사진을 찍다)

W You're right, but I'm scared.

09 대화 장소 파악

stay, room, view, service 등의 단어를 듣고 답을 유추한다.

대화를 듣고, 두 사람이 대화하는 장소로 가장 적절한 곳을 고르시오.

① 기차역
② 영화관
③ 호텔
④ 부동산 중개사무소
⑤ 관광안내소

M How did you like your stay, Madame? Was everything okay?

W Yes, thanks. It was a very pleasant stay.

M How was the room?

W Oh, the room was awesome. And it ________ ________ ________ ________. (경치가 좋았다.)

M I hope you're ________ ________ our service, too. (~에 만족하는)

W Hmm... Well, actually, it could be better...

M I'm sorry to hear that. Could you tell us more?

10 주제, 소재 파악

cat, vet 등의 단어를 힌트로 답을 찾는다.

대화를 듣고, 여자의 무엇에 관한 내용인지 가장 적절한 것을 고르시오.

① 건강 ② 동생
③ 어머니 ④ 장래희망
⑤ 반려동물

M Hyeri, what's wrong? You look down this morning.

W I think Bony is sick. She won't eat and ________ ________ ________. (계속 토하다)

M Bony is your cat, right? How long has she been like that?

W Yes. Since yesterday. My mom will ________ ________ ________ ________ ________, but I'm worried. (수의사에게 데려가다)

M Don't worry. She will be okay.

W I hope so.

11 특정 정보 파악 – 날짜

대화를 듣고, 아빠가 출장에서 돌아오는 요일을 고르시오.

① 화요일 ② 수요일
③ 월요일 ④ 토요일
⑤ 일요일

아빠가 출장을 떠난 날과 혼동하지 않도록 주의한다.

M Mom, when's Dad coming back from his business trip?

W He said it would be five days.

M When did he leave? Was it Tuesday or Wednesday?

W He ________ ________ ________. Why? What do you need him for?
(화요일에 떠났다.)

M I was wondering if we could ________ ________ ________ ________ on Sunday.
(야구 경기를 보다)

W He will be back before then. Let's all go together.

12 이유 파악

대화를 듣고, 여자가 내일 남자를 만날 수 없는 이유로 가장 적절한 것을 고르시오.

① 미리 통보를 받지 못해서
② 날짜를 잘못 알고 있어서
③ 축구 경기 구경을 가야 해서
④ 연극 관람을 가기로 해서
⑤ 연극 연습에 참가해야 해서

M Bye, Sunghee. See you at the soccer game tomorrow.

W Oh, sorry, I ________ ________ you. I can't make it.
(말하는 것을 잊었다)

M Really? Why not?

W You know there's a play competition next month, right?

M Yeah, I heard about it.

W I decided to ________ ________ ________ it, and we have our first practice tomorrow.
(~에 참여하다)

M Oh, I see. That's too bad I can't see you tomorrow, but good luck!

13 관계 파악

대화를 듣고, 두 사람의 관계로 가장 적절한 것을 고르시오.

① 교사 – 학생 ② 교사 – 학부모
③ 부모 – 자녀 ④ 가게 점원 – 손님
⑤ 변호사 – 고객

Susie가 학교 생활을 어떻게 하는지 묻고 답하는 대화에서 둘의 관계를 알 수 있다.

W Good afternoon, Mr. Smith. Can I come in?

M Yes, of course, Mrs. Kim. Please sit down.

W Thank you.

M So, how can I help you?

W I was wondering how Susie is doing in class. She doesn't talk much with me at home.

M Susie is doing well. She's ________ ________ ________, but she's a good student.
(조금 조용한)

W I ________ ________ ________ to hear that.
(매우 안심하다)

14 지도, 위치 파악

대화를 듣고, 여자가 가려고 하는 장소를 고르시오.

Library | Post office | Flower Shop | Book Store | ① | ③ | ⑤
Police Station | Bank | ② | ④ | Clothes Shop | Fire Station
You're Here

W Excuse me. Do you know where the National Art Gallery is?

M Yes, you should turn right ________ ________ ________ ________.
(다음 모퉁이에서)

W Turn right over there?

M Yes, and ________ ________ until you see the fire station on your right.
(계속 걸어라)

W Okay. Then?

M It's across from it. And it is also next to a flower shop.

W Thank you very much!

15 부탁하는 일 파악

부탁의 표현인 'Can you~?'를 집중하며 듣는다.

대화를 듣고, 여자가 남자에게 부탁한 일로 가장 적절한 것을 고르시오.

① 숙제 마저 끝내기 ② 바깥 활동하기
③ 쓰레기 버리기 ④ 재활용품 모으기
⑤ 집안 청소하기

W Tony, what are you doing?

B I just finished my homework. Can I go out to meet Insu?

W Sure, if you finished your homework. But can you ________ ________ ________ ________ first? (쓰레기를 버리다)

B Okay. Should I take out these plastic bottles for recycling?

W No, that's fine. I will take them out later with other things.

B Just this, then. Okay, see you later, Mom!

W ________ ________! (재미있게 놀아)

16 제안한 일 파악

제안의 표현인 'Would you~?'를 집중하며 듣는다.

대화를 듣고, 여자가 남자에게 제안한 것으로 가장 적절한 것을 고르시오.

① 세차 도와주기
② 아버지에게 부탁하기
③ 자전거 타러 가기
④ 공원에 소풍가기
⑤ 자전거 타는 법 가르쳐주기

W Tom, what are you doing for the long weekend?

M I promised my dad to ________ ________ ________ ________ ________ on Saturday or Sunday. But that's it. (그가 세차하는 것을 돕다)

W What about on Monday?

M Nothing much. I was thinking about ________ ________ ________. (자전거를 타는 것)

W Would you join us then? We're going to Main Park for a picnic.

M That sounds good. I could ride my bike there, too!

17 할 일 파악

대화를 듣고, 여자가 대화 직후에 할 일로 가장 적절한 것을 고르시오.

① 시험 공부하기
② 공책 가지러 가기
③ 수업내용 가르쳐주기
④ 복사하러 가기
⑤ 남자 기다리기

W Minoo, you're back. I heard you were sick yesterday. Are you better now?

M Yes, I am. Thank you. ________ ________ ________ ________? (내가 놓친 것 없어?)

W Well, we're going to have a test tomorrow in history.

M What? But I don't have my notes.

W I can ________ ________ ________ ________, if you want. (너에게 내 공책을 빌려주다)

M That would be great. I'll make a copy and give it right back.

W Okay, wait here and I'll get it.

18 직업 파악

대화를 듣고, 여자의 직업으로 가장 적절한 것을 고르시오.

① 우체국 직원 ② 집배원
③ 항공사 직원 ④ 공항 체크인 직원
⑤ 호텔 직원

화를 듣고, 두 사람이 대화하는 장소로 가장 적절한 것을 고르시오.

① 여행사 ② 공항
③ 우체국 ④ 건물 관리사무소
⑤ 호텔

package, by air, express mail 등을 듣고 답을 찾는다.

M Excuse me, can I send this package to Japan?

W Sure, there are two ways by air. The express mail _________ _________ _________ (이틀이 걸리다), and it costs $30.

M Oh, it's too expensive. What's the other way?

W It's called economy air. It's $15, and it takes four days.

M Is there anything cheaper?

W Yeah, you can _________ _________ _________ _________ (배로 보내다), but it can take up to two weeks.

19 알맞은 응답 찾기

[19~20] 대화를 듣고, 여자의 마지막 말에 이어질 남자의 응답으로 가장 적절한 것을 고르시오.

Man: ____________________

① It was really nice.
② I didn't go there.
③ Let's go together.
④ I will visit next week.
⑤ That's a great idea.

M What are you doing, Kate?

W I'm looking at this picture. It won the school photo contest this year.

M Can I _________ _________ _________ (한 번 보다), too?

W Sure. Isn't it really nice? I like this green field a lot.

M Yes, it's nice. And actually, I _________ _________ _________ (거기 가 봤다).

W Really? What was it like?

M ____________________

20 알맞은 응답 찾기

Man: ____________________

① I'm going there this week.
② Sure, I'd like to see that movie.
③ No, I don't want to go alone.
④ Oh, that's too bad.
⑤ Sure, that'd be great.

M You look very nice, Emily. I like your new jeans.

W Thank you. I bought these when I went shopping with my mom last weekend.

M Really? Where did you buy them?

W At the new mall downtown. _________ _________ _________ _________ (거기 가 본 적 있어?)?

M No, not yet. I haven't had a chance.

W It's _________ _________ _________ _________ (꽤 멋진 곳). Would you like to go with me someday?

M ____________________

답안 체크지

실전처럼 문항별 정답을 마킹해서 확인하세요.
틀린 문제는 다시 듣고 확인하세요.
*디딤돌 홈페이지에서 다운로드 받아 교재 안에 수록된 모든 회차의 모의고사 답안 마킹에 활용하세요.

......회	
번호	답 란
01	① ② ③ ④ ⑤
02	① ② ③ ④ ⑤
03	① ② ③ ④ ⑤
04	① ② ③ ④ ⑤
05	① ② ③ ④ ⑤
06	① ② ③ ④ ⑤
07	① ② ③ ④ ⑤
08	① ② ③ ④ ⑤
09	① ② ③ ④ ⑤
10	① ② ③ ④ ⑤
11	① ② ③ ④ ⑤
12	① ② ③ ④ ⑤
13	① ② ③ ④ ⑤
14	① ② ③ ④ ⑤
15	① ② ③ ④ ⑤
16	① ② ③ ④ ⑤
17	① ② ③ ④ ⑤
18	① ② ③ ④ ⑤
19	① ② ③ ④ ⑤
20	① ② ③ ④ ⑤
plus	① ② ③ ④ ⑤
plus	① ② ③ ④ ⑤

......회	
번호	답 란
01	① ② ③ ④ ⑤
02	① ② ③ ④ ⑤
03	① ② ③ ④ ⑤
04	① ② ③ ④ ⑤
05	① ② ③ ④ ⑤
06	① ② ③ ④ ⑤
07	① ② ③ ④ ⑤
08	① ② ③ ④ ⑤
09	① ② ③ ④ ⑤
10	① ② ③ ④ ⑤
11	① ② ③ ④ ⑤
12	① ② ③ ④ ⑤
13	① ② ③ ④ ⑤
14	① ② ③ ④ ⑤
15	① ② ③ ④ ⑤
16	① ② ③ ④ ⑤
17	① ② ③ ④ ⑤
18	① ② ③ ④ ⑤
19	① ② ③ ④ ⑤
20	① ② ③ ④ ⑤
plus	① ② ③ ④ ⑤
plus	① ② ③ ④ ⑤

......회	
번호	답 란
01	① ② ③ ④ ⑤
02	① ② ③ ④ ⑤
03	① ② ③ ④ ⑤
04	① ② ③ ④ ⑤
05	① ② ③ ④ ⑤
06	① ② ③ ④ ⑤
07	① ② ③ ④ ⑤
08	① ② ③ ④ ⑤
09	① ② ③ ④ ⑤
10	① ② ③ ④ ⑤
11	① ② ③ ④ ⑤
12	① ② ③ ④ ⑤
13	① ② ③ ④ ⑤
14	① ② ③ ④ ⑤
15	① ② ③ ④ ⑤
16	① ② ③ ④ ⑤
17	① ② ③ ④ ⑤
18	① ② ③ ④ ⑤
19	① ② ③ ④ ⑤
20	① ② ③ ④ ⑤
plus	① ② ③ ④ ⑤
plus	① ② ③ ④ ⑤

......회	
번호	답 란
01	① ② ③ ④ ⑤
02	① ② ③ ④ ⑤
03	① ② ③ ④ ⑤
04	① ② ③ ④ ⑤
05	① ② ③ ④ ⑤
06	① ② ③ ④ ⑤
07	① ② ③ ④ ⑤
08	① ② ③ ④ ⑤
09	① ② ③ ④ ⑤
10	① ② ③ ④ ⑤
11	① ② ③ ④ ⑤
12	① ② ③ ④ ⑤
13	① ② ③ ④ ⑤
14	① ② ③ ④ ⑤
15	① ② ③ ④ ⑤
16	① ② ③ ④ ⑤
17	① ② ③ ④ ⑤
18	① ② ③ ④ ⑤
19	① ② ③ ④ ⑤
20	① ② ③ ④ ⑤
plus	① ② ③ ④ ⑤
plus	① ② ③ ④ ⑤

......회	
번호	답 란
01	① ② ③ ④ ⑤
02	① ② ③ ④ ⑤
03	① ② ③ ④ ⑤
04	① ② ③ ④ ⑤
05	① ② ③ ④ ⑤
06	① ② ③ ④ ⑤
07	① ② ③ ④ ⑤
08	① ② ③ ④ ⑤
09	① ② ③ ④ ⑤
10	① ② ③ ④ ⑤
11	① ② ③ ④ ⑤
12	① ② ③ ④ ⑤
13	① ② ③ ④ ⑤
14	① ② ③ ④ ⑤
15	① ② ③ ④ ⑤
16	① ② ③ ④ ⑤
17	① ② ③ ④ ⑤
18	① ② ③ ④ ⑤
19	① ② ③ ④ ⑤
20	① ② ③ ④ ⑤
plus	① ② ③ ④ ⑤
plus	① ② ③ ④ ⑤

......회	
번호	답 란
01	① ② ③ ④ ⑤
02	① ② ③ ④ ⑤
03	① ② ③ ④ ⑤
04	① ② ③ ④ ⑤
05	① ② ③ ④ ⑤
06	① ② ③ ④ ⑤
07	① ② ③ ④ ⑤
08	① ② ③ ④ ⑤
09	① ② ③ ④ ⑤
10	① ② ③ ④ ⑤
11	① ② ③ ④ ⑤
12	① ② ③ ④ ⑤
13	① ② ③ ④ ⑤
14	① ② ③ ④ ⑤
15	① ② ③ ④ ⑤
16	① ② ③ ④ ⑤
17	① ② ③ ④ ⑤
18	① ② ③ ④ ⑤
19	① ② ③ ④ ⑤
20	① ② ③ ④ ⑤
plus	① ② ③ ④ ⑤
plus	① ② ③ ④ ⑤

______회	
번호	답 란
01	① ② ③ ④ ⑤
02	① ② ③ ④ ⑤
03	① ② ③ ④ ⑤
04	① ② ③ ④ ⑤
05	① ② ③ ④ ⑤
06	① ② ③ ④ ⑤
07	① ② ③ ④ ⑤
08	① ② ③ ④ ⑤
09	① ② ③ ④ ⑤
10	① ② ③ ④ ⑤
11	① ② ③ ④ ⑤
12	① ② ③ ④ ⑤
13	① ② ③ ④ ⑤
14	① ② ③ ④ ⑤
15	① ② ③ ④ ⑤
16	① ② ③ ④ ⑤
17	① ② ③ ④ ⑤
18	① ② ③ ④ ⑤
19	① ② ③ ④ ⑤
20	① ② ③ ④ ⑤
plus	① ② ③ ④ ⑤
plus	① ② ③ ④ ⑤

______회	
번호	답 란
01	① ② ③ ④ ⑤
02	① ② ③ ④ ⑤
03	① ② ③ ④ ⑤
04	① ② ③ ④ ⑤
05	① ② ③ ④ ⑤
06	① ② ③ ④ ⑤
07	① ② ③ ④ ⑤
08	① ② ③ ④ ⑤
09	① ② ③ ④ ⑤
10	① ② ③ ④ ⑤
11	① ② ③ ④ ⑤
12	① ② ③ ④ ⑤
13	① ② ③ ④ ⑤
14	① ② ③ ④ ⑤
15	① ② ③ ④ ⑤
16	① ② ③ ④ ⑤
17	① ② ③ ④ ⑤
18	① ② ③ ④ ⑤
19	① ② ③ ④ ⑤
20	① ② ③ ④ ⑤
plus	① ② ③ ④ ⑤
plus	① ② ③ ④ ⑤

______회	
번호	답 란
01	① ② ③ ④ ⑤
02	① ② ③ ④ ⑤
03	① ② ③ ④ ⑤
04	① ② ③ ④ ⑤
05	① ② ③ ④ ⑤
06	① ② ③ ④ ⑤
07	① ② ③ ④ ⑤
08	① ② ③ ④ ⑤
09	① ② ③ ④ ⑤
10	① ② ③ ④ ⑤
11	① ② ③ ④ ⑤
12	① ② ③ ④ ⑤
13	① ② ③ ④ ⑤
14	① ② ③ ④ ⑤
15	① ② ③ ④ ⑤
16	① ② ③ ④ ⑤
17	① ② ③ ④ ⑤
18	① ② ③ ④ ⑤
19	① ② ③ ④ ⑤
20	① ② ③ ④ ⑤
plus	① ② ③ ④ ⑤
plus	① ② ③ ④ ⑤

______회	
번호	답 란
01	① ② ③ ④ ⑤
02	① ② ③ ④ ⑤
03	① ② ③ ④ ⑤
04	① ② ③ ④ ⑤
05	① ② ③ ④ ⑤
06	① ② ③ ④ ⑤
07	① ② ③ ④ ⑤
08	① ② ③ ④ ⑤
09	① ② ③ ④ ⑤
10	① ② ③ ④ ⑤
11	① ② ③ ④ ⑤
12	① ② ③ ④ ⑤
13	① ② ③ ④ ⑤
14	① ② ③ ④ ⑤
15	① ② ③ ④ ⑤
16	① ② ③ ④ ⑤
17	① ② ③ ④ ⑤
18	① ② ③ ④ ⑤
19	① ② ③ ④ ⑤
20	① ② ③ ④ ⑤
plus	① ② ③ ④ ⑤
plus	① ② ③ ④ ⑤

______회	
번호	답 란
01	① ② ③ ④ ⑤
02	① ② ③ ④ ⑤
03	① ② ③ ④ ⑤
04	① ② ③ ④ ⑤
05	① ② ③ ④ ⑤
06	① ② ③ ④ ⑤
07	① ② ③ ④ ⑤
08	① ② ③ ④ ⑤
09	① ② ③ ④ ⑤
10	① ② ③ ④ ⑤
11	① ② ③ ④ ⑤
12	① ② ③ ④ ⑤
13	① ② ③ ④ ⑤
14	① ② ③ ④ ⑤
15	① ② ③ ④ ⑤
16	① ② ③ ④ ⑤
17	① ② ③ ④ ⑤
18	① ② ③ ④ ⑤
19	① ② ③ ④ ⑤
20	① ② ③ ④ ⑤
plus	① ② ③ ④ ⑤
plus	① ② ③ ④ ⑤

______회	
번호	답 란
01	① ② ③ ④ ⑤
02	① ② ③ ④ ⑤
03	① ② ③ ④ ⑤
04	① ② ③ ④ ⑤
05	① ② ③ ④ ⑤
06	① ② ③ ④ ⑤
07	① ② ③ ④ ⑤
08	① ② ③ ④ ⑤
09	① ② ③ ④ ⑤
10	① ② ③ ④ ⑤
11	① ② ③ ④ ⑤
12	① ② ③ ④ ⑤
13	① ② ③ ④ ⑤
14	① ② ③ ④ ⑤
15	① ② ③ ④ ⑤
16	① ② ③ ④ ⑤
17	① ② ③ ④ ⑤
18	① ② ③ ④ ⑤
19	① ② ③ ④ ⑤
20	① ② ③ ④ ⑤
plus	① ② ③ ④ ⑤
plus	① ② ③ ④ ⑤

회

번호	답 란
01	① ② ③ ④ ⑤
02	① ② ③ ④ ⑤
03	① ② ③ ④ ⑤
04	① ② ③ ④ ⑤
05	① ② ③ ④ ⑤
06	① ② ③ ④ ⑤
07	① ② ③ ④ ⑤
08	① ② ③ ④ ⑤
09	① ② ③ ④ ⑤
10	① ② ③ ④ ⑤
11	① ② ③ ④ ⑤
12	① ② ③ ④ ⑤
13	① ② ③ ④ ⑤
14	① ② ③ ④ ⑤
15	① ② ③ ④ ⑤
16	① ② ③ ④ ⑤
17	① ② ③ ④ ⑤
18	① ② ③ ④ ⑤
19	① ② ③ ④ ⑤
20	① ② ③ ④ ⑤
plus	① ② ③ ④ ⑤
plus	① ② ③ ④ ⑤

회

번호	답 란
01	① ② ③ ④ ⑤
02	① ② ③ ④ ⑤
03	① ② ③ ④ ⑤
04	① ② ③ ④ ⑤
05	① ② ③ ④ ⑤
06	① ② ③ ④ ⑤
07	① ② ③ ④ ⑤
08	① ② ③ ④ ⑤
09	① ② ③ ④ ⑤
10	① ② ③ ④ ⑤
11	① ② ③ ④ ⑤
12	① ② ③ ④ ⑤
13	① ② ③ ④ ⑤
14	① ② ③ ④ ⑤
15	① ② ③ ④ ⑤
16	① ② ③ ④ ⑤
17	① ② ③ ④ ⑤
18	① ② ③ ④ ⑤
19	① ② ③ ④ ⑤
20	① ② ③ ④ ⑤
plus	① ② ③ ④ ⑤
plus	① ② ③ ④ ⑤

회

번호	답 란
01	① ② ③ ④ ⑤
02	① ② ③ ④ ⑤
03	① ② ③ ④ ⑤
04	① ② ③ ④ ⑤
05	① ② ③ ④ ⑤
06	① ② ③ ④ ⑤
07	① ② ③ ④ ⑤
08	① ② ③ ④ ⑤
09	① ② ③ ④ ⑤
10	① ② ③ ④ ⑤
11	① ② ③ ④ ⑤
12	① ② ③ ④ ⑤
13	① ② ③ ④ ⑤
14	① ② ③ ④ ⑤
15	① ② ③ ④ ⑤
16	① ② ③ ④ ⑤
17	① ② ③ ④ ⑤
18	① ② ③ ④ ⑤
19	① ② ③ ④ ⑤
20	① ② ③ ④ ⑤
plus	① ② ③ ④ ⑤
plus	① ② ③ ④ ⑤

중학영어듣기 만점 솔루션

정답과 해설

영어듣기능력 진단평가 01 회

01 ③	02 ②	03 ①	04 ②	05 ④
06 ④	07 ⑤	08 ①	09 ④	10 ③
11 ②	12 ⑤	13 ③	14 ①	15 ①
16 ⑤	17 ③	18 ②	19 ⑤	20 ④

01 ③

W I have four legs and a long tail. I have thick skin. I also have very strong and sharp teeth. I can live both in the water and on the ground. What am I?

W 나는 네 개의 다리와 하나의 긴 꼬리를 가졌어요. 나는 두꺼운 피부를 가지고 있어요. 나는 또 아주 강하고 날카로운 이빨을 가지고 있습니다. 나는 물 속에서도 살 수 있고 땅 위에서도 살 수 있어요. 나는 무엇일까요?

02 ②

W May I help you?
M Yes. I'd like to buy a pair of slippers for my sister.
W Okay. How about these ones with bears on them?
M Not bad. But do you have any others?
W Hmm... We have slippers with ribbons.
M The ones with ribbons are good. I'll take them.

W 도와드릴까요?
M 네, 여동생을 위한 슬리퍼 한 켤레를 사고 싶습니다.
W 알겠습니다. 슬리퍼 위에 곰이 있는 건 어떠세요?
M 나쁘지 않네요. 하지만 다른 것도 있나요?
W 흠... 리본이 달린 슬리퍼도 있습니다.
M 리본이 들린 것이 좋겠네요. 그걸로 하겠습니다.

03 ①

M Good morning! Here is today's world weather forecast. In Tokyo, there will be rain all day long. In Bangkok, it'll be sunny. Paris will be windy and very cold. London will be very cloudy.

M 안녕하세요! 오늘의 세계 일기 예보입니다. 도쿄는 하루 종일 비가 내리겠습니다. 방콕은 맑겠습니다. 파리는 바람이 불고 매우 춥겠습니다. 런던은 매우 흐리겠습니다.

04 ②

M Jimin, look at these roses here.
W Wow! They're really beautiful.
M There are so many kinds of flowers in this park.
W I like those yellow tulips.
M Me, too. Let's take some photos there.
W Sure. That's a good idea.

M 지민, 여기 장미들을 봐.
W 와! 정말 아름답다.
M 이 공원에 아주 많은 종류의 꽃들이 있어.
W 저 노란색 튤립이 좋아.
M 나도. 거기서 사진을 좀 찍자.
M 물론이야. 좋은 생각이야.

05 ④

W Hi, everyone. I'd like to introduce my best friend, Sumi, to you. She goes to Brown Middle School. She has long curly hair. Her hobby is making things with paper. She is kind, so many people like her.

W 모두, 안녕. 내 가장 친한 친구 수미를 모두에게 소개하고 싶어. 그녀는 브라운 중학교에 다니고 있어. 그녀는 긴 곱슬머리를 가지고 있어. 그녀의 취미는 종이로 물건을 만드는 거야. 그녀는 친절해서 많은 사람들이 그녀를 좋아해.

06 ④

W Sam, did you buy a gift for Mother's Day?
M No. What about you?
W Not yet. Why don't we go shopping together?
M Okay. Let's meet tomorrow morning at 10.
W Um... That's a little early for me. Can we meet at 10:30 a.m.?
M No problem. See you tomorrow.

W 샘, 어머니의 날을 위한 선물 샀니?
M 아니. 너는?
W 아직. 같이 사러 가는 거 어때?
M 좋아. 내일 오전 10시에 만나자.
W 음... 나에게 좀 이른 시간인데. 10시 30분에 볼 수 있을까?
M 문제 없어. 내일 보자.

07 ⑤

W Stuart, you look a little tired.
M Yeah. I practiced tennis for 4 hours yesterday.
W Wasn't it hard?
M It was not easy, but I love tennis.
W Oh, I didn't know that.
M I actually want to become a famous tennis player.
W I hope your dream comes true.

W 스튜어트, 너 조금 피곤해 보인다.
M 응. 어제 테니스를 4시간 연습했어.
W 어렵지 않았니?
M 쉽지 않았지만, 난 테니스를 좋아해.
W 아, 몰랐어.

M 난 사실 유명한 테니스 선수가 되고 싶어.
W 네 꿈이 이루어지길 바란다.

08 ①

M Mom, it's finally picnic day this Friday!
W Great. I know you waited a long time for it. Do you need to bring lunch?
M Yes. Can you make gimbap for me? I really want to have it.
W Of course.
M Wow, I can't wait!

M 엄마, 이번주 금요일 드디어 소풍이에요!
W 잘됐네. 네가 오랫동안 기다렸다는 걸 알고 있어. 점심을 가져가야 하니?
M 네. 저를 위해 김밥을 만들어 주실 수 있나요? 진짜 먹고 싶어요.
W 물론이지.
M 와, 못 기다리겠어요!

09 ④

W Eric, let's go to the concert now.
M Okay. *[Pause]* Wait!
W What's wrong?
M I left my jacket in the restaurant.
W Are you sure?
M I think so. The tickets are in the jacket.
W Oh, no! What should we do?
M Wait here, and I'll go back to the restaurant right now.

W 에릭, 지금 콘서트에 가자.
M 좋아. *[멈춤]* 잠깐!
W 무슨 일이야?
M 식당에다 내 재킷을 두고 왔어.
W 확실해?
M 그런 거 같아. 표가 재킷 안에 있는데.
W 안 돼! 어떻게 해야 하지?
M 여기서 기다려, 내가 당장 식당에 가 볼게.

10 ③

W Nick, what are you doing?
M I'm looking on the Internet for volunteer work to do.
W What kind of work do you want to do?
M I want to play the violin for people.
W Hmm... Oh, look! You can play it for the patients at Nara Hospital.
M Excellent!

W 닉, 뭐 해?
M 인터넷으로 봉사활동을 찾고 있어.
W 네가 하고 싶은 일이 어떤 일인데?
M 사람들을 위해 바이올린을 연주하고 싶어
W 흠... 아, 봐! 나라 병원에서 환자들을 위해 바이올린을 연주할 수 있어.
M 잘됐다!

11 ②

M See you later, Mom. I'm going to the museum.
W How are you getting there, Joe?
M I'll walk there. It's not far.
W But it's raining outside. I'll take you by car.
M Thanks. That will be great.

M 나중에 봐요, 엄마. 저 박물관에 갈 거예요.
W 거기는 어떻게 갈 거니, 조?
M 걸어갈 거예요. 멀지 않아요.
W 그래도 밖에 비가 오고 있어. 차로 데려다줄게.
M 고마워요. 잘 됐네요.

12 ⑤

W Chris, can you do me a favor?
M What is it, Amy?
W Could you help me with my math homework at lunch time?
M I'd love to, but I can't. I have a club meeting in the art room then.
W Oh, I see.
M Why don't you ask Betty?
W Okay, I will. Thanks.

W 크리스, 부탁 좀 해도 될까?
M 무슨 일이야, 에이미?
W 점심시간에 내 수학 숙제를 도와줄 수 있니?
M 그러고 싶은데, 그럴 수 없어. 그땐 미술실에서 동아리 모임이 있어.
W 아, 알았어.
M 베티한테 부탁하는 거 어때?
W 알겠어, 그럴게. 고마워.

13 ③

M Hi, Dr. Yoon. I'm James King from ABA News.
W Good afternoon.
M Could you tell us about your new invention?
W I invented a cleaning robot to help busy people.
M I'm sure many people will love it.
W I hope this saves lots of time.
M Great. Thanks for the interview.

M 안녕하세요, 윤 박사님. 저는 ABA 뉴스의 제임스 킹입니다.
W 안녕하세요.
M 선생님의 새로운 발명에 대해 말씀해 주시겠어요?
W 저는 바쁜 사람들을 돕기 위한 청소 로봇을 발명했습니다.
M 많은 사람들이 좋아할 것이라 확신해요.
W 이것이 많은 시간을 절약하길 바랍니다.
M 굉장하네요. 인터뷰 감사드립니다.

14 ①

W Hi, Daniel. What's wrong?
M My cell phone is broken.
W Really? I know a good service center.
M Great! How can I get there?
W Go straight two blocks and turn left.
M Okay.
W It'll be on your right between the library and the shoe store.
M Oh, I see. Thanks.

W 안녕, 다니엘. 무슨 일이니?
M 내 휴대 전화가 망가졌어.
W 진짜? 나 좋은 서비스 센터를 알고 있어.
M 잘됐다! 거기 어떻게 가?
W 두 블록 쭉 간 다음에 왼쪽으로 꺾어.
M 알겠어.
W 네 오른편에 도서관이랑 신발 가게 사이에 있을 거야.
M 아, 알겠어. 고마워.

15 ①

M Carol, do you remember the plans for Tina's birthday?
W You mean the surprise party?
M Yes. Ben will bring a cake and I'll get some drinks.
W Then what do I need to bring?
M Can you buy some flowers for her?
W Sure. No problem.

M 캐롤, 티나의 생일을 위한 계획 기억해?
W 깜짝 파티 말하는 거야?
M 응. 벤이 케이크를 가져오고 내가 음료를 살 거야.
W 그럼 나는 무엇을 가져갈까?
M 그녀를 위해 꽃을 좀 살 수 있어?
W 물론. 문제 없어.

16 ⑤

M Wow! Mina, you're really good at dancing.
W Thank you for saying so.
M Where did you learn to dance?
W I joined a dancing club last year.
M Cool! I want to learn to dance, too.
W Then why don't you join our club?

M 와! 미나, 너 진짜 춤 잘 춘다.
W 그렇게 말해주니 고마워.
M 춤은 어디서 배웠어?
W 작년에 댄스 클럽에 가입했어.
M 멋지다! 나도 춤 추는 법을 배우고 싶어.
W 그럼 우리 클럽에 가입할래?

17 ③

M Mom, look! They are selling fruits over there.
W Yeah. Let's go get some.
M Hmm... These apples look delicious.
W Yeah. But we have apples at home.
M Then how about those strawberries?
W Okay. They look fresh. Let's buy some.

M 엄마, 봐요! 저기서 과일을 팔고있어요.
W 그래. 가서 좀 사자.
M 흠... 이 사과들은 맛있어 보이네요.
W 그래. 하지만 집에 사과가 있어.
M 그럼 저 딸기들은 어때요?
W 그래. 신선해 보이네. 좀 사자.

18 ②

M Good evening, ma'am. How did you like your steak?
W It was delicious, thank you.
M Great. Would you like some dessert?
W Yes. Could you show me the menu?
M Certainly. Here you are.
W Um... I'll have the chocolate cake, please.
M Sure. I'll bring it now.

M 안녕하세요. 스테이크 맛이 어떠셨나요?
W 맛있었어요. 고마워요.
M 잘됐네요. 디저트를 드시겠습니까?
W 네. 메뉴를 좀 보여 주시겠어요?
M 당연하죠. 여기 있습니다.
W 음... 초콜릿 케이크 부탁해요.
M 물론이죠. 곧 가져오겠습니다.

19 ⑤

W Hi, Dave. What are you doing here?
M I'm waiting for the bus to go home.
W But you left school early. Why are you still here?
M The bus didn't come yet.
W Really? Why don't you just walk home?
M I want to, but I hurt my foot yesterday.
W Oh, I'm sorry to hear that.

W 안녕, 데이브. 여기서 뭐하니?
M 집에 가려고 버스를 기다리고 있어.
W 그런데 너 학교에서 일찍 나왔잖아. 왜 아직도 여기에 있어?
M 버스가 아직도 안 왔어.
W 진짜? 그냥 집에 걸어가는 게 어때?
M 그러고 싶은데, 어제 다리를 다쳤어.
W 아, 안됐다.

① 만나서 반가워
② 그러고 싶은데, 그럴 수 없어.
③ 아니, 갖고 있지 않아.
④ 조언 고마워.

20 ④

W Hi, Suho. What will you do this summer vacation?
M I'm going to travel with my family.
W That's wonderful! Where will you go?
M We'll visit Ulleungdo.
W Oh, I went there last year.
M Really? What did you do in Ulleungdo?
W I had some delicious seafood.

W 안녕, 수호. 이번 여름 방학 때 뭐 할 거야?
M 가족과 여행을 갈 거야.
W 멋지다! 어디를 갈 거니?
M 울릉도에 방문할 거야.
W 아, 나 작년에 거기 갔었어.
M 진짜? 울릉도에서 뭐 했어?
W 맛있는 해산물을 먹었어.

① 난 14살이야.
② 나는 거기 기차를 타고 갈 거야.
③ 난 숙제를 하고 있어.
⑤ 수영 캠프에 가입할 거야.

영어듣기능력 진단평가 02회

01 ④	02 ②	03 ③	04 ①	05 ③
06 ③	07 ②	08 ⑤	09 ②	10 ④
11 ⑤	12 ⑤	13 ①	14 ④	15 ①
16 ②	17 ④	18 ⑤	19 ⑤	20 ④

01 ④

M Many people use this every day. You can do many things with this. You can watch video clips, take pictures, and play games on this. We can talk on this. Some people use this too much. We need to use this wisely.

M 많은 사람들이 매일 이것을 사용합니다. 여러분은 이것으로 많은 것을 할 수 있습니다. 여러분은 이것으로 비디오를 보고, 사진을 찍고, 게임을 할 수 있습니다. 우리는 이것에 대고 말을 할 수 있습니다. 몇몇 사람들은 이것을 너무 많이 사용합니다. 우리는 이것을 현명하게 사용할 필요가 있습니다.

02 ②

W Dad, did you see my blanket? I can't find it.
M What does it look like, Amy?
W It has a dog on it.
M Does it have anything else?
W It also has my name under the dog.
M Okay. Let's find it together.

W 아빠, 제 담요 봤어요? 찾을 수가 없네요.
M 어떻게 생겼니, Amy?
W 강아지가 그려져 있어요.
M 다른 건 없니?
W 강아지 밑에 제 이름이 있어요.
M 알겠다. 같이 찾아보자.

03 ③

W Here is the weather report for today and this weekend. It will rain all day long today. It will rain until Saturday. But, the air will be cleaner after the rain. On Sunday it will be sunny. You can go out and enjoy the sunshine.

W 오늘과 이번주말을 위한 일기 예보입니다. 오늘은 하루 종일 비가 오겠습니다. 비는 토요일까지 오겠습니다. 하지만 비가 내린 후 공기가 맑아지겠습니다. 일요일에는 맑겠습니다. 여러분들은 나가서 햇빛을 즐기실 수 있습니다.

04 ①

M Jane, who is dancing in this video?

W It's my friend. He was in a Hip-hop dance contest.
M Wow! He is a great dancer.
W Yes. He won the first prize at the dance contest.
M Why don't we invite him to our school festival?

M Jane, 이 비디오에서 춤 추는 사람 누구야?
W 내 친구야. 그는 힙합 댄스 대회에 나갔었어.
M 와! 진짜 춤 잘 춘다.
W 맞아. 그는 댄스 대회에서 1등상을 받았어.
M 그를 우리 학교 축제에 초대 하는 거 어때?

05 ③

M Let me tell you about our club activities. We read many kinds of books and talk about them. We make book posters, too. Once a month, our club has a street campaign for reading. We also read books to sick children in hospitals twice a year.

M 우리 동아리 활동을 말해 줄게. 우리는 많은 종류의 책을 읽고 그것에 대해 이야기해. 우리는 책 포스터를 만들기도 해. 한 달에 한번, 우리 동아리는 독서를 위한 길거리 캠페인을 해. 우리는 또 일 년에 두 번 병원에서 아픈 아이들에게 책을 읽어줘.

06 ③

M Mina, will you attend any after-school programs?
W Sure. I'm going to take the yoga class.
M Really? Me, too. When should I sign up?
W Sign up starts at 4 o'clock this afternoon.
M Thanks. When does the yoga class start?
W It begins at 4:30 p.m. every Friday.

M Mina, 방과 후 프로그램에 참여할 거니?
W 물론이야. 요가 수업을 들을 거야.
M 진짜? 나도. 언제 등록해야 해?
W 등록은 오늘 오후 4시부터 시작이야.
M 고마워. 요가 수업은 언제 시작해?
W 매주 금요일 오후 4시 30분에 시작해.

07 ②

M Hi, Joan, I have musical tickets. Would you like to come?
W Sure, when is it?
M It's this Friday.
W Um... I have an important piano contest on Friday.
M Oh... I didn't know that.
W Yes, I need to practice for the contest.
M Right.
W I want to be a good pianist.

M 안녕, Joan, 나 음악회 표가 있어. 갈래?
W 물론이야. 언제야?
M 이번 주 금요일.
W 음... 나 금요일에 중요한 피아노 대회가 있어
M 아...몰랐어.
W 응, 대회를 위해 연습을 해야 해.
M 알겠어.
W 나 훌륭한 피아니스트가 되고 싶어.

08 ⑤

M I can't wait for the class field trip tomorrow!
W Me, too. Do you want to play games together?
M Yeah, let's play Catch the Tail.
W Good idea. And how about Hide and Seek?
M Sounds great! Tomorrow will be fun.

M 내일 현장 학습 빨리 가고 싶어!
W 나도. 같이 게임 할래?
M 좋아. 꼬리잡기 하자.
W 좋은 생각이야. 그리고 숨바꼭질하는 거 어때?
M 좋아! 내일 재미있겠다.

09 ②

W Hi, Mike. How are you doing?
M I'm doing very well. Thanks.
W I'd like to tell you some good news.
M What is it?
W Emma won the first prize in the speech contest.
M Great! I will call her to congratulate her right now.

W 안녕, Mike. 잘 지내고 있니?
M 잘 지내. 고마워.
W 좋은 소식을 말하고 싶어.
M 뭐야?
W Emma가 웅변 대회에서 1등을 했어.
M 잘됐다! 지금 당장 축하한다고 전화해야지.

10 ④

M I have something good to tell you.
W What is that?
M Our homeroom teacher is going to get married this Saturday.
W Wow, that's surprising! Where is the wedding?
M It's at the "Happy Wedding Hall".
W What time is the wedding?
M It's at 3 p.m.
W Why don't we go and sing for her at the wedding?

M 나 좋은 소식이 있어.
W 뭐야?
M 우리 담임 선생님이 이번 주 토요일에 결혼을 하신대.
W 와, 놀랍다! 어디서?
M "Happy Wedding Hall"에서 열릴 거야.
W 결혼식은 몇 시야?
M 오후 3시야.
W 결혼식장에서 선생님을 위해 우리 노래를 부르는 거 어때?

11 ⑤

W Junho, What time does the concert begin?
M It begins at 7:30.
W 7:30? I think we should leave home now.
M It's too early. It's not even 6 o'clock yet.
W But there are lots of cars on the road around this time of the day.
M Yeah, then why don't we go by subway?
W You're right. Let's take the subway.

W Junho, 콘서트 언제 시작이야?
M 7시 30분에 시작해.
W 7시 30분? 지금 집에서 나와야 할 거 같아.
M 너무 이른 시간이야. 아직 6시도 안됐어.
W 하지만 이 시간에는 도로에 차가 많아.
M 맞아, 그럼 지하철을 타고 갈까?
W 맞아. 지하철을 타자.

12 ⑤

W Excuse me. You can't ride your bike in the park today.
M Really? Why not?
W We are having a Kimchi festival here.
M Oh, sorry! That's why there are so many people.
W That's right. The festival will be held until this Friday.
M Oh, I see. I should find another place then.

W 실례합니다. 오늘 공원에서 자전거를 탈 수 없습니다.
M 진짜요? 왜요?
W 여기서 김치 축제가 열립니다.
M 아, 죄송해요! 그래서 사람이 이렇게 많았군요.
W 맞아요. 축제는 이번 주 금요일까지 열립니다.
M 아, 알겠어요. 그럼 다른 장소를 찾아야 하겠네요.

13 ①

W Why is it so hot in this room?
M We just came back from P.E class. We are still sweating.
W Please open the windows and let's begin the class.
M Okay, Ma'am.
W Move your desks into groups of four. Let's start our history project.

W 이 방 왜 이렇게 덥지?
M 체육 수업 후에 막 돌아왔어요. 우린 아직 땀이 나고 있어요.
W 창문 좀 열고 수업을 시작하자.
M 네, 선생님.
M 책상을 4명 그룹으로 만들렴. 역사 프로젝트를 시작하자.

14 ④

M What are you looking for, Katie?
W Uhm... I can't find my cell phone.
M I think I saw it next to the computer this morning.
W But it's not there.
M Then why don't you use my cell phone to call yours?
W That's a good idea. *[Pause] [Phone Rings]* Oh... It's under the chair.

M 무엇을 찾고 있니, Katie?
W 음... 내 휴대 전화를 찾을 수가 없어.
M 오늘 아침에 컴퓨터 옆에 있는 걸 본 거 같은데.
W 하지만 거기 없어.
M 그럼 내 휴대 전화로 네 휴대 전화에 전화해 보는 거 어때?
W 좋은 생각이다. *[멈춤] [전화벨이 울린다]* 아... 의자 밑에 있어.

15 ①

W Dennis, what are you doing with these blocks?
M I'm making a bear with them.
W Wow, there are so many different sizes and colors.
M Oops. I lost one. Can you find it for me?
W Sure. What does it look like?
M It's the small, yellow one for the ear.
W Okay. I'll have a look.

W Dennis, 이 블록들로 뭐하고 있어?
M 곰을 만들고 있어.
W 와, 정말 많은 크기와 색깔들이 있네.
M 아, 하나를 잃어버렸어. 찾아 줄래?
W 물론이야. 어떻게 생겼어?
M 찾고, 귀 부분의 노란색이야.
W 응, 찾아 볼게.

16 ②

M Guess what, Lisa? I'm visiting Busan this Saturday.
W Sounds exciting! What will you do there?
M I'll look around the city.
W Are you going to take the city tour bus?
M I want to, but it is more expensive than I thought.
W Hmm... How about finding discount coupons online?
M That's a good idea.

M 그거 알아, Lisa? 나 이번 주 토요일에 부산에 간다.
W 재미있겠다! 거기서 무엇을 할 거야?
M 도시를 구경할 거야.
W 도시 여행 버스를 탈 거니?
M 그러고 싶은데, 내가 생각한 거 보다 비싸더라.
W 흠... 온라인에서 할인 쿠폰을 찾아보는 거 어때?
M 좋은 생각이야.

17 ④

M Diane, do you have any plans this weekend?
W Nothing special. Why?
M My club will have a "Clean the Earth" campaign and we need some help.
W What can I do to help you?

M I plan to draw some posters on Saturday. Are you good at drawing?
W Yes, I am. Let's do it together.

M Diane, 이번 주말에 무슨 계획이 있니?
W 특별히 없어. 왜?
M 우리 동아리에서 "Clean the Earth" 캠페인을 하는데 도움이 필요해.
W 무엇을 해야 하니?
M 토요일에 포스터를 그릴까 하거든. 너 그림 잘 그리니?
W 응, 잘 그려. 같이 하자.

18 ⑤

M Wow, Sumin. What a lovely dress!
W Actually, my mom made it for me.
M Really? I like that style.
W Thanks.
M Does she work in fashion?
W Yes, she designs children's clothes.
M That sounds great!

M 와, Sumin. 드레스 예쁘다!
W 사실, 엄마가 나를 위해 만들어 주셨어.
M 진짜? 스타일이 마음에 들어.
W 고마워.
M 어머니가 패션일에 종사하시니?
W 응, 엄마는 아동복을 디자인 해.
M 멋지다!

19 ⑤

W Are you going to join a school club, Matt?
M Yes, I want to join the drum club, but I can't play drums.
W That's okay. You can learn about it in the club.
M What about you, Mina? Do you want to join a club?
W Yeah, I'm going to join the photo club. What do you think?
M That's a good idea.

W 학교 동아리에 가입할 거니, Matt?
M 응, 난 드럼 동아리에 가입하고 싶은데, 내가 드럼을 잘 못 쳐.
W 괜찮아. 동아리에서 배울 수 있어.
M 너는 어때, Mina? 동아리에 가입하고 싶니?
W 응, 나는 피아노 동아리에 가입할 거야. 어떻게 생각해?
M 좋은 생각이야.
① 공평하지 않아
② 내 잘못이야.
③ 저거 내 책이야.
④ 여기서 드실 건가요 가지고 가실 건가요?

20 ④

W Hey, Kyle. How was your vacation?
M Good, I had a great time. How about you?
W I took a trip to Daejeon with my family.
M Wow, that's nice. I practiced B-boy dancing.
W Really? Where did you practice?
M I practiced at a dance school.

W Kyle, 휴가 어떻게 보냈어?
M 좋았어. 좋은 시간을 보냈어. 너는 어때?
W 나는 가족과 대전에 여행을 갔어.
M 와, 좋다. 나는 비보이 춤 연습을 했어.
W 진짜? 어디서 연습 했어?
M 춤 학교에서 연습 했어.
① 응, 나도 춤 추는 거 좋아해.
② 아니, 나는 춤을 잘 못 춰.
③ 나는 춤에 관심이 없어.
⑤ 나는 춤 대회에 나가고 싶어.

영어듣기능력 진단평가 03회

01 ①	02 ③	03 ①	04 ②	05 ④
06 ⑤	07 ④	08 ④	09 ④	10 ⑤
11 ③	12 ④	13 ⑤	14 ②	15 ②
16 ③	17 ①	18 ⑤	19 ⑤	20 ③

01 ①

M You can find me in Korean traditional stories. I live deep in the mountains and woods. I am a large animal. I am a good hunter. I have black lines on my body. I am a member of the cat family. What am I?

M 여러분은 나를 한국 전래 동화에서 찾을 수 있습니다. 나는 산과 숲 속 깊은 곳에 삽니다. 나는 큰 동물입니다. 나는 훌륭한 사냥꾼입니다. 나는 몸에 검정 줄무늬가 있습니다. 나는 고양이과 동물입니다. 나는 무엇일까요?

02 ③

M Jina, tomorrow is my sister's birthday. What should I buy for her?
W What about socks?
M Good! She told me she needed some socks.
W I think your sister will like the ones with trees and stars.
M Okay, I'll get those.

M Jina, 내일 내 여동생 생일이야. 무엇을 사야 할까?
W 양말 어때?
M 좋아! 그녀가 나에게 양말이 필요하다고 말했어.
W 네 여동생은 나무와 별이 있는 양말을 좋아할 거야.
M 그래. 그걸로 사자.

03 ①

W Good morning. Here's the weather report. It's raining a lot now, but it's going to stop tonight. After today's rain, it will be sunny tomorrow. The sky will not be cloudy anymore. You can enjoy outdoor activities.

W 안녕하세요. 일기 예보입니다. 지금 비가 많이 내리고 있지만 오늘밤 그칠 것입니다. 오늘 비 이후에, 내일은 맑겠습니다. 하늘은 더 없이 맑겠습니다. 여러분은 야외 활동을 즐길 수 있습니다.

04 ②

W Dad, I need a new school bag.
M Why, Jimin? You have a nice one.
W It's too small for me now. Please buy me a bigger one.
M Okay, I'll buy it for you this weekend.

W 아빠, 나 새로운 학교 가방이 필요해요.
M 왜, Jimin? 좋은 가방 가지고 있잖아.
W 지금 저에게 너무 작아요. 더 큰 걸로 사주세요.
M 알겠다. 이번 주말에 하나 사줄게.

05 ④

M I'd like to introduce my mom to you. She teaches music at Daehan Middle School. Mom goes to work early in the morning and comes back home at 6 p.m. She has short black hair and wears glasses. Her hobby is playing board games.

M 우리 엄마를 소개하겠습니다. 엄마는 대한중학교에서 음악을 가르치십니다. 엄마는 아침 일찍 출근하시고 6시에 집에 오십니다. 엄마는 짧은 검정 머리이고 안경을 쓰십니다. 그녀의 취미는 보드 게임입니다.

06 ⑤

[Cellphone rings.]
M Hello, Jessica!
W Hey, Sam! Where are you?
M I'm on my way to the concert hall now.
W I'm going there, too. But I will be a little late.
M No worries. It's 4 o'clock now.
W Then, let's meet at 4:30 in front of the ticket box.
M Okay.

[휴대 전화가 울린다.]
M 여보세요, Jessica!
W 어, Sam! 어디야?
M 지금 콘서트장에 가고 있어.
W 나도 가고 있어. 그런데 조금 늦을 거 같아.
M 걱정 마. 지금 4시야.
W 그럼, 4시 30분에 매표소 앞에서 보자.
M 그래.

07 ④

M Look at the cute dog. Do you like dogs, Emily?
W Yes, I love dogs. What about you?
M I like dogs very much.
W Do you like cats, too?
M Yes, I love all animals. So I want to be an animal doctor.
W I'm sure you will be a good animal doctor.

M 귀여운 개 좀 봐. 개를 좋아하니, Emily?
W 응, 개를 좋아해. 너는 어때?
M 나는 개를 아주 좋아해.
W 고양이도 좋아하니?
M 응, 난 모든 동물들을 사랑해. 그래서 나는 수의사가 되고 싶어.
W 네가 훌륭한 수의사가 될 거라고 확신해.

08 ④

W What's wrong, Mike?
M My mom told me to walk the dog yesterday.
W Then, what happened?
M When I talked with my friend, my dog ran away.
W Oh, no! Did you find your dog?
M No, I couldn't find it anywhere. What shall I do?

W 무슨 일이야, Mike?
M 엄마가 어제 개를 산책을 하라고 했어.
W 그런데, 무슨 일이야?
M 친구랑 대화할 때, 개가 달아났어.
W 이럴수가! 개는 찾았니?
M 아니, 어디서도 찾을 수 가 없어. 어쩌면 좋지?

09 ④

M Wow, this school festival is really fun.
W Yes, it is.
M What do you want to do next?
W Let's make a candle in the gym.
M But it will take too much time. Why don't we do face painting?
W Sounds good! Let's go right now.

M 와, 이 학교 축제 진짜 재미있다.
W 맞아. 재미있어.
M 다음에 뭐 하고 싶어?
W 체육관에서 초를 만들자.
M 하지만 시간이 너무 걸릴 거 같아. 페이스 페인팅 하는 거 어때?
W 좋아! 지금 바로 가자.

10 ⑤

W James, you look excited. What's new?
M Today my class will visit the Bike museum.
W Cool. What are you going to do there?
M We'll learn about the history of bikes.
W Will you do anything else?
M We'll also ride special bikes. It will be fun.

W James, 너 신나 보인다. 무슨 일 있어?
M 오늘 우리 반이 자전거 박물관에 가거든.
W 멋지네. 거기서 무엇을 할 거야?
M 우리는 자전거에 역사에 대해 배울 거야.
W 다른 거는 안 하니?
M 특별한 자전거도 탈 거야. 신날 거야.

11 ③

M How will you go to Jake's birthday party, Stella?
W I will walk there after my piano lesson. How about you?
M My mom said she would take me there by car.
W Okay, see you at the party.
M See you there.

M Jake의 생인 파티에 어떻게 갈 거야, Stella?
W 피아노 레슨이 끝나고 걸어갈 거야. 너는?
M 엄마가 차로 태워 주신다고 했어.
W 알겠어. 파티에서 보자.
M 거기서 봐.

12 ④

W Sangmin, you look tired. What did you do last night?
M I watched a soccer match on TV until 2 a.m.
W Really? Was it a big match?
M Yeah, it was the final match between Korea and Iran.
W Did Korea win?
M Yes, Korea won the match.

W Sangmin, 지쳐 보인다. 어젯밤 무엇을 했니?
M 새벽 2시까지 축구 경기를 봤어.
W 진짜? 큰 경기였어?
M 응, 한국과 이란의 결승전이었어.
W 한국이 이겼어?
M 응, 한국이 경기에서 이겼어.

13 ⑤

M Can I help you?
W I think there is something wrong with my car.
M Okay. Let me check your car.
W Is there any problem?
M Well, there is a small hole in the tire.
W How long will it take to fix the tire?
M It'll take about one hour.

M 도와드릴까요?
W 제 차에 문제가 생긴 거 같아요.
M 알겠습니다. 차를 확인해 보겠습니다.
W 무슨 문제가 있나요?
M 타이어에 작은 구멍이 하나 있네요.
W 타이어를 고치는데 얼마나 걸릴까요?
M 대략 한 시간 걸립니다.

14 ②

M Emily, do you know any good hair shops near here?
W Sure, there's the Smile Shop.
M Okay. How can I get there from here?
W Go straight two blocks. Then turn right.
M Oh, I see.
W You will see a bookstore on your left. It's next to the bookstore.
M Thanks.

M Emily, 이 근처에 괜찮은 미용실 아니?
W 물론이야, Smile Shop이 있어.
M 그래, 여기서 거기에 어떻게 갈 수 있니?
W 두 블록 쭉 가서 왼쪽으로 돌아.
M 아, 알겠어.
W 왼쪽에 서점이 있을 거야. 서점 옆이야.
M 고마워.

15 ②

W Jeff, how was your Christmas?
M It was great.
W What presents did you get?
M My parents gave me a jigsaw puzzle. What about you?
W I got Korean history books from my uncle.
M Really? I need those for my homework. Can you lend them to me?
W Sure.

W Jeff, 크리스마스 어땠어?
M 멋졌어.
W 무슨 선물 받았어?
M 부모님이 퍼즐을 주셨어. 너는?
W 나는 삼촌에게 한국사 책들을 받았어.
M 진짜? 나 숙제를 위해 그게 필요해. 나에게 빌려줄 수 있니?
W 물론이야.

16 ③

W What will you do on Mother's Day?
M I want to bake cookies for my mom.
W I was going to bake cookies for my mom, too.
M Really? Then let's make them together after school.
W Good idea. See you then.

W 어머니의 날에 뭐 할 거야?
M 엄마를 위해 쿠키를 굽고 싶어.
W 나도 엄마를 위해 쿠키를 구우려고 했어.
M 진짜? 그럼 방과 후에 같이 쿠키를 만들자.
W 좋은 생각이야. 그때 보자.

17 ①

W Alex, what are you looking for?
M We need a ruler for our math class, but I can't find mine.
W Maybe you left it at home.
M No, I used it in art class today.
W Then, we can share my ruler for this class.

W Alex, 무엇을 찾고 있니?
M 수학 시간에 쓸 자가 필요한데 내 것을 찾을 수가 없어.
W 집에 두고 왔겠지.
M 아니야, 오늘 미술 시간에 썼어.
W 그럼, 이번 수업에 내 자를 같이 쓰자.

18 ⑤

W Can I help you?
M Yes, I'm looking for the book, 'The Short Stories of Sherlock Holmes'.
W Let me check the book list. [Keyboard typing sound] Here it is.
M Can I borrow it now?
W Yes, do you have your ID card?
M Sure. Here you are.
W Please remember to bring it back by April 17th.

W 도와드릴까요?
M 네, 'The Short Stories of Sherlock Holmes'라는 책을 찾고 있어요.
W 책 목록을 확인해 보겠습니다. [키보드 소리] 여기 있네요.
M 지금 빌릴 수 있나요?
W 네, 신분증 갖고 계시나요?
M 물론이죠. 여기 있습니다.
W 4월 17일까지 갖고 오시는 거 기억하세요.

19 ⑤

W Hi, Minho. Did you see Youngmin today?
M No, he didn't come to school.
W What's the matter with him?
M He is sick in bed.
W Really? I didn't know that! I have something to give him.
M You do? Why don't we visit him after school together?
W That's a great idea.

W 안녕, Minho. 오늘 Youngmin을 봤니?
M 아니, 학교에 안 왔어.
W 무슨 일 있어?
M 아파서 누워 있대.
W 진짜? 몰랐어! 그에게 줄 게 있어.
M 그래? 방과 후에 같이 그를 방문할래?
W 좋은 생각이야.

① 내 잘못이야. ② 믿을 수가 없어.
③ 만나서 반가워. ④ 오랜만이야.

20 ③

W Hi, Minsu. What will you do after school?
M I will play badminton with my friends.
W I like badminton, too.
M Do you play any other sports?
W I also play table tennis.
M How often do you play table tennis?
W Three times a week.

W 안녕, Minsu. 방과 후에 뭐 할 거야?
M 친구들이랑 배드민턴 칠 거야.
W 나도 배드민턴 좋아해.
M 다른 스포츠도 하니?
W 탁구도 해.
M 탁구는 얼마나 자주 하니?
W 일주일에 3번.

① 걱정하지 마.
② 유감이다.
④ 체육관에서 해.
⑤ 물론이야. 여기

영어듣기능력평가 01 회

01 ⑤	02 ⑤	03 ②	04 ①, ➕③	05 ③
06 ②	07 ④	08 ③	09 ③, ➕②	10 ③
11 ⑤	12 ②	13 ③	14 ④	15 ②
16 ③	17 ②	18 ③	19 ⑤	20 ⑤

01 ⑤

W Are you planning to go camping with your family? Then you must have this. Spray this on your arms and legs. Mosquitos don't like the smell of this. They won't come near you. Protect your children from getting mosquito bites. Please do not spray it on your face. If you spray this in your eyes, wash them well and go to a doctor.

W 가족과 함께 캠핑을 계획 중이십니까? 그러시다면 이것을 가져가야 합니다. 이것을 당신의 팔과 다리에 뿌리십시오. 모기는 이 냄새를 좋아하지 않습니다. 그것들은 당신 근처에 오려고 하지 않을 것입니다. 아이들이 모기에 물리지 않도록 보호해 주십시오. 얼굴에는 이것을 뿌리지 마십시오. 만약 이것을 눈에 뿌린다면, 잘 씻은 후 병원에 가 보세요.

02 ⑤

W What should I wear for the field trip? I want to dress nicely.
M I suggest shorts and a T-shirt. The weather will be hot.
W I want to wear a dress. It's nice and cool.
M I don't think that's a good idea.
W Why not? My dress is comfortable.
M Yes, but you will walk a lot. Shorts and a T-shirt are better.
W Okay.

W 현장 학습 갈 때 무엇을 입어야 할까? 멋지게 입고 싶거든
M 반바지와 티셔츠가 좋을 거야. 날이 더울 테니까.
W 난 원피스를 입고 싶어. 예쁘고 시원하잖아.
M 그건 좋은 생각 같지가 않은데.
W 왜 아닌데? 내 원피스는 편해.
M 그래, 하지만 넌 많이 걷게 될 거야. 반바지와 티셔츠가 더 나아.
W 알았어.

만점 솔루션 남자가 반바지와 티셔츠를 입을 것을 제안했고 여자도 이에 동의했다.

03 ②

M 9 o'clock news weather update. It's cloudy all over the country now. Seoul will have another cloudy day tomorrow. The eastern part of the country including Gangrung and Sockcho, it will rain all day. It will be a chilly day in the east, too. Don't wash your car today. Your car will be wet again tomorrow if you live in Gangrung or Sockcho.

M 9시 뉴스의 날씨 속보입니다. 지금은 전국적으로 흐립니다. 서울은 내일도 흐린 날이 계속되겠습니다. 강릉과 속초를 포함한 동부 지역은 하루 종일 비가 오겠습니다. 또한 동부 지역은 추운 날이 될 것으로 예상됩니다. 오늘은 세차하지 마십시오. 강릉이나 속초에 사신다면 내일 다시 자동차가 젖을 것입니다.

04 ① | ➕ ③

M Soyoung, what are you going to do this weekend?
W Miran and I are going to study together at my house. Will you join us?
M Well, I wanted to ask you to go to see a movie together.
W There will be a science quiz on Wednesday. Did you finish studying?
M Well, not exactly, but I really want to go for a movie.
W Well, enjoy it.
M Thank you.

M 소영아, 이번 주말에 뭐 할 거니?
W 미란이와 나는 우리 집에서 함께 공부하려고 해. 같이 할래?
M 글쎄, 나는 같이 영화 보러 가자고 말하려고 했는데.
W 수요일에 과학 쪽지 시험이 있잖아. 공부는 다 했니?
M 저, 꼭 그렇지는 않지만, 난 그래도 정말 영화를 보러 가고 싶어.
W 그럼, 재미있게 보렴.
M 고마워.

만점 솔루션 여자는 주말에 다른 친구와 공부할 계획이라며 남자에게 함께 할 것을 제안하지만 남자는 영화를 보러 가고 싶다고 말하며 제안을 거절하고 있다.

05 ③

① **M** Do you have any brothers or sisters?
W No, I'm an only child.
② **M** What does your brother do?
W He's a college student.
③ **M** What is your sister like?
W She likes to cook.
④ **M** What is your favorite food?
W I like *bulgogi* most.
⑤ **M** Where can we meet?
W Let's meet at the bus stop.

① **M** 너는 형제나 자매가 있니?
W 아니, 나는 외동이야.
② **M** 너의 오빠는 무슨 일을 하시니?
W 대학생이야.
③ **M** 너의 언니는 어떤 분이시니?
W 요리하는 것을 좋아해.
④ **M** 네가 제일 좋아하는 음식은 뭐니?
W 나는 불고기를 가장 좋아해.
⑤ **M** 어디서 만날까?
W 버스 정류장에서 만나자.

만점 솔루션 ③ What is ~ like?는 사람의 성격이나 특징, 생김새를 묻는 말이

므로 She's nice and kind.(친절하고 좋은 사람이에요.) 또는 She's tall and funny.(키가 크고 재미있는 사람이에요.) 등으로 대답해야 한다.

06 ②

M When does the movie start? I don't want to be late.
W It starts at 7 o'clock. We have lots of time, don't worry.
M Should we leave at 6:30?
W Sure. Then we'll get there about ten minutes early.
M Good. We'll have enough time to get good seats.
W Yes, and we can buy some snacks.

M 그 영화 언제 시작해? 늦게 가고 싶지 않아.
W 7시에 시작해. 우린 시간이 많으니까, 걱정하지 마.
M 6시 30분에 떠나야 할까?
W 물론이지. 그럼 거기에 10분쯤 일찍 도착할 거야.
M 좋아. 좋은 자리를 잡을 충분한 시간도 있겠다.
W 그래, 그리고 간식도 좀 살 수 있고.

만점 솔루션 영화 시작 시각인 7시보다 10분 일찍 도착한다고 했으므로 도착 시각은 6시 50분이 된다.

07 ④

[Telephone rings.]
M Good afternoon. Green line Lost and Found. How can I help you?
W I left my bag behind on the subway this morning.
M What station did you get on and get off at?
W I got on at Suyoung station and got off at Seomyeon station.
M Can you tell me more about the bag?
W It's a black school backpack. A small teddy bear is hanging on the zipper.
M I'll check if it's here. Hold on, please.

[전화벨이 울린다.]
M 안녕하세요. 녹색 노선 분실물 보관소입니다. 무엇을 도와드릴까요?
W 오늘 아침에 제 가방을 지하철에 두고 내렸어요.
M 어느 역에서 승차하시고 하차하셨나요?
W 수영역에서 탔고 서면역에서 내렸어요.
M 그 가방에 대해 좀 더 설명해 주시겠습니까?
W 검은색 학교 가방이에요. 지퍼에 작은 곰인형이 달려 있어요.
M 그것이 여기에 있는지 확인해 보겠습니다. 기다리세요.

08 ③

M I have a short tail and long ears. I also have soft fur. I like eating vegetables, green grass, and flowers. But I don't eat meat. I like living in groups in the woods or forests. But sometimes, people have me as a pet. What am I?

M 나는 짧은 꼬리와 긴 귀를 가지고 있어요. 나는 또 부드러운 털을 가지고 있어요. 나는 채소, 초록 풀, 그리고 꽃을 먹는 것을 좋아해요. 하지만 나는 고기는 먹지 않아요. 나는 숲에서 집단으로 사는 것을 좋아해요. 하지만 가끔, 사람들은 나를 애완동물로 키웁니다. 나는 무엇일까요?

09 ③ | ⊕ ②

W I'm really busy these days. I have no free time.
M Why? Are you studying for a test?
W Actually, I am planning the class party. It's hard work.
M You mean the end-of-semester party?
W Yes, and there's so much to do. We are inviting the parents and siblings as well.
M That sounds like a huge responsibility. Could I help you with anything?
W That would be great. Can you make invitations for the parents?
M Sure, I would be glad to. Please email the information to me.

W 요즘 난 정말 바빠. 여가 시간이 없어.
M 왜? 시험공부 하고 있어?
W 사실, 내가 학급 파티를 계획하고 있거든. 힘든 일이야.
M 학기말 파티 말이야?
W 응, 그런데 할 일이 너무 많아. 우리는 부모님과 형제자매들도 초대할 거야.
M 책임이 큰 것처럼 들리는구나. 내가 뭐라도 도와줄까?
W 그러면 좋지. 부모님을 위한 초대장을 만들어 줄 수 있어?
M 물론이지, 기꺼이. 나에게 정보를 이메일로 보내 줘.

만점 솔루션 학급 파티를 계획 중인 여자는 남자에게 부모님들께 보낼 초대장을 만들어 달라고 부탁하고 있다.

10 ③

M What are you doing here? The bell already rang. You should go to your classroom.
W Well, I don't know where to go, sir.
M Where is your classroom?
W I think I have English now and the room is over there. But it's locked. Nobody's in there.
M Are you a new student?
W Yes, sir. Today is my second day here.
M Come to the teachers' office with me. I'll find out where you should go.

M 여기서 뭐 하고 있니? 종은 이미 울렸는데. 네 교실로 가야지.
W 저, 어디로 가야 할지 모르겠어요, 선생님.
M 교실이 어디니?
W 지금은 영어 시간이고, 교실은 저기 같은데요. 그런데 잠겨 있어요. 아무도 없고요.
M 새로 온 학생이니?
W 예, 선생님. 오늘이 여기 온 지 이틀째예요.
M 나와 함께 교무실에 가 보자. 네가 어디로 가야 할지 알아볼게.

만점 솔루션 여자의 첫 번째 말 I don't know where to go와 남자의 마지막 말 I'll find out where you should go.를 통해 여자가 가야 할 곳을 찾을 수 없는 상황임을 알 수 있다.

11 ⑤

M I'm Minsu. I'm 13 years old. I lived in Incheon when I was young. When I was 10, my family moved to Seoul. My relatives and my close friends live in Incheon, so I sometimes visit my hometown. There are my parents, one sister and one brother in my family. We have a dog, whose name is Mimi. I like to play soccer and basketball with my friends.

M 저는 민수입니다. 13살이에요. 저는 어릴 때 인천에서 살았습니다. 10살 때, 우리 가족이 서울로 이사왔어요. 제 친척들과 친한 친구들은 인천에 살고 있어서, 가끔 제 고향에 갑니다. 우리 가족은 부모님과 누나 한 명, 남동생 한 명이 있습니다. 강아지가 한 마리 있는데, 이름은 미미입니다. 저는 제 친구들과 축구와 농구하는 것을 좋아합니다.

12 ②

W Is something wrong? You don't look well.
M I'm very hungry. I can't wait until lunchtime.
W But it's only 10 in the morning.
M I didn't eat breakfast. I usually get up late and don't have time to eat.
W That's too bad. All scientists say that breakfast is important for your brain. It's not good to skip it.

W 무슨 일이 있니? 얼굴이 안 좋아 보여.
M 배가 너무 고파. 점심 시간까지 기다릴 수가 없어.
W 하지만 겨우 아침 10시야.
M 나는 아침을 못 먹었어. 나는 보통 늦게 일어나서 먹을 시간이 없어.
W 정말 안됐구나. 모든 과학자들이 그러는데 아침 식사가 뇌에 중요하대. 아침 식사를 거르는 것은 좋지 않아.

13 ③

W What should we have for dinner?
M Let's order something in. How about fried chicken?
W I'm tired of fried chicken. I had that last night.
M Then let's have pizza.
W Sounds good. And I already made something for dessert, too.
M That sounds great.
W Do you like chocolate cake?
M Are you kidding? Who doesn't?

W 저녁에 뭐 먹을까?
M 뭔가를 주문하자. 프라이드치킨 어때?
W 나는 프라이드치킨에 질렸어. 어젯밤에 그것을 먹었거든.
M 그럼 피자를 먹자.
W 좋아. 그리고 내가 후식으로 먹을 것도 이미 만들어 놨어.
M 멋진걸.
W 너 초콜릿 케이크 좋아해?
M 농담해? 누군들 안 좋아하겠어?

만점 솔루션 초콜릿 케이크를 좋아하냐는 말에 누군들 안 좋아하겠냐고 말하고 있다. 즉, 모든 사람이 초콜릿 케이크를 좋아한다는 긍정의 의미이다.

14 ④

M What are you going to do after school?
W My friends and I are practicing a dance for the school festival.
M A dance for school festival? That's great. When is the festival?
W It's on the last Thursday of October.
M Today is Thursday. You have only one week to practice.
W That's right. We're doing great. Come and see us.
M Of course.

M 방과 후에 뭐 할 거니?
W 친구들과 나는 학교 축제를 위한 춤 연습을 할 거야.
M 학교 축제를 위한 춤이라고? 굉장한걸. 축제가 언제니?
W 10월의 마지막 주 목요일이야.
M 오늘이 목요일이잖아. 연습할 날이 일주일밖에 안 남았네.
W 맞아. 우리는 아주 잘 할 거야. 구경하러 와.
M 물론이지.

만점 솔루션 10월 마지막 주 목요일이 축제인데, 오늘이 목요일이고 축제가 일주일 남았다고 했다. 따라서 오늘은 네 번째 주 목요일인 24일이 된다.

15 ②

M Good afternoon.
W Hi, I'd like to send this package to Sydney.
M By airmail or surface mail?
W By surface mail. The package has books in it.
M Put the box on this scale, please. Let me check how much it weighs.
W All right.
M Well, it'll cost $37.

M 어서 오십시오.
W 안녕하세요. 이 소포를 Sydney로 보내고 싶어요.
M 항공 우편으로 보낼까요, 해상 우편으로 보낼까요?
W 해상 우편으로 보내 주세요. 소포 안에 들어 있는 것은 책들이에요.
M 상자를 이 저울 위에 올려주세요. 무게가 얼마나 나가는지 확인하겠습니다.
W 좋습니다.
M 음, 비용은 37달러입니다.

16 ③

M I'm going out, honey. See you in the evening.
W Dan, why don't you bring your umbrella? It looks like it's going to rain.
M It won't rain today. The weather forecast said that.
W The weather forecast might be wrong. Look at the sky.

M I really don't want to carry an umbrella. Don't you remember I lost one the other day?
W All right. If you insist.

M 다녀올게요, 여보. 저녁에 봐요.
W Dan, 우산을 가져가지 그래요? 비가 올 것 같은데요.
M 오늘은 비가 오지 않을 거예요. 일기 예보에서 그렇게 말했어요.
W 일기 예보가 틀릴지도 몰라요. 하늘 좀 보세요.
M 난 정말 우산을 가지고 다니고 싶지 않아요. 요전에도 내가 하나 잃어버린 것 기억 안 나요?
W 알겠어요. 정 그렇다면.

만점 솔루션 남자의 마지막 말에서 우산을 잃어버릴까 봐 가지고 가기 싫어한다는 것을 알 수 있다.

17 ②

W Finally, it's Friday!
M You look happy. Do you have good plans for the weekend?
W Yes, I'm going to Wonderland with my family.
M Wow, that sounds interesting. You will have fun!
W Yes, I'm very excited. What about you, Minho?
M We're just going to go biking in the park.
W We? Who are you going with?
M With my brother. We are going to have a race.

W 드디어, 금요일이야!
M 행보해 보인다. 주말에 좋은 계획이라도 있니?
W 응, 가족들이랑 원더랜드에 갈 거야.
M 와, 신나겠다. 재미있게 보내고 와!
W 응, 진짜 신나. 너는 어때, 민호?
M 우리는 그냥 공원에 자전거 타러 갈 거야.
W 우리? 누구랑 같이 가?
M 남동생이랑. 우리는 경주를 할 거야.

18 ③

M Are you OK? You don't look very good today.
W Yeah, just feeling a little down today, that's all.
M Why? Did something happen to you?
W It's my puppy. He is very sick.
M Oh, no. Is it something serious?
W I hope not. I feel upset because he's sick.
M I'm sure he'll get better. Don't be upset.
W I will try not to.

M 너 괜찮아? 너 오늘 그리 좋아 보이지 않아.
W 응, 그냥 오늘 마음이 약간 우울할 뿐이야, 그게 다야.
M 왜? 너한테 무슨 일이 있었어?
W 내 강아지한테. 그가 많이 아파.
M 오, 이런. 심각한 거야?
W 그렇지 않기를 바라고 있어. 그가 아파서 속이 상해.
M 틀림없이 괜찮아질 거야. 속상해 하지 마.
W 그러지 않으려고 노력할게.

19 ⑤

M May I help you?
W Yes, I'm looking for jeans.
M Jeans for ladies are in the next row. Is there any particular style you want?
W I'd like a classic style with no decorations on them.
M These jeans over here have a basic design. What size do you wear?
W Size 4. Where can I try them on?
M ______________________

M 도와드릴까요?
W 예, 청바지를 찾고 있어요.
M 여성용 청바지는 다음 열에 있습니다. 원하시는 특별한 스타일이 있으세요?
W 장식이 없는 고전적인 스타일을 원해요.
M 여기에 있는 이 청바지들이 기본 디자인입니다. 몇 사이즈를 입으시나요?
W 4 사이즈입니다. 어디에서 그것을 입어 볼 수 있나요?
M 탈의실은 저쪽에 있습니다.

① 저희는 청바지를 팔지 않습니다.
② 검은색과 파란색이 있습니다.
③ 더 작은 것을 입어 보세요.
④ 다른 사이즈를 입어 보실 수 있습니다.

20 ⑤

[Telephone rings.]
W Hello. Jacobson and Brown. How may I help you?
M May I talk to Mr. Robinson?
W Who is this, please?
M This is Mr. James Callman.
W I'm sorry, Mr. Callman. He's talking on the phone right now. Can I take a message?
M ______________________

[전화벨이 울린다.]
W 여보세요. Jacobson and Brown 회사입니다. 무엇을 도와드릴까요?
M Robinson 씨와 통화할 수 있을까요?
W 누구세요?
M James Callman이라고 합니다.
W 죄송합니다, Callman 씨. 지금 다른 전화를 받고 계세요. 메시지를 남겨 드릴까요?
M 제가 다시 전화하겠다고만 전해 주세요.

① 통화 중입니다.
② 끊지 마세요.
③ 예, 나중에 그에게 전화하실 수 있습니다.
④ 제가 그분께 안부를 전해 드릴게요.

만점 솔루션 통화를 하려고 했던 상대방이 전화를 받을 수 없는 상황이고, 전화를 받은 사람이 메시지를 남겨 주겠다고 했으므로, 남자는 남길 메시지를 말하는 것이 가장 적절하다.

영어듣기능력평가 02회

01 ⑤	02 ②	03 ④	04 ③	05 ④
06 ④	07 ①	08 ④	09 ②	10 ①
11 ③	12 ③, ⊕①	13 ③, ⊕②	14 ③	15 ④
16 ④	17 ①	18 ①	19 ③	20 ④

01 ⑤

M Today, we drew pictures in art class. We had to draw pictures of the country. Some students drew mountains. Others drew rivers or lakes. But I drew a farm. It was my uncle's farm. I went there last summer vacation. There were many different kinds of animals. There were lots of cows. There were sheep, too. I helped my uncle feed the animals.

M 오늘, 우리는 미술 시간에 그림을 그렸어요. 우리는 시골 그림을 그려야 했습니다. 몇몇 학생들은 산을 그렸고, 다른 학생들은 강이나 호수를 그렸습니다. 하지만 저는 농장을 그렸습니다. 그것은 우리 삼촌의 농장이었습니다. 저는 그곳에 지난 여름 방학에 갔습니다. 그곳에는 많은 여러 종류의 동물들이 있었습니다. 그곳에는 많은 소가 있었고, 양도 있었습니다. 저는 우리 삼촌이 그 동물들에게 먹이 주는 것을 도와드렸습니다.

만점 솔루션 남자는 미술 시간에 지난 여름 방학 때 방문한 삼촌의 농장을 그렸다고 했다.

02 ②

M Where did you put the popcorn?
W It's in a bowl.
M Is it on the counter?
W Yes, beside the stove.
M I don't see the bowl. Is it next to the sink?
W No, it's on the other side of the stove.
M Oh, I see. There is a big bowl.
W Right, that one.

M 너 팝콘을 어디에 두었니?
W 그릇 안에 있어.
M 조리대 위에 있어?
W 응, 가스레인지 옆에.
M 그릇이 안 보여. 개수대 옆에 있니?
W 아니, 가스레인지의 다른 옆쪽이야.
M 오, 보인다. 큰 그릇이 있네.
W 맞아, 바로 그거야.

만점 솔루션 팝콘은 가스레인지 옆 큰 그릇 안에 들어 있다고 했다.

03 ④

W It's time for the weather report. It's snowing all over the country including Jeju Island. The snow will continue until tomorrow for most of the country. However, in the Gangwon area, it'll be sunny tomorrow with no snow. There will be showers in the some southern part of Gyoungsang province. And that's all.

W 일기 예보 시간입니다. 제주도를 포함하여 전국적으로 눈이 내리고 있습니다. 대부분의 지역에서 눈은 내일까지 계속 내리겠습니다. 하지만, 강원도 지역은, 내일 눈이 내리지 않고 화창할 것입니다. 경상도 남부의 일부 지역에서는 소나기가 올 것입니다. 이상입니다.

04 ③

W In two weeks, we'll have summer vacation.
M That's right. So, will you really learn scuba diving and tennis during this vacation?
W No. I changed my mind. I'll take a trip to Asia.
M Really? That's a wonderful plan. But I think you'll need a lot of money.
W Don't worry. I already saved enough.

W 2주만 지나면, 여름 방학이야.
M 맞아. 그래, 이번 방학 동안에 정말 스쿠버다이빙과 테니스를 배울 거니?
W 아니, 마음이 바뀌었어. 아시아로 여행을 갈 거야.
M 정말? 그거 멋진 계획이다. 하지만 돈이 많이 필요할 것 같은데.
W 걱정 마. 이미 충분히 저축해 두었어.

만점 솔루션 여자는 여름 방학 동안 스쿠버다이빙과 테니스를 배울 계획이었지만, 마음이 바뀌어 아시아로 여행을 갈 계획이라고 했다.

05 ④

① **W** Oh, this jacket looks nice. Where did you buy it?
M At the Sunshine Shopping Mall. It was only $30.
② **W** What are you reading, Sam?
M A detective story. It's very interesting.
③ **W** Excuse me, can you take a picture of me?
M Sure, no problem.
④ **W** Please put on your helmet before riding your bicycle.
M Okay, I'll buy this helmet.
⑤ **W** I'd like to send this package to Seattle.
M I see. Please put it on this scale.

① **W** 오, 이 재킷이 멋져 보이는데. 어디서 샀니?
M Sunshine 쇼핑 몰에서. 30달러밖에 안 했어.
② **W** Sam, 무엇을 읽고 있니?
M 탐정 소설. 정말 재미있어.
③ **W** 실례합니다, 사진 한 장만 찍어 주시겠어요?
M 그럼요, 문제없어요.
④ **W** 자전거를 타기 전에 헬멧을 착용하세요.
M 좋아요. 이 헬멧을 살게요.
⑤ **W** 이 소포를 Seattle로 보내고 싶어요.
M 알겠습니다. 이 저울에 올려놓으세요.

만점 솔루션 ④ 헬멧을 착용하라는 말에 헬멧을 사겠다는 대답은 어색하다.

06 ④

[Cellphone rings.]

W Hello? Angela speaking.

M Hi, Angela. Where are you now? It's almost two forty.

W I'm passing City Hall now.

M How long is it going to take from where you're at?

W Well... it will take about ten minutes, I think. I'll be there soon.

M Okay, see you soon.

[휴대 전화 벨이 울린다.]

W 여보세요? Angela입니다.

M 안녕, Angela. 지금 어디니? 거의 2시 40분이야.

W 지금 시청을 지나고 있어.

M 네가 있는 곳에서부터 얼마나 걸릴까?

W 음… 약 10분 걸릴 것 같아. 곧 그곳에 도착할 거야.

M 알았어, 곧 보자.

만점 솔루션 현재 2시 40분인데 10분 정도 후에 도착할 것이라고 했으므로 두 사람이 만날 예상 시각은 2시 50분이 된다.

07 ①

[Telephone rings.]

W Hello, Seven Star Home Shopping. How may I help you?

M Yes, please. I'd like to order the computer showing on TV now.

W I see. It costs $800. And you can get either a digital camera or a photo printer as a free gift.

M Well... I'll take the photo printer.

W I see. How would you like to pay?

M Credit card, please.

[전화벨이 울린다.]

W 여보세요, Seven Star 홈쇼핑입니다. 도와드릴까요?

M 예, 지금 TV에 방영되고 있는 컴퓨터를 주문하고 싶어요.

W 알겠습니다. 가격은 800달러입니다. 그리고 디지털 카메라 또는 포토 프린터를 사은품으로 받으실 수 있어요.

M 음… 포토 프린터로 할게요.

W 알겠습니다. 어떻게 지불하시겠어요?

M 신용카드로요.

08 ④

M You ride this to go to a place. This has a pair of wheels. You don't need any fuel. But you need to use your legs. It can be hard to go up a hill, but it's really easy to go down. What is this?

M 당신은 장소에 가기 위해 이것을 탑니다. 이것은 두 개의 바퀴가 있습니다. 연료는 필요 없습니다. 하지만 당신의 다리를 움직여야 합니다. 언덕을 올라가는 것이 어려울 수 있지만 내리막길은 정말 쉽습니다. 이것은 무엇일까요?

09 ②

W What do you want to be in the future?

M Well... I want to be a progammer or a computer programmer.

W I'm sure you'll be one of them. You're very good at computers.

M What about you, Stella? Do you still want to be a fashion designer?

W No, I changed my mind. Now I want to be a jewelry designer!

W 넌 장래에 무엇이 되고 싶니?

M 음… 프로 게이머나 컴퓨터 프로그래머가 되고 싶어.

W 네가 그것들 중의 하나가 될 거라고 확신해. 너는 컴퓨터를 아주 잘 하니까 말이야.

M 넌 어때, Stella? 여전히 패션 디자이너가 되고 싶니?

W 아니, 마음이 바뀌었어. 지금, 나는 보석 디자이너가 되고 싶어!

만점 솔루션 남자의 장래희망은 프로 게이머나 컴퓨터 프로그래머이고, 여자는 장래희망은 과거에는 패션 디자이너였으나 지금은 바뀌어서 보석 디자이너라고 했다.

10 ①

W Hi, do you remember me?

M Yes, I do. You bought a rubber tree last weekend, didn't you?

W Yeah, that's right. You have a good memory.

M Is it doing well?

W Yes, it is. But I think the pot is a little bit small for the tree. So, I'd like to buy a bigger pot.

M I see. Follow me, please. Pots are inside.

W 안녕하세요, 저 기억하세요?

M 예, 기억해요. 지난 주말에 고무나무를 사셨잖아요, 그렇죠?

W 예, 맞아요. 기억력이 좋으시네요.

M 고무나무는 잘 자라고 있나요?

W 예. 하지만, 나무에 비해서 화분이 약간 작은 것 같아요. 그래서, 좀 더 큰 화분을 사고 싶어요.

M 알겠습니다. 저를 따라 오세요. 화분은 안쪽에 있습니다.

11 ③

M Let me tell you something about myself. My name is Patrick Johnson and I'm 30 years old. This year, I'll teach you the most difficult subject, mathematics. I live in Green Apartments just next to the school. My hobby is playing tennis. I was a tennis player when I was in high school. I was pretty good and won a few medals at local competitions.

M 저에 대한 것을 말씀드릴게요. 제 이름은 Patrick Johnson이고, 나이는 30살입니다. 올해, 여러분에게 가장 어려운 과목인 수학을 가르칠 거예요. 저는 학교 바로 옆에 있는 Green 아파트에 살아요. 제 취미는 테니스 치는 거예요. 저는 고등학교 다닐 때 테니스 선수였어요. 저는 테니스를 상당히 잘 쳐서 지역 대회에서 메달을 몇 번 따기도 했어요.

12 ③ | ➕ ①

W Peter, did you finish your homework?
M Yes, I did it as soon as I came home.
W That's good, son. How about cleaning your room? I think your room is a little bit messy.
M OK. I'll do it now.
W Good! After cleaning your room, let's go out for dinner. I'll take you to a nice Chinese restaurant.
M Really? Oh, I like Chinese food.

W Peter, 숙제 다 했니?
M 예. 집에 오자마자 했어요.
W 잘했다, 얘야. 네 방 청소를 하는 게 어떠니? 네 방이 약간 지저분한 것 같은데.
M 알았어요. 지금 그것을 할게요.
W 좋아! 방을 청소한 다음에, 저녁 먹으러 나가자. 근사한 중국 식당에 너를 데리고 갈게.
M 정말요? 오, 저는 중국 음식을 좋아해요.

13 ③ | ➕ ②

M Judy, how about going to the amusement park with me tomorrow?
W Tomorrow? Sorry, I have to write my biology report.
M Didn't you finish it yet? Poor Judy. Then, how about Sunday? If you don't have any plans, let's go there on Sunday.
W Sorry, again. I have to work as a volunteer at a senior center.

M Judy, 내일 나와 함께 놀이 공원에 갈래?
W 내일? 미안, 난 생물 보고서를 작성해야 해.
M 너 아직 그것을 다 못 썼니? 불쌍한 Judy. 그럼, 일요일은 어때? 계획이 없으면, 일요일에 그곳에 가자.
W 또 미안해. 난 양로원에서 자원봉사자로 일해야 해.

14 ③

W John, you won't forget my birthday, will you?
M Sure! How can I forget your birthday? It's the end of November.
W Right! And your birthday is just the next day.
M That's right! Hey, why don't we have a birthday party together?
W That's a good idea.

W John, 내 생일 잊지 않을 거지, 그렇지?
M 물론이지! 어떻게 네 생일을 잊을 수 있겠니? 11월의 마지막 날이잖아.
W 맞아! 그리고, 네 생일은 바로 그 다음 날이고.
M 그래! 야, 우리 생일 파티 함께 할래?
W 그거 좋은 생각이다.

15 ④

M Did you finish your homework?
W Yes, but I need your help.
M OK. What is it?
W I don't understand number 9.
M Oh, don't worry. I'll explain the homework to everyone later in class.
W Then I'll just hand it in to you now.

M 숙제 다 했니?
W 예, 하지만 선생님의 도움이 필요해요.
M 좋아. 뭔데?
W 9번을 이해하지 못하겠어요.
M 오, 걱정 마라. 나중에 수업 시간에 모두에게 숙제를 설명해 줄 거야.
W 그럼 그냥 지금 선생님께 그것을 제출해야겠네요.

만점 솔루션 여자가 숙제에 관해 질문하고 있고, 남자가 수업 시간에 설명해 준다는 것으로 보아 두 사람은 학생과 교사 관계이며, '교실'이 대화 장소로 적절하다.

16 ④

W What should I do now?
M Did you clean the storeroom?
W Yes. Should I clean the store shelves?
M That's a good idea. And then please open all the boxes here.
W Are they newly-arrived items?
M Yes, they are. You need to put them on the shelves afterwards.
W When can I take a break?
M In about half an hour.

W 이제 제가 뭘 해야 하죠?
M 창고 청소 했나요?
W 예. 매장 선반을 청소해야 할까요?
M 좋은 생각이에요. 그러고 나서 여기 상자들을 모두 개봉해 주세요.
W 그것들은 신상품들인가요?
M 맞아요. 나중에 그것들을 선반에 놓아야 해요.
W 저는 언제 쉴 수 있는 거죠?
M 약 30분 후에요.

만점 솔루션 남자가 여자에게 창고와 매장 선반 청소 및 물품 진열 등에 관한 지시를 내리고 있으므로 상사와 직원의 관계임을 알 수 있다.

17 ①

W Okay, you don't have a fever. That's good news.
M Really? Does it mean I don't have the flu?
W Yes, that's right. But you are coughing a lot.
M Yeah, and I have a headache and a stuffy nose.
W You have a cold. You should drink lots of water, and you should get lots of rest.
M Are you going to give me any medicine?

W 좋아요, 열이 없네요. 좋은 소식예요.
M 정말요? 제가 독감이 아니라는 건가요?
W 네, 맞아요. 하지만 기침을 많이 하네요.
M 네, 그리고 두통이 있고 코가 막혀요.
W 감기에 걸렸네요. 물을 많이 마시고 휴식을 충분히 취해야 합니다.
M 어떤 약이든 처방해 주실 건가요?

18 ①

M Did you do anything fun yesterday?
W Kind of. We saw a movie.
M Was it a good movie?
W Not really. It was kind of boring.
M What movie was it?
W It was called *Battle of Planets*.
M I'm sorry to hear that you did not enjoy it.
W It's okay. I still had fun hanging out with my friends.

M 어제 재미있는 일을 했니?
W 약간은. 우리는 영화를 봤어.
M 영화 괜찮았어?
W 그렇지는 않았어. 조금 지루했어.
M 무슨 영화였는데?
W *Battle of Planets*였어.
M 그게 재미없었다니 유감이네.
W 괜찮아. 그래도 내 친구들과 어울리며 즐거운 시간을 보냈으니까.

19 ③

M Wow, look at the sea!
W Oh, it's really beautiful. The sea looks very nice.
M That's right. Anyway, hurry up. I want to swim in the sea right away.
W Me too. But we have to check into the hotel first.
M ______________________

M 와, 바다 좀 봐!
W 오, 정말 아름답다. 바다가 매우 멋있어 보여.
M 맞아. 어쨌든, 서둘러. 난 지금 당장 바다에서 수영하고 싶어.
W 나도 그래. 하지만 호텔 체크인을 먼저 해야 해.
M 좋아! 그럼, 지금 바로 호텔에 가자.

① 죄송합니다, 남은 객실이 없습니다.
② 좋아! 네게 수영을 가르쳐 줄게.
④ 여기서 해변까지 얼마나 걸리지?
⑤ 음… 스파게티가 먹고 싶어. 넌 어때?

20 ④

W How much is this computer program course for beginners?
M It's $80 a month.
W Well... that's not very cheap. Ah, do I have to buy a textbook?
M No, you don't have to. We'll give you one for free.
W That's good. Okay, I'll take the course.
M ______________________

W 이 컴퓨터 프로그램 초급 과정은 얼마죠?
M 한 달에 80달러입니다.
W 음… 그다지 저렴하지는 않네요. 아, 교재도 사야 하나요?
M 아니요, 사지 않으셔도 돼요. 교재를 무료로 드립니다.
W 잘됐군요. 알겠어요, 그 과정을 수강할게요.
M 감사합니다. 먼저 이 양식을 작성해 주세요.

① 그럼, 교재를 사셔야 합니다.
② 아니요, 이 프로그램을 배우고 싶지 않아요.
③ 잠시 당신 컴퓨터를 써도 되나요?
⑤ 정말요? 이 컴퓨터를 언제 샀나요?

만점 솔루션 컴퓨터 프로그램 과정에 수강 신청을 하는 상황이다. 마지막에 여자가 선택한 프로그램을 수강하겠다고 했으므로 남자는 필요한 양식을 작성해 달라고 말하는 것이 가장 적절하다.

영어듣기능력평가 03 회

01 ⑤	02 ①	03 ②, ⊕④	04 ③	05 ④
06 ④	07 ⑤	08 ②	09 ③	10 ④
11 ①	12 ④	13 ③	14 ⑤, ⊕③	15 ②
16 ③	17 ③	18 ②	19 ③	20 ②

01 ⑤

M You can use this to send a letter or a postcard. You put your letter or postcard in this, and then someone will pick it up later. The color of this is usually red. But not many people use this nowadays, because they use email. What is this?

M 편지나 엽서를 보낼 때 이것을 사용할 수 있습니다. 당신의 편지나 엽서를 이것 안에 넣으면 누군가가 나중에 그것을 가져갑니다. 이것의 색은 보통 빨간색입니다. 하지만 요즘에는 이메일을 사용하기 때문에 많은 사람들이 이것을 사용하지는 않습니다. 이것은 무엇일까요?

02 ①

M Mom, I can't find my memory stick.
W Did you check on your desk or on the bed?
M Yes, I did. I even checked under the bed, but I couldn't find it.
W Then check on the bookshelf. You usually put your things on it.
M Oh, here it is. Thank you, Mom.

M 엄마, 제 메모리 스틱을 찾을 수가 없어요.
W 책상 위나 침대 위를 확인했니?
M 예, 했어요. 침대 아래도 확인해 봤지만, 그것을 찾을 수가 없었어요.
W 그러면 책장 위를 확인해 보렴. 너는 보통 네 물건들을 그 위에 놓잖니.
M 오, 여기 있어요. 고마워요, 엄마.

03 ② | ⊕ ④

W Here's the channel 9 weather report. Today it was clear and sunny and not too cold. I think you had a great day if you did something outdoors. However, we'll have rain tomorrow morning. And it will start to get very cold. The rain will change to snow tomorrow afternoon. So don't forget to wear your coat.

W 채널 9번의 일기 예보입니다. 오늘은 청명하고 맑았으며 그다지 춥지 않았습니다. 실외에서 일을 하셨다면 좋은 하루를 보내셨으리라고 생각합니다. 하지만, 내일 아침에는 비가 올 것입니다. 그리고 매우 추워지기 시작할 것입니다. 비는 내일 오후에 눈으로 바뀔 것입니다. 그러니 외투 입는 것을 잊지 마시기 바랍니다.

04 ③

M Jihye, look at this photo. Isn't this your dad here?
W Yes, that's him. What is this?
M It's this month's city magazine. I got it from city hall.
W Cool, I didn't know he was in it.
M I didn't know he is a famous person. It's awesome.
W Yes, he designed some famous buildings in our city.
M Wow, that's great.

M 지혜, 이 사진 좀 봐. 여기 이 사람 너네 아빠 아니야?
W 응, 맞아. 이거 뭐야?
M 이번 달 시 잡지야. 시청에서 얻었어.
W 멋지다, 아빠가 여기 실린 줄 몰랐어.
M 너희 아빠가 유명한 사람인 줄 몰랐어. 멋지다.
W 응, 아빠가 우리 시의 몇몇 유명한 건물들을 디자인했거든.
M 와, 대단하다.

05 ④

W Honey. Did you send invitation cards to people for our party?
M Yes, I did.
W How many invitation cards did you send?
M I sent the invitation cards to twenty people.
W Did you send one to Tom and Mary?
M Oh, I forgot to send one to them. I'll send one to each of them tomorrow.
W OK.

W 여보. 우리 파티를 위한 초대장을 사람들에게 보냈나요?
M 예, 보냈어요.
W 초대장을 몇 장 보냈나요?
M 20명의 사람들에게 초대장을 보냈어요.
W Tom과 Mary에게 초대장을 보냈나요?
M 오, 그들에게 초대장을 보내는 것을 잊었어요. 내일 그들에게 각각 하나씩 보낼게요.
W 좋아요.

06 ④

M What are you doing now?
W Can you help me with this box? It won't take long.
M Sure. What do you want me to do with it?
W Could you move it for me? It's too heavy for me to lift.
M No problem at all. Where should I put it?
W Can you put it on the table?
M Of course. It's easy.
W Thank you.

M 지금 뭐 하고 있니?
W 이 상자 좀 도와줄 수 있어? 시간이 오래 걸리지 않을 거야.
M 물론이지. 내가 뭘 해 주기를 원하니?
W 나를 위해 그것을 옮겨 줄 수 있어? 내가 들기에는 너무 무거워.
M 전혀 문제없어. 그것을 어디에 두면 되는 거야?

W 탁자 위에 그것을 놓을 수 있니?
M 물론이지. 쉽네.
W 고마워.

07 ⑤

[Telephone rings.]
W Hello? This is Kim's Medical Clinic.
M This is Mr. Morgan.
W How can I help you, sir?
M I'd like to make an appointment with Dr. Kim tomorrow at two o'clock.
W I'm sorry. He has an appointment with another patient at that time.
M Then, how about three o'clock?
W I'm sorry. He isn't free then. He is free at three thirty. Is that OK with you, sir?
M Well, it's fine with me.

[전화벨이 울린다.]
W 여보세요? Kim's 의료원입니다.
M 저는 Mr. Morgan입니다.
W 어떻게 도와드릴까요, 손님?
M 내일 2시에 김 박사님과 약속을 하고 싶습니다.
W 죄송합니다. 박사님은 그 시간에 다른 환자분과 약속이 있습니다.
M 그러면, 3시는 어떤가요?
W 죄송합니다. 그때는 시간이 없습니다. 그는 3시 30분에 시간이 있습니다. 그 시간이 괜찮으신가요, 손님?
M 음, 좋습니다.

08 ②

① W What subject do you like best?
M I like history best.
② W When are you leaving for America?
M I just arrived at the airport.
③ W How's it going these days?
M I'm feeling good.
④ W Shall we go out for dinner?
M Really? I'd love to.
⑤ W You look tired. What's wrong?
M I stayed up all night yesterday.

① W 넌 어떤 과목을 가장 좋아하니?
M 난 역사가 가장 좋아.
② W 미국으로 언제 떠날 거니?
M 난 공항에 막 도착했어.
③ W 요즘 어떻게 지내니?
M 잘 지내고 있어.
④ W 저녁 먹으러 밖에 나갈까?
M 정말? 나도 그러고 싶어.
⑤ W 피곤해 보이네. 무슨 일이니?
M 어제 밤새 깨어 있었거든.

09 ③

W Honey, look at the road sign. We have to turn left.
M But the navigation system says we have to turn right.
W Let's trust the sign, honey.
M OK. *[Pause]* The sign was right. I can see the parking lot of the concert hall over there.
W We are almost there. Thank you for driving, honey.

W 여보, 도로 표지판을 보세요. 좌회전해야 해요.
M 그런데 네비게이션에서는 우회전해야 한다고 하네요.
W 표지판을 믿어 봐요, 여보.
M 알겠어요. *[잠시 후]* 그 표지판이 옳았어요. 저기 콘서트 홀 주차장이 보이네요.
W 거의 다 왔어요. 운전해 줘서 고마워요, 여보.

10 ④

W Do you have any plans for tomorrow?
M Yes, I am going to my friend's house tomorrow.
W Are you going to play games with him?
M No, he is having a birthday party.
W But you don't seem so happy. What's bothering you?
M I have a big test next week so I would like to stay home and study. But I can't miss the party. He's my best friend.
W Just enjoy. You can study later.

W 내일 무슨 계획이라도 있니?
M 응, 내일 내 친구네 집에 갈 거야.
W 그와 함께 게임 하기 위해 가는 거야?
M 아니, 그는 생일 파티를 열 거야.
W 하지만 넌 별로 좋아하는 것 같지가 않다. 고민거리라도 있니?
M 다음 주에 중요한 시험이 있어서 집에서 공부하고 싶거든. 하지만 파티를 빠질 수가 없어. 그는 내 가장 친한 친구이거든.
W 그냥 즐겨. 나중에 공부해도 되잖아.

만점 솔루션 남자는 내일 가장 친한 친구의 생일 파티 참석을 위해 친구의 집에 갈 예정이다.

11 ①

M Nora. Do you have a minute to talk with me?
W Sure. What do you want to talk about?
M Well, Tony and I are going to visit a hospital to sing some songs for patients. Would you like to join us?
W I'd love to join you guys.

M Nora, 나와 잠깐 이야기 할 시간이 있니?
W 물론이야. 무엇에 대해 이야기 하고 싶니?
M 음, Tony와 내가 환자들에게 노래를 몇 곡 불러 주기 위해 병원을 방문할 예정이야. 우리와 함께 할래?
W 나도 너희들과 함께 하고 싶어.

12 ④

W Hi, my name is Yura. There are four family members in

my family: My father, my mother, my younger sister, and me. My family likes to watch a baseball game together. My father is a high school teacher. My mother is a nurse. Everyone is very busy, but we have a nice family dinner every Sunday evening.

W 안녕, 내 이름은 유라야. 우리 가족은 아빠, 엄마, 여동생과 나, 이렇게 네 명이야. 우리 가족은 함께 야구 경기를 보는 것을 좋아해. 아빠는 고등학교 선생님이셔. 엄마는 간호사이시고. 모두가 아주 바쁘지만, 우리는 매주 일요일 저녁에 근사한 가족 저녁 식사를 해.

13 ③

[Telephone rings.]

M Hello?

W Hello, Daniel. This is Julie.

M Hi, Julie. What's up?

W Actually, I need your help. Can you help me put up festival posters around the school?

M No problem. Did you make the posters already?

W Yes, I did.

M Then, I can do that.

W Thank you.

[전화벨이 울린다.]

M 여보세요?

W 여보세요, Daniel. 나 Julie야.

M 안녕, Julie. 무슨 일이니?

W 사실, 네 도움이 필요해. 학교 주변에 축제 포스터 붙이는 것을 도와줄 수 있니?

M 물론이야. 포스터를 벌써 만들었니?

W 응, 만들었어.

M 그러면, 그 일을 할 수 있어.

W 고마워.

14 ⑤ | ➕ ③

M Where should I put this sofa, ma'am?

W Put it over here, please. Be careful.

M This sofa is the last thing. We've already moved your desk, books, and everything else.

W You did a good job!

M Thanks. Your new house is very nice.

W Thank you.

M 이 소파를 어디에 놓아야 하나요, 부인?

W 여기에 놓아 주세요. 조심하세요.

M 이 소파가 마지막 물건입니다. 우리는 이미 책상, 책들과 다른 모든 것들을 옮겼습니다.

W 잘하셨습니다!

M 감사합니다. 당신의 새 집이 아주 좋군요.

W 감사합니다.

15 ②

W Hi, Ujin. Where are you going?

M Well, I want to go to the library, but I'm lost.

W You have to walk one more block to the main street, and turn left.

M Oh, is it next to the bank?

W No, it's on the opposite side. It's between the flower shop and the convenience store.

M Now I got it. Thanks!

W 안녕, 우진. 어디 가고 있어?

M 음, 도서관에 가고 싶은데 길을 잃었어.

W 대로로 한 블록 더 걸어가야 해, 그리고 왼쪽으로 돌아.

M 아, 은행 옆에 있어?

W 아니, 반대편이야. 꽃집이랑 편의점 사이에 있어.

M 이제 알겠다. 고마워!

16 ③

W You should sit at the front seat in the classroom. And pay attention to your teacher. Take notes when the teacher speaks. Don't think about other things during the class. Think only about the lesson. These things will help you get a good grade.

W 당신은 교실에서 앞 자리에 앉아야 합니다. 그리고 선생님의 말씀에 주의를 기울이십시오. 선생님께서 말씀하실 때 필기를 하세요. 수업 중에는 다른 것에 대해 생각하지 마세요. 수업에 대해서만 생각하세요. 이러한 것들이 당신이 좋은 점수를 받도록 도와줄 것입니다.

17 ③

M Soft pretzels are delicious bread treats. They have knot-like shape and they are a little difficult to make. First, you make dough. Let it sit until it becomes bigger. Then roll the dough into long strings. You have to twist the dough. Next bake it. Pretzels are hard to make, but easy to eat!

M 부드러운 프레첼은 맛있는 빵 간식입니다. 그것은 매듭 모양이고, 그것을 만드는 것은 약간 어렵습니다. 우선, 반죽을 만드세요. 그것이 더 커질 때까지 그대로 두세요. 그 다음 반죽을 굴려서 긴 줄로 만듭니다. 그러고 나서 그 반죽을 꼬고 그것을 구우세요. 프레첼은 만들기 어렵지만, 먹기는 쉽습니다!

만점 솔루션 반죽이 커질 때까지 그대로 두라고 했다.

18 ②

W Finally the day is over.

M What's up? Did you have a hard day?

W Yes. My boss got mad at me.

M Were you late for work?

W No, but I broke a computer by mistake.

M Oh. Was it an accident?

W Of course. But he was still angry and made me cry.

M That's too bad. Well, sit down and rest now.

W 마침내 하루가 끝났어.
M 무슨 일이야? 힘든 하루였니?
W 응. 내 상사가 내게 화를 냈거든
M 회사에 늦었어?
W 아니, 하지만 난 실수로 컴퓨터를 망가뜨렸어.
M 이런. 사고였어?
W 물론이야. 하지만 그래도 그는 화를 냈고 나를 울게 만들었어.
M 너무 안됐다. 음, 이제 앉아서 쉬어.

만점 솔루션 실수로 회사 컴퓨터를 고장 낸 여자에게 상사가 화를 내서 슬퍼하고 있는 상황이다.

19 ③

M Where are you going?
W I'm going to run. Nowadays I'm afraid I'm gaining weight.
M Me too. So we need to exercise every day.
W Right. So I'm running around the park now. Do you want to join me?
M ______________________________

M 어디에 가고 있니?
W 달리기하러 갈 거야. 요즘 살이 찌고 있는 것 같거든.
M 나도 그래. 그러니까 우리는 매일 운동할 필요가 있어.
W 맞아. 그래서 지금 공원에서 달리기할 거야. 나와 함께 할래?
M 그래. 너와 함께 갈게.

① 오늘 달리기할 거니?
② 그래. 난 배가 아주 고파.
④ 너는 살이 찌고 있니?
⑤ 아니, 나는 먹는 걸 즐기지 않아.

20 ②

M It's already 2 o'clock. What time will we arrive at the City Park?
W I don't know. This is my first time to go there. How about you?
M Me too. I've never been there.
W How about asking the bus driver?
M ______________________________

M 벌써 2시네요. 우리는 몇 시에 City 공원에 도착할까요?
W 모르겠어요. 이번이 그곳에 처음 가는 거예요. 당신은 어때요?
M 저도 그래요. 그곳에 가 본 적이 없어요.
W 버스 기사에게 물어보는 것이 어떨까요?
M 좋은 생각이네요.

① 아주 친절하시군요.
③ 버스에서 내려요.
④ 저는 공원에서 걷는 것을 좋아해요.
⑤ 저를 도와줘서 고마워요.

영어듣기능력평가 04 회

01 ①	02 ②	03 ③	04 ③	05 ④
06 ③	07 ②, ➊⑤	08 ⑤	09 ⑤	10 ④
11 ④	12 ②, ➊⑤	13 ④	14 ③	15 ②
16 ④	17 ③	18 ①	19 ②	20 ⑤

01 ①

W This is a useful item when you use a computer. You can save files in it and carry it anywhere you want. It's small enough to put in your pocket. The files might be documents, video clips or MP3s. You can even put movies in it. Just connect this to any computer. You can access the files in it by clicking a folder.

W 이것은 컴퓨터를 사용할 때 유용한 물건입니다. 그 안에 파일을 저장할 수 있고 당신이 원하는 어느 곳이든 그것을 가지고 다닐 수 있습니다. 그것은 당신의 주머니에 들어갈 만큼 작습니다. 파일은 문서, 동영상이나 MP3 파일일 수도 있습니다. 영화를 그 안에 넣을 수도 있습니다. 어느 컴퓨터에든 연결하기만 하세요. 폴더를 클릭하여 그 안에 있는 파일에 접속할 수 있습니다.

02 ②

M Are you going to buy it?
W Yes, I need it to wake up in the morning.
M But don't you have a Cellphone? Doesn't it have an alarm?
W It does, but I always turn off the alarm and go to sleep again.
M Do you mean you can't turn off this one?
W It's not easy. Can you see the wheels? After it rings, it rolls around.

M 그것을 살 거니?
W 응, 나는 아침에 일어나기 위해 그것이 필요해.
M 하지만 넌 휴대 전화가 있지 않아? 알람 기능이 없니?
W 있어, 하지만 나는 늘 알람을 끄고 다시 자곤 해.
M 이것은 끌 수가 없다는 말이니?
W 쉽지 않아. 바퀴가 보이지? 이것은 울린 다음에, 굴러다니거든.

만점 솔루션 아침에 일어나기 위해 필요하며 바퀴가 있어서 알람이 울린 다음 굴러다닌다고 했으므로 바퀴가 달린 알람시계임을 알 수 있다.

03 ③

M Good morning. This is today's weather update. I'm your weather forecaster Steve Coyle. Today is Friday and it'll be mostly cloudy but it won't be raining. On the weekend, the weather will be nice and warm. On Monday, we are expecting rain but very little.

M 안녕하세요. 오늘의 날씨 속보입니다. 저는 기상 통보관인 Steve Coyle입니다. 오늘은 금요일이고 대부분 흐린 날이 되겠지만 비는 오지 않을 것입니다. 주말에는, 날씨가 좋고 포근할 것입니다. 월요일에는, 비가 오겠지만 양은 아주 적을 것으로 예상됩니다.

만점 솔루션 오늘이 금요일이므로 내일은 토요일이다. 토요일과 일요일이라는 말 대신 weekend라는 말을 사용했으며 주말에 날씨가 좋을 것이라고 예보했다.

04 ③

M What are you going to do this Saturday?
W I'm going to go shopping with my friend.
M Where are you going to go?
W To Dongdaemun. Do you want to come with us?
M I'd really like to, but I have a dental appointment on that day.

M 이번 토요일에 뭐 할 거니?
W 친구와 쇼핑하러 갈 거야.
M 어디로 갈 거니?
W 동대문에. 너도 우리와 같이 가고 싶니?
M 나도 정말 그러고 싶지만, 그 날 치과 진료 예약이 되어 있어.

05 ④

W Jason, what happened to your leg? Why do you have a cast on?
M I broke it.
W That's too bad. Did it happen yesterday?
M No, it was on Saturday.
W What happened? Did you go skiing?
M No. I slipped on the ice on my way home.

W Jason, 네 다리에 무슨 일이 생긴 거야? 왜 깁스를 하고 있니?
M 다리가 부러졌어.
W 정말 유감이구나. 어제 그런 거야?
M 아니, 토요일에.
W 무슨 일이야? 스키 타러 갔었어?
M 아니. 집에 오는 길에 얼음 위에서 넘어졌어.

만점 솔루션 남자는 집에 오는 길에 넘어져서 깁스를 한 상황이다.

06 ③

① M Did you like the movie?
W Yes, it was funny.
② M Is it 5 o'clock?
W Yes, it is.
③ M What should we eat?
W Yes, that's good.
④ M Where is the milk?
W It's in the fridge.
⑤ M What dose she do?
W She's an English teacher.

① M 그 영화 좋았어?
W 응, 재미있더라.
② M 5시야?
W 응, 그래.
③ M 뭘 먹을까?
W 그래, 그거 좋다.
④ M 우유 어디 있어?
W 냉장고 안에 있어.
⑤ M 그녀의 직업은 뭐니?
W 영어 선생님이셔.

07 ② | ⊕ ⑤

M Do you remember we are going to the concert tonight?
W Sure. When does the concert start?
M It begins at 7.
W Should we leave at 6:30? It will take about 15 minutes by car.
M That's too late. Before the concert, we have to eat something. Let's leave at a quarter past six.
W OK. Then we'll be able to have some snacks.
M All right. I'll pick you up at your house.

M 오늘 밤에 음악회 가기로 한 거 기억하지?
W 물론이지. 음악회가 언제 시작하지?
M 7시에 시작해.
W 6시 30분에 출발해야 할까? 차로 15분 정도 걸릴 거야.
M 그건 너무 늦어. 음악회 전에, 우리는 뭘 좀 먹어야 해. 6시 15분에 출발하자.
W 그래. 그럼 간식을 좀 먹을 수 있을 거야.
M 좋아. 너의 집으로 널 데리러 갈게.

만점 솔루션 음악회가 7시에 시작하니 6시 15분에 출발하자고 남자가 제안하자 여자도 이에 동의하고 있다.

08 ⑤

[Telephone rings.]
W Hello, Nick. This is Sandy.
M Hi, Sandy. What's up?
W Well, I asked you to send me the pictures. I mean the pictures of our field trip.
M I sent them. I sent an e-mail with an attachment an hour ago.
W Oh, did you? But I didn't get it. Can you send them one more time?
M OK. That's not difficult at all.

[전화벨이 울린다.]
W 여보세요, Nick. 나 Sandy야.
M 안녕, Sandy. 무슨 일이니?
W 나에게 사진을 보내달라고 부탁했었는데. 우리 현장 학습 사진 말이야.
M 보냈어. 한 시간 전에 첨부 파일로 붙여서 이메일을 보냈는 걸.

W 오, 그랬니? 하지만 난 못 받았어. 한 번만 다시 그것들을 보내 줄 수 있니?
M 그럴게. 전혀 어려운 일도 아닌데 뭐.

09 ⑤

M Hi, Miranda. Are you waiting for someone?
W Hi, Jack. I'm waiting for a bus to the gym. I'm taking swimming lessons.
M Wow. I'd like to go swimming, too. It's really hot.
W Where are you going?
M I'm going to my aunt's house. Oh, here comes the bus. See you around.
W See you. Bye.

M 안녕, Miranda. 누구 기다리고 있니?
W 안녕, Jack. 체육관에 가려고 버스를 기다리고 있어. 수영 수업을 듣고 있거든.
M 와. 나도 수영하러 가고 싶은 걸. 정말 덥잖아.
W 너는 어디 가는데?
M 나는 이모네 집에 가. 오, 버스가 온다. 또 보자.
W 또 만나. 안녕.

10 ④

M Did you enjoy the dinner?
W Yes, I did. The spaghetti was great.
M I'm glad you enjoyed the meal. What would you like for dessert? We have ice creams, pies and cakes.
W I don't want dessert. Can I just have some tea?
M Of course. Do you need sugar or milk for your tea?
W With milk, please.

M 식사는 맛있게 하셨습니까?
W 예, 맛있었어요. 스파게티가 훌륭했어요.
M 식사를 맛있게 하셨다니 기쁩니다. 후식은 무엇으로 하시겠어요? 아이스크림과 파이, 그리고 케이크가 있습니다.
W 후식은 먹고 싶지 않아요. 차만 마셔도 될까요?
M 물론이죠. 차에 설탕이나 우유를 넣으시겠습니까?
W 우유를 넣어 주세요.

11 ④

M I'm a kind of insect. I'm usually bigger than a fly or a mosquito. I have bright and colorful wings, and they come with many different patterns. I fly from one flower to another flower. I eat nectar from those flowers. What am I?

M 나는 곤충의 한 종류입니다. 나는 보통 파리나 모기보다 커요. 나는 밝고 화려한 날개를 가지고 있고 날개는 많은 다양한 패턴이 있어요. 나는 꽃과 꽃으로 날라갑니다. 나는 꽃으로부터 꿀을 먹어요. 나는 무엇일까요?

12 ② | ⊕ ⑤

W Bill, can you take this garbage out for me?
M But I'm late for school.
W It's only 8 o'clock and it won't take much time.
M All right.
W Don't forget to take your running shoes for your gym class. I washed them. They will be dry now.
M Oh, that's right. I almost forgot about them. Thank you.

W Bill, 이 쓰레기 좀 밖에 내다놓아 주겠니?
M 하지만 저는 학교에 늦었어요.
W 8시밖에 안 되었고 시간이 많이 걸리지도 않을 텐데.
M 알겠어요.
W 체육 수업이 있으니 운동화 가져가는 것을 잊지 마라. 내가 빨았지. 지금쯤이면 말랐을 거야.
M 오, 맞아요. 잊어버릴 뻔했어요. 감사합니다.

만점 솔루션 학교에 가기 전에 쓰레기를 버려달라고 부탁하고, 운동화 가져가는 것을 잊지 말라고 말하는 것으로 보아 아들과 엄마 관계임을 알 수 있다.

13 ④

M Janet, can I borrow your math textbook?
W Sure, but what happened to your book?
M It's totally wet. Kelly spilled water all over my desk.
W Oh, no. Can you dry it?
M I don't think so. I guess I have to get a new one.
W Maybe Kelly will buy you another one.

M Janet, 수학 책 좀 빌려주겠니?
W 물론이지, 하지만 네 책은 어떻게 되었는데?
M 완전히 젖었어. Kelly가 내 책상에 물을 엎질렀어.
W 저런. 말릴 수 있겠니?
M 안될 것 같아. 새 것을 사야 할까 봐.
W Kelly가 한 권 사 줄지도 모르지.

14 ③

M Excuse me, how can I get to the Saint George bus station?
W Walk up the street and turn right at the first corner. That's Willow Street. Walk down the street one block. The bus stop is on your left across Coles.
M Turn right on Willow Street and it's on the left across Coles.
W That's right.
M Thank you very much.

M 실례합니다만, Saint George 버스 정류장에 어떻게 갈 수 있나요?
W 이 길로 가시다가 첫 번째 모퉁이에서 오른쪽으로 도세요. 그곳이 Willow 거리입니다. 한 블록을 걸어가세요. 버스 정류장은 Coles 건너편 당신의 왼쪽에 있어요.
M Willow 거리에서 오른쪽으로 돌아서 Coels 건너편 왼쪽에 있다고요.
W 맞아요.
M 정말 감사합니다.

15 ②

W How long are you staying in Canada?
M A week.
W Which cities are you going to visit?
M I have a business meeting in Toronto on next Monday and Tuesday.
W What will you do after the meeting?
M I'll visit my friend in Ottawa and stay there for four days.
W Sounds great. Have a nice trip.

W 캐나다에 얼마나 머물 예정이니?
M 일주일.
W 어느 도시를 방문할 거니?
M Toronto에서 다음 주 월요일과 화요일에 업무 회의가 있어.
W 회의 이후에는 뭐 할 거니?
M Ottawa에 있는 친구네 집에서 나흘간 머물 거야.
W 멋지다. 여행 잘 다녀 와.

만점 솔루션 Toronto에서는 회의를 하기 위해 월요일과 화요일 이틀간 머물 것이라고 했다.

16 ④

W Fireflies get their names because they make light. Being able to light up has a few benefits for fireflies. Some fireflies use light to scare off animals. Other fireflies use light to catch other bugs to eat. But most fireflies use light to find true love.

W 반딧불이는 빛을 내기 때문에 그 이름을 갖게 되었습니다. 빛을 낼 수 있는 것은 반딧불이에게 몇 가지 이점이 있습니다. 어떤 반딧불이들은 동물들을 겁 주어 떼어내기 위해 빛을 사용합니다. 또 다른 반딧불이들은 다른 먹을 곤충들을 잡기 위해 빛을 사용합니다. 하지만 대부분의 반딧불이들은 자신들의 진정한 짝을 찾기 위해 빛을 사용합니다.

만점 솔루션 반딧불이가 빛을 내서 얻는 이점은 동물을 겁 주어 떼어내기, 먹을 곤충 잡기, 짝 찾기 등으로 설명하고 있는 담화이다.

17 ③

M I'll have a birthday party this Saturday.
W Really? Happy birthday, Paul.
M Can you come to the party?
W Thank you for inviting me, but my mom is in the hospital and I think I have to be home to take care of my sister.
M Oh, I didn't know that. I'm so sorry.
W That's all right. My mom will come home next week.

M 이번 토요일에 생일 파티를 해.
W 정말? 생일 축하해, Paul.
M 파티에 올 수 있니?
W 나를 초대해 줘서 고마워, 하지만 엄마가 병원에 입원해 계셔서 내 여동생을 돌보기 위해 집에 있어야 할 것 같아.
M 저런, 그런 줄은 몰랐어. 정말 유감이야.
W 괜찮아. 엄마는 다음 주에 퇴원하실 거야.

18 ①

M I'm so tired.
W But it's only 3 o'clock.
M I know. I am always tired.
W Maybe you should take a nap.
M But then I won't be able to sleep tonight.
W I think taking a nap helps relieve your stress.
M Do you think so?
W Sure. But do not take a nap for more than 30 minutes.
M OK. Wake me up in 30 minutes.

M 너무 피곤해.
W 하지만 겨우 3시야.
M 알아. 난 항상 피곤해.
W 낮잠을 자야 할 것 같구나.
M 하지만 그러면 오늘 밤에 잠을 못 잘 거야.
W 낮잠을 자는 게 네 스트레스를 풀어 주는 데 도움을 줄 거라고 생각해.
M 그렇게 생각하니?
W 물론. 하지만 30분 이상은 낮잠을 자지 마.
M 알았어. 30분 후에 나를 깨워 줘.

19 ②

M Where are you going this summer?
W I'm not sure. Do you have any suggestions?
M How about going to Jeju Island?
W Jeju Island? Sounds great.
M I was there last summer.
W Really? How did you like it?
M It was fantastic.
W ______________________

M 이번 여름에 어디에 갈 거니?
W 확실하지 않아. 어떤 의견이라도 있니?
M 제주도에 가는 것은 어때?
W 제주도? 멋진데.
M 내가 지난 여름에 거기에 갔었거든.
W 정말? 거기가 얼마나 좋았는데?
M 환상적이었지.
W 그럼, 이번 여름에는 거기에 가야겠다.

① 너는 좀 더 신중해야 해.
③ 나는 팝 콘서트에 가고 싶어.
④ 우리는 오늘 밤에 영화를 보러 갈 거야.
⑤ 너는 지금 바로 병원에 가 보는 게 좋겠어.

만점 솔루션 남자가 제주도에 가라고 하면서 작년에 갔었는데 환상적이라고 말했을 때 여자는 자신도 거기에 가겠다는 말을 하는 것이 가장 적절하다.

20 ⑤

W Good afternoon. May I help you, sir?
M Yes. I'm going to Macy's Department Store before I leave this hotel.

W Then what can I help you with?
M Can you look after these bags?
W Sure. How many bags do you have?
M Three.
W ______________________

W 안녕하세요. 도와드릴까요, 손님?
M 예. 이 호텔을 떠나기 전에 Macy's 백화점에 가 보려고요.
W 그럼 제가 뭘 도와드릴까요?
M 이 가방들을 봐 주시겠어요?
W 물론이죠. 몇 개의 가방들을 가지고 계신가요?
M 세 개요.
W 그 가방들을 이쪽 구석으로 놔 주세요.

① 제가 지금 바로 떠나야 하나요?
② 당신은 운동이 좀 필요한 것 같아요.
③ 백화점으로 운전해 갈까요?
④ 잠시 동안 공원에 산책하러 가는 건 어때요?

영어듣기능력평가 05 회

01 ①	02 ④	03 ④, ➕①	04 ④	05 ①
06 ②	07 ③	08 ⑤	09 ④, ➕③	10 ②
11 ②	12 ①	13 ④	14 ②	15 ⑤
16 ⑤	17 ④	18 ⑤	19 ④	20 ④

01 ①

M Wow, this lake is very beautiful.
W Yeah, I think so, too.
M Hey, why don't we swim in the lake? It'll be fun.
W John, look at the sign over there. It says we can't swim here.
M Oh, I didn't see it.

M 와, 이 호수는 매우 아름답다.
W 그래, 나도 그렇게 생각해.
M 야, 호수에서 수영할래? 재미있을 거야.
W John, 저기에 있는 표지판을 봐. 여기서는 수영을 할 수 없다고 되어 있잖아.
M 오, 그것을 못 봤어.

02 ④

W Sam, what about going bowling with me this Sunday?
M This Sunday? Sorry, I have something to do with my classmates.
W What are you going to do with them?
M We'll play basketball or soccer.
W Then, what about Saturday? If you're not busy, let's go bowling that day.
M Saturday? Okay, I'll go with you.

W Sam, 이번 주 일요일에 나와 볼링 치러 갈래?
M 이번 주 일요일? 미안, 난 반 친구들과 할 일이 있어.
W 그들과 무엇을 할 건데?
M 농구나 축구를 할 거야.
W 그럼, 토요일은 어때? 바쁘지 않으면, 그 날 볼링 치러 가자.
M 토요일? 좋아, 같이 갈게.

03 ④ | ➕①

M Now take a look at the weather for tomorrow. Seoul and the Gyoung gi area are going to have a clear and sunny Saturday. However, for the Chungcheong area, it will be cloudy and cold. If you are in Busan, please carry an umbrella. There'll be a heavy rain from tonight until tomorrow.

M 이제 내일 날씨를 살펴보겠습니다. 서울과 경기 지역은 맑고 화창한 토요일이 될 것입니다. 하지만, 충청 지역은 구름이 끼고 추울 것입니다. 부산에 계신다면, 우산을 챙기세요. 오늘 밤부터 내일까지 많은 비가 내릴 것입니다.

04 ④

W What's up? You look sad.
M Did you hear Melanie is moving soon?
W No, I didn't. Where will she go?
M Her family will go to America.
W When will they leave?
M In August. She said they'll move before the new semester starts.
W That's too bad. I'll miss her.

W 무슨 일이야? 슬퍼 보이네.
M Melanie가 곧 이사 간다는 얘기 들었어?
W 아니, 못 들었어. 그녀가 어디로 갈 거래?
M 그녀의 가족이 미국으로 간대.
W 언제 떠날 거래?
M 8월에. 새 학기가 시작하기 전에 이사한다고 하더라.
W 그거 정말 안됐다. 그녀가 보고 싶을 거야.

05 ①

W Hey, Jake. Are you going to the dance party?
M I don't know. I heard we have to dress up.
W Yes. Don't you have a suit?
M No. I have to buy one.
W It might be expensive, but it is worth buying one.
M You are right. I will need it, anyway.

W 이봐, Jake. 댄스 파티에 갈 거야?
M 모르겠어. 옷을 차려 입어야 한다고 들었어.
W 맞아. 너 정장이 없니?
M 없어. 한 벌 사야 해.
W 비싸겠지만, 한 벌 살 가치는 있어.
M 네 말이 맞아. 어쨌든, 그것이 필요할 테니까.

만점 솔루션 비싸도 정장을 한 벌 살 만한 가치가 있다는 여자의 말에 남자가 동의하고 있다.

06 ②

W Great! My package finally arrived!
M Did it take a long time to get here?
W Yes, almost two months. I thought it would take one month.
M You waited for a long time.
W Yes. I can't wait to open it.
M Me too. I want to see it.

W 좋았어! 내 소포가 마침내 도착했네!
M 여기 도착하는 데 오래 걸렸어?
W 응, 거의 두 달. 한 달 정도 걸릴 거라고 생각했거든.
M 너 오래 기다렸구나.
W 맞아. 빨리 그것을 열어 보고 싶어.
M 나도 그래. 나도 그것을 보고 싶어.

만점 솔루션 여자는 두 달 동안 기다려 받은 소포를 어서 열어 보고 싶어 흥분한 상태이다.

07 ③

W Peter, is there something wrong with you? You don't look good.
M Do I? Nothing special.
W Hey, tell me. Did you get a bad score on the biology test?
M No. In fact, I lost my digital camera in the afternoon.
W Really? You bought it just a week ago, didn't you?
M Yeah. I don't know why I am so careless.

W Peter, 무슨 나쁜 일 있니? 안 좋아 보여.
M 내가? 특별한 일 없어.
W 야, 말해 봐. 생물 시험에서 나쁜 점수를 받았니?
M 아니. 사실, 오후에 내 디지털 카메라를 잃어버렸어.
W 정말? 겨우 일주일 전에 그것을 샀잖아, 그렇지 않니?
M 그래. 나는 왜 이렇게 부주의한지 모르겠어.

08 ⑤

① M Are you busy tomorrow?
W Yes, I am. I have to study all day for an English test.
② M Oh, the sky is getting darker and darker.
W Right. It will rain soon.
③ M How about having seafood spaghetti for lunch?
W That's a good idea!
④ M Hey, where are you going now?
W To the post office.
⑤ M How was your trip to London?
W Sorry, I can't go with you this time.

① M 내일 바빠?
W 응. 하루 종일 영어 시험공부를 해야 해.
② M 오, 하늘이 점점 더 어두워지고 있어.
W 그래. 곧 비가 올 거야.
③ M 점심 식사로 해산물 스파게티 먹는 게 어때?
W 좋은 생각이야!
④ M 야, 지금 어디 가니?
W 우체국에.
⑤ M 런던 여행 어땠니?
W 미안, 이번에는 너와 같이 갈 수 없어.

만점 솔루션 ⑤ 런던 여행이 어땠는지 묻는 말에 대한 응답으로는 '좋았어.' 또는 '나빴어.' 등의 대답이 와야 자연스럽다.

09 ④ | ⊕ ③

W My apartment is too messy.
M Why don't you clean it?

W I don't have time these days. I have extra work.
M You can find a cleaning lady online.
W Really? I should do that tonight.
M I can help you. I found one through the website the other day.

W 내 아파트가 너무 지저분해.
M 왜 청소하지 않는 거야?
W 요즘 내가 시간이 없어. 초과 근무를 하거든
M 인터넷에서 청소해 주는 아주머니를 찾아 볼 수 있어.
W 정말? 오늘 밤에 알아봐야겠네.
M 내가 널 도와줄 수 있어. 나도 며칠 전에 웹사이트를 통해 한 명 찾았거든.

만점 솔루션 초과 근무 때문에 집 청소를 못하는 여자에게 남자가 인터넷을 통해 청소해 주는 아주머니를 구할 수 있다는 말을 하자, 여자는 오늘 밤에 알아보기로 했다.

10 ②

M Stella, what time does the musical start?
W At 7 o'clock sharp.
M Then, let's meet in front of the theater one hour before the show starts.
W Don't you think it's too early?
M No. To have dinner, we need more than 30 minutes.
W Maybe you're right. I see. See you later at the theater.

M Stella, 뮤지컬이 몇 시에 시작하지?
W 7시 정각에.
M 그럼, 뮤지컬이 시작하기 1시간 전에 극장 앞에서 만나자.
W 너무 이르다고 생각하지 않니?
M 아니. 저녁을 먹기 위해서는, 30분 이상 필요해.
W 네 말이 맞을 것 같구나. 알았어. 있다가 극장에서 보자.

만점 솔루션 뮤지컬은 7시 정각에 시작하지만, 저녁을 먹기 위해 1시간 전에 극장 앞에서 만나자고 남자가 제안했고 여자가 동의했으므로, 두 사람은 6시에 만날 것이다.

11 ②

M Many people use this in the summer. It has an electric motor, and it moves the blades. Then, because the air moves in the room, you feel cooler. You can have this on the floor, on the wall, or even on the ceiling. What is this?

M 많은 사람들이 여름에 이것을 사용합니다. 이것은 전동기가 있고 날개를 움직입니다. 공기가 방 안에서 움직이기 때문에 여러분은 더 시원하다고 느낍니다. 여러분은 이것을 바닥에 두거나, 벽에 걸거나, 심지어 천장에 둘 수 있습니다. 이것은 무엇일까요?

12 ①

M Oh, I'm really full. I can't eat any more.
W Me too. So, how was the *bulgogi*? Was it delicious?
M Yes, it was. I think you're a really good cook.
W My pleasure! I am glad you enjoyed the meal.
M Let me wash the dishes. You just rest and watch TV.
W Oh, thank you.

M 오, 정말 배가 불러. 더 이상 못 먹겠어.
W 나도 마찬가지야. 그래, 불고기 어땠어? 맛있었니?
M 그래, 맛있었어. 넌 정말 요리를 잘 하는 것 같아.
W 천만에! 네가 음식을 맛있게 먹었다니 기뻐.
M 내가 설거지를 할게. 넌 그냥 쉬면서 TV를 봐.
W 오, 고마워.

만점 솔루션 남자의 마지막 말 Let me wash the dishes.를 통해 남자가 설거지를 할 것임을 알 수 있다.

13 ④

W Excuse me, is there a drugstore around here?
M Hmm... let me think, yes! Go straight one block and turn right.
W Go straight and... Sorry?
M Turn right after walking one block from here, and walk about 20 meters.
W Okay, thanks, and?
M It'll be on your left side, across from the police station.

W 실례합니다. 여기 근처에 약국이 있나요?
M 흠.. 생각 좀 해보고요, 네! 한 블록 쭉 가서 오른쪽으로 도세요.
W 쭉 가서... 뭐라고요?
M 여기서 한 블록 걸어간 뒤에 오른쪽으로 도세요, 그리고 20미터 걸어가세요.
W 알겠습니다, 고마워요, 그리고요?
M 당신 왼쪽에 약국이 있어요, 경찰서 건너편이요.

14 ②

M Sara, what do you want to be in the future?
W Well... I want to become a fashion model or a jewelry designer.
M Wow, that's cool!
W What about you, Jason? Do you still want to be a teacher?
M No. I have a new dream. I want to be a novelist.
W Oh, that's good. As you are good at writing, you'll become a good writer.

M Sara, 넌 장래에 무엇이 되고 싶니?
W 음… 패션 모델이나 보석 디자이너가 되고 싶어.
M 와, 멋지다!
W 넌 어때, Jason? 여전히 선생님이 되고 싶니?
M 아니. 난 새로운 꿈이 생겼어. 난 소설가가 되고 싶어.
W 오, 멋진데. 넌 글을 잘 쓰니까, 훌륭한 작가가 될 거야.

15 ⑤

W What time is it now?

M It's 5:40.
W Only 5:40? Oh, we still have to wait for one hour before taking the train.
M Yeah, you're right. The train leaves at 6:40.
W Hey, why don't we eat something? I feel a little bit hungry.
M Why not? Let's go downstairs. There are some restaurants there.

W 지금 몇 시야?
M 5시 40분.
W 겨우 5시 40분? 오, 기차를 타려면 아직도 한 시간을 더 기다려야 해.
M 그래, 맞아. 기차가 6시 40분에 출발하니까 말이야.
W 야, 뭐라도 먹을래? 약간 배가 고파.
M 좋아. 아래층으로 가자. 거기에 식당이 몇 개 있어.

16 ⑤

W Did you try them on? What do you think?
M I'm not sure. I think they're a little too tight.
W Would you like to try a bigger size?
M Yes, please.
W What size did you just try?
M Thirty. Actually, can I try both 31 and 32?
W Sure, hold on a second. I will be right back.

W 입어 보셨어요? 어떠세요?
M 잘 모르겠어요. 너무 딱 맞는 거 같아요.
W 더 큰 사이즈로 입어보시겠어요?
M 네, 부탁해요.
W 방금 무슨 사이즈를 입어보셨죠?
M 30이요. 31과 32 두 사이즈를 입어볼 수 있을까요?
W 물론이죠, 잠시만요. 바로 돌아오겠습니다.

17 ④

W Can I talk to you for a minute, Mr. Brown?
M Sure! What's up?
W Well... my parents are going to visit me tomorrow from England.
M Oh, I didn't know that your parents live there.
W They moved there last year. So, can I have a day off tomorrow and go to the airport to see them?
M Sure, you can. Instead of coming to the office tomorrow, just go to the airport.
W Thank you.

W Brown 씨, 잠시 이야기 나눌 수 있을까요?
M 그럼요! 무슨 일이죠?
W 저… 내일 부모님이 영국에서 저를 보러 오시거든요.
M 오, 부모님이 그곳에 사시는 줄 몰랐어요.
W 그분들은 작년에 그곳으로 이사하셨어요. 그래서, 내일 하루 휴가 내서 부모님을 마중하러 공항에 갈 수 있을까요?
M 물론, 그러세요. 내일은 사무실에 오는 대신에, 바로 공항으로 가세요.
W 고맙습니다.

18 ⑤

W Could you drive today?
M Why? I thought you liked driving.
W Sometimes, but I don't know this area.
M OK, then. Can you check the map for me?
W Sure. Shall I tell you which way to go?
M Yes, please. Only in the city, though.
W Do you know where to go on the highway?
M Yeah, I've been here before.

W 오늘 네가 운전할래?
M 왜? 네가 운전하는 거 좋아하는 줄 알았는데.
W 가끔은. 하지만 난 이 지역을 잘 모르거든.
M 좋아. 그럼, 나를 위해 지도를 확인해 줄 수 있어?
W 물론이지. 너에게 어느 길로 가야 하는지 말해 줘야 하는 거야?
M 응. 하지만, 시내에서만.
W 고속도로에서는 어디로 가야 하는지 알아?
M 응. 전에 여기 온 적이 있어.

만점 솔루션 운전을 대신 해 주기로 한 남자는 여자에게 시내에서 지도를 보고 가야 할 길을 말해 달라고 부탁하고 있다.

19 ④

M Oh, I feel hungry. Do you have anything to eat?
W Just wait a minute. I'll make a sandwich for you.
M Thanks, Mom. If you need my help, please tell me.
W Then, can you go to the mart and buy a jar of mayonnaise?
M Sure! I can go to the mart right away.
W ______________________

M 오, 배가 고파요. 먹을 것이 있어요?
W 잠시만 기다려라. 샌드위치를 만들어 주마.
M 고마워요, 엄마. 제 도움이 필요하면, 말씀하세요.
W 그럼, 가게에 가서 마요네즈 한 통을 사다 줄래?
M 물론이죠! 지금 바로 가게에 갈 수 있어요.
W 좋아! 마요네즈 값 10달러 여기 있다.

① 나도 마요네즈를 좋아하지 않아.
② 물론이죠! 저는 햄 샌드위치를 아주 좋아해요.
③ 정말 맛있어요. 엄마는 요리를 잘 하세요.
⑤ 저녁 먹기 전에 먼저 손부터 씻어라.

만점 솔루션 엄마가 아들에게 마요네즈를 사다 달라고 하자 아들이 바로 다녀오겠다고 했으므로, 아들에게 돈을 주며 하는 말이 엄마의 대답으로 가장 적절하다.

20 ④

M Alice, why don't we go to the Seven Star Concert Hall this evening?
W To the Seven Star Concert Hall?
M Yeah, I have free tickets for a rock concert.
W Really? I like rock music a lot. Thank you, Andy.
M Don't mention it.

W What time does the concert start?
M At 7 o'clock.
W ______________________

M Alice, 오늘 저녁에 Seven Star 콘서트 홀에 갈래?
W Seven Star 콘서트 홀에?
M 그래, 록 콘서트 무료 입장권이 있거든.
W 정말? 나 록 음악 아주 좋아해. 고마워, Andy.
M 천만에.
W 콘서트가 몇 시에 시작하니?
M 7시에.
W 그럼, 6시 30분에 홀 앞에서 만나자.

① 좋아, 너를 위해 내가 표를 살게.
② 그럼, 어젯밤에 어디 갔었니?
③ 미안하지만, 이번에는 너를 도와줄 수 없어.
⑤ 정말? 하지만 너는 록 음악을 좋아하잖아, 안 그래?

영어듣기능력평가 06 회

01 ⑤	02 ④	03 ②	04 ③	05 ②
06 ④	07 ①	08 ②	09 ⑤, ➊①	10 ③
11 ⑤	12 ①	13 ④	14 ③	15 ②, ➊④
16 ⑤	17 ②	18 ③	19 ③	20 ③

01 ⑤

M You can use one of these when the power goes out. It will give you some light in a dark room. Or, you can use these on your birthday. After your friends sing "Happy Birthday," you make a wish and blow these out. What are these?

M 여러분은 전기가 나갔을 때 이것들 중 하나는 사용할 수 있습니다. 이것은 어두운 방 안에 약간의 빛을 줄 것입니다. 여러분은 이것들을 생일에 사용할 수도 있습니다. 친구들이 생일축하 노래를 부른 뒤, 당신은 소원을 빌고 이것들을 꺼트립니다. 이것들은 무엇일까요?

02 ④

M What are you drawing for homework?
W I don't know. I was going to draw a bicycle at first. But I changed my mind.
M Why?
W I thought it was too hard for me.
M Then, how about apples or hands?
W My friends are drawing them. So I will draw a bottle.
M Sounds good.

M 숙제로 무엇을 그릴 거니?
W 모르겠어. 처음에는 자전거를 그릴 예정이었어. 하지만 마음을 바꿨어.
M 왜?
W 그게 나에겐 너무 어렵다고 생각했거든.
M 그럼, 사과나 손은 어때?
W 내 친구들이 그것들을 그릴 거야. 그래서 나는 병을 그릴 거야.
M 괜찮은데.

03 ②

W Good evening. Here's the weather forecast. Today was nice enough to go out. But tomorrow will be a little different. It will be very windy all day and you will feel very cold. But you don't have to take your umbrella with you when you go out. We will not have rain tomorrow.

W 안녕하세요. 일기 예보입니다. 오늘은 외출하기에 충분히 날씨가 좋았습니다. 하지만 내일은 약간 다를 것입니다. 하루 종일 바람이 아주 많이 불고 매우 추울 것입니다. 하지만 외출할 때 우산을 가지고 가실 필요는 없습니다. 내일은 비가 오지 않을 것입니다.

04 ③

M Is there anything I can do for you, honey?
W Well, we need to order some meat online today.
M Why is that?
W My parents will visit us this Saturday. We're going to have a barbecue party.
M I see. How much meat should I order?
W Order three kilograms, please.
M Okay. I'll do it right away.

M 여보, 제가 도와줄 일이 있나요?
W 음, 오늘은 인터넷에서 고기를 좀 주문해야겠어요.
M 왜 그렇죠?
W 부모님이 이번 주 토요일에 우리를 방문하실 거예요. 우리는 바비큐 파티를 할 예정이에요.
M 알겠어요. 고기를 얼마나 주문해야 하죠?
W 3킬로그램을 주문해 주세요.
M 알겠어요. 지금 바로 그렇게 할게요.

만점 솔루션 여자는 토요일에 바비큐 파티를 할 예정이라며 남자에게 고기를 주문해 달라고 부탁하는 상황이다.

05 ②

① **W** Would you tell me the way to the post office?
M Sure. Turn right and it's on your left.
② **W** I want to take violin lessons.
M Really? I just bought this violin.
③ **W** Can I get you something to eat?
M Thank you. I'm so hungry.
④ **W** What time do you have?
M It's 9:30.
⑤ **W** I enjoyed the party. Thank you for inviting me.
M I am so happy to hear that.

① **W** 우체국에 가는 길 좀 알려 주시겠어요?
M 그러죠. 우회전하면 당신의 왼편에 있습니다.
② **W** 바이올린 수업을 받고 싶습니다.
M 정말요? 저는 이 바이올린을 방금 샀습니다.
③ **W** 먹을 것 좀 가져다 드릴까요?
M 고맙습니다. 아주 배가 고프군요.
④ **W** 몇 시죠?
M 9시 30분입니다.
⑤ **W** 파티가 즐거웠습니다. 초대해 주셔서 감사합니다.
M 그 말을 들으니 기분이 아주 좋네요.

06 ④

W Hurry up! We are late for the class. It's already 10:10!
M Don't worry. We have time.
W Are you kidding? The class started at 10:00, didn't it?
M No, we still have five minutes left.
W Are you sure?
M It starts later because his 9 o'clock class ends at 10:10.
W I see. That gives us five minutes to get to class.
M Right. The class is a bit longer than ours.

W 서둘러! 우린 수업에 늦었어. 벌써 10시 10분이야!
M 걱정 마. 우린 시간이 있어.
W 농담해? 수업이 10시에 시작했어, 그렇지 않니?
M 아니, 아직 5분 남았어.
W 확실해?
M 그의 9시 수업이 10시 10분에 끝나서 그 후에 시작해.
W 그렇군. 그럼 수업에 가는 데 5분이 있는 거네.
M 맞아. 그 수업이 우리 수업보다 조금 더 길어.

만점 솔루션 현재 시각은 10시 10분인데 수업까지 5분이 남았다고 했으므로, 수업 시작 시간은 10시 15분이 된다.

07 ①

[Telephone rings.]
W Hello.
M Hi! Jenny. It's me, Tom.
W Hi, Tom. Are you getting better? How's your cold?
M I'm feeling better. Thank you for asking. By the way, I'm calling to ask you about the math homework.
W Let me tell you about it. The math teacher told us to solve the problems on page 16.
M Did he say just one page?
W Yes. We were so happy to hear that.

[전화벨이 울린다.]
W 여보세요.
M 안녕! Jenny. 나야, Tom.
W 안녕, Tom. 건강이 좋아지고 있는 거니? 네 감기는 어때?
M 좋아지고 있어. 물어봐 줘서 고맙다. 그건 그렇고, 너에게 수학 숙제에 대해 물어보려고 전화했어.
W 그것에 대해 말해 줄게. 수학 선생님이 16쪽에 있는 문제들을 풀라고 말씀하셨어.
M 겨우 한 페이지라고 말씀하셨니?
W 그래. 그 말을 듣고 우리는 기분이 아주 좋았지.

08 ②

W You look lost. Do you need any help?
M Oh, yes, please. I'm looking for White Lion.
W Oh, I know that restaurant. Go straight to Baker Street, and turn left at the corner.
M White Lion is on Baker Street?
W Yes, it is. After you turn left, walk one more block. Then cross the street. It's next to the big post office and across from a bank.
M Thank you so much.

W 길을 잃은 거 같네요. 도와드릴까요?
M 아, 네, 부탁드립니다. 화이트 라이온을 찾고 있습니다.
W 아, 그 레스토랑 알아요. 베이커 가로 쭉 가신 다음에 모퉁이에서 왼쪽으로 도세요.

M 화이트 라이온이 베이커 가에 있나요?
W 네. 왼쪽으로 돈다음에 한 블록 더 걸어가세요. 그리고 길을 건너세요. 큰 우체국 옆, 큰 은행 건너편에 있어요.
M 정말 감사합니다.

09 ⑤ | ➕ ①

M Sarah, what do you want to study in the university?
W I want to study math. What about you?
M When I was young I wanted to major in history or language. But later I changed my mind.
W So what do you want to study?
M I want to study computer engineering.
W Sounds interesting.

M Sarah, 너는 대학교에서 무엇을 공부하고 싶니?
W 수학을 공부하고 싶어. 너는 어때?
M 어렸을 때는 역사학이나 언어학을 전공하고 싶었어. 하지만 이후에는 마음을 바꾸었어.
W 그러면 무엇을 공부하고 싶은데?
M 컴퓨터 공학을 공부하고 싶어.
W 재미있겠다.

10 ③

M You look so happy. Please tell me the reason. I want to share your happiness with you.
W Guess what, Henry.
M You got a good grade in math, or you got a new boyfriend?
W Well, no. It's more than that. Let me give you a hint. It's about my writing.
M Did you win the first prize in the Book Report Contest?
W Exactly! I'm so happy about that.

M 기분이 아주 좋아 보이는데. 이유를 말해 줘. 네 기쁨을 함께 나누고 싶어.
W 그게 무엇인지 맞혀 봐, Henry.
M 수학에서 좋은 점수를 받았거나 아니면 새로운 남자 친구가 생겼지?
W 음, 아니. 그것보다 더한 거야. 힌트를 하나 줄게. 나의 작문에 관한 거야.
M 독후감 대회에서 우승했니?
W 정확해! 그래서 너무 기뻐.

11 ⑤

M Nice to meet you all. My name is Jack Tyler. I'm in the first grade of middle school. I joined this biking club to make good friends. Someday I want to be a TV reporter. I will interview famous people. I like to play basketball on weekends. I want to play basketball with you guys sometime in the future.

M 너희 모두를 만나게 되어 기뻐. 내 이름은 Jack Tyler야. 나는 중학교 1학년이야. 나는 좋은 친구들을 사귀기 위해 이 자전거 동아리에 가입했어. 언젠가 나는 TV 기자가 되고 싶어. 나는 유명한 사람들을 인터뷰할 거야. 주말에는 농구하는 것을 좋아해. 앞으로 언제든 너희들과 농구를 하고 싶어.

12 ①

M These days my hair is falling out. I don't know why.
W Do you wash your hair every day?
M Not every day, but once every two days.
W Then how about changing your shampoo into this one?
M Would it help?
W Well, this shampoo stops your hair from falling out.

M 요즘 머리카락이 빠지고 있어요. 그 이유를 모르겠어요.
W 매일 머리를 감나요?
M 매일은 아니지만 이틀에 한 번은 감죠.
W 그렇다면 당신의 샴푸를 이것으로 바꾸는 게 어떨까요?
M 그것이 도움이 될까요?
W 음, 이 샴푸는 당신의 머리카락이 빠지는 것을 막아 줘요.

만점 솔루션 여자는 how about~?이라는 표현을 이용하여 샴푸를 바꾸어 볼 것을 제안하고 있다.

13 ④

W What are you doing, Matt?
M I'm looking for my notebook. I think I lost it.
W Is this your notebook?
M Oh! Yes. Where did you find it?
W In the classroom. You left it there yesterday.
M Thank you, Mrs. Olsen.
W Be careful not to misplace your things.

W 무엇을 하고 있니, Matt?
M 제 공책을 찾고 있어요. 그것을 잃어버린 것 같아요.
W 이게 네 공책이니?
M 오! 그래요. 어디서 그것을 찾으셨나요?
W 교실에서. 그것을 어제 거기에 놓고 갔더구나.
M 고맙습니다. Olsen 선생님.
W 물건을 잘못 놓고 다니지 않도록 주의하렴.

14 ③

M I can't wait for our school's sports day next week.
W Same here. What date is today?
M It's May 12th. We have five days to go.
W I feel excited.
M Me too. This is my first sports day in middle school.
W I'm sure we'll have a lot of fun on that day.

M 다음 주 학교 체육대회가 정말 기다려져.
W 나도 그래. 오늘이 며칠이지?
M 5월 12일이야. 앞으로 5일 남았어.
W 흥분이 돼.
M 나도 그래. 이번이 중학교에서 하는 첫 번째 체육대회잖아.
W 난 우리가 그 날 아주 재미있는 시간을 보낼 거라고 확신해.

만점 솔루션 오늘은 5월 12일이고 체육대회까지 5일 남았으므로 5월 17일이 체육대회 날짜이다.

15 ② | ⊕ ④

W May I help you?
M Yes. I have a project and I need the book *The Family*.
W Well, let me check. [*pause*] I'm sorry, but somebody has already checked out the book. You have to wait for a few days.
M A few days? Exactly how long do I have to wait for?
W It is going to come back next Monday. I mean, you have to wait for four days.
M I see.

W 도와드릴까요?
M 예. 프로젝트가 있어서 'The Family'라는 책이 필요합니다.
W 음, 확인해볼게요. *[잠시 후]* 미안하지만, 이미 누군가가 그 책을 대출했네요. 며칠 기다리셔야 해요.
M 며칠이라고요? 정확히 제가 얼마나 기다려야 하나요?
W 그것은 다음 주 월요일에 반납될 거예요. 그러니까, 4일 동안 기다리셔야 해요.
M 알겠습니다.

만점 솔루션 남자가 찾는 책이 이미 대출되었다고 하는 것으로 보아 '도서관'에서 나누는 대화임을 알 수 있다.

16 ⑤

W I can't wait for Friday.
M Because of the field trip?
W Yes, I've always wanted to go to the new zoo!
M Oh, didn't you hear? The school changed the field trip.
W No way, what do you mean?
M The weather forecast says it'll rain Friday, so we're going to the science museum instead.
W What? That sounds boring!

W 금요일이 기다려진다.
M 현장 학습때문에?
W 응, 나 새로 생긴 동물원에 항상 가고 싶었어.
M 아, 못 들었어? 학교가 현장 학습을 변경했어.
W 안돼, 무슨 뜻이야?
M 일기 예보에서 금요일에 비가 온다고 해서 대신에 과학 박물관에 가게 되었어.
W 뭐라고? 진짜 지루하겠네!

17 ②

W Hello, Mr. Johnson. How do you feel today?
M A little better. But I still have a stomachache.
W Did the medicine I gave you yesterday help you?
M Yes, I think so. I don't have a headache anymore.
W In that case, keep taking it and see me tomorrow.
M Yes, I'll do that.

W John 씨, 안녕하세요. 오늘은 기분이 어떠세요?
M 조금 더 나아요. 하지만 여전히 복통이 있어요.
W 제가 어제 드린 약이 도움이 되셨나요?
M 예, 그런 것 같아요. 더 이상 두통은 없어요.
W 그럼, 그것을 계속 복용하시고 내일 다시 보시죠.
M 예, 그럴게요.

만점 솔루션 약을 처방해 주고 병세를 묻고 답하는 것으로 보아, 의사와 환자의 관계임을 알 수 있다.

18 ③

M Can you make copies of this document?
W Sure. How many copies do you need?
M 10 copies. But it's only 2 pages long.
W Do you want the copies on both sides?
M Yes. Then we don't have to staple it.
W That's good. Then we will only need 10 pieces of paper.
M Yes, I'd like to save paper whenever possible.
W OK. They will be ready in about 5 minutes.

M 이 서류를 복사해 줄 수 있어요?
W 물론이죠. 몇 부 필요하세요?
M 10부요. 하지만 겨우 2페이지짜리에요.
W 양면 복사를 원하세요?
M 예. 그럼 스테이플로 그것을 고정시킬 필요가 없죠.
W 좋아요. 그럼 10장의 종이만 필요할 거예요.
M 예, 가능하면 종이를 절약하고 싶어요.
W 알겠어요. 약 5분 후면 준비될 거예요.

만점 솔루션 남자는 여자에게 2페이지짜리 서류를 10부 양면 복사해 달라고 부탁하고 있으므로 10장의 종이가 필요할 것이다.

19 ③

M Which language are you taking this semester?
W I'm thinking of taking French. Do you want to take it with me?
M I think it's too difficult for me.
W Actually my family is planning to take a trip to France this summer.
M Sounds nice. That's the reason you want to take French.
W ______________________

M 이번 학기에는 어떤 언어를 수강할 거니?
W 나는 불어를 수강할까 생각 중이야. 나랑 그것을 함께 들을래?
M 그게 나에겐 너무 어려운 것 같아.
W 사실 우리 가족이 이번 여름에 프랑스로 여행을 갈 계획이야.
M 좋겠다. 그게 네가 불어를 수강하고 싶어 하는 이유구나.
W 맞아. 그때 내 불어를 연습할 수 있잖아.

① 프랑스에서 재미있는 시간을 보냈어.

② 불어는 나에게도 쉽지 않아.
④ 그래. 여행을 위해 쇼핑하러 가야 해.
⑤ 좋아. 나는 함께 여행을 하고 싶어.

20 ③

W What's wrong with the computer?
M It doesn't start at all.
W Maybe it's because there is a lot of dust in the computer. Before you take it to the repair shop, try to vacuum out all the dust in it.
M Did you have the same experience?
W ______________________

W 컴퓨터에 무슨 문제가 있나요?
M 전혀 작동이 안 돼요.
W 아마도 컴퓨터 안에 먼지가 많기 때문일 거예요. 그것을 수리점에 가지고 가기 전에, 그 안에 있는 먼지를 진공청소기로 다 빨아들여 보세요.
M 같은 경험을 해 보셨나요?
W 예. 제것은 진공청소기로 먼지를 빨아들인 후에 괜찮아졌어요.

① 아니요. 저는 진공청소기로 청소하는 것을 잘 못해요.
② 좋아요. 저는 똑같은 것을 사고 싶어요.
④ 맞습니다. 컴퓨터가 작동하지 않을 거예요.
⑤ 예. 당신은 그것을 수리점에 가지고 갈 필요가 있어요.

만점 솔루션 남자의 컴퓨터가 작동되지 않는다고 하자 여자는 컴퓨터 안의 먼지를 진공청소기로 빨아들일 것을 충고한다. 이에 남자는 같은 경험이 있었느냐고 물었으므로 이에 대한 여자의 응답은 자신의 경험을 말하는 것이 가장 적절하다.

영어듣기능력평가 07회

01 ②	02 ①	03 ①	04 ③, ⊕⑤	05 ④
06 ①, ⊕③	07 ②	08 ⑤	09 ⑤	10 ①
11 ②	12 ①	13 ④	14 ②	15 ③
16 ②	17 ④	18 ③	19 ⑤	20 ③

01 ②

M I am a bird, but I can't fly. Instead of flying, I can swim very well. I catch fish while I swim. When I lay an egg, I have to keep it warm. It's hard work for parents because I live in a cold place. You can see me standing on snow with thousands of my friends. I have a black back and black wings, but my belly is white.

M 저는 새이지만, 날지는 못합니다. 나는 것 대신, 저는 수영을 아주 잘 합니다. 저는 수영하는 동안 물고기를 잡습니다. 제가 알을 낳으면, 그것을 따뜻하게 유지해 주어야 합니다. 저는 추운 곳에 살기 때문에 그것은 부모들에게 힘든 일입니다. 여러분은 제가 수천 명의 제 친구들과 함께 눈 위에 서 있는 것을 볼 수 있습니다. 저는 검은색 등과 검은색 날개를 가졌지만, 저의 배는 흰색입니다.

02 ①

W Look, I got it from my sister for my birthday present.
M Do you use it every morning?
W Of course. You might not need it. You have short hair, so it dries quickly. But my hair is long. I need it to dry my hair every morning.
M I sometimes use it to dry my hair, too.

W 이것 좀 봐. 언니한테 이것을 생일 선물로 받았어.
M 넌 그것을 매일 아침마다 사용하니?
W 물론이지. 너는 필요하지 않을지도 모르겠다. 너는 머리가 짧으니까, 금세 마르잖아. 하지만 나는 머리가 길어. 내 머리를 말리기 위해 매일 아침 그것을 사용해야 해.
M 나도 가끔은 내 머리를 말리는 데 그것을 사용해.

03 ①

M Good morning. This is Jim Kelly from the weather center. We are having hot dry summer days. Today, will be another hot and sunny day in the morning, but there is good news: A rain shower in the afternoon. Let's hope it will cool us down in this hot dry weather. Thank you for listening.

M 안녕하십니까. 기상청의 Jim Kelly입니다. 덥고 건조한 여름 날이 계속되고 있습니다. 오늘 아침 역시 또 하루의 덥고 맑은 날이 되겠지만, 좋은 소식이 있습니다. 오후에는 소나기 소식이 있습니다. 이 덥고 건조한 날씨를 시원하게 식혀 주기를 기대해 봐야겠습니다. 들어주셔서 감사합니다.

04 ③ | ⊕ ⑤

M What do you usually do on weekends?

W My grandmother lives alone, so my family visits her on Saturdays.

M Wow. That's great. Saturday is my basketball day. My friends and I usually meet at the gym.

W How about on Sunday?

M I go to church.

M 넌 주말에 주로 무엇을 하니?

W 할머니가 혼자 사셔서, 우리 가족은 토요일마다 할머니 댁에 가.

M 와. 대단한 걸. 토요일은 내가 농구하는 날이야. 친구들과 나는 보통 체육관에서 만나.

W 일요일은 어떤데?

M 교회에 가지.

05 ④

W The Eiffel Tower is a famous building. It is an iconic symbol of France. It is 324 meters tall. It was built in 1889, and it was the tallest building in Paris at that time. Today there are many buildings taller than the Eiffel, but it is still the tallest tower in Paris. Since the Eiffel Tower opened, more than 200 million visitors have visited the landmark.

W 에펠탑은 유명한 건물입니다. 그것은 프랑스의 상징물입니다. 그 높이는 324미터입니다. 그것은 1889년에 만들어졌고, 그 당시 파리에서 가장 높은 건물이었습니다. 오늘날 에펠탑보다 더 높은 많은 건물들이 있지만, 그것은 여전히 파리에서 가장 높은 탑입니다. 에펠탑이 문을 연 이래로, 2억 명 이상의 방문객이 그 역사적 건물을 다녀갔습니다.

만점 솔루션 Eiffel Tower보다 더 높은 건물들은 많지만, 파리에서 가장 높은 탑은 Eiffel Tower라고 했다.

06 ① | ⊕ ③

[Cellphone rings.]

W Hello. This is Amanda.

M Hello. This is Jackson in A&T Co. I'd like to ask if you can draw a picture for us.

W Sure. What do you want to use it for?

M I need it for an advertisement that will be in a magazine.

W What would you like to advertise?

M I want to advertise our new sneakers. We need a nice drawing for them. I'll email you some details.

W Fine. I'll call you back after I review them.

[휴대 전화 벨이 울린다.]

W 여보세요. Amanda입니다.

M 여보세요. A&T 회사의 Jackson입니다. 우리를 위해 그림을 그려 주실 수 있는지 여쭤 보고 싶어서요.

W 물론이죠. 그것을 어디에 사용하고 싶으신가요?

M 잡지에 실릴 광고를 위해 그것이 필요합니다.

W 어떤 광고를 하기를 원하시나요?

M 우리의 새 신발을 광고하고 싶어요. 우리는 그것들의 멋진 그림이 필요해요. 몇 가지 자세한 사항은 이메일로 보내드릴게요.

W 좋아요. 그것들을 검토해 보고 나서 다시 전화 드릴게요.

만점 솔루션 남자가 여자에게 그림을 그려 달라고 부탁하고 있으므로 여자의 직업이 '화가'임을 알 수 있다.

07 ②

① **W** Can I borrow your pen?
M Sure. Here you go.

② **W** How long is this desk?
M It is over an hour.

③ **W** Where did you get that backpack?
M I bought it downtown.

④ **W** Do you think we should leave now?
M No, let's wait for Jenny to come.

⑤ **W** It's a nice day today, isn't it?
M Yes, it's warm and sunny.

① **W** 네 펜을 빌릴 수 있을까?
M 물론이지. 여기 있어.

② **W** 이 책상 길이가 얼마나 되니?
M 한 시간 이상이야.

③ **W** 저 배낭 어디서 났어?
M 난 그것을 시내에서 샀어.

④ **W** 우리가 지금 떠나야 한다고 생각해?
M 아니, Jenny가 오기를 기다리자.

⑤ **W** 오늘 날씨 좋지, 그렇지 않아?
M 맞아, 따뜻하고 화창해.

만점 솔루션 ② 책상의 길이를 묻고 있으므로 미터 혹은 센티미터 등의 길이로 답해야 한다.

08 ⑤

[Telephone rings.]

W Hello.

M Helen, this is Dad. I need your help. Can you turn on the computer?

W All right, Dad. I'm turning it on.

M Open the "my document" folder. There is a powerpoint presentation file. The name of the file is "September presentation."

W Yes, I found it.

M Good. Can you email the file to me?

W All right.

[전화벨이 울린다.]

W 여보세요.

M Helen, 아빠다. 네가 좀 도와줬으면 좋겠구나. 컴퓨터를 켤 수 있겠니?

W 그럼요, 아빠. 켜고 있어요.

M '내 문서' 폴더를 열어라. 파워포인트 프레젠테이션 파일이 있단다. 파일 이름은 '9월 프레젠테이션'이야.

W 예, 찾았어요.

M 그래. 그 파일을 나에게 전자우편으로 보내 주겠니?
W 그럴게요.

09 ⑤

M Do you know that the Earth is getting warmer?
W I know. Global warming is a real big issue these days.
M There are floods and droughts all over the world. I believe pollution is the reason for that.
W I agree with you. We should know that there is only one Earth and we have to protect it.

M 지구가 점점 더워지고 있다는 것을 아니?
W 알아. 지구 온난화는 요즘 정말 큰 논쟁거리야.
M 세계 도처에 홍수와 가뭄이 있어. 나는 공해가 그것의 원인이라고 생각해.
W 네 말에 동의해. 지구는 하나뿐이라는 것을 알고 우리는 그것을 보호해야 해.

만점 솔루션 지구 온난화에 대해 언급하며 지구를 보호해야 한다고 말하고 있으므로, 대화의 주제로는 '환경 보호'가 가장 적절하다.

10 ①

M You use these to listen to music or the radio. You put these on your head. If you use these, only you can hear the music. That is good because you won't disturb other people. But you have to be careful, because you can't hear other noises. What are these?

M 여러분은 이것을 음악이나 라디오를 들을 때 사용해요. 여러분은 이것을 머리에 써요. 이것을 이용하면 음악만 들을 수 있어요. 여러분이 다른 사람들을 방해하지 않으니 좋습니다. 하지만 다른 소리를 들을 수 없으니까 조심해야 해요. 이것은 무엇일까요?

11 ②

M Hey, Sara. What are you doing here? Can you help us and come to the school library?
W School library? For what?
M We are cleaning the library today. Didn't you know that?
W Oh, no. I forgot that. Just wait a minute. I'll call my piano teacher and tell her I'll be late for the lesson.
M All right. I'll see you at the library.

M 이봐, Sara. 여기서 뭐 하고 있니? 우리를 도와주러 학교 도서관에 올 수 있니?
W 학교 도서관? 왜?
M 우리는 오늘 도서관을 청소하고 있어. 몰랐니?
W 저런. 잊어버렸어. 잠시만 기다려. 피아노 선생님께 전화해서 수업에 늦는다고 말씀드려야겠다.
M 좋아. 도서관에서 보자.

12 ①

[Cellphone rings.]
W Hello. This is Ann. Everybody there?
M Not quite.
W Hasn't Bob arrived there yet?
M No, he's late as usual.
W I can't believe it! I was sure he would be there by now.
M It is not surprising, though. He's late every day.
W But he promised me that he would be on time today.
M No way.

[휴대 전화 벨이 울린다.]
W 여보세요. 나 Ann이야. 모두 왔니?
M 물론 아니지.
W Bob이 아직 거기 도착 안 했어?
M 아니, 그는 항상 그렇듯이 늦고 있어.
W 믿을 수가 없어! 지금쯤이면 거기 도착했을 거라고 확신했는데.
M 뭐, 놀랄 일도 아니지. 그는 매일 늦잖아.
W 하지만 그가 오늘은 제 시간에 올 거라고 내게 약속했거든.
M 말도 안 돼.

만점 솔루션 남자의 마지막 말은 Bob이 제 시간에 올 리가 없다는 부정의 의미이다.

13 ④

[Telephone rings.]
M Hello.
W Hello, this is the HBS radio quiz show, "Quiz Quiz." Who are you and where are you calling from?
M I'm Juwon from Gwangju.
W Thanks for calling and nice to meet you, Juwon. Please hang on. We are talking to another person for today's show. Juwon, are you ready to meet your partner?
M Yes, I am.

[전화벨이 울린다.]
M 여보세요.
W 여보세요. HBS의 라디오 퀴즈 쇼 '퀴즈 퀴즈'입니다. 어디에 사시는 누구신가요?
M 광주에 사는 주원입니다.
W 주원 씨, 전화 주셔서 감사하고 만나게 되어 반갑습니다. 끊지 말고 기다리세요. 오늘 쇼를 위해 또 다른 한 분과 이야기할 거예요. 주원 씨, 상대방을 만날 준비가 되셨나요?
M 예.

14 ②

W Excuse me, where is the City Information Center?
M Go straight. You will meet Ann Street.
W Go to the Ann Street.
M And turn right. You can see the Information Center on your left. It's across from the police station, between a coffee shop and a cinema.
W Thank you.

W 실례합니다, 도시 안내 센터가 어디인가요?
M 곧장 가시면 Ann 거리가 나올 거예요.
W Ann 거리까지 가라고요.
M 그리고 우회전하세요. 안내 센터가 당신의 왼편에 보일 겁니다. 경찰서 건너편, 커피숍과 영화관 사이에 있죠.
W 감사합니다.

15 ③

W When will the fireworks show start?
M It should begin at 10 o'clock.
W How long will it last?
M It's usually half an hour long.
W So it will be over by 10:30?
M Yes, that's how it's scheduled as long as the weather is nice this evening.
W It looks like we'll have clear skies tonight, but what happens if the weather is bad?
M It depends. They might cancel the show or finish it early.

W 불꽃놀이 쇼는 언제 시작해?
M 10시 정각에 시작할 거야.
W 얼마나 오랫동안 하는 거지?
M 보통은 30분 정도야.
W 그럼 10시 30분이면 끝나겠네?
M 응, 오늘 밤에 날씨가 괜찮기만 하면 그렇게 예정되어 있어.
W 오늘 밤에는 하늘이 맑을 것 같은데, 날씨가 안 좋으면 어떻게 되는 거야?
M 상황에 따라 달라. 쇼가 취소되거나 일찍 끝날 수도 있어.

만점 솔루션 오늘 밤에는 날씨가 좋다고 했으므로 불꽃놀이 쇼는 10시 30분에 끝날 것이다.

16 ②

W Paul, please come here and help me.
M What's the matter?
W The computer monitor suddenly went black.
M Push the reset button.
W No way. I'm working on an important file. If I push the button, I'll lose the file.
M Do you mean you didn't save it?
W I didn't. Oh, please, what should I do?

W Paul, 이리 와서 저 좀 도와줘요.
M 무슨 일인데요?
W 컴퓨터 모니터가 갑자기 까맣게 되었어요.
M 리셋 버튼을 눌러봐요.
W 안 돼요. 중요한 파일을 작업 중이에요. 제가 그 버튼을 누르면, 그 파일을 잃어버리게 되잖아요.
M 그 파일을 저장하지 않았단 말이에요?
W 안 했어요. 오, 제발요, 어떻게 해야 하죠?

17 ④

[Cellphone rings.]
W Hi, Steve. I'm leaving for your house. Can you tell me your address?
M How are you coming?
W I'm driving. I have a GPS car navigation system.
M Well, I don't think you can come in time for the party if you drive.
W Why not? Because of the traffic?
M That's right. Why don't you take the subway? It'll only take 40 minutes.
W All right. I don't want to be late. Thanks for your advice.

[휴대 전화 벨이 울린다.]
W 안녕, Steve. 너의 집으로 출발할 거야. 주소 좀 알려 줄래?
M 어떻게 올 거니?
W 운전하고 갈 거야. GPS 자동차 네비게이션이 있거든.
M 음, 네가 운전하고 오면 파티 시간에 맞춰서 오기 힘들 것 같아.
W 왜 힘들지? 교통 체증 때문에?
M 맞아. 지하철을 타는 게 어때? 40분밖에 안 걸릴 텐데.
W 알았어. 나도 늦기는 싫어. 충고 고마워.

18 ③

W Good afternoon, I'd like to borrow this book.
M Can I see your student library card?
W Here it is.
M Oh, you have already borrowed three books.
W Have I?
M Yes. Students can't borrow books more than three at a time. You have to return one of the books you've borrowed.

W 안녕하세요. 이 책을 빌리고 싶어요.
M 학생 도서관 대출 카드를 보여 주시겠어요?
W 여기 있습니다.
M 저런, 이미 3권을 빌리셨네요.
W 제가요?
M 예. 학생은 한 번에 3권 이상 빌릴 수 없어요. 이미 빌린 책들 중에서 1권을 반납하셔야 해요.

만점 솔루션 학생에게는 한 번에 3권 이상 대출해 줄 수 없는데, 이미 3권을 빌렸기 때문에 1권을 더 빌리려면 이미 빌렸던 책 중에서 1권을 반납해야 한다고 말하고 있다.

19 ⑤

W Hold the elevator, please!
M No problem.
W Thank you.
M What floor are you going to?
W Oh, the 5th please.
M Do you live here?
W ______________________

W 엘리베이터 좀 세워 주세요!
M 그럴게요.

W 감사합니다.
M 몇 층에 가시죠?
W 5층입니다.
M 여기에 사시나요?
W 예. 지난 주 토요일에 이사 왔어요.

① 아니요, 괜찮습니다.
② 아니요, 5층이에요.
③ 예, 집에 가는 중이에요.
④ 아니요, 저는 엘리베이터를 싫어해요.

20 ③

W Hi, Arnold. It's been a long time!
M It sure has. How are you doing?
W I'm doing fine. I'm working at a bank.
M Great. Do you like it?
W ____________________

W 안녕, Arnold. 오랜만이야!
M 정말 그렇구나. 잘 지내니?
W 잘 지내고 있어. 난 은행에서 근무하고 있어.
M 잘됐구나. 그 일이 마음에 드니?
W 좋은 직업인 것 같아.

① 나는 그가 정말 좋아.
② 항상 바쁘지 뭐.
④ 나는 은행 매니저가 되고 싶어.
⑤ 네 차례를 기다려야 해.

만점 솔루션 Do you like it?은 직장이 마음에 드는지 묻는 말이므로 직장이 좋은지 어떤지에 대해 말하는 것이 가장 적절하다.

영어듣기능력평가 08 회

01 ③	02 ③	03 ③, ➕③	04 ⑤	05 ④
06 ①	07 ①	08 ⑤	09 ②	10 ①
11 ①	12 ④	13 ②	14 ⑤	15 ④
16 ④, ➕④	17 ①	18 ②	19 ⑤	20 ⑤

01 ③

M We can usually see this in the bathroom of almost every house, apartment, or building. Its shape is round or rectangular, and it is a little bit hard. However, once you put water on this, it becomes soft. You can use this when you wash your body; especially your face and hands.

M 일반적으로 거의 모든 집, 아파트, 또는 건물의 욕실에서 이것을 볼 수 있습니다. 그것의 모양은 둥글거나 직사각형이고, 그것은 약간 단단합니다. 하지만, 일단 이것이 물에 닿으면, 그것은 부드러워집니다. 당신의 몸, 특히 얼굴과 손을 씻을 때 이것을 사용할 수 있습니다.

02 ③

M What's wrong? What are you looking for?
W I forgot my bag. Can you go back and get it for me?
M Did you leave it on the chair?
W No, it's sitting on the table.
M Is it beside the flower vase or the lamp?
W I think it's between the flower vase and the lamp.
M OK. I'll be back with it in a few minutes.

M 무슨 일이야? 뭘 찾고 있는 거야?
W 내 가방을 깜빡했어. 나를 위해 다시 가서 가져올 수 있어?
M 그것을 의자 위에 두고 온 거야?
W 아니, 탁자 위에 있어.
M 꽃병 옆이야, 아니면 전등 옆이야?
W 꽃병과 전등 사이인 것 같아.
M 알았어. 곧 그것을 가지고 올게.

만점 솔루션 여자는 가방을 탁자 위 꽃병 옆과 전등 사이에 두었다고 했다.

03 ③ | ➕ ③

W Now, let's move on to tomorrow's weather in East area. Boston will be mostly sunny. However, in New York it'll rain with strong winds. And, it'll be quite windy in the Washington area. Same story for Philadelphia. Finally, Delaware will have partly cloudy skies. That's all for today's weather forecast.

W 이제, 동부 지역의 내일 날씨를 알아보겠습니다. Boston은 대부분 화창할 것입니다. 하지만, New York의 날씨는 강풍을 동반한 비가 올 것입

니다. 그리고, Washington 지역에는 바람이 많이 불 것입니다. Philadelphia도 마찬가지입니다. 마지막으로, Delaware는 부분적으로 구름이 낄 것입니다. 이상, 오늘의 일기 예보였습니다.

04 ⑤

M I'm the biggest among all the land mammals. My favorite food is a banana. I can peel my own bananas, because I'm very clever. I have a special trunk. I can use my trunk to drink, smell, pick up food, and touch things. What am I?

M 나는 육지 포유류 중에 가장 큽니다. 내가 가장 좋아하는 음식은 바나나예요. 나는 매우 똑똑하기 때문에 바나나 껍질을 벗길 수도 있어요. 나에게는 특별한 코가 있어요. 나는 내 코를 이용하여 마시고, 냄새를 맡고, 음식을 집고 그리고 물건들을 느낄 수 있어요. 나는 무엇일까요?

05 ④

M Excuse me, how long does it take from here to the Express Way?
W To the Express Way? It'll take about 20 minutes.
M Then, from the Express Way, how long does it take to Disney Land?
W About one and half hours. It's not that far.
M I see. Thank you very much.

M 실례합니다. 여기서 고속도로까지 얼마나 걸리나요?
W 고속도로까지요? 약 20분 정도 걸릴 거예요.
M 그럼, 고속도로에서 디즈니랜드까지는 얼마나 걸리나요?
W 약 한 시간 반이요. 그다지 멀지 않아요.
M 알겠습니다. 정말 감사합니다.

만점 솔루션 현재 있는 곳에서 고속도로까지 20분, 고속도로에서 디즈니랜드까지 1시간 30분 걸리므로, 총 1시간 50분이 걸릴 것이다.

06 ①

M Wow! I can't believe you have this book. Where did you get it?
W I bought it online. Why?
M It was a bestseller for 237 weeks in Britain. I wanted to read it, but it's all sold out at bookstores.
W I believe it. I thought it was really good.
M If you're done, could I read it?
W Sure. You can borrow it now.

M 와! 네가 이 책을 가지고 있다니 믿어지지 않는다. 어디서 구했어?
W 인터넷에서 샀어. 왜?
M 그 책은 영국에서 237주 동안 베스트셀러였어. 나도 그 책을 읽고 싶었는데, 서점에서는 전부 품절이야.
W 그런 것 같아. 그 책 정말 좋은 것 같아.
M 네가 다 읽었으면, 내가 그 책을 읽어도 돼니?
W 물론이지. 지금 그것을 빌려도 돼.

만점 솔루션 베스트셀러 책을 구입하지 못한 남자는 여자에게 책을 다 읽으면 빌려달라고 부탁하고 있다.

07 ①

M Mom, I'm home!
W You're a little late. I was wondering where you were.
M Sorry, Mom. I'm late because I bought this for you on the way home.
W What is this?
M Tomorrow's your birthday!
W Wow, thank you, son. I thought you forgot.
M I could never forget your birthday. I hope you like it.

M 엄마, 나 집에 왔어요!
W 조금 늦었구나. 네가 어디 있는지 궁금했어.
M 죄송해요, 엄마. 집에 오는 길에 엄마를 위해 이걸 사느라 늦었어요.
W 이게 뭐니?
M 내일 엄마 생일이잖아요!
W 와, 고맙구나, 아들. 네가 잊었다고 생각했어.
M 엄마 생일을 어떻게 잊어요. 엄마가 좋아했으면 좋겠어요.

08 ⑤

① **M** Which do you like more, cats or dogs?
W I like dogs more than cats.
② **M** May I speak to Jennifer?
W This is Jennifer. Who is speaking?
③ **M** Why don't you have one more sandwich?
W No, thanks. I'm really full.
④ **M** Will you go bowling with me tomorrow?
W That sounds interesting. What time shall we meet?
⑤ **M** Can you lend me your digital camera?
W Oh, this picture is very good. Where did you take it?

① **M** 고양이와 개 중에서 어느 것을 더 좋아하세요?
W 고양이보다 개가 더 좋아요.
② **M** Jennifer와 통화를 할 수 있을까요?
W 제가 Jennifer에요. 누구시죠?
③ **M** 샌드위치 한 개 더 드시겠어요?
W 아니요, 정말 배가 불러요.
④ **M** 내일 나와 함께 볼링 치러 갈래?
W 재미있겠는데. 몇 시에 만날까?
⑤ **M** 나에게 디지털 카메라 좀 빌려 줄래?
W 오, 이 사진은 정말 멋지구나. 어디서 그것을 찍었니?

09 ②

W It's so hot today. There are so many people here.
M It's always really crowded on days like today.
W I can see why. I like swimming in hot weather.
M There are a lot of people sitting in the sand, too.
W I guess they like sun tanning.
M Not me. I prefer the cool salt water.

W 오늘 너무 더워. 여기 사람이 아주 많구나.
M 오늘 같은 날은 항상 정말 사람이 많아.

W 왜 그런지 알겠다. 난 더운 날씨에 수영하는 것이 좋아.
M 모래에 앉아 있는 사람도 많아.
W 그들은 선탠을 좋아하는 것 같아.
M 난 아니야. 난 시원한 바닷물이 더 좋아.

만점 솔루션 sand, sun tanning, salt water 등의 표현에서 두 사람은 '해변'에 있다는 것을 알 수 있다.

10 ①

M Lucy, did you go to the ABC Shopping Mall in the afternoon?
W Yes, I did. But I couldn't buy anything.
M Why? Was the shopping mall closed today?
W No. I lost my wallet on the way to the mall. I feel so bad now.
M I'm sorry to hear that.

M Lucy, 오후에 ABC 쇼핑몰에 갔었니?
W 응, 갔어. 하지만 아무 것도 못 샀어.
M 왜? 오늘 쇼핑몰이 문을 닫았니?
W 아니. 쇼핑몰 가는 길에 내 지갑을 잃어버렸거든. 지금 기분이 너무 안 좋아.
M 그 말을 들으니 유감이네.

11 ①

W Oh, you skate very well. When did you learn to skate?
M When I was in elementary school. I took lessons for more than three years.
W Wow, you're great! Hey, if you don't mind, can you teach me how to skate? I'd like to skate as well as you do.
M Um... if you want, I'll teach you.

W 오, 너 스케이트 정말 잘 탄다. 언제 스케이트를 배웠니?
M 초등학교 때. 3년 이상 수업을 받았어.
W 와, 대단하다! 야, 괜찮으면, 나에게 스케이트 타는 법 좀 가르쳐 줄래? 나도 너처럼 스케이트를 잘 타고 싶어.
M 음… 네가 원하면, 가르쳐 줄게.

12 ④

W Hi, I'd like to introduce myself to you. I'm from Brazil and I'm 14 years old now. I was born in Sao Paulo and my family moved to Rio De Janeiro when I was five. Since then, we have lived here in Rio De Janeiro. Like any other Brazilian girl, my hobby is playing and watching soccer. I'm really happy to meet all of you.

W 안녕하세요, 제 소개를 할게요. 저는 브라질 출신이고 지금 14살이에요. 저는 Sao Paulo에서 태어나서 5살 때 가족이 Rio De Janeiro로 이사 왔어요. 그때부터, 우리는 여기 Rio De Janeiro에 계속 살고 있어요. 다른 브라질 소녀처럼, 제 취미는 축구를 하고 보는 것이에요. 여러분 모두를 만나서 정말 반가워요.

13 ②

[Cellphone rings.]
W Hello? Sally speaking.
M Hi, Sally. It's me, Tom. Did you know Issac is in hospital now?
W Yeah, I heard that he got in a car accident.
M That's right. He is in Saint Maria Hospital. Sally, why don't we visit him this evening?
W Okay, let's go together.

[휴대 전화 벨이 울린다.]
W 여보세요? 저는 Sally입니다.
M 안녕, Sally. 나야, Tom. Issac이 지금 입원해 있다는 소식 들었니?
W 응, 그 애가 자동차 사고가 났다는 소식을 들었어.
M 맞아. 지금 Saint Maria 병원에 있어. Sally, 오늘 저녁에 Issac에게 병문안 가는 게 어때?
W 좋아, 같이 가자.

만점 솔루션 남자가 자동차 사고가 나서 병원에 입원해 있는 친구의 병문안을 같이 가자고 제안하자 여자가 이를 수락하는 상황이다.

14 ⑤

W David, did you ever think about what you want to be?
M Sure! I want to be an announcer or a reporter. What about you, Jessica?
W Well... about a month ago, I wanted to become a nurse or a doctor. But I have a new dream.
M Really? What's your new dream?
W I want to be a tour guide. I want to travel all around the world.

W David, 넌 무엇이 되고 싶은지 생각해 본 적이 있니?
M 물론이지! 아나운서나 기자가 되고 싶어. 너는 어때, Jessica?
W 음… 한 달 전쯤에는 간호사나 의사가 되고 싶었거든. 하지만 새로운 꿈이 생겼어.
M 정말? 너의 새로운 꿈이 뭐니?
W 난 관광 안내원이 되고 싶어. 전 세계를 여행하고 싶거든.

15 ④

M Cathy, you look always healthy.
W Do I? Thank you for saying so.
M If you have a secret way to stay healthy, please let me know it. I want to be as healthy as you are.
W Well... then, why don't you jog every morning? You'll be healthy.
M I see. Thank you for the tip.

M Cathy, 넌 항상 건강해 보여.
W 내가? 그렇게 말해 줘서 고마워.
M 건강을 유지하는 비결이 있으면, 나에게 알려 줘. 나도 너처럼 건강해지고 싶어.
W 음… 그럼 매일 아침 조깅을 하는 게 어때? 넌 건강해질 거야.
M 알았어. 조언 고마워.

16 ④ | ⊕ ④

M Alice, you said you wanted to see the musical, *Happy House*, didn't you?
W Yeah, I really want to see it.
M Good! Then, let's go see the musical. I have free tickets for this Friday.
W This Friday? Oh, no! I have to visit my grandmother in Florida on that day. Can you get tickets for Sunday?
M No. Well... I have to ask another friend to go with me.

M Alice, 너 뮤지컬 *Happy House* 보고 싶다고 말했지, 그렇지 않니?
W 그래, 정말로 그것을 보고 싶어.
M 좋아! 그럼, 그 뮤지컬을 보러 가자. 이번 주 금요일 무료 입장권이 있거든.
W 이번 주 금요일? 오, 안 돼! 그 날에는 Florida에 계시는 할머니 댁을 방문해야 해. 일요일 공연 표를 구할 수 있니?
M 아니. 음··· 다른 친구에게 나와 함께 가자고 물어봐야겠네.

17 ①

W A group of scientists made an exciting discovery in a T-Rex bone in 2005. They found some blood cells! There was no DNA, but there was some protein. Scientists used the protein to see which animals today are similar to the dinosaur. Can you guess the closest relative? Maybe you think alligators or giant lizards, but it is chickens! Think about that next time you eat chicken.

W 한 무리의 과학자들이 2005년에 티아노사우루스 렉스의 뼈에서 흥미로운 발견을 했습니다. 그들은 약간의 혈액 세포를 발견했습니다! DNA는 없었지만, 약간의 단백질이 있었습니다. 과학자들은 그 단백질을 사용해서 오늘날 어떤 동물이 그 공룡과 비슷한지를 알아보았습니다. 가장 가까운 친척을 추측할 수 있나요? 아마도 당신은 악어나 거대한 도마뱀을 생각할 수도 있지만, 그것은 닭이었습니다! 다음 번에 닭을 먹을 때 그것을 생각해 보세요.

만점 솔루션 2005년에 과학자들이 T-Rex에서 혈액 세포를 발견했다고 했다.

18 ②

M Are you interested in learning Korean? Are you thinking about studying Korean? Then, visit our Korean academy right now! We're waiting for you. We have lots of good teachers and all of them are from Korea. Once you learn Korean here from us, you'll be a good Korean speaker soon.

M 한국어 배우기에 관심이 있으세요? 한국어를 공부하려고 생각 중이세요? 그럼, 지금 바로 저희 한국어 학원을 방문하세요! 저희는 여러분을 기다리고 있습니다. 이곳에는 훌륭한 선생님들이 많이 계시고, 그분들 모두 한국 출신입니다. 일단 여기서 저희에게 한국어를 배우시면, 여러분은 곧 한국어를 잘 하게 되실 것입니다.

만점 솔루션 Then, visit our Korean academy right now! We're waiting for you. 등의 표현을 통해 한국어 학원을 광고하고 있음을 알 수 있다.

19 ⑤

M Sally, when are you going to Jeju Island?
W This Sunday. I am very excited now.
M Yeah, you look very happy now. What are you going to do there?
W I will swim at the beach. And I'll climb up Halla Mountain.
M ______________________

M Sally, 제주도에는 언제 가니?
W 이번 주 일요일에. 나는 지금 너무 흥분돼.
M 그래, 너 지금 매우 행복해 보여. 거기서 무엇을 할 거니?
W 해변에서 수영할 거야. 그리고 한라산에 오를 거야.
M 와! 거기서 재미있는 시간을 보내겠구나.

① 정말 고마워, Sally.
② 나도 그래. 나는 등산이 싫어.
③ 미안, 하지만 너와 함께 갈 수 없어.
④ 정말? 언제 서울에 갔는데?

20 ⑤

M Cindy, do you like playing tennis?
W Yes, I do. Tennis is one of my favorite sports. You know, I once won a tennis contest.
M Really? When?
W When I was an elementary school student.
M Oh, I didn't know that. Then, how about playing tennis with me?
W That's a great idea. When do you want to play?
M ______________________

M Cindy, 너 테니스 치는 거 좋아하니?
W 응, 좋아해. 테니스는 내가 가장 좋아하는 운동 중 하나야. 너 아니, 나 테니스 대회에서 우승도 했어.
M 정말? 언제?
W 초등학생이었을 때.
M 오, 그건 몰랐는 걸. 그럼, 나와 테니스를 치는 것은 어때?
W 그거 좋은 생각이야. 언제 치고 싶니?
M 이번 주 토요일 오후 어때?

① 미안, 네 테니스 공을 잃어버렸어.
② 넌 어떤 운동을 가장 좋아하니?
③ 좋아, 난 이 테니스 라켓을 살 거야.
④ 응, 난 축구보다는 테니스가 더 좋아.

영어듣기능력평가 09 회

01 ⑤	02 ②	03 ②	04 ③	05 ②
06 ④	07 ③, ⊕②	08 ③	09 ⑤	10 ①, ⊕③
11 ②	12 ③	13 ④	14 ②	15 ②
16 ⑤	17 ③	18 ⑤	19 ①	20 ④

01 ⑤

W This is my new house. What do you think?
M It's quite big.
W It is a two-story house.
M I see. Each floor has two windows only.
W Yes, it isn't many, but it's enough for me. I can open the windows and take a deep breath of fresh air every morning.
M I like it. I think it's a lovely house.

W 여기가 내 새 집이야. 어때?
M 꽤 크다.
W 2층 집이야.
M 그렇구나. 각 층에 2개의 창문만 있네.
W 응, 많지 않아. 하지만 나한테는 충분해. 나는 매일 아침마다 창문을 열고 신선한 공기를 깊이 들이 마실 수 있어.
M 마음에 든다. 좋은 집인 것 같아.

만점 솔루션 여자의 집은 2층 집으로, 각 층마다 2개의 창문이 있다고 했다.

02 ②

M Hey, would you raise one hand?
W Like this? Should I stand beside the chair or sit on the chair?
M Stand for a moment, please. And would you look at your hand in the air?
W OK. Like this?
M Yes. Now I'm going to take a picture of you.

M 저, 한 손을 들어줄래요?
W 이렇게요? 의자 옆에 서 있어야 하나요, 아니면 의자에 앉아야 하나요?
M 잠시 동안 서 계세요. 그리고 허공에 있는 당신의 손을 봐 주시겠어요?
W 알겠어요. 이렇게요?
M 그래요. 이제 당신의 사진을 찍겠습니다.

03 ②

M Good morning, everyone. This morning we have thick fog around the Seoul area. But the fog will go away around noon. In the afternoon, we'll have a little bit of wind and rain and it'll be colder than it is now. So take your umbrella with you and be sure to wear your coat.

M 안녕하세요, 여러분. 오늘 아침에는 서울 지역 전역에 짙은 안개가 꼈습니다. 하지만 안개는 정오쯤에 사라질 것입니다. 오후에는, 약간의 바람이 불고 비가 와서 지금보다 더 춥겠습니다. 그러니 우산을 가져가시고 반드시 외투를 입으시기 바랍니다.

04 ③

W When people think of hospital jobs, they think of doctors and nurses. But there are many other jobs in the hospital. There are people working in laboratories. They do blood tests and X-rays. Some people take care of medicine. Pharmacists dispense prescription medicine and sell over-the-counter drugs. And there are many who do office work, or do cleaning. These are all important jobs.

W 사람들이 병원의 직업에 대해 생각할 때, 의사와 간호사를 떠올립니다. 그러나 병원에는 많은 다른 직업들이 있습니다. 실험실에서 일을 하는 사람들이 있습니다. 그들은 혈액 테스트와 X-선 촬영을 합니다. 어떤 사람들은 약을 처리합니다. 약사들은 처방전이 필요한 약을 조제하고 의사의 처방 없이 팔 수 있는 약을 판매합니다. 그리고 사무 일을 하거나 청소 일을 하는 많은 사람들이 있습니다. 이것들은 모두 중요한 일입니다.

만점 솔루션 의사, 간호사 외에 병원 내의 다양한 직업군인 실험실 연구원, 약사, 사무직원, 청소직원 등을 소개하고 있는 담화이다.

05 ②

W Did you choose a club to join?
M Yes. I'm going to join the tennis club. How about you?
W Well, I'm thinking of joining the travel club, but I also want to join the dance club.
M But you always said you want take trips all over the country.
W Right. Hmm.... I'll choose the travel club.

W 가입할 동아리를 골랐니?
M 응. 나는 테니스 동아리에 가입할 거야. 너는 어때?
W 음, 나는 여행 동아리에 가입할까 생각 중이야. 하지만 난 춤 동아리에도 가입하고 싶어.
M 하지만 너는 전국을 여행하고 싶다고 항상 말했잖아.
W 맞아. 흠…. 여행 동아리를 선택해야겠다.

만점 솔루션 여자는 춤 동아리와 여행 동아리 중에서 고민하다가 마지막에 여행 동아리를 선택했다.

06 ④

① **M** How was your day, honey?
W It was great as usual.
② **M** Can I have your name?
W My name is Kim Bora.
③ **M** Why don't we go see a movie tonight?
W Sorry. I'm busy tonight.

④ **M** Are you going there by car?
W I bought a new car yesterday.
⑤ **M** Would you give me two tickets for the 3 o'clock show?
W The tickets are all sold out.

① **M** 오늘 하루 어땠어요, 여보?
W 여느 때처럼 좋았어요.
② **M** 성함을 말씀해 주시겠어요?
W 제 이름은 김보라입니다.
③ **M** 오늘 밤에 영화 보러 가는 게 어때요?
W 미안해요. 오늘 밤에는 제가 바빠요.
④ **M** 그곳에 차로 갈 예정이에요?
W 나는 어제 새 차를 샀어요.
⑤ **M** 3시 공연 입장권 2장 주시겠어요?
W 표가 모두 매진이에요.

07 ③ | ➕ ②

W Did Mr. Kim arrive yet?
M Not yet. He just called me. He said that he would be thirty minutes late.
W Really? What time is it now?
M It's 2 o'clock.
W Then, we have thirty minutes left until he comes.
M Yes.

W 김 선생님이 벌써 도착하셨나요?
M 아직 아니에요. 그분이 방금 전화하셨어요. 30분 늦을 거라고 말씀하셨어요.
W 정말요? 지금 몇 시죠?
M 2시예요.
W 그러면, 그가 올 때까지 30분 남았군요.
M 그래요.

만점 솔루션 현재 시각은 2시이고 Mr. Kim이 올 때까지 30분 남았다고 했으므로 Mr. Kim이 도착할 시각은 2시 30분이 된다.

08 ③

[Telephone rings.]
M Hello, may I speak to Jenny, please?
W Speaking.
M This is Brooks. Do you have some time to help me now?
W Yes, I do.
M Would you come to my place and help me with math? I can't solve some math problems.
W OK. I'll be there soon.

[전화벨이 울린다.]
M 여보세요. Jenny 좀 바꿔 주시겠어요?
W 전데요.
M 나 Brooks야. 지금 나를 도와줄 시간이 좀 있니?
W 응, 있어.
M 우리 집에 와서 수학 좀 도와줄래? 수학 문제 몇 개를 풀 수가 없어.
W 알겠어. 곧 그곳으로 갈게.

09 ⑤

W I can't wait to see the actor. He's so handsome.
M You're always saying that.
W Sorry. We should have gotten some popcorn and Coke before sitting down.
M You're right. But I'll go and get them.
W Thanks. Hurry back. The movie's going to start in a few minutes.

W 그 배우를 빨리 보고 싶어. 너무 잘생겼거든.
M 너는 항상 그렇게 말하더구나.
W 미안해. 앉기 전에 약간의 팝콘과 콜라를 사 왔어야 했는데.
M 네 말이 맞아. 하지만 내가 가서 사 올게.
W 고마워. 빨리 돌아와. 영화가 곧 시작할 예정이야.

10 ① | ➕ ③

W What do you have there?
M It's my science project. I'm building a model.
W What kind of a model is it?
M I'm trying to make a miniature rocket. What are you doing?
W I might do a project about making electricity.
M That could be fun. It sounds like you have some research to do.
W That's right. I'll start looking up information online.

W 거기 있는 게 뭐야?
M 내 과학 프로젝트야. 난 모형을 만들고 있어.
W 그건 어떤 종류의 모형이야?
M 난 축소 모형 로켓을 만들려고 하고 있어. 넌 뭐 하고 있어?
W 난 전기 만드는 것에 관한 프로젝트를 할까 해.
M 그거 재미있겠다. 넌 해야 할 조사가 있는 것처럼 들리는구나.
W 맞아. 인터넷에서 정보 찾는 것을 시작할 거야.

만점 솔루션 과학 프로젝트로 남자는 축소 모형 로켓을, 여자는 전기를 만들려고 계획하고 있다.

11 ②

M You can find this in any public place or on a bus or a train. In fact, the law requires that every building should have this. If there is a fire, you can use this to put the fire out. What is this?

M 여러분은 이것을 어느 공공장소나 버스 안이나 기차 안에서 발견할 수 있습니다. 사실, 법적으로 모든 건물에는 이것이 있어야 합니다. 불이 나면, 여러분은 이것을 불을 끄는 데 사용할 수 있습니다. 이것은 무엇일까요?

12 ③

M Christine, can you understand my lesson?
W It's a little hard for me, but I think I can do it.
M I'm happy to hear that. If you don't give up, you can get a good grade.

W I'm trying. Nowadays, I am trying hard to take good notes in your class.
M That's a good way to follow the class.

M Christine, 내 수업을 이해할 수 있니?
W 저에겐 약간 어렵지만, 할 수 있을 것 같아요.
M 그 말을 들으니 기쁘구나. 네가 포기하지 않으면, 너는 좋은 성적을 받을 수 있단다.
W 노력하고 있어요. 요즘, 선생님 수업 시간에 필기를 잘 하려고 열심히 노력하고 있어요.
M 그것이 수업을 따라가는 좋은 방법이지.

만점 솔루션 남자는 자신의 수업을 이해하고 있는지 물으면서 포기하지 않으면 좋은 성적을 받을 것이라고 말하고, 여자는 필기를 잘 하려고 노력하고 있다고 말하는 것으로 보아, 교사와 학생의 관계임을 알 수 있다.

13 ④

M Excuse me.
W Yes. What can I help you with?
M There is a hair in my soup.
W Oh, really? I'm so sorry. Let me bring you another bowl of soup.
M You don't have to do that. I don't want to eat anything here. I feel terrible.
W I'm really sorry, sir.

M 실례합니다.
W 예. 무엇을 도와드릴까요?
M 제 수프에 머리카락이 있네요.
W 오, 정말요? 정말 죄송합니다. 다른 수프를 가져다 드리겠습니다.
M 그럴 필요 없습니다. 이곳에서 어떤 것도 먹고 싶지 않습니다. 기분이 아주 안 좋네요.
W 정말 죄송합니다, 손님.

14 ②

W Excuse me. Would you tell me where Wilson Bank is?
M Go straight one block. And turn left at Maple Street.
W Turn left at Maple Street?
M That's right. And you will see the library on your right.
W The library on my right? Is it across from the library?
M No, the bank is right next to the library.
W Now I see. Thank you very much.

W 실례합니다. Wilson 은행이 어디에 있는지 알려 주시겠어요?
M 한 블록 직진하세요. 그리고 Maple 거리에서 좌회전하세요.
W Maple 거리에서 좌회전하라고요?
M 맞습니다. 그러면 오른쪽에 도서관이 보일 겁니다.
W 오른쪽에 도서관이요? 그것이 도서관 맞은편에 있나요?
M 아니요, 은행은 도서관 바로 옆에 있습니다.
W 이제 알겠습니다. 정말 감사합니다.

15 ②

M When are you leaving for your grandmother's house?
W I'm leaving next Monday.
M When will you come back?
W I'm staying there until Friday of the same week.
M I see. I hope you have a good time there.
W Thanks.

M 언제 할머니 댁으로 떠날 거니?
W 다음 주 월요일에 떠날 거야.
M 언제 돌아올 거니?
W 같은 주의 금요일까지 그곳에서 머무를 거야.
M 알겠어. 그곳에서 좋은 시간을 보내길 바랄게.
W 고마워.

16 ⑤

M Why did you open the window?
W I wanted to get some fresh air. It's stuffy in here.
M Just turn on the air conditioner.
W But I don't like air conditioning. It's too cold.
M On a hot day, I think air conditioning is perfect.
W I prefer to open the window and use a fan.
M Alright. It's not too hot anyway.

M 왜 창문을 연 거야?
W 신선한 공기를 좀 마시고 싶었어. 이 안은 답답해서.
M 그냥 에어컨을 켜.
W 하지만 난 에어컨이 싫어. 너무 추워.
M 더운 날에는, 에어컨을 켜는 것이 최고인 것 같아.
W 난 창문을 열고 선풍기를 사용하는 게 더 좋아.
M 알았어. 어쨌든 밖이 너무 덥지는 않으니까.

만점 솔루션 남자는 에어컨 켜는 것을 좋아하고 여자는 창문을 열고 선풍기 켜는 것을 좋아한다.

17 ③

M Jane! Was there a problem? You're thirty minutes late.
W Sorry. I thought the musical would start at six.
M No, it starts at five.
W It's my mistake. I'm terribly sorry. I'll buy you dinner tonight.
M Anyway let's go into the theater. The musical will start soon.

M Jane! 문제가 있었니? 너는 30분 늦었어.
W 미안해. 뮤지컬이 6시에 시작하는 줄 알았어.
M 아니야, 그것은 5시에 시작해.
W 내 실수야. 정말 미안해. 오늘 밤에 저녁은 내가 살게.
M 어쨌든 극장으로 들어가자. 뮤지컬이 곧 시작할 거야.

만점 솔루션 여자가 뮤지컬이 6시에 시작하는 줄 알았다고 하자 남자는 5시에 시작한다고 말한다. 따라서 여자가 늦은 이유는 공연 시간을 잘못 알았기 때문이다.

18 ⑤

M I have an important meeting at 2, but my tie's got a stain on it.
W Do you have an extra tie?
M No, I didn't bring one.
W What are you going to do? Are you going to take it to the cleaner?
M Not really. Maybe I should go and buy a new tie.
W You don't have enough time. Is there someone you could borrow a tie from?
M That's a good idea. Who's here today?
W I'll ask Tim. He always wears a tie.

M 2시에 중요한 회의가 있는데, 내 넥타이에 얼룩이 졌어.
W 여분의 넥타이가 있니?
M 없어, 가져오지 않았거든.
W 어떻게 하려고? 그것을 세탁소에 가져갈 거니?
M 그건 아니야. 가서 새 넥타이를 사야 할 것 같아.
W 시간이 충분치 않아. 넥타이를 빌릴 수 있는 사람이 있니?
M 그거 좋은 생각이야. 오늘 여기 누가 있지?
W 내가 Tim에게 물어볼게. 그는 항상 넥타이를 매거든.

만점 솔루션 넥타이에 얼룩이 묻어 걱정하는 남자에게 여자는 시간이 없으니 다른 사람의 넥타이를 빌리라고 제안하고 있다.

19 ①

W Tony. Would you come here for a minute?
M Is there anything I can help you with, Mom?
W Yes. Would you take out this garbage bag to the front of the house?
M That's no problem. I'll do it right away.
W ______________________

W Tony. 잠깐만 이곳에 와 주겠니?
M 제가 도와드릴 일이 있나요, 엄마?
W 그래. 이 쓰레기 봉투를 집 앞에 내다놓아 주겠니?
M 물론이에요. 바로 그 일을 할게요.
W 고맙구나.

② 죄송하지만, 할 수 없어요.
③ 천만에요.
④ 그것을 적을게요.
⑤ 그건 저에게는 너무 어려워요.

20 ④

W Honey, what are you doing this Saturday?
M I have nothing to do.
W We have to paint the front door. It looks too old. So I already bought some paint.
M You're so diligent. And how about paintbrushes?
W ______________________

W 여보, 이번 주 토요일에 무엇을 할 건가요?
M 할 일이 없어요.
W 우리는 현관 문에 페인트칠을 해야 해요. 너무 낡아 보여서요. 그래서 저는 이미 페인트를 좀 사다 놓았어요.
M 정말 부지런하군요. 그러면 페인트 붓은요?
W 물론이죠. 그것들도 사다 놓았어요.

① 당신은 페인트칠을 잘 하는군요.
② 나를 도와줘서 고마워요.
③ 내가 당신에게 페인트칠 하는 방법을 가르쳐 줄게요.
⑤ 이 페인트 붓은 아주 비싸요.

만점 솔루션 여자가 페인트를 사다 놓았다고 하자 남자는 페인트 붓도 있는지 묻고 있으므로, 그것도 사다 놓았다는 말을 하는 것이 가장 적절하다.

영어듣기능력평가 10회

01 ②	02 ②	03 ④	04 ⑤	05 ①
06 ⑤	07 ④	08 ②	09 ④, ⊕④	10 ③
11 ①	12 ④	13 ③	14 ②, ⊕⑤	15 ②
16 ③	17 ①	18 ④	19 ⑤	20 ③

01 ②

W ① She is planting a tree.
② She is watering a plant.
③ She is buying some flowers.
④ She is picking flowers.
⑤ She is carrying a flowerpot.

W ① 여자가 나무를 심고 있다.
② 여자가 식물에 물을 주고 있다.
③ 여자가 꽃을 좀 사고 있다.
④ 여자가 꽃을 꺾고 있다.
⑤ 여자가 화분을 옮기고 있다.

02 ②

W Look at the cute kittens. I'd like to have one.
M Ask your mom to have a pet.
W She doesn't like cats, dogs and hamsters.
M My mom didn't like pets, either. But she likes Ming Ming now.
W When did you get her?
M A year before. She was a tiny little puppy then.

W 귀여운 아기고양이들 좀 봐. 나도 한 마리 있으면 좋겠다.
M 엄마에게 애완동물을 키우자고 부탁해 봐.
W 엄마는 고양이, 강아지, 햄스터를 싫어하셔.
M 우리 엄마도 애완동물을 싫어하셨어. 하지만 지금은 Ming Ming을 좋아하셔.
W 언제 그것을 샀는데?
M 1년 전에. 그때는 아주 작은 강아지였어.

03 ④

W Good morning. This is Kim Jisu from HBS weather center. It is cloudy all around the peninsula. In Seoul and Incheon, we are expecting rain soon. However, in the southeastern part of the country in Pohang and Daegu, it will start snowing in the late afternoon. It will be the first snow this year. It will also snow in Jeju.

W 안녕하세요. HBS 기상센터의 김지수입니다. 한반도 전체가 흐립니다. 서울과 인천은, 곧 비가 올 것으로 예상됩니다. 하지만, 우리나라 남동 지역인 포항과 대구는, 오후 늦게 눈이 내리기 시작할 것입니다. 올해 첫 눈이 되겠네요. 제주에도 눈이 오겠습니다.

04 ⑤

M Where is the meeting place?
W In front of Mega World ticket booth.
M Can we take the subway?
W It's not very far from here. Why don't we take a taxi?
M Isn't it too expensive?
W It won't be that expensive if we pay together.
M Good idea.

M 모이는 장소가 어디지?
W Mega World 매표소 앞이야.
M 지하철을 탈까?
W 여기에서 별로 멀지 않아. 택시를 타는 게 어때?
M 너무 비싸지 않을까?
W 같이 내면 그렇게 비싸지 않을 거야.
M 좋은 생각이야.

05 ①

W You are the next speaker, Larry. Are you ready?
M I am really nervous. I think I will forget everything as soon as I stand on the stage.
W You can't forget it because you practiced so much. Look at people's eyes and speak clearly. Don't talk fast.
M Okay.
W I know you are going to do great, Larry. Go for it!

W Larry, 네가 다음 연설자야. 준비됐니?
M 정말 긴장돼요. 무대에 서자마자 모든 것을 잊어버릴 것 같아요.
W 넌 연습을 아주 많이 했기 때문에 잊어버릴 리가 없어. 사람들 눈을 쳐다보고 또렷하게 말하도록 해. 빨리 말하지 말고.
M 알겠습니다.
W 넌 아주 잘 할 거라는 것을 알아, Larry. 잘해 봐!

06 ⑤

W Mr. Gang, I think I have to go home now.
M What's the problem, Nara?
W I think I have a fever. I feel cold now.
M Oh, I see. I'll call your mom. Go straight home.
W Mr. Gang, what if it is H1N1?
M You'll be okay if you take medicine. Take good care of yourself.
W Yes, I will.

W 강 선생님, 저 지금 집에 가야 할 것 같아요.
M 나라야, 무슨 일이니?
W 열이 있는 것 같아요. 지금 추워요.
M 오, 알겠다. 내가 어머니께 전화를 드리마. 곧장 집으로 가거라.
W 강 선생님, 만약 신종플루면 어쩌죠?
M 약을 먹으면 괜찮을 거야. 몸을 잘 돌봐라.
W 예, 그럴게요.

만점 솔루션 여자는 열이 나고 있으며, 신종플루에 걸렸을지도 몰라 걱정하고 있다.

07 ④

W Ryan! Where are you?
M I'm fixing the car in the garage.
W Can you come and carry this? It's too heavy.
M Oh, I can't. My hands and clothes are really dirty now. I can't come inside the house right now.
W When do you think you can finish it?
M Well, it won't take long.

W Ryan! 어디 있어요?
M 차고에서 자동차를 고치고 있어요.
W 와서 이것 좀 옮겨 줄래요? 너무 무거워요.
M 저런, 안 돼요. 내 손과 옷이 지금 정말 더러워요. 지금 당장은 집 안으로 들어갈 수가 없어요.
W 언제 끝날 것 같아요?
M 음, 오래 걸리진 않을 거예요.

08 ②

M You can see this in playgrounds, parks, or schools. First, you climb up the stairs, and sit down at the top. Then, you slide all the way down. It is fun, because you can go down fast. What is this?

M 여러분은 이것을 놀이터, 공원 또는 학교에서 볼 수 있습니다. 우선, 여러분은 계단을 오르고 꼭대기에서 앉습니다. 그런 후 여러분은 미끄러져 내려옵니다. 아래로 빠르게 내려올 수 있기 때문에 재미있습니다. 이것은 무엇일까요?

09 ④ | ➕ ④

W Do you like watching documentaries on TV?
M Yes, I like nature shows. I enjoy watching what animals do.
W I like those, but I prefer history shows.
M History shows about wars are interesting.
W I'd rather watch shows about kings and queens.
M I know you watch the history channel a lot. Can you recommend one?
W Sure.

W TV에서 다큐멘터리 보는 것을 좋아하니?
M 응, 난 자연 프로그램을 좋아해. 난 동물들이 하는 일을 보는 것을 즐겨.
W 난 그것도 좋지만, 역사 프로그램이 더 좋아.
M 전쟁에 관한 역사 프로그램은 흥미롭지.
W 난 오히려 왕과 여왕에 관한 프로그램을 보는데.
M 네가 역사 채널을 많이 본다는 것을 알고 있지. 하나 추천해 줄래?
W 물론이야.

만점 솔루션 TV 다큐멘터리 중 남자는 자연 프로그램, 여자는 역사 프로그램을 좋아한다며, 각자 좋아하는 다큐멘터리에 관해 대화를 나누고 있다.

10 ③

M Jenny, your Cellphone has a message.
W Oh, thank you.
M What does it say?
W It's my mother. She said I have to be at home before 8 o'clock.
M What time is it now?
W It's 7 o'clock. I have to leave in 30 minutes.
M Okay. Let's practice just two more times and finish today's practice.

M Jenny, 네 휴대 전화에 메세지가 왔어.
W 오, 고마워.
M 뭐라고 써 있니?
W 우리 엄마야. 8시 전에 집으로 와야 한다고 하셔.
M 지금 몇 시지?
W 7시야. 30분 후에 출발해야 해.
M 좋아. 두 번만 더하고 오늘 연습을 마치자.

만점 솔루션 in 30 minutes는 '30분 후에'라는 의미이다.

11 ①

M May I help you?
W Yes, I'd like to buy a pack of A4 copy paper.
M It's 2,500 won.
W And this wrapping paper, too.
M It's 1,000 won.
W Here's 5,000 won.
M And here is your change. Thank you.

M 도와드릴까요?
W 예, A4 복사 용지 한 팩을 사고 싶어요.
M 2,500원입니다.
W 그리고 이 포장지도 주세요.
M 1,000원입니다.
W 여기 5,000원이요.
M 거스름돈 여기 있습니다. 감사합니다.

만점 솔루션 여자는 A4 복사 용지 한 팩(2,500원)과 포장지(1,000원)를 구입하며 5,000원을 지불했으므로, 거스름돈은 1,500원이 된다.

12 ④

M Do we have any flour?
W I think I put it in the fridge. Check the middle part.
M I checked there already, but it wasn't there.
W Really? Hmm, what about the cupboard right above the fridge?
M Let me check. *[pause]* It's not here, either.
W Then it must be in one of the other upper cupboards.
M Yes, I found it. It was in the cupboard on the far right.

M 우리 밀가루 있나?
W 냉장고에 넣어둔 거 같은데. 중간 부분을 확인해봐.

M 거긴 이미 확인했는데, 없었어.
W 진짜? 흠, 냉장고 바로 위에 있는 찬장은 어때?
M 한번 확인해 볼게. *[멈춤]* 여기도 없어.
W 그럼 다른 찬장들 중에 있는게 확실해.
M 응, 찾았어. 가장 오른쪽에 있는 찬장에 있었어.

13 ③

W This is your tour guide, Jane. We are arriving in front of the Botanical Gardens. We are staying here for 2 hours. It's 10 o'clock now, so you have to come back to the bus by 12 o'clock. When you get off the bus, I'll give you a ticket for the Botanical Gardens. You can't bring food in the Gardens, but water bottles are okay.

W 여러분의 관광 안내원 Jane입니다. 우리는 식물원 앞에 도착할 것입니다. 이곳에 2시간 동안 머물 예정이고요. 지금이 10시니까, 12시까지 버스로 돌아오셔야 합니다. 버스에서 내리실 때, 식물원 입장권을 드리겠습니다. 식물원에 음식물을 가지고 들어가실 수 없지만, 물병은 괜찮습니다.

만점 솔루션 I'll give you a ticket for the Botanical Gardens.라고 했으므로 입장권은 각자 구입하는 것이 아니라 관광 안내원이 제공하는 것임을 알 수 있다.

14 ② | ⊕ ⑤

W George, what kind of job do you want to have?
M I'd like to be an actor.
W I believe you will make a great actor.
M My father doesn't think so. He wants me to be a doctor.
W Just like him?
M That's right. But I don't have any interest in medicine.

W George, 너는 어떤 직업을 갖고 싶니?
M 나는 배우가 되고 싶어.
W 너는 훌륭한 배우가 될 거야.
M 우리 아버지는 그렇게 생각하지 않으셔. 그분은 내가 의사가 되길 원하시지.
W 그분처럼?
M 맞아. 하지만 나는 의학에는 전혀 관심이 없어.

15 ②

W Good afternoon, sir. How may I help you?
M Good afternoon. I would like to check in.
W Sure. Do you have a reservation?
M Yes, under Ben Johnson.
W I have it here, Mr. Johnson. A single, for three nights?
M Yes, that's correct.
W OK, here's your key card. It's room 731.
M Thank you.

W 안녕하세요. 손님. 무엇을 도와드릴까요?
M 안녕하세요. 입실하고 싶어요.
W 알겠습니다. 예약하셨나요?
M 예, Ben Johnson이라는 이름으로요.
W 여기 있네요, Johnson 씨. 1인실이시고, 3일 동안이죠?
M 예, 맞아요.
W 좋습니다, 여기 키 카드가 있습니다. 731호실입니다.
M 감사합니다.

16 ③

W Do you have some free time tomorrow?
M Sure. What do you have in mind?
W Actually, I need your help.
M What do you want me to do?
W I have to go shopping for my sister's housewarming party. But my car is in for repair.
M Do you want me to drive to the department store?
W That would be great.
M No problem.
W Thanks a lot. I'll see you tomorrow morning.

W 내일 여유 시간이 있니?
M 물론. 뭔가 생각하고 있는 거라도 있니?
W 사실, 네 도움이 필요해.
M 내가 뭘 해 주기를 원하니?
W 내 여동생 집들이를 위해 쇼핑을 가야 하거든. 그런데 내 차가 수리중이야.
M 넌 내가 백화점에 차로 태워다 주기를 원하는 거니?
W 그렇게 해 주면 좋지.
M 문제없어.
W 정말 고마워. 내일 아침에 보자.

만점 솔루션 여자는 내일 쇼핑을 해야 하는데 차가 수리중이라 남자에게 차를 태워 줄 것을 부탁하고 있는 상황이다.

17 ①

W Good afternoon. Can I have your prescription?
M Here it is.
W Thank you. Just wait for a moment while your medicine is being prepared.
M I'd like to buy this band-aid, too.
W OK. Let me tell you about your medicine. Take this pink syrup four times a day. Take these pills three times a day after a meal. It's 4,500 won including the band-aid.
M Here you are.

W 어서 오세요. 처방전을 주시겠어요?
M 여기 있습니다.
W 감사합니다. 당신의 약이 준비되는 동안 잠시 기다리세요.
M 이 일회용 반창고도 사고 싶어요.
W 알겠습니다. 제가 당신의 약에 대해 말씀드릴게요. 이 분홍색 시럽은 하루에 네 번 드세요. 이 알약들은 하루에 세 번 식후에 드세요. 일회용 반창고를 포함해서 4,500원입니다.
M 여기 있습니다.

18 ④

W I'm having a problem with my neighbor.
M Why? What is he doing to you?
W Things from his home keep blowing onto my lawn.
M You mean garbage? Maybe you should discuss it with him.
W I thought a fence would help.
M It might not. Anyway, he may not even know there is a problem.
W I guess you're right. But I'm just a little shy.
M I know you are, but you should let him know it.

W 내 이웃하고 문제가 있어.
M 왜? 그 사람이 네게 어떻게 하고 있는데?
W 그의 집 물건들이 계속 내 잔디밭으로 불어 넘어오고 있어.
M 쓰레기 말이야? 그와 그것에 대해 이야기 해 봐야 할 것 같구나.
W 난 울타리가 도움이 될 거라고 생각했어.
M 그렇지 않을지도 몰라. 어쩌면, 그가 문제가 있다는 것조차 모를 수도 있어.
W 네 말이 맞을 수도 있겠다. 하지만 내가 약간 낯을 가려서.
M 네가 그렇다는 것은 알지만, 넌 그가 그 문제를 알게 해야 해.

만점 솔루션 이웃의 쓰레기가 바람에 날려 자신의 집으로 넘어오는 것이 불만인 여자에게 남자는 그 사람과 이야기 해 볼 것을 제안하고 있다.

19 ⑤

[Telephone rings.]
W Hello.
M Hello, Maggie. This is Thomas. Are you going to Greg's birthday party today?
W Yes. I thought you were coming, too.
M Actually, I called you because of that. I can't come to the party.
W Why not?
M ______________________

[전화벨이 울린다.]
W 여보세요.
M 안녕, Maggie. 나 Thomas야. 오늘 Greg의 생일 파티에 갈 거니?
W 응. 너도 올 거라고 생각했는데.
M 사실, 그것 때문에 너에게 전화했어. 나는 그 파티에 갈 수 없어.
W 왜 못 오는데?
M 이모 결혼식에 가야 해.

① 난 늦고 싶지 않아.
② 6시 전에 그곳으로 가야 해.
③ 친구들도 모두 올 거야.
④ 내 선물을 Greg에게 전해 줄래?

20 ③

M Excuse me. Can I come in?
W Of course. Welcome to the newspaper club.
M I'd like to join this club.
W That's great. What's your name?
M I'm Lee Hun in 1st grade.
W Nice to meet you, Hun. You look like someone in the second grade. Do you have any brothers or sisters?
M ______________________

M 실례합니다. 들어가도 될까요?
W 물론입니다. 신문 동아리에 오신 걸 환영해요.
M 이 동아리에 가입하고 싶어요.
W 좋아요. 이름이 뭔가요?
M 1학년 이훈입니다.
W 만나서 반가워요. 훈. 2학년의 누군가를 닮은 것 같은데요. 형이나 누나가 있어요?
M 아니요. 저는 외동이에요.

① 아니요. 형은 저를 좋아하지 않아요.
② 예. 저는 형을 아주 좋아해요.
④ 예. 저는 형이 있으면 좋겠어요.
⑤ 아니요. 저는 이 동아리에 아는 사람이 없어요.

영어듣기능력평가 11 회

01 ①	02 ③	03 ①	04 ②, ➕⑤	05 ③
06 ③	07 ②	08 ④	09 ⑤	10 ②
11 ②	12 ④, ➕④	13 ③	14 ③	15 ①
16 ④	17 ①	18 ⑤	19 ③	20 ⑤

01 ①

W This is one of our favorite outdoor activities. Unlike other activities such as hang gliding or scuba diving, this doesn't need anything special. For this you need only a pair of good shoes and your health. When you do this, you climb up a mountain. When you reach the top of the mountain, you will feel refreshed.

W 이것은 우리가 가장 좋아하는 야외 활동 중의 하나입니다. 행글라이딩이나 스쿠버 다이빙 같은 다른 활동들과는 달리, 이것은 특별한 것을 필요로 하지 않습니다. 이것을 위해서는 단지 좋은 신발 한 켤레와 건강만 있으면 됩니다. 이것을 할 때, 당신은 등산을 합니다. 산의 정상에 오르면, 당신은 기분이 상쾌해질 것입니다.

02 ③

W Can I help you?
M Well, I need sandals for a trip. I'm planning to go to the beach.
W What about these? I think these are better than sandals for your trip.
M They look like sneakers.
W They're not. We call them water shoes. You can use them in water, and they dry really quickly.
M Can I wear them out of water?
W Of course. They cover your feet well and they're good for walking in mountains.
M Okay, I'll take them.

W 도와드릴까요?
M 저, 여행을 위한 샌들이 필요해요. 해변으로 갈 계획이거든요.
W 이것은 어떨까요? 당신의 여행에는 샌들보다 이것이 더 좋을 것 같아요.
M 운동화처럼 보이는군요.
W 그렇지 않아요. 아쿠아 슈즈라고 합니다. 그것을 물 속에서 사용할 수 있고, 정말 빨리 말라요.
M 물 밖에서도 신을 수 있는 건가요?
W 물론이죠. 발을 잘 감싸서 산에서 걷기에도 좋아요.
M 좋아요. 그것으로 할게요.

만점 솔루션 운동화처럼 생겼지만 물 속이나 물 밖에서 모두 신을 수 있고 아주 빨리 마른다고 했다.

03 ①

W Taking a look at the weather for Saturday, we'll have clear and sunny skies in the Seoul area. It will be sunny also in Daegu and Gwangju. However, in Daejeon, there will be strong chance of snow. In the Busan area, it'll be partly cloudy in the morning and it will snow or rain in the evening. That's all. I'm Jina Shin. Thank you.

W 토요일 날씨를 보면, 서울 지역은 하늘이 맑고 화창하겠습니다. 대구와 광주 지역도 화창하겠습니다. 하지만, 대전에서는 눈이 올 확률이 높겠습니다. 부산 지역은, 오전에는 부분적으로 흐리고 저녁에는 눈 또는 비가 내리겠습니다. 이상입니다. 저는 신진아입니다. 감사합니다.

04 ② | ➕ ⑤

W Where are you going, David? Lunch will be ready soon.
M I'm going to the bookstore. Dad asked me to buy a sports magazine.
W Really? Then can you buy some milk at the mart next to the bookstore?
M Sure, no problem.
W Thank you. Here is $3 for the milk.

W 어디에 가니, David? 점심이 곧 준비되는데.
M 서점에 가요. 아빠가 스포츠 잡지를 사 오라고 부탁하셨거든요.
W 정말? 그럼 서점 옆에 있는 마트에서 우유를 좀 사다 줄래?
M 물론이죠, 문제없어요.
W 고맙구나. 여기 우유 값 3달러 있다.

만점 솔루션 여자의 말 Then can you buy some milk ~?를 통해 여자가 우유를 사다 줄 것을 부탁했음을 알 수 있다.

05 ③

① **W** Did you ever try *gimchi*?
M Yes, of course. It was spicy but good.
② **W** I'd like to stay at your hotel.
M How many days are you going to stay?
③ **W** Can I use your mobile phone?
M I'm sorry, but I don't know his phone number.
④ **W** Can you speak Korean?
M A little bit. I learned Korean last winter.
⑤ **W** The sky is so dark. It will rain soon.
M I think so. We have to get an umbrella.

① **W** 김치 먹어 봤니?
M 그럼, 물론이지. 맵지만 맛있었어.
② **W** 이 호텔에 묵고 싶습니다.
M 며칠이나 묵으실 건가요?
③ **W** 네 휴대 전화를 사용해도 될까?
M 미안하지만, 난 그의 전화번호를 몰라.
④ **W** 한국어 할 줄 아니?
M 약간. 지난 겨울에 한국어를 배웠거든.

⑤ W 하늘이 너무 어두워. 곧 비가 올 것 같아.
M 내 생각도 그래. 우산을 챙겨야겠어.

만점 솔루션 ③ 휴대 전화를 사용해도 되는지 묻는데 그 사람의 전화번호를 모른다는 응답은 어색하다.

06 ③

M Excuse me, I'd like to book a ticket to London for this Saturday.
W I'm sorry, but there are no flights on Saturday.
M How about Sunday?
W Let me check. We have two flights. One departs at 10 in the morning, and the other departs at 5:20 in the afternoon.
M Then, I'll book the morning flight.
W Fine.

M 실례합니다, 이번 주 토요일 런던행 표를 예약하고 싶은데요.
W 죄송합니다만, 토요일에는 항공편이 없습니다.
M 일요일은요?
W 확인해 볼게요. 두 개의 항공편이 있습니다. 한 편은 오전 10시에 출발하고, 나머지 한 편은 오후 5시 20분에 출발합니다.
M 그럼, 오전 항공편을 예약할게요.
W 좋습니다.

만점 솔루션 토요일에는 항공편이 없고, 일요일에는 오전 10시와 오후 5시 20분 항공편이 있다고 하자, 남자는 오전에 출발하는 항공편을 예약하겠다고 했다.

07 ②

[Telephone rings.]
W Rainbow Hotel. How can I help you?
M Hi, I booked your hotel through the Internet. My reservation number is 2024.
W Wait a minute, please. Yes, you booked a single room for three nights.
M That's right. But, I'd like to cancel my reservation.
W No problem. Let me cancel your reservation.

[전화벨이 울린다.]
W Rainbow 호텔입니다. 무엇을 도와드릴까요?
M 안녕하세요, 인터넷으로 이 호텔을 예약했는데요. 제 예약 번호는 2024입니다.
W 잠시만 기다리세요. 예, 1인실로 3일 동안 예약하셨네요.
M 맞아요. 그런데, 제 예약을 취소하고 싶습니다.
W 문제없습니다. 예약을 취소해 드리겠습니다.

08 ④

M Excuse me, I'd like to have these dress shirts dry-cleaned.
W It costs $3 per shirt. How many shirts do you have?
M I have 5 shirts. Can I pay when I get them back?
W Yes, you can. Please let me know your name or phone number.
M My name is Bob Morgan.

M 실례합니다, 이 드레스 셔츠들을 드라이클리닝하고 싶은데요.
W 셔츠 한 벌당 3달러입니다. 셔츠가 모두 몇 벌이죠?
M 셔츠 다섯 벌이에요. 찾을 때 돈을 지불해도 되나요?
W 그럼요. 이름이나 전화번호를 알려 주세요.
M 제 이름은 Bob Morgan입니다.

09 ⑤

W Roger, can you meet me after school?
M All right. Do you want to talk about the presentation for history class?
W That's right. You and I are a team for that.
M I'm happy to be a team with you. You are a queen of history.
W I'm glad to work with you, too. I heard you are really good at making presentation slides. I need to learn from you.
M Okay. See you after school.

W Roger, 방과 후에 나를 만날 수 있니?
M 좋아. 역사 수업 발표에 관해 이야기 하고 싶니?
W 맞아. 너와 내가 그것을 위한 팀이잖아.
M 너와 한 팀이 돼서 기뻐. 넌 역사의 여왕이잖아.
W 나도 너와 같이 하게 돼서 기뻐. 난 네가 발표 슬라이드를 정말 잘 만든다고 들었어. 난 너에게 배워야 해.
M 좋아. 방과 후에 보자.

만점 솔루션 남자와 여자는 한 팀으로 역사 수업 시간에 발표를 하게 되었고, 여자는 그것을 준비하기 위해 방과 후에 만나자고 제안하는 상황이다.

10 ②

W Hi, Peter!
M Hi, Susan! Nice to see you!
W Oh, you look quite good. Did you get an A⁺ on the test?
M Well... don't be surprised. I finally got a part-time job.
W Really? Congratulations, Peter. Where are you going to work?
M At a Korean restaurant on Oxford Street. I start to work next Monday.

W 안녕, Peter!
M 안녕, Susan! 만나서 반가워!
W 오, 너 아주 좋아 보인다. 시험에서 A⁺를 받았니?
M 음… 놀라지 마. 나 드디어 시간제 일자리를 구했어.
W 정말? 축하해, Peter. 어디에서 일하게 되었는데?
M Oxford 거리에 있는 한국 식당에서. 다음 주 월요일부터 일을 시작해.

11 ②

M You can find me near water like ponds and streams. You can see me the most in summer. I have smooth skin and big eyes. I can jump far because I have long back legs. But my front legs are short. I eat flies and mosquitos. What am I?

M 여러분은 연못이나 개울 같은 물 근처에서 날 찾을 수 있습니다. 나를 여름에 주로 볼 수 있을 겁니다. 나는 부드러운 피부와 큰 눈을 가지고 있습니다. 나에게는 긴 뒷다리가 있어서 멀리 뛸 수 있습니다. 하지만 나의 앞다리는 매우 짧습니다. 나는 파리와 모기들을 먹습니다. 나는 무엇일까요?

12 ④ | ⊕ ④

M Please open your mouth and say "Ah...."
W Ah....
M Okay, that's all. Fortunately, you don't have to have any teeth pulled out.
W Whew... what a relief!
M But you should brush your teeth after every meal. Otherwise, you'll be in a big trouble.
W I see. I'll follow your advice.

M 입을 벌리고 '아…'해 보세요.
W 아….
M 좋아요, 다 됐습니다. 다행히, 치아를 뽑지 않아도 될 것 같습니다.
W 휴… 다행이네요!
M 하지만 매 식사 후에는 반드시 양치질을 하셔야 해요. 그렇지 않으면, 큰 문제가 생길 거예요.
W 알겠습니다. 당신의 충고를 따를게요.

13 ③

W May I help you?
M I'd like to get the ticket. I booked it online.
W Can I have your name, sir?
M My name's Paul Kim.
W We have you here. Did you book two tickets for the 7 o'clock play?
M That's right.
W Well, here's your tickets. Enjoy the play.
M Thanks.

W 도와드릴까요?
M 표를 받고 싶어요. 인터넷에서 표를 예매했거든요.
W 성함을 말씀해 주시겠어요, 손님?
M 제 이름은 Paul Kim입니다.
W 여기 있네요. 7시 연극표 2장을 예매하셨죠?
M 맞습니다.
W 음, 표 여기 있습니다. 연극 즐겁게 관람하세요.
M 감사합니다.

만점 솔루션 남자가 인터넷에서 예매한 연극표를 요청하자 여자가 명단에서 확인한 뒤 표를 주는 것으로 보아, 극장 매표원과 손님의 관계임을 알 수 있다.

14 ③

M I heard that you're going on a business trip to Korea.
W Yeah, I'll leave for Korea this Friday.
M How long are you going to stay there?
W Well... I'll stay at Seoul for a week. And then, I have to go to Daejeon. I'm going to stay there for five days.
M Then, you will come back here, won't you?
W Yeah, that's right.

M 한국으로 출장 간다는 소식 들었어.
W 그래, 이번 주 금요일에 한국으로 출발할 거야.
M 거기서 며칠이나 머물 거니?
W 글쎄… 서울에서 일주일 머물 거야. 그러고 나서, 대전으로 가야 해. 나는 그곳에서 5일 동안 머물 거야.
M 그러고 나서, 이곳으로 돌아오는 거지, 그렇지?
W 응, 맞아.

만점 솔루션 여자는 한국에 출장을 가서 서울에서 일주일, 대전에서 5일 머문다고 했다. 따라서 여자가 한국에 머무는 기간은 총 12일이 된다.

15 ①

W David, look at all those people! It's really crowded.
M It's Saturday night. Everyone wants to enjoy their time just like us.
W So, did you decide which movie to see?
M Yes, I did. What about *Avatar*?
W That's what I want to see, too. Okay, I'll go buy the tickets now. You buy some popcorn and drinks over there.
M Good! I'll get soda and popcorn.

W David, 저 사람들 좀 봐! 정말 복잡하다.
M 토요일 밤이잖아. 모든 사람들이 바로 우리처럼 토요일 밤을 즐기고 싶은 거야.
W 그래, 어떤 영화를 볼지 결정했니?
M 응. '아바타' 어때?
W 내가 보고 싶은 것도 바로 그거야. 좋아, 내가 지금 가서 표를 사 올게. 너는 저쪽에서 팝콘과 음료수를 좀 사.
M 좋아! 난 청량음료와 팝콘을 사 올게.

16 ④

W Robert, you look excited. Is there something interesting?
M Yes, there is. Tomorrow, I'm going to go fishing in the Colorado River with Robin and Lucy.
W Go fishing in the Colorado River? Sounds exciting.
M Hey, Susan, why don't you join us? If you do, we'll have much more fun.
W I'd love to join you, but I can't. I have to do some volunteer work at an orphanage tomorrow.
M Do you? Oh, I didn't know you did such good things.

W Robert, 너 들떠 보인다. 무슨 재미있는 일이라도 있니?
M 응, 있어. 내일, Robin과 Lucy와 함께 Colorado 강으로 낚시를 갈 거야.

W Colorado 강으로 낚시하러 간다고? 재미있겠구나.
M 야, Susan, 우리와 함께 하는 게 어때? 네가 같이 가면, 훨씬 더 재미있을 거야.
W 나도 너와 같이 가고는 싶지만, 갈 수 없어. 내일 고아원에서 자원봉사 활동을 해야 하거든.
M 그래? 오, 네가 그렇게 좋은 일을 하는지 몰랐어.

17 ①

M Suyeon, what's wrong? You look worried.
W I might have to change the topic of my presentation.
M You mean for the science class?
W Yes, I was going to do it on electric current, but it's not going well.
M Have you talked to Mr. Brown about it?
W Not yet, I'm afraid he will be angry.
M No, he is always happy to help us.

M 수연, 무슨 일이야? 걱정 있어 보여.
W 나 내 발표 주제를 바꿔야 할 거 같아.
M 과학 수업 발표 말하는 거야?
W 응, 전류에 대해서 하고 있었는데 잘 안돼.
M 그것에 대해 브라운 선생님이랑 말해봤어?
W 아직, 그가 화낼까 두려워.
M 아니야, 그는 언제나 우릴 돕는 걸 좋아하잖아.

18 ⑤

W Good afternoon. How can I help you?
M I'd like to send this box to Britain.
W Okay. What do you have inside?
M It's a book.
W Would you put it on the scale there?
M All right. How long will it take to get there?
W It'll take a week. It's 6,000 won.
M Here it is.

W 안녕하세요. 무엇을 도와드릴까요?
M 이 상자를 영국으로 보내고 싶어요.
W 알겠습니다. 안에 무엇이 들어 있죠?
M 책입니다.
W 저기 저울 위에 그것을 올려 놓아 주시겠어요?
M 알겠습니다. 그곳에 도착하는 데 얼마나 걸릴까요?
W 일주일 걸릴 거예요. 6,000원입니다.
M 여기 있습니다.

만점 솔루션 남자는 책이 든 상자를 영국으로 보내고 싶다며 도착하는 데 걸리는 시간을 묻고 있으므로 '우체국'에서 이루어지는 대화임을 알 수 있다.

19 ③

W Did you clean your room, Daniel?
M No, I didn't. I was busy because of my homework.
W Then when will you clean your room?
M I'll do it right after I have dinner. By the way, what's for dinner this evening?
W I'm going to make chicken curry and tomato salad.
M ______________________

W 방 청소했니, Daniel?
M 아니요, 못 했어요. 숙제하느라 바빴거든요.
W 그럼 방 청소를 언제 할 거니?
M 저녁 먹자마자 바로 할게요. 그런데, 오늘 저녁 식사는 뭐예요?
W 치킨 카레와 토마토 샐러드를 만들 거란다.
M 좋아요! 저는 두 음식 모두 좋아해요.

① 맞아요, 저는 아침을 안 먹었어요.
② 좋아요, 치킨 카레를 주문할게요.
④ 맞아요, 이 식당은 유명해요.
⑤ 맘껏 드세요, 모두 당신을 위한 거예요.

20 ⑤

W Excuse me, I'd like to buy tickets for the movie, *King Kong*.
M I see. What time do you want to see it?
W At 5:30. I need two tickets. How much is it altogether?
M It's $25. How would you like to pay?
W I'll pay in cash. Here is $25.
M ______________________

W 실례합니다, 영화 King Kong 표를 사고 싶어요.
M 알겠습니다. 몇 시에 그 영화를 보고 싶으신가요?
W 5시 30분이요. 2장 주세요. 모두 얼마죠?
M 25달러입니다. 어떻게 지불하시겠어요?
W 현금으로 지불할게요. 여기 25달러 있습니다.
M 표 여기 있습니다. 영화 재미있게 보세요.

① 걱정 마세요, 제가 25달러 빌려 줄게요.
② 당신은 영화를 보기에는 너무 어려요.
③ 아니요, 저는 Harry Potter는 보고 싶지 않아요.
④ 좋아요, 내일 그 영화를 보러 가요.

만점 솔루션 영화표를 구입하기 위해 요금을 지불한 손님에게 극장 매표원은 표를 건네주며 영화 재미있게 보라는 말을 하는 것이 가장 적절하다.

영어듣기능력평가 12회

01 ③	02 ④	03 ④	04 ④	05 ③
06 ④	07 ④	08 ⑤	09 ④, ➊②	10 ④
11 ⑤, ➊②	12 ②	13 ②	14 ③	15 ③
16 ⑤	17 ⑤	18 ③	19 ①	20 ③

01 ③

M What are you buying Mary for her birthday? I'm going to buy her a key chain.
W Well, I didn't decide yet. What do you think of a teddy bear?
M I don't think it's a good idea. She's a middle school student.
W Then, how about a picture frame?
M That's better.
W Then, I'll get one for her.

M Mary의 생일 선물로 무엇을 살 거니? 나는 열쇠고리를 사 줄 거야.
W 음, 난 아직 결정하지 못했어. 테디 베어에 대해 어떻게 생각하니?
M 그건 좋은 생각이 아닌 것 같아. 그 애는 중학생이잖아.
W 그럼, 사진 액자는 어때?
M 그게 더 낫다.
W 그럼, 나는 그녀에게 그것을 사 줘야겠다.

02 ④

M This is the living room of my house. There is a big sofa in the middle of the room. A coffee table is in front of the sofa. I usually read newspapers there. Can you see the newspaper on the sofa? My mom will not be happy with that. I have to put it away right now. I have a plant. It's next to the sofa. Behind the sofa, there is a three-tiered bookshelf. It's a small living room, but I like to be here.
M 여기가 우리 집 거실이에요. 거실 중앙에 큰 소파가 있어요. 커피 탁자가 소파 앞에 있고요. 나는 보통 거기에서 신문을 읽어요. 소파 위에 신문 보이죠? 어머니는 좋아하지 않으실 거예요. 지금 당장 치워야겠어요. 우리는 화분도 있어요. 그것은 소파 옆에 있죠. 소파 뒤에, 3단 짜리 책꽂이가 있어요. 작은 거실이지만, 나는 여기에 있는 것이 좋아요.

만점 솔루션 주로 소파에서 신문을 읽는다고 했으며 지금도 소파 위에 신문이 있어서 치워야겠다고 했으므로 ④가 담화의 내용과 일치하지 않는다.

03 ④

W We are going to have a snowstorm next Monday. It will bring us a lot of snow. I'm afraid we'll have a hard time cleaning up the snow. The snow will continue until next Wednesday. However, this weekend we'll have just a little bit of wind. The weather will be good enough for outdoor activities.

W 다음 주 월요일에는 눈보라가 칠 것입니다. 그 때문에 많은 눈이 내리게 될 것입니다. 그 눈을 치우는 데 어려움을 겪게 될 것 같습니다. 눈은 다음 주 수요일까지 계속될 것입니다. 그러나, 이번 주말에는 약간의 바람만 불 것입니다. 날씨는 야외 활동을 하기에 충분히 좋을 것입니다.

04 ④

M You can use this when you clean your house. It's a kind of electric machine. You hold this with your hand, turn the switch on, and move it around on the floor. Then, this sucks all the dust and dirt from the floor. What is this?

M 여러분이 집 청소를 할 때 이것을 사용할 수 있습니다. 이것은 전기기기의 한 종류입니다. 여러분은 손에 이것을 쥐고 전원을 켜고 바닥을 따라 움직입니다. 그러면 이것이 바닥의 모든 먼지를 빨아들입니다. 이것은 무엇일까요?

05 ③

M Good afternoon. My name is Jason Lee. This is my first time at this camp, but I want to be close to you guys during this camp. I'm good at listening to others, so tell me all the troubles you have. In the future, I want to be a counselor for young people.

M 안녕하세요. 제 이름은 Jason Lee입니다. 이번 캠프에는 처음이지만, 저는 이 캠프 동안 여러분들과 친해지고 싶습니다. 저는 다른 사람들의 말을 잘 경청합니다. 그러니 여러분이 가지고 있는 모든 어려움을 제게 말씀해 주세요. 장래에, 저는 젊은이들을 위한 상담가가 되고 싶습니다.

06 ④

W Would you hurry and get on the bus, please? The bus driver is waiting.
M What's the next place to see?
W We're going to see Tora Castle. That's the most famous place in this area.
M Really? Why is it famous?
W When the bus starts going, I will explain to everyone the history of the castle.
M OK. Thank you. I'm really enjoying this tour.

W 서둘러 버스에 탑승해 주시겠어요? 버스 기사님이 기다리고 계십니다.
M 구경할 다음 장소는 어디인가요?
W 우리는 Tora 성을 구경할 예정입니다. 그곳은 이 지역에서 가장 유명한 곳입니다.
M 정말요? 그곳이 왜 유명한가요?
W 버스가 출발하면, 그 성의 역사에 대해 모두에게 설명해 드리겠습니다.
M 알겠습니다. 감사합니다. 저는 이 여행이 정말로 즐거워요.

만점 솔루션 여자의 말 get on the bus, explain to everyone the history of the castle 등을 통해 여자의 직업이 '관광 안내원'임을 추론할 수 있다.

07 ④

① W What does your mother do?
M She's working for a food company.
② W How's the weather today?
M It's partly cloudy.
③ W What's wrong with you?
M I have a little bit of a headache.
④ W Who are you waiting for?
M He will be back soon.
⑤ W Do you want to go out for dinner?
M Yes. I really want to go out.

① W 너의 어머니의 직업은 무엇이니?
M 식품 회사에 다니셔.
② W 오늘 날씨가 어떠니?
M 부분적으로 구름이 꼈어.
③ W 무슨 일이 있니?
M 두통이 약간 있어.
④ W 너는 누구를 기다리고 있니?
M 그는 곧 돌아올 거야.
⑤ W 저녁 식사하러 나가기를 원하니?
M 응. 정말 나가고 싶어.

08 ⑤

W How was your trip to Europe?
M We had a good time there. Especially our guide was great. She guided us to many wonderful places.
W Sounds great. Would you give me her email address?
M Why not? Are you going there?
W Yes, in a few weeks.
M Great. I'm sure she'll do a great job for you, too.

W 유럽 여행은 어땠니?
M 그곳에서 좋은 시간을 보냈어. 특히 우리 안내원이 좋았어. 그녀는 우리를 많은 훌륭한 장소들로 안내해 주었지.
W 좋았겠다. 나에게 그녀의 이메일 주소를 알려 줄래?
M 그럴게. 너도 그곳에 갈 거니?
W 응, 몇 주 후에.
M 잘됐다. 그녀가 네게도 틀림없이 잘해 줄 거야.

만점 솔루션 여자의 말 Would you give me her email address?를 통해 여자가 부탁하는 일이 안내원의 이메일 주소를 알려달라는 것임을 알 수 있다.

09 ④ | ➕ ②

M Mina, are you studying English even during a break?
W I'm memorizing English words for my essay writing.
M Do you mean the writing test for English class? Can't we use a dictionary?
W Yes. You can use a dictionary if you want, but it would be much easier if I know all the words I'm going to use in the essay, wouldn't it?
M It makes sense. Can I borrow your dictionary?
W Sure, but it's not mine. I borrowed it from the library.
M Okay. I'll return it after I use it. Thanks.

M 미나야, 너는 쉬는 시간에도 영어 공부를 하고 있는 거니?
W 에세이 쓰기를 위해서 영어 단어를 외우고 있는 중이야.
M 영어 시간의 쓰기 평가 말이야? 우리가 사전을 사용할 수 없니?
W 응. 원하면 사전을 사용해도 되지만, 내가 에세이에 사용할 단어를 모두 알면 훨씬 더 쉽지 않겠어?
M 말이 되네. 네 사전 좀 빌려도 될까?
W 물론이지, 하지만 내 것이 아냐. 도서관에서 빌렸어.
M 알았어. 내가 사용한 뒤에 반납할게. 고마워.

10 ④

M Excuse me. How can I get to the train station?
W Oh, you have to take a bus.
M Where should I take the bus?
W Go straight one block and turn right.
M One block and turn right.
W Yes, then walk two more blocks.
M Should I cross the intersection?
W Yes, then you can take the bus in front of Star Pharmacy.

M 실례합니다. 기차역을 어떻게 가야하나요?
W 아, 버스를 타야 합니다.
M 버스는 어디서 타야 하나요?
W 한 블록 더 가셔서 오른쪽으로 도세요.
M 한 블록 더 가서 오른쪽으로 돌아라.
W 네, 그리고 두 블록을 더 가세요.
M 교차로를 건너야 하나요?
W 네, 그럼 스타 약국 앞에서 버스를 탈 수 있어요.

11 ⑤ | ➕ ②

M Is that your bicycle?
W Yes, but I haven't ridden it for a few months. I'm afraid it's not working well.
M Then, let me check it. I think the chain needs some oil.
W Oh, really? Then I can ride it more easily, right?
M It will help. Let me give the chain some oil for you.
W While you're doing that, I'll get a cup of coffee for you.

M 저것이 네 자전거니?
W 응, 하지만 그것을 몇 달 동안 타지 않았어. 작동이 잘 될지 모르겠어.
M 그렇다면, 내가 점검해 볼게. 체인에 기름칠이 좀 필요한 것 같은데.
W 오, 정말? 그러면 자전거 타기가 좀 더 쉬워지겠구나, 그렇지?
M 그게 도움이 될 거야. 내가 너를 위해 체인에 기름칠을 해 줄게.
W 네가 그것을 하는 동안, 난 커피 한 잔 사 올께.

만점 솔루션 남자는 여자의 자전거에 기름칠이 필요하다고 하면서 기름칠을 해 주겠다고 말하고 있다.

12 ②

W Oh, Tom. I heard you broke your leg. What happened?
M Well, I tried to jump over the fence around the parking lot, but wasn't successful.
W I saw some boys sometimes jump over it. I always thought it was dangerous.
M You're right. I learned the lesson the hard way. I won't do that again.

W 오, Tom. 다리가 부러졌다고 들었어. 무슨 일이 있었니?
M 저, 주차장 둘레의 철조망을 뛰어넘으려고 했는데, 성공하지 못했어요.
W 몇몇 남자 아이들이 가끔 그것을 뛰어넘는 것을 보았지. 난 항상 그것이 위험하다고 생각했어.
M 맞아요. 저는 어렵게 교훈을 얻었어요. 다시는 그러지 않을게요.

만점 솔루션 남자는 울타리를 뛰어넘으려다 다리가 부러졌으며 다시는 그러지 않겠다고 했으므로, 자신이 한 일에 대해 후회하고 있음을 알 수 있다.

13 ②

W Jack, how about playing tennis this Saturday?
M I'd like to do that, but I can't.
W Why is that? Do you have homework to do?
M No, my grandmother is in hospital. I have to take care of her.
W Sorry to hear that.

W Jack, 이번 주 토요일에 테니스를 치는 게 어때?
M 그러고 싶지만, 그럴 수가 없어.
W 왜 그런데? 해야 할 숙제가 있니?
M 아니, 할머니께서 병원에 계셔. 할머니를 간호해야 하거든.
W 그 말을 들으니 유감이다.

14 ③

W Excuse me, where is Kim's Company?
M Go straight for two blocks along Olsen Street. You'll see the bookstore on your left.
W Two blocks and the bookstore is on my left, right?
M Yes. Kim's Company is right across from the bookstore. So the building is on your right.
W Now I see. Thank you very much.

W 실례합니다, Kim's 회사가 어디에 있나요?
M Olsen 거리를 따라 두 블록 직진하세요. 왼편으로 서점이 보일 겁니다.
W 두 블록을 가면 서점이 제 왼쪽에 있다는 말씀이시죠, 그렇죠?
M 예. Kim's 회사는 그 서점 바로 건너편에 있습니다. 그러니까 그 건물은 당신의 오른편에 있는 거죠.
W 이제 알겠습니다. 정말 감사합니다.

15 ③

W When will Randy's plane arrive?
M He said it would arrive at six.
W Then, we have two hours left.
M Yes. We're leaving for the airport at five. I can't wait to see Randy.
W Me too. I haven't seen him for two years.

W Randy의 비행기가 언제 도착하지?
M 비행기가 6시에 도착할 거라고 말했어.
W 그러면, 2시간 남았구나.
M 응. 우리는 공항으로 5시에 출발할 거야. Randy가 정말 보고 싶다.
W 나도 그래. 그를 2년 동안 보지 못했어.

16 ⑤

W Paul, what do you have in your hand?
M It's a picture book I made. I did it in English class.
W Great. Let me see it. Did you write the story, too?
M Yes, but it is not very good. You know, I'm not an artistic person.
W I think the pictures are nice. Believe your mom, honey. You did a great job.

W Paul, 손에 있는 것이 뭐니?
M 제가 만든 그림책이에요. 영어 시간에 만들었어요.
W 훌륭하구나. 좀 보여 다오. 네가 이야기도 썼니?
M 예, 하지만 그렇게 잘된 것은 아니에요. 아시잖아요, 저는 예술적인 사람이 아니에요.
W 내 생각에는 그림이 좋구나. 아들아, 엄마를 믿으렴. 아주 잘 했어.

만점 솔루션 여자는 아들이 만든 작품을 보고 기뻐하며 칭찬하고 있는 상황이다.

17 ⑤

W London is the capital city of the United Kingdom. People from around the world come to London to travel, to study or to live. It is said that more than 300 languages are spoken in London. London is known as a rainy city. It rains a lot in summer and it rains a lot even in winter. The city hosted the Olympic Games three times. The latest one was in 2012. The city has a subway system. It is called London Underground. It is the oldest subway system in the world.

W 런던은 영국의 수도입니다. 전 세계의 사람들이 여행을 하거나 공부를 하거나 또는 살기 위해 런던으로 옵니다. 런던에서는 300개 이상의 언어들이 사용된다고 합니다. 런던은 비가 많이 오는 도시로 알려져 있습니다. 여름에 비가 많이 오고 겨울에도 비가 많이 옵니다. 그 도시는 3번 올림픽 경기를 개최했습니다. 가장 최근의 경기는 2012년이었습니다. 그 도시에는 지하철 시스템이 있습니다. 그것은 런던 지하철이라고 불립니다. 그것은 세계에서 가장 오래된 지하철 시스템입니다.

만점 솔루션 마지막 부분에서 London의 지하철 시스템에 대해 말하고 있으며, 2층 버스에 대한 언급은 나와 있지 않다.

18 ③

W How was my singing? Was I good?
M You sounded a little tired.

W Actually, I'm very tired. Is today's schedule over now?
M No, you have to go to Mr. Larry's Show to sing a song there.
W Is that my last appointment today?
M Yes, but tomorrow is busy too. Sorry about that.

W 제 노래가 어땠나요? 괜찮았나요?
M 약간 피곤하게 들렸어요.
W 사실, 전 아주 피곤해요. 이제 오늘 일정이 끝났나요?
M 아니요, Mr. Larry 쇼에 노래를 부르러 가야 해요.
W 그것이 오늘 마지막 약속인가요?
M 예, 하지만 내일도 바빠요. 미안해요.

19 ①

M Thank you for giving me a ride home.
W My pleasure.
M How long have you lived in this town?
W For more than 10 years.
M It's hard to talk. Would you mind turning the radio off?
W ______________________

M 집까지 저를 태워 주셔서 감사해요.
W 천만에요.
M 이 마을에 얼마나 오래 사셨어요?
W 10년이 넘었어요.
M 이야기 하기가 어렵군요. 라디오 끄는 것을 꺼리시나요?
W 아니요, 제가 끌게요.

② 그것을 켜도 괜찮아요.
③ 라디오는 나의 좋은 친구에요.
④ 나는 운전할 때 보통 라디오를 꺼 두죠.
⑤ 예, 소리를 올려야겠네요.

만점 솔루션 Would you mind ~?에 대해 요청을 수락할 때는 No, I don't mind. 또는 Not at all. 등의 부정으로, 요청을 거절할 때는 긍정으로 한다.

20 ③

W Do you know how to play this card game?
M Yeah, actually, it's one of my favorite games.
W Sounds great! We're going to have a wonderful time this evening.
M I think so. Let's get started right away.
W ______________________

W 이 카드 게임을 하는 방법을 알고 있니?
M 응, 사실, 그것은 내가 가장 좋아하는 게임들 중 하나야.
W 잘됐다! 오늘 저녁에 우리는 멋진 시간을 보내겠는 걸.
M 나도 그렇게 생각해. 지금 바로 시작하자.
W 좋아. 난 게임할 준비가 되었어.
① 이제 네 차례야.
② 나는 이 게임을 좋아하지 않아.
④ 좋아. 나는 곧 나갈 거야.

영어듣기능력평가 13회

01 ③	02 ⑤	03 ⑤	04 ①, ⊕③	05 ③
06 ④	07 ③	08 ②	09 ①, ⊕③	10 ⑤
11 ④	12 ②	13 ②	14 ⑤	15 ③
16 ②	17 ④	18 ④	19 ⑤	20 ④

01 ③

M I live in Australia. I can jump fast with my back legs. I have a long, strong tail. It helps me balance when I jump. When I was a little baby, my mother carried me in the pouch of her stomach. What am I?

M 나는 호주에 살고 있어요. 나는 뒷다리로 빠르게 뛸 수 있어요. 나는 길고 강한 꼬리를 가지고 있어요. 꼬리는 내가 뛸 때 균형을 잡도록 도와줍니다. 내가 아기 였을 때는, 엄마 복부에 있는 주머니 안에 날 넣고 다녔어요. 나는 무엇일까요?

02 ⑤

M Mom, I left my Cellphone on the sofa. Can you get it for me?
W Well, it isn't on the sofa.
M Then it may be on the table in the kitchen.
W No, it isn't there. Wait. Let me call your phone.
M I can hear the Cellphone ringing. It's on the coffee table in front of the TV.

M 엄마, 제 휴대 전화를 소파 위에 놓고 왔어요. 좀 가져다주시겠어요?
W 음, 소파 위에 없는데.
M 그러면 부엌 식탁 위에 있을지도 몰라요.
W 아니, 거기에도 없구나. 잠깐만. 네 전화기에 전화를 해 볼게.
M 휴대 전화가 울리는 게 들려요. TV 앞에 있는 커피 탁자 위에 있어요.

03 ⑤

W Good afternoon. This is Lee Yunjin with the weather update. The rain will stop soon and we'll be able to see the full moon at night. Temperatures will go up to 25 degrees. It will be foggy throughout the country tomorrow morning. In the afternoon, it will be sunny and nice.

W 안녕하세요. 기상 속보의 이윤진입니다. 비가 곧 그치고 밤에는 보름달을 보실 수 있을 것입니다. 기온은 25도까지 오를 것입니다. 내일 아침에는 전국적으로 안개가 끼겠습니다. 오후에는, 맑고 청명한 날씨가 되겠습니다.

04 ① | ⊕ ③

M Last Saturday, there was no class at school. Minju wanted

to go to a bookstore with her best friend, Hyuna, but Hyuna got a cold. She had to stay at home. Minju visited her sick friend and they went to see a doctor together. They watched TV at Hyuna's house. In the afternoon, Minju came home and did her homework. She helped her mom cook dinner and set the table.

M 지난 토요일에, 학교 수업이 없었습니다. 민주는 가장 친한 친구 현아와 서점에 가고 싶었지만, 현아는 감기에 걸렸습니다. 그녀는 집에 있어야만 했습니다. 민주는 그녀의 아픈 친구네 집에 가서 병원에 함께 갔습니다. 그들은 현아의 집에서 TV를 보았습니다. 오후에 민주는 집에 와서 숙제를 했습니다. 그녀는 엄마가 저녁 식사 준비를 하고 식탁 차리는 것을 도와드렸습니다.

05 ③

G Oh, no, I left my Cellphone at home.
M Again? I can't believe it.
G Sorry, but can I go back and get it?
M But we'll be late for the reservation.
G I'm really sorry. Could you call the restaurant, and tell them we will be a little late?
M Okay. I guess I'll have to.
G Thank you, Dad! I'll be back soon.

G 안돼, 휴대폰을 집에 두고 왔어요.
M 또? 믿을 수가 없네.
G 미안해요, 하지만 돌아가서 갖고 오면 안될까요?
M 하지만 예약 시간에 늦을 거야.
G 진짜 미안해요. 식당에 전화해서 조금 늦는다고 말하면 안될까요?
M 알겠어. 그래야겠다.
G 고마워요 아빠! 금방 돌아올게요.

06 ④

W School soccer tournament starts next Monday. Each class must select 11 players and at least two of them must be girls. The homeroom teacher can play in a team. Games will start at 8 o'clock every morning. The final match will be on school sports day. We hope everybody enjoys the games.

W 교내 축구 토너먼트 대회가 다음 주 월요일에 시작됩니다. 각 학급은 11명의 선수를 선발해야 하며 선수들 중 적어도 2명은 반드시 여학생이어야 합니다. 담임선생님도 팀에서 경기를 할 수 있습니다. 경기는 매일 아침 8시에 시작될 것입니다. 결승전은 학교 체육 대회 날 있을 예정입니다. 모두가 경기를 즐기시기 바랍니다.

만점 솔루션 Games will start at 8 o'clock every morning.에서 경기는 매일 아침 8시에 시작됨을 알 수 있다.

07 ③

M How about going to the City Swimming Pool tomorrow?
W Sounds good. They say tomorrow will be a really hot day.
M Let's go early before a lot of people come.
W Great. What time can you make it?
M Can you come at 8 o'clock?
W The swimming pool opens at nine and closes at seven.
M Then let's make it at 8:30. It will be really hot after nine.
W All right.

M 내일 City 수영장에 가는 게 어때?
W 좋아. 내일은 정말 더운 하루가 될 거래.
M 사람들이 많이 오기 전에 일찍 가자.
W 좋아. 몇 시에 만날까?
M 8시에 올 수 있니?
W 수영장은 9시에 열고 7시에 닫아.
M 그러면 8시 30분에 만나자. 9시가 넘으면 정말 더울 거야.
W 좋아.

만점 솔루션 남자가 8시에 만나자고 제안했지만 수영장이 9시에 문을 열어 결국 8시 30분에 만나기로 했다.

08 ②

① **M** Please, have a seat.
W Thank you.
② **M** Can I take your order?
W You have to stand in line here.
③ **M** Can I help you?
W Yes, I'm looking for snow boots.
④ **M** Where is the nearest bus stop?
W It's just around the corner.
⑤ **M** What season do you like most?
W I like summer because I can swim.

① **M** 앉으세요.
W 감사합니다.
② **M** 주문하시겠습니까?
W 여기에 줄을 서야 합니다.
③ **M** 도와드릴까요?
W 예, 눈 장화를 사려고 합니다.
④ **M** 가장 가까운 버스 정류장이 어디인가요?
W 바로 모퉁이 부근에 있습니다.
⑤ **M** 어느 계절이 가장 좋으세요?
W 수영을 할 수 있어서 여름이 가장 좋아요.

만점 솔루션 ② Can I take your order?는 식당 종업원이 손님에게 식사 주문을 받기 위해 하는 말이므로 손님은 I'll have ~. 또는 I'd like ~. 등과 같은 표현을 사용하여 주문할 메뉴를 말하는 것이 자연스럽다.

09 ① | ⊕ ③

M So... what do you think of this apartment?
W It's really clean and nice. How much is it?
M It's $800 a month.
W Wow, the rent is too expensive for me. Do you have any cheaper place?

M Yes, I do have one. Do you want to go and have a look?
W Yes, please. How far is it from here?

M 그래서... 이 아파트에 대해서 어떻게 생각하세요?
W 정말 깨끗하고 좋네요. 얼마죠?
M 한달에 800달러입니다.
W 와, 집세가 저에게 너무 비싸네요. 더 저렴한 곳은 없나요?
M 네, 하나 있습니다. 가서 한번 보실래요?
W 네. 여기서 얼마나 먼가죠?

10 ⑤

M I need to go to history class now. I have a couple of things to ask before the class starts.
W Wow, Fred. I didn't know you liked history so much. Do you have a girl friend in the class?
M No. It's because of the teacher. Mr. Miller makes the class really interesting.
W You're right. I enjoy listening to his storytelling about historical events.
M I have to go. See you in the class.

M 지금 역사 수업에 가야 해. 수업이 시작하기 전에 몇 가지 질문할 것이 있거든.
W 와, Fred. 나는 네가 역사를 그렇게 좋아하는 줄 몰랐어. 그 수업에 여자 친구라도 있니?
M 아니. 그건 선생님 때문이야. Miller 선생님은 수업을 정말 재미있게 하셔.
W 네 말이 맞아. 나도 선생님이 이야기 해 주시는 역사적 사건들을 듣는 게 즐거워.
M 이제 가야겠어. 수업 때 보자.

11 ④

M You look tired.
W Yes, I am. The final exam's starting next week.
M I'm tired, too. I had to finish writing a paper last night.
W On the other hand, it means the summer vacation is just around the corner.
M Oh, you're right. I'm really looking forward to it. I can't wait.

M 피곤해 보이는구나.
W 그래. 기말고사가 다음 주에 시작되잖아.
M 나도 피곤해. 어젯밤에 보고서 작성을 끝내야 했거든.
W 한편으로, 그것은 여름 방학이 바로 코앞에 다가왔다는 것을 의미하기도 하지.
M 오, 네 말이 맞아. 나는 그것을 손꼽아 기다리고 있어. 너무 기대돼.

만점 솔루션 look forward to, can't wait는 무엇인가를 몹시 기다리고 바랄 때 쓰는 표현이므로 남자의 기대하는 마음을 엿볼 수 있다.

12 ②

M Where are you going?
W I'm going to Thomson Library.
M How are you going there?
W Which way is better, bus or subway?
M You'd better take the subway. But if you are in a hurry, take a taxi.
W Well, I am not in a hurry. So I'll take the subway.

M 어디 가는 중이니?
W Thomson 도서관에 가는 중이야.
M 그곳에 어떻게 갈 거니?
W 버스나 지하철 중에서 어떻게 가는 게 더 낫니?
M 지하철을 타는 게 나아. 하지만 급하면, 택시를 타.
W 음, 난 급하지 않아. 그러니까 지하철을 탈 거야.

13 ②

W Excuse me, sir. Would you take a picture for me? This place is very beautiful.
M Sure. This is my first time in such a beautiful place. Anyway, do you want to have the whole building in your picture?
W Yes, please. You can press this button.
M Okay. On the count of three. One, two, three.
W Oh, thank you very much.
M You're welcome.

W 실례합니다, 선생님. 제 사진을 좀 찍어 주시겠어요? 이 장소가 정말 아름답네요.
M 물론이죠. 저도 이렇게 아름다운 곳은 처음이에요. 어쨌거나, 사진에 건물 전체가 들어가게 하고 싶으신가요?
W 예, 그렇게 해 주세요. 이 버튼을 누르시면 됩니다.
M 알겠습니다. 셋을 셀게요. 하나, 둘, 셋.
W 오, 정말 감사합니다.
M 천만에요

만점 솔루션 관광지에서 여자가 남자에게 사진을 찍어 달라고 부탁하는 상황으로, 대화의 처음에서 Excuse me, sir.로 시작한 것으로 보아 두 사람은 잘 모르는 사이임을 알 수 있다.

14 ⑤

[Telephone rings.]
W Hello.
M Hello, Helen. This is Charley.
W Hi, Charley. You called me at a bad time.
M Oh, I'm sorry. What are you doing?
W I'm watching the drama, *Ghost*. Aren't you watching it?
M No, I'm doing my homework. Helen, do you have James's phone number? I called you to ask for his number.
W Well, I think I have it on my phone. Wait. I'll look for it.
M Thanks.

[전화벨이 울린다.]
W 여보세요.
M 안녕, Helen. 나 Charley야.
W 안녕, Charley. 통화하기 힘들 때 전화를 했군.

M 오, 미안해. 뭐 하고 있는데?
W 드라마 Ghost를 보고 있어. 너는 그것을 안 보니?
M 아니, 나는 숙제를 하고 있어. Helen, 너 James 전화번호 가지고 있니? 그의 전화번호를 물어보려고 전화했어.
W 글쎄, 내 전화기에 있을 거야. 기다려 봐. 찾아볼게.
M 고마워.

만점 솔루션 남자의 말 I called you to ask for his number.를 통해 남자가 전화를 건 목적이 James의 전화번호를 물어보기 위해서라는 것을 알 수 있다.

15 ③

M Mary, what are you interested in?
W There are so many sick people in the hospital. I'd like to help sick people.
M Do you want to be a doctor?
W No, I want to take care of sick people, give medicine and assist doctors in the operating room.
M Then this would be a nice job for you.

M Mary, 너는 무엇에 관심이 있니?
W 병원에는 아픈 사람들이 아주 많아. 나는 아픈 사람들을 돕고 싶어.
M 너는 의사가 되고 싶니?
W 아니, 나는 아픈 사람들을 돌보고, 약을 주고, 수술실에서 의사들을 돕고 싶어.
M 그럼 이것이 네게 좋은 직업일 것 같다.

만점 솔루션 여자는 의사가 되고 싶지는 않다고 했으며 환자를 돌보고 약을 주고 의사를 돕고 싶다고 했으므로 '간호사'가 장래 희망임을 알 수 있다.

16 ②

W Did you finish packing for the trip?
M It's almost done. When are we going to leave tomorrow?
W We have to arrive at the airport before 9 o'clock.
M Then we have to leave around 6 o'clock.
W Isn't it too early? We need to eat breakfast, too. How about 7 o'clock?
M I think we can have breakfast at the airport. I don't want to be late.
W All right. I'll set the alarm at 5 o'clock.

W 여행을 위해서 짐은 다 쌌니?
M 거의 다 되었어. 내일 언제 출발할 거야?
W 공항에 9시 전에 도착해야 해.
M 그러면 6시경에 출발해야겠네.
W 너무 이른 것 아닐까? 아침 식사도 해야 할 텐데. 7시는 어떨까?
M 공항에서 아침 식사를 할 수 있을 거야. 나는 늦고 싶지 않아.
W 알겠어. 내가 5시에 자명종을 맞춰 놓을게.

만점 솔루션 여자는 아침 식사를 하고 출발하려고 했으나 남자는 공항에서 아침 식사를 할 수 있으므로 늦지 않도록 일찍 출발하자고 말하고 있다.

17 ④

W Welcome to Korea Department Store. For your safety, inline skates and roller shoes are not allowed anywhere in the shopping mall. Also on the 2nd floor where food corners are located, pets are not allowed. It's for everybody's comfortable shopping. Thank you for your cooperation.

W 한국 백화점에 오신 것을 환영합니다. 여러분의 안전을 위해, 인라인 스케이트와 바퀴달린 신발은 쇼핑몰 어느 곳에서도 허용되지 않습니다. 또한 음식점이 위치하고 있는 2층에서는 애완동물은 출입할 수 없습니다. 모든 분들의 편안한 쇼핑을 위한 것입니다. 여러분의 협조에 감사드립니다.

만점 솔루션 인라인 스케이트를 금지하고, 애완동물의 출입을 제한하는 내용이므로, 백화점과 쇼핑몰 등에서 들을 수 있는 안내 방송임을 알 수 있다.

18 ④

W I have a beautiful daughter. Five years ago, she was sick and in the hospital for three months. She was very weak. After she came home, she started to learn swimming for her health. At first, she could swim only 10 minutes. However, she didn't give up. She went to the swimming pool three times a week for 5 years. Now she is a wonderful swimmer. She is on the swimming team in her school.

W 저에게는 예쁜 딸이 한 명 있습니다. 그 애는 5년 전, 아파서 병원에 3개월 동안 입원해 있었어요. 그 애는 매우 약했습니다. 퇴원 후, 그 애는 건강을 위해 수영을 배우기 시작했어요. 처음에는, 10분밖에 수영할 수 없었어요. 하지만, 그 애는 포기하지 않았죠. 5년 동안 일주일에 세 번씩 수영장에 갔어요. 지금 그 애는 훌륭한 수영 선수입니다. 그 애는 학교의 수영팀에 소속되어 있어요.

만점 솔루션 여자는 몸이 아팠던 딸이 건강해져 훌륭한 수영 선수가 된 것을 자랑스러워 하고 있다.

19 ⑤

M Excuse me. Would you take a picture for me?
W Sure.
M Thank you.
W Which button do I have to push?
M Push the big round button. Push it until you hear the 'click' sound.
W Pardon?
M ________________

M 실례합니다. 사진 좀 찍어 주시겠어요?
W 물론이죠.
M 감사합니다.
W 어느 버튼을 눌러야 하나요?
M 큰 동그란 버튼을 누르세요. '찰칵'하는 소리가 날 때까지 그것을 누르세요.

W 뭐라고 하셨죠?
M '찰칵'하는 소리가 날 때까지 그 버튼을 누르세요.

① 저는 사진을 잘 찍지 못해요.
② "지금"이라고 말할 때까지 기다리세요.
③ 아니요. 미안해 할 필요 없어요.
④ 조심하세요. 비싼 카메라거든요.

만점 솔루션 Pardon? / Sorry? / Excuse me? 등은 상대방의 말을 알아듣지 못했을 때, 다시 한 번 말해 달라고 부탁하는 표현이다.

20 ④

M Mom, did you see my MP3 player?
W I think I saw it on your desk this morning.
M It's not there.
W Did you check your bag?
M I did. I checked the pockets of my jacket, too.
W Well, when is the last time you saw it?
M ______________________

M 엄마, 제 MP3 플레이어 보셨어요?
W 오늘 아침에 네 책상 위에서 본 것 같구나.
M 거기에 없어요.
W 가방도 확인해 봤니?
M 확인해 봤어요. 제 재킷 주머니도 확인해 봤어요.
W 음, 언제 그것을 마지막으로 봤니?
M 아침 식사하기 전에 책상 위에 놓은 게 확실해요.

① 반짝거리는 검정색이에요.
② 저는 그것으로 음악을 들어요.
③ 7학년 때부터 제 것이었어요.
⑤ 그것은 Margaret 이모가 생일 선물로 저에게 주신 거예요.

만점 솔루션 마지막으로 본 것이 언제냐고 물었으므로 MP3 플레이어를 마지막으로 보았던 때를 말하는 것이 가장 적절하다.

영어듣기능력평가 14회

01 ①	02 ①	03 ②	04 ①	05 ⑤
06 ③	07 ④	08 ①	09 ①, ➊①	10 ③
11 ②	12 ③, ➊②	13 ④	14 ⑤	15 ②
16 ②	17 ④	18 ④	19 ①	20 ①

01 ①

M ① He is making a snowman with his friend.
② He is walking on the beach with his mom.
③ He is going to school in the morning.
④ He is brushing his teeth.
⑤ He is watching a movie with his brother.

M ① 그는 친구와 함께 눈사람을 만들고 있다.
② 그는 엄마와 함께 해변을 걷고 있다.
③ 그는 아침에 학교에 가고 있다.
④ 그는 양치질을 하고 있다.
⑤ 그는 형과 함께 영화를 보고 있다.

02 ①

M Alice, can you take a picture of me in front of the sculpture?
W Hey, you can't take a picture here.
M Why not?
W Look at the sign over there! The sign says no picture taking here.
M Oops. I didn't see it. Thank you for telling me.

M Alice, 조각상 앞에서 사진을 찍어 줄래?
W 야, 여기서는 사진을 찍을 수 없어.
M 왜 안 되는데?
W 저쪽에 있는 표지판을 봐! 여기서 사진을 찍을 수 없다고 되어 있잖아.
M 이런. 못 봤어. 말해 줘서 고마워.

03 ②

W Let's move on to other parts of Asia for tomorrow's weather. Beijing is mainly cloudy and it will be much colder with the strong wind. Tokyo's looking at some clouds and a high of 13. And there's a 40% chance of thunderstorms expected in Bangkok, and a very strong chance of showers in Singapore. Taipei continues to be windy with a few snow in the evening.

W 아시아 다른 지역들의 내일 날씨를 알아보겠습니다. Beijing은 전반적으로 흐리고 강한 바람과 함께 훨씬 더 추워지겠습니다. Tokyo는 약간의 구름이 끼겠고 최고 기온은 13도가 되겠습니다. 그리고 Bangkok

에서는 천둥을 동반한 폭우가 올 확률이 40% 정도입니다. 그리고 Singapore에서는 소나기가 올 확률이 아주 높습니다. Taipei에는 저녁에 몇 차례의 눈과 함께 바람이 계속해서 불겠습니다.

04 ①

W It's 6 o'clock. How about having dinner together?
M Sounds good! Do you have anything special to eat?
W Well... what about Italian food? There is a good Italian restaurant on Alex Street.
M Good! But the sky is so dark. It'll rain soon, I think.
W Yeah, that's right. Just wait a minute here. I'll bring an umbrella.

W 6시야. 함께 저녁 먹는 게 어때?
M 좋아! 특별히 먹고 싶은 음식이 있니?
W 음… 이탈리아 음식 어때? Alex 거리에 좋은 이탈리아 식당이 있거든.
M 좋아! 하지만, 하늘이 너무 어둡다. 곧 비가 내릴 것 같아.
W 그래, 맞아. 여기서 잠깐만 기다려. 우산을 가져올게.

만점 솔루션 마지막 여자의 말 I'll bring an umbrella.를 통해 여자가 할 일이 우산을 가져오는 일임을 알 수 있다.

05 ⑤

M You can use this to buy various products. For example, you can buy snacks, beverages, tickets, and so on. To use this, you put money in first. Next you simply press a button to choose your item. Then, the item comes out. What is this?

M 여러분은 여러 물건들을 사기 위해 이것을 사용할 수 있습니다. 예를 들어, 과자, 음료, 표 등을 살 수 있습니다. 이것을 사용하기 위해서 여러분은 우선 돈을 집어 넣어야 합니다. 그리고 단순히 물건을 고르기 위해 버튼을 누릅니다. 그러면 물건이 나옵니다. 이것은 무엇일까요?

06 ③

① **W** What did you do last weekend?
M I went fishing on Saturday with my family.
② **W** John, you look excited. What happened to you?
M I got A+ on the math test!
③ **W** What do you think about my new hair style?
M I see. I'll go with you tomorrow.
④ **W** Have a seat, please. What made you come here?
M I think I have a cold.
⑤ **W** Did you finish your biology report?
M Sure, I did. I finished it last night.

① **W** 지난 주말에 무엇을 했니?
M 토요일에 가족과 함께 낚시하러 갔었어.
② **W** John, 들떠 보이는데. 무슨 일 있었니?
M 수학 시험에서 A+를 받았어!
③ **W** 내 새로운 머리 모양에 대해 어떻게 생각하니?
M 알았어. 내일 내가 너와 함께 갈게.
④ **W** 앉으세요. 이곳에 무엇 때문에 오셨죠?
M 감기에 걸린 것 같아요.
⑤ **W** 생물 보고서 다 썼니?
M 물론이지. 어젯밤에 다 썼어.

07 ④

W Sam, when did you come back from your trip to Korea?
M Last weekend. It was a really wonderful trip.
W Was it? So did you visit Seoul?
M Of course, I did. I stayed there for five days. And I also visited Daejeon for three days.
W How about Busan? You wanted to stay there for about three days.
M It was canceled. After Daejeon, I just came back home.

W Sam, 한국 여행에서 언제 돌아왔니?
M 지난 주말에. 정말 멋진 여행이었어.
W 그랬니? 그래, 서울은 방문했어?
M 물론이지. 그곳에서 5일 동안 머물렀어. 그리고 3일 동안 대전도 방문했어.
W 부산은? 부산에서 3일 정도 머물고 싶어 했잖아.
M 그것은 취소됐어. 대전을 방문한 다음에, 방금 집으로 돌아온 거야.

만점 솔루션 남자는 한국 여행에서 서울에 5일, 대전에 3일을 머물렀다고 했으므로 총 8일 동안 머물렀다. 부산에서의 일정은 취소되었다고 했으므로 포함시키지 않도록 유의한다.

08 ①

[Cellphone rings.]
W Hello? Cindy speaking!
M Hi, Cindy. It's me, Brad.
W Hi, Brad. I heard that you're going camping with your brother during this weekend.
M Right. And that's why I'm calling you. Cindy, if you don't mind, can I borrow your tent?
W Sure, no problem. I'll lend it to you.

[휴대 전화 벨이 울린다.]
W 여보세요, Cindy입니다!
M 안녕, Cindy. 나야, Brad.
W 안녕, Brad. 이번 주말에 네 형과 캠핑하러 간다는 소식 들었어.
M 맞아. 그래서 네게 전화한 거야. Cindy, 괜찮으면, 너의 텐트를 빌려 줄래?
W 물론이지. 그것을 너에게 빌려 줄게.

09 ① | ⊕ ①

W Hi, have a seat please. What seems to be the problem?
M I think I have a bad cold. I have a runny nose and a fever.
W Let me take your temperature. Wait a minute.... Well... you are 37.2 degrees.
M Is it serious?

W Well... it's not that serious. Take medicine and have a good rest, and then you'll get better.

W 안녕하세요. 여기 앉으세요. 어떻게 오셨죠?
M 심한 감기에 걸린 것 같아요. 콧물이 나오고 열이 있어요.
W 체온을 재 볼게요. 잠시만요…. 음… 37.2도군요.
M 심각한가요?
W 음… 그다지 심각하지는 않아요. 약을 복용하고 푹 쉬세요. 그러면 더 좋아지실 거예요.

10 ③

M Oh, no. Is today already the 22nd?
W Yes, it is. Why?
M The vacation is almost over! I haven't finished my homework.
W But there are still five days left.
M Yeah, but actually I haven't even started it.
W Really? What did you do all this time?
M I don't know. Time just flew. Can you help me with it, please?

M 안돼. 오늘이 벌써 22일이야?
W 응. 왜?
M 방학이 거의 끝나가잖아! 아직 숙제 다 못했는데.
W 하지만 아직 5일이 남았어.
M 그래. 하지만 사실 아직 시작도 안 했어.
W 진짜? 방학 내내 뭘 한 거야?
M 모르겠어. 시간이 그냥 흘렀어. 나 좀 도와줄래?

11 ②

W Hi, I'd like to go to Detroit this Friday. Are there any tickets left?
M On this Friday? Sorry, we don't have any tickets. Instead, we have tickets on Saturday and Sunday.
W Then, I'll buy tickets for Saturday. What time does the train leave?
M There are three trains on Saturday. One is 9:00 in the morning, another is 2:30 in the afternoon, and the other is 6:00 in the evening.
W Um... I'll buy the earliest one. How much is it?
M It's $80.

W 안녕하세요. 이번 주 금요일에 Detroit에 가려고요. 표가 남아 있나요?
M 이번 주 금요일이요? 죄송합니다, 표가 없어요. 대신에, 토요일과 일요일에는 표가 있어요.
W 그럼, 토요일 표를 살게요. 기차가 몇 시에 출발하죠?
M 토요일에는 3편의 기차가 있어요. 하나는 아침 9시, 다른 하나는 오후 2시 30분, 그리고 나머지 하나는 저녁 6시입니다.
W 음… 가장 이른 기차표를 살게요. 얼마죠?
M 80달러입니다.

만점 솔루션 여자는 토요일에 출발하는 3편의 기차 중 가장 일찍 출발하는 기차표를 구입하겠다고 했으므로, 오전 9시 기차를 탈 것이다.

12 ③ | ⊕ ②

[Cellphone rings.]
M Hello, Laura. I'm in the building now.
W Oh, Jack. Where did you park your car?
M The parking area on the 4th floor. Where are you now?
W I'm on the 2nd floor looking for a jacket for me.
M Okay, where can we meet?
W Let's meet at the snack corner on the 3rd floor. We can eat something there.
M All right. I'll be there right away.

[휴대 전화 벨이 울린다.]
M 여보세요, Laura. 나 지금 건물 안에 있어.
W 오, Jack. 차는 어디에 주차했니?
M 4층 주차장에. 너는 지금 어디에 있니?
W 내 재킷을 보느라 2층에 있어.
M 알았어. 어디서 만날까?
W 3층의 스낵 코너에서 만나자. 거기서 뭔가 먹을 수 있어.
M 좋아. 당장 그곳으로 갈게.

만점 솔루션 남자는 건물에 들어와 4층 주차장에 차를 주차했고, 여자는 재킷을 보느라 2층에 있으며, 두 사람은 3층 스낵 코너에서 만나기로 했다.

13 ④

M Oh, Mina, would you stop doing that?
W Stop doing what?
M You're checking your Cellphone every other minute.
W I am not.
M You are. You keep looking at it and touching it. It's hard to talk with you.
W Oh, I'm sorry. I'll put it in my bag.

M 오, 미나야, 그것을 하는 것을 그만두겠니?
W 뭘 그만두라는 거니?
M 너는 네 휴대 전화를 2분마다 확인하고 있어.
W 그렇지 않아.
M 넌 그러고 있어. 넌 계속 그것을 쳐다보고 만지고 있잖아. 너와 이야기하기가 힘들어.
W 오, 미안해. 그것을 가방 안에 넣어둘게.

만점 솔루션 남자는 여자가 계속 휴대 전화를 쳐다보고 만지는 동작을 반복하고 있어 대화하기 힘들다고 불평하고 있다.

14 ⑤

[Someone knocks the door.]
W The door is open. Please come in.
M Hi!
W Hi, have a seat, please. So what's the problem with your pet?
M My pet dog has a fever. And she hasn't eaten anything since last night.

W Well... I think she has a cold now. Let me take her temperature first. Can you hold on her for a moment?
M Yes, I can.

[누군가가 문을 두드린다.]
W 문 열려 있습니다. 들어오세요.
M 안녕하세요!
W 안녕하세요. 앉으세요. 그래, 당신의 애완동물에게 무슨 문제가 있나요?
M 저의 애완견이 열이 있어요. 그리고 어젯밤부터 아무 것도 먹지 않고요.
W 음… 지금 감기에 걸린 것 같아요. 먼저 체온을 재 볼게요. 잠시 애완견을 잡아 주시겠어요?
M 예.

15 ②

M Mmm... Your pie was so good. What did you make it with?
W I put chicken, green onions, bell peppers, and some spices. Did you like it?
M Yes, it was really delicious. Thank you again for inviting me.
W You're welcome. Thank you for coming. Would you like some more?
M I would love to, but I'm full now.

M 음... 네 파이 정말 맛있다. 뭘로 만든 거야?
W 닭고기, 파, 피망, 그리고 약간의 향신료를 넣었어. 맘에 들어?
M 응, 진짜 맛있어. 나를 초대해 줘서 다시 한번 고마워.
W 천만에. 와줘서 고마워. 더 먹을래?
M 그러고 싶은데, 지금 배가 불러.

16 ②

W Albert, you look happy. Did something good happen?
M Yeah, something did. You know, I got a phone call from my brother a minute ago.
W You mean, your older brother, Jason in San Diego?
M That's right. He'll come here to see me this Friday.
W Wow, you must be very happy.

W Albert, 기분이 좋아 보인다. 좋은 일이라도 생겼니?
M 응, 좋은 일이 생겼어. 있잖아, 방금 전에 내 형한테 전화를 받았어.
W San Diego에 있는 형, Jason을 말하는 거니?
M 맞아. 형이 이번 주 금요일에 나를 보러 여기 올 거야.
W 와, 정말 행복하겠구나.

17 ④

W Rodger, are you feeling all right?
M I don't feel very well. I have a sore throat. It hurts every time I swallow something.
W I think you should drink some hot tea.
M Does it help?
W Of course. Haven't you heard that cold doesn't like hot drinks?
M I haven't, but it seems to be a good idea.

W Rodger, 너 기분 괜찮니?
M 몸이 별로 좋지 않아. 목이 아파. 무언가를 삼킬 때마다 아파.
W 너는 따뜻한 차를 좀 마셔야 할 것 같아.
M 그게 도움이 되니?
W 물론이지. 감기는 따뜻한 음료를 싫어한다는 것을 들어 보지 못했니?
M 들어 보지는 못했지만, 좋은 생각인 것 같아.

만점 솔루션 남자가 무언가를 삼킬 때마다 목이 아프다고 하자 여자는 따뜻한 차를 마셔 볼 것을 제안하고 있다.

18 ④

M Hi, students. I'm your homeroom teacher, Robert Jackson. I'm 46 years old and I have a wife and a 14-year-old son like you. I graduated from this middle school. So, I'm your senior. My hobby is reading, especially detective stories. I have read more than 100 detective stories. So if you want to read one, please tell me. I'll lend them to you.

M 안녕하세요, 학생 여러분. 저는 여러분의 담임선생님인 Robert Jackson입니다. 저는 46살이고 아내와 여러분과 같은 14살 된 아들이 한 명 있어요. 저는 이 중학교를 졸업했어요. 그러니, 저는 여러분의 선배죠. 제 취미는 독서, 특히 탐정 소설 읽기에요. 100권도 넘는 탐정 소설을 읽었어요. 그러니 탐정 소설을 읽고 싶다면, 저에게 말하세요. 책들을 여러분에게 빌려 줄게요.

19 ①

W Kevin, can I ask you a favor?
M Sure! What is it?
W You have a digital camera, don't you?
M Yes, I do. Ah, do you want to use my digital camera?
W That's right. I'm going to take a trip to Grand Canyon tomorrow. But my digital camera is broken at the moment.
M ______________________

W Kevin, 부탁 하나 해도 돼?
M 물론! 그게 뭔데?
W 너 디지털 카메라 있지, 그렇지 않니?
M 응. 있어. 아, 내 디지털 카메라를 사용하려고 하는구나?
W 맞아. 내일 Grand Canyon으로 여행을 가는데. 내 디지털 카메라가 지금 고장 났거든.
M 좋아, 내 것을 너에게 빌려 줄게.

② 하지만 난 그것의 사용법을 몰라.
③ 걱정 마. 네 사진을 찍어 줄게.
④ 네 디지털 카메라를 어디에 두었니?
⑤ 실례합니다, 이 디지털 카메라는 얼마죠?

만점 솔루션 여자가 여행을 가는데 자신의 카메라가 고장났다고 했으므로 남자는 자신의 카메라를 빌려 주겠다는 말을 하는 것이 가장 적절하다.

20 ①

W Ralph, I called you this afternoon. But you didn't answer.
M I'm sorry. Maybe you called me while I was watching a movie.
W Watching a movie? What did you see?
M I saw *Spider Man 3*. I saw it with my family.
W Oh, I heard that it was an interesting movie. Did you enjoy it?
M ________________________

W Ralph, 오늘 오후에 전화했었어. 하지만 전화를 안 받더라.
M 미안. 아마 내가 영화를 보고 있는 동안에 전화를 했나 보구나.
W 영화를 봤다고? 무엇을 봤는데?
M *Spider Man 3*을 봤어. 가족들과 함께 봤지.
W 오, 그 영화 재미있다고 들었어. 재미있었니?
M 물론! 너도 그것을 보는 게 좋을 거야.

② 좋아! 네 표도 내가 살게.
③ 맞아, 나는 영화 배우가 되고 싶어.
④ 아니, 그렇지 않았어. 나는 점심을 안 먹었어.
⑤ 내일 쇼핑하러 갈래?

영어듣기능력평가 15회

01 ⑤	02 ④	03 ③, ⊕①	04 ④	05 ②
06 ⑤	07 ③	08 ③	09 ②	10 ④
11 ①	12 ⑤	13 ③	14 ③	15 ①, ⊕⑤
16 ④	17 ②	18 ⑤	19 ②	20 ③

01 ⑤

M Oh, you're making the invitation card for your birthday.
W Yes, dad. I put my face in the middle. I have a big smile.
M Yes. I can see your teeth. You look good.
W Thanks. Under my face, I wrote the words, "Happy Birthday!"
M Good. I hope you have a great birthday party.

M 오, 너는 생일 초대장을 만들고 있구나.
W 예, 아빠. 제 얼굴을 가운데에 넣었어요. 제가 활짝 웃는 얼굴이에요.
M 그래. 네 이가 보이는구나. 좋아 보이는데.
W 고마워요. 제 얼굴 아래에 "Happy Birthday!"라는 단어를 썼어요.
M 좋은데. 네가 멋진 생일 파티를 하기를 바란다.

02 ④

W This is my room. Everything in this room is too old. The light is not bright enough. The wallpaper is dark and dirty. I'd like to change them. The bookshelf is too small. I need a bigger one. I think I need a new desk, too. I want to put my desktop computer on the desk. The chair was the birthday present from my parents. I like it.

W 여기가 제 방이에요. 이 방의 모든 것이 너무 낡았어요. 전등은 충분히 밝지 않아요. 벽지는 어둡고 더러워요. 저는 그것들을 바꾸고 싶어요. 책꽂이는 너무 작아요. 저는 더 큰 것이 필요해요. 저는 새 책상도 필요한 것 같아요. 책상 위에 데스크톱 컴퓨터를 놓고 싶어요. 의자는 부모님께 받은 생일 선물이었어요. 저는 그것이 좋아요.

만점 솔루션 부모님께 받은 생일 선물인 의자는 마음에 든다고 하므로 바꾸지 않을 것이다.

03 ③ | ⊕ ①

M Good evening. This is Matt Kim. For Seoul's weather tomorrow, tomorrow will start with a little bit of rain, so don't forget to take your umbrella with you. In the afternoon, the rain will stop but we will have a strong wind all afternoon.

M 안녕하세요. 저는 Matt Kim입니다. 내일의 서울 날씨를 말씀드리면, 내일은 약간의 비로 시작할 것입니다. 그러니 우산 챙기는 것을 잊지 마시기 바랍니다. 오후에는, 비가 멈추지만 오후 내내 강한 바람이 불 것입니다.

04 ④

M What are all these things? There are coins, spoons, and postcards.
W I got those things when I traveled around the world.
M Wow.
W Do you collect anything?
M I collect stamps. That's my hobby.
W That's a good hobby.

M 이것들이 뭐니? 동전들, 숟가락들, 그리고 우편엽서들이네.
W 내가 전 세계를 여행했을 때 그것들을 샀어.
M 와.
W 너도 수집하는 것이 있니?
M 나는 우표를 모아. 그게 내 취미야.
W 그거 좋은 취미구나.

05 ②

W Dad, can I ask you a favor?
M What is it?
W I want to have a pet dog.
M But you have an allergy to fur. I don't think having a pet dog is a good idea.
W Then can I have Chihuahua? It has short fur.
M I'm sorry, but I don't want you to be sick.

W 아빠, 부탁 하나 드려도 돼요?
M 그게 뭐니?
W 애완견을 기르고 싶어요.
M 하지만 너는 털에 대한 알레르기가 있잖아. 애완견을 기르는 것은 좋은 생각이 아닌 것 같구나.
W 그럼, 치와와를 기를 수 있을까요? 그건 털이 짧잖아요.
M 미안하지만 나는 네가 아픈 것을 원하지 않는다.

06 ⑤

W How was your dance contest?
M I don't want to talk about it.
W Why? Did you make some mistakes?
M You know, I prepared for the contest so hard. But I couldn't move my body well.
W That's too bad.
M I don't know why I did that.

W 너의 춤 경연대회는 어땠니?
M 그것에 대해 말하기 싫어.
W 왜? 실수라고 한 거니?
M 알다시피, 나는 아주 열심히 그 경연대회를 준비했어. 하지만 내 몸을 잘 움직일 수 없었어.
W 정말 안됐구나.
M 내가 왜 그랬는지 모르겠어.

만점 솔루션 남자는 춤 경연대회에서 몸을 잘 움직일 수 없었다고 말하며 자신이 왜 그렇게 했는지 모르겠다며 자책하고 있는 상황이다.

07 ③

M Sojin, are you coming to the club meeting?
W Sorry, I can't. I have to go to the migrant worker center.
M What's the migrant worker center?
W It's a center for the workers from other countries.
M Why are you going there?
W I volunteered to help doctors and nurses take care of the workers.

M 소진아, 동아리 모임에 올 거니?
W 미안해, 갈 수 없어. 나는 이주민 노동자 센터에 가 봐야 해.
M 이주민 노동자 센터가 뭐야?
W 다른 나라에서 온 노동자들을 위한 센터야.
M 네가 거기에 왜 가는데?
W 난 의사와 간호사들이 노동자들을 돌보는 것을 도와주려고 자원했어.

08 ③

① **M** How much does this basket cost?
W It costs two dollars.
② **M** May I have your order?
W Would you recommend something?
③ **M** Would you tell me where Green Bank is?
W It takes fifteen minutes on foot.
④ **M** You don't look good today.
W I think I have a cold.
⑤ **M** What can I call you?
W You can call me Jennifer.

① **M** 이 바구니는 얼마죠?
W 2달러입니다.
② **M** 주문하시겠어요?
W 추천 좀 해 주시겠어요?
③ **M** Green 은행이 어디에 있는지 알려 주시겠어요?
W 도보로 15분 걸립니다.
④ **M** 오늘 표정이 좋아 보이지 않는구나.
W 감기에 걸린 것 같아요.
⑤ **M** 당신을 뭐라고 부를까요?
W Jennifer라고 불러 주세요.

09 ②

W Chulsu, what are you doing this weekend?
M My parents and I are going to my grandmother's house.
W Where does she live?
M She lives on Jeju Island. We're going there by ship.
W Not by plane?
M Yes. I think taking a ship will be fun even though it takes a long time.

W 철수야, 이번 주말에 뭐 할 거니?
M 부모님과 나는 할머니 댁에 갈 예정이야.
W 그분이 어디에 사시는데?
M 제주도에 사셔. 우리는 배로 그곳에 갈 거야.

W 비행기로 가지 않고?
M 그래. 시간이 오래 걸려도 배를 타는 것이 재미있을 것 같아.

10 ④

[Telephone rings.]
M Hello?
W Hello? This is Sumi. You're Minsu, right?
M Yes. Are you calling on the train?
W No. I thought the train would leave at two, but I was wrong.
M Then what time does your train leave?
W They say it leaves at three.

[전화벨이 울린다.]
M 여보세요?
W 여보세요? 난 수미야. 너 민수, 맞지?
M 그래. 기차에서 전화를 거는 거니?
W 아니. 나는 기차가 2시에 출발할 거라고 생각했어. 하지만 내가 틀렸어.
M 그러면 기차가 몇 시에 출발하니?
W 3시에 출발한다고 하더라고.

11 ①

M You can buy this in a grocery store. And you should keep this in a cool place. You can cook this, and use it in many different dishes. You can boil or fry it. And you can mix it with other ingredients. If you fry this, you should break the shell first. What is this?

M 여러분은 이것을 식료품점에서 살 수 있습니다. 그리고 여러분은 이것을 시원한 곳에 보관해야 합니다. 여러분은 이것을 요리할 수도 있고 많은 다른 요리에 사용할 수 있습니다. 여러분은 이것을 끓이거나 튀길 수 있습니다. 그리고 다른 재료들과 섞을 수 있습니다. 이것을 튀기려면 껍질을 우선 깨트려야 합니다. 이것은 무엇일까요?

12 ⑤

[Telephone rings.]
W Hello, Nori Communication.
M Hello? This is Mr. Lee from Yukee Company. May I speak to Mr. Kinsley?
W He just went out and he'll be back at three.
M Would you tell me his Cellphone number?
W Sorry, I can't. But I can leave him a message.
M OK. Then, ask him to call me at 555-6236.
W What time should he call you back?
M Around 4 o'clock.

[전화벨이 울린다.]
W 여보세요, Nori 통신사입니다.
M 여보세요. 저는 Yukee 회사의 Mr. Lee입니다. Kinsley 씨 좀 바꿔 주시겠어요?
W 방금 나가셨는데 3시에 돌아오실 거예요.
M 그의 휴대 전화 번호를 저에게 알려 주시겠어요?
W 알려드릴 수 없어서 죄송합니다. 하지만 그에게 메시지를 남겨 드릴 수 있어요.
M 알겠습니다. 그러면, 그에게 555-6236번으로 저에게 전화해 달라고 전해 주세요.
W 몇 시에 전화 드려야 하나요?
M 4시경에요.

13 ③

W This Saturday, we're having a Children's Basketball Day at Clinton park. The event will begin at nine in the morning and finish at three in the afternoon. This event is free for all children. This will be a good opportunity for the children to play basketball with each other.

W 이번 주 토요일에, 저희는 Clinton 공원에서 '아이들을 위한 농구의 날'을 열 예정입니다. 행사는 오전 9시에 시작해서 오후 3시에 끝날 것입니다. 이 행사는 모든 어린이들에게 무료입니다. 이번 행사가 아이들이 서로 농구를 할 수 있는 좋은 기회가 될 것입니다.

만점 솔루션 행사는 오전 9시에 시작하여 오후 3시에 끝난다고 했다.

14 ③

W Your bag looks heavy. What do you have in there?
M It's my camera and lenses. They are heavy.
W Are you a camera man for news reports?
M No, I take pictures of food for magazines. I work with many cooks. When a cook make a dish, I take the picture of it.
W Wow, do you get to taste the food?
M Sometimes.

W 가방이 무거워 보여요. 그 안에 무엇이 들어 있나요?
M 제 카메라와 렌즈들이에요. 그것들은 무겁죠.
W 당신은 뉴스 기사를 찍는 카메라맨이신가요?
M 아니요. 저는 잡지용 음식 사진을 찍어요. 많은 요리사들과 함께 일하죠. 요리사가 음식을 만들면, 저는 그 사진을 찍어요.
W 와, 당신은 음식을 맛 보기도 하나요?
M 가끔은요.

만점 솔루션 남자는 무거운 렌즈와 카메라를 들고 다니며 요리사가 음식을 만들면 그것의 사진을 찍는다고 했으므로 '사진작가'임을 알 수 있다.

15 ① | ⊕ ⑤

W Tommy, are you going out?
M Yes. I'm going to the post office. I have to mail this letter.
W Before you go out, would you try this soup? I made it. Have a seat at the dinner table.
M Thanks, Mom. Would you pass me the spoon?
W Oh, I forgot. Here it is.

W Tommy, 너 외출할 거니?
M 예. 우체국에 가려고요. 이 편지를 부쳐야 하거든요.
W 외출하기 전에, 이 수프를 먹어 보겠니? 내가 만들었단다. 식탁에 앉아라.

M 고마워요, 엄마. 숟가락 좀 주시겠어요?
W 오, 깜빡했구나. 여기 있어.

만점 솔루션 남자는 편지를 부치러 나가다가 엄마가 만든 수프를 먹기 위해 식탁에 앉았으므로 '부엌'에 있음을 알 수 있다.

16 ④

M ① Violin Class A begins at nine.
② Violin Class B begins at eleven.
③ Violin Class C begins one hour later than Violin Class A.
④ Ron teaches Violin Class A and C.
⑤ Sam teaches his class in room number 202.

M ① 바이올린 수업 A는 9시에 시작한다.
② 바이올린 수업 B는 11시에 시작한다.
③ 바이올린 수업 C는 바이올린 수업 A보다 한 시간 늦게 시작한다.
④ Ron은 바이올린 수업 A와 C를 가르친다.
⑤ Sam은 자신의 수업을 202호실에서 가르친다.

17 ②

W John, it's time to pick up Barry.
M OK. I'm ready. What time does his school finish?
W It finishes at two. Our Barry is doing well these days.
M Really?
W Yes. He began to be interested in studying.
M I'm so happy to hear that. And I'm proud of our son.
W Me too.

W John, Barry를 태우러 갈 시간이에요.
M 알겠어요. 준비됐어요. 그의 학교는 몇 시에 끝나죠?
W 2시에 끝나요. 우리 Barry가 요즘 잘 하고 있어요.
M 정말요?
W 예. 그 애가 공부에 흥미를 갖기 시작했어요.
M 그 말을 들으니 기분이 정말 좋군요. 그리고 우리 아들이 자랑스러워요.
W 저도 그래요.

18 ⑤

W Brad, would you help me with my book report this Saturday?
M Sorry, I can't. I have to do something on Saturday.
W Are you going somewhere?
M No, but I have to show my cousin around the city. He's coming on Friday.
W It'll be fun to guide your cousin around the city.
M That's right.

W Brad, 이번 주 토요일에 내가 독후감 쓰는 것을 도와주겠니?
M 미안해, 도와줄 수가 없어. 토요일에 해야 할 일이 있거든.
W 어디 가기라도 하니?
M 아니, 하지만 내 사촌에게 도시 구경을 시켜 줘야 해. 그 애가 금요일에 오거든.
W 네 사촌에게 도시를 안내해 주는 일은 재미있겠구나.
M 맞아.

19 ②

M Mrs. Evans, can James and I stay at the gym after school today?
W What are you guys going to do?
M James will help me practice volleyball serves.
W Hmm, are you practicing for the match?
M Well, you know, I made several service mistakes during the last games. I can't do that anymore. I believe practice will make perfect.
W ______________________

M Evans 선생님, James와 제가 오늘 방과 후에 체육관에 남아도 될까요?
W 너희들은 무엇을 할 예정이니?
M James가 제가 배구 서브 연습하는 것을 도와줄 거예요.
W 흠, 시합을 위해 연습하는 거니?
M 저, 아시다시피, 저는 이전 시합에서 서브 실수를 몇 번 했어요. 더 이상 그렇게 할 수는 없어요. 연습을 하면 완벽해질 거라고 믿어요.
W 바로 그런 정신이 중요해.

① 네 맘대로 하렴.
③ 부끄럽구나.
④ 자업자득이구나.
⑤ 잘 했다.

만점 솔루션 열심히 연습을 해서 같은 실수를 반복하지 않겠다는 남자의 말에 여자는 격려하는 말을 하는 것이 가장 적절하다.

20 ③

W How was your interview?
M I'm afraid I made a lot of mistakes. I was so nervous.
W You prepared for the interview a lot.
M Right. But I didn't know what to say at that time.
W Don't worry. Everybody makes mistakes.
M Do you really think so?
W ______________________

W 면접은 어땠니?
M 실수를 많이 한 것 같아. 너무 긴장했었거든.
W 너 면접 준비 많이 했잖아.
M 맞아. 하지만 그 당시에는 뭐라고 말해야 할지 모르겠더라고.
W 걱정하지 마. 모두가 실수를 해.
M 정말 그렇게 생각하니?
W 그럼, 나도 실수를 하는 걸.

① 그렇게 말해 줘서 고마워.
② 맞아. 나는 그곳에 가지 않을 거야.
④ 그래. 그 면접은 쉬웠어.
⑤ 아니. 나는 면접을 잘 못해.

영어듣기능력평가 16회

01 ③	02 ⑤	03 ④, ➕③	04 ④, ➕①	05 ③
06 ④	07 ①	08 ②	09 ②	10 ④
11 ⑤	12 ⑤	13 ②	14 ⑤	15 ⑤
16 ④	17 ④	18 ①	19 ④	20 ②

01 ③

W You can put it on the wall or on your desk. There are numbers on it. It tells you days and dates. It shows holidays, too. You can circle important days. When you look at this, you will not forget what you should do that day.

W 여러분은 그것을 벽에 또는 책상 위에 둘 수 있습니다. 그것에는 숫자들이 있습니다. 그것은 여러분에게 요일과 날짜를 알려 줍니다. 그것은 공휴일도 알려 줍니다. 중요한 날에는 동그라미를 해 둘 수 있습니다. 이것을 보면, 여러분이 그 날 무엇을 해야 하는지 잊지 않을 것입니다.

02 ⑤

W You've got a new fish tank! Are they guppies?
M Yes. Four guppies and one algae eater. They say algae eater lives at the bottom of the tank and cleans the water.
W Some are hiding behind the water plant.
M One is here. Beside the shell.
W Did you pick the shell from the beach?
M No, I bought one. I bought the light, too. I didn't know I need a light for the fish.
W It seems to make the fish tank more beautiful.

W 어항을 새로 샀구나! 그것들은 구피니?
M 응. 구피 네 마리와 청소 물고기 한 마리야. 청소 물고기는 어항 바닥에 살면서 물을 청소해 준데.
W 몇 마리는 수초 뒤에 숨어 있네.
M 한 마리는 여기에 있어. 조개껍질 옆에.
W 조개껍질은 바닷가에서 주워 왔니?
M 아니, 하나 샀어. 형광등도 샀어. 물고기에게 형광등이 필요한 줄 몰랐어.
W 그것이 수족관을 더 아름답게 보이게 하는 것 같아.

03 ④ | ➕③

M This is today's weather update. Are you enjoying the nice warm weather today? The temperature is higher than average this week. We are going to have this warm weather until the weekend. On Sunday night, however, the temperature will drop down and it will rain through the whole country on Monday.

M 오늘의 기상 속보입니다. 오늘 맑고 따뜻한 날씨를 즐기고 계시죠? 이번 주의 기온은 평년 기온보다 높습니다. 이러한 따뜻한 날씨는 주말까지 계속되겠습니다. 하지만 일요일 밤에는, 기온이 떨어질 것이고 월요일에는 전국적으로 비가 내리겠습니다.

04 ④ | ➕①

M How was your English test?
W It wasn't that hard. I think I did quite well.
M That's good. Can we play computer games together? You know, the test is finished.
W Oh, can we do it tomorrow? I have to go shopping with my mom now.
M All right. Let's do it tomorrow afternoon. I'll send you a text message.

M 영어 시험은 어땠니?
W 별로 어렵진 않았어. 꽤 잘한 것 같아.
M 잘됐네. 같이 컴퓨터 게임을 할까? 시험도 끝났잖아.
W 오, 내일 하면 어떨까? 지금은 엄마와 쇼핑하러 가야 해.
M 좋아. 내일 오후에 그것을 하자. 내가 문자 메시지를 보낼게.

05 ③

① **M** Are we there yet?
W Not yet, honey.
② **M** How much did you pay for it?
W It was 25 dollars.
③ **M** Do you mind turning off the volume?
W That's not mine but I'll turn it on.
④ **M** Who's the man over there?
W He's our new English teacher.
⑤ **M** What sport do you like best?
W I'm a big fan of baseball.

① **M** 다 왔나요?
W 아직이예요, 여보.
② **M** 그것을 얼마 주고 샀니?
W 25달러였어.
③ **M** 소리 좀 줄여 줄래?
W 내 것은 아니지만 내가 그것을 켤게.
④ **M** 저기 있는 남자는 누구지?
W 그분은 새로 오신 우리 영어 선생님이셔.
⑤ **M** 너는 어떤 운동을 가장 좋아하니?
W 나는 야구 열성팬이야.

06 ④

W How long will it take to get to Seoul Station?
M Around twenty minutes. But you know, taxi drivers can't tell time on Saturday afternoon. Look at the traffic!
W Oh, I have to be there by three. My train will leave at three twenty.
M It's two thirty now. I think we can make it.

W 서울역에 도착하는 데 얼마나 걸릴까요?

M 20분쯤 걸려요. 하지만 아시다시피, 택시 운전사들은 토요일 오후 시간에 대해서는 장담할 수가 없어요. 교통 상황 좀 보세요!
W 오, 3시까지는 거기에 가야 해요. 기차가 3시 20분에 출발하거든요.
M 이제 2시 30분인 걸요. 시간 맞춰 갈 수 있을 거예요.

만점 솔루션 현재 시각은 2시 30분이고, 기차가 출발하는 시각은 3시 20분이다. 3시는 여자가 서울역에 도착해야 하는 시각이다.

07 ①

M Sarah, how's your father doing?
W He's getting better. He'll come home next Monday.
M That's great. Can I visit him today?
W Of course. He'll be happy to see you.
M What time is good?
W Can you come before 8 o'clock?
M All right. I'll be there around 6.

M Sarah, 아버지는 좀 어떠시니?
W 좋아지고 계셔. 다음 주 월요일이면 퇴원하실 거야.
M 잘됐구나. 오늘 그분을 문병해도 될까?
W 물론이지. 널 보시면 기뻐하실 거야.
M 몇 시가 좋을까?
W 8시 이전에 올 수 있겠니?
M 좋아. 6시쯤에 갈게.

08 ②

M I look like a big fish, but actually I'm not a fish. I live in the sea, but I'm a mammal, like humans. I live all around the world. But you can also see me in some aquariums. I do interesting shows there. What am I?

M 나는 큰 물고기처럼 생겼지만 사실은 물고기가 아닙니다. 나는 바다에 살지만 사람과 같은 포유류예요. 나는 전세계에 살고 있어요. 하지만 여러분은 나를 몇몇의 수족관에서도 볼 수 있어요. 나는 그곳에서 흥미로운 쇼를 하지요. 나는 무엇일까요?

09 ②

M I think you're interested in cooking.
W I am. I'd like to be a hotel chef.
M I think you'll make a good chef.
W I know what you are going to be. Don't you want to be a TV producer?
M Well, actually I want to be a talk show host.
W A talk show host like Oprah Winfrey?
M That's right.

M 너는 요리에 관심이 있는 것 같아.
W 맞아. 나는 호텔 주방장이 되고 싶어.
M 너는 훌륭한 주방장이 될 거야.
W 나는 네가 무엇이 되려는지 알아. 너는 TV 프로듀서가 되고 싶지 않니?
M 글쎄, 사실 나는 토크 쇼 진행자가 되고 싶어.
W 오프라 윈프리 같은 토크 쇼 진행자 말이니?
M 맞아.

만점 솔루션 여자는 요리에 관심이 있어 호텔 주방장이 되고 싶고, 남자는 오프라 윈프리 같은 토크 쇼 진행자가 되고 싶다고 말했다.

10 ④

W Nice to meet you, everyone. I'm Mrs. Jones, your English conversation teacher. You will have English class with me every Wednesday. My first name is Gloria but I want you to call me Mrs. Jones. I like to play racquetball and tennis.

W 만나서 반갑습니다, 여러분. 저는 Mrs. Jones이고 여러분의 영어 회화 선생님입니다. 여러분은 매주 수요일에 제 영어 수업을 받게 될 것입니다. 제 이름은 Gloria이지만 Mrs. Jones라고 불러 주시길 바랍니다. 저는 라켓볼과 테니스를 치는 것을 좋아합니다.

11 ⑤

M Where are you going, Mary?
W To the clubroom. Our band practices every Friday and Saturday, you know.
M Well, Mary. I've just met Zoe and she said there was no practice today.
W Did she? But nobody told me about it.
M Didn't you get the text message?
W No, I didn't. This is not right. Somebody should have told me about it.
M I agree.

M Mary, 어디에 가고 있니?
W 동아리방에. 너도 알다시피, 매주 금요일과 토요일에 밴드 연습을 하잖아.
M 저, Mary. 방금 Zoe를 만났는데 오늘은 연습이 없다고 하던데.
W 그래? 하지만 아무도 그것에 대해 내게 말해 주지 않았어.
M 문자 메시지를 못 받았니?
W 아니, 못 받았어. 이건 아닌데. 누구든 내게 그것에 대해 말을 해 줬어야 했어.
M 맞아.

만점 솔루션 동아리 밴드 연습을 위해 연습실로 가는 여자에게 남자가 오늘은 연습이 없다는 것을 알려 주고 있는 상황으로, 여자는 아무도 연습이 취소된 것을 알려 주지 않아 화가 나 있다.

12 ⑤

M A-choo!
W Bless you. Brian, look at you! Your hair is still wet.
M Because I washed it just before I came out.
W You might get a bad cold.
M You're right. Oh, my hair is frozen.
W That's why you keep sneezing.
M I didn't have time to dry it.
W It won't take much time if you use a hair drier.

M 에취!

W 저런. Brian, 너 좀 봐! 네 머리카락이 아직도 젖어 있어.
M 나오기 직전에 머리를 감았거든.
W 감기에 심하게 걸릴지도 몰라.
M 맞아. 오, 내 머리카락이 얼었다.
W 그래서 네가 계속 재채기를 하는 거야.
M 머리카락을 말릴 시간이 없었어.
W 헤어 드라이어를 사용하면 별로 오래 걸리지 않을 거야.

13 ②

M Last week, my class went on a three-day camp trip. First day, we enjoyed rafting in Dong-Gang River. We got all wet on the rafts. It was exciting. The second day, we visited a famous cave. It was hot outside, but inside the cave, it was cool. We visited the beach and played there before we left for home. It was a great trip.

M 지난주에, 우리 반은 3일간의 캠프 여행을 갔습니다. 첫째 날, 우리는 동강에서 래프팅을 즐겼습니다. 우리는 뗏목 위에서 완전히 젖었습니다. 그것은 재미있었습니다. 둘째 날, 우리는 유명한 동굴을 방문했습니다. 바깥은 더웠지만, 동굴 안은 시원했습니다. 우리는 바닷가에 들러서 놀다가 집으로 출발했습니다. 정말 즐거운 여행이었습니다.

만점 솔루션 3일간의 캠프 여행에서 있었던 일들을 말하고 있는 담화이다.

14 ⑤

M Summer vacation is just around the corner.
W I know. But I should come to school anyway during the vacation.
M Do you have summer school classes?
W I do. My class begins July 19th.
M That's the first day of vacation. Doesn't our vacation start on the 19th?
W You're right.
M Oh, that's too bad. It's not a vacation for you at all.

M 여름 방학이 코앞에 다가왔어.
W 알아. 하지만 방학 동안에도 나는 학교에 나와야 해.
M 여름 학기 수업이 있니?
W 응. 7월 19일에 수업이 시작돼.
M 방학 시작 첫 날이잖아. 우리 방학이 19일에 시작하지 않니?
W 맞아.
M 오, 정말 안됐다. 너에게는 전혀 방학이 아니구나.

15 ⑤

W Tom, my Cellphone's broken. Do you know a good repair shop near here?
M Sure, I know one. It's called Fine Repair.
W Can you tell me where it is?
M Go straight to Green Street, and turn right.
W Turn right? Okay.
M Walk one more block, then you will see Smile Bank. Keep walking straight, and it's just past the bank.
W Thanks!

W 톰, 내 휴대 전화가 고장났어. 이 근처에 좋은 수리점 알고 있니?
M 물론, 하나 알고 있어. 파인 리페어라는 곳이야.
W 어디에 있는지 알려줄래?
M 그린 가까지 쭉 간 다음에 오른쪽으로 돌아.
W 오른쪽으로? 알겠어.
M 한 블록 더 가면 스마일 은행이 보일 거야. 계속 쭉 가. 수리점은 은행 바로 지나면 나와.
W 고마워!

16 ④

M Oh, this is bad. My Cellphone is dead.
W It looks like the battery ran out.
M Can I use your Cellphone, Yolanda? I'll send just one text message.
W I'm sorry, Mark. I don't have a Cellphone. Why don't we use the pay phone over there?

M 오, 이런. 내 휴대 전화가 작동하지 않네.
W 배터리가 다 된 것 같아.
M Yolanda, 네 휴대 전화를 써도 될까? 문자 메시지 하나만 보낼게.
W 미안해, Mark. 나는 휴대 전화가 없어. 저기 있는 공중전화를 사용하면 어떨까?

17 ④

M That was a really good meal. So, shall we go?
W Oh, no, wait. Where is my wallet?
M Your wallet?
W Yes, I can't find my wallet in my purse. I don't know where it is.
M Maybe you left it at home?
W No, I used it to pay for the bus when I came here.
M Oh, no. Maybe you should check the washroom.

M 정말 맛있는 식사였어. 이제 갈까?
W 아니, 잠깐. 내 지갑이 어디 있지?
M 지갑?
W 응, 가방 안에 지갑을 못 찾겠어. 어디 있는지 모르겠어.
M 집에 두고 온 거 아니야?
W 아니야, 여기로 올 때 버스 요금 낼 때 사용했어.
M 이런. 화장실을 살펴봐.

18 ①

W It's raining outside. Take your umbrella.
M Oh, I hate rainy days. I don't like it when the shoes get all wet.
W If you don't like wet shoes on a rainy day, you can get a pair of rain boots.
M Aren't they for girls?

W I don't think so. I saw a lot of rain boots for boys.
M Okay, Mom.

W 밖에 비가 오고 있어. 우산을 가져가라.
M 오, 저는 비 오는 날이 싫어요. 신발이 완전히 젖어버리는 게 싫거든요.
W 비 오는 날 젖은 신발이 싫다면, 장화를 한 켤레 살 수 있어.
M 그것은 여자 아이들이 신는 것 아닌가요?
W 나는 그렇게 생각하지 않는다. 남자 아이들을 위한 장화도 많이 봤어.
M 좋아요, 엄마.

만점 솔루션 남자가 비가 오는 날 신발이 젖는 것이 싫다고 하자 여자는 장화를 구입할 것을 제안하고 있다.

19 ④

M Have some French fries. Aren't you eating?
W No, thank you. I'm on a diet.
M Why are you on a diet?
W Well, I'd like to lose some weight.
M Oh, would you? What else do you do to lose weight?
W ______________________

M 감자튀김 좀 먹어. 안 먹을 거니?
W 고맙지만, 안 먹을래. 다이어트 중이야.
M 왜 다이어트를 하는데?
W 음, 몸무게를 줄이고 싶어.
M 오, 그래? 넌 몸무게를 좀 줄이기 위해 다른 어떤 것을 하니?
W 저녁마다 공원에서 달리기를 해.

① 계속 다이어트 할 거야.
② 해야만 하니까.
③ 그 말 명심할게.
⑤ 살을 빼는 것은 결코 쉬운 일이 아니야.

20 ②

M What club are you interested in?
W Well, I'm thinking of joining a dancing club.
M All the girls seem to try to get into the dancing club.
W You're right. That's why there will be an audition.
M Which club are you going to join if you can't get in the dancing club?
W ______________________

M 어느 동아리에 관심이 있니?
W 글쎄, 춤 동아리에 가입하려고 생각 중이야.
M 모든 여학생들이 춤 동아리에 들어가려고 하는 것 같아.
W 맞아. 그래서 오디션이 있지.
M 춤 동아리에 들어가지 못하면, 어느 동아리에 가입할 거니?
W 연극 동아리를 생각하고 있어.

① 나는 네가 잘 해내길 바라.
③ 춤 동아리가 매우 인기가 있어.
④ 나는 오디션을 위해 최선을 다 할 거야.
⑤ 나는 오디션을 위해 연습을 해야 해.

영어듣기능력평가 17회

01 ①	02 ⑤	03 ①	04 ③	05 ⑤
06 ④	07 ⑤	08 ②	09 ①	10 ④
11 ④	12 ⑤	13 ⑤	14 ⑤	15 ③
16 ⑤	17 ⑤, ⊕③	18 ②, ⊕①	19 ④	20 ①

01 ①

M You can see this in many rooms. People use this to block the sunlight in hot weather, or to keep the room warm in cold weather. Sometimes, people use it to decorate a room. The room can look cozier and nicer with this. This is usually made of fabric. What is this?

M 여러분은 이것은 많은 방에서 볼 수 있습니다. 사람들은 뜨거운 날씨에 햇빛을 가리기 위해, 또는 추운 날씨에 방을 따뜻하게 하기 위해 이것을 사용합니다. 가끔, 사람들은 방을 꾸미기 위해 이것을 사용합니다. 이것으로 방이 더 아늑하고 좋아 보일 수 있습니다. 이것은 주로 천으로 만들어 집니다. 이것은 무엇일까요?

02 ⑤

W Tomorrow we're leaving for home at last.
M Right. I miss my family.
W Me too. By the way, did you buy anything for your family?
M Yes. I bought T-shirts and postcards. How about you?
W I got a small lady doll for my sister. Here it is.
M She's so pretty.

W 내일 우리는 드디어 집으로 떠나는구나.
M 맞아. 가족들이 보고 싶어.
W 나도 그래. 그건 그렇고, 가족들을 위해 뭐라도 샀니?
M 응. 티셔츠와 우편엽서를 샀어. 너는?
W 나는 여동생을 위해 작은 여자 인형을 샀어. 여기 있어.
M 아주 예쁘게 생겼다.

03 ①

M The rain will start this afternoon and continue until around midnight. Rainfall will be from between 1 and 2 inches across parts of Seoul area. However, Seoul will experience a pleasant June day tomorrow. You can enjoy a lot of sunshine, a good day for a picnic.
M 오늘 오후에 비가 오기 시작하여 자정 무렵까지 계속될 것입니다. 서울의 일부 지역에서 강수량은 1인치와 2인치 사이가 될 것입니다. 그러나, 내일 서울은 쾌청한 6월의 날이 될 것입니다. 햇빛이 많이 나고, 소풍 가기에 좋은 날이 될 것입니다.

04 ③

W Ryan, do you have time tomorrow evening?
M Well, I have to go to an evening class at the cultural center.
W What class are you taking? A drawing class?
M No. I'm learning how to cook Italian food.
W Sounds interesting.

W Ryan, 내일 저녁에 시간이 있니?
M 음, 문화센터에서 하는 저녁 수업에 가야 해.
W 넌 어떤 수업을 듣고 있니? 그림 그리기 수업?
M 아니. 이탈리아 음식을 요리하는 방법을 배우고 있어.
W 재미있겠다.

05 ⑤

W Let me tell you about our next meeting. We'll have the meeting at the Wilmar center, room number 201 next Wednesday 5 PM. It will finish at 7 PM. The topic of the meeting is about how to prepare for the field trip. I hope every member will come to the meeting.

W 우리의 다음 모임에 대해 말씀드리겠습니다. 우리는 다음 주 수요일 오후 5시에 Wilmar 센터, 201호실에서 모임을 갖겠습니다. 모임은 오후 7시에 끝날 것입니다. 모임의 주제는 현장 학습을 준비하는 방법에 관한 것입니다. 모든 회원이 그 모임에 오시길 바랍니다.

06 ④

W Excuse me, sir.
M Yes. What can I help you with?
W Would you help me find this book? I need it for my history class.
M Let me see. You're lucky. Nobody has checked it out yet. Go down the aisle and it's on the last shelf.
W Thank you for your help.

W 안녕하세요, 선생님.
M 그래. 무엇을 도와줄까?
W 제가 이 책을 찾는 것을 도와주시겠어요? 제 역사 수업 때문에 그 책이 필요하거든요.
M 어디 보자. 너는 운이 좋구나. 아무도 그 책을 아직 대출해 가지 않았거든. 통로를 따라가면 맨끝 책장에 있단다.
W 도와주셔서 감사합니다.

만점 솔루션 여자는 역사 수업에 필요한 책을 찾고 있고, 남자는 그 책이 있는 위치를 설명해 주고 있다. 또한 그 책을 아무도 대출해 가지 않았다는 말로 보아, 남자의 직업은 '도서관 사서'임을 알 수 있다.

07 ⑤

① **M** How old is your younger sister?
W She's eleven years old.
② **M** What can I do for you?
W Move this baggage over there, please.
③ **M** I have a little bit of a fever.
W You'd better go see a doctor.
④ **M** I can't solve this math problem.
W Let me help you with it.
⑤ **M** Can I borrow your pencil?
W Thank you for helping me.

① **M** 네 여동생은 몇 살이니?
W 11살이야.
② **M** 무엇을 도와드릴까요?
W 이 짐을 저쪽으로 옮겨 주세요.
③ **M** 난 열이 조금 있어.
W 병원에 가 보는 게 좋겠구나.
④ **M** 이 수학 문제를 못 풀겠어.
W 내가 그것을 도와줄게.
⑤ **M** 네 연필을 빌릴 수 있을까?
W 나를 도와줘서 고마워.

08 ②

W Hi, Mr. Jackson. What can I do for you?
M Well, my family is taking a trip. We'll be back on next Monday. So would you take care of our cat while we're gone?
W That's no problem. I love cats.
M Thank you for your help.
W I hope you and your family have a good trip.

W 안녕하세요, Jackson 씨. 무엇을 도와드릴까요?
M 음, 저희 가족이 여행을 떠나서, 다음 주 월요일에 돌아올 거예요. 그래서 저희가 없는 동안 우리 고양이를 돌봐 주시겠어요?
W 그러죠. 저는 고양이를 정말 좋아한답니다.
M 도와주셔서 감사합니다.
W 당신과 가족이 즐거운 여행을 하시기를 바랍니다.

만점 솔루션 가족 여행을 가는 남자가 여자에게 고양이를 돌봐 줄 것을 부탁하고 있는 상황이다.

09 ①

W Honey, where do you want to visit first?
M Well, how about the palace near the train station?
W That would be nice. Let me see the map. Hmm... the palace is not far from the Natural History Museum.
M You're right. We can spend the whole afternoon in the museum. I've always wanted to visit there.
W Do we have to reserve a hotel for the night?
M Actually I already booked a hotel. It'll take about 30 minutes from the museum.
W That's great. I'm so excited.

W 여보, 어디를 먼저 방문하고 싶으세요?
M 음, 기차역 근처에 있는 궁전이 어떨까요?
W 그게 좋겠네요. 제가 지도를 보게 해 주세요. 흠… 그 궁전은 자연사 박물관에서 멀지 않군요.

M 맞아요. 오후 내내 그 박물관에서 보낼 수 있겠어요. 나는 항상 그곳이 가 보고 싶었거든요.
W 밤에 묵을 호텔을 예약해야 하지 않나요?
M 사실 이미 호텔을 하나 예약했어요. 그 박물관에서 30분쯤 걸릴 거예요.
W 멋진걸요. 너무 흥분돼요.

만점 솔루션 지도를 보고 어디를 갈지 정하고, 항상 가 보고 싶었던 곳을 가게 되어 즐거워하고 있으며, 호텔을 예약해 두었다는 내용으로 보아, '여행 계획'에 대해 대화하고 있음을 알 수 있다.

10 ④

M Sophie, how many T-shirts do we have to make for the festival?
W Well, we'll give one to every student in the school. So I think 500 will be good.
M But you missed our teachers. There are 20 teachers.
W You're right. Is that all?
M Well, I want to make 100 more to sell to our guests.
W That's a great idea.

M Sophie, 축제를 위해 티셔츠를 몇 장 만들어야 하지?
W 음, 우리는 학교의 모든 학생들에게 한 장씩 줄 거야. 그러니까 500장이 좋을 것 같아.
M 하지만 선생님들을 빠뜨렸다. 20명의 선생님들이 계시잖아.
W 네 말이 맞아. 그게 전부니?
M 음, 손님들에게 판매할 100장을 더 만들고 싶어.
W 좋은 생각이구나.

만점 솔루션 학생들에게 제공할 500장, 선생님들에게 제공할 20장, 손님들에게 판매할 100장이 필요하다고 했으므로, 티셔츠는 총 620장이 필요하다.

11 ④

W It's nice weather! Let's take a walk, Tom.
M I want to, but I have to go buy a book.
W Really? Can I come along? I need to buy a new novel.
M Why not?
W I can give you a ride to the bookstore.
M That's good.

W 날씨가 좋네! 산책하러 가자, Tom.
M 그러고 싶지만, 나는 책을 사러 가야 해.
W 정말? 내가 함께 가도 되니? 나는 새로운 소설책을 사야 하거든.
M 좋아.
W 내가 서점까지 너를 태워 줄게.
M 잘됐다.

12 ⑤

W Dad, I have something to say to you.
M What is it?
W I want to go camping with my friends next week.
M How many nights will you go for?
W Just one night. And we go with our teacher, Miss Kim.
M Then you can go there.

W 아빠, 드릴 말씀이 있어요.
M 그게 뭐니?
W 다음 주에 친구들과 캠핑하러 가고 싶어요.
M 며칠 동안 갈 거니?
W 겨우 하루에요. 그리고 저희 선생님이신 김 선생님과 함께 가요.
M 그렇다면 그곳에 가도 좋다.

13 ⑤

M What are you doing on the Internet?
W I'm trying to download my favorite song, but it's not doing well.
M Then, let me help you.
W Thanks. This is my first time to download.
M I'll show you how to do it. Next time it will be easy for you.
W You're so kind.

M 넌 인터넷에서 무엇을 하고 있니?
W 내가 가장 좋아하는 노래를 다운로드 하려고 하는 중이야. 그런데 잘 안 되네.
M 그럼, 내가 너를 도와줄게.
W 고마워. 이번이 내가 처음으로 다운로드하는 거야.
M 내가 그것을 하는 방법을 보여줄게. 다음 번에는 너에게도 쉬울 거야.
W 넌 정말 친절하구나.

14 ⑤

M Excuse me, where is the flower shop?
W Go straight and turn left at Pine Street.
M Turn left at Pine Street?
W Yes. And then go straight one block. It's on the left corner next to the post office.
M One block and it's on the left corner?
W That's right.

M 실례합니다, 꽃가게가 어디에 있나요?
W 직진하시다가 Pine 거리에서 좌회전하세요.
M Pine 거리에서 좌회전하라고요?
W 예. 그런 다음 한 블록 직진하세요. 그것은 우체국 옆 왼쪽 모퉁이에 있습니다.
M 한 블록 가면 왼쪽 모퉁이에 있다는 말씀이시죠?
W 맞습니다.

15 ③

M Let's go pick up Tommy, honey.
W We don't have to leave now. His swimming class finishes at 5:30.
M Really? I thought his class would finish at 4:00.

W His class schedule was changed.
M I didn't know that.
W We can leave home thirty minutes before his class finishes.
M I see.

M Tommy를 태우러 갑시다, 여보.
W 지금 출발할 필요가 없어요. 그 애의 수영 수업은 5시 30분에 끝나요.
M 그래요? 나는 그의 수업이 4시에 끝난다고 생각했어요.
W 그의 수업 일정이 바뀌었어요.
M 난 그걸 몰랐어요.
W 우리는 그 애의 수업이 끝나기 30분 전에 집에서 출발해도 돼요.
M 알겠어요.

만점 솔루션 Tommy의 수영 수업은 5시 30분에 끝나고, 두 사람은 수업이 끝나기 30분 전에 집을 나서기로 했으므로, 두 사람이 집을 나서는 시각은 5시가 된다.

16 ⑤

M Did you bring my book?
W Yes. Let me take it out of my bag.
M That's my sister's book and I promised to give it back to her today.
W Well, I can't find the book. I thought it was in my bag.
M Could you double check in your bag?

M 내 책을 가져왔니?
W 응. 그거 내 가방에서 꺼낼게.
M 그것은 내 여동생의 책이어서 오늘 돌려주기로 약속했거든.
W 음, 그 책을 찾을 수가 없네. 그 책이 내 가방에 있다고 생각했는데.
M 네 가방 속을 다시 한 번 확인해 볼래?

17 ⑤ | ⊕ ③

M I have to finish this report today and the computer isn't working well.
W Oh, what can be the problem?
M I think I need a new computer. This one's too old.
W It can't be. We bought it only last year.
M I checked for viruses and it doesn't have any. I rebooted it several times, but it is still acting strange.
W Why don't you just turn it off and wait some time? That computer might have been on for too long.

M 이 보고서를 오늘 끝내야 하는데 컴퓨터가 잘 작동되질 않아요.
W 저런, 문제가 뭘까요?
M 새 컴퓨터가 필요한 것 같아요. 이것은 너무 오래 되었어요.
W 그럴 리가요. 우리는 이것을 겨우 작년에 샀는걸요.
M 바이러스를 검사했는데 전혀 없어요. 여러 번 그것을 재 작동시켜 봤지만, 여전히 이상해요.
W 그냥 전원을 끄고 좀 기다려 보면 어때요? 그 컴퓨터가 너무 오래 켜져 있었는지도 몰라요.

만점 솔루션 컴퓨터가 고장 난 상황에서 남자는 컴퓨터를 새로 사야 한다고 했지만, 여자는 컴퓨터를 끄고 잠시 둘 것을 제안하고 있다.

18 ② | ⊕ ①

W Mr. Brown, I'd like to thank you.
M Thank me for what?
W You always tried your best for your students.
M That's my job. Thank you anyway for saying so. And you were also a good student.
W Thanks. Here is a small present for you.

W Brown 선생님, 선생님께 감사드리고 싶어요.
M 뭐가 감사하다는 거지?
W 선생님께서는 항상 학생들을 위해 최선을 다하셨잖아요.
M 그게 내 일인걸. 그렇게 말해 주니 어쨌든 고맙구나. 그리고 너도 좋은 학생이었단다.
W 감사합니다. 여기 선생님께 드리는 작은 선물이 있습니다.

19 ④

W Fred, we're having interviews for the new members of the club.
M Interviews for the new members?
W Yes, twenty freshmen are expected to come for the interview.
M Wow. I didn't know that our club is that popular. When is the interview?
W It's the day after tomorrow.
M On Thursday? Oh, sorry, Jenny. I'm afraid I can't come.
W Why's that?
M ____________________

W Fred, 우리 동아리 새내기 회원을 뽑는 인터뷰를 할 예정이야.
M 새내기 회원을 뽑는 인터뷰라고?
W 맞아, 20명의 1학년들이 인터뷰를 기다리고 있어.
M 와. 우리 동아리가 그렇게 인기 있는 줄 몰랐는걸. 인터뷰가 언제야?
W 내일 모레야.
M 목요일이라고? 오, 미안해, Jenny. 나는 갈 수 없겠어.
W 그건 왜지?
M 나는 그 날 치과 예약이 있어.

① 인터뷰를 하게 되어 기뻐.
② 나는 우리가 새내기 회원이 필요하다고 생각하지 않아.
③ 우리가 정말 새내기 회원이 필요하기 때문이지.
⑤ 왜냐하면 네가 올해 동아리 회장이잖아.

만점 솔루션 Why's that?은 이유를 묻는 말이므로 남자는 인터뷰에 가지 못하는 이유를 말하는 것이 가장 적절하다.

20 ①

W John, I want to pay for today's dinner.
M No, you don't have to do that.
W I really want to pay for it. You helped me with a lot of things for the week.
M Are you serious?
W Yes, I really want to do that.

M ______________________

W John, 오늘 저녁은 제가 사고 싶어요.
M 아니에요, 그러실 필요 없어요.
W 저녁을 정말 사고 싶어요. 당신이 이번 주에 저를 많이 도와주셨잖아요.
M 진심이에요?
W 그래요, 정말 그렇게 하고 싶어요.
M 좋아요. 그러면 다음 번에 제가 대접할게요.

② 맞아요. 이곳의 음식이 맛있어요.
③ 그것이 얼마인지 말해 줄래요?
④ 음식에 무슨 문제가 있나요?
⑤ 정말이에요. 이번에 여기 처음 왔어요.

만점 솔루션 남자의 사양에도 불구하고 여자가 계속 저녁을 사겠다고 하는 상황이므로 남자는 수락의 말을 하는 것이 가장 적절하다.

영어듣기능력평가 18회

01 ①	02 ⑤	03 ②	04 ④	05 ①
06 ④	07 ①	08 ③	09 ⑤, ➕⑤	10 ⑤
11 ⑤	12 ⑤	13 ②	14 ④, ➕③	15 ④
16 ②	17 ⑤	18 ①	19 ①	20 ⑤

01 ①

M This is a kind of electronic machine. You can use this when drinking water. People think that tap water is not good enough to drink. So they use this machine to make tap water better. You can get both cold water and hot water from this. As this is an electronic machine, you can not use this without electricity.

M 이것은 일종의 전자 제품입니다. 물을 마실 때 이것을 사용할 수 있습니다. 사람들은 수돗물이 마시기에 괜찮다고 생각하지 않습니다. 그래서, 그들은 수돗물을 더 좋게 만들기 위해 이 기계를 이용합니다. 이것으로부터 차가운 물과 뜨거운 물 모두를 얻을 수 있습니다. 이것은 전자 기계이기 때문에, 전기가 없으면 사용할 수 없습니다.

02 ⑤

M Honey, did you see my wallet? I can't find it.
W Didn't you put it next to the computer?
M No, it wasn't there.
W Did you check your pants or jacket?
M I already did. But....
W How about under the bed or in your drawer of the desk?
M Oh, I got it. I found it in the drawer. Thank you, honey.

M 여보, 내 지갑 봤어요? 찾을 수가 없네요.
W 컴퓨터 옆에 두지 않았나요?
M 아니요, 거기에 없어요.
W 바지나 재킷을 확인해 봤어요?
M 벌써 봤어요. 하지만….
W 침대 아래나 책상 서랍 속은요?
M 오, 찾았어요. 서랍 속에서 찾았어요. 고마워요, 여보.

03 ②

W Taking a look at the weather now. We have cloudy skies this morning with a 50% chance of showers this afternoon. High temperatures today will reach up to 11 degrees. Lows tonight will drop to around zero. However, tomorrow will be warmer and sunnier. You can enjoy outdoor activities in the nice weather. The current temperature in Seoul is 5 degrees.

W 이제 날씨를 알아보겠습니다. 오늘 아침에는 흐리겠고 오후에는 소나기가 올 가능성이 50%입니다. 오늘의 최고 기온은 11도까지 오르겠습니다. 오늘 밤 최저 기온은 0도까지 떨어질 것입니다. 하지만, 내일은 더 따뜻해지고 더 화창해질 것입니다. 화창한 날씨 속에서 야외 활동을 즐기실 수 있습니다. 서울의 현재 기온은 5도입니다.

04 ④

W Your dad is visiting us on October 17th, right?
M He planned to, but I just got a call from him and he said he got something to do for his company suddenly.
W So does he want to delay the date from October 17th? By how much? A week?
M Well, he said that five days would be enough for him to finish his work.
W You mean, he'll visit us October 22nd.
M Yes.

W 당신 아버지께서 10월 17일에 우리를 방문하시는 거죠, 그렇죠?
M 그럴 계획이셨지만, 아버지께 방금 전화를 받았는데 갑자기 회사에서 해야 할 일이 생겼다고 말씀하셨어요.
W 그러니까 10월 17일에서 날짜를 연기하려고 하신다는 거죠? 얼마나요? 일주일요?
M 음, 아버지께서 일을 끝마치시는 데 5일이면 충분할 거라고 말씀하셨어요.
W 그러니까, 10월 22일에 우리를 방문하시겠다는 거네요.
M 맞아요.

05 ①

M I have two legs and a beak. People usually think I'm yellow, but I can be a different color. I like eating worms, bugs, seeds, and grains. I come from an egg, and it takes 21 days for me to hatch. What am I?

M 나는 두 개의 다리와 하나의 부리를 갖고 있어요. 사람들은 보통 내가 노란색이라고 생각하지만 난 여러가지 색일 수 있어요. 나는 벌레, 곤충, 씨앗 그리고 곡물들 먹는 것을 좋아해요. 나는 알에서 태어나고 깨어나는데 21일이 걸려요. 나는 무엇일까요?

06 ④

W Albert, do you know when your mother's birthday is?
M Of course, it's April 20th.
W Then, what about your father's birthday? Do you remember it, too?
M Yes, of course. My father's birthday is just two days later than my mother's birthday.
W Really? Oh, that's easy to remember.

Question When is Albert's father's birthday?

W Albert, 너의 어머니 생신이 언제인지 아니?
M 당연하지, 4월 20일이야.
W 그럼, 너의 아버지 생신은? 그것도 기억하니?
M 그럼, 물론이지. 아버지의 생신은 어머니의 생신보다 겨우 이틀 늦거든.
W 정말? 오, 기억하기 쉽구나.

07 ①

W Ted, you don't look good. What's wrong with you?
M It's because of my parents. They want me to become a lawyer or a professor.
W Really? But you already have your own dream, don't you?
M You're right. I want to be a singer. I really like singing and dancing.
W Don't worry about it too much. Someday your parents will understand you.

W Ted, 너 안 좋아 보인다. 무슨 일이니?
M 부모님 때문에. 부모님은 내가 변호사나 교수가 되기를 원하셔.
W 정말? 하지만 이미 넌 네 꿈이 있잖아, 안 그래?
M 맞아. 난 가수가 되고 싶어. 노래하고 춤 추는 것이 정말 좋거든.
W 너무 걱정하지 마. 언젠가 너희 부모님께서 너를 이해해 주실 거야.

08 ③

① **W** If you don't use the computer, why don't you turn it off?
M OK. I'll turn it off right now.
② **W** Did you buy a birthday present for Jessica?
M No, I didn't. What about you?
③ **W** Can you tell me the way to the Green Department Store?
M No. I don't want to work there.
④ **W** Oh, I feel hungry. Is there something to eat?
M There is some pizza on the kitchen table.
⑤ **W** I'd like to borrow these two books.
M Can I see your library card, please?

① W 컴퓨터를 사용하지 않으면, 전원을 끄는 게 어때?
M 알았어. 지금 바로 끌게.
② W Jessica에게 줄 생일 선물 샀니?
M 아니, 안 샀어. 너는?
③ W Green 백화점에 가는 길을 알려 주시겠어요?
M 아니요. 전 그곳에서 일하고 싶지 않아요.
④ W 오, 배고프다. 먹을 것이 있니?
M 부엌 식탁 위에 피자가 좀 있어.
⑤ W 이 두 권의 책을 빌리고 싶어요.
M 도서관 대출 카드를 보여 주시겠어요?

09 ⑤ | ⊕ ⑤

W What seems to be the problem with Bella?
M She doesn't eat. She hasn't eaten for the whole day.
W Let me check her eyes and teeth. Hmm... her eyes are okay and her teeth seem to be okay, too. Maybe she just ate something bad.
M She might have eaten something from the garbage or from the ground while I was walking her in the park.
W That's what dogs do. She will be okay in a couple of days but I think she needs to be in the hospital tonight.
M Okay. I'll come again tomorrow.

W Bella의 문제가 뭔가요?

M 먹지를 않아요. 하루 종일 아무 것도 안 먹었어요.

W 눈과 이빨을 확인해 볼게요. 흠… 눈은 괜찮고 이빨도 괜찮아 보여요. 아마 그냥 안 좋은 것을 먹었을지도 모르겠네요.

M 공원에서 산책시키는 동안 쓰레기나 땅에서 뭔가를 먹었을지도 몰라요.

W 개들이 원래 그렇죠. 이틀 정도 있으면 괜찮아지겠지만, 오늘 밤은 병원에 있어야 할 것 같아요.

M 알겠습니다. 내일 다시 올게요.

만점 솔루션 여자의 말 That's what dogs do.(개들이 원래 그렇죠.)라는 말로 미루어 보아 Bella는 개임을 알 수 있으므로 '동물병원'에서의 대화로 볼 수 있다.

10 ⑤

M Hi, I bought these two books yesterday. Here's the receipt.

W Yeah, I remember you. You bought them for your daughter.

M That's right. But my daughter already read one. So, can I exchange this book for another book?

W Yes, you can. How about this one? Young girls think it's interesting.

M 안녕하세요, 어제 이 책 두 권을 샀는데요. 영수증 여기 있어요.

W 예, 기억나요. 따님께 주려고 사셨잖아요.

M 맞아요. 그런데, 딸이 이미 그것을 읽었어요. 그래서, 이 책을 다른 책으로 교환할 수 있을까요?

W 예, 그러실 수 있습니다. 이 책은 어떠세요? 여자 아이들이 재미있어 하더라고요.

11 ⑤

[Cellphone rings.]

M Hello.

W Hello, honey. Are you coming home now?

M I need to talk with my boss a little bit, but I'm coming home soon.

W That's good. Can you swing by the dry cleaner's on your way home? I got the message that our clothes were ready last week, but I didn't have time to pick them up.

M Okay. What do I have to pick up?

W Your suits, my winter coat and my pants.

M All right. I'll get them.

W Thanks, honey.

[휴대 전화 벨이 울린다.]

M 여보세요.

W 여보세요. 여보. 지금 집에 오고 있어요?

M 상사와 이야기를 좀 해야 해요. 하지만 곧 집에 갈 거예요.

W 잘됐네요. 집에 오는 길에 세탁소에 들를 수 있어요? 지난주에 우리 옷이 준비되었다는 메시지를 받았지만, 그것을 가져올 시간이 없었어요.

M 좋아요. 무엇을 가져와야 하죠?

W 당신 양복과 제 겨울 코트 그리고 제 바지예요.

M 알겠어요. 제가 그것들을 가져갈게요.

W 고마워요. 여보.

만점 솔루션 여자는 남자에게 집에 오는 길에 드라이클리닝 맡겼던 세탁물을 찾아와 달라고 부탁하고 있다.

12 ⑤

W Hi, nice to meet you. My name is Jennifer Johnson and I'm 14 years old. I moved here last weekend from Seattle. My favorite subject is history and my hobby is playing the violin. I belonged to a violin club at my previous school. I hope to have a good time with all of you. Thank you.

W 안녕, 만나서 반가워. 내 이름은 Jennifer Johnson이고 14살이야. 나는 지난 주말에 Seattle에서 이곳으로 이사 왔어. 내가 가장 좋아하는 과목은 역사이고 내 취미는 바이올린을 켜는 거야. 이전 학교에서 바이올린 동아리에 속해 있었어. 너희 모두와 좋은 시간을 갖기를 바라. 고마워.

13 ②

[Cellphone rings.]

W Carol speaking.

M Hi, Carol. This is John. Do you have any plans this weekend?

W This weekend? No, nothing special. Why?

M Then, will you join us? Robert, Susan, Jessica, and I are going to take a trip to the Redwood National Park.

W Really? That sounds interesting. Okay, I'll join you.

[휴대 전화 벨이 울린다.]

W Carol입니다.

M 안녕, Carol. 나 John이야. 이번 주말에 무슨 계획 있니?

W 이번 주말? 아니, 특별한 건 없어. 왜?

M 그럼, 우리와 함께 할래? Robert, Susan, Jessica와 나는 Redwood 국립공원으로 여행을 갈 거야.

W 정말? 재미있겠다. 좋아, 나도 같이 갈게.

만점 솔루션 남자의 말 Then, will you join us? 뒤에 전화를 건 목적이 이어진다. 즉, 몇몇 친구들과 국립공원으로 여행을 갈 것이라며 여자에게 함께 갈 것을 제안하고 있는 상황이다.

14 ④ | ➕ ③

W Randy, can we go to a movie tonight?

M Sounds great. I've wanted to watch the newly released 3D movie.

W What time do you finish work today?

M Today, I can leave no later than 6.

W All right. I'll get the tickets for the 8 o'clock showing so that we can have dinner before the movie.

M Perfect. There's a spaghetti house just across from the movie theater.

W Can we meet there at 7 o'clock, then?

M Let's make it at 6:30.

W Okay. Don't make me wait for you.

W Randy, 오늘 밤에 영화 보러 갈까?
M 좋지. 나는 새로 나온 3D 영화가 보고 싶었어.
W 오늘 몇 시에 일이 끝나니?
M 오늘은, 늦어도 6시에는 나올 수 있어.
W 좋아. 영화 전에 저녁을 먹을 수 있도록 내가 8시 영화표를 사 놓을게.
M 완벽해. 영화관 바로 건너편에 스파게티 식당이 있어.
W 그럼, 거기서 7시에 만날까?
M 6시 30분으로 하자.
W 좋아. 나를 기다리게 하지 마.

만점 솔루션 여자는 식당에서 7시에 만나자고 했지만 남자가 6시 30분에 만나자고 하자 여자도 그 제안에 동의했다.

15 ④

W Hi, Jack. Where are you going?
M I'm going to the hospital to visit Younghun.
W Is he in the hospital? Why?
M You didn't know? He got injured while playing soccer.
W No way. That's too bad.
M Yeah, he has to stay there for two weeks. Would you like to come with me?
W Sure, I'd love to. I'm free now anyway.

W 안녕, 잭. 어디 가?
M 영훈이 만나서 병원에 가고 있어.
W 영훈이가 병원에 있어? 왜?
M 몰랐어? 축구 하다가 다쳤잖아.
W 말도 안돼. 안됐다.
M 응, 병원에 2주동안 입원해야 한대. 너도 나랑 같이 갈래?
W 물론, 같이 가자. 지금 할 일도 없었고.

16 ②

M Almost every student wants good grades. But only some students study well and get good grades. Here are some simple basic secrets of studying well. First, you have to study regularly. Try to study even at least 30 minutes every day. Second, focus your mind while you're studying. Third, listen to your teacher in the classroom. If you keep these simple rules, you'll be a good student before long.

M 거의 모든 학생들이 점수를 잘 받기를 원합니다. 하지만, 일부 학생들만이 공부를 잘 하고 좋은 점수를 받습니다. 여기 공부를 잘 하는 몇 가지 간단한 기본적인 비결이 있습니다. 먼저, 규칙적으로 공부해야 합니다. 매일 적어도 30분씩 공부하려고 노력하세요. 둘째, 공부하는 동안에 집중하십시오. 셋째, 교실에서 선생님 말씀에 귀를 기울이세요. 이러한 간단한 규칙들을 지킨다면, 여러분도 머지않아 훌륭한 학생이 될 것입니다.

17 ⑤

W Welcome to the Children's Zoo. For the safety of the animals in the zoo, we ask for your cooperation. Please don't feed the animals. Animals in the zoo are fed regularly by us. Because of the food people give them, animals may become seriously ill or even die. Parents, please don't let your children give anything to the animals. Thank you for your help and enjoy your visit.

W 어린이 동물원에 오신 것을 환영합니다. 동물원의 동물들의 안전을 위해, 여러분의 협조를 구합니다. 동물들에게 먹이를 주지 마세요. 동물원의 동물들은 저희들에 의해 규칙적으로 먹이를 얻고 있습니다. 사람들이 주는 음식 때문에, 동물들이 심각하게 아프거나 죽기도 합니다. 부모님들께서는 아이들이 동물들에게 아무 것도 주지 못하도록 해 주십시오. 협조해 주셔서 감사하고 즐거운 방문되시기 바랍니다.

만점 솔루션 동물원의 동물들이 관람객이 주는 음식으로 병이 나거나 죽는다고 경고하며 동물들의 안전을 위해 먹이를 주지 말 것을 부탁하는 내용으로, 동물원 사육사가 관람객에게 하는 안내 방송이다.

18 ①

W I'm planning to go to Australia next month. I'm really looking forward to it. I'll enjoy summer there.
M I think you can try ocean sports. The city is famous for them.
W Such as scuba diving? I'm staying there for four days only. Do you think I can learn it in a day or two?
M How about snorkeling? It doesn't need any special trainings.
W That sounds interesting.
M You'll be able to enjoy the beautiful tropical sea life.

W 난 다음 달에 호주에 갈 계획이야. 그것을 정말 고대하고 있어. 거기서 여름을 즐길 거야.
M 넌 해양 스포츠를 해 볼 수 있을 것 같은데. 그 도시는 그것들로 유명하거든.
W 스쿠버 다이빙 같은 것 말이니? 난 겨우 4일 동안 머물 거야. 하루 이틀 안에 내가 그것을 배울 수 있다고 생각하니?
M 스노클링은 어때? 그것은 특별한 훈련이 필요 없어.
W 재미있을 것 같구나.
M 넌 아름다운 열대 해양 생물을 즐길 수 있을 거야.

만점 솔루션 여자가 호주로 여행을 간다는 말에 남자는 해양 스포츠를 즐겨 보라며 구체적으로 스노클링을 제안하고 있다.

19 ①

M What do you think about this hotel?
W It's nice. But I think $200 a day is too expensive for us.
M But you want to stay at a hotel near the beach, don't you?
W Well... that's true. But I don't want to spend $200 for just one day.
M ______________________

M 이 호텔에 대해 어떻게 생각하니?
W 좋아. 하지만 하루에 200달러는 우리에게는 너무 비싼 것 같아.
M 하지만 너는 해변 근처에 있는 호텔에 머물고 싶어 했잖아, 안 그래?
W 음… 그건 사실이야. 하지만 단지 하루 머무는 데 200달러를 쓰고 싶지

는 않아.

M 그렇다면, 다른 호텔을 찾아 볼게.

② 너는 이 호텔을 왜 좋아하니?
③ 좋아. 이 호텔에 투숙하자.
④ 오늘 이 호텔에 머무를 수 있을까요?
⑤ 아니, 난 호텔에서 일하고 싶지 않아.

20 ⑤

W James, I have a good news for you. An Italian restaurant needs a waiter. I think it's just for you.

M Really? Where is it? I can't work at a restaurant far from school.

W Don't worry. It's very close to school. It's only a 5 minute walk.

M That's good. How much do they pay per hour?

W It's $10 an hour. You know, that's really good money.

M ______________________

W James, 너에게 좋은 소식이 하나 있어. 이탈리아 식당에서 종업원을 구한데. 너에게 딱 맞는 것 같아.

M 정말? 그게 어디에 있는데? 학교에서 먼 식당에서는 일을 할 수가 없어.

W 걱정하지 마. 학교에서 아주 가까워. 걸어서 겨우 5분 거리야.

M 좋은데. 시간당 얼마나 주는데?

W 시간당 10달러야. 알잖아. 정말로 좋은 벌이야.

M 오, 그 식당에 지금 당장 가 봐야겠어.

① 미안, 너에게 10달러를 빌려 줄 수 없어.
② 좋아, 난 비프 스테이크를 주문할게.
③ 괜찮아. 점심은 내가 살게.
④ 네 덕분에, 식사 맛있게 했어.

만점 솔루션 여자는 이탈리아 식당에 시간제 일자리가 있다며 남자에게 소개하고 있다. 학교와 가까운 식당의 위치와 임금이 시간당 10달러라는 좋은 조건에 대해 들은 남자는 그 식당에 당장 가 봐야겠다는 말을 하는 것이 가장 적절하다.

영어듣기능력평가 19회

01 ②	02 ④	03 ⑤	04 ③	05 ③
06 ④, ➕①	07 ⑤, ➕②	08 ④	09 ②	10 ②
11 ④	12 ⑤	13 ③	14 ①	15 ④
16 ②	17 ⑤	18 ⑤	19 ③	20 ③

01 ②

M I am a computer's friend. Whenever I move on the pad, an arrow on the screen moves along too. Click me twice fast with the arrow on an icon on the screen. You can open a program by doing that. I am called as the name of an animal because I look like that animal.

M 저는 컴퓨터의 친구입니다. 제가 패드 위에서 움직일 때마다, 화면 위의 화살표 또한 따라 움직입니다. 화면 위에 있는 아이콘에 화살표를 놓은 채 저를 두 번 빠르게 클릭하세요. 그렇게 함으로써 프로그램을 열 수 있습니다. 저는 동물처럼 생겼기 때문에 그 동물의 이름으로 불립니다.

02 ④

W Peter, why don't we play tennis tomorrow?

M Well... I played tennis yesterday. What about swimming?

W The weather is too cold to swim, I think.

M Then, what do you want to do?

W How about an indoor sport such as table tennis or badminton?

M I don't know how to play table tennis. So, I want to play badminton.

W Okay! I'll follow you.

W Peter, 내일 테니스 치는 게 어때?

M 음… 어제 테니스를 쳤어. 수영은 어때?

W 수영하기에는 날씨가 너무 추운 것 같아.

M 그럼, 무엇을 하고 싶니?

W 탁구나 배드민턴 같은 실내 운동 어때?

M 나는 탁구를 칠 줄 몰라. 그래서, 배드민턴을 치고 싶어.

W 좋아! 네 의견을 따를게.

03 ⑤

W Good morning. Here's the weather forecast for tomorrow. Yesterday we had much snow all over the country. Fortunately the snow has stopped today. We're expecting no more snow. Today in Seoul we'll have partly cloudy skies, and in Busan we'll have a little bit of rain. For Busan citizens, be sure to take an umbrella with you.

W 안녕하세요. 내일의 일기 예보입니다. 어제는 전국적으로 눈이 많이 왔습니다. 다행히 눈은 오늘 멈추었습니다. 더 이상의 눈은 오지 않을 것

으로 예상됩니다. 오늘 서울은 부분적으로 흐린 하늘이겠고, 부산에는 약간의 비가 내리겠습니다. 부산 시민께서는, 우산을 챙기시기 바랍니다.

04 ③

W What are you going to do this afternoon?

M I'm going to buy a book about dieting at the bookstore. How about you?

W Actually, I just called one of my friends to meet her, but she said she has to go for a job interview.

M Then, why don't you come with me?

W Sounds great.

W 오늘 오후에 뭐 할 거니?

M 서점에서 식이요법에 관한 책을 살 거야. 너는?

W 사실, 나는 내 친구들 중 한 명을 만나기 위해 전화했지만, 그 애가 취업 면접에 가야 한다고 말했어.

M 그럼, 나와 함께 가는 게 어때?

W 좋아.

05 ③

① **W** What a lovely day!
M How about going on a picnic?

② **W** How about playing tennis this afternoon?
M I'd love to, but it looks like rain.

③ **W** When does the movie start?
M I think it was a very sad movie.

④ **W** What can I do for you, sir?
M Can you recommend a shampoo for dry hair?

⑤ **W** Could you turn down your TV?
M I'll turn it down right away.

① **W** 날씨가 참 좋아요!
M 소풍 가는 것이 어때요?

② **W** 오늘 오후에 테니스를 치는 것이 어때요?
M 그러고 싶지만, 비가 올 것 같아요.

③ **W** 그 영화가 언제 시작하죠?
M 그것이 아주 슬픈 영화였다고 생각해요.

④ **W** 무엇을 도와드릴까요, 손님?
M 건조한 머리에 맞는 샴푸를 추천해 주시겠어요?

⑤ **W** TV 소리를 줄여 주시겠어요?
M 지금 바로 줄이겠습니다.

06 ④ | ➕ ①

M Jane, how about meeting at two in front of your school?

W Well, let me check my schedule. My last class ends at 2:30, but I have a club meeting after class.

M When does the meeting finish? We have to arrive at Grandma's house by five.

W It will be finished at four o'clock.

M Then let me give you thirty minutes more just in case.

W Okay, Dad. I'll meet you thirty minutes after the club meeting.

M Jane, 너의 학교 앞에서 2시에 만나는 게 어떠니?

W 음, 제 일정을 확인해 볼게요. 마지막 수업이 2시 30분에 끝나지만, 방과 후에 동아리 모임이 있어요.

M 그 모임은 언제 끝나니? 5시까지 할머니 댁에 도착해야 하거든.

W 모임은 4시에 끝날 거예요.

M 그러면 만일을 대비해서 너에게 30분을 더 줄게.

W 알겠어요, 아빠. 동아리 모임 끝나고 30분 뒤에 만나요.

만점 솔루션 여자의 동아리 모임이 4시에 끝난다고 하자 남자는 만일의 경우를 대비해서 여자에게 30분을 더 주기로 했으므로, 두 사람이 만날 시각은 4시 30분이 된다.

07 ⑤ | ➕ ②

[Telephone rings.]

M Hi, Mrs. Schoolings. This is Tim Lopez. I'm calling to inform you that your daughter Lynda didn't come to school today.

W Good afternoon, Mr. Lopez. Lynda couldn't come to school today. She has a fever.

M Oh, have you taken her to see the doctor?

W She has an appointment with the doctor at 2.

M Oh, I see. I hope she'll get well soon.

W I'm sorry for not calling you first.

M That's okay. I hope I can see her tomorrow. Good bye, Mrs. Schoolings.

W Thank you for calling, Mr. Lopez.

[전화벨이 울린다.]

M 안녕하세요, Schoolings 부인. 저는 Tim Lopez입니다. 따님 Lynda가 오늘 학교에 오지 않았다는 것을 알려드리려고 전화했어요.

W 안녕하세요, Lopez 선생님. Lynda가 오늘 학교에 갈 수 없었어요. 열이 있거든요.

M 저런, 병원에 데려가셨나요?

W 2시에 의사와 예약이 되어 있어요.

M 오, 그렇군요. 그 애가 곧 회복되길 바랍니다.

W 먼저 전화 드리지 못해 죄송합니다.

M 괜찮습니다. 내일 그 애를 볼 수 있기를 바랍니다. 안녕히 계십시오, Schoolings 부인.

W 전화 주셔서 감사합니다, Lopez 선생님.

만점 솔루션 남자는 Lynda의 선생님이고 여자는 Lynda의 어머니로, 남자는 Lynda가 학교에 오지 않은 것을 알려 주며 무슨 일이 있는지 묻고 있는 상황이다.

08 ④

M This is a tool we use a lot in our daily lives. This has two parts. One part works as a handle, and the other part has two sharp metal blades. These blades are screwed together, and cut thin things like paper or cloth. What is this?

M 이것은 우리 일상생활에서 많이 쓰이는 도구입니다. 이것은 두 부분이 있습니다. 한 부분은 손잡이고 다른 한 부분은 두 개의 날카로운 금속 칼날입니다. 이 칼날은 같이 나사로 고정되어 있고 종이나 천 같은 얇은 것들을 자릅니다. 이것은 무엇일까요?

09 ②

W Thanksgiving Day is just one week away from now.
M Yes. I'm looking forward to seeing my family.
W So how are you going home? By bus or by train?
M Well, at first I was thinking of going by car, but I thought it would be tiring to drive. So I decided to take a bus.
W But I think the plane is better than the bus.
M I think so, but the airport is a little far from my house. The bus stops near my house and it's easy for my dad to pick me up.
W I see.

W 추수감사절이 지금부터 딱 일주일 남았어.
M 맞아. 난 가족들을 만나는 것을 고대하고 있어.
W 그런데 넌 집에 어떻게 갈 거니? 버스로 아니면 기차로?
M 음, 처음에는 자동차로 갈까 생각했었어. 하지만 운전하는 것이 피곤할 거라고 생각했어. 그래서 버스를 타기로 결심했어.
W 하지만 비행기가 버스보다 더 좋을 것 같은데.
M 나도 그렇게 생각하지만, 공항이 우리 집에서 좀 멀어. 게다가 버스가 우리 집 근처에서 서니까 아빠가 나를 태우러 오시기가 쉽거든.
W 그렇구나.

10 ②

W You look happy today, Kevin.
M Do I look happy? I have a good reason for that.
W Tell me what made you so happy.
M Well, I measured my weight and found out that I lost 5 kilograms at last.
W Congratulations. You succeeded on your diet. I envy you. You have a strong will.
M Thank you for saying so.

W Kevin, 너 오늘 기분 좋아 보인다.
M 내가 기분 좋아 보이니? 그럴 만한 충분한 이유가 있어.
W 무엇 때문에 그렇게 기분이 좋은지 말해 봐.
M 음, 내 몸무게를 재어 봤는데 마침내 5킬로그램이 빠졌다는 것을 알게 되었어.
W 축하해. 식이요법에 성공했네. 부럽다. 너는 의지가 강하구나.
M 그렇게 말해 줘서 고마워.

11 ④

W Hello, everyone. Today I'd like to make an announcement about the Green Concert. First I'd like to thank you for buying tickets. The concert will be at the Baron High School gym at six o'clock on the evening of April 16th. The concert is for the benefit of poor people in the neighborhood. For the concert, we invited singer John Doran and the Baron High School orchestra. I am sure you will have fun.

W 안녕하세요, 여러분. 오늘 저는 Green 콘서트에 대해 말씀을 드리고자 합니다. 우선 입장권을 구입해 주신 것에 대해 여러분께 감사드리고 싶습니다. 콘서트는 4월 16일 저녁 6시에 Baron 고등학교 체육관에서 있을 예정입니다. 콘서트는 이웃의 가난한 사람들을 위한 것입니다. 콘서트를 위해서, 우리는 가수 John Doran과 Baron 고등학교 관현악단을 초대했습니다. 틀림없이 즐거운 시간을 보내실 것입니다.

12 ⑤

W What are you doing, Jack?
M My bag got dirty and I'm trying to clean it up with this towel.
W Let me see. I'm afraid you won't get it cleaned with only a towel.
M Then what should I do?
W Put some alcohol on the towel and rub your bag with it. That will really work.
M Thanks for the tip. I'll try it right away.

W 뭐 하고 있니, Jack?
M 내 가방이 더러워져서 이 수건으로 닦으려던 중이었어.
W 어디 보자. 너는 수건만으로는 그것을 닦아내지 못할 것 같은데.
M 그럼 어떻게 해야 하지?
W 수건에 알코올을 약간 묻혀서 그것으로 네 가방을 문질러 봐. 그렇게 하면 정말 효과가 있을 거야.
M 조언 고마워. 바로 그렇게 해 볼게.

13 ③

M We're having the Spring Book Festival this coming Friday. Students are coming to school with their favorite books. In the morning, we are going to make a poster to advertise their chosen books. After that, students will be asked to present about their favorite books to their classmates with the poster. After lunch, all students are coming to the auditorium to watch a play. The drama club prepared a wonderful play for the festival. I hope all of you enjoy the wonderful book festival.

M 다가오는 금요일에 '봄맞이 책 축제'가 있습니다. 학생들은 자신이 가장 좋아하는 책을 들고 학교에 올 것입니다. 오전에는, 자신이 선택한 책을 광고하기 위한 포스터를 만들 것입니다. 그 후에, 학생들은 그 포스터를 가지고 자신이 가장 좋아하는 책을 반 친구들에게 소개하도록 요청받을 것입니다. 점심 식사 후에는, 모든 학생들이 연극 관람을 위해 강당으로 올 것입니다. 연극반이 그 축제를 위해 멋진 연극을 준비했습니다. 여러분 모두 멋진 책 축제를 즐기시기 바랍니다.

만점 솔루션 오전에는 학생들이 가져온 책에 대한 포스터를 만들고 그것을 가지고 반 친구들에게 책을 소개한다고 했다.

14 ①

W Excuse me but can you show me how to get to the Modern theater?

M Modern theater? That's just a 10 minute walk from here. You are on the Oak Street. Walk two blocks down the street and turn left on 6th Avenue.

W Okay, walk two blocks and turn left.

M Just walk another block along the 6th Avenue and turn left. You will find the building on your right.

W Thank you very much.

M My pleasure.

W 실례지만 Modern 극장에 가는 길을 알려 주시겠어요?

M Modern 극장이요? 여기서 10분만 걸으면 돼요. 당신은 Oak 거리에 있어요. 이 거리를 따라 두 블록을 걸어서 6번가에서 좌회전하세요.

W 알겠어요, 두 블록을 걸어서 좌회전이요.

M 6번가를 따라서 한 블록을 더 걸어가서 좌회전하세요. 그 건물은 당신의 오른편에 있을 거예요.

W 정말 고맙습니다.

M 천만에요.

15 ④

W What do you think about this one? I really like the color.

M Do you know about the painter? It must have taken a long time to complete the work.

W Can I take a picture of this?

M You can, but do not use the flash. The sudden bright light is not good for paintings.

W Okay. Can you hold my coffee while I take a picture?

M Actually, food and drinks are not allowed here. Please remember that next time.

W Oh, I'm sorry.

W 이것에 대해 어떻게 생각해? 난 색이 정말 맘에 들어.

M 그 화가에 대해 아니?

M 틀림없이 그 작품을 완성하는 데 시간이 많이 걸렸을 거야.

W 이것을 사진으로 찍어도 될까?

M 찍어도 돼, 하지만 플래시를 사용하지 마. 갑작스러운 밝은 빛이 그림에는 좋지 않거든.

W 알았어. 내가 사진 찍는 동안 내 커피 좀 들고 있어 줄래?

M 사실, 여기에 음식과 음료수는 허용되지 않아. 다음 번에는 그것을 기억해.

W 오, 미안해.

만점 솔루션 그림과 화가에 대해 이야기하고 있고, 플래시를 사용하지 말고 사진을 찍어야 하며, 음식물을 가지고 올 수 없다고 했으므로, '미술관'에서의 대화임을 알 수 있다.

16 ②

M Hi, Marie! Where did you buy those sneakers? They're very nice.

W Thanks. They're from XYZ Shoe Store.

M Where is that?

W You know Water Street, right? Go straight to there, and turn left.

M Okay, turn left on Water Street, and then?

W Walk until you see the post office on your left. It's just across from it.

M Thanks! I'll go check right now.

M 안녕, 마리! 이 운동화 어디서 샀어? 아주 멋지다.

W 고마워. XYZ신발 가게에서 샀어.

M 그게 어디에 있어?

W 워터 가 알지? 거기로 쭉 간다음에 왼쪽으로 돌아.

M 알겠어, 워터 가에서 왼쪽으로 돈다음에?

W 네 왼편에 우체국이 보일 때까지 걸어. 바로 그 건너편에 있어.

M 고마워! 지금 바로 확인해봐야겠다.

17 ⑤

W What's wrong with you, Tom? You look so sad. You were so happy to join the team finally. What's wrong?

M I made a big mistake during practice.

W Tell me what happened.

M Our team had its first soccer practice today. I kicked the ball into our own goal by mistake. Can you believe it?

W Anybody can make a mistake. They'll see soon that you are a good player.

W 무슨 일 있니, Tom? 아주 슬퍼 보이는구나. 마침내 팀에 들어가게 되어 아주 기뻐했었잖아. 뭐가 문제니?

M 연습하다가 큰 실수를 했어요.

W 무슨 일이 있었는지 말해 보렴.

M 우리 팀이 오늘 첫 번째 축구 연습을 했어요. 제가 실수로 공을 우리 팀의 골대로 차 넣었어요. 믿어지세요?

W 누구나 실수를 할 수 있단다. 네가 좋은 선수라는 것을 사람들이 곧 알게 될 거야.

만점 솔루션 남자가 우울해 하는 이유가 I kicked the ball into our own goal by mistake.에 잘 나타나 있다. 즉, 팀의 첫 번째 연습 경기에서 실수로 자신의 팀의 골대에 골을 넣어 우울해하고 있다.

18 ⑤

W I'd like to visit the museum when we're there.

M Can we do that on the second day? I want to rest first.

W But I want to check out the local market on the second day.

M We can go to the museum in the morning and the market in the afternoon.

W I guess that could work.

M What about on our third day? Do you have any ideas?

W 우리가 거기 갔을 때 박물관을 방문하고 싶어.

M 둘째날에 갈 수 있을까? 나 우선 쉬고 싶어.

W 하지만 둘째날에는 지역 시장을 확인해보고 싶어.
M 오전에 박물관에 갔다가 오후에 시장에 갈 수 있어.
W 그래도 되겠다.
M 셋째날은 어떻게 할까? 좋은 생각 있어?

19 ③

M Why are you looking so unhappy?
W It's about my hair. I wanted it to be dyed brown.
M But your hair is red now.
W Well, I asked my hairdresser to dye it brown.
M You mean, he made a mistake, right?
W Yes. What am I supposed to do now?
M What were you doing while he was dying it red?
W ______________________

M 너 왜 그렇게 기분이 안 좋아 보이니?
W 내 머리 때문이야. 나는 갈색으로 염색하기를 원했거든.
M 그런데 지금 네 머리는 빨간색이잖아.
W 음, 나는 미용사에게 갈색으로 염색해 달라고 요청했었어.
M 그러니까 그가 실수를 했다는 거구나, 맞지?
W 그래. 이제 나는 어쩌지?
M 그가 빨간색으로 머리를 염색하는 동안 너는 무엇을 하고 있었니?
W 운이 나쁘게도 나는 잠이 들었어.

① 나는 내 스타일에 만족해.
② 내 미용사는 아주 좋아.
④ 나는 빨간색보다 갈색을 더 좋아해.
⑤ 나는 거울을 보고 있었어.

20 ③

W You're playing the computer game again.
M I just started. I studied for two hours. Please believe me, Mom.
W Okay. I believe you this time. And did you finish your homework?
M Not yet, but I did half of it. Please give me just thirty minutes.
W ______________________

W 너는 또 컴퓨터 게임을 하고 있구나.
M 막 시작했어요. 저는 2시간 동안 공부한 걸요. 믿어 주세요, 엄마.
W 알겠다. 이번에는 너를 믿어 주마. 그런데 네 숙제는 끝냈니?
M 아직 못 끝냈지만 절반은 했어요. 저에게 30분만 주세요.
W 좋아. 게임 후에 숙제를 끝내야 한다.
① 나는 막 컴퓨터를 켰단다.
② 이 말을 해야겠구나. 정말 잘했어.
④ 맞아요. 숙제하러 제 방으로 가야겠어요.
⑤ 정말 미안하다. 함께 놀 시간이 충분하지 않구나.

만점 솔루션 숙제를 절반밖에 하지 않은 아들이 엄마에게 게임할 시간 30분을 달라고 했으므로 게임을 한 후에 숙제를 끝내라는 말이 엄마의 대답으로 가장 적절하다.

영어듣기능력평가 20회

01 ①	02 ③	03 ②	04 ③	05 ⑤
06 ④	07 ⑤	08 ③	09 ④	10 ②
11 ③, ➕①	12 ⑤, ➕④	13 ⑤	14 ⑤	15 ⑤
16 ②	17 ②	18 ①	19 ⑤	20 ②

01 ①

M You can easily see this in the kitchen of your house. This is an electronic machine. When you want to keep food fresh, you put it in this. Also, when you want to make ice, you can use this. If you put water in this, the water turns into ice. In modern life, many people say that we can't live without this.

M 여러분은 이것을 집의 부엌에서 쉽게 볼 수 있습니다. 이것은 전자 제품입니다. 음식을 신선하게 보관하고 싶을 때, 음식을 이것에 넣습니다. 또한, 얼음을 만들고 싶을 때, 이것을 이용할 수 있습니다. 이것에 물을 넣으면, 물은 얼음으로 변합니다. 현대 사회에서, 많은 사람들이 이것 없이는 살 수 없다고 말합니다.

02 ③

W ① I'm in line. Stand behind me.
② Wait for your turn. Don't cut in line.
③ Do not run in the hall way. Safety first.
④ Can I have more of the soup?
⑤ What's for lunch today?

W ① 나는 줄 서 있어. 내 뒤에 서.
② 네 차례를 기다려. 새치기 하지 마.
③ 복도에서 뛰지 마. 안전이 먼저야.
④ 수프 좀 더 받을 수 있을까요?
⑤ 오늘 점심 메뉴가 뭐지?

만점 솔루션 ③ 복도에서 학생들에게 뛰지 말라는 내용이므로, 식당에서 줄을 서서 급식을 받고 있는 상황에는 어울리지 않는 말이다.

03 ②

M ① It will be raining on Monday, Tuesday and Thursday.
② The temperature will be the highest on Tuesday.
③ On Wednesday, it's not going to rain.
④ It will be rainy on Saturday morning, but the rain will stop soon.
⑤ On the weekend, the weather will be okay for outdoor activities.

M ① 월요일, 화요일, 그리고 목요일에는 비가 올 것이다.

② 기온은 화요일에 가장 높을 것이다.
③ 수요일에는, 비가 오지 않을 것이다.
④ 토요일 아침에는 비가 오겠지만, 그 비는 곧 그칠 것이다.
⑤ 주말에, 날씨는 야외 활동을 해도 괜찮을 것이다.

04 ③

M You might use this almost every day at home. You can control other devices with this. By pressing buttons on this, you can turn the devices on or off. You can also control the volume or change the channels with this. What is this?

M 여러분은 아마 집에서 이것을 매일 사용할 것입니다. 이것으로 다른 장치를 조절할 수 있습니다. 이것의 버튼을 눌러서 여러분은 장치를 켜고 끌 수 있습니다. 여러분은 이것으로 소리를 조절하거나 채널을 바꿀 수 있습니다. 이것은 무엇일까요?

05 ⑤

W Honey, we need to buy some winter socks.
M Clothes sections are over there. Oh, look at this. They're having a bundle sale.
W Hmm... $10 for three pairs of socks. That's not bad.
M If we buy six pairs, it would be $19. Look at the prices.
W Is it going to be cheaper if we buy more?
M I think so. $28 for nine pairs and $37 for twelve pairs.
W Nine pairs would be enough. Did you say $27?
M No, that would be $28.

W 여보, 우리 겨울 양말을 좀 사야 해요.
M 의류 코너는 저쪽이에요. 오, 이것 좀 봐요. 묶음 할인 판매를 하고 있어요.
W 흠… 양말 3켤레에 10달러라. 나쁘지 않은 걸요.
M 6켤레를 사면, 19달러예요. 가격을 봐요.
W 더 많이 사면 더 싸지는 건가요?
M 그런 것 같아요. 9켤레에 28달러이고 12켤레에는 37달러예요.
W 9켤레면 충분할 거예요. 27달러라고 했나요?
M 아니요, 28달러예요.

만점 솔루션 3켤레에 10달러를 기준으로 더 많은 묶음으로 살수록 가격이 더 싸지고 있다. 두 사람은 9켤레를 사기로 했고 가격은 28달러라고 했다.

06 ④

① **M** When did you see the concert?
W Last weekend. It was really good.
② **M** What do you want to be in the future?
W A math teacher. I want to be a math teacher.
③ **M** Which do you like better, classical or rock music?
W Well... I like rock music more than classical music.
④ **M** How many books do you read a month?
W Yeah, I like reading poems most.
⑤ **M** Is this your MP3 player?
W Yeah, I bought it last weekend.

① **M** 그 콘서트 언제 봤니?
W 지난 주말에. 정말 좋았어.
② **M** 너는 장래에 무엇이 되고 싶니?
W 수학 선생님. 난 수학 선생님이 되고 싶어.
③ **M** 클래식 음악과 록 음악 중에서 어느 것을 더 좋아하니?
W 음… 클래식 음악보다는 록 음악이 더 좋아.
④ **M** 너는 한 달에 몇 권의 책을 읽니?
W 그래, 나는 시 읽는 것을 가장 좋아해.
⑤ **M** 이것이 네 MP3 플레이어니?
W 그래, 지난 주말에 샀어.

07 ⑤

[Cellphone rings.]
W Hello, Linda speaking!
M Mom, it's me, Kevin! Where are you now?
W At home. I'm washing the dishes now. Why?
M Mom, I'm sorry, but I left my history report at home.
W You should be more careful. Where is the report?
M It's on my desk in my room. Can you bring it to me now?
W Yes, I can. I'll go to your school right now.

[휴대 전화 벨이 울린다.]
W 여보세요, Linda입니다!
M 엄마, 저예요, Kevin! 지금 어디세요?
W 집이란다. 지금 설거지를 하고 있어. 왜 그러니?
M 엄마, 죄송하지만, 제가 집에 역사 보고서를 두고 왔어요.
W 좀 더 조심성이 있어야지. 보고서가 어디에 있는데?
M 제 방 책상 위에 있어요. 지금 제게 그것을 가져다주시겠어요?
W 그래, 그러지. 지금 바로 학교로 갈게.

08 ③

W Mr. Jackson, what was my time today?
M 4 minutes 37 seconds.
W Really? Oh, that's great. I ran about 20 seconds faster than last month.
M That's right. But to become the champion, you must run even faster.
W How fast do I have to run to win the gold medal?
M Well.... As you know, your today's record is 4 minutes 37 seconds. I think you must be 10 seconds faster than this record.
W 10 seconds! Okay, I see. I'll do my best to run that fast!

W Jackson 감독님, 오늘 제 기록이 어땠나요?
M 4분 37초야.
W 정말요? 오, 대단한데요. 지난달보다 20초 정도 더 빨리 달렸어요.
M 맞아. 하지만 챔피언이 되기 위해서는, 훨씬 더 빨리 달려야 해.
W 금메달을 따기 위해서 제가 얼마나 더 빨리 달려야 하죠?
M 음…. 알다시피, 네 오늘 기록이 4분 37초잖아. 이 기록보다 10초 더 빨라야 할 것 같구나.
W 10초요! 좋아요, 알겠습니다. 그만큼 빨리 달리기 위해서 최선을 다할 거예요!

만점 솔루션 4분 37초의 기록을 낸 여자에게 남자는 금메달을 따기 위해서는 오늘보다 10초 더 빨리 달려야 한다고 말했으므로, 여자가 목표로 하는 기록은 4분 27초가 된다.

09 ④

M Alice, you don't look good. What's wrong with you?
W It's because of my sister, Jane.
M Your sister, Jane? Why? Tell me in more detail.
W She lost my MP3 player.
M Again? She lost your digital camera last month, didn't she?
W Yeah, that's right. She's really careless.

M Alice, 너 안 좋아 보인다. 무슨 일이니?
W 내 여동생 Jane 때문이야.
M 네 여동생 Jane? 왜? 좀 더 자세히 말해 봐.
W 그 애가 내 MP3 플레이어를 잃어버렸어.
M 또? 지난달에는 네 디지털 카메라를 잃어버렸잖아, 그렇지 않니?
W 그래, 맞아. 그 애는 정말 조심성이 없어.

10 ②

W It's already 4:30. Don't you feel hungry?
M Yes, a little bit.
W Then, I'll make a sandwich for you. What about a tomato sandwich?
M OK. That's fine. Ah, can you also bring me a glass of orange juice?
W Sorry, we don't have any orange juice. How about milk?
M Sure, no problem.

W 벌써 4시 30분이야. 배고프지 않니?
M 응, 약간.
W 그럼, 내가 너에게 샌드위치를 만들어 줄게. 토마토 샌드위치 어때?
M 응, 좋아. 아, 오렌지 주스도 한 잔 가져다줄래?
W 미안, 오렌지 주스가 없어. 우유는 어때?
M 좋아, 괜찮아.

만점 솔루션 여자는 배가 고프다는 남자의 말에 I'll make a sandwich for you.라고 말하였으므로, 여자는 남자를 위해 샌드위치를 만들어 줄 것임을 알 수 있다.

11 ③ | ⊕ ①

W Oh, the winter vacation is coming soon.
M Yeah, that's right. So, will you really learn swimming during the vacation?
W Yes, I will. What about you, Pedro? Are you going to learn scuba diving?
M No, I changed my mind.
W Then, what are you going to do this vacation?
M Well... I'll get a job and save some money.
W What do you want to save money for?
M I'm going to take a trip to Korea next summer vacation!

W 오, 겨울 방학이 곧 다가오고 있어.
M 응, 맞아. 그래, 넌 이번 방학 동안에 정말 수영을 배울 거니?
W 응, 배울 거야. 넌 어때, Pedro? 스쿠버 다이빙을 배울 거니?
M 아니, 나는 마음이 바뀌었어.
W 그럼, 이번 방학에 무엇을 할 거니?
M 음… 일자리를 구해서 돈을 좀 모을 거야.
W 무엇 때문에 돈을 모으려고 하니?
M 내년 여름 방학에 한국으로 여행을 갈 거야!

12 ⑤ | ⊕ ④

W So, did you say you want regular volunteer job?
M Yes, Mrs. Hong. I'd like to find volunteer work that I can do regularly.
W There is Clean River campaign on every Saturday morning. How about that?
M Oh, no. I have baseball practice every Saturday morning.
W Do you? Then, how about Sunday afternoon?
M What kind of work is it?
W You can help doctors and nurses treating foreign workers at a hospital. It opens only on Sunday afternoon.
M That would be very good for me. Thank you.

W 그래, 너는 정기적인 자원봉사 활동을 원한다고 했지?
M 예, 홍 선생님. 저는 규칙적으로 할 수 있는 자원봉사 활동을 찾고 싶어요.
W 토요일 아침마다 '깨끗한 강 만들기' 캠페인이 있어. 그것은 어떠니?
M 저런, 안돼요. 토요일 오전마다 야구 연습이 있어요.
W 그래? 그럼, 일요일 오후는 어떠니?
M 어떤 종류의 일이죠?
W 병원에서 의사들과 간호사들이 외국인 근로자들을 치료하는 것을 도울 수 있어. 그 병원은 일요일 오후에만 문을 열거든.
M 제게 아주 좋은 것 같아요. 감사합니다.

만점 솔루션 여자는 정기적인 자원봉사 활동을 원하는 남자의 일정을 고려하여 그에 알맞은 자원봉사 프로그램을 소개해 주고 있다.

13 ⑤

M I heard that you will go on a business trip to China on July 13th. Is it true?
W Half right, half wrong.
M What do you mean by that?
W Well... I'll leave for China, but not on the 13th.
M Then, when are you leaving?
W It's on the 15th. There were no airline tickets on the 13th.

M 7월 13일에 중국으로 출장을 간다는 소식 들었어. 정말이니?
W 절반은 맞고 절반은 틀려.
M 그게 무슨 뜻이니?
W 음… 중국에 가긴 갈 거야. 하지만 13일은 아니야.
M 그럼, 언제 가는데?
W 15일에. 13일에는 비행기 표가 없었거든.

14 ⑤

W Hi, George. What a surprise to see you here!
M It is. I didn't expect to see someone I know here.
W Are you here for a swimming lesson?
M No, I'm taking a badminton lesson. How about you?
W I'm taking a yoga class. The doctor recommended me to do yoga regularly.
M Good for you. So, is your class over?
W Yes. The class ended at 7:30.
M Mine begins at 8. Would you like something to drink? I have a little bit of time before the class.
W Great.

W 안녕, George. 여기서 너를 만나다니 놀라운데!
M 정말 그렇군. 여기서 내가 아는 사람을 만나리라고는 기대하지 않았는데.
W 이곳에 수영 수업을 받으러 오니?
M 아니, 나는 배드민턴 수업을 받고 있어. 너는 어때?
W 나는 요가 수업을 받고 있어. 의사가 요가를 규칙적으로 하라고 권해 줬거든.
M 잘 됐다. 그래, 수업은 끝났니?
W 응. 수업은 7시 30분에 끝났어.
M 내 수업은 8시에 시작해. 뭐 좀 마시겠니? 수업 전에 시간이 좀 있어.
W 좋아.

만점 솔루션 수영 수업, 배드민턴 수업, 요가 수업을 함께 들을 수 있는 곳은 '스포츠 센터'이다.

15 ⑤

M Oh, is this trophy yours?
W No, it is Angela's, my sister. She won it in a tennis competition last year.
M Is your sister a good tennis player?
W Yes, she is. She is really good at playing tennis.
M Sounds good! When did she learn to play tennis?
W When she was an elementary school student.
M What about you? Can you also play tennis well?
W No, I can't. I should have learned to play it when I was little like my sister.

M 오, 이 트로피가 네 것이니?
W 아니, Angela 언니 것이야. 작년에 언니가 테니스 대회에서 받았어.
M 너의 언니는 테니스를 잘 치니?
W 응, 그래. 언니는 테니스를 정말 잘 쳐.
M 잘 됐구나! 그녀는 언제 테니스를 배웠니?
W 초등학생이었을 때.
M 넌 어때? 너도 테니스를 잘 칠 수 있니?
W 아니, 난 못 쳐. 나도 언니처럼 어렸을 때 테니스 치는 것을 배웠어야 했는데.

16 ②

W Sam, can I talk to you for a minute?
M Sure! What is it?
W Well, a part of the fence around the farm is broken. Do you know that?
M Yeah, I saw it. I'll take care of it tomorrow.
W Good! Ah, we need more food for the cows. Can you buy some this afternoon?
M I see. After lunch, I'll go buy some.
W Thank you. The car keys are on the table in the kitchen.

W Sam, 잠시 이야기 할 수 있겠어요?
M 그럼요! 무슨 일이죠?
W 저, 농장 주변 울타리 일부가 파손되었어요. 알고 있어요?
M 예, 봤어요. 내일 그것을 살펴볼게요.
W 좋아요! 아, 소 먹이가 더 필요해요. 오늘 오후에 좀 사 올래요?
M 알겠어요. 점심 먹고 나서, 좀 사러 갈게요.
W 고마워요. 자동차 열쇠는 부엌 식탁 위에 있어요.

17 ②

W Excuse me, I'm looking for Green Hotel. Is it around here?
M Yes, it's on White Street.
W Where is that?
M Go straight two blocks and turn left.
W Turn left?
M Yes, and walk a little bit, then you will see White Street. Then turn right, and the hotel is just next to the post office.
W Do I have to cross the street?
M No, you don't have to.

W 실례합니다. 그린 호텔을 찾고 있습니다. 이 근처에 있나요?
M 네, 화이트 가에 있습니다.
W 어디에 있나요?
M 두 블록 쭉 가셔서 왼쪽으로 도세요.
W 왼쪽으로요?
M 네, 그리고 조금만 걸으면 화이트 가가 보일 겁니다. 그러면 오른쪽으로 도세요. 우체국 바로 옆이 호텔입니다.
W 길을 건너야 하나요?
M 아니요, 그럴 필요 없습니다.

18 ①

W Where are you going, Hyunsu?
M Hi, Maya! I'm going home.
W Home? But you have club activities on Thursdays, don't you?
M Yes, but my grandparents are coming home today. I want to go wait for them.
W Where are they coming from?
M They live in Canada, and they always bring nice gifts for me.
W Ah, now I see why you are skipping your club activities.

W 어디 가고 있어, 현수?
M 안녕, 마야! 나 집에 가고 있어.

W 집? 하지만 목요일마다 동아리 활동 있지 않았어?
M 맞아, 그런데 오늘 조부모님이 집에 오시기로 하셨어. 집에 가서 기다리고 싶어.
W 어디서 오시는 거야?
M 캐나다에 사시는데 나를 위해서 항상 좋은 선물을 갖고 오셔.
W 아, 이제 왜 네가 동아리 활동을 빼먹는지 알겠다.

19 ⑤

W Daniel, you have a new bicycle. When did you buy it?
M Two days ago. You know, it's one of the newest ones on the market.
W Wow, it looks very good. How much did you pay for it?
M Don't be surprised! It's only $80.
W Only $80? That's great! I'd like to buy one as well. Where did you buy it?
M At the ABC Bike Shop. It's on Lake Street.
W ______________________

W Daniel, 새 자전거를 가지고 있네. 그것을 언제 샀니?
M 이틀 전에. 있잖아, 이 자전거는 시중에 판매되는 가장 최신형 자전거 중 하나야.
W 와, 매우 좋아 보인다. 그것에 얼마를 지불했니?
M 놀라지 마! 겨우 80달러야.
W 겨우 80달러? 대단하다! 나도 하나 사고 싶다. 어디서 그것을 샀니?
M ABC 자전거 가게에서. Lake 거리에 있어.
W 좋아. 난 내일 그 가게에 갈 거야.

① 알았어. 지금 바로 너를 도와줄게.
② 됐어. 난 좋은 자전거가 있어.
③ 걱정 마. 네 잘못이 아니야.
④ 맞아. 난 어제 자전거를 잃어버렸어.

만점 솔루션 저렴한 가격에 자전거를 구입한 남자에게 여자는 어디서 자전거를 구입했는지 묻자 남자는 Lake 거리에 있는 ABC 자전거 가게에서 샀다고 말했으므로, 여자는 그곳에 가 보겠다는 말을 하는 것이 가장 적절하다.

20 ②

M Oh, this Saturday is Kevin's birthday.
W Yeah, that's right. What should we buy our son?
M He likes sports a lot. How about a baseball glove or a soccer ball?
W That's a good idea. Then, let's buy both of them for him!
M Buy both of them? Well... aren't they too expensive?
W No, I know where we can buy them cheaply.
M I see. Then make sure you buy them tomorrow.
W ______________________

M 오, 이번 주 토요일이 Kevin의 생일이에요.
W 맞아요. 우리 아들에게 무엇을 사 주죠?
M 그애가 운동을 아주 좋아하잖아요. 야구 글러브나 축구공은 어때요?
W 그거 좋은 생각이에요. 그럼, 그 애에게 그것들 둘 다 사 줘요!
M 그것들 둘 다 사자고요? 음… 그것은 너무 비싸지 않을까요?
W 아니요. 그것들을 싸게 살 수 있는 곳을 알아요.
M 알았어요. 그럼 내일 꼭 그것들을 사 오세요.
W 그럴게요! Kevin이 우리의 선물을 좋아할 거예요.

① 제 야구 글러브를 사용해도 괜찮아요.
③ 당신 때문에, 제 일을 끝냈어요.
④ 어젯밤에 축구 경기장에 갔어요.
⑤ 아니요. 저는 야구와 축구 둘 다 좋아하지 않아요.

고난도 영어듣기능력평가

01 ⑤	02 ③	03 ①	04 ①, ➕⑤	05 ④
06 ②	07 ②	08 ⑤	09 ③	10 ⑤
11 ④	12 ⑤	13 ②	14 ⑤	15 ③
16 ④	17 ②	18 ①, ➕③	19 ①	20 ⑤

01 ⑤

M You can see this in a kitchen. Usually, this looks like a large big spoon with a long handle and a deep bowl. This can be made of metal, wood, or plastic. You use this when you serve a liquid form of food, such as soup or sauce. What is this?

M 여러분은 이것을 부엌에서 볼 수 있습니다. 보통, 이것은 긴 손잡이와 깊은 그릇이 달린 큰 숟가락처럼 생겼습니다. 이것은 금속, 목재 또는 플라스틱으로 만들어질 수 있습니다. 여러분은 이것을 국이나 소스 같은 액체의 음식을 제공할 때 사용합니다. 이것은 무엇일까요?

02 ③

W Hey, Nick, do you know a good electronics service center?
M What's the problem?
W My laptop is broken. There is no sound at all.
M Did you look into the sound control panel?
W Yes, but it didn't work.
M How about the sound driver? You can turn it off and on.
W Really? Let me try. *[pause]* Oh, wow, it's working again. Thanks!
M You're welcome.

W 안녕, 닉. 너 괜찮은 전자제품 서비스 센터 알고 있어?
M 무슨 문제 있어?
W 내 노트북이 망가졌어. 소리가 전혀 안 나와.
M 음성 제어판 확인해봤어?
W 응, 그런데 안돼.
M 음성 드라이버는 어때? 껐다 켤 수 있잖아.
W 진짜? 한 번 해볼게. *[멈춤]* 아, 이제 된다. 고마워!
M 천만에.

03 ①

W Good morning! Here is tomorrow's world weather forecast. In Seoul, it will be cloudy but warm. In Tokyo, it'll start to rain in the afternoon. In New York, it'll be sunny and mild. London will have some rain, and Paris will be cloudy and windy. Sydney will be snowy and cold.

W 안녕하세요! 내일의 세계 일기 예보입니다. 서울은 흐리지만 따뜻하겠습니다. 도쿄는 오후에 비가 오겠습니다. 뉴욕은 맑고 화창하겠습니다. 런던은 약간의 비가 오겠고, 파리는 구름이 끼고 바람이 불겠습니다. 시드니는 눈이 오고 춥겠습니다.

04 ① | ➕ ⑤

[Phone rings.]
W Restaurant Ciel. How may I help you?
M Hi, could I make a reservation for tomorrow?
W Certainly. For what time, and how many people, sir?
M For four people. Will 6:30 be okay?
W I'm really sorry, sir, but I'm afraid we're already full at that time. What about 8 o'clock?
M Hmm.... it's a bit late, but I guess I can't help.

[전화벨이 울린다.]
W 레스토랑 씨엘입니다. 무엇을 도와드릴까요?
M 안녕하세요, 내일 예약을 하고 싶습니다.
W 네. 몇 시에 몇 분이 오실 건가요?
M 네 명입니다. 6시 30분 괜찮나요?
W 죄송합니다만 그 시간은 이미 예약이 다 찼습니다. 8시 어떠세요?
M 흠... 좀 늦지만 어쩔 수 없네요.

만점 솔루션 여자가 제안하는 시간에 만족하지는 않지만 어쩔 수 없이 그 제안을 받아들이고 있다. 'I can't help.'가 '도울 수 없다.'라는 뜻이 아닌, '어쩔 수 없다.'라는 의미인 것을 알면 더 쉽게 풀 수 있다.

05 ④

W I'd like to introduce my cousin Ann. She lives in Los Angeles, California. She is one year older than me. Her mother is my mother's younger sister. I like Ann because she's very friendly and outgoing. She's tall, and she has short brown hair. She likes to play beach volleyball with her friends.

W 내 사촌 앤을 소개하겠습니다. 그녀는 캘리포니아의 로스앤젤레스에서 살고 있습니다. 그녀는 나보다 한 살 많습니다. 그녀의 어머니는 나의 어머니의 동생입니다. 앤은 매우 다정하고 활발하기 때문에 그녀를 좋아합니다. 그녀는 키가 크고 짧은 갈색 머리는 가졌습니다. 그녀는 그녀의 친구들과 비치발리볼하는 것을 좋아합니다.

06 ②

M Hi, Chris. Do you still want to go bowling on Sunday?
W Sure, why not? What time would you like to go?
M What about six?
W Isn't it too late? We have school on Monday, you know.
M Okay, then what about two?
W It's too early. I usually finish my lunch at two.
M Then at three or four? I'm okay either way.
W Three sounds good. See you then!

M 안녕, 크리스. 너 아직도 일요일에 볼링을 치러 가길 원하니?
W 당연하지. 몇 시에 갈까?
M 6시 어때?

W 너무 늦지 않아? 월요일에 학교도 가야하고.
M 알겠어, 그럼 2시 어때?
W 그건 너무 일러. 보통 점심을 2시에 끝마치는데.
M 그럼 3시나 4시? 난 둘 다 좋아.
W 3시가 괜찮겠다. 그때 보자!

07 ②

W Hi, Tony, did you have a good weekend?
M Yes, I helped my mom make kimchi, and it was fun!
W I didn't know you have an interest in cooking.
M Yes, I want to be a famous chef one day.
W Really? I want to be a TV show host. Maybe, I'll invite you to my show.
M Sounds great. I hope our dreams come true.

W 안녕, 토니. 주말 잘 보냈니?
M 응, 엄마가 김치 담그는 걸 도왔는데, 재미 있었어!
W 네가 요리에 흥미를 갖고 있는지 몰랐네.
M 응, 나 언젠가 유명한 요리사가 되고 싶어.
W 진짜? 난 TV쇼 진행자가 되고 싶어. 내가 널 내 쇼에 초대할지도 모르겠다.
M 멋진데. 우리 꿈이 이루어졌으면 좋겠다.

만점 솔루션 장래 희망을 나타내는 표현을 알고 있다면 쉽게 풀 수 있는 문제이다. 남자는 'I want to be ~.'표현을 사용하여 유명한 요리사가 되고 싶다고 했고, 여자는 'I want to be ~.'표현을 사용하여 TV쇼 진행자가 되고 싶다고 말했다.

08 ⑤

M Look over there! Isn't that David Shaw?
W What? Are you serious? It can't be!
M Yes, I'm sure it's him. Why don't you go say hi? You're a fan, right?
W Yeah, but I'm afraid he'll run away.
M Come on. A chance like this doesn't come often.
W I'd like to, but.... I'm not ready.
M Who knows? Maybe you could take a picture with him.
W You're right, but I'm scared.

M 저기 봐! 저 사람 데이비드 쇼 아니야?
W 뭐? 진짜? 그럴 수 없어!
M 그래, 그가 확실해. 인사하는 거 어때? 너 팬이잖아, 맞지?
W 응, 그런데 그가 달아날까 두려워.
M 이봐. 이런 기회가 자주 오지 않는다고.
W 인사하고 싶은데... 준비가 안됐어.
M 누가 알아? 같이 사진을 찍을 수도 있잖아.
W 네 말이 맞지만 무서워.

만점 솔루션 남자는 여자가 데이비드 쇼의 팬이라는 것을 알고 우연히 보게 된 그 사람에게 인사하길 권하지만 여자는 계속해서 준비가 안 됐다며 다가가고 있지 못하는 상황이다.

09 ③

M How did you like your stay, Madame? Was everything okay?
W Yes, thanks. It was a very pleasant stay.
M How was the room?
W Oh, the room was awesome. And it had a great view.
M I hope you're happy with our service, too.
W Hmm... Well, actually, it could be better...
M I'm sorry to hear that. Could you tell us more?

M 머무시는 건 어떠셨나요? 다 괜찮나요?
W 네, 감사합니다. 아주 만족스러웠어요.
M 방은 어떠셨나요?
W 아, 방이 아주 좋았어요. 풍경도 훌륭했고요.
M 저희 서비스에도 만족하셨기를 바랍니다.
W 흠... 사실, 약간 아쉬움이 있습니다.
M 유감입니다. 더 말씀해 주시겠습니까?

10 ⑤

M Hyeri, what's wrong? You look down this morning.
W I think Bony is sick. She won't eat and keeps throwing up.
M Bony is your cat, right? How long has she been like that?
W Yes. Since yesterday. My mom will take her to the vet, but I'm worried.
M Don't worry. She will be okay.
W I hope so.

M 혜리, 무슨 일이야? 오늘 아침 기분 안 좋아 보여.
W 보니가 아픈 거 같아. 먹지도 않고 계속 토해.
M 보니는 네 고양이 맞지? 그렇게 한지 얼마나 됐어?
W 맞아. 어제부터. 엄마가 수의사에게 데려갈 건데 걱정돼.
M 걱정하지만. 괜찮을 거야.
W 그러길 바라.

11 ④

M Mom, when's Dad coming back from his business trip?
W He said it would be five days.
M When did he leave? Was it Tuesday or Wednesday?
W He left on Tuesday. Why? What do you need him for?
M I was wondering if we could watch a baseball game on Sunday.
W He will be back before then. Let's all go together.

M 엄마, 아빠가 출장에서 언제 돌아와요?
W 아빠는 5일이라고 말했어.
M 아빠가 언제 떠났죠? 화요일인가요 수요일인가요?
W 화요일에 떠났지. 왜? 뭐 때문에 아빠가 필요하니?
M 일요일에 야구경기를 같이 볼 수 있을까 궁금해서요.
W 그 전에는 돌아올 거야. 다같이 가자.

12 ⑤

M Bye, Sunghee. See you at the soccer game tomorrow.
W Oh, sorry, I forgot to tell you. I can't make it.

M Really? Why not?

W You know there's a play competition next month, right?

M Yeah, I heard about it.

W I decided to take part in it, and we have our first practice tomorrow.

M Oh, I see. That's too bad I can't see you tomorrow, but good luck!

M 잘 가, 성희. 내일 축구 경기에서 보자.

W 아, 미안, 너에게 말하는 거 깜빡했어. 나 내일 못 가.

M 진짜? 왜?

W 다음 달에 연극 대회가 있는 거 알고 있지?

M 응, 들었어.

W 거기 참여하기로 했는데, 첫 연습이 내일이야.

M 아, 알겠어. 내일 못 본다고 하니 안됐지만 행운을 빌게.

만점 솔루션 이유를 묻는 남자의 'Why not?'이후 여자의 말에 주목한다. 연극을 뜻하는 'play'와 '~에 참여하다'를 의미하는 'take part in' 표현을 안다면 쉽게 답을 고를 수 있다.

13 ②

W Good afternoon, Mr. Smith. Can I come in?

M Yes, of course, Mrs. Kim. Please sit down.

W Thank you.

M So, how can I help you?

W I was wondering how Susie is doing in class. She doesn't talk much with me at home.

M Susie is doing well. She's a bit quiet, but she's a good student.

W I feel so relieved to hear that.

W 안녕하세요, 스미스 선생님. 들어가도 될까요?

M 네, 물론입니다. 앉으세요.

W 감사해요.

M 무엇을 도와드릴까요?

W 수지가 학급에서 어떻게 하고 있나 궁금해서요. 집에서는 말을 많이 안 해요.

M 수지는 잘 하고 있습니다. 조금 조용하지만 좋은 학생입니다.

W 그 말을 들으니 마음이 놓이네요.

14 ⑤

W Excuse me. Do you know where the National Art Gallery is?

M Yes, you should turn right at the next corner.

W Turn right over there?

M Yes, and keep walking until you see the fire station on your right.

W Okay. Then?

M It's across from it. And it is also next to a flower shop.

W Thank you very much!

W 실례합니다. 국립 미술관이 어디 있는지 아시나요?

M 네, 다음 모퉁이에서 오른쪽으로 도세요.

W 저기서 오른쪽으로요?

M 네, 그리고 오른쪽에 소방서가 보일 때까지 계속 걸으세요.

W 알겠습니다. 그런 다음에요?

M 그 건너편에 있습니다. 꽃집 옆입니다.

W 정말 감사합니다.

15 ③

W Tony, what are you doing?

B I just finished my homework. Can I go out to meet Insu?

W Sure, if you finished your homework. But can you take out the garbage first?

B Okay. Should I take out these plastic bottles for recycling?

W No, that's fine. I will take them out later with other things.

B Just this, then. Okay, see you later, Mom!

W Have fun!

W 토니, 뭐하고 있니?

B 저 방금 숙제를 끝냈어요. 나가서 인수를 만나도 되나요?

W 물론, 숙제를 끝냈다면. 하지만 우선 쓰레기를 버려줄 수 있겠니?

B 네. 재활용을 위한 이 플라스틱 통들도 버릴까요?

W 아니, 괜찮아. 나중에 내가 다른 것들과 같이 버릴 거야.

B 그럼 이것만. 알겠어요. 나중에 봐요 엄마!

W 재미있게 놀으렴!

만점 솔루션 부탁할 때 쓰이는 'Can you ~?'표현과 '밖에 내놓다'라는 의미의 'take out'을 알면 쉽게 풀 수 있는 문제이다. 소년은 이미 숙제를 끝냈고(just finished my homework) 재활용을 위한 플라스틱 통은 여자가 나중에 처리하기로 했다. (I will take them out later ~.)

16 ④

W Tom, what are you doing for the long weekend?

M I promised my dad to help him wash his car on Saturday or Sunday. But that's it.

W What about on Monday?

M Nothing much. I was thinking about riding a bike.

W Would you join us then? We're going to Main Park for a picnic.

M That sounds good. I could ride my bike there, too!

W 톰, 긴 주말 동안 뭐 할 거야?

M 아빠랑 토요일이나 일요일에 아빠차를 세차하는 걸 돕기로 약속했어. 그냥 그거 뿐이야.

W 월요일에는?

M 특별히 없어. 자전거를 탈까 생각했어.

W 그럼 우리랑 같이 놀래? 우리 메인 공원에 소풍 갈 거야.

M 재미있겠는데. 거기서 자전거도 탈 수 있겠다!

17 ②

W Minoo, you're back. I heard you were sick yesterday. Are you better now?

M Yes, I am. Thank you. Did I miss anything?
W Well, we're going to have a test tomorrow in history.
M What? But I don't have my notes.
W I can lend you my notebook, if you want.
M That would be great. I'll make a copy and give it right back.
W Okay, wait here and I'll get it.

W 민우, 돌아왔구나. 어제 아팠다고 들었어. 지금 괜찮아?
M 응, 고마워. 내가 뭐 놓친 건 없어?
W 내일 역사 시험이 있어.
M 뭐? 하지만 난 필기를 안 했는데.
W 네가 원하면 내 공책을 빌려줄게.
M 잘됐다. 복사한 다음에 돌려줄게.
W 응, 여기서 기다려 갖고 올게.

18 ① | ➕ ③

M Excuse me, can I send this package to Japan?
W Sure, there are two ways by air. The express mail takes two days, and it costs $30.
M Oh, it's too expensive. What's the other way?
W It's called economy air. It's $15, and it takes four days.
M Is there anything cheaper?
W Yeah, you can send it by ship, but it can take up to two weeks.

M 실례합니다. 이 소포를 일본에 보낼 수 있을까요?
W 물론입니다. 공항 우편은 두 가지가 있습니다. 속달 우편은 이틀이 걸리고 30달러입니다.
M 너무 비싸네요. 다른 하나는 뭔가요?
W 이코노미 우편입니다. 15달러이고 나흘이 걸립니다.
M 너 저렴한 건 없나요?
W 네, 배로 보낼 수도 있지만 2주까지 걸릴 수 있습니다.

19 ①

M What are you doing, Kate?
W I'm looking at this picture. It won the school photo contest this year.
M Can I have a look, too?
W Sure. Isn't it really nice? I like this green field a lot.
M Yes, it's nice. And actually, I have been there.
W Really? What was it like?
M ______________________

M 뭐하고 있니, 케이트?
W 이 사진을 보고 있어. 이번 해에 학교 사진 대회에서 우승한 거야.
M 나도 볼 수 있을까?
W 물론. 진짜 좋지 않니? 이 녹색 들판이 진짜 좋아.
M 응, 좋다. 사실, 나 거기 가본 적 있어.
W 진짜? 어땠어?
M 진짜 좋았어.

② 나 거기 안 갔어.
③ 같이 가자.
④ 다음 주에 방문할 거야.
⑤ 그거 좋은 생각이다.

만점 솔루션 남자가 사진 속의 장소를 가보았다고 말하자 여자가 어땠냐고 묻고 있으므로, 그 물음에 대한 남자의 대답은 장소에 대한 감상을 말하는 것이 옳다.

20 ⑤

M You look very nice, Emily. I like your new jeans.
W Thank you. I bought these when I went shopping with my mom last weekend.
M Really? Where did you buy them?
W At the new mall downtown. Have you been there?
M No, not yet. I haven't had a chance.
W It's a pretty cool place. Would you like to go with me someday?
M ______________________

M 너 정말 멋져 보인다, 에밀리. 네 새 바지 마음에 들어.
W 고마워, 지난 주말에 엄마랑 쇼핑 갔을 때 샀어.
M 진짜? 어디서 샀어?
W 시내에 새로 생긴 몰에서. 가본 적 있어?
M 아니, 아직. 기회가 없었어.
W 꽤 멋진 곳이야. 언제 나랑 같이 가볼래?
M 물론, 그럼 좋지.

① 이번주에 거길 갈 거야.
② 물론, 그 영화 보고 싶어.
③ 아니, 혼자 가고 싶지 않아.
④ 아, 그거 참 안됐다.

만점 솔루션 새로 생긴 몰에 함께 가자고 제안하고 있는 여자의 물음에 대한 남자의 대답으로는 거절이나 승낙이 올 수 있다.

만점 듣기 표현

24회

Plus Book

다락원

영어듣기능력평가 01 회

만점 듣기 표현

Step 1 우리말 보면서 영어 듣기

		1회	2회	3회
1	얼굴에는 이것을 뿌리지 마십시오.	☐	☐	☐
2	그건 좋은 생각 같지가 않은데.	☐	☐	☐
3	오늘은 세차하지 마십시오.	☐	☐	☐
4	이번 주말에 뭐 할 거니?	☐	☐	☐
5	네가 제일 좋아하는 음식은 뭐니?	☐	☐	☐
6	그 영화 언제 시작해?	☐	☐	☐
7	그 가방에 대해 좀 더 설명해 주시겠습니까?	☐	☐	☐
8	나는 짧은 꼬리와 긴 귀를 가지고 있어요.	☐	☐	☐
9	내가 뭐라도 도와줄까?	☐	☐	☐
10	네가 어디로 가야 할지 알아볼게.	☐	☐	☐
11	저는 제 친구들과 축구와 농구하는 것을 좋아합니다.	☐	☐	☐
12	모든 과학자들이 그러는데 아침 식사가 뇌에 중요하대.	☐	☐	☐
13	저녁에 뭐 먹을까?	☐	☐	☐
14	방과 후에 뭐 할 거니?	☐	☐	☐
15	무게가 얼마나 나가는지 확인하겠습니다.	☐	☐	☐
16	일기 예보가 틀릴지도 몰라요.	☐	☐	☐
17	주말에 좋은 계획이라도 있니?	☐	☐	☐
18	그가 아파서 속이 상해.	☐	☐	☐
19	몇 사이즈를 입으시나요?	☐	☐	☐
20	메시지를 남겨 드릴까요?	☐	☐	☐

영어듣기능력평가 01 회

Step 2 듣고 따라 말하기

		1회	2회	3회
1	Please do not spray it on your face.	☐	☐	☐
2	I don't think that's a good idea.	☐	☐	☐
3	Don't wash your car today.	☐	☐	☐
4	What are you going to do this weekend?	☐	☐	☐
5	What is your favorite food?	☐	☐	☐
6	When does the movie start?	☐	☐	☐
7	Can you tell me more about the bag?	☐	☐	☐
8	I have a short tail and long ears.	☐	☐	☐
9	Could I help you with anything?	☐	☐	☐
10	I'll find out where you should go.	☐	☐	☐
11	I like to play soccer and basketball with my friends.	☐	☐	☐
12	All scientists say that breakfast is important for your brain.	☐	☐	☐
13	What should we have for dinner?	☐	☐	☐
14	What are you going to do after school?	☐	☐	☐
15	Let me check how much it weighs.	☐	☐	☐
16	The weather forecast might be wrong.	☐	☐	☐
17	Do you have good plans for the weekend?	☐	☐	☐
18	I feel upset because he's sick.	☐	☐	☐
19	What size do you wear?	☐	☐	☐
20	Can I take a message?	☐	☐	☐

영어듣기능력평가 02회

만점 듣기 표현

Step 1 우리말 보면서 영어 듣기

		1회	2회	3회
1	그곳에는 많은 여러 종류의 동물들이 있었습니다.	☐	☐	☐
2	너 팝콘을 어디에 두었니?	☐	☐	☐
3	눈이 내리지 않고 화창할 것입니다.	☐	☐	☐
4	아시아로 여행을 갈 거야.	☐	☐	☐
5	사진 한 장만 찍어 주시겠어요?	☐	☐	☐
6	약 10분 걸릴 것 같아.	☐	☐	☐
7	어떻게 지불하시겠어요?	☐	☐	☐
8	당신은 장소에 가기 위해 이것을 탑니다.	☐	☐	☐
9	넌 장래에 무엇이 되고 싶니?	☐	☐	☐
10	기억력이 좋으시네요.	☐	☐	☐
11	저에 대한 것을 말씀드릴게요.	☐	☐	☐
12	네 방 청소를 하는 게 어떠니?	☐	☐	☐
13	난 생물 보고서를 작성해야 해.	☐	☐	☐
14	어떻게 네 생일을 잊을 수 있겠니?	☐	☐	☐
15	숙제 다 했니?	☐	☐	☐
16	저는 언제 쉴 수 있는 거죠?	☐	☐	☐
17	기침을 많이 하네요.	☐	☐	☐
18	조금 지루했어.	☐	☐	☐
19	난 지금 당장 바다에서 수영하고 싶어.	☐	☐	☐
20	교재도 사야 하나요?	☐	☐	☐

영어듣기능력평가 02회

Step 2 듣고 따라 말하기

		1회	2회	3회
1	There were many different kinds of animals.	☐	☐	☐
2	Where did you put the popcorn?	☐	☐	☐
3	It'll be sunny tomorrow with no snow.	☐	☐	☐
4	I'll take a trip to Asia.	☐	☐	☐
5	Can you take a picture of me?	☐	☐	☐
6	It will take about ten minutes, I think.	☐	☐	☐
7	How would you like to pay?	☐	☐	☐
8	You ride this to go to a place.	☐	☐	☐
9	What do you want to be in the future?	☐	☐	☐
10	You have a good memory.	☐	☐	☐
11	Let me tell you something about myself.	☐	☐	☐
12	How about cleaning your room?	☐	☐	☐
13	I have to write my biology report.	☐	☐	☐
14	How can I forget your birthday?	☐	☐	☐
15	Did you finish your homework?	☐	☐	☐
16	When can I take a break?	☐	☐	☐
17	you are coughing a lot.	☐	☐	☐
18	It was kind of boring.	☐	☐	☐
19	I want to swim in the sea right away.	☐	☐	☐
20	Do I have to buy a textbook?	☐	☐	☐

영어듣기능력평가 03회

만점 듣기 표현

Step 1 우리말 보면서 영어 듣기

		1회	2회	3회
1	이것의 색은 보통 빨간색입니다.	☐	☐	☐
2	책상 위나 침대 위를 확인했니?	☐	☐	☐
3	외투 입는 것을 잊지 마시기 바랍니다.	☐	☐	☐
4	여기 이 사람 너네 아빠 아니야?	☐	☐	☐
5	초대장을 몇 장 보냈나요?	☐	☐	☐
6	내가 뭘 해 주기를 원하니?	☐	☐	☐
7	그는 3시 30분에 시간이 있습니다.	☐	☐	☐
8	난 공항에 막 도착했어.	☐	☐	☐
9	운전해 줘서 고마워요.	☐	☐	☐
10	내일 내 친구네 집에 갈 거야.	☐	☐	☐
11	나와 잠깐 이야기 할 시간이 있니?	☐	☐	☐
12	우리 가족은 함께 야구 경기를 보는 것을 좋아해.	☐	☐	☐
13	포스터를 벌써 만들었니?	☐	☐	☐
14	여기에 놓아 주세요.	☐	☐	☐
15	도서관에 가고 싶은데 길을 잃었어.	☐	☐	☐
16	선생님께서 말씀하실 때 필기를 하세요.	☐	☐	☐
17	그것이 더 커질 때까지 그대로 두세요.	☐	☐	☐
18	힘든 하루였니?	☐	☐	☐
19	우리는 매일 운동할 필요가 있어	☐	☐	☐
20	그곳에 가 본 적이 없어요.	☐	☐	☐

영어듣기능력평가 03회

Step 2 듣고 따라 말하기

		1회	2회	3회
1	The color of this is usually red.	☐	☐	☐
2	Did you check on your desk or on the bed?	☐	☐	☐
3	Don't forget to wear your coat.	☐	☐	☐
4	Isn't this your dad here?	☐	☐	☐
5	How many invitation cards did you send?	☐	☐	☐
6	What do you want me to do with it?	☐	☐	☐
7	He is free at three thirty.	☐	☐	☐
8	I just arrived at the airport.	☐	☐	☐
9	Thank you for driving.	☐	☐	☐
10	I am going to my friend's house tomorrow.	☐	☐	☐
11	Do you have a minute to talk with me?	☐	☐	☐
12	My family likes to watch a baseball game together.	☐	☐	☐
13	Did you make the posters already?	☐	☐	☐
14	Put it over here, please.	☐	☐	☐
15	I want to go to the library, but I'm lost.	☐	☐	☐
16	Take notes when the teacher speaks.	☐	☐	☐
17	Let it sit until it becomes bigger.	☐	☐	☐
18	Did you have a hard day?	☐	☐	☐
19	We need to exercise every day.	☐	☐	☐
20	I've never been there.	☐	☐	☐

영어듣기능력평가 04 회

만점 듣기 표현

Step 1 우리말 보면서 영어 듣기

		1회	2회	3회
1	영화를 그 안에 넣을 수도 있습니다.	☐	☐	☐
2	나는 아침에 일어나기 위해 그것이 필요해.	☐	☐	☐
3	대부분 흐린 날이 되겠지만 비는 오지 않을 것입니다.	☐	☐	☐
4	너도 우리와 같이 가고 싶니?	☐	☐	☐
5	집에 오는 길에 얼음 위에서 넘어졌어.	☐	☐	☐
6	그녀의 직업은 뭐니?	☐	☐	☐
7	차로 15분 정도 걸릴 거야.	☐	☐	☐
8	한 번만 다시 그것들을 보내 줄 수 있니?	☐	☐	☐
9	체육관에 가려고 버스를 기다리고 있어.	☐	☐	☐
10	식사는 맛있게 하셨습니까?	☐	☐	☐
11	나는 보통 파리나 모기보다 커요.	☐	☐	☐
12	운동화 가져가는 것을 잊지 마라.	☐	☐	☐
13	수학 책 좀 빌려주겠니?	☐	☐	☐
14	이 길로 가시다가 첫 번째 모퉁이에서 오른쪽으로 도세요.	☐	☐	☐
15	대부분의 반딧불이들은 자신들의 진정한 짝을 찾기 위해 빛을 사용합니다.	☐	☐	☐
16	어느 도시를 방문할 거니?	☐	☐	☐
17	나를 초대해 줘서 고마워.	☐	☐	☐
18	낮잠을 자야 할 것 같구나.	☐	☐	☐
19	이번 여름에 어디에 갈 거니?	☐	☐	☐
20	제가 뭘 도와드릴까요?	☐	☐	☐

영어듣기능력평가 04회

Step 2 듣고 따라 말하기

		1회	2회	3회
1	You can even put movies in it.	☐	☐	☐
2	I need it to wake up in the morning.	☐	☐	☐
3	It'll be mostly cloudy but it won't be raining.	☐	☐	☐
4	Do you want to come with us?	☐	☐	☐
5	I slipped on the ice on my way home.	☐	☐	☐
6	What dose she do?	☐	☐	☐
7	It will take about 15 minutes by car.	☐	☐	☐
8	Can you send them one more time?	☐	☐	☐
9	I'm waiting for a bus to the gym.	☐	☐	☐
10	Did you enjoy the dinner?	☐	☐	☐
11	I'm usually bigger than a fly or a mosquito.	☐	☐	☐
12	Don't forget to take your running shoes	☐	☐	☐
13	Can I borrow your math textbook?	☐	☐	☐
14	Walk up the street and turn right at the first corner.	☐	☐	☐
15	Most fireflies use light to find true love.	☐	☐	☐
16	Which cities are you going visit?	☐	☐	☐
17	Thank you for inviting me.	☐	☐	☐
18	Maybe you should take a nap.	☐	☐	☐
19	Where are you going this summer?	☐	☐	☐
20	What can I help you with?	☐	☐	☐

영어듣기능력평가 05회

만점 듣기 표현

Step 1 우리말 보면서 영어 듣기

		1회	2회	3회
1	호수에서 수영할래?	☐	☐	☐
2	난 반 친구들과 할 일이 있어.	☐	☐	☐
3	오늘 밤부터 내일까지 많은 비가 내릴 것입니다.	☐	☐	☐
4	그녀의 가족이 미국으로 간대.	☐	☐	☐
5	옷을 차려 입어야 한다고 들었어.	☐	☐	☐
6	너 오래 기다렸구나.	☐	☐	☐
7	무슨 나쁜 일 있니?	☐	☐	☐
8	하늘이 점점 더 어두워지고 있어.	☐	☐	☐
9	요즘 내가 시간이 없어.	☐	☐	☐
10	극장 앞에서 만나자	☐	☐	☐
11	공기가 방 안에서 움직이기 때문에 여러분은 더 시원하다고 느낍니다.	☐	☐	☐
12	내가 설거지를 할게.	☐	☐	☐
13	여기 근처에 약국이 있나요?	☐	☐	☐
14	여전히 선생님이 되고 싶니?	☐	☐	☐
15	뭐라도 먹을래?	☐	☐	☐
16	더 큰 사이즈로 입어보시겠어요?	☐	☐	☐
17	당신 부모님이 그곳에 사시는 줄 몰랐어요.	☐	☐	☐
18	나를 위해 지도를 확인해 줄 수 있어?	☐	☐	☐
19	제 도움이 필요하면, 말씀하세요.	☐	☐	☐
20	콘서트가 몇 시에 시작하니?	☐	☐	☐

영어듣기능력평가 05 회

Step 2 듣고 따라 말하기

		1회	2회	3회
1	Why don't we swim in the lake?	☐	☐	☐
2	I have something to do with my classmates.	☐	☐	☐
3	There'll be a heavy rain from tonight until tomorrow.	☐	☐	☐
4	Her family will go to America.	☐	☐	☐
5	I heard we have to dress up.	☐	☐	☐
6	You waited for a long time.	☐	☐	☐
7	Is there something wrong with you?	☐	☐	☐
8	The sky is getting darker and darker.	☐	☐	☐
9	I don't have time these days.	☐	☐	☐
10	Let's meet in front of the theater.	☐	☐	☐
11	Because the air moves in the room, you feel cooler.	☐	☐	☐
12	Let me wash the dishes.	☐	☐	☐
13	Is there a drugstore around here?	☐	☐	☐
14	Do you still want to be a teacher?	☐	☐	☐
15	Why don't we eat something?	☐	☐	☐
16	Would you like to try a bigger size?	☐	☐	☐
17	I didn't know that your parents live there.	☐	☐	☐
18	Can you check the map for me?	☐	☐	☐
19	If you need my help, please tell me.	☐	☐	☐
20	What time does the concert start?	☐	☐	☐

영어듣기능력평가 06 회

만점 듣기 표현

Step 1 우리말 보면서 영어 듣기

		1회	2회	3회
1	여러분은 이것들을 생일에 사용할 수도 있습니다.	☐	☐	☐
2	처음에는 자전거를 그릴 예정이었어.	☐	☐	☐
3	외출할 때 우산을 가지고 가실 필요는 없습니다.	☐	☐	☐
4	부모님이 이번 주 토요일에 우리를 방문하실 거예요.	☐	☐	☐
5	먹을 것 좀 가져다 드릴까요?	☐	☐	☐
6	아직 5분 남았어.	☐	☐	☐
7	너에게 수학 숙제에 대해 물어보려고 전화했어.	☐	☐	☐
8	큰 우체국 옆, 큰 은행 건너편에 있어요.	☐	☐	☐
9	너는 대학교에서 무엇을 공부하고 싶니?	☐	☐	☐
10	네 기쁨을 함께 나누고 싶어.	☐	☐	☐
11	언젠가 나는 TV 기자가 되고 싶어.	☐	☐	☐
12	매일 머리를 감나요?	☐	☐	☐
13	물건을 잘못 놓고 다니지 않도록 주의하렴.	☐	☐	☐
14	앞으로 5일 남았어.	☐	☐	☐
15	며칠 기다리셔야 해요.	☐	☐	☐
16	금요일이 기다려진다.	☐	☐	☐
17	제가 어제 드린 약이 도움이 되셨나요?	☐	☐	☐
18	가능하면 종이를 절약하고 싶어요.	☐	☐	☐
19	나는 불어를 수강할까 생각 중이야.	☐	☐	☐
20	선혀 식동이 안 돼요.	☐	☐	☐

영어듣기능력평가 06회

Step 2 듣고 따라 말하기

		1회	2회	3회
1	You can use these on your birthday.	☐	☐	☐
2	I was going to draw a bicycle at first.	☐	☐	☐
3	You don't have to take your umbrella with you when you go out.	☐	☐	☐
4	My parents will visit us this Saturday.	☐	☐	☐
5	Can I get you something to eat?	☐	☐	☐
6	We still have five minutes left.	☐	☐	☐
7	I'm calling to ask you about the math homework.	☐	☐	☐
8	It's next to the big post office and across from a bank.	☐	☐	☐
9	What do you want to study in the university?	☐	☐	☐
10	I want to share your happiness with you.	☐	☐	☐
11	Someday I want to be a TV reporter.	☐	☐	☐
12	Do you wash your hair every day?	☐	☐	☐
13	Be careful not to misplace your things.	☐	☐	☐
14	We have five days to go.	☐	☐	☐
15	You have to wait for a few days.	☐	☐	☐
16	I can't wait for Friday.	☐	☐	☐
17	Did the medicine I gave you yesterday help you?	☐	☐	☐
18	I'd like to save paper whenever possible.	☐	☐	☐
19	I'm thinking of taking French.	☐	☐	☐
20	It doesn't start at all.	☐	☐	☐

영어듣기능력평가 07 회

만점 듣기 표현

Step 1 우리말 보면서 영어 듣기

		1회	2회	3회
1	여러분은 제가 수천 명의 제 친구들과 함께 눈 위에 서 있는 것을 볼 수 있습니다.	☐	☐	☐
2	내 머리를 말리기 위해 매일 아침 그것을 사용해야 해.	☐	☐	☐
3	이 덥고 건조한 날씨를 시원하게 식혀 주기를 기대해 봐야겠습니다.	☐	☐	☐
4	친구들과 나는 보통 체육관에서 만나.	☐	☐	☐
5	그것은 1889년에 만들어졌고, 그 당시 파리에서 가장 높은 건물이었습니다.	☐	☐	☐
6	그것을 어디에 사용하고 싶으신가요?	☐	☐	☐
7	우리가 지금 떠나야 한다고 생각해?	☐	☐	☐
8	컴퓨터를 켤 수 있겠니?	☐	☐	☐
9	지구가 점점 더워지고 있다는 것을 아니?	☐	☐	☐
10	다른 소리를 들을 수 없으니까 조심해야 해요.	☐	☐	☐
11	피아노 선생님께 전화해서 수업에 늦는다고 말씀드려야겠다.	☐	☐	☐
12	그가 오늘은 제 시간에 올 거라고 내게 약속했거든.	☐	☐	☐
13	상대방을 만날 준비가 되셨나요?	☐	☐	☐
14	안내 센터가 당신의 왼편에 보일 겁니다.	☐	☐	☐
15	얼마나 오랫동안 하는 거지?	☐	☐	☐
16	중요한 파일을 작업 중이에요.	☐	☐	☐
17	네가 운전하고 오면 파티 시간에 맞춰서 오기 힘들 것 같아.	☐	☐	☐
18	학생 도서관 대출 카드를 보여 주시겠어요?	☐	☐	☐
19	몇 층에 가시죠?	☐	☐	☐
20	오랜만이야!	☐	☐	☐

영어듣기능력평가 07회

Step 2 듣고 따라 말하기

		1회	2회	3회
1	You can see me standing on snow with thousands of my friends.	☐	☐	☐
2	I need it to dry my hair every morning.	☐	☐	☐
3	Let's hope it will cool us down in this hot dry weather.	☐	☐	☐
4	My friends and I usually meet at the gym.	☐	☐	☐
5	It was built in 1889, and it was the tallest building in Paris at that time.	☐	☐	☐
6	What do you want to use it for?	☐	☐	☐
7	Do you think we should leave now?	☐	☐	☐
8	Can you turn on the computer?	☐	☐	☐
9	Do you know that the Earth is getting warmer?	☐	☐	☐
10	You have to be careful, because you can't hear other noises.	☐	☐	☐
11	I'll call my piano teacher and tell her I'll be late for the lesson.	☐	☐	☐
12	He promised me that he would be on time today.	☐	☐	☐
13	Are you ready to meet your partner?	☐	☐	☐
14	You can see the Information Center on your left.	☐	☐	☐
15	How long will it last?	☐	☐	☐
16	I'm working on an important file.	☐	☐	☐
17	I don't think you can come in time for the party if you drive.	☐	☐	☐
18	Can I see your student library card?	☐	☐	☐
19	What floor are you going to?	☐	☐	☐
20	It's been a long time!	☐	☐	☐

영어듣기능력평가 08 회

만점 듣기 표현

Step 1 우리말 보면서 영어 듣기

		1회	2회	3회
1	일단 이것이 물에 닿으면, 그것은 부드러워집니다.	☐	☐	☐
2	그것을 의자 위에 두고 온 거야?	☐	☐	☐
3	New York의 날씨는 강풍을 동반한 비가 올 것입니다.	☐	☐	☐
4	나는 매우 똑똑하기 때문에 바나나 껍질을 벗길 수도 있어요.	☐	☐	☐
5	약 20분 정도 걸릴 거예요.	☐	☐	☐
6	네가 이 책을 가지고 있다니 믿어지지 않는다.	☐	☐	☐
7	네가 어디 있는지 궁금했어.	☐	☐	☐
8	내일 나와 함께 볼링 치러 갈래?	☐	☐	☐
9	오늘 같은 날은 항상 정말 사람이 많아.	☐	☐	☐
10	쇼핑몰 가는 길에 내 지갑을 잃어버렸어.	☐	☐	☐
11	나도 너처럼 스케이트를 잘 타고 싶어.	☐	☐	☐
12	제 취미는 축구를 하고 보는 것이에요.	☐	☐	☐
13	그 애가 자동차 사고가 났다는 소식을 들었어.	☐	☐	☐
14	넌 무엇이 되고 싶은지 생각해 본 적이 있니?	☐	☐	☐
15	나도 너처럼 건강해지고 싶어.	☐	☐	☐
16	이번 주 금요일 무료 입장권이 있어.	☐	☐	☐
17	가장 가까운 친척을 추측할 수 있나요?	☐	☐	☐
18	한국어를 공부하려고 생각 중이세요?	☐	☐	☐
19	거기서 무엇을 할 거니?	☐	☐	☐
20	나와 테니스를 치는 것은 어때?	☐	☐	☐

영어듣기능력평가 08 회

Step 2 듣고 따라 말하기

		1회	2회	3회
1	Once you put water on this, it becomes soft.	☐	☐	☐
2	Did you leave it on the chair?	☐	☐	☐
3	In New York it'll rain with strong winds.	☐	☐	☐
4	I can peel my own bananas, because I'm very clever.	☐	☐	☐
5	It'll take about 20 minutes.	☐	☐	☐
6	I can't believe you have this book.	☐	☐	☐
7	I was wondering where you were.	☐	☐	☐
8	Will you go bowling with me tomorrow?	☐	☐	☐
9	It's always really crowded on days like today.	☐	☐	☐
10	I lost my wallet on the way to the mall.	☐	☐	☐
11	I'd like to skate as well as you do.	☐	☐	☐
12	My hobby is playing and watching soccer.	☐	☐	☐
13	I heard that he got in a car accident.	☐	☐	☐
14	Did you ever think about what you want to be?	☐	☐	☐
15	I want to be as healthy as you are.	☐	☐	☐
16	I have free tickets for this Friday.	☐	☐	☐
17	Can you guess the closest relative?	☐	☐	☐
18	Are you thinking about studying Korean?	☐	☐	☐
19	What are you going to do there?	☐	☐	☐
20	How about playing tennis with me?	☐	☐	☐

영어듣기능력평가 09회

만점 듣기 표현

Step 1 우리말 보면서 영어 듣기

		1회	2회	3회
1	나는 매일 아침마다 창문을 열고 신선한 공기를 깊이 들이 마실 수 있어.	☐	☐	☐
2	이제 당신의 사진을 찍겠습니다.	☐	☐	☐
3	우산을 가져가시고 반드시 외투를 입으시기 바랍니다.	☐	☐	☐
4	병원에는 많은 다른 직업들이 있습니다.	☐	☐	☐
5	나는 여행 동아리에 가입할까 생각 중이야.	☐	☐	☐
6	성함을 말씀해 주시겠어요?	☐	☐	☐
7	그가 올 때까지 30분 남았군요.	☐	☐	☐
8	우리 집에 와서 수학 좀 도와줄래?	☐	☐	☐
9	영화가 곧 시작할 예정이야.	☐	☐	☐
10	넌 해야 할 조사가 있는 것처럼 들리는구나.	☐	☐	☐
11	여러분은 이것을 불을 끄는 데 사용할 수 있습니다.	☐	☐	☐
12	네가 포기하지 않으면, 너는 좋은 성적을 받을 수 있단다.	☐	☐	☐
13	다른 수프를 가져다 드리겠습니다.	☐	☐	☐
14	은행은 도서관 바로 옆에 있습니다.	☐	☐	☐
15	그곳에서 좋은 시간을 보내길 바랄게.	☐	☐	☐
16	난 창문을 열고 선풍기를 사용하는 게 더 좋아.	☐	☐	☐
17	뮤지컬이 6시에 시작하는 줄 알았어.	☐	☐	☐
18	가서 새 넥타이를 사야 할 것 같아.	☐	☐	☐
19	이 쓰레기 봉투를 집 앞에 내다놓아 주겠니?	☐	☐	☐
20	힐 일이 없어요.	☐	☐	☐

영어듣기능력평가 09 회

Step 2 듣고 따라 말하기

		1회	2회	3회
1	I can open the windows and take a deep breath of fresh air every morning.	☐	☐	☐
2	Now I'm going to take a picture of you.	☐	☐	☐
3	Take your umbrella with you and be sure to wear your coat.	☐	☐	☐
4	There are many other jobs in the hospital.	☐	☐	☐
5	I'm thinking of joining the travel club.	☐	☐	☐
6	Can I have your name?	☐	☐	☐
7	We have thirty minutes left until he comes.	☐	☐	☐
8	Would you come to my place and help me with math?	☐	☐	☐
9	The movie's going to start in a few minutes.	☐	☐	☐
10	It sounds like you have some research to do.	☐	☐	☐
11	You can use this to put the fire out.	☐	☐	☐
12	If you don't give up, you can get a good grade.	☐	☐	☐
13	Let me bring you another bowl of soup.	☐	☐	☐
14	The bank is right next to the library.	☐	☐	☐
15	I hope you have a good time there.	☐	☐	☐
16	I prefer to open the window and use a fan.	☐	☐	☐
17	I thought the musical would start at six.	☐	☐	☐
18	Maybe I should go and buy a new tie.	☐	☐	☐
19	Would you take out this garbage bag to the front of the house?	☐	☐	☐
20	I have nothing to do.	☐	☐	☐

영어듣기능력평가 10회

만점 듣기 표현

Step 1 우리말 보면서 영어 듣기

		1회	2회	3회
1	여자가 나무를 심고 있다.	☐	☐	☐
2	엄마에게 애완동물을 키우자고 부탁해 봐.	☐	☐	☐
3	올해 첫 눈이 되겠네요.	☐	☐	☐
4	택시를 타는 게 어때?	☐	☐	☐
5	무대에 서자마자 모든 것을 잊어버릴 것 같아요.	☐	☐	☐
6	약을 먹으면 괜찮을 거야.	☐	☐	☐
7	내 손과 옷이 지금 정말 더러워요.	☐	☐	☐
8	아래로 빠르게 내려올 수 있기 때문에 재미있습니다.	☐	☐	☐
9	전쟁에 관한 역사 프로그램은 흥미롭지.	☐	☐	☐
10	두 번만 더하고 오늘 연습을 마치자.	☐	☐	☐
11	거스름돈 여기 있습니다.	☐	☐	☐
12	가장 오른쪽에 있는 찬장에 있었어.	☐	☐	☐
13	12시까지 버스로 돌아오셔야 합니다.	☐	☐	☐
14	나는 의학에는 전혀 관심이 없어.	☐	☐	☐
15	예약하셨나요?	☐	☐	☐
16	내가 뭘 해 주기를 원하니	☐	☐	☐
17	제가 당신의 약에 대해 말씀드릴게요.	☐	☐	☐
18	난 울타리가 도움이 될 거라고 생각했어.	☐	☐	☐
19	나는 그 파티에 갈 수 없어.	☐	☐	☐
20	당신 2학년의 누군가를 닮은 것 같은데요.	☐	☐	☐

영어듣기능력평가 10회

Step 2 듣고 따라 말하기

		1회	2회	3회
1	She is planting a tree.	☐	☐	☐
2	Ask your mom to have a pet.	☐	☐	☐
3	It will be the first snow this year.	☐	☐	☐
4	Why don't we take a taxi?	☐	☐	☐
5	I think I will forget everything as soon as I stand on the stage.	☐	☐	☐
6	You'll be okay if you take medicine.	☐	☐	☐
7	My hands and clothes are really dirty now.	☐	☐	☐
8	It is fun, because you can go down fast.	☐	☐	☐
9	History shows about wars are interesting.	☐	☐	☐
10	Let's practice just two more times and finish today's practice.	☐	☐	☐
11	Here is your change.	☐	☐	☐
12	It was in the cupboard on the far right.	☐	☐	☐
13	You have to come back to the bus by 12 o'clock.	☐	☐	☐
14	I don't have any interest in medicine.	☐	☐	☐
15	Do you have a reservation?	☐	☐	☐
16	What do you want me to do?	☐	☐	☐
17	Let me tell you about your medicine.	☐	☐	☐
18	I thought a fence would help.	☐	☐	☐
19	I can't come to the party.	☐	☐	☐
20	You look like someone in the second grade.	☐	☐	☐

영어듣기능력평가 11 회

만점 듣기 표현

Step 1 우리말 보면서 영어 듣기

		1회	2회	3회
1	이것은 특별한 것을 필요로 하지 않습니다.	☐	☐	☐
2	그것을 물 속에서 사용할 수 있고, 정말 빨리 말라요.	☐	☐	☐
3	눈이 올 확률이 높겠습니다.	☐	☐	☐
4	서점 옆에 있는 마트에서 우유를 좀 사다 줄래?	☐	☐	☐
5	며칠이나 묵으실 건가요?	☐	☐	☐
6	오전 항공편을 예약할게요.	☐	☐	☐
7	제 예약을 취소하고 싶습니다.	☐	☐	☐
8	이름이나 전화번호를 알려 주세요.	☐	☐	☐
9	나도 너와 같이 하게 돼서 기뻐.	☐	☐	☐
10	다음 주 월요일부터 일을 시작해.	☐	☐	☐
11	나에게는 긴 뒷다리가 있어서 멀리 뛸 수 있습니다.	☐	☐	☐
12	매 식사 후에는 반드시 양치질을 하셔야 해요.	☐	☐	☐
13	7시 연극표 2장을 예매하셨죠?	☐	☐	☐
14	나는 그곳에서 5일 동안 머물 거야.	☐	☐	☐
15	너는 저쪽에서 팝콘과 음료수를 좀 사.	☐	☐	☐
16	네가 그렇게 좋은 일을 하는지 몰랐어.	☐	☐	☐
17	나 내 발표 주제를 바꿔야 할 거 같아.	☐	☐	☐
18	그곳에 도착하는 데 얼마나 걸릴까요?	☐	☐	☐
19	방 청소를 언제 할 거니?	☐	☐	☐
20	어떻게 지불하시겠어요?	☐	☐	☐

영어듣기능력평가 11회

Step 2 듣고 따라 말하기

		1회	2회	3회
1	This doesn't need anything special.	☐	☐	☐
2	You can use them in water, and they dry really quickly.	☐	☐	☐
3	There will be strong chance of snow.	☐	☐	☐
4	Can you buy some milk at the mart next to the bookstore?	☐	☐	☐
5	How many days are you going to stay?	☐	☐	☐
6	I'll book the morning flight.	☐	☐	☐
7	I'd like to cancel my reservation.	☐	☐	☐
8	Please let me know your name or phone number.	☐	☐	☐
9	I'm happy to be a team with you.	☐	☐	☐
10	I start to work next Monday.	☐	☐	☐
11	I can jump far because I have long back legs.	☐	☐	☐
12	You should brush your teeth after every meal.	☐	☐	☐
13	Did you book two tickets for the 7 o'clock play?	☐	☐	☐
14	I'm going to stay there for five days.	☐	☐	☐
15	You buy some popcorn and drinks over there.	☐	☐	☐
16	I didn't know you did such good things.	☐	☐	☐
17	I might have to change the topic of my presentation.	☐	☐	☐
18	How long will it take to get there?	☐	☐	☐
19	When will you clean your room?	☐	☐	☐
20	How would you like to pay?	☐	☐	☐

영어듣기능력평가 12회

만점 듣기 표현

Step 1 우리말 보면서 영어 듣기

		1회	2회	3회
1	그건 좋은 생각이 아닌 것 같아.	☐	☐	☐
2	소파 위에 신문 보이죠?	☐	☐	☐
3	날씨는 야외 활동을 하기에 충분히 좋을 것입니다.	☐	☐	☐
4	이것이 바닥의 모든 먼지를 빨아들입니다.	☐	☐	☐
5	저는 이 캠프 동안 여러분들과 친해지고 싶습니다.	☐	☐	☐
6	그곳은 이 지역에서 가장 유명한 곳입니다.	☐	☐	☐
7	두통이 약간 있어.	☐	☐	☐
8	나에게 그녀의 이메일 주소를 알려 줄래?	☐	☐	☐
9	내가 사용한 뒤에 반납할게.	☐	☐	☐
10	기차역을 어떻게 가야하나요?	☐	☐	☐
11	그게 작동이 잘 될지 모르겠어.	☐	☐	☐
12	저는 어렵게 교훈을 얻었어요.	☐	☐	☐
13	해야 할 숙제가 있니?	☐	☐	☐
14	왼편으로 서점이 보일 겁니다.	☐	☐	☐
15	그를 2년 동안 보지 못했어.	☐	☐	☐
16	손에 있는 것이 뭐니?	☐	☐	☐
17	여름에 비가 많이 오고 겨울에도 비가 많이 옵니다.	☐	☐	☐
18	그것이 오늘 저의 마지막 약속인가요?	☐	☐	☐
19	집까지 저를 태워 주셔서 감사해요.	☐	☐	☐
20	이 카드 게임을 하는 방법을 알고 있니?	☐	☐	☐

영어듣기능력평가 12회

Step 2 듣고 따라 말하기

		1회	2회	3회
1	I don't think it's a good idea.	☐	☐	☐
2	Can you see the newspaper on the sofa?	☐	☐	☐
3	The weather will be good enough for outdoor activities.	☐	☐	☐
4	This sucks all the dust and dirt from the floor.	☐	☐	☐
5	I want to be close to you guys during this camp.	☐	☐	☐
6	That's the most famous place in this area.	☐	☐	☐
7	I have a little bit of a headache.	☐	☐	☐
8	Would you give me her email address?	☐	☐	☐
9	I'll return it after I use it.	☐	☐	☐
10	How can I get to the train station?	☐	☐	☐
11	I'm afraid it's not working well.	☐	☐	☐
12	I learned the lesson the hard way.	☐	☐	☐
13	Do you have homework to do?	☐	☐	☐
14	You'll see the bookstore on your left.	☐	☐	☐
15	I haven't seen him for two years	☐	☐	☐
16	What do you have in your hand?	☐	☐	☐
17	It rains a lot in summer and it rains a lot even in winter.	☐	☐	☐
18	Is that my last appointment today?	☐	☐	☐
19	Thank you for giving me a ride home.	☐	☐	☐
20	Do you know how to play this card game?	☐	☐	☐

영어듣기능력평가 13회

만점 듣기 표현

Step 1 우리말 보면서 영어 듣기

		1회	2회	3회
1	엄마 복부에 있는 주머니 안에 날 넣고 다녔어요.	☐	☐	☐
2	TV 앞에 있는 커피 탁자 위에 있어요.	☐	☐	☐
3	비가 곧 그치고 밤에는 보름달을 보실 수 있을 것입니다.	☐	☐	☐
4	그녀는 엄마가 저녁 식사 준비를 하고 식탁 차리는 것을 도와드렸습니다.	☐	☐	☐
5	예약 시간에 늦을 거야.	☐	☐	☐
6	결승전은 학교 체육 대회 날 있을 예정입니다.	☐	☐	☐
7	사람들이 많이 오기 전에 일찍 가자.	☐	☐	☐
8	주문하시겠습니까?	☐	☐	☐
9	더 저렴한 곳은 없나요?	☐	☐	☐
10	나는 네가 역사를 그렇게 좋아하는 줄 몰랐어.	☐	☐	☐
11	나는 그것을 손꼽아 기다리고 있어.	☐	☐	☐
12	지하철을 타는 게 나아.	☐	☐	☐
13	이렇게 아름다운 곳은 처음이에요.	☐	☐	☐
14	그의 전화번호를 물어보려고 전화했어.	☐	☐	☐
15	병원에는 아픈 사람들이 아주 많아.	☐	☐	☐
16	내일 언제 출발할 거야?	☐	☐	☐
17	여러분의 협조에 감사드립니다.	☐	☐	☐
18	저에게는 예쁜 딸이 한 명 있습니다.	☐	☐	☐
19	사진 좀 찍어 주시겠어요?	☐	☐	☐
20	언제 그것을 마지막으로 봤니?	☐	☐	☐

영어듣기능력평가 13회

Step 2 듣고 따라 말하기

		1회	2회	3회
1	My mother carried me in the pouch of her stomach.	☐	☐	☐
2	It's on the coffee table in front of the TV.	☐	☐	☐
3	The rain will stop soon and we'll be able to see the full moon at night.	☐	☐	☐
4	She helped her mom cook dinner and set the table	☐	☐	☐
5	We'll be late for the reservation.	☐	☐	☐
6	The final match will be on school sports day.	☐	☐	☐
7	Let's go early before a lot of people come.	☐	☐	☐
8	Can I take your order?	☐	☐	☐
9	Do you have any cheaper place?	☐	☐	☐
10	I didn't know you liked history so much.	☐	☐	☐
11	I'm really looking forward to it.	☐	☐	☐
12	You'd better take the subway.	☐	☐	☐
13	This is my first time in such a beautiful place.	☐	☐	☐
14	I called you to ask for his number.	☐	☐	☐
15	There are so many sick people in the hospital.	☐	☐	☐
16	When are we going to leave tomorrow?	☐	☐	☐
17	Thank you for your cooperation.	☐	☐	☐
18	I have a beautiful daughter.	☐	☐	☐
19	Would you take a picture for me?	☐	☐	☐
20	When is the last time you saw it?	☐	☐	☐

영어듣기능력평가 14회

만점 듣기 표현

Step 1 우리말 보면서 영어 듣기

		1회	2회	3회
1	그는 엄마와 함께 해변을 걷고 있다.	☐	☐	☐
2	저쪽에 있는 표지판을 봐!	☐	☐	☐
3	강한 바람과 함께 훨씬 더 추워지겠습니다.	☐	☐	☐
4	함께 저녁 먹는 게 어때?	☐	☐	☐
5	이것을 사용하기 위해서 여러분은 우선 돈을 집어 넣어야 합니다.	☐	☐	☐
6	이곳에 무엇 때문에 오셨죠?	☐	☐	☐
7	한국 여행에서 언제 돌아왔니?	☐	☐	☐
8	괜찮으면, 너의 텐트를 빌려 줄래?	☐	☐	☐
9	체온을 재 볼게요.	☐	☐	☐
10	아직 5일이 남았어.	☐	☐	☐
11	기차가 몇 시에 출발하죠?	☐	☐	☐
12	차는 어디에 주차했니?	☐	☐	☐
13	넌 계속 그것을 쳐다보고 만지고 있잖아.	☐	☐	☐
14	당신의 애완동물에게 무슨 문제가 있나요?	☐	☐	☐
15	나를 초대해 줘서 다시 한번 고마워.	☐	☐	☐
16	좋은 일이라도 생겼니?	☐	☐	☐
17	너는 따뜻한 차를 좀 마셔야 할 것 같아.	☐	☐	☐
18	저는 이 중학교를 졸업했어요.	☐	☐	☐
19	부탁 하나 해도 돼?	☐	☐	☐
20	그 영화 재미있다고 들었어.	☐	☐	☐

영어듣기능력평가 14회

Step 2 듣고 따라 말하기

		1회	2회	3회
1	He is walking on the beach with his mom.	☐	☐	☐
2	Look at the sign over there!	☐	☐	☐
3	It will be much colder with the strong wind.	☐	☐	☐
4	How about having dinner together?	☐	☐	☐
5	To use this, you put money in first.	☐	☐	☐
6	What made you come here?	☐	☐	☐
7	When did you come back from your trip to Korea?	☐	☐	☐
8	If you don't mind, can I borrow your tent?	☐	☐	☐
9	Let me take your temperature.	☐	☐	☐
10	There are still five days left.	☐	☐	☐
11	What time does the train leave?	☐	☐	☐
12	Where did you park your car?	☐	☐	☐
13	You keep looking at it and touching it.	☐	☐	☐
14	What's the problem with your pet?	☐	☐	☐
15	Thank you again for inviting me.	☐	☐	☐
16	Did something good happen?	☐	☐	☐
17	I think you should drink some hot tea.	☐	☐	☐
18	I graduated from this middle school.	☐	☐	☐
19	Can I ask you a favor?	☐	☐	☐
20	I heard that it was an interesting movie.	☐	☐	☐

영어듣기능력평가 15회

만점 듣기 표현

Step 1 우리말 보면서 영어 듣기

		1회	2회	3회
1	네가 멋진 생일 파티를 하기를 바란다.	☐	☐	☐
2	이 방의 모든 것이 너무 낡았어요.	☐	☐	☐
3	우산 챙기는 것을 잊지 마시기 바랍니다.	☐	☐	☐
4	너도 수집하는 것이 있니?	☐	☐	☐
5	애완견을 기르는 것은 좋은 생각이 아닌 것 같구나.	☐	☐	☐
6	그것에 대해 말하기 싫어.	☐	☐	☐
7	다른 나라에서 온 노동자들을 위한 센터야.	☐	☐	☐
8	추천 좀 해 주시겠어요?	☐	☐	☐
9	우리는 배로 그곳에 갈 거야.	☐	☐	☐
10	기차에서 전화를 거는 거니?	☐	☐	☐
11	여러분은 이것을 시원한 곳에 보관해야 합니다.	☐	☐	☐
12	그에게 메시지를 남겨 드릴 수 있어요.	☐	☐	☐
13	이 행사는 모든 어린이들에게 무료입니다.	☐	☐	☐
14	저는 잡지용 음식 사진을 찍어요.	☐	☐	☐
15	숟가락 좀 주시겠어요?	☐	☐	☐
16	바이올린 수업 A는 9시에 시작한다.	☐	☐	☐
17	그 애가 공부에 흥미를 갖기 시작했어요.	☐	☐	☐
18	내 사촌에게 도시 구경을 시켜 줘야 해.	☐	☐	☐
19	시합을 위해 연습하는 거니?	☐	☐	☐
20	너 면접 준비 많이 했잖아.	☐	☐	☐

영어듣기능력평가 15회

Step 2 듣고 따라 말하기

		1회	2회	3회
1	I hope you have a great birthday party.	☐	☐	☐
2	Everything in this room is too old.	☐	☐	☐
3	Don't forget to take your umbrella with you.	☐	☐	☐
4	Do you collect anything?	☐	☐	☐
5	I don't think having a pet dog is a good idea.	☐	☐	☐
6	I don't want to talk about it.	☐	☐	☐
7	It's a center for the workers from other countries.	☐	☐	☐
8	Would you recommend something?	☐	☐	☐
9	We're going there by ship.	☐	☐	☐
10	Are you calling on the train?	☐	☐	☐
11	You should keep this in a cool place.	☐	☐	☐
12	I can leave him a message.	☐	☐	☐
13	This event is free for all children.	☐	☐	☐
14	I take pictures of food for magazines.	☐	☐	☐
15	Would you pass me the spoon?	☐	☐	☐
16	Violin Class A begins at nine.	☐	☐	☐
17	He began to be interested in studying.	☐	☐	☐
18	I have to show my cousin around the city.	☐	☐	☐
19	Are you practicing for the match	☐	☐	☐
20	You prepared for the interview a lot.	☐	☐	☐

영어듣기능력평가 16회

만점 듣기 표현

Step 1 우리말 보면서 영어 듣기

		1회	2회	3회
1	중요한 날에는 동그라미를 해 둘 수 있습니다.	☐	☐	☐
2	조개껍질은 바닷가에서 주워 왔니?	☐	☐	☐
3	이번 주의 기온은 평년 기온보다 높습니다.	☐	☐	☐
4	같이 컴퓨터 게임을 할까?	☐	☐	☐
5	그것을 얼마 주고 샀니?	☐	☐	☐
6	교통 상황 좀 보세요!	☐	☐	☐
7	아버지는 좀 어떠시니?	☐	☐	☐
8	여러분은 나를 몇몇의 수족관에서도 볼 수 있어요.	☐	☐	☐
9	너는 요리에 관심이 있는 것 같아.	☐	☐	☐
10	여러분은 매주 수요일에 제 영어 수업을 받게 될 것입니다.	☐	☐	☐
11	문자 메시지를 못 받았니?	☐	☐	☐
12	그래서 네가 계속 재채기를 하는 거야.	☐	☐	☐
13	우리는 유명한 동굴을 방문했습니다.	☐	☐	☐
14	여름 방학이 코앞에 다가왔어.	☐	☐	☐
15	이 근처에 좋은 수리점 알고 있니?	☐	☐	☐
16	저기 있는 공중전화를 사용하면 어떨까?	☐	☐	☐
17	어디 있는지 모르겠어.	☐	☐	☐
18	남자 아이들을 위한 장화도 많이 봤어.	☐	☐	☐
19	몸무게를 줄이고 싶어.	☐	☐	☐
20	춤 동아리에 가입하려고 생각 중이야.	☐	☐	☐

영어듣기능력평가 16회

Step 2 듣고 따라 말하기

		1회	2회	3회
1	You can circle important days.	☐	☐	☐
2	Did you pick the shell from the beach?	☐	☐	☐
3	The temperature is higher than average this week.	☐	☐	☐
4	Can we play computer games together?	☐	☐	☐
5	How much did you pay for it?	☐	☐	☐
6	Look at the traffic!	☐	☐	☐
7	How's your father doing?	☐	☐	☐
8	You can also see me in some aquariums.	☐	☐	☐
9	I think you're interested in cooking.	☐	☐	☐
10	You will have English class with me every Wednesday.	☐	☐	☐
11	Didn't you get the text message?	☐	☐	☐
12	That's why you keep sneezing.	☐	☐	☐
13	We visited a famous cave.	☐	☐	☐
14	Summer vacation is just around the corner.	☐	☐	☐
15	Do you know a good repair shop near here?	☐	☐	☐
16	Why don't we use the pay phone over there?	☐	☐	☐
17	I don't know where it is.	☐	☐	☐
18	I saw a lot of rain boots for boys.	☐	☐	☐
19	I'd like to lose some weight.	☐	☐	☐
20	I'm thinking of joining a dancing club.	☐	☐	☐

영어듣기능력평가 17회

만점 듣기 표현

Step 1 우리말 보면서 영어 듣기

		1회	2회	3회
1	사람들은 방을 꾸미기 위해 이것을 사용합니다.	☐	☐	☐
2	가족들을 위해 뭐라도 샀니?	☐	☐	☐
3	오늘 오후에 비가 오기 시작하여 자정 무렵까지 계속될 것입니다.	☐	☐	☐
4	내일 저녁에 시간이 있니?	☐	☐	☐
5	모든 회원이 그 모임에 오시길 바랍니다.	☐	☐	☐
6	제가 이 책을 찾는 것을 도와주시겠어요?	☐	☐	☐
7	나를 도와줘서 고마워.	☐	☐	☐
8	저희가 없는 동안 우리 고양이를 돌봐 주시겠어요?	☐	☐	☐
9	오후 내내 그 박물관에서 보낼 수 있겠어요.	☐	☐	☐
10	축제를 위해 티셔츠를 몇 장 만들어야 하지?	☐	☐	☐
11	내가 서점까지 너를 태워 줄게.	☐	☐	☐
12	며칠 동안 갈 거니?	☐	☐	☐
13	내가 가장 좋아하는 노래를 다운로드 하려고 하는 중이야.	☐	☐	☐
14	꽃가게가 어디에 있나요?	☐	☐	☐
15	그의 수업 일정이 바뀌었어요.	☐	☐	☐
16	네 가방 속을 다시 한 번 확인해 볼래?	☐	☐	☐
17	그냥 전원을 끄고 좀 기다려 보면 어때요?	☐	☐	☐
18	뭐가 감사하다는 거지?	☐	☐	☐
19	우리 동아리가 그렇게 인기 있는 줄 몰랐는걸.	☐	☐	☐
20	당신이 이번 주에 저를 많이 도와주셨잖아요.	☐	☐	☐

영어듣기능력평가 17회

Step 2 듣고 따라 말하기

		1회	2회	3회
1	People use it to decorate a room.	☐	☐	☐
2	Did you buy anything for your family?	☐	☐	☐
3	The rain will start this afternoon and continue until around midnight.	☐	☐	☐
4	Do you have time tomorrow evening?	☐	☐	☐
5	I hope every member will come to the meeting.	☐	☐	☐
6	Would you help me find this book?	☐	☐	☐
7	Thank you for helping me.	☐	☐	☐
8	Would you take care of our cat while we're gone?	☐	☐	☐
9	We can spend the whole afternoon in the museum.	☐	☐	☐
10	How many T-shirts do we have to make for the festival?	☐	☐	☐
11	I can give you a ride to the bookstore.	☐	☐	☐
12	How many nights will you go for?	☐	☐	☐
13	I'm trying to download my favorite song.	☐	☐	☐
14	Where is the flower shop?	☐	☐	☐
15	His class schedule was changed.	☐	☐	☐
16	Could you double check in your bag?	☐	☐	☐
17	Why don't you just turn it off and wait some time?	☐	☐	☐
18	Thank me for what?	☐	☐	☐
19	I didn't know that our club is that popular.	☐	☐	☐
20	You helped me with a lot of things for the week.	☐	☐	☐

영어듣기능력평가 18회

만점 듣기 표현

Step 1 우리말 보면서 영어 듣기

		1회	2회	3회
1	물을 마실 때 이것을 사용할 수 있습니다.	☐	☐	☐
2	바지나 재킷을 확인해 봤어요?	☐	☐	☐
3	내일은 더 따뜻해지고 더 화창해질 것입니다.	☐	☐	☐
4	당신 아버지께서 10월 17일에 우리를 방문하시는 거죠, 그렇죠?	☐	☐	☐
5	나는 알에서 태어나고 깨어나는데 21일이 걸려요.	☐	☐	☐
6	너의 어머니 생신이 언제인지 아니?	☐	☐	☐
7	이미 넌 네 꿈이 있잖아, 안 그래?	☐	☐	☐
8	먹을 것이 있니?	☐	☐	☐
9	개들이 원래 그렇죠.	☐	☐	☐
10	이 책을 다른 책으로 교환할 수 있을까요?	☐	☐	☐
11	그것을 가져올 시간이 없었어요.	☐	☐	☐
12	내가 가장 좋아하는 과목은 역사이고 내 취미는 바이올린을 켜는 거야.	☐	☐	☐
13	이번 주말에 무슨 계획 있니?	☐	☐	☐
14	오늘 밤에 영화 보러 갈까?	☐	☐	☐
15	너도 나랑 같이 갈래?	☐	☐	☐
16	매일 적어도 30분씩 공부하려고 노력하세요.	☐	☐	☐
17	아이들이 동물들에게 아무 것도 주지 못하도록 해 주십시오.	☐	☐	☐
18	난 겨우 4일 동안 머물 거야.	☐	☐	☐
19	이 호텔에 대해 어떻게 생각하니?	☐	☐	☐
20	너에게 좋은 소식이 하나 있어.	☐	☐	☐

영어듣기능력평가 18회

Step 2 듣고 따라 말하기

		1회	2회	3회
1	You can use this when drinking water.	☐	☐	☐
2	Did you check your pants or jacket?	☐	☐	☐
3	Tomorrow will be warmer and sunnier.	☐	☐	☐
4	Your dad is visiting us on October 17th, right?	☐	☐	☐
5	I come from an egg, and it takes 21 days for me to hatch.	☐	☐	☐
6	Do you know when your mother's birthday is?	☐	☐	☐
7	You already have your own dream, don't you?	☐	☐	☐
8	Is there something to eat?	☐	☐	☐
9	That's what dogs do.	☐	☐	☐
10	Can I exchange this book for another book?	☐	☐	☐
11	I didn't have time to pick them up.	☐	☐	☐
12	My favorite subject is history and my hobby is playing the violin.	☐	☐	☐
13	Do you have any plans this weekend?	☐	☐	☐
14	Can we go to a movie tonight?	☐	☐	☐
15	Would you like to come with me?	☐	☐	☐
16	Try to study even at least 30 minutes every day.	☐	☐	☐
17	Please don't let your children give anything to the animals.	☐	☐	☐
18	I'm staying there for four days only.	☐	☐	☐
19	What do you think about this hotel?	☐	☐	☐
20	I have a good news for you.	☐	☐	☐

영어듣기능력평가 19회

만점 듣기 표현

Step 1 우리말 보면서 영어 듣기

		1회	2회	3회
1	그렇게 함으로써 프로그램을 열 수 있습니다.	☐	☐	☐
2	수영하기에는 날씨가 너무 추운 것 같아.	☐	☐	☐
3	어제는 전국적으로 눈이 많이 왔습니다.	☐	☐	☐
4	오늘 오후에 뭐 할 거니?	☐	☐	☐
5	TV 소리를 줄여 주시겠어요?	☐	☐	☐
6	그 모임은 언제 끝나니?	☐	☐	☐
7	먼저 전화 드리지 못해 죄송합니다.	☐	☐	☐
8	이것은 우리 일상생활에서 많이 쓰이는 도구입니다.	☐	☐	☐
9	난 가족들을 만나는 것을 고대하고 있어.	☐	☐	☐
10	그럴 만한 충분한 이유가 있어.	☐	☐	☐
11	콘서트는 이웃의 가난한 사람들을 위한 것입니다.	☐	☐	☐
12	조언 고마워.	☐	☐	☐
13	학생들은 자신이 가장 좋아하는 책을 들고 학교에 올 것입니다.	☐	☐	☐
14	그 건물은 당신의 오른편에 있을 거예요.	☐	☐	☐
15	내가 사진 찍는 동안 내 커피 좀 들고 있어 줄래?	☐	☐	☐
16	네 왼편에 우체국이 보일 때까지 걸어.	☐	☐	☐
17	우리 팀이 오늘 첫 번째 축구 연습을 했어요.	☐	☐	☐
18	좋은 생각 있어?	☐	☐	☐
19	이제 나는 어쩌지?	☐	☐	☐
20	저에게 30분만 주세요.	☐	☐	☐

영어듣기능력평가 19회

Step 2 듣고 따라 말하기

		1회	2회	3회
1	You can open a program by doing that.	☐	☐	☐
2	The weather is too cold to swim, I think.	☐	☐	☐
3	Yesterday we had much snow all over the country.	☐	☐	☐
4	What are you going to do this afternoon?	☐	☐	☐
5	Could you turn down your TV?	☐	☐	☐
6	When does the meeting finish?	☐	☐	☐
7	I'm sorry for not calling you first.	☐	☐	☐
8	This is a tool we use a lot in our daily lives.	☐	☐	☐
9	I'm looking forward to seeing my family.	☐	☐	☐
10	I have a good reason for that.	☐	☐	☐
11	The concert is for the benefit of poor people in the neighborhood.	☐	☐	☐
12	Thanks for the tip.	☐	☐	☐
13	Students are coming to school with their favorite books	☐	☐	☐
14	You will find the building on your right.	☐	☐	☐
15	Can you hold my coffee while I take a picture?	☐	☐	☐
16	Walk until you see the post office on your left.	☐	☐	☐
17	Our team had its first soccer practice today.	☐	☐	☐
18	Do you have any ideas?	☐	☐	☐
19	What am I supposed to do now?	☐	☐	☐
20	Please give me just thirty minutes.	☐	☐	☐

영어듣기능력평가 20 회

만점 듣기 표현

Step 1 우리말 보면서 영어 듣기

		1회	2회	3회
1	이것에 물을 넣으면, 물은 얼음으로 변합니다.	☐	☐	☐
2	새치기 하지 마.	☐	☐	☐
3	기온은 화요일에 가장 높을 것이다.	☐	☐	☐
4	이것으로 다른 장치를 조절할 수 있습니다.	☐	☐	☐
5	묶음 할인 판매를 하고 있어요.	☐	☐	☐
6	너는 장래에 무엇이 되고 싶니?	☐	☐	☐
7	제가 집에 역사 보고서를 두고 왔어요.	☐	☐	☐
8	금메달을 따기 위해서 제가 얼마나 더 빨리 달려야 하죠?	☐	☐	☐
9	무슨 일이니?	☐	☐	☐
10	배고프지 않니?	☐	☐	☐
11	무엇 때문에 돈을 모으려고 하니?	☐	☐	☐
12	토요일 오전마다 야구 연습이 있어요.	☐	☐	☐
13	언제 가는데?	☐	☐	☐
14	수업 전에 시간이 좀 있어.	☐	☐	☐
15	그녀는 언제 테니스를 배웠니?	☐	☐	☐
16	자동차 열쇠는 부엌 식탁 위에 있어요.	☐	☐	☐
17	길을 건너야 하나요?	☐	☐	☐
18	오늘 조부모님이 집에 오시기로 하셨어.	☐	☐	☐
19	그것에 얼마를 지불했니?	☐	☐	☐
20	야구 글러브나 축구공은 어때요?	☐	☐	☐

Step 2 듣고 따라 말하기

		1회	2회	3회
1	If you put water in this, the water turns into ice.	☐	☐	☐
2	Don't cut in line.	☐	☐	☐
3	The temperature will be the highest on Tuesday.	☐	☐	☐
4	You can constrol other devices with this.	☐	☐	☐
5	They're having a bundle sale.	☐	☐	☐
6	What do you want to be in the future?	☐	☐	☐
7	I left my history report at home.	☐	☐	☐
8	How fast do I have to run to win the gold medal?	☐	☐	☐
9	What's wrong with you?	☐	☐	☐
10	Don't you feel hungry?	☐	☐	☐
11	What do you want to save money for?	☐	☐	☐
12	I have baseball practice every Saturday morning.	☐	☐	☐
13	When are you leaving?	☐	☐	☐
14	I have a little bit of time before the class.	☐	☐	☐
15	When did she learn to play tennis?	☐	☐	☐
16	The car keys are on the table in the kitchen.	☐	☐	☐
17	Do I have to cross the street?	☐	☐	☐
18	My grandparents are coming home today.	☐	☐	☐
19	How much did you pay for it?	☐	☐	☐
20	How about a baseball glove or a soccer ball?	☐	☐	☐

고난도 영어듣기능력평가

만점 듣기 표현

Step 1 우리말 보면서 영어 듣기

		1회	2회	3회
1	이것은 긴 손잡이와 깊은 그릇이 달린 큰 숟가락처럼 생겼습니다.	☐	☐	☐
2	내 노트북이 망가졌어.	☐	☐	☐
3	오후에 비가 오겠습니다.	☐	☐	☐
4	좀 늦지만 어쩔 수 없네요.	☐	☐	☐
5	그녀는 나보다 한 살 많습니다.	☐	☐	☐
6	몇 시에 갈까?	☐	☐	☐
7	주말 잘 보냈니?	☐	☐	☐
8	이런 기회는 자주 오지 않는다.	☐	☐	☐
9	저희 서비스에도 만족하셨기를 바랍니다.	☐	☐	☐
10	오늘 아침 기분 안 좋아 보여.	☐	☐	☐
11	일요일에 야구경기를 같이 볼 수 있을까 궁금해서요.	☐	☐	☐
12	내일 축구 경기에서 보자.	☐	☐	☐
13	그 말을 들으니 마음이 놓이네요.	☐	☐	☐
14	오른쪽에 소방서가 보일 때까지 계속 걸으세요.	☐	☐	☐
15	재활용을 위한 이 플라스틱 통들도 버릴까요?	☐	☐	☐
16	긴 주말 동안 뭐 할 거야?	☐	☐	☐
17	내일 역사 시험이 있어.	☐	☐	☐
18	이 소포를 일본에 보낼 수 있을까요?	☐	☐	☐
19	나 거기 가본 적 있어.	☐	☐	☐
20	기회가 없었어.	☐	☐	☐

Step 2 듣고 따라 말하기

		1회	2회	3회
1	This looks like a large big spoon with a long handle and a deep bowl.	☐	☐	☐
2	My laptop is broken.	☐	☐	☐
3	It'll start to rain in the afternoon.	☐	☐	☐
4	It's a bit late, but I guess I can't help.	☐	☐	☐
5	She is one year older than me.	☐	☐	☐
6	What time would you like to go?	☐	☐	☐
7	Did you have a good weekend?	☐	☐	☐
8	A chance like this doesn't come often.	☐	☐	☐
9	I hope you're happy with our service, too.	☐	☐	☐
10	You look down this morning.	☐	☐	☐
11	I was wondering if we could watch a baseball game on Sunday.	☐	☐	☐
12	See you at the soccer game tomorrow.	☐	☐	☐
13	I feel so relieved to hear that.	☐	☐	☐
14	Keep walking until you see the fire station on your right.	☐	☐	☐
15	Should I take out these plastic bottles for recycling?	☐	☐	☐
16	What are you doing for the long weekend?	☐	☐	☐
17	We're going to have a test tomorrow in history.	☐	☐	☐
18	Can I send this package to Japan?	☐	☐	☐
19	I have been there.	☐	☐	☐
20	I haven't had a chance.	☐	☐	☐

중요 어휘 및 표현

24회 Plus Book

영어듣기능력평가 01 회

중요 어휘 및 표현

01	
□ spray	(분무기로) 뿌리다, 살포하다
□ mosquito	모기
□ protect A from B	A를 B로부터 보호하다
□ bite	물다; 물기, 물린 상처
□ wash	(물로) 씻다
02	
□ field trip	현장 학습
□ dress	옷을 입다
□ cool	멋진
□ comfortable	편안한
03	
□ weather	날씨
□ update	최신 정보
□ all over the country	전국적으로
□ eastern	동쪽의, 동부의
□ including	~을 포함하여
□ chilly	쌀쌀한, 추운
□ wash a car	세차하다
□ wet	젖은
04	
□ be going to	~할 예정이다
□ join	함께 하다
□ go to see a movie	영화 보러 가다
□ science	과학
□ exactly	꼭, 정확히
05	
□ only child	(형제자매가 없는) 외동아이
□ college	대학(교)
□ favorite	가장 좋아하는
□ Let's meet at ~.	~에서 만나자. (제안)
06	
□ lots of	많은
□ worry	걱정하다
□ leave	출발하다
□ enough	충분한
□ snack	간식
07	
□ lost and found	분실물 보관소
□ leave	남기다(-left-left)
□ get on	승차하다(↔get off 하차하다)
□ station	역
□ teddy bear	곰 인형, 테디 베어
□ zipper	지퍼
□ hold on	(전화를) 끊지 않고 기다리다
08	
□ fur	털
□ vegetable	채소
□ group	집단
09	
□ free time	여가 시간
□ end-of-semester party	학기말 파티
□ invite	초대하다
□ sibling	형제자매
□ responsibility	책임
□ invitation	초대장
□ information	정보
□ I would be glad to.	기꺼이.
10	
□ already	이미, 벌써
□ ring	(종이) 울리다
□ where to go	어디로 가야 할지
□ over there	저쪽에
□ lock	잠그다
□ new student	새로 온 학생
□ teachers' office	교무실
□ find out	알아내다
11	
□ move	이사하다, 이동하다
□ relative	친척
□ close	가까운, 친한
□ sometimes	가끔, 때때로

□ hometown	고향
□ play soccer	축구를 하다
12	
□ look well	좋아 보이다, 건강해 보이다
□ lunchtime	점심 시간
□ usuallly	보통, 대개
□ get up	(잠자리에서) 일어나다
□ scientist	과학자
□ brain	뇌
□ skip	거르다, 빼먹다
13	
□ order	주문하다
□ be tired of	~에 질리다
□ dessert	후식
□ kid	농담하다
14	
□ after school	방과 후에
□ practice	연습하다
□ festival	축제
□ October	10월
□ week	주
□ That's right.	맞아.
15	
□ package	소포
□ airmail	항공 우편
□ surface mail	(항공 우편이 아닌) 일반 우편
□ put on	~ 위에 놓다
□ scale	저울
□ weigh	무게가 ~ 나가다
□ cost	(가격이) ~이다
16	
□ look like	~할 것 같다, ~처럼 보이다
□ forecast	예측, 예상; 예보(예측)하다
□ wrong	틀린, 잘못된(↔ right)
□ look at	~을 보다
□ carry	가지고 다니다

□ insist	주장하다, 고집하다
17	
□ That sounds interesting.	재미있겠다.
□ have a race	경주하다
18	
□ down	(의기 등이) 침체하여
□ happen	(일이) 일어나다
□ serious	심각한
□ upset	속상한
□ get better	더 나아지다
□ try	노력하다
19	
□ jeans for ladies	여성용 청바지
□ row	줄, 열
□ particular	특별한, 독특한
□ decoration	장식
□ try on	입어 보다, 써 보다
□ fitting room	탈의실
20	
□ right now	지금, 당장
□ take a message	메시지를 받다
□ call back	다시 전화하다

영어듣기능력평가 02회 중요 어휘 및 표현

01	
□ draw	그리다
□ art class	미술 시간
□ country	시골
□ river	강
□ lake	호수
□ farm	농장
□ lots of	많은
□ sheep	양
□ feed	먹이를 주다
02	
□ bowl	그릇
□ counter	조리대
□ stove	가스레인지
□ next to	~ 옆에
□ sink	개수대
03	
□ It's time for ~.	~할 시간이다.
□ all over the country	전국적으로
□ including	~을 포함하여
□ island	섬
□ continue	계속되다, 지속하다
□ shower	소나기
□ southern	남쪽의, 남부의
□ province	(행정 단위) 도, 주
04	
□ in two weeks	2주일 후에
□ vacation	방학, 휴가
□ change one's mind	마음이 바뀌다
□ take a trip	여행하다
□ save	저축하다
□ enough	충분히; 충분한
05	
□ detective story	탐정 소설
□ take a picture	사진을 찍다
□ put on	착용하다, 입다(=wear)
□ ride	(자전거 등을) 타다
□ send	보내다
□ package	소포
□ scale	저울
06	
□ Where are you now?	지금 어디니?
□ almost	거의
□ pass	지나가다, 통과하다
□ City Hall	시청
□ take	(시간 등이) 걸리다
07	
□ would like to	~하고 싶다
□ order	주문하다
□ either A or B	A와 B 둘 중 하나
□ cost	(가격이) ~이다
□ free gift	사은품
□ How would you like to pay?	어떻게 지불하시겠어요?
08	
□ fuel	연료
□ hill	언덕
09	
□ in the future	미래에, 장래에
□ pro gamer	프로 게이머
□ be good at	~을 잘하다(↔ be poor at)
□ fashion designer	패션 디자이너
□ jewelry designer	보석 디자이너
10	
□ rubber tree	고무나무
□ You have a good memory.	기억력이 좋으시네요.
□ pot	화분, 냄비
□ Follow me, please.	따라 오세요.
□ inside	안에(↔ outside)
11	
□ difficult	어려운(↔ easy)
□ subject	과목

□ mathematics	수학(=math)
□ hobby	취미
□ just next to	~ 바로 옆에
□ local competition	지역 대회
12	
□ finish one's homework	숙제를 끝내다
□ as soon as	~하자마자
□ How about ~?	~은 어때?
□ a little bit	약간
□ clean	청소하다
□ messy	지저분한, 뒤범벅의
□ go out for dinner	저녁을 외식하다
13	
□ amusement park	놀이 공원
□ biology report	생물 보고서
□ volunteer	자원봉사자
□ senior center	양로원, 요양원
14	
□ forget	잊어버리다(↔remember)
□ the end of November	11월 마지막 날
□ just the next day	바로 그 다음 날
□ have a party	파티를 하다
15	
□ help	도움
□ worry	걱정하다
□ understand	이해하다
□ explain	설명하다
□ in class	수업 시간에
□ hand in	제출하다
16	
□ storeroom	창고
□ shelve	선반
□ newly-arrived	새롭게 들어온
□ item	물건
□ afterwards	그 후, 곧 이어
□ take a break	휴식을 취하다

17	
□ flu	독감
□ cough	기침하다
□ get rest	휴식을 취하다
18	
□ Kind of.	어느 정도는 그렇다.
□ boring	지루한
□ battle	전투
□ planet	행성
□ hang out with	~와 어울리다
19	
□ anyway	어쨌든
□ hurry up	서두르다
□ right away	지금 바로, 당장
□ check into the hotel	호텔 투숙 절차를 밟다, 호텔에서 체크인을 하다
20	
□ beginner	초보자
□ textbook	교과서, 교재
□ don't have to	~할 필요가 없다 (= need not)
□ for free	무료로, 공짜로
□ I'll take the course.	이 과정을 수강할게요.

영어듣기능력평가 03회

중요 어휘 및 표현

01	
□ postcard	엽서
□ nowadays	요즘
02	
□ memory	기억
□ stick	막대, 막대기
□ check	확인하다
□ under	~ 밑에, ~ 아래에
□ bookshelf	책장
□ put	~을 놓다, 두다
03	
□ weather report	일기예보
□ clear	맑은
□ sunny	햇빛이 비치는
□ have a great day	즐거운 하루를 보내다
□ outdoors	실외에서(↔indoors)
□ however	그러나
□ change to snow	눈으로 바뀌다
□ forget to	~할 것을 잊다
04	
□ city hall	시청
□ awesome	멋진
05	
□ send	보내다(-sent-sent)
□ invitation card	초대장
□ each of	~ 각자
06	
□ help A with B	A가 B하는 것을 돕다
□ take	시간이 걸리다
□ move	옮기다
□ heavy	무거운
□ lift	들어올리다
07	
□ medical clinic	의료 진료소
□ make an appointment	(병원에) 예약하다
□ patient	환자
□ at that time	그 시간에, 그때에
□ free	자유로운, 시간이 있는
□ Is that OK with you?	당신에게 괜찮습니까?
08	
□ subject	과목
□ history	역사
□ leave for	~를 향해 떠나다
□ How's it going?	어떻게 지내니?
□ these days	요즈음
□ go out for dinner	저녁을 외식하다
□ would love to	~하고 싶다
□ look tired	피곤해 보이다
□ stay up all night	밤새 (잠들지 않고) 깨어 있다
09	
□ road sign	도로 표지판
□ turn left	좌회전하다
□ navigation system	네비게이션 시스템
□ turn right	우회전하다
□ trust	믿다, 신뢰하다
□ parking lot	주차장
□ over there	저쪽에
10	
□ plan	계획
□ bother	성가시게 하다
□ stay	머무르다
□ miss	빠지다
□ later	나중에
11	
□ have a minute to talk	이야기할 시간이 조금 있다
□ hospital	병원
□ sing songs	노래를 부르다
□ patient	환자
□ join	함께 하다, 참여하다
□ guy	친구, 녀석
12	
□ family member	가족 구성원

□ watch	구경하다, 관람하다
□ nurse	간호사
□ every Sunday evening	매주 일요일 저녁
13	
□ What's up?	무슨 일이니?
□ need	~이 필요하다
□ Can you help me ~?	내가 ~하는 것 좀 도와줄래?
□ put up	붙이다
□ festival poster	축제 포스터
□ already	이미, 벌써
□ No problem.	물론이야.
14	
□ sofa	소파
□ Be careful.	조심하세요.
□ last	마지막의
□ move	옮기다, 이동시키다
□ everything else	다른 모든 것
□ You did a good job!	잘 했어요! (칭찬)
15	
□ lost	길을 잃은
□ convenience store	편의점
□ I got it.	알겠어.
16	
□ at the front seat	앞 자리에
□ pay attention to	~에 주의를 기울이다
□ take notes	노트 필기하다
□ during the class	수업 중에
□ lesson	수업
□ get a good grade	좋은 점수를 받다
17	
□ pretzel	프레첼(막대 모양 또는 B자 모양으로 묶은 크레커의 일종)
□ treat	간식
□ knot-like shape	매듭 모양
□ dough	반죽
□ roll	굴리다

□ string	끈, 줄
□ twist	꼬다
□ bake	굽다
18	
□ be over	끝나다
□ break	고장나다
□ hard	힘든
□ get mad	화를 내다
□ by mistake	실수로
□ accident	사고
□ rest	쉬다
19	
□ I'm afraid ~.	(유감이지만) ~인 것 같다.
□ gain weight	살이 찌다(↔lose weight)
□ need to exercise	운동할 필요가 있다
□ around	~ 주위에
□ park	공원
20	
□ arrive at	~에 도착하다
□ How about ~?	~는 어때?
□ bus driver	버스 기사

영어듣기능력평가 04회 중요 어휘 및 표현

01	
□ useful	쓸모 있는, 유용한
□ item	품목, 물품
□ save	저장하다
□ carry	가지고 다니다
□ anywhere	어느 곳이나
□ small enough to put in	~에 들어갈 만큼 충분히 작은
□ document	문서
□ connect	접속시키다, 연결하다
□ access	(컴퓨터에) 접속하다, 접근하다
□ click	(마우스를) 클릭하다
02	
□ wake up	(잠에서) 깨다
□ alarm	자명종 (시계)
□ turn off	전원을 끄다(↔ turn on)
□ wheel	바퀴
□ ring	울리다
□ roll around	굴러다니다
03	
□ weather forecaster	일기 예보관
□ mostly	대부분, 주로
□ cloudy	흐린
□ expect	예상하다, 기대하다
04	
□ go shopping	쇼핑하러 가다
□ dental	치과의
□ I'd really like to, but ~.	정말 그러고 싶지만 ~.
□ have an appointment	예약(약속)이 있다
05	
□ leg	다리
□ cast	깁스
□ go skiing	스키 타러 가다
□ slip	미끄러지다
□ on one's way	도중에
06	
□ movie	영화
□ funny	재미있는
□ fridge	냉장고
□ What does she do?	그녀는 직업이 뭐니?
07	
□ remember	기억하다(↔forget)
□ leave	떠나다
□ quarter	15분
□ past	지나서
□ pick up	태워주다
08	
□ What's up?	무슨 일이야?
□ ask A to B	A에게 B해 달라고 부탁하다
□ send	보내다
□ field trip	현장 학습
□ one more time	한 번 더
□ attachment	첨부 문서
□ not ~ at all	전혀 ~하지 않다
09	
□ wait for	~를 기다리다
□ gym	체육관(= gymnasium)
□ take a lesson	수업을 받다
□ Here comes ~.	~이 온다.
□ See you around.	(헤어질 때) 또 보자.
10	
□ enjoy	~을 즐기다
□ dinner	식사
□ spaghetti	스파게티
□ meal	끼니, 식사
□ tea	차
□ sugar	설탕
11	
□ insect	곤충
□ mosquito	모기
□ nectar	꿀
12	
□ take garbage out	쓰레기를 밖에 내다놓다

□ take much time	시간이 많이 걸리다
□ gym class	체육 수업
□ wash	(물로) 씻다
□ almost	거의
13	
□ borrow	빌리다
□ textbook	교과서
□ happen	(일이) 일어나다
□ totally wet	완전히 젖은
□ spill	엎지르다
□ dry	말리다
□ another	또 다른
14	
□ How can I get to ~?	~에 어떻게 가나요?
□ walk up(down)	죽 걸어가다
□ turn right	우회전하다
□ at the corner	모퉁이에서
□ bus stop	버스 정류장
□ across	~을 가로질러
15	
□ How long are you staying?	얼마나 머물 건가요?
□ city	도시
□ visit	방문하다
□ business meeting	업무 회의
□ Have a nice trip.	즐거운 여행 되세요.
16	
□ firefly	반딧불이
□ light up	빛을 내다
□ benefit	이점
□ scare	놀라게 하다
□ catch	잡다
□ bug	곤충
□ true	진정한
17	
□ invite	초대하다
□ be in hospital	입원하다
□ take care of	~를 돌보다
□ That's all right.	괜찮아.
18	
□ be tired	피곤해하다
□ take a nap	낮잠 자다
□ relieve	풀어 주다
□ stress	스트레스
□ more than	~ 이상
□ wake up	깨우다
19	
□ summer	여름
□ suggestion	제안, 제의
□ island	섬
□ last	지난
□ fantastic	환상적인
□ careful	조심하는, 주의 깊은
20	
□ department store	백화점
□ leave	떠나다
□ look after	~를 돌보다
□ exercise	운동
□ for a walk	산보 삼아(서)

영어듣기능력평가 05 회

중요 어휘 및 표현

01	
□ lake	호수
□ swim	수영하다
□ It'll be fun.	재미있을 거야.
□ look at	~을 보다
□ sign	게시판
□ say	(표지 등이) ~라고 쓰여 있다
02	
□ What about ~?	~하는 게 어때?
□ go bowling	볼링 치러 가다
□ have something to do	할 일이 있다
□ classmate	반 친구
03	
□ take a look at	~을 보다
□ area	지역
□ cloudy	구름이 낀, 흐린
□ cold	추운
□ carry	가지고 다니다, 운반하다
□ umbrella	우산
□ heavy rain	폭우, 많은 비
04	
□ move	이사 가다
□ family	가족
□ leave	떠나다
□ semester	학기
□ miss	그리워하다
05	
□ have to	~해야 한다
□ dress up	차려 입다
□ suit	정장
□ worth	~할 가치가 있는
□ any way	어쨌든
06	
□ package	소포
□ finally	드디어, 마침내
□ arrive	도착하다
□ almost	거의
□ I can't wait to ~.	나는 몹시 ~하고 싶다.
07	
□ look good	좋아 보이다
□ Nothing special.	특별한 일 없어.
□ score	점수
□ biology	생물
□ careless	부주의한
08	
□ busy	바쁜
□ clean	청소하다
□ get darker and darker	점점 더 어두워지다
□ It will rain soon.	곧 비가 올 거야.
□ seafood spaghetti	해산물 스파게티
□ for lunch	점심 식사로
□ That's a good idea!	좋은 생각이야!
□ post office	우체국
09	
□ too	너무나
□ messy	지저분한
□ clean	청소하다
□ extra	추가의
□ find	찾다
□ online	온라인으로
□ tonight	오늘 밤
□ through	~을 통해
□ the other day	요전 날
10	
□ sharp	정각에
□ in front of	~ 앞에
□ theater	극장
□ more than	~보다 많이, 이상
11	
□ electric	전기의
□ blade	날
□ ceiling	천장

12

□ I'm really full.	정말 배부르다.
□ not ~ anymore	더 이상 ~ 않다
□ delicious	맛있는
□ My pleasure.	천만에.
□ Let me wash the dishes.	설거지는 내가 할게.
□ rest	휴식하다, 쉬다

13

□ drugstore	약국
□ police station	경찰서

14

□ in the future	미래에, 장래에
□ jewelry designer	보석 디자이너
□ cool	멋진
□ novelist	소설가
□ be good at	~을 잘하다(↔be poor at)
□ writer	작가

15

□ wait for	~를 기다리다
□ take the train	기차를 타다
□ leave	출발하다, 떠나다
□ downstairs	아래층으로(↔upstairs)

16

□ tight	딱 맞는
□ try	입어보다
□ Hold on a second.	잠시만 기다리세요.

17

□ for a minute	잠시, 잠깐
□ be going to	~할 것이다, ~할 예정이다
□ have a day off	하루 휴가를 내다
□ airport	공항
□ instead of	~ 대신에
□ office	사무실

18

□ drive	운전하다
□ area	지역
□ map	지도
□ where+to부정사	어디로 ~할지
□ highway	고속도로

19

□ feel hungry	배고프다
□ wait	기다리다
□ make a sandwich	샌드위치를 만들다
□ a jar of	한 통의 ~
□ right away	곧바로, 즉시
□ cook	요리사

20

□ free ticket	무료 입장권
□ rock music	록 음악
□ a lot	많이
□ Don't mention it.	천만에.
□ What time does the concert start?	그 콘서트가 몇 시에 시작하니?

영어듣기능력평가 06 회

중요 어휘 및 표현

01	
□ make a wish	소원을 빌다
□ blow out	끄다
02	
□ draw	(그림을) 그리다
□ at first	처음에
□ change one's mind	~의 생각을 바꾸다
□ bottle	병
03	
□ weather forecast	일기예보
□ enough to	~할 만큼 충분히 …한
□ go out	외출하다
□ windy	바람이 부는
□ all day	하루 종일
□ take one's umbrella	우산을 가지고 가다
04	
□ need to	~할 필요가 있다
□ order	주문하다
□ meat	고기, 육류
□ have a barbecue party	바비큐 파티를 하다
□ I'll do it right away.	그것을 바로 할게요.
05	
□ tell one the way to	…에게 ~으로 가는 길을 알려 주다
□ turn right	우회전하다
□ on the left	왼쪽에
□ take lessons	수업을 듣다
□ Can I get you something to eat?	먹을 것 좀 가져다 드릴까요?
□ What time do you have?	몇 시죠?
□ invite	초대하다
06	
□ already	벌써, 이미
□ class	수업
□ kid	농담하다
□ later	이후에, 나중에
□ a bit	약간
07	
□ get better	좋아지다, 회복되다
□ cold	감기; 추운
□ I'm feeling better.	더 좋아지고 있어.
□ by the way	그런데, 그건 그렇고
□ math	수학(=mathematics)
□ solve	풀다
08	
□ look for	~을 찾다
□ at the corner	모퉁이에서
09	
□ university	대학교
□ What about you?	너는 어때?
□ major in	~을 전공하다
□ history	역사(학)
□ language	언어(학)
□ computer engineering	컴퓨터 공학
10	
□ reason	이유
□ share A with B	A를 B와 나누다, 공유하다
□ Guess what.	알아맞혀 봐.
□ get a good grade	좋은 점수를 받다
□ give a hint	힌트를 주다
□ win the first prize	일등상을 받다, 우승하다
□ book report contest	독후감 대회
□ exactly	정확히, 꼭
11	
□ first grade	1학년
□ join	가입하다, 합류하다
□ someday	언젠가
□ reporter	기자
□ interview	인터뷰하다
□ famous	유명한
□ play basketball	농구를 하다

□ on weekends	주말마다
□ sometime	언젠가
12	
□ hair is falling out	머리가 빠지다
□ wash one's hair	머리를 감다
□ every day	매일
□ once every two days	이틀에 한 번
□ change A into B	A를 B로 바꾸다
□ stop A from -ing	A가 ~하지 못하게 하다
13	
□ look for	~을 찾다
□ lose	잃어버리다(-lost-lost)
□ classroom	교실
□ leave	남기다, 놓다(-left-left)
□ Be careful.	주의하세요.
□ misplace	잘못 두다
14	
□ can't wait for	~을 무척 고대하다
□ sports day	체육대회, 운동회 날
□ Same here.	나도 그래. (동의)
□ What date is it today?	오늘이 며칠이니?
□ have five days to go	앞으로 5일 남았다
□ have fun	재미있는 시간을 보내다
15	
□ project	과제, 프로젝트
□ check	확인하다
□ already	이미, 벌써
□ check out the book	책을 대출하다
□ for a few days	며칠 동안
□ come back	돌아오다
□ I see.	알겠어요.
16	
□ field trip	현장 학습
□ weather forecast	일기 예보
17	
□ How do you feel today?	오늘 기분이 어떠세요?
□ stomachache	복통
□ medicine	약
□ headache	두통
□ not ~ anymore	더 이상 ~않다
18	
□ make copies	복사하다
□ document	서류
□ staple	~을 스테이플로 고정시키다
□ save	절약하다
19	
□ semester	학기
□ take French	불어를 수강하다
□ actually	사실
□ take a trip	여행하다
□ prepare for	~을 준비하다
20	
□ What's wrong with ~?	~에 대해 무엇이 잘못되었나요?
□ It doesn't start at all.	전혀 작동이 되지 않아요.
□ dust	먼지
□ repair shop	수리점, 정비 공장
□ vacuum out	진공청소기로 빨아내다
□ same	같은
□ experience	경험

영어듣기능력평가 07회

중요 어휘 및 표현

01	
□ instead of	~ 대신에
□ catch	잡다
□ lay an egg	알을 낳다
□ keep ~ warm	~을 따뜻하게 유지하다
□ hard work	힘든 일
□ thousands of	수천의
□ wing	날개
□ belly	배
02	
□ every morning	매일 아침
□ might not	~가 아닐지도 모른다
□ quickly	빨리
□ dry	말리다
□ sometimes	가끔, 때때로
□ use	사용하다
03	
□ another	또 하나의
□ rain shower	소나기
□ Let's hope ~.	~하기를 바랍시다.
□ cool down	식히다, 서늘해지다
04	
□ on weekends	주말마다
□ visit	방문하다
□ gym	체육관(=gymnasium)
□ go to church	식히다, 서늘해지다
05	
□ tower	탑
□ iconic	전통적인
□ symbol	상징
□ since	~이래로
□ more than	~ 이상
□ visitor	방문객
□ landmark	역사적 의의가 있는 건물
06	
□ Co.	회사(=Company)
□ draw	(그림을) 그리다
□ advertisement	광고
□ magazine	잡지
□ advertise	광고하다
□ sneakers	운동화
□ details	세부사항
□ review	검토하다
07	
□ borrow	빌리다
□ Here you go.	자, 여기 있어.
□ over	~ 이상
□ backpack	배낭
□ downtown	시내에서
□ sunny	맑은
08	
□ turn on	(전원을) 켜다(↔turn off)
□ document	서류, 문서
□ presentation file	발표 파일
□ September	9월
□ email	전자우편을 보내다
09	
□ get warmer	점점 더워지다
□ global warming	지구 온난화
□ issue	쟁점, 이슈
□ flood	홍수
□ drought	가뭄
□ all over the world	전 세계에
□ pollution	공해, 오염
□ reason	이유
□ agree with	~에 동의하다
□ protect	보호하다
10	
□ disturb	방해하다
□ careful	조심하는
11	
□ library	도서관

□ For what?	왜?, 무엇 때문에?
□ forget	잊어버리다(↔remember)
□ Just wait a minute.	잠깐만 기다려.
□ call	~에게 전화하다
□ be late for	~에 늦다
12	
□ as usual	언제나처럼
□ I can't believe it!	믿을 수 없어!
□ promise	약속하다
□ on time	정시에
□ No way.	말도 안 돼.
13	
□ call	전화 걸다
□ hang on	(전화를) 끊지 않고 기다리다
□ be ready to	~할 준비가 되다
□ partner	상대방, 짝
14	
□ information center	안내 센터
□ across from	~의 건너편에
□ police station	경찰서
□ cinema	극장
15	
□ firework	불꽃놀이
□ last	지속하다
□ usually	대개
□ schedule	예정하다
□ as long as	~하는 한
□ It depends.	상황에 따라 다르다.
16	
□ suddenly	갑자기
□ push	누르다
□ reset button	(컴퓨터 재부팅을 위한) 리셋 버튼
□ lose	잃어버리다(–lost–lost)
□ Do you mean ~?	~라는 말이니?
□ save	저장하다

17	
□ leave for	~를 향해 출발하다
□ address	주소
□ in time	시간에 맞춰서
□ drive	운전하다
□ traffic	교통
□ take the subway	지하철을 타다
□ advice	충고, 조언
18	
□ student library card	학생 도서 대출증
□ already	이미, 벌써
□ more than	~ 이상
□ at a time	한 번에
□ return	되돌려주다, 반납하다
19	
□ hold	잡고 있다, 유지하다
□ elevator	엘리베이터
□ floor	층
□ move in	이사 오다
20	
□ It's been a long time!	오랜만이다!
□ work at	~에서 일하다
□ bank	은행
□ manager	관리인
□ turn	차례

영어듣기능력평가 08회

중요 어휘 및 표현

01

□ usually	보통, 대개
□ bathroom	욕실
□ building	건물
□ shape	모양, 형태
□ rectangular	직사각형의, 직각의
□ once	일단 ~하면
□ soft	부드러운
□ especially	특히

02

□ forget	잊어버리다(↔remember)
□ chair	의자
□ beside	~ 옆에
□ flower vase	꽃병
□ between A and B	A와 B 사이에

03

□ move on	~로 이동하다
□ mostly	주로, 대부분
□ quite windy	바람이 많이 부는
□ finally	마침내, 마지막으로
□ weather forecast	일기예보

04

□ mammals	포유류
□ peel	껍질을 벗기다
□ clever	영리한
□ trunk	코

05

□ How long does it take ~?	~하는 데 (시간이) 얼마나 걸리나요?
□ from A to B	A부터 B까지
□ express way	고속도로
□ It's not that far.	그다지 멀지 않아요.

06

□ believe	믿다
□ bestseller	베스트셀러
□ Britain	영국
□ sold out	매진인
□ bookstore	서점
□ borrow	빌리다

07

□ on the way home	집에 오는 길에
□ forget	잊다

08

□ full	배가 부른
□ go bowling	볼링 치러 가다
□ lend	빌려 주다
□ What time shall we meet?	몇 시에 만날까?

09

□ hot	더운
□ crowded	붐비는
□ sit	앉다
□ guess	추측하다
□ sand	모래
□ tan	(피부를) 햇볕에 태우다
□ prefer	선호하다
□ salt water	바닷물

10

□ mall	쇼핑몰, 쇼핑센터
□ be closed	문을 닫다
□ lose	잃어버리다(–lost–lost)
□ wallet	지갑
□ on the way to	~로 가는 길에
□ I'm sorry to hear that.	안됐다.

11

□ skate	스케이트(를 타다)
□ elementary school	초등학교
□ take lessons	수업을 받다
□ more than	~ 넘게, ~ 이상
□ If you don't mind, ~	괜찮으시다면, ~
□ how to skate	스케이트 타는 법

12

□ introduce oneself	자신을 소개하다

□ be from	~ 출신이다
□ be born	태어나다
□ move	이사하다
□ since then	그때부터, 그때 이후로
□ hobby	취미
13	
□ be in hospital	입원해 있다
□ get in a car accident	자동차 사고를 입다
□ visit	병문안 가다
14	
□ think about	~에 대해 생각하다
□ announcer	아나운서
□ reporter	기자
□ dream	꿈
□ tour guide	여행 가이드, 관광 안내원
□ travel	여행하다
□ all around the world	전 세계로
15	
□ look healthy	건강해 보이다
□ Thank you for ~.	~해서 고마워.
□ secret	비밀, 비결
□ stay healthy	건강을 유지하다
□ Please let me know it.	그것을 알려 주세요.
□ jog	조깅하다, 달리기하다
□ tip	조언
16	
□ free ticket	무료 입장권
□ on that day	그 날에
□ ask	물어보다, 요청하다
□ another	또 하나의
17	
□ T-Rex	티아노사우루스 렉스
□ blood	혈액
□ cell	세포
□ protein	단백질
□ similar to	~와 비슷한
□ dinosaur	공룡
□ closest	가장 가까운
□ relative	친척
□ alligator	악어
□ lizard	도마뱀
□ chicken	닭
18	
□ be interested in	~에 관심이 있다
□ learn	배우다
□ academy	학원
□ wait for	~를 기다리다
□ lots of	많은(=a lot of)
□ once	일단 ~하면
19	
□ excited	들뜬, 흥분된
□ look happy	행복해 보이다
□ at the beach	해변에서
□ climb up	~에 오르다
20	
□ favorite	가장 좋아하는
□ once	예전에
□ elementary school student	초등학생
□ That's a great idea.	좋은 생각이야.(동의)

영어듣기능력평가 09회

중요 어휘 및 표현

01	
□ quite	꽤
□ story	층
□ enough	충분한
□ breath	숨, 호흡
□ fresh	신선한
02	
□ raise one hand	한 손을 들다
□ beside the chair	의자 옆에
□ for a moment	잠시 동안
□ look at	~을 보다
□ in the air	허공에, 공중에
□ take a picture	사진을 찍다
03	
□ thick fog	짙은 안개
□ area	지역
□ go away	사라지다
□ around the noon	정오 무렵에
□ a little bit	약간의
□ wind	바람
□ be sure to	반드시 ~하다
□ wear coat	외투를 입다
04	
□ laboratory	실험실
□ blood	혈액
□ take care of	~을 처리하다
□ pharmacist	약사
□ dispense	조제하다
□ prescription	처방전
□ medicine	약
□ over-the-counter	의사의 처방 없이 팔 수 있는
□ office work	사무 일
05	
□ choose	선택하다
□ club	동아리
□ I'm thinking of	~에 대해 생각 중이다
□ take a trip	여행하다
□ all over the country	전국적으로
06	
□ as usual	평상시처럼
□ Can I have your name?	성함을 말씀해 주시겠어요?
□ Why don't we ~?	~하는 게 어때?
□ go see a movie	영화 보러 가다
□ tonight	오늘 밤
□ ticket	표, 입장권
□ sold out	매진된
07	
□ arrive	도착하다
□ yet	아직
□ call	전화하다
□ left	남은
08	
□ May I speak to ~?	(전화) ~를 바꿔 주시겠어요?
□ Speaking.	(전화) 접니다.
□ place	집, 장소
□ solve	풀다, 해결하다
□ math problem	수학 문제
□ I'll be there soon.	곧 그곳으로 갈게.
09	
□ public place	공공장소
□ require	요구하다
□ put out	끄다
10	
□ project	프로젝트
□ build	만들다
□ miniature	축소 모형
□ electricity	전기
□ research	연구, 조사
□ look up	~을 찾아 보다
11	
□ public place	공공장소
□ require	공공장소

□ put out	끄다
12	
□ understand	이해하다
□ lesson	수업
□ give up	포기하다
□ get a good grade	좋은 성적을 받다
□ take good notes	필기를 잘 하다
□ follow	이해하다, 알아듣다
13	
□ What can I help you with?	무엇을 도와드릴까요?
□ bring	가지고 오다
□ bowl	그릇, 통
□ feel terrible	기분이 매우 나쁘다
14	
□ go straight one block	한 블록 곧장 가다
□ turn left	좌회전하다
□ on the right	오른편에
□ across from	~ 맞은편에
□ next to	~ 옆에
15	
□ leave	떠나다, 출발하다
□ come back	돌아오다
□ stay	머무르다
□ until	~까지
□ the same week	같은 주
□ have a good time	즐거운 시간을 보내다
16	
□ stuffy	답답한
□ turn on	(전원을) 켜다(↔turn off)
□ air conditioner	에어컨
□ perfect	완벽한
□ prefer	선호하다
□ fan	선풍기
□ anyway	어쨌든
17	
□ thirty minutes late	30분 늦은
□ mistake	실수
□ terribly	대단히, 몹시
□ go into	들어가다
□ theater	극장
18	
□ tie	넥타이
□ stain	얼룩
□ extra	여분의
□ cleaner	세탁소
□ borrow	빌리다
□ wear	입다, 착용하다
19	
□ for a minute	잠시 동안
□ take out	가지고 나가다, 가지고 가다
□ garbage bag	쓰레기 봉투
□ front	앞
□ That's no problem.	그것은 문제가 되지 않아요.
□ right away	즉시
20	
□ have nothing to do	할 일이 없다
□ paint	페인트칠 하다
□ the front door	앞문, 정문
□ look old	낡아 보이다
□ diligent	부지런한
□ paintbrush	페인트 붓

영어듣기능력평가 10회

중요 어휘 및 표현

01	
□ plant	(식물을) 심다
□ water	물을 주다
□ pick	(꽃, 과일 등을) 따다
□ carry	나르다, 운반하다
□ flowerpot	화분
02	
□ kitten	아기 고양이
□ hamster	햄스터
□ pet	애완동물
□ puppy	강아지
03	
□ weather center	기상청
□ peninsula	반도
□ expect	예상하다, 기대하다
□ southeastern	남동쪽의
□ in the late afternoon	오후 늦게
04	
□ ticket booth	매표소
□ take the subway	지하철을 타다
□ far from	~에서 먼
□ Why don't we ~?	~하는 게 어때?(제안)
□ expensive	비싼(↔cheap)
□ pay	지불하다
05	
□ speaker	연설자
□ nervous	긴장된, 초조한
□ as soon as	~하자마자
□ stand the stage	무대에 서다
□ practice	연습하다
□ clearly	분명하게
□ fast	빨리
□ Go for it!	힘 내!, 파이팅!
06	
□ have a fever	열이 있다
□ go straight	~로 곧장 가다
□ What if ~?	~라면 어쩌죠?
□ H1N1	신종 인플루엔자
□ take medicine	약을 먹다
□ take good care of	~를 잘 돌보다
07	
□ fix a car	차를 고치다
□ garage	주차장, 차고
□ carry	옮기다
□ heavy	무거운(↔light)
□ clothes	옷, 의복
□ inside	~의 안에(↔outside)
□ take long	(시간이) 오래 걸리다
08	
□ playground	운동장, 놀이터
□ climb up	~을 오르다
09	
□ documentary	다큐멘터리
□ nature	자연
□ perfer	선호하다
□ history	역사
□ a lot	많이
□ recommend	추천하다
10	
□ message	메시지, 문자
□ practice	연습(하다)
□ leave	떠나다, 출발하다
□ in 30 minutes	30분 후에
□ finish	끝마치다
11	
□ pack	꾸러미, 한 상자
□ copy paper	복사 용지
□ wrapping paper	포장지
□ change	거스름돈, 잔돈
12	
□ flour	밀가루
□ fridge	냉장고

□ cupboard	찬장
13	
□ tour guide	관광 안내원
□ arrive	도착하다
□ in front of	~ 앞에
□ botanical garden	식물원
□ get off	하차하다, 내리다(↔get on)
□ water bottle	물병
14	
□ What kind of job do you want to have?	어떤 직업을 갖고 싶니?
□ actor	배우
□ just like	~와 똑같은
□ interest	관심, 관심사
□ medicine	의학, 약
15	
□ check in	입실하다(↔check out)
□ reservation	예약
□ single	1인실
□ correct	옳은
□ key card	키 카드
16	
□ free time	여가 시간
□ have in mind	염두에 두다
□ housewarming party	집들이
□ in for repair	수리중인
□ department store	백화점
17	
□ prescription	처방전
□ wait for a moment	잠시 기다리다
□ medicine	약
□ band-aid	반창고
□ syrup	물약, 시럽
□ four times a day	하루에 네 번
□ pill	알약
□ after meal	식후에

□ including	~을 포함하여
18	
□ neighbor	이웃
□ keep -ing	계속 ~하다
□ blow	불다
□ garbage	쓰레기
□ discuss	논의하다
□ fence	울타리
□ shy	부끄러워하는
19	
□ actually	사실
□ because of	~ 때문에
□ Why not?	왜 안 되는데?
□ present	선물
20	
□ welcome to	~에 온 것을 환영하다
□ join a club	동아리에 가입하다
□ look like	~처럼 보이다
□ second grade	2학년
□ only child	외동아이

영어듣기능력평가 11회

중요 어휘 및 표현

01	
□ favorite	가장 좋아하는
□ outdoor activity	야외 활동
□ unlike	~와는 달리
□ such as	~와 같은
□ a pair of shoes	신발 한 켤레
□ health	건강
□ climb up	~에 오르다
□ reach the top of	~의 정상에 오르다
□ refreshed	기분이 상쾌한
02	
□ sandal	샌들
□ plan to	~할 계획이다
□ beach	해변
□ trip	여행
□ sneakers	운동화
□ dry	마르다
□ quickly	빨리
□ wear	입다, 신다
□ cover	감싸다
□ take	선택하다, 사다
03	
□ take a look at	~을 한 번 보다
□ area	지역, 영역
□ strong chance	높은 확률, 높은 가능성
□ partly	부분적으로
04	
□ be ready	준비가 되다
□ bookstore	서점
□ magazine	잡지
□ next to	~ 옆에
05	
□ try	~을 먹어 보다, 시도하다
□ spicy	매운
□ How many days ~?	며칠 동안 ~?
□ It will rain soon.	곧 비가 올 거야.
□ umbrella	우산
06	
□ book a ticket	표를 예매하다
□ flight	항공편
□ Let me check.	확인해 볼게요.
□ depart	출발하다, 떠나다
□ one ~, the other ...	(둘 중) 하나는 ~, 나머지 하나는 …
07	
□ rainbow	무지개
□ through the Internet	인터넷으로, 인터넷을 통해서
□ reservation number	예약 번호
□ single room	1인실
□ cancel	취소하다
08	
□ dry-clean	드라이클리닝하다
□ cost	(비용이) ~ 나가다, (가격이) ~이다
□ pay	지불하다
□ get back	되찾다
□ Let me know your name.	성함을 알려 주세요.
09	
□ presentation	발표, 프레젠테이션
□ history	역사
□ be happy to	~하게 되어 기쁘다
□ be good at	~을 잘하다
□ slide	슬라이드
□ learn	배우다
10	
□ Nice to meet you!	만나서 반가워!
□ Don't be surprised.	놀라지 마.
□ get a part-time job	아르바이트 일자리를 구하다
□ Congratulations.	축하해.
11	
□ stream	개울
□ smooth	부드러운

12	
□ fortunately	다행히도
□ don't have to	~할 필요가 없다(=need not)
□ have any teeth pulled out	이를 뽑다
□ relief	안도, 안심
□ brush one's teeth	양치질을 하다
□ otherwise	그렇지 않으면
□ in trouble	곤경에 빠져서
□ advice	충고, 조언
13	
□ online	온라인으로(↔off-line)
□ book	예약하다
□ play	연극
□ Enjoy the play.	연극 즐겁게 관람하세요.
14	
□ go on a business trip	출장 가다
□ stay	머무르다
□ come back	돌아오다
15	
□ crowded	복잡한, 붐비는
□ enjoy	즐기다
□ everyone	모든 사람
□ just like	꼭 ~처럼
□ decide	결심하다, 결정하다
□ drink	음료수
□ That's what I want to see.	내가 보고 싶은 것이 바로 그거야.
16	
□ look excited	흥분되어 보이다
□ go fishing	낚시하러 가다
□ Why don't you ~?	~하는 게 어때?
□ volunteer work	자원봉사 활동
□ orphanage	고아원
17	
□ topic	주제
□ electric current	전류
18	
□ How can I help you?	무엇을 도와드릴까요?
□ Britain	영국
□ send	보내다
□ inside	안에
□ scale	저울
□ take	(시간이) 걸리다
19	
□ clean	청소하다
□ because of	~ 때문에
□ right after	~하자마자 바로
□ be going to	~할 예정이다
20	
□ altogether	모두 합해서
□ How would you like to pay?	어떻게 지불하시겠어요?
□ pay in cash	현금으로 지불하다

영어듣기능력평가 12회

중요 어휘 및 표현

01	
□ key chain	열쇠 고리
□ decide	결정하다
□ What do you think of ~?	~에 대해 어떻게 생각하니?
□ middle school student	중학생
□ picture frame	사진 액자
02	
□ in the middle of	~의 중앙에
□ in front of	~ 앞에
□ usually	보통
□ happy with	~가 마음에 드는
□ put ~ away	~을 치우다
□ plant	식물, 작은 나무
□ next to	~ 옆에
□ three-tiered	3단의
□ bookshelf	책꽂이
03	
□ snowstorm	눈보라
□ bring	~을 초래하다, ~을 데려오다
□ have a hard time -ing	~하는 데 어려움을 겪다
□ clean up	~을 치우다, 청소하다
□ continue	계속하다
□ outdoor activity	야외 활동
04	
□ electric machine	전기기기
□ suck	빨아들이다
□ dust	먼지
05	
□ first time	처음
□ close	가까운, 친한
□ be good at	~을 잘하다
□ trouble	고민거리, 문제
□ in the future	미래에, 장래에
□ counselor	상담가
06	
□ hurry	서두르다
□ get on	~에 타다
□ next place	다음 장소
□ famous	유명한
□ area	지역
□ explain	설명하다
□ history	역사
□ castle	성
□ tour	여행, 관광
07	
□ work for	~에서 일하다
□ company	회사
□ partly cloudy	부분적으로 흐린
□ a little bit of	약간의 ~
□ headache	두통
□ go out for dinner	저녁을 외식하다
08	
□ have a good time	즐거운 시간을 보내다
□ especially	특히
□ guide	안내, 여행 안내원; 안내하다
□ address	주소
□ Why not?	그럴게. (동의)
□ in a few weeks	몇 주 후에
09	
□ break	휴식, 쉬는 시간
□ memorize	암기하다
□ essay	에세이
□ use	사용하다
□ dictionary	사전
□ much	훨씬
□ make sense	말이 되다
□ borrow	빌리다
□ library	도서관
□ return	반납하다
10	
□ train station	기차역
□ take a bus	버스를 타다

□ intersection	교차로
11	
□ ride	(자전거 등을) 타다(–rode–ridden)
□ for a few months	몇 달 동안
□ work well	작동이 잘 되다
□ Let me check.	내가 점검할게.
□ It will help.	그것이 도움이 될 것이다.
□ a cup of	한 잔의 ~
12	
□ break	부러지다
□ jump	뛰어넘다
□ fence	울타리
□ parking lot	주차장
□ successful	성공적인
□ dangerous	위험한
□ hard way	고생해서
13	
□ homework	숙제
□ be in hospital	입원하다
□ take care of	~를 돌보다
□ Sorry to hear that.	그 말을 들으니 유감이다.
14	
□ company	회사
□ go straight	직진하다, 곧장 가다
□ along	~을 따라
□ on the left	왼편에
□ right across	~의 바로 건너편에
15	
□ plane	비행기(=airplane)
□ leave for	~로 떠나다
□ airport	공항
□ I can't wait ~.	나는 몹시 ~하고 싶다.
16	
□ artistic	예술적인
□ write	쓰다
□ believe	믿다

17	
□ capital	수도
□ travel	여행하다
□ more than	~ 이상
□ language	언어
□ be known as	~로 알려지다
□ host	개최하다
□ latest	최근의
□ underground	(the) 지하철
18	
□ sound	~하게 들리다
□ be over	끝나다
□ schedule	스케줄, 일정
□ last	마지막의
□ appointment	약속
19	
□ give ~ a ride	~를 차로 태워다 주다
□ My pleasure.	천만에요.
□ hard	힘든
□ mind	싫어하다, 꺼리다
□ turn off	(전원을) 끄다(↔turn on)
20	
□ how to play	경기하는 방법
□ actually	사실
□ have a wonderful time	아주 재미있는 시간을 보내다
□ get started	시작하다

영어듣기능력평가 13회

중요 어휘 및 표현

01

□ strong	강한
□ pouch	주머니
□ stomach	복부

02

□ leave	두다, 놓다(-left-left)
□ ring	(벨이) 울리다
□ in front of	~앞에

03

□ update	최신 정보
□ be able to	~할 수 있다(=can)
□ full moon	보름달
□ temperature	온도, 기온
□ go up	오르다
□ degree	(온도계의) 도
□ foggy	안개가 낀
□ throughout	~의 전체에 걸쳐

04

□ class	수업
□ bookstore	서점
□ get a cold	감기에 걸리다
□ see a doctor	병원에 가다
□ do one's homework	숙제하다
□ set the table	식탁을 차리다

05

□ leave	~을 두고 오다(left-left)
□ reservation	예약

06

□ tournament	토너먼트
□ select	선발하다
□ at least	적어도
□ homeroom teacher	담임선생님
□ final match	결승전
□ school sports day	체육대회

07

□ How about -ing?	~하는 게 어때?
□ pool	수영장
□ before	~ 전에(↔after)
□ a lot of	많은
□ make it	시간에 맞추어 도착하다
□ close	문을 닫다(↔open)

08

□ have a seat	자리에 앉다, 착석하다
□ take one's order	주문을 받다
□ stand in line	줄을 서다
□ look for	~을 찾다, 구하다
□ near	가까운
□ around	가까이에
□ corner	모퉁이
□ season	계절

09

□ rent	집세
□ expensive	비싼
□ have a look	한번 보다

10

□ a couple of	한두 개의 ~, 몇몇의 ~
□ because of	~ 때문에
□ storytelling	이야기하기
□ historical	역사적인
□ event	사건

11

□ look	~하게 보이다
□ final exam	기말고사
□ be (just) around the corner	코앞에 있는, 목전에 있는
□ look forward to	~을 학수고대하다
□ I can't wait.	너무 기대돼.

12

□ library	도서관
□ subway	지하철
□ You'd better ~.	~하는 게 더 낫다.
□ if you are in a hurry	급하다면

□ take a taxi	택시를 타다

13

□ take a picture	사진을 찍다
□ place	장소
□ anyway	어쨌든
□ whole	전체의
□ press	누르다
□ count	계산

14

□ at a bad time	난처한 때에, 안 좋은 때에
□ ghost	영혼, 유령
□ ask for	~을 요청하다, 부탁하다
□ look for	~을 찾다

15

□ be interested in	~에 흥미가 있다
□ sick	아픈
□ take care of	~를 돌보다
□ medicine	약
□ assist	도와주다
□ operating room	수술실
□ job	직업

16

□ pack	짐을 싸다
□ almost	거의
□ leave	출발하다
□ arrive at	~에 도착하다
□ around	~경, 쯤
□ alarm	자명종

17

□ department store	백화점
□ safety	안전
□ be not allowed	허용되지 않다
□ anywhere	아무데도
□ be located	(~에) 위치하고 있다
□ pet	애완동물
□ comfortable	편안한
□ cooperation	협조

18

□ be in the hospital	입원하다
□ weak	약한(↔ strong)
□ give up	포기하다
□ three times a week	일주일에 세 번
□ swimmer	수영 선수, 수영하는 사람

19

□ button	버튼
□ push	누르다
□ click	'찰칵'하는 소리
□ photographer	사진사
□ don't have to	~할 필요가 없다
□ expensive	비싼
□ Pardon?	뭐라고 하셨죠?

20

□ check	확인하다
□ last time	마지막
□ shiny	반짝이는
□ sure	틀림없는

영어듣기능력평가 14회

중요 어휘 및 표현

01	
□ make a snowman	눈사람을 만들다
□ beach	해변
□ brush one's teeth	양치질을 하다
□ watch	~을 시청하다, 보다
02	
□ take a picture	사진을 찍다
□ in front of	~ 앞에
□ sculpture	조각상
□ look at	~을 보다
□ sign	게시판
□ Thank you for ~.	~ 해줘서 고마워.
03	
□ mainly	주로, 전반적으로
□ cloudy	흐린
□ strong wind	강풍
□ chance	확률
□ thunderstorm	천둥을 동반한 폭우
□ expect	예상하다, 기대하다
□ shower	소나기
□ continue	계속되다
04	
□ together	함께
□ anything	어떤 것
□ special	특별한
□ Italian	이탈리아의; 이탈리아인
□ It'll rain soon.	곧 비가 올 거야.
□ wait a minute	잠깐 기다리다
□ umbrella	우산
05	
□ various	다양한
□ beverage	음료
□ choose	선택하다
06	
□ last weekend	지난 주말
□ look excited	들떠 보이다
□ have a seat	자리에 앉다, 착석하다
□ What made ~?	왜 ~?
□ have a cold	감기에 걸리다
□ finish	끝마치다
□ biology	생물
07	
□ come back	돌아오다
□ trip	여행
□ stay	머무르다
□ visit	방문하다
□ cancel	취소하다
08	
□ during	~ 동안에
□ That's why ~.	그것이 ~하는 이유이다.
□ if you don't mind	괜찮으시다면
□ borrow	빌리다
□ lend	빌려주다
09	
□ have a runny nose	콧물이 나오다
□ fever	열
□ temperature	체온, 온도
□ degree	(온도계의) 도
□ serious	심각한, 진지한
□ take medicine	약을 먹다
□ have a good rest	편히 쉬다
□ get better	나아지다
10	
□ vacation	방학
□ fly	시간이 빨리 흐르다(flew-flown)
11	
□ would like to	~하고 싶다
□ instead	대신에
□ leave	떠나다, 출발하다
□ one ~, another ..., and the other ~	하나는 ~, 다른 하나는 …, 나머지 하나는 ~

12	
□ park	주차하다
□ parking area	주차 구역
□ look for	~을 찾다.
□ right away	지금 바로
13	
□ stop -ing	~하는 것을 멈추다
□ check	확인하다
□ every other	하나 걸러 (두 번마다 한 번씩)
□ keep -ing	계속 ~하다
□ touch	만지다
14	
□ pet	애완동물
□ have a fever	열이 있다
□ since	~ 이래로
□ first	먼저, 우선
□ hold on	붙잡다
□ for a moment	잠깐 동안
15	
□ Thank you for coming.	와줘서 고마워.
□ full	배가 부른
16	
□ look happy	행복해 보이다
□ get a phone call	전화를 받다
□ a minute ago	방금 전에
□ older brother	오빠, 형
□ must	~임에 틀림없다
17	
□ feel all right	(몸 상태가) 좋다
□ soar throat	목이 부은 상태
□ hurt	아프다
□ every time	~할 때마다
□ swallow	삼키다
□ tea	차
□ cold	감기
□ drink	음료수

18	
□ homeroom teacher	담임선생님
□ like	~같은
□ graduate from	~를 졸업하다
□ senior	상급생, 선배(↔junior)
□ especially	특히
□ detective story	탐정 소설
□ more than	~ 이상(=over)
□ lend	빌려 주다
19	
□ Can I ask you a favor?	부탁 하나 해도 되나요?
□ use	사용하다
□ take a trip	여행하다
□ broken	고장 난
□ at the moment	현재, 지금
20	
□ answer	대답하다, 응답하다
□ maybe	아마도
□ while	~하는 동안에
□ interesting	재미있는, 흥미있는
□ enjoy	즐기다

영어듣기능력평가 15회

중요 어휘 및 표현

01	
□ invitation card	초대장
□ in the middle	중앙에, 가운데에
□ have a big smile	활짝 웃다
□ tooth	이빨, 치아
□ under one's face	~의 얼굴 아래에
02	
□ light	전등
□ bright	밝은
□ enough	충분히
□ wallpaper	벽지
□ bookshelf	책꽂이
□ desktop computer	데스크톱 컴퓨터(*cf.* laptop computer 노트북 컴퓨터)
03	
□ a little bit of	약간의 ~
□ forget+to부정사	~할 것을 잊다
□ take one's umbrella	우산을 가져가다
□ have a strong wind	강한 바람이 불다
□ all afternoon	오후 내내
04	
□ coin	동전
□ postcard	우편엽서
□ travel around the world	전 세계를 여행하다
□ collect	수집하다, 모으다
□ stamp	우표
05	
□ Can I ask you a favor?	부탁 하나 해도 될까요?
□ pet dog	애완견
□ allergy	알레르기, 이상 민감증
□ fur	(동물의) 털
□ sick	아픈
06	
□ dance contest	춤 경연대회
□ make mistakes	실수하다
□ prepare	준비하다
□ hard	열심히
□ move	움직이다, 이사하다
07	
□ migrant	이주민
□ worker	노동자
□ volunteer	자원하다
□ take care of	~를 돌보다
08	
□ cost	(값이) ~이다, (비용이) ~들다
□ May I have your order?	주문하시겠어요?
□ recommend	추천하다
□ on foot	걸어서
□ look good	좋아 보이다
□ have a cold	감기에 걸리다
□ What can I call you?	당신을 뭐라고 부를까요?
09	
□ island	섬
□ by plane	비행기로
□ take a ship	배를 타다
□ fun	재미있는
□ even though	비록 ~일지라도
□ take	(시간이) 걸리다
10	
□ call	전화하다
□ leave	떠나다, 출발하다
□ wrong	틀린, 잘못된
11	
□ the same A as B	B와 같은 A
□ expensive	비싼
□ pay for	대금을 지불하다
□ discount	할인, 할인액
□ Good for you.	좋겠다., 잘됐다.
12	
□ communication	통신, 의사소통
□ company	회사

□ May I speak to ~?	~와 통화할 수 있을까요?
□ go out	외출하다
□ be back	돌아오다
□ leave a message	메시지를 남기다
□ call back	다시 전화하다
13	
□ event	행사
□ finish	끝나다
□ free for	~에게 무료인
□ opportunity	기회
□ each other	(둘 사이)서로서로
14	
□ look	~하게 보이다
□ lense	렌즈
□ heavy	무거운
□ camera man	카메라맨
□ report	기사
□ take pictures	사진을 찍다
□ cook	요리사
□ magazine	잡지
□ dish	음식
□ taste	맛 보다
15	
□ grocery store	식료품점
□ keep	보관하다
□ boil	끓이다
□ ingredient	재료
□ shell	껍질
16	
□ class	수업
□ begin	시작하다
□ later	뒤에
□ teach	가르치다
17	
□ It's time to ~.	~할 시간이다.
□ pick up	(차로) 태우러 가다
□ these days	요즈음
□ be interested in	~에 관심이 있다
□ be proud of	~를 자랑스러워하다
18	
□ help A with B	A가 B하는 것을 돕다
□ book report	독후감
□ cousin	사촌
□ city	도시
□ guide	안내하다
19	
□ gym	체육관
□ volleyball	배구
□ practice	연습(하다)
□ serve	서브(하는 법)
□ match	시합, 경기
□ mistake	실수
□ perfect	완벽한
□ suit	~에게 맞추다
□ spirit	정신
□ It serves you right.	자업자득이다.
20	
□ interview	면접, 인터뷰
□ a lot of	많은(=lots of)
□ nervous	긴장한, 초조한
□ at that time	그 당시에
□ Don't worry.	걱정하지 마.

영어듣기능력평가 16회

중요 어휘 및 표현

01	
□ on the wall	벽에
□ date	날짜
□ holiday	공휴일, 휴가
□ circle	동그라미(를 그리다)
02	
□ fish tank	수족관
□ guppy	구피(송사릿과의 열대어)
□ algae	말, 조류(藻類)
□ eater	부식물
□ algae eater	청소 물고기
□ bottom	바닥
□ hide	숨다
□ behind	~ 뒤에
□ water plant	수초
□ beside	~ 옆에
□ shell	조개껍질
03	
□ temperature	온도, 기온
□ average	평균; 평균의
□ drop down	(기온이) 떨어지다, 내려가다
□ through the whole country	전국적으로
04	
□ quite	꽤, 상당히
□ finish	끝마치다
□ go shopping	쇼핑 가다
□ send	보내다
05	
□ Are we there yet?	다 왔나요?
□ pay for	대금을 지불하다
□ turn off the volume	소리를 낮추다
□ turn on	(전원을) 켜다
□ big fan	열성팬
06	
□ How long ~?	얼마나 오래 ~?
□ get to	~에 도착하다
□ station	역, 정거장
□ around	대략, ~쯤
□ look at	~을 보다
□ traffic	교통(량)
□ leave	떠나다, 출발하다
□ make it	시간에 맞추어 도착하다
07	
□ get better	좋아지다, 회복되다
□ visit	병문안 가다
□ Of course.	물론이지.
08	
□ look like	~인 것처럼 보이다
□ aquarium	수족관
09	
□ be interested in	~에 관심이 있다
□ chef	주방장
□ producer	제작자, 생산자
□ actually	사실은, 실제로
□ talk show host	토크 쇼 진행자
10	
□ everyone	모든 사람
□ conversation	회화, 대화
□ first name	이름
□ want to	~하기를 원하다
□ racquetball	라켓볼
11	
□ clubroom	동아리방
□ practice	연습(하다)
□ nobody	아무도 ~ 없다
□ text message	문자 메시지
□ This is not right.	이건 옳지 않아.
□ agree	동의하다
12	
□ Bless you.	몸조심 하세요., 저런.
□ still	아직도, 여전히

□ wet	젖은, 축축한(↔dry)
□ wash	(물로) 씻다
□ frozen	언, 냉동한
□ keep sneezing	계속 재채기하다
□ dry	말리다, 건조시키다
□ use	사용하다
13	
□ rafting	래프팅
□ raft	뗏목
□ exciting	흥분한
□ famous	유명한
□ outside	밖에서(↔inside)
□ cave	동굴
□ beach	바닷가
14	
□ vacation	방학, 휴가
□ just around the corner	바로 근처에, 임박하여
□ during	~ 동안에
□ begin	시작하다
□ You're right.	맞아.
□ That's too bad.	정말 안됐다.
□ not ~ at all	전혀 ~ 아니다
15	
□ repair shop	수리점
□ past	지나서
16	
□ dead	작동을 하지 않는, 죽은
□ battery	건전지, 배터리
□ run out	다 쓰다, 다 떨어지다
□ pay phone	공중전화
17	
□ meal	식사
□ check	살펴보다
□ washroom	화장실
18	
□ take	가지고 가다
□ rainy	비오는
□ get wet	젖다
□ a pair of	한 켤레의 ~
□ rain boots	장화
19	
□ on a diet	다이어트 중인
□ lose weight	살을 빼다(↔gain weight)
20	
□ join	가입하다
□ get into	~에 들어가다
□ seem to	~인 것 같다
□ audition	오디션

영어듣기능력평가 17회

중요 어휘 및 표현

01	
□ block	가리다, 차단하다
□ decorate	장식하다
□ cozy	아늑한
□ fabric	천
02	
□ at last	드디어, 마침내
□ miss	그리워하다
□ by the way	그런데(화제 전환)
□ postcard	우편엽서
03	
□ continue	계속되다, 지속되다
□ around midnight	자정 무렵
□ rainfall	강수량
□ between A and B	A와 B 사이에
□ area	지역
□ experience	경험(하다)
□ pleasant	(날씨가) 좋은, 쾌적한
□ sunshine	햇빛
04	
□ tomorrow evening	내일 저녁
□ evening class	저녁 수업
□ cultural center	문화센터
□ drawing class	그림 그리기 수업
□ how to cook	요리하는 방법
05	
□ next meeting	다음 모임
□ finish	끝마치다
□ topic	주제
□ how to prepare	준비하는 방법
□ field trip	현장 학습
□ member	회원
06	
□ find	찾다
□ history	역사
□ lucky	운좋은
□ check out	(책을) 대출하다
□ aisle	통로
□ shelf	선반, 책꽂이
07	
□ younger sister	여동생(=little sister)
□ move	옮기다
□ baggage	짐
□ fever	열
□ had better	~하는 게 낫다
□ solve	풀다, 해결하다
□ math problem	수학 문제
□ borrow	빌리다
08	
□ What can I do for you?	무엇을 도와드릴까요?
□ take a trip	여행하다
□ be back	돌아오다
□ take care of	~를 돌보다
□ That's no problem.	문제 없어요.
09	
□ visit	방문하다
□ palace	궁전
□ train station	기차역
□ far from	~에서 멀리 떨어진
□ Natural History Museum	(영국 런던의) 자연사 박물관
□ whole	전체의
□ reserve	예약하다
□ book	예약하다
□ excited	흥분된
10	
□ festival	축제
□ miss	빠뜨리다, 놓치다
□ sell	팔다(↔buy)
□ guest	손님(↔host)
11	
□ weather	날씨

□ take a walk	산책하다
□ come along	~을 따라가다
□ novel	소설
□ give ~ a ride	~를 차로 태워 주다
□ bookstore	서점
12	
□ I have something to say to you.	드릴 말씀이 있어요.
□ go camping	캠핑하러 가다
□ next week	다음 주
13	
□ try to	~하려고 노력하다
□ download	다운로드 하다
□ favorite	가장 좋아하는
□ first time	처음
□ how to do	~하는 방법
14	
□ flower shop	꽃가게
□ go straight	직진하다
□ turn left	좌회전하다
□ on the left corner	왼쪽 모퉁이에 있는
□ next to	~ 옆에
□ post office	우체국
15	
□ go pick up	태우러 가다
□ don't have to	~할 필요가 없다
□ swimming class	수영 수업
□ class schedule	수업 일정
□ change	바꾸다, 변하다
16	
□ bring	~을 가져오다
□ promise	약속하다
□ give back	~을 돌려주다
□ double check	다시 한 번 확인하다
17	
□ work	작동하다
□ can't	~일 리가 없다
□ virus	바이러스
□ reboot	시스템을 재 작동시키다
□ several	몇몇의
□ times	번
□ act	작동하다
□ strange	이상하게
□ turn off	(전원을) 끄다(↔turn on)
□ wait	기다리다
18	
□ always	항상
□ try one's best	최선을 다하다(=do one's best)
□ job	일, 직업
□ anyway	어쨌든
□ present	선물(=gift)
19	
□ freshman	1학년
□ popular	인기 있는
□ the day after tomorrow	내일 모레
□ dental appointment	치과 진료 약속
20	
□ pay for	~을 지불하다
□ serious	진심의

영어듣기능력평가 18회

중요 어휘 및 표현

01	
□ electronic	전자의
□ machine	기계
□ use	사용하다
□ tap water	수돗물
□ enough to	~하기에 충분한
□ both A and B	A와 B 둘 다
□ without	~ 없이
□ electricity	전기, 전력
02	
□ wallet	지갑
□ next to	~ 옆에
□ pants	바지
□ drawer	서랍
03	
□ take a look at	~을 보다
□ chance of showers	소나기가 올 확률
□ high temperature	최고 기온
□ up to	~까지
□ degree	(온도계의) 도
□ drop	떨어지다
□ outdoor activity	야외 활동
□ current	현재의
04	
□ plan to	~할 것을 계획하다
□ get a call	전화를 받다
□ company	회사
□ suddenly	갑자기
□ delay	연기하다, 지연하다
□ mean	의미하다, 뜻하다
05	
□ beak	부리
□ hatch	부화하다
06	
□ What about ~?	~하는 게 어때?
□ remember	기억하다
□ later	이후의
□ That's easy to ~.	~하기는 쉽다.
07	
□ It's because of ~.	이것은 ~ 때문이다.
□ lawyer	변호사
□ professor	교수
□ Don't worry about ~.	~에 대해 걱정하지 마라.
□ someday	(미래의) 언젠가
□ understand	이해하다
08	
□ turn off	(전원을) 끄다(↔turn on)
□ Can you tell me the way to ~?	~에 가는 길을 알려 주시겠어요?
□ department store	백화점
□ feel hungry	배고프다
□ borrow	빌리다
□ library card	도서관 대출 카드
09	
□ whole day	하루 종일
□ garbage	쓰레기
□ ground	땅
□ walk a dog	개를 산책시키다
□ a couple of	한두 개의
□ be in the hospital	입원하다
10	
□ receipt	영수증
□ already	이미, 벌써
□ exchange	교환하다
□ another	또 다른, 또 하나의
11	
□ boss	상사
□ pick up	(맡긴 물건 등을) 찾아오다
□ laundry	세탁물, 빨래
□ swing by	잠시 ~에 들르다
□ on one's way home	집에 오는 길에
□ suit	양복, 정장

12	
□ favorite	가장 좋아하는
□ subject	과목
□ belong to	~에 속하다, ~의 소유이다
□ previous	이전의
□ hope to	~을 희망하다
□ have a good time	즐거운 시간을 보내다
13	
□ plan	계획
□ Nothing special.	특별한 것은 없어.
□ join	합류하다, 함께 하다
□ take a trip	여행하다
14	
□ newly	새롭게
□ released	발표된
□ no later than	늦어도
□ showing	상영
□ so that ~ can	~할 수 있도록
□ perfect	완벽한
15	
□ get injured	부상을 당하다
□ That's too bad.	안됐다.
16	
□ get a good grade	좋은 점수를 받다
□ basic	기본적인
□ secret	비밀, 비결
□ regularly	규칙적으로
□ at least	적어도, 최소한
□ focus one's mind	집중하다
□ rule	규칙
□ before long	곧, 머지 않아
17	
□ safety	안전
□ cooperation	협조
□ feed	먹이를 주다(-fed-fed)
□ seriously	심각하게

18	
□ look forward to	~을 학수고대하다
□ ocean	해양의
□ be famous for	~로 유명하다
□ training	훈련
□ tropical	열대의
□ sea life	해양 생물
19	
□ What do you think about ~?	~에 대해 어떻게 생각하니?
□ stay	머무르다
□ near beach	바닷가 근처에
□ spend	소비하다, 쓰다
20	
□ good news	좋은 소식
□ far from	~에서 멀리 떨어진
□ Don't worry.	걱정하지 마.
□ close	가까운
□ It's only a 5 minutes walk.	걸어서 겨우 5분 거리이다.
□ per	~마다, ~당

영어듣기능력평가 19회

중요 어휘 및 표현

01	
□ whenever	~할 때마다
□ move	움직이다, 이동하다
□ arrow	화살, 화살표
□ click	(마우스를) 클릭하다, 누르다
□ twice	두 번
□ look like	~처럼 보이다
02	
□ Why don't we ~?	~하는 게 어때?
□ indoor sports	실내 운동
□ such as	~와 같은
□ how to do	~하는 방법
□ follow	~을 따르다
03	
□ weather forecast	일기예보
□ all over the country	전국적으로
□ fortunately	다행히도
□ expect	예상하다, 기대하다
□ partly cloudy	부분적으로 흐린
□ citizen	시민
04	
□ dieting	식이요법
□ bookstore	서점
□ job interview	취업 면접
05	
□ lovely	(날씨가) 아주 좋은, 사랑스러운
□ go on a picnic	소풍을 가다
□ would love to	~하고 싶다
□ recommend	추천하다
□ dry	건조한
□ turn down	(소리를) 줄이다
□ right away	바로, 지금 당장
06	
□ in front of	~ 앞에
□ check one's schedule	일정을 확인하다
□ last class	마지막 수업
□ club meeting	동아리 모임
□ after class	방과 후에
□ arrive	도착하다
□ just in case	만일을 대비해서
07	
□ inform	알리다, 통지하다
□ fever	열
□ appointment	약속
□ get well	나아지다
08	
□ tool	도구
□ blade	날
□ screw	나사로 고정시키다
09	
□ Thanksgiving Day	추수감사절
□ look forward to	~할 것을 고대하다
□ at first	처음에
□ tiring	피곤하게 하는
□ decide	결정하다, 결심하다
□ take a bus	버스를 타다
□ airport	공항
□ pick up	~를 (차로) 태우러 가다
10	
□ reason	이유
□ measure	측정하다
□ at last	마침내, 드디어
□ Congratulations.	축하해.
□ succeed	성공하다
□ envy	부러워하다
□ strong	강한(↔weak)
□ will	의지
11	
□ grocery store	식료품점
□ keep	보관하다
□ boil	끓이다
□ ingredient	재료

□ shell	껍질
12	
□ get dirty	더러워지다
□ clean up	깨끗하게 하다, 청소하다
□ towel	수건
□ What should I do?	어떻게 해야 하지?
□ alcohol	알코올
□ rub	문지르다
□ tip	조언, 요령
13	
□ poster	포스터
□ advertise	광고하다
□ be asked to	~하도록 요구되다
□ present	발표하다
□ auditorium	강당
□ play	연극
□ prepare	준비하다
14	
□ Can you show me how to get to ~?	~에 가는 길을 알려 주시겠어요?
□ theater	극장
□ turn left	좌회전하다
□ avenue	~가, 대로
□ along	~을 따라
15	
□ painter	화가
□ must have p.p.	~했음에 틀림없다
□ complete	완성하다
□ work	작품
□ take a picture	사진을 찍다
□ sudden	갑작스러운
□ bright	밝은
□ light	빛
□ painting	그림
□ hold	잡고 있다
□ while	~하는 동안

16	
□ post office	우체국
□ check	확인하다
17	
□ join	가입하다, 합류하다
□ soccer	축구
□ kick	(발로) 차다
□ goal	골대, 골, 득점
□ by mistake	실수로
□ Can you believe it?	믿어지세요?
18	
□ local	지역의
□ work	(계획 등이) 잘되어 가다
19	
□ dye	염색하다
□ hairdresser	미용사
□ be supposed to	~하기로 되어 있다
20	
□ play computer games	컴퓨터 게임을 하다
□ believe	믿다, 신뢰하다
□ half	절반, 2분의 1

영어듣기능력평가 20회 중요 어휘 및 표현

01	
□ easily	쉽게
□ electronic machine	전자 제품, 전기 기계
□ make ice	얼음을 만들다
□ turn into	~로 변하다
□ modern	현대의
□ without	~ 없이
02	
□ be in line	줄을 서 있다
□ stand	서다
□ behind	~의 뒤에
□ turn	순서, 차례
□ cut in line	새치기 하다
□ hall way	복도
□ safety	안전
03	
□ temperature	온도, 체온
□ rainy	비오는
□ outdoor activity	야외 활동
04	
□ control	조절하다
□ device	장치
05	
□ clothes	옷
□ section	구역
□ over there	저쪽에
□ bundle	묶음, 꾸러미
□ bundle sale	묶음 할인 판매
□ pair	두 개가 짝을 이루는 쌍
□ enough	충분한
06	
□ in the future	미래에, 장래에
□ math	수학
□ classical music	클래식 음악, 고전 음악
□ more than	~ 이상
□ poem	시

07	
□ wash the dishes	설거지하다
□ leave	~을 남겨놓다(-left-left)
□ history	역사
□ careful	조심스러운, 신경을 쓰는
□ right now	지금, 바로
08	
□ minute	(시간 단위) 분
□ second	(시간 단위) 초
□ become the champion	챔피언이 되다
□ even	훨씬
□ win the gold medal	금메달을 따다
□ record	기록
□ do one's best	최선을 다하다
09	
□ What's wrong with you?	무슨 일이니?
□ It's because of ~.	그것은 ~ 때문이다.
□ in detail	자세히, 상세히
□ careless	부주의한
10	
□ already	이미, 벌써
□ feel hungry	배고프다
□ a little bit	약간의
□ a glass of	한 잔의 ~
□ No problem.	문제 없어., 괜찮아.
11	
□ winter vacation	겨울 방학
□ That's right.	맞아.
□ What about you?	넌 어때?
□ change one's mind	~의 마음이 바뀌다
□ save	모으다, 저장하다
□ take a trip	여행하다
12	
□ regular	규칙적인
□ volunteer	자원봉사

□ regularly	규칙적으로
□ campaign	캠페인
□ practice	연습
□ treat	치료하다, 처치하다
□ foreign	외국의
□ worker	노동자
□ open	문을 열다(↔ close)
13	
□ go on a business trip	출장 가다
□ Is it true?	정말이야?
□ What do you mean by that?	그게 무슨 뜻이야?
□ airline ticket	항공권
14	
□ What a surprise to see you here!	너를 여기서 만나다니 놀랍다!
□ expect	기대하다, 예상하다
□ recommend	추천하다, 권하다
□ be over	끝나다(=end)
□ begin	시작하다
15	
□ trophy	트로피
□ competition	대회, 경기
□ be good at	~을 잘하다
□ Sounds good.	좋아. (동의)
□ elementary school	초등학교
□ like	~처럼
16	
□ for a minute	잠시 동안
□ a part of	~의 일부
□ fence	울타리
□ farm	농장
□ broken	파손된, 부서진
□ take care of	~를 돌보다
□ cow	암소, 젖소
17	
□ look for	~을 찾다
□ next to	~옆에
18	
□ club activities	동아리 활동
□ bring	가져오다
□ skip	빼먹다
19	
□ newest	최신의
□ on the market	시중에 판매되는
□ pay for	대금을 지불하다
□ Don't be surprised!	놀라지 마!
□ would like to	~하고 싶다
□ as well	또한, 역시
20	
□ How about ~?	~은 어때?
□ both	둘 다
□ expensive	비싼(↔cheap)
□ cheaply	싸게, 저렴하게
□ make sure	확실히 ~하다

고난도 영어듣기능력평가

중요 어휘 및 표현

01	
□ look like	~처럼 보이다
□ serve	제공하다
□ liquid	액체 형태의
02	
□ electronics service center	전자제품 서비스 센터
□ broken	고장 난
□ Let me try.	해 볼게.
□ work	작동되다[기능하다]
03	
□ weather forecast	일기 예보
□ mild	화창한
04	
□ make a reservation	예약하다
□ full	가득한, 빈 공간이 없는
□ I can't help.	어쩔 수 없네요.
05	
□ introduce	소개하다
□ friendly	다정한
□ outgoing	활발한
06	
□ go bowling	볼링 치러 가다
□ usually	보통

07	
□ interest	관심, 흥미
□ chef	요리사
□ come true	이루어지다, 실현되다
08	
□ Are you serious?	정말이야?
□ chance	기회
□ take a picture	사진을 찍다
09	
□ pleasant	쾌적한
□ awesome	멋진
□ view	풍경
□ I'm sorry to hear that.	유감입니다.
10	
□ down	우울한
□ throw up	토하다
□ vet	수의사
11	
□ business trip	출장
□ leave	떠나다
12	
□ forget to	~하는 것을 잊다
□ competition	대회

□ practice	연습
13	
□ quiet	조용한
□ relieved	안도하는
14	
□ keep -ing	계속 ~하다
□ fire station	소방서
15	
□ recycling	재활용
□ Have fun!	재미있게 놀아!
16	
□ wash	씻다
□ Nothing much.	별일 없어.
□ ride a bike	자전거를 타다
17	
□ better	(몸이) 나은
□ miss	놓치다
□ lend	빌려주다
□ make a copy	복사를 하다
18	
□ package	소포
□ express mail	속달 우편
□ up to	~까지

19	
□ look at	~을 보다
□ win	우승하다(won-won)
20	
□ have a chance	기회를 갖다
□ pretty	꽤
□ someday	언젠가